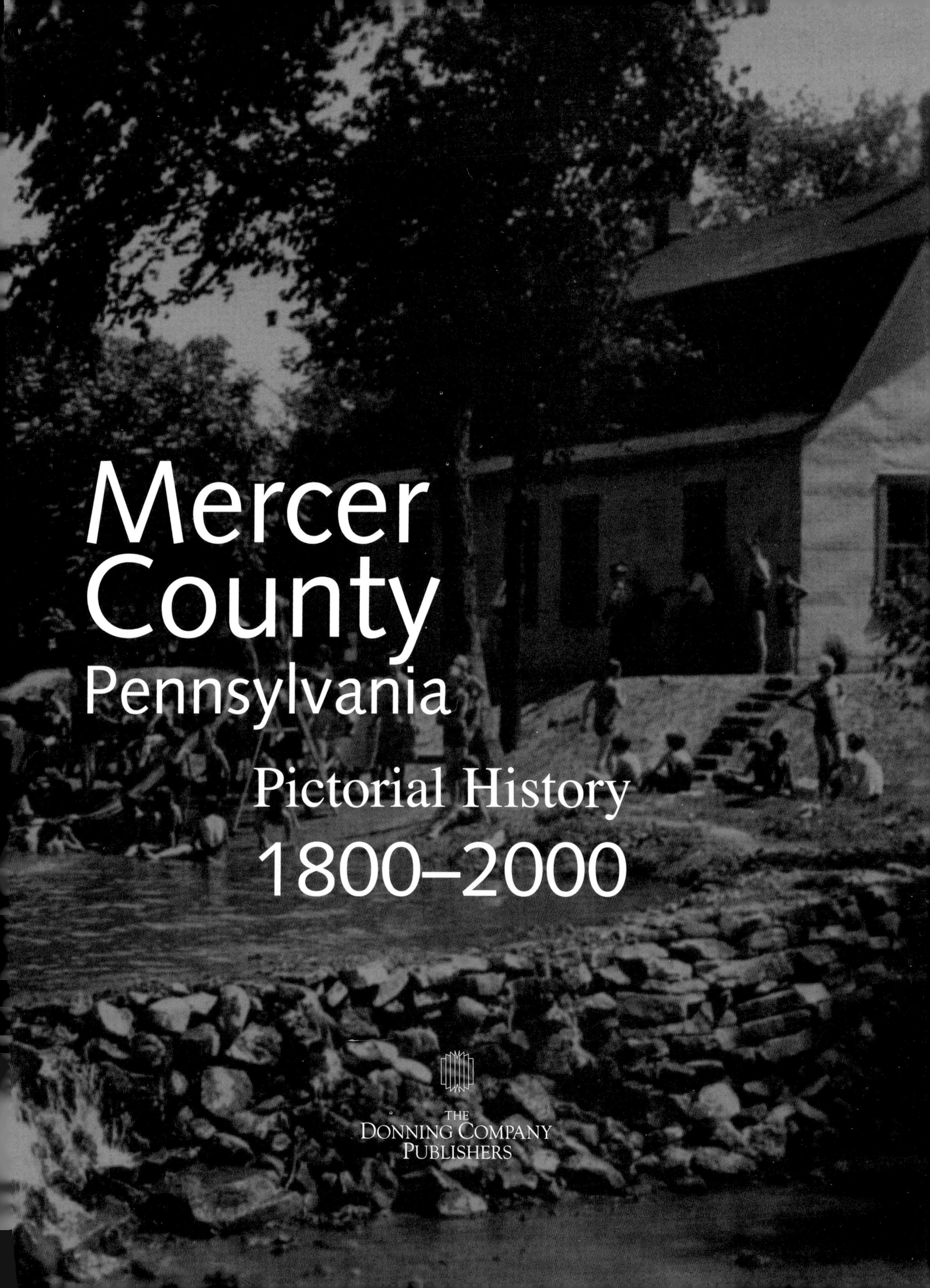

Mercer County
Pennsylvania

Pictorial History
1800–2000

THE
DONNING COMPANY
PUBLISHERS

This term...	Identifies who...
Caption	Wrote the text for the caption
Photo *or* Postcard	Loaned the picture for use in this publication
Contributor	Wrote the text and loaned the picture
Photographer	Took the photograph
When no owner is identified...	*The photograph or item belongs to the Mercer County Historical Society archives.*
When no credit is given for a caption...	*The caption was compiled from various sources.*

Copyright © 2001 by the Mercer County Historical Society

All rights reserved, including the right to reproduce this work in any form whatsoever without permission in writing from the publisher, except for brief passages in connection with a review. For information, write:

The Donning Company Publishers
184 Business Park Drive, Suite 206
Virginia Beach, VA 23462

Steve Mull, *General Manager*
Mary Taylor, *Project Director*
Lori Kennedy and Susan Adams, *Project Research Coordinators*
Dawn V. Kofroth, *Assistant General Manager*
Sally Clarke Davis, *Editor*
Rick Vigenski, *Graphic Designer*
John Harrell, *Imaging Artist*
Elizabeth Vigenski, *Layout Artist*
Scott Rule, *Senior Marketing Coordinator*
Patricia Peterson, *Marketing Coordinator*

Library of Congress Cataloging-in-Publication Data

Available upon request

Printed in the United States of America

Contents

Foreword	7
Preface	9
Contributors	11
Recommended Reading	15
Introduction: Prelude to the 1800s	19
Chapter 1: The 1800s	29
Chapter 2: 1900–1910	131
Chapter 3: 1911–1920	177
Chapter 4: 1921–1930	229
Chapter 5: 1931–1940	281
Chapter 6: 1941–1950	333
Chapter 7: 1951–1970	389
Chapter 8: 1971–1990	445
Chapter 9: 1991–2000	483
Appendix A: Government	529
Color Pictures	542
Appendix B: Military	563
Index	583

Foreword

COMMISSIONERS' OFFICE

CLOYD E. BRENNEMAN, CHAIRMAN
BRIAN W. SHIPLEY
OLIVIA M. LAZOR

County of Mercer
103 Courthouse
Mercer, PA 16137

(724) 662-3800
(724) 962-5711

As we celebrate Mercer County's Bicentennial in the year 2000, it is a time for reflection and for vision. Established on March 12, 1800 with a 675 square mile area carved out of the northern portion of Allegheny County, Mercer County began as the U.S. Census shows with 3,228 residents. Today, our population has grown to approximately 121,000. Mercer County was named for the Revolutionary War hero General Hugh Mercer who was killed at the Battle of Princeton in 1777.

The county became one of 67 in the Commonwealth and there are eight classes of Pennsylvania counties. Our county is a fifth class county; one of 8 in this population category. Made up of 48 political subdivisions or municipalities, Mercer County is comprised of three cities, 14 boroughs, and 31 townships of a second class. In the 1990 U.S. Census, Sharon remained the largest city, Shenango the largest township, Grove City the largest borough and Sheakleyville the smallest. There will certainly be some changes as a result of the year 2000 census.

Mercer Borough was established as the county seat and the first courthouse was built in 1807. Today's courthouse, built in 1911, is the third building, fires having destroyed two previous structures. This magnificent building is the people's heritage. Leadership has devoted time and money to keep it maintained and there are plans for future renovations in order to restore its original beauty and preserve it for future generations.

The courthouse serves not only as the Hall of Justice, but also as the seat for administering county government. Upon entering the building, one senses our rich history. But the government that dwells beneath the dome today, is far different than the one that began in 1800. As an agent for the Commonwealth, the county's annual budget has grown to more than 40 million dollars and employs more than 350 people who are required to deliver a multitude of services.

Just as county government has grown and changed over these 200 years, so has the county economy. At its founding, the major industry was farming, then quickly turning to iron and coal. Today, we have diversification with agriculture, tourism, industrial, commercial and service industries. There are over 56,000 people employed, 19,000 public school students and 1,280 farms in Mercer County. The people who have settled here also symbolize our diversity for Mercer County's roster of nationalities reads like the League of Nations.

Truly our rich heritage is embodied within the pages of this history book. In this year of celebrating Mercer County's Bicentennial to honor our past accomplishments we, the Board of Commissioners, have found it to be a great testimony to the strength of its people.

Mercer County Board of Commissioners

Cloyd E. Brenneman, Chairman

Brian W. Shipley, Vice-Chairman

Olivia M. Lazor, Secretary

Hutchinson School (Shenango Township), 1940s. (The school closed in 1952.)

Preface

This publication is not a textbook. It's more of a scrapbook with bits and pieces of history as one might record one's own life—lots of good stories, some sad, some folksy, and many unique. One reason we took this approach is that a separate book could be written about all the subjects mentioned on these pages. In fact, books have already been written on farming, one-room schools, Wendell August Forge, East Lackawannock Township, Wilmington Township, Grove City, Jamestown, Sheakleyville, and even the Billy Whitla kidnapping. Furthermore, detailed manuscripts were submitted on aviation, railroads, Shenango Valley, Clark, Stoneboro, Worth Township, Lakeview High School, and several churches and families. Combined as submitted, these manuscripts would have exceeded the word-count limits of this project. (All of the submitted material is on file at the Mercer County Historical Society, and readers are encouraged to visit the society's library for more details.)

Featured in this book are people who were the first to do something, who did something for a long time, who did something on a grand scale, or who took the time to reminisce and document their memories. In some cases, anecdotes are personal, yet represent an era or group of people. In many cases, the histories are extensive and the result of many hours of research. The society thanks all the authors for their contributions, and we salute all the unsung residents who have contributed to our beautiful corner of the world.

Because three books already document the county's history in the 1800s, this book's introduction and Chapter 1 set the stage for the rest of the book, which focuses on the 1900s. (For brevity, "now" is used throughout this book to mean "in 2000" or "at the time this publication went to press" or thereabouts.)

At first glance, the book may seem disjointed, with many disparate pieces. However, as you read the text and captions, you will begin to see how interlocked the pieces are. We have tried hard to include information about as many places in the county as possible as a reminder to all readers that Mercer County consists of many diverse, yet interwoven, parts. Plus, although justifiably proud of our connections to Mercer County, we must remember that we do not live in a vacuum. From our economy to our personal family ties, Mercer County's reach stretches worldwide, and this book gives a few examples.

Who knows what aspects of today's lifestyle will be important fifty or one hundred years from now. Maybe cooking will be a hobby as gardening has become. In the 1800s and early 1900s, many people had vegetable gardens. Now, the convenience of supermarket shopping with its efficient trucking and distribution system makes *buying* vegetables more popular than *growing* them. In our fast-paced world, cooking meals may be losing ground to eating out and simply heating up already prepared dishes.

Please take time out of your hectic schedule to pause and reflect on your past and heritage. Use this book to see where your history fits in with your neighbors and other residents of our county. Then, when the speed of your routine slows and you have time to collect your family photographs and anecdotes, it may be time to compile another book. In the meantime, enjoy this pictorial history of Mercer County's first two hundred years.

The Prime Outlets of Grove City, Exit 31 off Interstate 79 in Springfield Township. (1999 aerial: **The Herald***)*

Contributors

BICENTENNIAL COMMISSION EXECUTIVE COMMITTEE

John G. "Jerry" Johnson, Chairman

Kathryn Lima, Vice Chairperson

Catherine Mack, Secretary

Robert Jazwinski, Treasurer

James Cattron

Jane Leyde

Walter Matthews

Sue Corbett Moore

Barry Nelson

David Shaffer

Judge John Q. Stranahan

Richard Werner

Donna Winner

MERCER COUNTY HISTORICAL SOCIETY STAFF

William Philson, executive director

Margo Glaser Letts, office manager

James K. Sewall, library manager (volunteer)

Marge Crompton, preservationist (volunteer)

OTHER CONTRIBUTORS

In addition to the people listed above, special thanks goes to the handful of volunteers, many of them also contributing authors, who scurried around in the final stages of this project: **Autumn L. Buxton, Richard S. Christner, Michael Coulter and his students, Gail Habbyshaw, Frederick N. Houser, Delber L. McKee, Vonda Minner, Ruth Z. Woods, Joyce M. Young,** and especially **Tom Darby**, who scanned the majority of the 650 or so black and white photos.

Contributors continued

Evelyn Anderson
Margaret Anderson
Henry Andrae
Ila Ayre
Alan J. Baldarelli
Roland C. Barksdale-Hall
Genevieve Bartholomew
Linda Bennett
Mae "Joannie Appleseed" Beringer
James E. Bickell, Sr.
Mrs. W. S. Blair
Lois Blake
Margaret Pizor Bower
Mary Bowlin
Cloyd E. Brenneman
Jean Brown
Mark Brown
Marilyn McCutchen Byerley
Eli J. Byler
James M. Campbell
K. Joshua Christiansen
Nathan S. Clark
Janis Clarke
Arlene Comher
Betsy Cooper
Monica Copley
William E. Cowan, Jr.
Rachel Darby
Ernie Desu
Marilyn Dewald
Woodrow S. Dixon

Adeline Drennen
Jerry Drew
Helen Duby
Lucille Eagles
Bruce Engelhardt
Richard H. Fahnline
Bill Finney
Judy Finney
Jean Fleet
Norma Fischer Furey
Robert B. Fuhrman
John George, Jr.
Serena Ghering
Jeff Gill
Jimmy Gill
Casey J. Glockner
Sharon L. Gran
Lee Greenfield
Josh Grubbs
Helen Hall
John Hamelly
James Hansen
Kelly Elizabeth Hedglin
Eileen Hendrickson
Ethel Hildebran
Janet Hills
Rita Kreidle Holler
Joseph Hood
Edward W. Hoagland, Jr.
George Hostetter
Lloyd W. Hughes
Bill Hugo
Julia Stamm Hugo
Barbara A. Hunter

Margaret Hunter
Suzanne Hutto
Peter Iacino
Ellsworth Jamison
Raymond Jamison
Aaron C. Jarvinen
Henrietta Jazwinski
John Jefferis
Cynthia Snodgrass Jones
Patricia Jones
Gene Jordan
Pete J. Joyce
Mike Kalpich
Theo Karfes
Sondra Kasbee
Ralph Kilgore
Brian Krall
Evelyn Kriedle
Carrol R. Lacey
Robert F. Lark
Olivia M. Lazor
Pat Leali
Norma Leary
John Leslie
Donald Lewis
Janice Liao
Gwen A. Lininger
William Lombardo
Frank Lord
Ed Loreno
Jennifer L. Mahurin
Dorothy Malloy
Helen Marenchin
Pauline Marsh

Cris Martin
Daniel V. Maurice
Maria Mayerchak
Doug Mays
Madeleine McBride
Milford L. "Miff"
   McBride, Jr.
Howard McCartney
Idella McConnell
Celia McCoy
William Menzies
Lloyd Meyer
John Milan
David Miller
Shirley Minshull
Don Mitchell
Howard Mitchell
Mary Mitchell
Clyde Moffett
Kathryn Miles
   Moorehouse
Mary Ellen Moreland
William A. Morocco, Sr.
John Moser
Chris Mullins
Matt Musko
Edith Myers
Barry Nelson
Dorothy Cookson Nutt
Rose Elizabeth O'Hare
Audley Olson
Robert Olson
Robert Osborn

Dewitt Palmer
Maxine Patterson
Carolyn Phillips
Valarie Phillips
William J. Phillips, Sr.
Roberta A. Bleakney
   Philson
Kathy Pompa
Nick Pompa
George F. Reeher
Jennifer Reinhart
Lydia Manteau Regula
E. Jane Rhodes
Abby Rissler
Michael Ristvey, Jr.
Dick Rose
Donna Rose
Shane Rosenfelder
Ray Rossi
George Hardy Rowley
Mary Sample
Rosanne Seafuse
Esther Shaffer
Jeremy Shankle
Richard Sherbondy
Brian Shipley
Nick Sicilina
Vinson F. Skibo
Jim Smartz
Marce Smigel
Virginia N. Snyder

Catherine Sok
Jeff Spanogle
Teresa Spatara
Betty Harter Spence
Tom Stanton
Frances Steese
Sharon Steindurf
Richard Stevenson
T. D. Stewart
Julia Swaelon
Jean E. Thompson
Deanna Tuttle
Eileen Urmson
Al Vermeire
Esther Viglio
Shirley Vinton
Wally Wachter
Gilbert A. Walters
Michael P. Walton
Betty Whitehouse
Eleanora Wiand
Cinda S. Wilpula
Mary Wilson
Daniel J. Wininsky
Mairy Jayn Woge
Sarah L. Wright
Sharon L. Wright
Jacob Yount

Coordinating editor
Diane W. Lacey

Kelly's blacksmith shop, West Middlesex, about 1900.

Recommended Reading

"A Brief History of the Mercer County Bench and Bar"

"A Century for Christ, 1879–1979. A History of the East Main United Presbyterian Church of Grove City, Pennsylvania," Dorothy Cookson Nutt

"Anna Garrett: The Hannah More of America," Gail Habbyshaw

Area Friends Remember When: A Collection of Nostalgic Memories of Times Gone By, James Mennell (editor)

"Brief History of The Good Shepherd Parish," Henrietta Jazwinski

Clarksville Remembered: The Birth, Life, Death and Rebirth of a Town, Helen H. Hall

Clarksville/Clark: Past to Present 1848–1998, Phyliss Parshall and Janet Moats

Erie Extension Canal: Hike With History, Fred Brenner

"First Presbyterian Church, Sharpsville, PA"

Frontier Farmer: Autobiography and Family History of Aaron A. Boylan, Katherine Lytle Sharp (editor)

Furrows of the Past: A History of Mercer County Agriculture, Vonda L. Minner

"Grace United Methodist Church History, Grove City, Pennsylvania," Katherine Griffith, Alice Hoffman, Kathryn Urey, Joan Stuck, Betty McCracken, Jean Brown

"Greenville Newspapers," Teresa Spatara

"Grove City College," Jennifer L. Mahurin

Hail Temple Built to Justice: A History of Mercer Count's Court Houses, Robert B. Fuhrman

"The Herald," Teresa Spatara

"History of Central Community Church," Autumn L. Buxton

History of East Lackawannock Township, Mercer County, Pennsylvania 1900–2000, Ruth Z. Woods

"History of First Assembly of God," Pat Leali

History of Mercer County, Pennsylvania, 1888

"History of Mercer County Railroad," Frederick N. Houser

"History of Pine Township (1851–1999)"

"History of Sacred Heart Church, Sharon, Pennsylvania," William E. Cowan, Jr.

History of the Barnes Families in Jackson Township Mercer County, Pennsylvania, Beatrice Barnes McClelland

"History of the Borough of Stoneboro," Frederick N. Houser

History of the Clarksville Presbyterian Church & Faith United Presbyterian Church: 1837–1981

History of Wilmington Township, Mercer County 1900–2000, Delber McKee

Indian Paths of Pennsylvania, Paul A. W. Wallace

"John Hoge," Gail Habbyshaw

"Johnny Oakes," Gail Habbyshaw

"Lakeview High School," Serena Ghering, Jerry Drew, and John Hamelly

Mercer As Its Citizens Remember It, James E. Mennell

Mercer County History, journal of the Mercer County Historical Society

Mercer County One-Room School Story: 1800–1960, Joannie Appleseed

'Mid the Pines, David M. Dayton

"New Virginia United Methodist Church: A Brief History," Virginia N. Snyder

"Newspapers in the Grove City Area," Teresa Spatara

On Polar Trails, John W. Goodsell (Donald Whisenhunt, editor)

"Our Inheritance: History of Holy Trinity Evangelical Lutheran Church of Grove City"

Sewall Family of Mercer Co., Pa.—Clement Sewall of Mercer Co., Pa. His Ancestors and His Descendants, James Kerr Sewall

Sheakleyville, Ethel Hildebran (editor)

"Shenango Valley History," Mairy Jayn Woge

Small Manuscript Files, Mercer County Historical Society

St. Anthony's Church, 75th Anniversary: 1924–1999

"Stoneboro and St. Columbkille's Church, 1874–1999," Henry Andrae

"The Borough of Clark (formerly Clarksville)," Clyde Moffett

"The County After 1800," Pete J. Joyce

The Mother Church, William Lombardo

"The Old Order of Amish of Mercer County, Pennsylvania," Norma Fischer Furey

"The Twin City Elks Lodge: A Unifying Force in Farrell's African American Community," Roland C. Barksdale-Hall

"The 200 Year History of the Fairfield Presbyterian Church"

Through the Arch: A Jamestown and Jamestown Area History to Commemorate Our Nation's Bicentennial in 1976, Norma Leary

Wolf Creek Legacy I and II, Lillian Reynolds Reeher

"Worth Township," Idella McConnell and Lucille Eagles

"Zion's Reformed United Church of Christ," Gwen A. Lininger

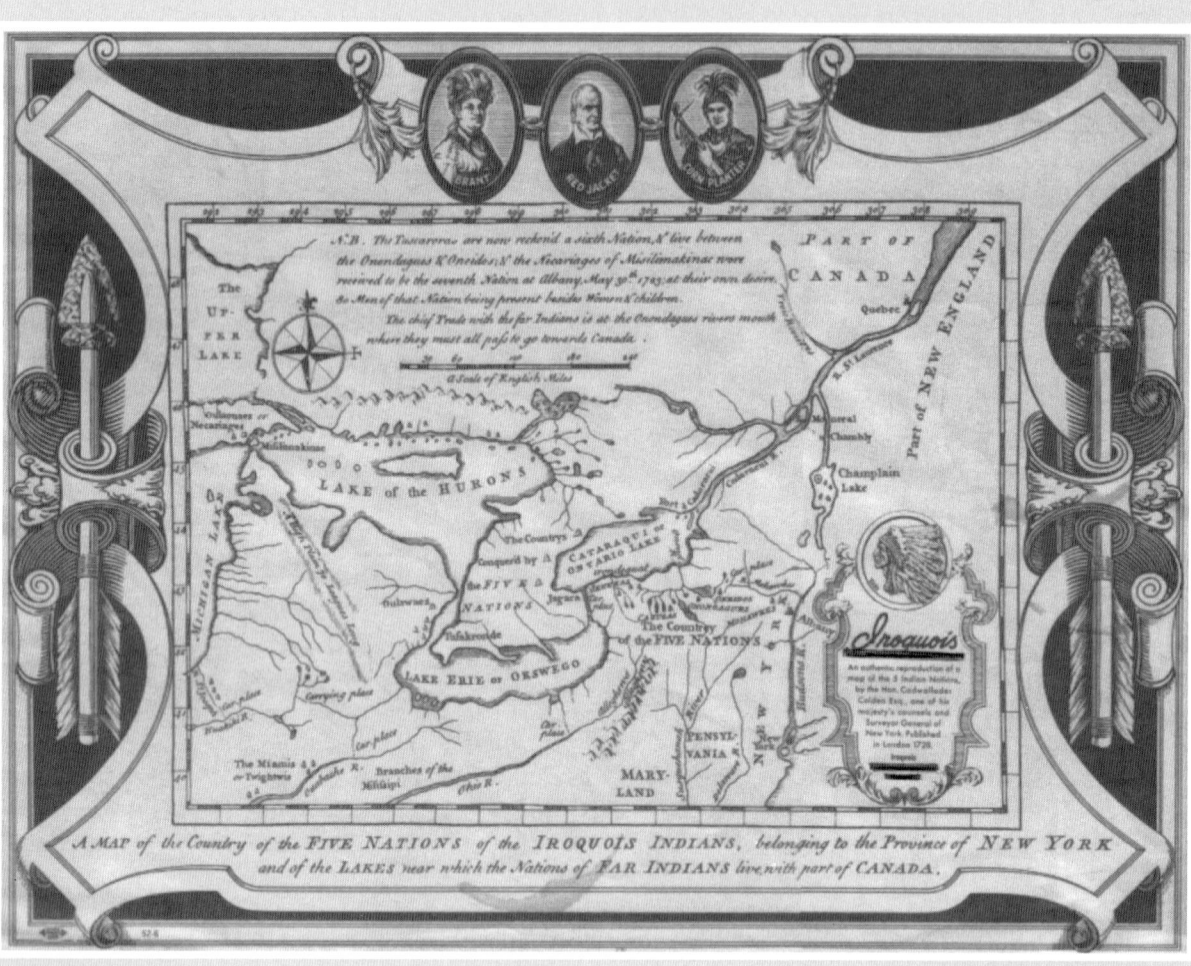

Introduction: Prelude to the 1800s

EARLY HISTORY
By William Philson

Imagine walking in an old woods, with large, tall trees. Their bushiness blocks out most of the sunlight. Only where a tree has fallen, been struck by lightning, or died does enough sunlight reach the ground and allow seedlings to grow. The tall trees keep much of the summer's heat out, too, and act as a wind break. Imagine walking in the shade of these trees on a hot summer day. Then, imagine on a cold winter day how good the sun feels since the bare branches let in the sunlight, and the force of the wind is still cut by the trees. These pictures are how much of what is now Mercer County looked to its first inhabitants, the Indians.

According to recent archaeological thought, Indians came to the American continents during several Ice Ages beginning 30,000 to 40,000 years ago and ending about 8,000 years ago. These Indians probably came over a land bridge and glacier formations that connected Asia with Alaska, presumably following game. If Indians followed the line of glacial activity and waterways, they probably came to what is now western Pennsylvania fairly quickly. Moraine State Park and the moraine line through this region mark the farthest advance of the glaciers of the last Ice Age and served as a fairly direct pathway.

The most recent findings suggest that Indians moved into this area over 10,000 years ago. These Paleo-Indians (pre-7,000 BC) were nomadic, yet left evidence of dwellings, fire pits, and many types of artifacts indicating that they traveled this area extensively.

The first evidence of permanent Indian habitation in what is now western Pennsylvania is over 5,000 years old. These Indians were of the Monongahela culture. They were probably descendants of some of the wandering bands of Paleo-Indians. Sites of their villages, burials, and their trash piles—pottery, flint arrowheads, and other Neolithic items—give a picture of what they were like. Evidence suggests they were forced to move, or were destroyed, by war about 1620.

Perhaps, the Mound Builders displaced the Monongahela culture. These tribes built mounds to celebrate religious ceremonies, bury their dead, and remember those dead. Sometime between 1542 and 1650, they quit building mounds. Evidence suggests that they had migrated from the southwest, across the Mississippi River, and up the Ohio Valley until they reached this area and as far north as what is now New York. The mounds may have been primitive versions of the great pyramids that the Aztec-Toltec and Mayan civilizations of ancient Mexico built. (During the late 1800s, an Indian mound was reportedly discovered in Greenville, but scavengers looking for souvenirs destroyed it. Between 9,000 and 10,000 mounds have been found, with the nearest and best known remaining mounds as close as Ohio.)

The next group that claimed control of this region is the Erie Indians, or the Cat Nation (Eriehronon). The Erie controlled the area during the early and mid-1600s. In 1656 the power of the Erie tribe was destroyed by the Six Nations of the Iroquois Confederation. Trade with Europe had brought on the war between the Eriehronon and the Iroquois. The Iroquois wanted a monopoly of trade with the Europeans for their weapons.

Therefore, they needed many trading goods, primarily animal pelts. To gather more pelts, the Iroquois ranged farther than their traditional hunting and trapping grounds, intruding on the lands of other tribes, including the Eriehronon. This war saw European weapons used against inferior, Neolithic, and traditional weapons.

After 1656, the area that became Mercer County was under Iroquois control and was used for a hunting preserve. It was sparsely populated for the better part of a century. Hunting and trapping parties visited, and it was a main crossing grounds of Indian paths. By 1722, without Iroquois approval, some Delaware (Lenni Lenape) and Shawnee started to migrate into the region. By 1747 the Lenape, with Iroquois permission, continued to migrate into this area. Their capital in the Ohio Valley region was located at Kuskuski (near present-day New Castle), which until 1849 was the southern border of Mercer County. Along with these Indians, a Wyandot tribe of about one hundred families moved into the surrounding regions, on or near the Shenango River. Their move westward demonstrates the constant pressure the settlers were putting on the Indians for their lands. Before the summer of 1753, the Iroquois had subjugated every other tribe as far west as the Mississippi. The Iroquois denied most of these tribes independent status, regarding them as mere hunters on territory actually belonging to the Six Nations. The fact that four tribal groups—the Iroquois, the Lenni Lenape, the Shawnee, and the Wyandot—shared an area that had not been populated completely for many years shows the extent of this pressure.

Southern and western Pennsylvania played a leading role in the French and Indian War (1754–1763). The Six Nations refused to commit to either side of the European power struggle. During the early part of the French and Indian War, they sided with neither the French or British. They watched both parties. The Indians in the Ohio Valley, however, viewed the French intrusion into "their" land with deep concern since over the years, the Iroquois and the Colonies had displaced them from the East Coast. From late 1753 until early 1754, Lieutenant Governor Robert Dinwiddie (Virginia) sent a young George Washington on a risky journey to the French forts in western Pennsylvania to protest the French occupation of these still contested lands. At this time, travel into western Pennsylvania during the best weather was slow. A two-and-a-half-month trek during the fall and winter was almost inconceivable. Add hostile Indians and French soldiers, and many considered it folly. Washington volunteered and traveled mostly by horse, foot, and canoe through a Pennsylvania covered by forest. Washington carried a letter from Dinwiddie demanding the French leave British territory. The French rejected the British claim, and the stage was set for the first truly world war. On his trip to deliver Dinwiddie's letter to the French, Washington may have passed through Mercer County. At very least he probably stopped at, passed through, or passed by an Indian village in Mercer County.

By 1756, the area that became Mercer County is again mentioned in European texts—from the viewpoint of an Indian captive. The Lenni Lenape captured eight-year-old John McCullough in the valley of the Conococheague in 1756. His adoptive family lived in Shenango Town, near present-day West Middlesex. He reported that the Indians led an austere life. However, his remembrances are of a well-intentioned people who laughed and had a rough camaraderie.

"The next summer I had like to lose my life. All the Indians of the town, except one man and one woman, were out at their cornfields, leaving the young ones to take care of their houses. About 10 o'clock of the day, four of the little fellows and I went into the creek to bathe ourselves. The creek is perhaps about 60 or 70 yards wide. There is a ridge of rocks that reaches across the stream, where I had often observed the Indians wading across the stream, the water being deep at each side. I ventured to wade over, and made out very well, until I got about a rod off the shore on the opposite side. When the water began to get too deep for me. I turned about, proud of my performance. When I got about half way back, I missed my course, and all at once stepped over the edge of the rocks and went down over head and ears. I made a few springs as high as I could above the water. At last I swallowed so much water, and not having yet learned to swim, I was obliged to give over. When the little fellows who came to bathe along with me saw that I had given myself up, they raised the scream. The woman who I mentioned before came running to the bank to see what was the matter. They told her that Isting-go-weh-hing (that was the name they gave me) and was drowned. She immediately ran to the house and awakened her husband who came as quickly as possible (as they told me afterward) to my relief. As I kept afloat all the time, he waded up to his chin before he could get a hold of me by the leg. He then trailed me through the water until he got to the rocks that I had stepped over. He then laid me over his shoulder and brought me out to the bank where he threw me down, supposing that I was dead. It so happened that my head was downhill. The water gushed out of my mouth and nose. He previously had sent off one of the little boys to inform my friends of the accident. After some time I began to show some signs of life. He then took me by the middle, clasping his hands across my belly, and shook me, the water still running plentifully out of my mouth and nose. By the time my friends arrived, I began to breathe more freely. They carried me up to the bank to a week-a-waum, or house, and laid me down on a deer skin where I lay till about the middle of the afternoon. At last I awoke out of sleep and was surprised to see a great number of Indians of both sexes standing around me. I raised my head. My old brother advanced toward me and said, 'au moygh-t-ha-hee a-moigh,' that is, 'Rise, go and bathe yourself.' I then recollected what I had been doing. He then told me that if he would see me in the creek again, he would drown me outright. However, the very next day I was paddling in the water again."

McCullough's account of his captivity gives today's reader a view of life with Indians in western Pennsylvania before 1800. Their culture was different, but allowed the Indians to prosper. In fact, for over 12,000 years, Indians had used this region for their needs. With the coming of the French and British, that practice changed forever.

Two Indian chiefs left a lasting impression on history and have Mercer County connections: Custaloga and Guyasutha.

Custaloga was one of three principal chiefs of the Lenape after 1760. During the French and Indian War, he was made a captain by the French and signed many peace treaties with the English. Later, he fought against the English in the failed Pontiac's (Guyasutha's) Rebellion. He exerted significant control over land between French Creek and the Kuskuskies. Although seminomadic, his primary village seems to have been where French Creek and Deer Creek meet. In French Creek Township, the former Heydrick farm (on which the Indian village sat) is now Custaloga Town, a Boy Scout camp.

Guyasutha was a Seneca chief during the same period that Custaloga was active. Guyasutha guided George Washington to visit the French and visited him when he was in the Ohio Valley in the 1780s. Guyasutha tried to lead his people through a troubling period in peace. He was the principal orator during many conferences and treaties and was offered a colonial commission during the American Revolution in 1776. The Seneca chose to side with the British, but Guyasutha and the territory he controlled sat out the war. Guyasutha met with General "Mad" Anthony Wayne as he marched toward the Battle of Fallen Timbers. In 1793, his surprise testimony for Captain Samuel Brady led to Brady's acquittal on charges of murdering several Indians.

By 1777 the American Revolution was in full gear, and Indians were making choices that would affect them after the war was over. During the war, only Indians, especially the Lenape, inhabited the area that became Mercer County. Although no direct conflict occurred in Mercer County during the Revolution, the actions outside the area affected population patterns among the Indians. The Squaw Campaign of 1778, as it became known, resulted from a failed American mission to take British provisions on the Cuyahoga River. The Westmoreland County Colonial Militia, failing to reach their objective due to February weather, turned their attention on friendly Delaware encampments— kidnapping, killing, and scalping women and boys. The effect of this raid turned the Lenape hostile against the Americans. The Lenape moved from western Pennsylvania into Ohio to be away from the Americans and left a void, which was filled by the Seneca.

After the Revolution, Indian affairs grew steadily worse. The Indians were not given choices that might have brought peace and coexistence between them and their white neighbors. Treaties were one-sided and gave the Indian chiefs and nations no real hope. Many times the Indians chose war out of sheer frustration.

The Fort McIntosh (now Beaver) Treaty of 1785 continued the effort of the new United States to render the Indian Confederation untenable. This treaty dealt with the Lenape, the Wyandot tribes, and a few wandering members of other tribes. The United States stripped the Indians of all land except south central Ohio above the Ohio River and between the Cuyahoga and the Maumee Rivers.

By 1789 the whole area beyond the Appalachians was at the brink of war. The Indians had hoped for British help, but little was forthcoming. By 1793, "Mad" Anthony Wayne had led his men through what is now eastern Mercer County against the Indians. By the time the Battle of Fallen Timbers, located south of present-day Toledo, Ohio, was won by General Wayne in 1794, the organized Indian threat was over in the region that would become Mercer County. Until this time, the threat had been real enough to keep settlers afraid and out of the region.

When early settlers moved into the area that would become Mercer County, the Indians that inhabited the area were primarily Cornplanter Indians, a division of the Seneca. The Cornplanter Indians took their name from Cornplanter, who had become the leader of the tribe after Guyasutha. The Seneca in western Pennsylvania did not have the permanent towns of the Lenape, but rather semipermanent hunting and seasonal farming camps.

By 1790, the Indians had a reasonable population, but no gatherings of more than one hundred families. Smaller bands of Indians lived in many places, the outskirts of present-day Mercer among them and another at the Pine Swamp in Jackson Township. East of Mercer, just outside the borough limits, at the junction where Mill and Otter Creeks form the Neshannock Creek, at least a dozen Indian habitations existed and perhaps as many as seventy at one time.

Benjamin Stokely was the first permanent settler around the area to become Mercer County. Nine months after the Battle of Fallen Timbers, Stokely was in the county surveying the land for the government to distribute as payment for duties performed during the Revolutionary War.

"On the 11th day of May [1795] I started to the District [where Mercer is now located] to survey and lay those warrants. In this summer the Indians were committing murders. By the advice of Captain Heath of Fort Franklin we desisted from our surveying, and on the 9th of June we left the country and went home. A letter received from Captain Heath, commanding Fort Franklin, and dated June 6th, 1795, giving notice of two men killed by the Indians near Conneaut and advising me of the danger we were in from hostile Indians induced me to take the measures I then adopted. This letter was sent to me by the hand of a friendly Indian and was received the next day by me."

Many Indians and tribes did not go to war and were considered friendly by the settlers, but accounts of these Indians were not related as often as ones of the warring Indians.

The situation was changing rapidly. Less than a year and a half later, Stokely moved his family to what would soon be Mercer County with apparent ease into this region. Others moved with him, but moved away before winter and the Stokely family was the only white family in the area.

"Our neighbors who had come out to the country during that year all left the country, and when winter set in we had no one to associate with but the Indians and wild beasts . . . . The first succor I ever got after my settlement was the 19th December, 1796, when I received six hundred pounds of flour and three hundred pounds of Indian meal which cost me about seventy dollars or eight dollars a hundred. The same winter I purchased from the Indians about three thousand pounds of venison at about a cent a pound and paid it chiefly in powder at two dollars a pound, lead at fifty cents and flour at one shilling a quart. I purchased from them also rough tallow at six cents and sold it in Pittsburgh at twenty cents per pound when rendered. Skins I bought at one dollar for a buck and fifty cents for a doe skin. Venison hams I sold on the road to Pittsburgh at one dollar a pair, or six cents a pound."

Pioneer families had many ways to make ends meet, and capitalism was alive and well on the frontier. Stokely was not just a pioneer, but also a soldier, a surveyor, a trader, a storekeeper, among other things. In the fall of 1797, Stokely planted the first known wheat in the area that became Mercer County. This area was beginning to grow. Stokely began to get neighbors. Throughout 1798 and 1799, Stokely made his living being a surveyor for the increasing population that surrounded his homestead. In 1800, a severe frost wiped out almost all corn and potatoes, the first missionaries came to the county, and an area of wilderness was carved out on the western border of Pennsylvania. Mercer County was created out of Allegheny County on March 12, 1800.

In 1792, before the Indian difficulties were entirely settled, the legislature of Pennsylvania enacted that all the lands north and west of the Ohio and Allegheny Rivers and Conewango Creek, not yet reserved for public or charitable uses, should be offered for sale to persons to cultivate, improve, and settle. Pennsylvania also sold plots at $20 per 100 acres with certain stipulations: The settlers must clear, fence, and cultivate two acres out of each one hundred; build and reside in a home there for at least five years; and accept the rule that new tenants could claim the home and plot if the fireplace was cold and no signs of residency were found. To hold the premises, when desirable, neighbor friends would travel miles on foot to keep up fires for those unavoidably absent on business or visiting their friends.

David Leyde found a well-watered and rolling farm of 180 acres that was affordable. The farm (Springfield Township) had a few clear acres and a small log cabin with no door or window. It could be entered by crawling under one side. The cabin was empty and cold, with no fire going and Leyde occupied it, according to the law. The settlement had been built by a man named Forrest. When Forrest returned later with his family, he found his belongings outside of the cabin, as it was now occupied by Leyde. Leyde stayed, worked on the land, put in a few acres of rye. Each Saturday he walked about four miles to spend the Sabbath with his grandfather, Old John Leyde, and his aunt and uncle, the Isaac Roses. Young Leyde worked to prepare the farm for his family, which he brought in the spring of 1810.

Secluded in woods near Leesburg are the Leesburg Falls. Near Neshannock Woods Refinishing (furniture and antiques) off Route 19, the falls are hard to find, but rewarding once found. During the 1990s, the wooded hill near the falls was the site of controversy when a developer pursued an idea of building a resort there. Although he obtained many of the required permits, he abandoned the idea because the local resistance to the project was strong. (Photographer: Marilyn Dewald)

*W. Walter Braham, former Lawrence County judge, believes that George Washington passed through Lawrence and Mercer Counties about 1754 almost directly using an eastern route. If he is correct, Washington very possibly slept in or near one of the three major Indian villages in Mercer: Shenango Town, Pymatuning Town, or Custaloga's Town. Braham theorizes that Washington's party chose to avoid the Allegheny River due to high water and bad weather. He uses mileage from Washington and Christopher Gist, Washington's frontier scout, and modern topography to make his case. Braham proposes that Washington's group passed close to both Shenango and Pymatuning and passed just north of present-day Jackson Center on the Venango Trail. Paul A. W. Wallace bases his theory on the fact that Washington was a surveyor and would keep accurate records of his travels. Wallace believed that Washington traveled by a more direct route—through present-day Wesley, Franklin, and Custaloga's Town to Meadville and beyond. In any case, George Washington was most likely here. (Map: **Indian Paths of Pennsylvania**; caption: William Philson)*

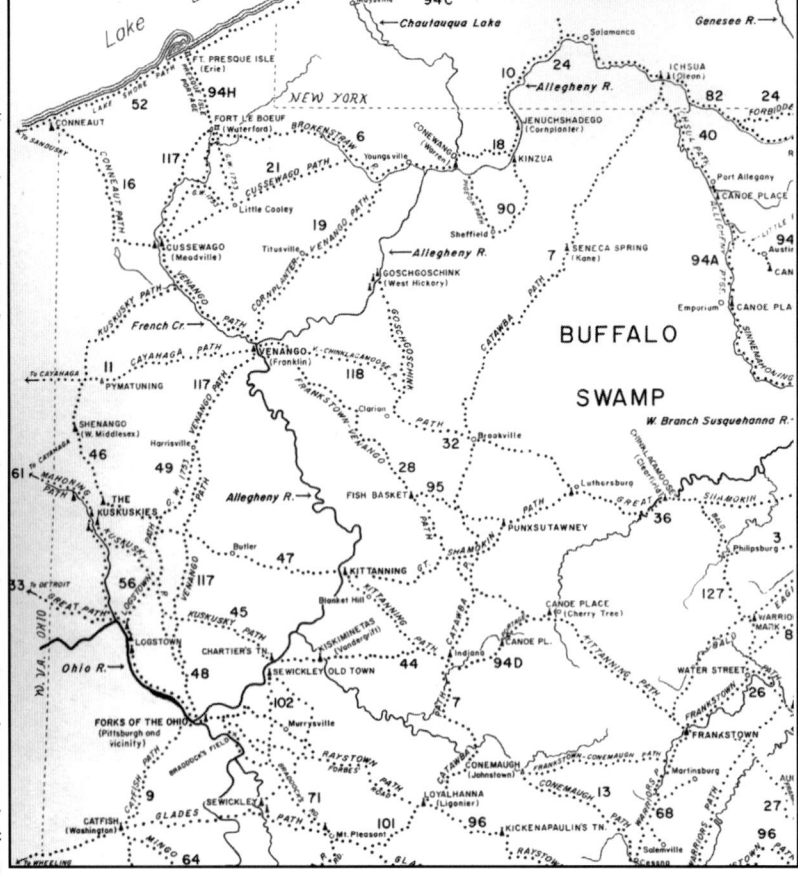

Reputed to be the oldest house in the county, a log cabin was built on a 500-acre tract (near Fredonia) in 1786 by Absalom Baird, a surgeon who had received the land as a Revolutionary War grant. The property was patented in 1807 to Jacob Stroud as Hunter's Choice. In 1913, George Hinckley bought the property and nicknamed it Yellow Breeches Farm. (Hinckley was one of the engineers who designed the Roosevelt Dam.) Later it was sold to Donald and Valeria Dukelow. Made of oak and poplar logs, the house had a loft that was converted to bedrooms. A porch and kitchen were later additions to the original structure. (Photographer: Marilyn Dewald)

The Main Street bridge and lower dam (pictured, in 1997) on Wolf Creek are near where Valentine Cunningham built a grist mill in 1778 and started a settlement known as Pine Grove (now Grove City). (Photographers: Nick and Kathy Pompa)

25

In the 1930s under a Works Progress Administration (WPA) project, a group of workers opened, closed, and labeled graves in an Indian cemetery located at the French Creek Council of Boy Scouts' Custaloga Camp (French Creek Township). A marker on one of the graves indicates Guyasutha was buried there. Guyasutha was a guide for George Washington while Washington was warning French officials at Fort LeBoeuf (now Waterford, Erie County) and Fort Venango (now Franklin, Venango County) in 1753 that they were trespassing on land that belonged to the English. Guyasutha, who later became chief of the Wolf Clan of the Senecas, lived near Sharpsburg (Allegheny County). However, based on further research, the Indian buried here may actually be Custaloga, whose town was just south of Meadville. A monument (pictured, in 2000) was erected by descendents of Charles Heydrick, who in 1787 acquired the property where the burial grounds lie as payment for his Revolutionary War service. A home (pictured, in 2000), built in 1871 by one of Heydrick's descendants, still stands nearby. (Photographer: Marilyn Dewald; caption: Mairy Jayn Woge)

Most villages in Mercer County started by a river or stream with a mill. Grist mills were usually first so farmers could grind their grain. Sawmills often followed when housing and other building activity increased as additional settlers arrived. Examples include Victor Mills (pictured) in West Middlesex and the grist mill in Wheatland (which still stands now, although the railroad tracks in the foreground of the photograph have been removed). Around 1798, Pine Grove (now Grove City) had Valentine Cunningham's mills, and Sheakleyville had William Byers's sawmill. Pine Township had James Graham's grist mill at Shaw's Dam on Wolf Creek in 1806. About 1831, Otter Creek Township had a sawmill built by the Carr brothers and a grist mill built by John Young and Adam Thompson. Mill Creek Township had Glenn Mill (built in 1815 and still standing in 1966 when photographed inside and out), Jefferson Township had Pearson Mill (pictured) at Lackawannock Crossing on the Mercer-Clarksville Road (formerly Plank Road), and Sharon had Clark's Mill (pictured). Thomas Clark purchased 200 acres along the Shenango River for growing grain for his mill. It was the most convenient grist mill for early Shenango Valley residents. After Clark died in 1875, the mill was kept open; and Frank H. Buhl bought the property in 1896 when he built the Sharon Steel Company. (Wheatland Mill photo: Vinson Skibo)

The 1896–1897 class of Fredonia Institute.

Chapter 1: The 1800s

TOWNSHIPS

In 1801, Mercer County had only four townships: Salem, Sandy Lake, Coolspring, and Neshannock. When creating Mercer County, the legislature also declared that a Court of Justice be established not greater than five miles from the center of the county. The population was 3,228 people.

Over the next few years, the boundaries of the county and the subdivision into townships changed several times until the county had fifteen townships. By 1805, the county court system and board of commissioners were in place with the county seat located in the borough of Mercer (which was at least in the center of the county from east to west). In the mid-1800s, more townships were created until the county had thirty-one. (As late as 1914, South Pymatuning was created bringing the count to thirty-two, but Hickory Township was absorbed by the creation of the city of Hermitage in 1976. As a result, now the county has thirty-one townships.)

Also during the 1800s, the borders of the county changed to give a strip of land to Crawford County (in 1808) and to help form Lawrence County (in 1849). In the latter change, Mercer County lost one-third of its population.

Coolspring Township formed one of the original four townships that composed Mercer County at its formation in 1800. In 1801, Coolspring was the name chosen to designate the southeast quarter of the new county. In 1802, the township was divided into the four townships known now, namely, Coolspring, Jackson, Fairview, and Lake. The name for Coolspring was taken from the fact that within its borders were a number of constantly flowing springs of cool and crystal waters. The rich bottom lands yield fine farming, and two streams cross the area: Otter Creek and Coolspring. Many early businesses were grist mills and sawmills, which took advantage of these waters. Coolspring Presbyterian was established in 1800 in Coolspring Township by Reverend Samual Tait (two years after Mercer County's first church was established in that township, the Old Salem Methodist Church).

East Lackawannock Township has been predominantly rural and residential. Its name is derived from the Delaware Indian name meaning "the place of the forks of the stream." Another source given for the name states that "Lac" is the French word for a "deep lake" found in its northern region, which was known to have been home to the Indian Chief Wannock and his tribe. Rocky terrain carpets its rolling hills and fertile valleys. The township was once the eastern part of Lackawannock Township, but was separated from Lackawannock Township in 1849 at the meandering Little Neshannock Creek line. In 1838, the Iron City Furnace was built by William Wallace on Bestwick Road. It operated until 1856 and was the last iron-works to survive in the township. Bog ore was used to manufacture the iron, but the iron was difficult to transport to market on dirt roads that were reduced to mud during the rainy season.

The first permanent settlers in ***Lackawannock Township*** were two families that came in 1798, the Youngs and Cozadds. The Youngs were well prepared to establish their new

VILLAGE OF GREENFIELD

By Genevieve Bartholomew

In southern Lackawannock Township lies the village of Greenfield. In 1820, Archelaus Wilkins cleared the spot that later became Greenfield. In the midst of this fine farming country, Wilkins built its first cabin.

A small frame school was built in 1834, near the village. D. C. Byers constructed a building that served as the first store and hotel. In the next forty years, small shops, a hotel, and a dry goods store were built. In 1865, a natural gas line was laid from Venango County into Shenango Valley and provided Greenfield with gas for cooking and lighting. About 1870, the village was laid out with roads, public alleys, and lots.

Greenfield eventually became the commercial center of the township. By 1900, this growing village had much to boast, including established doctors' offices that served the surrounding families.

In 1903, Lackawannock Township decided to build a two-room school in Greenfield. One room was for elementary students and the other for a three-year high school. The first class to graduate from this school, in 1907, included Glennie McCullough, Harry Thompson, Ernest Campbell, Charles Miller, Conrad Anderson, and Jess Sowers. The second—and last—graduating class, in 1908, included Ethel Bridgett, Minerva Stewart, Olive Somerville, Hayes Thompson, Harry Bartholomew, and Dan Phythyon. The two graduating classes of the school owe their education to Professor Mahle, the sole teacher and principal.

Also, at this time, the Byers brothers built large additions to their dry goods store and helped to establish the town even more. Priscilla Miller, the Byers's sister, built a home on what is now the Bartholomew parking lot. Rooms were rented out to Greenfield High School students from 1904 through 1910.

In 1921, Elmer Bartholomew purchased eighty acres of pastureland from Priscilla Miller. The first iron ore in Mercer County was taken from these eighty acres. Eventually, this land was cleared and cultivated with fruit trees.

In the 1800s, Greenfield was a busy village with more than two hundred people. Due to the closing of the several mines and businesses, the population has gradually decreased. Now, except for the continued traffic through the town from Route 318, Greenfield is a quiet village of only a few more than fifty people.

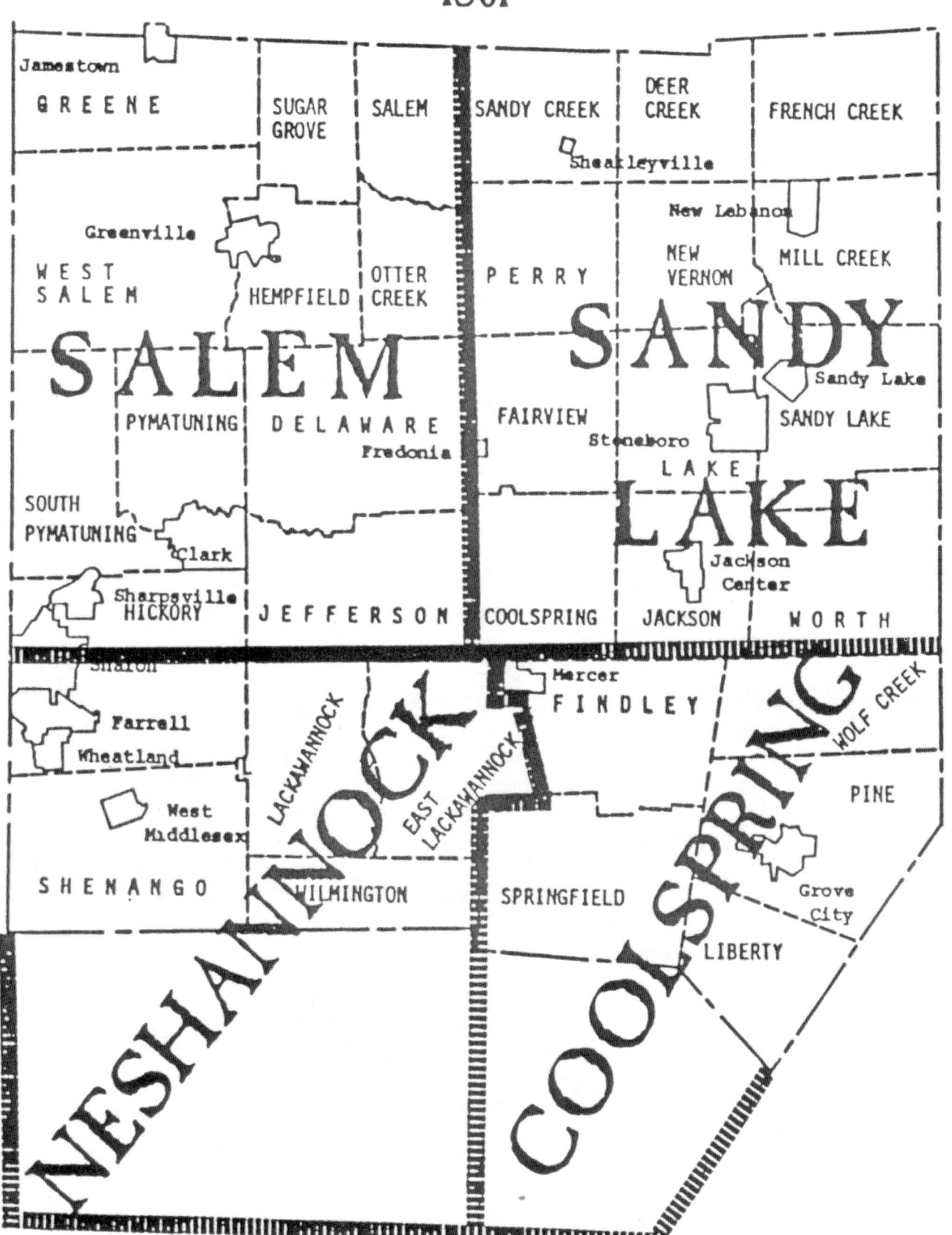

home. They came with domestic animals and the necessary tools to conquer the wilderness. The first birth was a son of James Young, Jonathan, on January 8, 1800. (Descendants of the Youngs now living in Mercer County include Paul Traposso and Helen Traposso Harrison.) The first wedding was between Betsy Cozadd and John Ritchie. The Cozadds, however, eventually faced poverty and soon left. Their land was taken over by the Yarian family. The Indians were, for the most part, friendly and helpful. They would stop at the settlers' homes for food and show their appreciation later by returning with venison. Gradually, Lackawannock Township became a first-rate farming area (and continues now to have a number of dairy farms). Early settlers soon realized their need for proper education. As a result, the township's first school was built of logs in 1805 on the Mercer-Pulaski Road. By 1834, school directors divided the township into eight portions, with about a three-mile distance between schools: Bell, Bethel, Blackstone, Frogtown, Greenfield, Love, Marquis, and Zuver. The community of Bethel was incorporated as a borough in 1872; however, it later surrendered its charter and became a part of the township again.

Although *Liberty Township* was not created until 1851, a village called North Liberty was laid out by James Foster in 1821 after the Mercer-Butler Turnpike (now Route 258) was established. The turnpike became the Main Street of the village. Forty lots were measured out, and until fairly recent time, none were added. The first house was built by Robert Waddell that year, occupied partly by a post office. Numerous other buildings followed

CEMETERIES

By Mairy Jayn Woge and Delber McKee

Oakwood Cemetery has been located in current Hermitage since 1876. The early burials there were from the West Hill in Sharon where pioneer William Budd had given land for cemeteries for the Baptist and Methodist Episcopal congregations. Dr. John Irvine of Sharon believed burying bodies in the borough was unhealthful for residents. He obtained an enactment from the Pennsylvania legislature that barred cemeteries from Sharon. Transferring remains from the West Hill in carts pulled by donkeys is said to have taken ten years. During that time, a small Presbyterian cemetery immediately east of Brooklyn Avenue was closed by authorities. Some persons who live in that neighborhood said they have found bones and parts of tombstones while digging in their yards.

The Mercer County Genealogical Society has a set of books listing the county cemeteries and the names of persons buried in each. Loretta DeSantis, coauthor of these books, states that Hermitage has twenty-five burial grounds, mostly related to denominations of churches or nationality groups. No other cities or boroughs in the Shenango Valley are known to have cemeteries.

Most townships and other county municipalities have cemeteries, however. In fact, now Mercer County has 187 (not including the Indian gravesites) according to the genealogical society's books. The county's oldest known gravestone of a settler is dated 1800 for Margaret Cunningham in the Presbyterian Cemetery (Pine Township).

closely, namely a store, hotel or tavern where travelers from Pittsburgh to Erie stayed overnight, cobbler's shop, tailor's shop, wagon shop, school, church, gun shop in William Foster's home, and homes for residents. Early on, a military company, known as the "Wolf Creek Rangers," was organized, met for drill training in a field near North Liberty, but disbanded by 1848. At Amsterdam (first called Yellow Horse), a village in the western part of the township, a blacksmith shop and a wagon shop were opened by Charlie Wingard about 1874. The Lawrence Grange Patrons of Husbandry was organized there about the same year. The township's population was 634.

Otter Creek Township is a rural community with some small home businesses. Its name is taken from a small stream that runs through the township. The first settler of the township was James Williamson, a Revolutionary War veteran who built a small cabin about 1797 on a farm (now A. Williamson Road area). Indians were numerous when Williamson made his settlement and for some years afterward. They belonged to the Cornplanter tribe and were friendly. Other early settlers were Thomas Jolly, who located on the land known as the McKean farm (on Route 358, now owned by the Baer family). A sawmill was located in the southern part of the township (at the end of Kitch and Bush roads) about 1831 by two brothers named Carr. In the same year, on the bank of the Little Shenango River, John Young and Adam Thompson built the township's first grist mill (on Log Cabin Road). (David Loreno now owns this property.) A stone quarry was worked on land owned by J. Dunham (now owned by Phillip Curtin) on Linn-Tyro Road. Stones from this quarry were used for many building foundations in the township.

Pymatuning was the name of an Indian who wandered near Clarksville (now Clark) during the time of early white settlement in the area. *Pymatuning Township* was named for him in 1802, the year the township was formed from part of Salem Township. Pioneers described the Indian Pymatuning as grumpy and inhospitable. Orvis Anderson (Sharpsville) said, when translated into English, Pymatuning means "crooked mouthed man," indicating Pymatuning either was dishonest or suffered from a defect that distorted his lips.

Robert Osborn documented his memories about the Freelands, early settlers in *Salem Township*. "I have been told by old relations of the Freelands that there was Indian blood involved. I am inclined to believe this, as I think about their physical features. All of them that I ever saw were tall, raw-boned, and had long pointed noses. The Freelands were not really hard working, unless there was work that really had to be done. They were very calm and not excitable. They were also very intelligent and shrewd—more inclined to work with their heads, instead of their hands. They were not fanatical about religion, but they had righteous principles. Anyone that came to their door was helped as best they could provide. Grandchildren were used the same as their own; and no matter how busy they were, they would always take time for anyone—regardless. You could be a 'bum' or unable to talk English, but you would still be helped. Many who visited could barely be understood, but they were welcomed as visitors. Charlie Freeland was the original Freeland in Salem Township, or in this part of the state, as far as I ever knew. . . . Freeland had quite a large family. His sons were John, Gary, Mike, and one who died of typhoid fever in Camp Oliver during the Civil War. . . . Charlie gave each of his sons a farm. The present home of Earl Campbell was given by Charlie to my Great-Granddad, John [who] . . . . was married twice. His first wife died from an operation for what was thought to be large tumor, but turned out to be a large baby. Both died. The surgery was performed in the parlor where Earl Campbell lives, today. John then married Elizabeth Reash, and they had Margaret, Saide, William, John, Mabel, and Elma. . . . [The younger] John married Lottie Roberts and had two sons and one daughter, Max, Edwin, and Melda. Today, there isn't a male around that carries the name Freeland. Edwin Freeland's son was the last."

Shenango Township took its name from an Indian name for black water or bull thistles, depending on whether it was derived from the Iroquoian or Algonquian languages. The Algonquian language was used by the Delawares who lived in the Shenango Valley under the supervision of the Iroquois confederation who claimed the land along the Shenango River in Mercer County.

Sugar Grove Township was established in 1856. However, in 1808, the first school in Sugar Grove Township was built at Kennard. Three years later, another school was erected at Riley's Corners.

Wilmington Township was formed in 1849, when Mercer County was reduced in size to allow the formation of Lawrence County. Nearly everyone in the township became "Republican" during the Civil War era because they were largely antislavery. Education received special attention from the township's beginning. Four school districts supported four one-room schools for grades one to eight: Ligo, Donaldson, Mercer (or Bend, Elliott, or Head), and Angell. Amish children attended school along with the others. In 1842, White Chapel Church was formed. It began as a Presbyterian Church, but drifted over time and became Methodist in 1880.

Hickory Township *(by Mairy Jayn Woge).* When Hickory Township was formed in 1832, from equal parts of Pymatuning and Shenango Townships, it contained almost thirty-nine square miles, including the sites of Sharon, Farrell, Sharpsville, Wheatland, and part of Bethel. The organization of the villages and boroughs and annexations over the ensuing years trimmed ten miles from the township.

The first settler in Hickory Township was Thomas Canon in about 1796. Henry Hoagland farmed on the west side of the township (now known as Patagonia) in 1798. The township's first school was built by Hoagland and his neighbor, Daniel Hull, in 1800 on land belonging to Hoagland along North Water Avenue. The school, built of logs, was in Pymatuning Township until Hickory Township was formed. An addition was added to the school before 1815. Classes were conducted at a Hoagland school in Patagonia until the beginning of World War I.

Hickory Township was a farm community until the 1830s when Isaac Patterson found coal cropping from a slope on his property there. When Joel Curtis, a Mercer businessman, heard about the discovery, he bought the Patterson farm. From 1835 until his death, Curtis was involved in coal mining in Hickory Township and Sharon.

To obtain coal for the mills, the Sharon & Greenfield narrow-gauge railway was built from Sharon Iron to the west side of Christy Road in Hickory Township where the company had opened a successful mine. General James Pierce's Sharpsville-Wilmington Railroad, also narrow gauge, transported coal to Pierce mills in Sharpsville from mines at New Virginia, Neshannock, and Bethel.

During the coal boom in Hickory Township, in the 1870s and 1880s, the population of the township was between 5,900 and 7,700. After industries opened in all the communities in the Valley, the Hickory miners got jobs there and either moved or commuted. The coal that could be reached by the equipment that was available at the time was exhausted by 1920.

Pine Township. A division of old Wolf Creek Township in 1851, dvided into three parts at the extreme southeastern corner of Mercer County, created a central portion called Pine Grove, lying between the new Wolf Creek Township on the north and newly formed Liberty Township on the south. The township of Pine Grove (now Pine) was so named from a small cluster of pine trees that stood on a hill just west of the settlement of Pine Grove (now Grove City).

Early in 1796, John Sutherland procured 400 acres of land by "settlers rights." He was the first known pioneer of the township, who sold 200 acres of land to John Perry, a Revolutionary War veteran, who cleared the land and built a cabin. Adjacent to the Sutherland tract, another 400 acres was settled by Philip Hoon about the same time. John White settled about 1800; David, Matthew, and son Robert McDowell about 1798 in Cranberry Plain; William Buchanan about 1797 with 400 acres; James Glenn on a farm in the western part of the township in 1798; John Miller on 150 acres with brother James; and William Daugherty, another Revolutionary War veteran, on a 400-acre tract about 1800.

In 1798, Ephraim and James Rose settled in the northwestern part of the township. Adjacent to the Rose tract was a small farm settled by Benjamin Woods. Thomas Dunlap came from Ireland and in 1826, with son John, came to the northern part of Pine Township. John McConnell, William McBride, John Cochran, and the Gibsons were also early settlers.

Interesting landmarks are the early mills. Probably the first one was built in 1806 by James Graham, who having settled here in 1798 was the brother-in-law of Valentine Cunningham. This grist mill on Shaw's Dam located on Wolf Creek supplied the water necessary to power the motor operating the millstones that ground the grain. Shaw's Dam was also the site of a sawmill built in 1812 by Robert Moore. The millwright in charge was James McCoy. William Perry built the second sawmill in 1842 for J. T. Hurst and later operated by J. C. Shaw located near Graham's grist mill. The capacity of this mill was something over 100,000 feet yearly because the hemlock timber was of fine quality, straight, and free from knots. This activity generated considerable income at the time, not only for the mill, but the landowner as well. (The industrial center at Shaw's Dam and growing settlement known as Hallville (Slabtown) is located off Route 173 north on Route 208 toward Barkeyville.) Third Island, located upstream from Shaw's Dam, was accessible by boat for swimming and picnickers. Hallville not only included the grist mill and

This recruiting notice for the War of 1812 was taken from a copy of the WESTERN PRESS dated — Mercer, Pa., Tuesday, November 2, 1813.

(Source: **Mercer Sesquicentennial 1803–1953**)

ATTENTION MEN OF COURAGE

A recruiting rendezvous is now open in Mercer for the 42 Regt. U. S. inf'y where able bodied men of patriotism, courage and enterprise can have an opportunity of entering the service of their country — hasten, I say hasten: or the laurels will be all Won ere you reach the soil in which they grow. The terms are truly inviting. To each man will be given, a bounty of **Forty Dollars,** eight dollars per month and abundant supply of good and handsome clothing with everything necessary for his subsistence, What more could be wished for? Yet in addition to the above every soldier who shall receive a regular discharge shall at the time of receiving such discharge be entitled to receive three Months extra pay and a farm of 160 acre of land. Hasten then, to reap your share of the laurels in the honorable cause of defending those sacred rights which have been purchased, secured, and handed to you by your fathers under the protection of divine providence.

John Junkin, capt.
42nd regt. U.S. infantry
Mercer, Oct. 18.

ANNA GARRETT
By Gail Habbyshaw

Anna Bevan Pearson Garrett conducted a private school in the early 1800s in Mercer. She was admired as an intelligent woman and a gifted teacher who instilled in her students a lifelong love for reading. Garrett was born in Darby, Pennsylvania, in 1774, a daughter of John Pearson and his first wife, Anne Bevan.

Pearson, a Revolutionary War veteran, arrived in Mercer in 1803, with one son. The twosome returned home with such impressive reports that the Pearson family decided in 1806 to relocate to Mercer. Among the family members who moved were two more sons and Anna Bevan Pearson Garrett, their widowed sister, and her two children.

Garrett's school was located in her home, a two-story log structure on North Pitt Street. Although no existing documentation states that Garrett's school was only for girls, the fact that her curriculum focused on sewing, embroidery, and such skills in addition to the ordinary subjects of education implies she aimed her efforts at young women. Garrett died at age eighty-two in 1856.

Many children in Mercer and the surrounding area were among Garrett's students. One student, Mary Brown (Norton) recalled when she was snowbound at the school by a severe winter storm in 1817. She was eight years old, and her brother had to carry her home from Garrett's house on his back. She was unable to return to school for six weeks because the snow fell so heavily during that time.

sawmill, but also a shoe shop, opened in 1874 by the Miller brothers who also had a tannery. The first store was opened by Hiram McCoy in 1866. The only blacksmith shop was opened by Henry McCutcheon. Hallville also had a hotel, bar, and shoe repair shop.

At the railroad station called Reed, grist and saw milling became the nucleus of a little settlement founded by Thomas McCoy, now known as the McCoytown area.

The population of Pine Township in 1870 was 1,235 residents.

Before 1888, salt, quarrying of building stone, and brick clay were found throughout the township and looked promising as marketable industries along with the coal, timber, and the agricultural products of the area. Good quality coal was mined in the township quite early due to the fact it burned readily. Veins averaged three to four feet in thickness and the seams increased as one progressed in a northerly direction from Liberty Township. These mines were the main source of employment in the early years. Coal was transported from the area by the Shenango & Allegheny Railway and later by the Beaver & Lake Erie Railroad.

In the Perry neighborhood, James White taught in a schoolhouse, which was built of round logs about 1805. In the Rose and McDowell neighborhood, an octagon schoolhouse was built around 1834 after the law was passed establishing free schools. James Tidball taught in this schoolhouse for the first two months. Thirteen one-room schools in Pine Township from the period of 1800 through 1960 included Chestnut Ridge, Cranberry, Galloway, Gregg, Hallville, Hemlock, Kerr, McConnell, McCoytown, Pinch-a-Long, Pine Top, Sutherland, and Whitaker. In 1877, ten schools in Pine Township averaged an enrollment of 356 school children and the value of school property was $6,000.

The first church in the township was built of pine logs on the Moore farm near Cranberry School in the western part of the township about 1801 by the Presbyterians. The first preacher was Reverend William Woods, the fourth preacher in Mercer County. A second church was built in 1806 from a split of the congregation. The old cemetery stands near the spot on the Glenn estate of 1877. The third church in the vicinity was a brick structure near the site of the old ones called "Center Church" built in 1837 and 1838 costing $1,800. A Methodist church was built on a hill above Shaw's Mill about 1842. The Presbyterians built another church at the northeastern part of Pine Township sometime between 1850 and 1855.

Worth Township *(by Idella McConnell and Lucille Eagles)*. The Henderson family settled in Worth Township around 1795. They have owned many businesses in Worth Township throughout the years. The village at the intersection of Route 965 and Hendersonville Road is now called Henderson (formerly Hendersonville). Earl Henderson was born in 1892 and graduated from Grove City College, the University of Pennsylvania, and the University of Minnesota. He took his postgraduate work in surgery at the Mayo Clinic. As a doctor, he was on the board at George Junior Republic and Grove City College. His son Robert also became a surgeon, at Jamison Hospital, and his other son Jon became a judge in Lawrence County. Carroll Henderson, a brother of Earl, was born in 1894 and also graduated from Grove City College. After also finishing at the University of Pittsburgh, he served in France as a Second Lieutenant in World War I. Another brother, Roy, operated the Henderson Clover Farm Store.

The Hendersonville United Methodist Church is on Route 965. The original congregation was organized and held meetings in the home of Robert Henderson. A log schoolhouse was erected in 1812 and the services were held there as early as 1833 and perhaps before that. The first church building was erected in 1839 and in 1871 was sold for $33.75 to make up a total of $2,266.56 to make possible the building of a new church on the same site of the same year. A church parsonage was built in 1839.

The Irwin Presbyterian Church was organized as Cumberland Presbyterian Church in 1838. At first, the congregation met in homes, and then land was purchased across from the present location. In 1868,

The report card of Lulu Bower (Delaware Township) from the Fredonia Institute, 1897. (Contributor: Autumn Buxton)

37

land was purchased for the present structure, which was also erected in 1868 at a cost between $2,000 and $3,500. In 1890 some members of the Amity Presbyterian Church met in the union hall (now the Grange hall) to form a new congregation, then known as the Rehobeth Presbyterian Church. Twelve families made up the membership of sixty-one members. A church was soon built across the street from the Wesleyan Methodist Church in Millbrook in 1892 and became known as the Millbrook Presbyterian Church.

The Millbrook Schoefield United Methodist Church, on Route 173, in the early 1800s was called Fairview. In 1898, the church building became unsafe so the congregation built a new building. The timber for the new church came from Sandy Lake by horse and wagon. Behind the church was a open-front building where the horses could be sheltered on Sunday morning, out of the weather. There was a millstone out front that the ladies could step out of the buggy and not get their shoes or the hems of their dresses dirty. To heat the church, the men dug out a place under the floor in the middle of the church to put the furnace, which had a large grate from which the heat rose. Their only source of light for the church was the oil lamps that hung from the ceiling. (About 1930, electricity was installed.)

Born in 1899, Samual D. Kilgore lived most of his life on the same farm on which he grew up. His family goes back several generations in the area with his great grandfather, John J. Kilgore, who was outstanding in public offices including the legislature. The village Kilgore was named for John J.

Worth Township had seven one-room schools: Carmichael, Henderson, Lamb, Millbrook, Perrine, St. John, and St. Paul. County records dating back to 1861 show that six months of school were taught. The two male teachers were paid $22 monthly while the twelve female teachers were pay $15.71 monthly. The monthly cost of teaching each student was $42. Elizabeth McFarland Northcote, of a family of four boys and three girls said, however, they learned their ABCs in the Fairview Meeting House. (The local schools were consolidated into the newly formed Lakeview School District in 1955.)

Municipalities

Along with the townships, several villages, boroughs, and cities developed in the 1800s:

Clark *(by Clyde Moffett).* The borough of Clark, originally known as Clarksville, lay along the banks of the Shenango River, about midway between Sharon and Greenville. The original site is now partially inundated. Prior to 1800 the area was a primeval forest teeming with game such as deer, raccoon, wolves, and rabbits. The Shenango River contained fish of many species, including catfish that could grow as large as forty pounds. Near the area of what would become Clarksville was a small settlement of Indians of the Seneca tribe who had established a more or less permanent village of natives known as the Cornplanters.

After Samuel Clark brought his family to the area in 1804, the next arrival seems to have been Samuel Koonce who came in 1808. Other settlers soon came to the little community, including John and William Fruit in 1811. A Methodist Church was organized in 1837. In 1829, Samuel Clark made the first village plat and sold forty-nine lots. In 1832, a post office was established and John Fruit became the first postmaster.

The early 1800s was an era of canal building and the Shenango Valley saw the construction of the Erie Extension Canal which began operations in 1844. This was a great impetus to the growth and development of Clarksville and the whole Valley. The waterway was important to the growing iron industry of western Pennsylvania. Clarksville became a hub of activity with businesses flourishing along the canal.

WILLIAM LEVER (GREENVILLE)

By Woodrow Dixon (grandson)

William Lever followed his older brother Charles to Greenville in 1887. William brought his wife Mary Ann (Cowley) and their three small sons with him to escape the poor conditions of Swindon, England. While living in the company house of the Carnegie Steel Mill, Mrs. Lever became so homesick she was ready to return to England, but in the meantime her mother and sister Edith had sold the home and sailed for the United States where they joined the Levers. William and Charles worked in several of the steel mills located in the Greenville area before 1900. William listed "working as a puddler for the Kimberly Mills" as his occupation. At that time, Greenville boasted several other mills and foundries that have disappeared along with a woolen mill where the Lever boys first found employment.

William "Robert," Sidney, and George came to Greenville with their parents while Edith, John "Wesley," Frank, and Sara were all born in the family home on Lever Street. The Levers lived in an area of Greenville where many Welsh and English families settled before 1900, on the west hill near Clarksville and Homer streets (and Lever Street).

Robert, Sid, and Frank later moved to California. George died young from an accident. Edith, Wesley, and Sara remained in Greenville. William died in 1936 and Mary Ann in 1937, both in their home on Lever Street.

Helen H. Hall, in her 1976 Bicentennial publication of Clarksville's history, described the fledgling town as follows: "Merchandise was shipped and received by way of the canal which had a loading dock behind the house last occupied by the Cubbisons. There was at least one more dock. It was behind the McKnight house. . . . William Fruit who was an influential promoter of the canal, shipped coal from his mines; farmers brought grain and livestock. Passengers there were on the packets, some bent on shopping in the town stores, some merely sightseers. The town resounded with the shouts of the drivers and the braying of their mules. Clarksville must have been lively indeed. In 1848 the town was incorporated into a borough."

But Clarksville's booming economy as a major hub on the Erie Extension Canal came to an abrupt end in 1871 with the building of a railroad a mile west of the town. Hall recalled the abandoning of the canal as a disaster. Referring to the busy canal days as Clarksville's time of glory and the subsequent coming of the railroad which ended the canal's role as a highway of commerce and Clarksville's role as a shipping and receiving point in that commerce, the residents of the little town were heard "mournfully . . . recounting to children and grandchildren that Clarksville had been the largest town between Erie and Pittsburgh." This statement is confirmed by old residents of the Valley. But with the abandoning of the canal in 1871, hard times fell upon the community. The coming of the railroad "seemed to preclude any hope of seeing the town becoming the dreamed of great city." So it declined but it never became a ghost town. According to

Another family that helped put Greenville on the map was the Biglers. The Bigler brothers made history by being the first to become governors of two states, Pennsylvania (William) and California (John), simultaneously (from 1852 until 1855). Their parents' house (pictured with Mae Beringer, in 1992) still stands in Delaware Township about three miles outside of Greenville. Nearby are the graves of the parents, John (died in 1827) and Susan (died in 1851).

Phyliss Parshall and Janet Moats in *Clarksville/Clarke: Past to Present 1848–1998*, "Hotels, several general stores, a butcher shop, blacksmiths and barbers, not affected by the decline of the canal, were mainstays of the town's business district."

Fredonia. The name Fredonia means "free donation." The town took this name because of the two donation tracts that William Simmons purchased for the town. Friends of this Delaware man wished to name it Simmonsville in honor of his generosity, but he refused this praise. Around the year 1834, at the center of Mercer County, Simmons built a country store, which also served as a makeshift post office. He accepted and transferred mail to residents prior to the institution of the first post office in 1870.

Within two years of each other, the citizens of Fredonia erected two churches: Fredonia Methodist and Fredonia United Presbyterian in 1873 and 1875, respectively. The Methodist church received a great honor when Andrew Carnegie donated an organ to the congregation.

Greenville *(by Gwen Lininger)*. Situated along the Shenango and Little Shenango Rivers is the community of Greenville. The first settlers came around 1796 or 1797. The first plot of land was auctioned off to Tobias Shank, who built a large two-story log structure known as "Shank's Tavern." Undoubtedly, Shank's venture proved to be very advantageous in the wilderness country, providing food and rest for weary travelers and as a way station for transportation. The town was on the "road from the lake to the city," the "lake" being Lake Erie and Warren, Ohio as the "city." A canal that traversed five counties gave people a new way to travel and transport goods. The waterway was known as the Erie Extension Canal. In 1826 or 1828 the town became "West Greenville."

A prominent businessman and medical doctor, Daniel Berry Packard, influenced the establishment of West Greenville. In fact, it was Packard's nephew, J. Randall, who eventually petitioned and successfully dropped the suffix, "West," resulting in the name of "Greenville." In 1858, Packard and Randall built a large brick building in the middle of Greenville, known as "Packard Commercial Block," which is still in use today. Several other businesses in Greenville were owned, operated, or leased by members of the Packard family. Randall also was responsible for sponsoring a public park, much of which is now part of Riverside Park. (Baseball and softball are still played on Packard's fields.)

Founded in 1885, the Pearce Woolen Mill was best known throughout the Eastern States for fine woolen blankets. The rights of production to the Pearce blankets were obtained by a man named Rich. (His firm is still operating; fine Woolrich products are well known nationwide.)

Sheakleyville. As Mary McDowell Vermeire remembers the history, "In the early 1800s it was called Culbertson, then Georgetown. Around 1850 it was named Exchangeville as the stage coach stopped there to exchange horses and drivers on old Route 19 going from Pittsburgh to Erie."

Stoneboro *(by Frederick Houser).* In Sandy Lake Township after the community of Liberia, peopled predominantly by former slaves, disbanded, ownership of the land changed several times until it was sold in the 1850s to John F. Hogue and William Shields. The men had purchased the land knowing about geological surveys that revealed three coal seams. The uppermost of the seams was four feet thick.

About the same time, Amasa Stone, Jr. (president of the Cleveland, Painesville, & Ashtabula Railroad) began looking for a source of coal. He had authorized conversion of one of the steam locomotives to burn coal due to the money it would save over wood. In 1863, the Cleveland, Painesville, & Ashtabula incorporated the Mercer Iron and Coal Company. Mercer Iron and Coal was authorized to hold five thousand acres of mineral lands in Mercer and Venango Counties and planned to connect with the Jamestown & Franklin Railroad.

The Jamestown & Franklin was leased to the Cleveland, Painesville, & Ashtabula in 1864, just as the first steps were being taken to open Mercer Iron and Coal Mine No. 1 near the top of what would soon be Franklin Street in Stoneboro. Former U.S. Secretary of War P. H. Watson supervised the opening. (He had moved to this area in 1864 because ill health forced him to seek an outdoor occupation away from wartime Washington.) During these early stages, coal was removed from the mine by local teamsters and sold for up to $15 per ton that winter. Watson remained mine supervisor for the year it took Mine No. 1 to reach full production.

In 1865 the Jamestown & Franklin reached Mine No. 1. Five days later, the first five carloads of coal were shipped via this new railroad. For the next year 15,000 tons of coal were moved, adding up to 650,000 tons over the next ten years. Mercer Iron and Coal then concentrated on exploiting its other two thousand acres. During 1865, the company's surveyor laid out the site for a new community. Since Amasa Stone was the president of both the railroad and the mining company, the new town was named after him. With the signatures of 103 local residents, the Mercer County Court ordered that the Borough of Stoneboro be incorporated on August 25, 1866.

In 1867, Colonel Henry B. Blood succeeded P. H. Watson as station agent for the Jamestown & Franklin. (He was one of many Civil War veterans who came to Stoneboro as merchants, managers, and miners.) Blood was named the first burgess (mayor). First council members were F. M. Finney, J. Cornwell, A. S. Throop, Samuel Custer, and J. C. Nolan. Blood was also made the town's first postmaster a year later. The post office opened in 1868, the same year the community's two-room schoolhouse was built. Another veteran, John P. Hines, came to Stoneboro in 1871 to purchase an existing drug store that he and his descendents operated for nearly a century. He also became postmaster in 1885 and was associated with other business enterprises in the community.

The Methodist Episcopal Church, organized in 1869, initially met in Stoneboro's two-room schoolhouse as did other new congregations when they came into existence. (The site of the Stoneboro United Methodist Church now, at the corner of Lake and Chestnut

Streets, was donated to its Methodist Episcopal predecessor by the Mercer Iron and Coal Company in 1873, and the building was completed in 1874. (The original structure has been enlarged and rebuilt several times; the most recent expansion took place in 1991.)

Stoneboro has always had several tourist attractions, often related to the lovely Sandy Lake. Foremost is the Stoneboro Fair, started in 1868 and continuing even now. Other attractions had their heyday, but did not survive. The "Picnic House" is shown on the 1873 map of the community. It was located just north of John Gumfory's Lake House, then one of the area's best-known hotels with a reputable dining hall and ballrooms. These attractions were located next to the Jamestown & Franklin Railroad station. (The station was essential until the 1920s, when the automobile was fulfilling the function of transportation.)

The Stoneboro Presbyterian Church was organized in 1878 with a lot at the corner of Franklin and Linden Streets donated to the congregation by Jeremiah Bonner. Its first building was completed there in 1883 and expanded in 1909. In 1923, following a community union Thanksgiving service, the structure and its contents were completely

MARQUIS DE LAFAYETTE IN MERCER

By William Philson

In 1776, the Marquis de Lafayette arrived in America and volunteered his services to the new United States. Eventually, he was assigned as an aide to General George Washington. Lafayette suffered through the winter at Valley Forge with Washington, was wounded at the Battle of Brandywine, and became instrumental in convincing the French to join the American cause.

In 1824, the federal government invited the Marquis de Lafayette to tour the United States. Taking thirteen months, Lafayette's tour included traveling through western Pennsylvania during the late spring of 1825. His entourage left Pittsburgh for Butler. In Butler, a committee of two was appointed to accompany the French general to Mercer.

On June 2, 1825, Lafayette arrived in Mercer to the sounds of the stagecoach horn and a shotgun salute from Dr. James Magoffin. As he had inspired patriotic fervor everywhere on his trip, Lafayette was enthusiastically welcomed in Mercer. The Marquis stayed at the Hackney Tavern at the corner of North Diamond and Pitt Streets in room twelve on the second floor.

Lafayette was especially interested in Mercer, as it was named after a man he knew of so well, but had never met. Joseph Smith was the master of ceremonies at the reception and introduced the Marquis to the people of the area. Everyone was anxious to meet the Marquis, and he was cordial to all.

A boy at the time of Lafayette's visit, eighty-three-year-old John Bingham reported in the Mercer Dispatch in 1898 that he was one of many school children who greeted the Marquis by passing in review. Each child wore a white ribbon with the word "welcome" printed on it. Not satisfied to bow as he passed, Bingham offered his hand to Lafayette. The general shook the boy's hand and laid his hand on the boy's head.

destroyed by fire. The sandstone building that replaced it was dedicated in 1926. The congregation is today affiliated with the United Presbyterian Church.

In 1879 St. Paul's Primitive Methodist Church was organized and then the so-called "Little Jim" Church on Oak Street was built in 1881. This structure was subsequently used by the Church of God after the Primitive Methodist congregation disbanded. The Stoneboro First Church of God moved to Stoneboro from near Hendersonville in the 1890s and purchased the "Little Jim" building. (It continued to use the building until the congregation completed its new building on Beech Street in 1912. In the 1960s, this congregation was reorganized as the Lakeview Church of God and built a new church on Route 62 across from Lakeview High School. Its original building was then converted into apartments.)

On June 2, 1890, Stoneboro's first amusement park opened. George P. Griffith was the owner of Lake Side Park, located on the northwest corner of Sandy Lake. Visitors were amused by performances by prominent entertainers at the pavilion and boat races on the lake. A "Moonlight Party" was held in July and attracted eight hundred people arriving on

---

After the reception, Lafayette was escorted across the street to meet some of the women of Mercer. Several callers, who had fought in the Revolution, followed and spoke to Lafayette. One older gentleman was smoking an old pipe with a "rather loud" odor and apologized by saying, "I suppose gentlemen in France smoke finely flavored cigars and not pipes." Lafayette reportedly replied quickly, "Gentlemen in France never smoke, sir."

The people in attendance would have stayed until daybreak as Lafayette was apparently too polite to take his leave. Major Hackney took pity on the fatiguing Marquis and appeared in the doorway of the hotel, holding candles aloft in his hands. At the "delicate hint" the townspeople withdrew and the travelers retired. Early the next morning, the stagecoach driver sounded his horn, and the sixty-eight-year-old Lafayette left Mercer for Meadville and Erie.

Aaron Hackney built and ran the Hackney House for many years. It became the American House and later the Hotel Humes. The bedroom of Lafayette became a well-known historic room. An unverified story tells that the bed was thrown out the window to save it from a fire in the 1840s and a leg was broken. The bed was definitely removed in 1916, again saved from the fire that destroyed the Humes. George Humes bought the Reznor Hotel at the south corner of West Market Street and Erie, renaming it the New Hotel Humes.

The Lafayette bed remained in the hotel until the furniture was auctioned in 1964. Dr. Karl Blake (Mercer) bought the bed and had it restored. He lent the bed to the Mercer County Bicentennial Commission and the Mercer County Historical Society for display. Two chairs handmade by John Sloss at his Mercer chair factory in the early 1800s and an Oriental rug that once adorned the office of Judge Leo McKay were also displayed for the Bicentennial.

special trains. Griffith had purchased a steam launch to shuttle patrons from the south shore railroad station to his park. The Jamestown & Franklin Railroad was later extended around the head of the lake so excursion trains could deliver their passengers directly to Lake Side Park. Although the park never saw 1900, the tracks leading into it are still identifiable.

In 1877 John Kelly opened a bakery, which he continued to run until 1910. In that same house at the corner of Franklin and Walnut Streets, he set up his justice of the peace office when appointed to that position in 1890 and continued to serve in that capacity until his death in 1944. (He was 94 then and had just received a new commission after holding the office for nearly fifty-five years.)

POSTAL SERVICE

According to a May 12, 1939, article in *The Mercer Dispatch and Republican*, "The early settlers in Mercer county had no mail service until 1801 when a through route was established between Erie and Pittsburgh, via Meadville and Franklin, to operate once a week. Volunteer messengers carried mail from Meadville into Mercer county until 1805. On July 1, that year, a post office was established in Mercer, with Cunningham S. Semple as the first postmaster. For 15 years this was the only post office in the county.

"In 1806, the mail route between Erie and Pittsburgh was changed to pass through Mercer. It was still but once a week service. Later it reached such proportions that two horses were employed, one for the postman, the other for the mail. Stage coaches came next, carrying both passengers and mail."

NEWSPAPERS
By Teresa Spatara

Greenville's newspapers survive in the *Record-Argus* now (see Chapter 7), early Sharon papers contributed to *The Herald* of today (see Chapter 9), and several communities' papers consolidated to form the *Allied News* in the Grove City area (see Chapter 8).

Several other newspapers helped to inform people of the events of the various communities although they did not last throughout the past two centuries. Probably the most significant of these was the *Sharpsville Advertiser*, which Walter Pierce (Sharpsville) founded in 1870. Printed in the office of the *Sharon Times*, it started as an avenue for the

---

POWER OF NEWSPAPER EDITORS
By Teresa Spatara

Early in the 1800s, a small-town newspaper editor had the power to describe events as he saw them and to influence public thought. He had no competition from metropolitan papers or the electronic media in those days, so he could be biased toward his favorite party. As a result, political papers started. Each party that had a point of view published its own paper. Usually, these papers existed until the end of a particular political campaign and then sold out or quit operating. Political and private causes, ranging from the support or opposition of slavery to the temperance movement, were espoused in such special publications as *The Whig*, *The Republican*, or *The Democrat*. Mercer County had its share of these papers.

advertising of Sharpsville businessmen and expanded to a four-page, eight-column newspaper, which later was printed in the offices of the *Greenville Advance*.

Pierce bought the *Signal*, which William McKnight had started in Mercer just a few months earlier. He kept it only a short time, then organized the Sharpsville Printing Co. and hired P. J. Bartleson from the *Greenville Argus* as editor.

Pierce published his first edition under the new Sharpsville firm in 1871. The paper did well and copies of the *Sharpsville Advertiser* printed in the early 1900s now appear on the walls of the Veterans of Foreign Wars building in Sharpsville.

Another paper in Sharpsville, founded in 1887 by M. W. Thompson and S. W. Hazen, was the *Sharpsville Times*, which in its short existence, devoted itself to local and personal news.

D. L. Calkins and his wife were publisher and editor of the *Jamestown Sun*, which they started in 1873 in Jamestown. But that paper lasted only for six years.

F. S. and F. A. Alden left Cleveland in 1870 to start another newspaper, the *Jamestown Era*, which they published until 1874. Then they leased it to DeWitt & Nichols who changed its name to the *Jamestown Democrat* and published it for one year. At that time, F. A. Alden took over and published the paper as the *Jamestown Sentinel*. Alden sold his interest in the paper to F. W. McCoy and J. B. Robinson, both of Sheakleyville, who ran it successfully for a number of years.

Other papers that came and went in Mercer County were the *Sandy Lake News* and the *Lake Local*, both in Sandy Lake. The former was established as an anti-alcohol publication and circulated well among the temperance community. The *Lake Local* circulated for many years under the ownership of W. R. Eckles. Another small paper that circulated in the early 1900s was *The Searchlight*, published by the Searchlight Club of Journalism of Fredonia.

Early Greenville newspapers. In addition to the early newspapers that led to the *Record-Argus*, which is now published in Greenville, a variety of newspapers were published there during the 1800s. The first was the *West Greenville Gazette*, a four-column, nonpartisan sheet started in 1830 when Richard Hill brought his portable press to Greenville. (The community then was known as West Greenville, and the "West" prefix remained until the Civil War era.) A great controversy was in progress at that time and Hill joined the anti-Masonic group, continuing his publication for three years. Hard times came and Hill discontinued his paper.

But that time was important in the economic development of Greenville because the Erie Extension Canal was being built through the town. Seeing a newspaper as a necessity, Hill returned and started another newspaper which he called the *Visitor*, publishing it for a while as a Whig advocate. However, when the Jacksonian doctrine gained power, Hill changed his allegiance to that side and continued to publish the paper for a few more years.

The *Greenville Progress* was started as a five-column daily in 1877 by William Orr Jr., proprietor and editor. It was the first and only daily issued in Greenville then. A month later, the *Weekly Progress* was started as an offshoot of the daily. It was issued by Yeakel and Orr as a Jeffersonian Democratic paper, advocating local self-government and honesty in office. The paper started during the great labor strike of 1877. Yeakel and Orr ran the paper for three months. Orr retired in November 1877 and A. D. Gillespie and Yeakel, publisher, took over the management. They announced that the existence of two Republican papers in Greenville was reason for a Democratic publication. Gillespie became sole owner in 1889 when Yeakel retired. Gillespie employed W. F. Harpst as foreman of the office. Harpst and Frank C. Huling bought the paper from Gillespie in 1891. They owned, managed, and edited the paper, enlarging it to a nine-column folio. The *Progress* was recognized as one of the best newspapers in the county. Before 1898, the *Progress* occupied the Goodwin Building at the corner of Main and North Race Streets. The Progress Building, which still stands, was erected on Main Street at North Water Street by Harpst. That site was used until 1909 when later owners Moser and Cutler moved the business to the Vaughn block on Canal Street.

(Fred D. Moser and John D. Cutler acquired the paper from Harpst in 1907 and operated as partners until 1921 when Moser bought Cutler's interest. Moser always had been a Democrat. Born in Greenville in 1874, he attended the local public schools and graduated from Thiel College. He was appointed Greenville postmaster during the Franklin Roosevelt administration, serving until 1951. Moser resigned as editor of the newspaper when he became postmaster, saying that "it was not feasible to run a business you cannot devote your full time to." After Moser stepped down as publisher, his son, Marvin, took over the role and remained until 1941 when Mr. and Mrs. A. Leroy "Spike" Johnson took over the paper. Johnson, a former *Record-Argus* composing room employee, and his wife published the *Progress* until 1946 when fire destroyed the plant. Johnson always took pride in the fact that, throughout World War II, he provided free copies of the *Progress* to all Greenville servicemen. After the fire, the company relocated at 62 Clinton Street and became a job shop operation. In 1967, Johnson turned the business over to his son-in-law Victor Jones and to William Carley, another one-time *Record-Argus* printer. Jones and Carley both retired in August of 1989.)

D. B. Robbins founded the *Shenango Valley News* in 1882 and sold it to William H. H. Dumars in the summer of that year. In the gubernatorial election of 1882 it advocated the cause of the Independent wing of the Republican party and became one of the party's staunchest local advocates.

Austin H. Robbins established the *Independent of Greenville* in 1885 as a four-column quarto, issued weekly at fifty cents a year. Robbins (Delaware Township) had learned his trade in the *Record-Argus* office and assisted his brother in establishing the *Shenango Valley News* in 1882.

Early Sharon newspapers. A. Walter (Dude) McDowell (later publisher and chairman of the board of *The Herald*) developed an interest in printing early when he and his brother, William C. (later treasurer of *The Herald*) published a junior journal, *The Sharon Star* from 1892 to 1898. It had a paid circulation of eight hundred copies a week. (Later McDowell also became known as a cartoonist for several metropolitan newspapers.)

A competitor with *The Sharon Star* was *The Sharon Hustler*, published by Fred Service and Ralph Heilman. Service later became a lawyer and a state senator. Heilman later went into medical practice and was supreme medical examiner of Protected Home Circle. When they published the July 4, 1882, edition of the paper, Service was 16 years old, and Heilman, 12. They sold their paper for a penny a copy or fifty cents a year. They served as publishers-reporters-newsboys who also were editors and advertising solicitors,

LEGEND OF HELL'S HOLLOW
By Cinda S. Wilpula

Circulating since the mysterious disappearance of an Indian, Harthegig, has been the popular folktale known as the Legend of Hell's Hollow. Like any other legend, several variations have spiraled from this mystery. The story has had humorous renditions, romanticized versions, and different characters as the "real murderer" of Harthegig. One Mercer County resident, F. F. Yarian, born in 1872, recounted a story he had heard in his childhood days about a murder that allegedly took place in the ravine two miles west of Mercer, known as Hell's Hollow. A white man supposedly murdered an Indian, and the Indian's spirit could not rest and would return to haunt the scene of the crime.

Another account of the legend was researched from the 1888 History of Mercer County. In this version from the family history of Samuel Pew (Findley Township), the legend receives a detailed description of the events preceding the disappearance of Harthegig. A murder is suspected when a man named John Johnston discovers a large human skeleton near Yankee Ridge (which is up the hill from Hell's Hollow) about nine years after Harthegig's disappearance. This rendition of the legend alludes to a possible murder suspect, an eccentric James Jeffers. Evidence to support this version is given in yet another tale of deadly encounter between Jeffers and the Indians.

Like other folktales, the legend's historical objectivity is not important compared to keeping the legend alive. Accepted by local residents as historical in origin, although not verifiable, the Legend of Hell's Hollow is entertaining and intriguing.

spending most of the night writing and printing the paper then devoting the next day to distributing it.

With advertising as their chief source of income, the young journalists noted that they got so much advertising that people complained that the paper was "all ads," but they would take all the advertising they could get. Among the advertisers was "the popular summer resort—Trout Island," with "good baseball grounds, good row boats and fishing tackle and dancing platform." William Steese, proprietor, guaranteed a good time for all. The paper listed itself as "independent in politics." No records could be found of when it ceased to publish.

TRANSPORTATION
By Mairy Jayn Woge

The first transportation in the county was walking, small boats, horses, donkeys, and mules. Wagons and buggies followed, but often bogged down in the mud that was the surface of the roads. The stagecoach stopped in Mercer among other places. Traveling from Mercer to Sharon required two days. Lawyers from the Shenango Valley and the other corners of the county going to the courthouse were frequent travelers. Overnight stays were at inns in houses along main roads. In 1806, Mercer County officials appointed six men to determine the feasibility and route of a forty-foot-wide road between Mercer and the

From 1844 to 1871, the Erie Extension Canal was a busy corridor of traffic between Lake Erie to the north and the Ohio River near Beaver to the south. Fare for a trip on the Reed Packet Line cost $4, including sleeping accommodations, meals, and sometimes entertainment. (Pictured are two scenes of the canal in the Sharon area.) After the aqueduct that carried the canal over Elk Creek in Erie County collapsed in 1871, the canal closed, although commercial and residential traffic continued from the Shenango Valley to Beaver at least until 1926. Dorothy Pitts (Sharon) recalls that, in 1926, she and others rode a boat on the canal to Beaver for an outing. (Caption: Mairy Jayn Woge)

Ohio line, the latter at the site of the future Sharon. The course chosen by the viewers zigzagged through Hell's Hollow west of Mercer. After the north-south route was adjusted near Yankee Ridge, it followed current Route 62. Initially, the road was dirt and without bridges at crossings over creeks.

RAILROADS
By Frederick Houser

Before 1846, several railroads had been proposed to traverse Mercer County. In 1846, the Pittsburgh & Erie Railroad Company was incorporated to go from Pittsburgh to Erie. Only two years earlier, the Erie Extension Canal had been completed so passengers and freight could, for the first time, move by water between the Ohio River and Lake Erie. An obvious drawback of the canal was that it froze and had to be shut down for several months. No railroad construction had been undertaken by 1849 when, on November 1, residents met in Greenville to push the building of the Pittsburgh & Erie Railroad. Citizens of Clarksville (now Clark) echoed this same sentiment at their own railroad rally, which they held just two days later. The Erie Extension Canal went through both communities; however, it was not living up to early expectations. The residents felt that the prospect of all-year transportation would help develop the Shenango Valley.

Late in 1849, work on the Pittsburgh & Erie Railroad actually did start. Surveys were made and, in 1851, the chief engineer estimated that a 103-mile line from the Beaver River to Lake Erie would cost almost $1,730,000. That same year, the Pittsburgh & Erie charter became a pawn in a series of events that would eventually produce both of Mercer County's first railroads: the Erie & Pittsburgh and the Atlantic & Great Western.

These events came about when Ohio railroad promoters suggested that the somewhat general terms of the Pittsburgh & Erie charter might enable the New York & Erie Railroad to build from New York state into the Midwest. Pennsylvania held to the idea that all traffic passing east from Ohio should go the full width of the state, from the headwaters of the Ohio River at Pittsburgh to the banks of the Delaware River at Philadelphia. It had first built the state-owned canal system (which also included some railroad mileage, plus several inclined planes) to carry this traffic. In 1846, the Commonwealth chartered a private company to build a railroad from Harrisburg to Pittsburgh and then to Erie. By 1852, the Pennsylvania Railroad had a continuous line from Philadelphia to Pittsburgh.

The Commonwealth had also acted to prevent easy access to out-of-state railroads seeking to traverse the forty-mile corridor where Pennsylvania reaches the Lake Erie shore. Entrepreneurs began to look at a plan to circumvent this restrictive policy. The Pittsburgh & Erie charter was used to build a branch through Meadville via Mercer County that could link up with lines in Ohio to the west and New York in the north.

A young Meadville attorney, Cyrus K. Holliday, who subsequently went to Kansas to found the Atchison, Topeka & Santa Fe Railway and become its first president, had assisted in drawing up the charter for the Pittsburgh & Erie and then turned his attention to promotion of its Meadville branch. On August 19, 1853, ground was broken at Meadville for this railroad, estimated to cost $1.25 million.

However, the project encountered opposition to the methods used for raising money, resulting in a scandal involving Crawford County. The City of Erie then entered with its proposition, demanding the immediate completion of the Pittsburgh & Erie to its harbor so it would not be bypassed by a northeast-west railroad through Meadville. The building of the Pittsburgh & Erie and its Meadville Branch came to a halt.

By 1856, with none of the Pittsburgh & Erie track yet laid, its charter was again altered so that the portion of the route from the Mercer County coal fields to Erie could be constructed by the Erie & North East Railroad.

However, in 1857, the Meadville Railroad was organized, ostensibly to build from any railroad in Erie County to the Mercer County coal fields via Meadville. This railroad acquired the charter of the Pittsburgh & Erie, along with the right of way that had already been graded for a few miles southwest out of Meadville. The Meadville Railroad was soon renamed the Atlantic & Great Western of Pennsylvania, part of the extension that one day would be the Erie Railroad main line from New York state into the Midwest. The original north-south configuration of the Pittsburgh & Erie was transformed into essentially an east-west alignment between Salamanca, New York, and Kent, Ohio. All of it would soon be known, simply, as the Atlantic & Great Western.

With the Atlantic & Great Western Railroad trying to reach the Midwest, the Erie & North East was authorized to take over unused portions of the Pittsburgh & Erie right of way to construct a north-south railroad from Erie to the Mercer County coal fields via Jamestown. To accomplish this task, the Erie & Pittsburgh Railroad was incorporated. Its line was to run from a junction on the Cleveland, Painesville & Ashtabula in Erie County, just west of Girard, Pennsylvania, to New Castle. By 1859, the track had been completed through Erie and Crawford Counties to Jamestown, the first point in Mercer County ever to have a railroad.

After three years, an Erie & Pittsburgh extension south of Jamestown was authorized and early in 1862 a contract was made with W. L. Scott and Co. for construction south to West Middlesex. Despite the labor shortage during the Civil War a large number of workers were soon grading previously ungraded sections of the roadbed and laying track. The line from Jamestown to Greenville was opened at the end of November 1862 and service to that point began. In 1863 a contract for the remainder of the line from West Middlesex to New Castle was also awarded to the Scott firm. By the end of that year, track was completed to Sharon and passenger service began to that point on January 4, 1864. By that time track was completed to West Middlesex; it reached New Castle on June 15, 1864, when connection was made with the New Castle & Beaver Valley Railroad. Michael D. Scurry, a Coolspring Township farmer and contractor, had the subcontract for a substantial part of the Erie & Pittsburgh extension. Following the Erie & Pittsburgh project he continued as a railroad contractor, building several lines in the area including the Shenango & Allegheny and Sharon Railway.

The Erie & Pittsburgh opened for through service over the ninety-eight miles between Erie and New Castle on October 31, 1864—using the track of the Cleveland, Painesville & Ashtabula between Erie and Girard Junction. Now all the towns along the Shenango River in Mercer County had railroad service and the Erie Extension Canal was soon feeling the effects of this competition.

By January 1863, the Atlantic & Great Western Railroad crossed Mercer County and was built to a gauge of 6 feet between the rails. This gauge matched the gauge of its eastern connection into western New York state. The Erie & Pittsburgh (and all other major Mercer County railroads), however, were built to a gauge of about 4 feet 8.5 inches between the rails. As time passed, this smaller gauge became the standard for virtually all tracks in North America. The broader gauge of the Atlantic & Great Western became such a detriment to future development that the entire system was converted to standard gauge over a *single* weekend in June 1880.

As built, however, the county's first two railroads were not of the same track gauge. They crossed each other two miles south of Greenville and then ran side by side for four more miles before the Atlantic & Great Western turned northwest into Ohio, away from the Erie & Pittsburgh, which continued south toward Sharon. Because of the differing gauges, the two railroads had to manually transfer freight between their respective freight cars. Thus, the station—and the community around it—became known as Transfer.

Up to this point in the Erie & Pittsburgh Railroad's development, it had been a subsidiary in the evolving rail system along the south shore of Lake Erie. It was built by the Erie & North East Railroad and from the beginning it utilized 16.5 miles of trackage rights over the Cleveland, Painesville & Ashtabula (which ran between Cleveland and Erie) for its entry into Erie. In a reversal of roles in 1864, when Cleveland, Painesville & Ashtabula's subsidiary Jamestown & Franklin Railroad began to build from Jamestown to Stoneboro and Franklin and, ultimately, Oil City, the Jamestown & Franklin obtained trackage rights for its trains over the Erie & Pittsburgh from Jamestown to Girard Junction. This arrangement lasted for many years. In a series of mergers from 1867 to about 1869, the parent companies had become part of the Lake Shore & Michigan Southern Railway, one of Commodore Cornelius Vanderbilt's holdings.

In 1870, the Erie & Pittsburgh was leased to the Pennsylvania Railroad, the major competitor with Vanderbilt's railroad system between the East Coast and the Midwest. Erie & Pittsburgh, however, were soon in financial trouble. An immediate expenditure was for acquisition of the Erie Extension Canal, which the Erie & Pittsburgh was driving out of business. The railroad operated the canal for another year, until the Elk Creek aqueduct at Girard collapsed. In disposing of the canal property, Erie & Pittsburgh sold segments that later provided rights of way for two other Mercer County railroads—today's Bessemer & Lake Erie from Greenville north into Erie County and a now-abandoned Erie Railroad branch between Sharon and New Castle.

By the 1870s, the amalgamation of short lines and regional railroads into trunk lines between the East Coast and the Midwest started to involve most of the Mercer County railroads. The Lake Shore & Michigan Southern was operated progressively more closely with the other major Vanderbilt railroad, the New York Central & Hudson River (until outright merger of the two as the New York Central Railroad took place in 1914).

From the time of its construction, the Atlantic & Great Western, because of its broad gauge, was allied (at least informally) with the Erie Railroad and its predecessors. The broad-gauge equipment the two roads used could move unimpeded only over their lines between the Hudson River and Cincinnati. The Atlantic & Great Western was merged into the Erie & Pittsburgh lines in 1883. The Pennsylvania Railroad's 1870 acquisition of the Erie & Pittsburgh gave the Pennsylvania Railroad its initial entry into Mercer County. The

The Number 2 Mine of Sharon Coal & Limestone Company.

Pennsylvania Railroad also acquired the Western New York & Pennsylvania in the eastern portion of the county in 1900 (from New Castle, through Mercer and Stoneboro, into western New York state).

MINING

When Lackawannock Township was yet a wilderness, the William Buchanan family settled about three miles south of the village of Greenfield. The family became quite wealthy after they found that their farm was rich in bituminous coal. Rumors abound that they had no bank account. Instead, they changed all their money into gold pieces and hid the gold on the farm. The business head of the family, Baxter, was known to lend money, even thousands of dollars, always in gold. On his deathbed in 1900, Baxter summoned his brother, James, supposedly to tell him of the hiding place. However, he died before James arrived. James apparently never knew where the gold was hidden and died a poor man.

Edward P. Dresch, president of the Hickory Township school board when Maple Drive High School opened, in 1909, recalled in a diary he wrote that the Nine Month Coal Strike that began in 1873 closed the mines in Hickory Township. Dresch wrote that his parents and other mine families moved to Austintown, Ohio, where the men dug coal. Dresch's family returned to Neshannock in 1874. According to Dresch, "the coal strike was still in progress and there was a great deal of poverty and distress among the mine folk." When the strike ended in the summer of 1874, having lasted beyond the nine months, Dresch's father began working at Mount Pleasant mine operated in Neshannock by Samuel Kimberly and Enoch Filer. (Filer, who had arrived in Hickory in 1852, introduced the first major shaft mine in Hickory in 1859. He had also devised a lift that carried miners in and out of mines and brought coal out.) The mine where Dresch's father worked in 1874 was east of South Keel Ridge Road and accessed by a spur of the Sharpsville-Oakland Railroad. (When Dresch was elected to serve as school director, he dealt with complaints from former neighbors in the southeastern Hickory Township coal fields about pupils from the west side of Hickory (Patagonia) being transported to Maple Drive High School by a cart while pupils from the New Virginia area walked five to eight miles to and from the school each weekday to attend classes.)

Strikes like the ones at coal mines in the Shenango Valley were not unusual, but few ended in victories. One Friday in 1899, employees of a Sharon mill met with their foremen and plant management to seek extra pay for overtime work on Fridays. Nothing was accomplished. The employees reported to work the following Monday, without having made any progress. According to a story in a Sharon newspaper, the instigators were fired.

Near Stoneboro, the Mercer Iron and Coal Company opened its No. 2 Mine along Fredonia Road in the early 1870s at a site just east of today's Wesleyan camp ground. The original No. 1 Mine was soon phased out, but by the 1880s the No. 3 Mine was operating in the southeastern corner of the borough. The Coal Branch track of the Jamestown & Franklin Railroad was extended to serve both of these mining operations and in 1883 was run south through Lake and Jackson Townships to reach newer Mercer Iron and Coal mines and those of other coal producers. The 1887 report of Pennsylvania's secretary of internal affairs shows that Stoneboro No. 2 Mine that year produced 66,536 tons of coal with 125 miners and the No. 3 Mine's output was 20,402 tons with 48 miners.

Pine Township. Westerman Filer Company successfully operated three mines: No. 2, No. 3, and Trout Mine in Pine Township near Grove City for many years. Partnered by Frank Filer and Mr. Westerman, their company employed over 700 men, some living in the areas of Hallville, Kerr School, and Diamond Corners. These mines produced between 1,200 and 1,500 tons daily.

Grove City Limestone Mine.

The Large Railroad Mine at Chestnut Ridge (Irishtown Road), owned by the Westerman Filer Company, opened in 1864 shortly after the Pardoe Mine and employed as many as 500 to 600 men. The Beaver & Lake Erie Railroad carried the high-quality coal to the steel mills of Sharpsville. Approximately one hundred homes built up around the mine with a population of around 1,800 people.

The Grove Coal Company, owned and supervised by David D. Morris, began in 1892, operated two mines at Enterprise and Hallville located just east of Grove City, produced 100,835 tons, and employed 150 men in 1906.

Hallville Mine first opened in 1882 by a man named Hall and closed in 1902. Good-quality coal was loaded on the Beaver & Lake Erie along present-day Forrest Drive, the spur built from the main line to Hallville. Many of the miners working this mine were of Italian descent.

Enterprise Mine, the second mine, had great success not only because of its good coal, but also because of its good source of fire clay found immediately underneath the coal. This clay was mined, crushed, and sold to brick factories in New Castle and Sharon. A large patch of homes (called Miner's Patch) built up around the mine before its closing in 1918.

The Pinchalong Mine opened in 1882; and after only fourteen years and one-third of the coal acreage removed, the depression of 1894, 1895, and 1896 combined with bad conditions (too much water in the mine and a bad roof) closed the mine in 1896. Located on the property now known as the Odd Fellows, owners James Spears and E. A. Wheeler leased five hundred acres and sank a shaft along the railroad in the village of Pinchalong and mined toward and underlying Grove City College buildings. Pinchalong was aptly named from the men who wanted their money before pay day and owner Spears who would tell them, "Pinch along, boys; just pinch along till pay day."

The Center Coal Company under the management of Walter and Lee Kimes was located at the Cranberry Road.

Hassell Mine, with a shaft opening of about thirty-five feet, was owned by Pete Hassell. Located south of Chestnut Ridge Crossroads (Irishtown Road), it employed ten to twelve men. In 1904, water and sand broke into the shaft and it was never worked again.

Bowie Coal Company operated twelve coal mines including the Pine Township Mine north of Grove City and the McCoytown Mine.

Diamond Coal Mine, located in the southeast section of Pine Township, and a huge watercourse that had flowed under the mine were recalled by retired miner William Teare in the *Grove City Reporter-Herald* (February 15, 1938, issue). While developing a coal field in a southeast direction near Kerr School, the coal seam and the overlying strata (what miners call the roof) was cut off as though an immense circular saw cut through the earth. Teare did not know how far below the coal level the bed of the river lay for no water was present and the washed-in material was solid (not a particle of sand and stone, which was as smooth as glass, was disturbed). An opening they cut into was ten feet wide in which a log was found. Coal on the east side of this ancient river was nineteen feet lower than the coal on the west side. Teare's friend Mr. Stubbs found wood in the Pine Township Mine located north of where Teare found wood, causing him to deduct that an old river had flowed around Grove City.

UTILITIES
By Mairy Jayn Woge

Enoch Filer and his sons opened the first electric plant in the Shenango Valley in Sharon in 1890. The first electric generating plant in Sharon opened in 1897. At that time, most industries used coal to produce power. Telegraph service came with the early railroads, around 1870.

The first telephones rang in Sharon in 1885 at downtown stores. The Shenango Valley had two telephone companies, Bell and Citizens. Each distributed skinny directories containing two digit numbers. The consequence of the competing telephone companies was that residents who subscribed to one service often walked next door or up the street to make or receive a call. Businesses subscribed to both Citizens and Bell and advertised in both directories.

UNDERGROUND RAILROAD
By Casey Glockner, James Sewall, and Gail Habbyshaw

Slavery was accepted in nearly every part of the world as the norm until the late 1700s when European sociopolitical philosophers, such as Montesquieu, began to advocate abolishing it. The Anti-Slavery Society of Mercer County was organized in 1835, following a lecture on abolition by the Reverend Nathaniel West at the First Presbyterian Church in Mercer. Many influential citizens were on its membership rolls.

During the height of abolitionist activity, slaveholding was still practiced by a few households in the county. Through entries in the federal census records, it is possible to glimpse one such household: that of John Robbins. The 1830 census showed Robbins living near Charleston (Jefferson Township) with a household that included several slaves and free blacks. In the next census, in 1840, only free blacks were counted among the Robbins household. Did Robbins lend his assistance to the underground railroad? Or did he come to Mercer County from the South with his slaves; and, in accordance with Pennsylvania law, they became free? We do not know. (Pennsylvania's gradual abolition law did not permit persons of color beyond the age of 28 to be held in bondage.)

Although the Fugitive Slave Act of 1850 imposed severe fines and imprisonment on citizens who helped, or failed to apprehend, runaway slaves, some families in the county accepted the risks involved in assisting runaway slaves to escape via the underground railroad. Connected by blood, marriage, or longstanding friendship, these families were largely of Presbyterian background and tended to be well educated, financially comfortable,

In 1818, Richard Travis, a black free man, bought 150 acres to farm on the shore of Sandy Lake for $2. By the 1840 Census, over two dozen nonwhites were residents of Sandy Lake Township. Many were escaped slaves and Native Americans. This colony of people became known as Liberia and existed until the revised Fugitive Slave Law was passed in 1850. Then, many fled to Canada to ensure freedom. Escaped slaves who died before this relocation are buried in a cemetery on Route 62 across from the Stoneboro Fairground entrance. Now, the cemetery's location is marked by a historical marker. Richard Travis died in 1843, and his land changed hands several times before John F. Hogue and William Shields purchased it for its three coal seams. The uppermost of the seams was four feet thick. (Caption: Frederick Houser)

and regarded as community leaders. They belonged to the ranks of doctors, lawyers, and businessmen.

The existence of the underground railroad in the county, more likely than not, was an open secret. With the large number of people involved, it would have been nearly impossible to have kept an undertaking of such magnitude concealed in small communities.

The underground railroad was neither underground, nor a railroad, but rather a network of escape routes and hideouts, known as "stations," maintained for the benefit of runaway slaves. All underground railroad "lines" began on various plantations in the South and ran along rivers, through valleys, across mountains to points on the Ohio and upper Mississippi rivers, and on to the North.

The most frequently used underground railroad lines through Mercer County were reportedly present-day Route 19, a path from Ohio to Greenville and Jamestown, a trail through the foothills from Franklin (Venango County) to Stoneboro, and from New Castle (Lawrence County) to Indian Run via Mercer and on to Sheakleyville.

Slaves fled with the realization the trek to freedom was wrought with physical danger and the risk of being captured and returned to their masters, a dreaded prospect. Auntie Strange, who resided in Liberia, a colony of runaway slaves that existed in present-day Stoneboro until the passage of the Fugitive Slave Law in 1850, fled her Southern master, but was captured; as a punishment, her fingers were amputated.

Since most runaway slaves were transported from one station to another during the night, life for an underground railroad "conductor" and his family was fraught with nocturnal adventures. A tap at night on the window of a house serving as a "station" signaled that runaway slaves were being delivered and galvanized the conductor and his family into action.

Elizabeth Breckinridge, a daughter of underground railroad conductor James Kilgore of Mercer, vividly recalled when John Young, her mother's uncle, transported thirteen fugitive slaves in a hay wagon, shrouded by darkness, and unloaded them beneath a tree near the cellar door. Young operated an underground railroad station at Indian Run (East Lackawannock Township).

Breckinridge explained that "a certain number of knocks" in a specific pattern on the cellar door of her childhood home at night "would let my father know that runaway slaves were there. He would take them in, feed them, and let them rest until the next night, when they would travel on to the next station, giving them minute instructions."

PANDENARIUM
By Ruth Woods

Indian Run is the name of a creek which flows through the southeastern section of East Lackawannock Township. It is also the place where an experiment in freedom was attempted in the late 1800s. By 1900, however, only two ex-slaves remained of the thirty-nine who were granted their freedom in 1848 on the death of their master, Charles Everett, a wealthy Virginia physician and plantation owner. Convinced that slavery was a sin, Everett's will liberated all his slaves and provided for their needs. He had planned a modern Utopia, complete with a restaurant, inn, church, school, and hospital. He also secretly arranged for his slaves to purchase the freedom of their spouses and children from other masters. Everett's estate was left to his nephew, C. D. Everett, a wealthy Philadelphia physician who carried out his uncle's wishes as best he could. He decided in 1853 to locate the ex-slaves in the North. The Indian Run community was selected because of its location in a slavery-free state and southern Mercer County's strong abolitionist activity. For example, an Anti-Slavery Society, referred to as the "Holy Ridgers," had built an independent church on John Young's farm at Indian Run, naming it White Chapel. Young had learned of the horrors of slavery from hearing stories told by ex-slave, Margaret Johnson. Inherited by Young's parents from relatives in Maryland, she and her children had moved with the Youngs to the Indian Run area in 1798. They had been treated as free Negroes, who lived and worshipped with the Young family at White Chapel.

Everett bought fifty acres of Young's farm and arranged for the Pennsylvania legislature to pass a law guaranteeing the freedom of the new arrivals. He also contracted to prepare sites and build homes. Three Mercer County abolitionists, Joseph Black, John Stewart, and George Hamilton, supervised the project. They built twenty-four two-story dwellings in a row with a small church. Wells were dug, gardens and orchards were planted, and the road was graded.

Although the community of Big Bend did not survive after the close of the Erie Extension Canal in 1871, people, like Will Weller (pictured, date unknown), continued to live in the area.

No. 324.

AN ACT

To authorize and empower the Court of Common Pleas of Mercer county to legitimate certain persons who were emancipated by the last will and testament of Dr. C. D. Everett, late of Albemarle county, Virginia.

WHEREAS, Dr. C. D. Everett, late of Albemarle county, state of Virginia, by his last will and testament provided for the manumission of his slaves, and for their maintenance and support:

And whereas, The executor of said decedent, under the powers of said will, purchased certain real and personal estate to and for the use of his said slaves, situate in the county of Mercer, in this Commonwealth:

And whereas, Doubts may arise as to the legitimacy of some or all of said manumitted slaves, and their children; therefore,

SECTION 1. *Be it enacted by the Senate and House of Representatives of the Commonwealth of Pennsylvania in General Assembly met, and it is hereby enacted by the authority of the same,* That the court of common pleas of said county of Mercer, are hereby specially authorized to entertain, on petition of one or more of the following persons, the reputed manumitted slaves, to wit: of Joe Duke, Lucy Myers, George W. Duke, Nancy Bell, Winsor Duke, Letitia Robertson, Rose Allen, James Duke, John Allen, George W. Lewis, children of Joe Duke; Tom Bell, Lucy Jane Bell, Milly Bell, Nelly Bell, Rachel Bell, Susan Bell, Judy Bell, Jackson Bell, William Bell, children of Nancy Bell; Sally Watson, Margaret Watson, Hannah Watson, Amanda Watson, Frank Robertson, Joe Robertson, Louisa Robertson, Alexander Robertson, Richmond Robertson, children of Letitia Robertson; Francis Allen, John Allen, Ann Allen, children of Rose Allen; William C. Rives, Edward Watson, Henry Myers, Susan Myers, children of Lucy Myers; Nick Myers, Lucy A. Myers, children of Susan Myers; Reuben Duke, Charles Duke, Joseph Duke, children of G. W. Duke; William Myers, Jerry Myers, children of Henry Myers; Henrietta Bell, daughter of Rachel Bell; Samuel J. Duke, son of James Duke; Willis Lewis and Mary J. Lewis, grand-children of Lucy Myers; manumitted slaves or descendants of manumitted slaves, and in a full hearing of all parties in interest, on notice prescribed by said court, and taking into view, as well recognized and reputed marriages, and parentage, as the same may be acknowledged or proved, to make a decree or decrees, severally or generally, to legitimate any or all of said persons, whereby they shall severally have and enjoy such rights and privileges, for the enjoyment, transmission and inheritance of property from their parents or reputed parents, or other relatives, as in the sound judgment and discretion of said court shall seem just and proper; whereupon such decree or decrees shall have the same force and effect in law and equity, as if herein specially set forth and provided for, for the legitimacy of any or all of said persons, and as if the descendants of any parents or other relationships so ascertained, had legitimately stood in such relationships by the laws of Pennsylvania.

HENRY K. STRONG,
Speaker of the House of Representatives.
WM. M. HIESTER,
Speaker of the Senate.

APPROVED—The twenty-sixth day of April, Anno Domini one thousand eight hundred and fifty-five.

JAS. POLLOCK.

No. 325.

AN ACT

Relative to the approving of bonds given by applicants for tavern licenses in the city of Philadelphia.

SECTION 1. *Be it enacted by the Senate and House of Representatives of the Commonwealth of Pennsylvania in General Assembly met, and it is hereby enacted by the authority of the same,* That for approving the securities on the bonds of applicants for tavern licenses in the city of Philadelphia, fifty cents for each shall be paid by the applicant to the officer authorized to examine and approve the same.

HENRY K. STRONG,
Speaker of the House of Representatives.
WM. M. HIESTER,
Speaker of the Senate.

APPROVED—The twenty-sixth day of April, Anno Domini one thousand eight hundred and fifty-five.

JAS. POLLOCK.

On arrival, the scene was recalled by one ex-slave as being "just like heaven," for the country roads were golden with the fallen leaves, Indian summer had cast a warm, though temporary spell, and antislavery neighbors welcomed them openly. The freed slaves visited around the neighborhood in their tan and blue muslin shirts, trousers, and dresses (cut from the same bolts of cloth) and new shoes, all of which were provided by the Everett estate. Each head-of-household was given $1,000 to sustain the family for three to four years until they would be self-sufficient and the deed to two acres of land. Among the group were farmers and tradesmen, including carpenters, plasterers, painters, mechanics, shoemakers, and a blacksmith.

Still in packing crates, waiting at each front door, were identical chairs, tables, beds, sheeting, blankets, and flower seeds for next spring's planting. Although the ex-slaves were accustomed to raising cotton and rice, their first harvest in the North was potatoes and corn. Milk and pork were also abundantly available locally. The creek flowed nearby and was not only a source of recreation, but also convenient for bathing and laundry.

Provided only with summer clothing and accustomed to a warmer climate, however, the colony was ill-prepared when a winter storm hit with a rush of blinding snow. Huddled together around their wood-burning stoves, many ex-slaves developed severe colds and pneumonia.

Weather continued to be a problem when spring finally arrived and the creek flooded twice, soaking household items and rusting machinery. The health of the colony at Pandenarium deteriorated; and within two years, many developed tuberculosis, which threatened to wipe out the village. Fearing for their lives, some families retraced their way south. With the start of the Civil War, two of the 15-year-olds enlisted.

Unaccustomed to handling finances, the ex-slaves fell easy prey to white investors and swindlers who lit on them, once it was learned that they had money and land. This fate foreseen, Everett had specified in his will that the land could be transferred only within the family, except through petitioning his estate. Thus, at least, their land was secure. Eventually, five families moved to Mercer, living in a row of homes on the south side of town. However, some families remained at Indian Run until early in the 1900s, bought

The most elegant house in the Hickory Township part of Sharpsville was built for Jonas Pierce in 1865. Pierce had returned to Sharpsville after serving as a captain during the Civil War. The house is second empire style with Italianate Victorian architectural features. It is capped by a large tower and mansard roof. A ballroom is inside. (By 1988, the Pierce mansion had been occupied by two generations of Pierce's descendants and rented by several families. It fell into poor condition. Now, it is unoccupied and for sale.) Jonas Pierce, who died in 1913, was the great-grandfather of Barbara Bush who visited Sharpsville in 1982 while her husband George was U.S. vice president. (Caption: Mairy Jayn Woge)

more property, cultivated larger farms, and ripped away most traces of the original Pandenarium. Some tradesmen worked for hire in the community. Charlie Allen and Wally Robinson worked at Billy Black's sawmill at Indian Run. Dan Bell is remembered as a jolly, hardworking field hand.

A grandson of one of the original freed slaves, Charlie Robinson was born at Pandenarium in 1870 and was the last Negro to leave there. Robinson's daughter Ellen, who lived at Pandenarium until she was six, recalled the springhouse where her grandmother churned butter. Charlie's cousin, Hazel Allen Atkinson, lived at the settlement until she was sixteen. She recalled attending the Mayne School, where the boys sat on one side of the room and the girls on the other. In the winter when the snow was too deep to walk, they were picked up at school by a big horse-drawn bobsled.

Now, the site of Pandenarium has been converted to farmland. The stone foundations have been removed, and the wells have been filled in. The many wooden grave markers in its small cemetery have disappeared, leaving no visible reminder of the liberated slaves and their families who were buried there. The White Chapel Church continues to thrive, however, as a constant reminder of its origin and of the right of all persons to be free.

GENERAL JAMES PIERCE
By Mairy Jayn Woge

General James Pierce was born in New Hampshire. He sold clocks, wool, and other merchandise in Crawford and Erie Counties before he moved to Clarksville (now Clark) in 1847. He became a prominent businessman by opening coal mines in Hickory and Pymatuning Townships, starting several blast furnaces in Sharpsville, and building a railroad to haul coal to Sharpsville from southeastern Hickory Township. He also purchased the bulk of the Erie Extension Canal between Crawford and Lawrence Counties in anticipation of building a major railroad on the towpath. Pierce and his wife Chloe had five children: Jonas J., twins Walter and Wallace, Frank, and James B.

After David Thompson died in the early 1840s, his estate, containing 120 acres of farmland and coal mines and a rectangular two-story red brick house with poplar floors and farm buildings (all located along North Keel Ridge Road), was worth just shy of his debts. He owed $932 to the Western Reserve Bank in Trumbull County, but his neighbors owed him just slightly less than that for coal and farm goods. The household and farm implements and animals were sold at two auctions. The house, outbuildings, and acreage were also auctioned, and the high bidder, for $2,500, was General Pierce. Pierce built a large, brick house with teardrop windows in the attic and red and yellow glass flanks beside the front door and connected that house, on the rear, to the former Thompson residence. The real estate was named Mount Hickory. Pierce raised prize-winning cattle in the fields. From there, he built a tram road that carried coal to the docks of the Erie Extension Canal and blast furnaces in Sharpsburg (now Sharpsville). With William Scott of Erie and coal mine operators, Pierce laid out the Sharpsville & Oakland Railroad to Oakland mine south of New Virginia that was owned by Pierce and Scott. The railroad later was extended to Wilmington Township. Investors in the railroad were mine owners who were serviced by spurs that transported coal to the main line of the railroad. (When the railway closed in 1929, it was part of the Baltimore & Ohio Railroad.)

General Pierce bought an old school building that Vincent, Himrod, and the McClures built to educate children of the blast furnaces workers they employed. Pierce tore down the old school and replaced it with a four-room schoolhouse about 1870. The school was in Hickory Township when Sharpsville was organized in 1874, and the Hickory school board donated the school to Sharpsville.

In 1845, Vincent and Himrod built Clay Furnace, named for Henry Clay. The furnace was in Delaware Township at that time and later located in Jefferson Township. It had the first successful use of raw bituminous coal, in place of charcoal, in 1846 and of unmixed Lake Superior iron ore in 1856. By 1861, it was abandoned (pictured, date unknown).

In 1873, General Pierce and James W. Ormsby designated a half acre of land for Schoolhouse #6 in Hickory, named Pierce School. The one-room school building was along current North Hermitage Road east of Irishtown where many of the builders for the Sharpsville-Oakland (Wilmington) coal railroad lived. The bulk of them were Irish. (The school was closed in 1937 and in 1941 bought by John and Ruth Miglin who added a second story in the process of making the school their home. Now, the former school belongs to the Recreation Center that provides miniature golf and other amusements.)

The Iron Banking Company was established in Sharpsville by General Pierce. His son, Frank, was president. In 1883, the bank was reorganized with Frank continuing as president and his brothers, Walter, Wallace, and James B. serving on the board with Charles E. Agnew whose father, David, was General Pierce's bookkeeper. (Iron Banking became the Sharpsville National Bank and now is a branch of the National City Bank.) The Sharpsville office is at the corner of Shenango Street and Mercer Avenue. The building was formerly the Pierce Opera House. Concerts, conventions, and school graduations were held there.

When the weather was bad or he experienced a long workday, General Pierce stayed in a house he had bought in Sharpsville. In 1871, he commissioned the construction of a mansion along Shenango Street. At the time, his financial worth was said to be $50 mil-

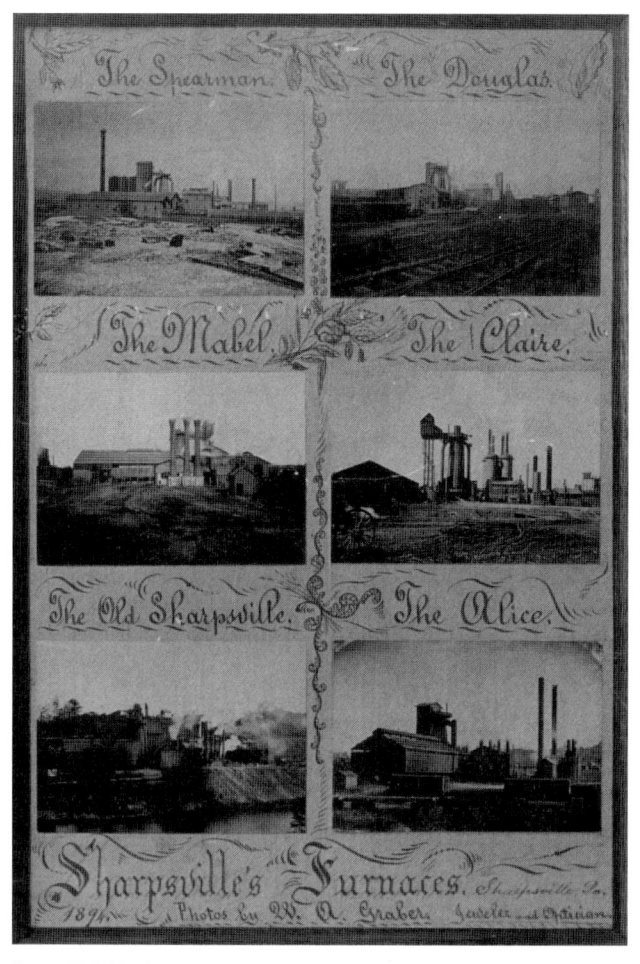

From 1853 until 1897, members of the Pierce family were involved in the operation of several blast furnaces around Sharpsville: Spearman, Douglas, Sharpsville, and Alice. In addition, the Mabel and Claire furnaces were prosperous near Sharpsville and Clarksville. According to one observer at the time, "Coal was the only leading business fifty years ago. I can mind when Clarksville was ahead of Sharon in shipping coal and merchandising. I can remember when a man started a livery stable in Sharon and could not stand it and moved to Clarksville and made money. I mention these things just to show how changes take place. This valley took a start for improvement some fifty four years ago, at that time they commenced building stone piles they called furnaces until there were over a score in Mercer Co. They run for a while then all crumbled down only two being rebuilt today standing on the sites. One at Sharpsville and one between Sharpsville and Sharon called now the Sharon Furnace. Nothing left of original ones except the ground they stood on." (Source: 1891–1893 diary of Sebastain Runser, transcribed by Margo Letts)

lion. While inspecting the almost complete mansion in 1874, he tripped and fell down the cellar stairs. He was taken to Mount Hickory where he died.

Chloe Pierce died in the Sharpsville mansion in 1888. She left Mount Hickory to two of her sons. They sold the property, and now Steven T. and Boel Johnson own Mount Hickory. They have repaired and restored the historic house and outbuildings.

BIG BEND
Sources: Unidentified newspaper clippings

The town of Big Bend no longer exists, but its location was at what is now the eastern end of Shenango River Reservoir about 5.5 miles east of Clark on Route 18. The town was initially recorded as "Shenango," but soon took its name from its location at a hairpin bend in the Shenango River, commonly referred to as Big Bend. This site had been a small Seneca Indian village in the late 1700s, but the last Indians left the area about 1810. Records show Joseph Morrison of Philadelphia bought a 500-acre site from a Revolutionary War captain in 1807 and laid out a small town named "Shenango" in 1808 that covered both sides of the river. It never developed to Morrison's expectations. In fact, little was built until the Erie Extension Canal opened up in 1840.

As a point on the canal, Big Bend prospered. By the mid-1850s, it boasted an iron furnace, a couple of nearby woolen and lumber mills, a hotel, warehouses, a church, a school, a blacksmith, two grocers, a teacher, and a butcher. Most of the population was of Irish and German descent, attracted to work on the canal. It was a major shipping and destination point along the canal for this portion of the county, and an eight-mile plank road linked Big Bend to Mercer. Because it was so far from other population centers in the county, however, it never developed beyond the canal trade. When the canal shut down in 1871, so did more of Big Bend. By 1900, it had virtually disappeared. The U.S. Army Corps of Engineers razed what was left when it built the Shenango Dam in the 1960s.

The canal towpath has remained largely in tact and is now the Shenango Trail, a hiking trail linking Big Bend to Kidd's Mill covered bridge in Transfer.

William P. "Pat" Brown (Cleveland, Ohio) worked on the canal during its entire thirty-one years of activity, as a driver, bowsman, steerer, and boat owner. He steered a boat that took Company F soldiers up the canal in 1861 to join other troops in the Civil War. "Plenty of whiskey aboard—just knocked in the head of a barrel of it, and hung tin cups around it on shingle-nails. Koonce of Clarksville furnished the roast ox. We took them as far as Rochester." That trip would generally take two days if they stopped for the night; otherwise, with two crews, it could be made in one day. The canal boats were "88 feet long and 15 wide. They'd carry from 65 to 70 tons. Two, sometimes three horses or mules, hitched tandem, hauled. The driver usually had a saddle on the hind one and drove the leader with lines. At night he jumped the team aboard, fed and bedded them, and he slept in the bow. The boats drew about three feet of water, maybe a little more."

Erie Extension Canal Locks
By Mairy Jayn Woge

Beginning in 1844, the Erie Extension Canal provided transportation between Lake Erie and the Ohio River in Beaver County. The first boats that used it carried coal. William Fruit of Clarksville hauled some coal to the port at Erie in 1843 with the hope of selling the fuel to propel lake boats. Joel B. Curtis of Sharon took a canal boat of coal to New Castle in 1842.

Locks were the lifelines of canals. Gates on locks that opened and closed, lifted and lowered boats to the level of the slack water they left to the level of the water they entered. There were six locks and a basin along the canal in the Valley. The basin was alongside Jennyburg Hill in Sharon. Boats were parked or repaired there. Two canal boat captains lived in Sharon. Jennyburg Hill was named for the donkeys or jennies that grazed on the hill when they were not pulling boats from towpaths.

The farthest north lock in the Valley was Number 10 in Sharpsville. Lock 9 is off Furnace Road near Thornton Run and the site of the former Boyce and Rawle iron furnace, named Sharon Furnace.

According to Ferd Dab (Shenango Valley) a complete lock is underground at the site of the former Wishart Lumber Company on Dayton Way, off Rena Street. Tracks for the Erie Railroad were laid along the towpath. A two-story lockkeeper's house, a stone building, was alongside the lock until it was torn down around 1960. Lock 7 was on the Ulp Farm at the south end of Farrell. It was destroyed by workers who were updating the sewer disposal plant south of Broadway Avenue. Lock 6 is on the property of the Satterfield family (Hickory Township), south of Broadway. Sections of the stone wall for the lock are thought to remain although much of the stone was removed to be used for construction of a railroad bridge. Lock 5 is south of Broadway where Bobby Run flowed into the canal and Shenango River. Water lies in the section of the canal under the bridge on Main Street in West Middlesex. Lock 4 was in West Middlesex and Lock 3 is a mile and a half south of the borough.

Mary Jones Hawthorne

By Kathryn Miles Moorehouse (granddaughter)

"William Jones, father of Mary Catterson Jones, was a wheelwright and was employed in building the Erie [Extension] Canal to keep the machinery in working order. His wife did the cooking for the crew. Little Mary, about six, helped her mother. There were benches around the long table. When she was given silver to put at the places, she ran around the table on the wooden benches and put it at the places. . . .

"One story: The men were working in the forest and Mary was sent with a message or a lunch. Trotting along the pathway, she heard a noise behind her, looked around, and saw a wolf following. She ran faster and faster and screamed louder and louder. As she ran faster, the wolf ran faster; when she ran slower, it slowed up a little. When she came near enough for the men to hear her screams, they grabbed their guns, which were always kept near at hand, and ran to meet her. They shot the wolf.

"Another story: Little Mary was on her way to where the men were making charcoal. She carried her kitten. Trotting alone the pathway through the forest, she stopped suddenly because there was a small log across the path. She couldn't remember of its being there before. She had been warned of the possibility of snakes, and she wondered whether this was a stick or a snake. She thought to herself, 'if it moves when my kitten touches it, I'll know it's a snake.' She dropped her kitten on it; both the kitten and the snake moved fast. Mary went along and delivered her message, and then she ran home as fast as she could because she was worried about her kitten. When she got back to the house, the kitten was sitting on the step washing its face with its paw. Mary's heart was filled with gladness as she picked the kitten up and hugged it.

"When Mary grew up, she married John Donnell Hawthorne and lived in Lackawannock Township. They had three children: Eva, my mother; Charles; and James. James died when a small child. Eva told us stories of her childhood that we enjoyed. She had a pet chipmunk that slept in her pocket. She had a pet raccoon. She came in from the woods one day and reported having seen a big yellow cat lying on a branch of a tree. Her father took his gun and went to look. It was a lynx and he killed it. Eva could remember the day a neighbor came to report that Lincoln had been shot. She was born September 10, 1855. Lincoln died April 15, 1865."

Blast Furnaces
By Mairy Jayn Woge

Sharpsville Furnace was also called Blanche Furnace and had been built in 1848 by Vincent and Himrod of Erie and Joseph and John McClure of Clarksville (now Clark). The contractor for the stone and brick blast furnace was Joseph Arbuckle, a mason living in Hickory Township. The proprietors of Blanche built wood houses near the furnace for their employees and a small school. Because it was difficult to obtain and keep mill hands, most Valley furnaces erected company houses to attract and accommodate personnel.

Railroad accidents often brought out the best efforts by local photo studios, in this case a Sharpsville photographer and a runaway train on the local Sharpsville Railroad. During switching in Hickory Township in October 1886 by a southbound mixed train (the line's lone passenger coach and four loads of pig iron, all unbraked) ran away down the three-mile steep grade until crashing into a boxcar in downtown Sharpsville. Although the coach was destroyed, only one of its five passengers sustained a slight cut; fortunately, the loads of pig iron (right) did not crush the passenger car. (Contributor: Frederick Houser)

The *1888 Mercer County History* states Blanche/Sharpsville Furnace closed in 1852 and was sold the next year to David and John P. Agnew. David had been one of the partners in the Sharon Blast Furnace at Deweyville when it went out of business in 1852. The Agnews operated Sharpsville Furnace for two blasts. General Pierce subsequently assumed the ownership of the furnace in 1853 and replaced the machinery in it. In 1859, he hired John J. Spearman as manager of the furnace. Spearman was a longtime iron furnace operator. By melting Lake Superior ore with Sharon block coal, Spearman reportedly produced red short iron. In 1862, Jonas J. Pierce followed Spearman as manager of Sharpsville Furnace. The furnace was torn down and rebuilt in 1882. By then, Sharpsville and West Middlesex were described as the Valley's furnace towns.

General Pierce and William Scott (Erie), partners in Oakland Coal mine south of New Virginia (Hickory Township), built the two-stack Mount Hickory Furnace on the site of Sharpsville in 1868 and 1869. In 1900, Mount Hickory Furnace produced 40,000 tons of iron. (Mount Hickory Furnace was torn down in 1970.)

In 1869, Jonas J. Pierce purchased fifty acres along the Pittsburgh & Erie Railroad in Hickory Township. The next year, he and George D. Kelly (Pittsburgh) opened Douglas

Furnace with one stack. A second stack was installed in 1872 after General Pierce and his son Wallace became involved in the business. By 1879, Douglas produced Bessemer, foundry, and forge pig iron.

Also in Sharpsville at the time was a furnace operated by Francis Allen and another built by James W. Ormsby and sold to banker Simon Perkins. Mark A. Hanna, a member of the Ohio group who manipulated Republican politics during the Warren G. Harding presidency, acted as sales agent for the Perkins Furnace from his office in Cleveland. The Spearman Furnace was built in 1870 in the part of Hickory Township that became Sharpsville. Alice Furnace opened in Sharpsville in 1865.

In 1896, Jonas Pierce and, in 1897, Walter, Frank, and James B. Pierce and principals in Spearman and Perkins furnaces, sold their shares in blast furnaces to Shenango Furnace Company, a firm organized by William A. Snyder (Pittsburgh). Operations at Shenango Furnace began in 1906. Shenango rebuilt Douglas Furnace making it the most modern in Pennsylvania as of 1910.

SEBASTAIN RUNSER
From 1891–1893 diary of Sebastain Runser, transcribed by Margo Letts

In the 1840s Sebastain Runser moved to Sharpsville to apprentice with his brother Andrew who had rented "the shop"—probably a blacksmith shop—from the Sharpsville Furnace in which to do the company's work and custom work for the neighborhood. Runser, born in 1828, had immigrated with his family from France in the 1830s and during his apprenticeship was paid $40 annually plus board.

". . . I had two years to serve yet to finish my time of apprenticeship, some call it to finish my trade, but I look on it different and claim a man never finishes his trade till he dies for there is always something to learn."

Delivered as the Civil War was starting, Erie & Pittsburgh No. 1, also named "Union," was the first locomotive produced for Mercer County's first railroad. The Erie & Pittsburgh Railroad acquired a fleet of twenty-nine locomotives, most of them much like this one, before being taken over by the Pennsylvania Railroad in 1870. (Contributor: Frederick Houser)

After completing his training, Runser visited his parents who had settled in Ohio. "I packed an old feed sack with shirts and socks and started on my journey, on foot, a distance of nearly 250 miles which took me thirteen days, the walking bad. I stayed at home some time, during which I helped to get the material for a hewedlog house for my folks then living in a round pole house about 15 square feet and in it there was two beds, a shoemaker shop, kitchen and parlor all in one room, yet we were all happy and contented."

After returning to Sharpsville in 1848, "I engaged to work at what is now called Sharon Furnace (then was called Bell furnace). J. J. Spearman was the Superintendent. I worked there two years at one dollar a day and board which was good wage at the time. I did all the smelting for the furnace, besides custom work for the turns that were engaged hauling ore and charcoal, no bituminous coal being used at that time nor any Lake ore. A furnace made about from three to five tons a day. In the Spring of 1850 my brother Andrew concluded to take some of his household goods out to Hardin Co. [Ohio] where he had purchased a farm and calculating later to move on same. . . . I had two horses which I used in hauling his wagon and goods out there and came home on foot. . . . At that time on my arrival home I rented the shop that my brother had occupied and went in business for myself to accommodate the trade that he had and stayed in Sharpsville. . . . I was married to Adeline Dunham, living on the road from Sharpsville to Trout Corners and afterwards bought a piece of land from her father. On the same road now owned by Albin Dunham, here I erected a small shop to do custom work for the neighborhood and after one years work I found the custom rather limited. I then added a wagon shop to same. This increased my work considerable and I soon had work for several men. I continued till the spring of 1862 at which I purchased some property from C. G. Carver in Sharon and the same fall moved my family there to a house that stood on a lot now owned by F. D. Runser. My shops were located on Dock St. near where Wallace and Carley's shops now are. I continued the business for three years and then in company with Carver and Trout, we formed the Empire Planning [probably Planing] Mill known as Runser, Carver and Trout and continued same until the spring of 1868, at which time I sold my interest to my partners, intending to go west. I changed my mind and the same spring in company with James Westerman, Wm. McGilvery, Sam Kimberly and myself founded the Sharon Boiler Works under the firm name of S. Runser and Co. and continued the business for some years during which time we put the irons in Mercer Jail. We built several blast furnaces and oil tanks in different parts of the country. In 1875 I sold my interest to R. J. Manison who is still in the business."

ERIE RAILROAD
By Frederick Houser

Evolution of what became the only trunk line railroad across Mercer County, that of the Erie Railroad between New York City and Chicago, goes back to the Atlantic & Great Western Railway. The Atlantic & Great Western was pushed across the county, from Meadville through Greenville and Orangeville, in 1863. The following year, it became a link—with an affiliated Ohio line—in a through route to Dayton. Also in 1864, Atlantic & Great Western built a branch from Meadville to Franklin, which was extended to Oil City in 1866. This branch along French Creek crossed the northeastern corner of Mercer County at Carlton. It promptly became the most profitable segment of the Atlantic & Great Western, with its tremendous volume of crude oil traffic. The oil bonanza lasted on the railroad for a decade, until pipelines were completed from Pennsylvania's Oil Region to the refineries at Cleveland.

In 1863, the Atlantic & Great Western leased the Cleveland & Mahoning Railroad between Cleveland, Youngstown, and Hubbard, Ohio. In 1865, the separate Atlantic & Great Western companies in the states of New York, Pennsylvania, and Ohio merged into, simply, the Atlantic & Great Western Railway. In 1868, the Atlantic & Great Western leased the Westerman Coal & Iron Railroad, a private coal railroad built in 1864 and operated by the Coleman, Westerman and Company from its Sharon furnace across the state line to the Brookfield Coal Company. It was soon connected to the Cleveland & Mahoning line at Hubbard. The first passenger train from Cleveland through to Sharon arrived on April 1, 1869.

Still missing at that time was a route from Sharon to the Atlantic & Great Western main line at Transfer for traffic moving toward Meadville and, ultimately, east to the New York area. A first possible link was incorporated in June 1870 as the Sharpsville, Wheatland, Sharon & Greenfield Railway. This line was to operate between Sharpsville and West Middlesex, with a branch from Sharon to Hickory Township coal mines. A narrow-gauge segment actually was built from Spearman Furnace in Sharpsville to a connection with the former Westerman railroad and east toward Keel Ridge. Some grading was also done south toward Wheatland and West Middlesex, but not completed.

In 1873, however, the Sharon Railway was organized specifically to fill the gap between the Atlantic & Great Western's former Westerman line at Sharon and the Atlantic & Great Western main line near Transfer. The Sharon Railway acquired the Sharpsville, Wheatland, Sharon & Greenfield in 1875 as a segment of this link. It also constructed the remaining, missing section during 1875. The new line joined the Atlantic & Great Western main line one mile south of Transfer, at the point where the original route curved sharply up the valley of Pymatuning Creek toward Orangeville. The railroad named this location Pymatuning Junction.

During this time, the unprofitable Atlantic & Great Western went through receivership, emerging in 1880 as the New York, Pennsylvania & Ohio (or, popularly, the NYPANO). Also in 1880, the entire Atlantic & Great Western system was finally converted from its original 6 foot gauge to the standard gauge of 4 feet 8.5 inches. Additionally, in 1880, the former Erie Railway—after its 1875 reorganization—had become the New York, Lake Erie & Western Railway. In 1883, the Atlantic & Great Western was leased to the New York, Lake Erie & Western as part of its New York-Chicago main line. The New York, Lake Erie & Western was again reorganized as the Erie Railroad in 1895, after failing in the Panic of 1893. The next year, the new Erie Railroad acquired all the capital stock of the Atlantic & Great Western and ultimately dissolved that historic corporation.

Under NYPANO management, the final extension of what would become the Erie Railroad in Mercer County was completed, incorporating what had started as the New Castle & Northern Railroad in 1868. The New Castle & Northern was to have run from Mahoningtown, in Lawrence County, to Sharpsville. It was actually built between New Castle and West Middlesex, making liberal use of the abandoned former Erie Extension Canal towpath for its grade. As the New Castle & Shenango Valley Railroad (of 1887), the track was extended north through Sharon to Sharpsville, apparently using part of the Sharpsville, Wheatland, Sharon & Greenfield right of way. The New Castle & Shenango Valley was leased to the NYPANO in 1889, eventually becoming the Erie Railroad's New Castle Branch.

The Erie Railroad developed into a major competitor for traffic between Chicago and New York and New England. It was especially noted for the high volume of Western fresh fruit and vegetable traffic it handled between these points. Standard operating procedure through Mercer County was for through freight trains to use the original A&GW route through Orangeville and Transfer. Erie's passenger trains and some through freights operated via Sharon and Youngstown, both of which generated considerable mail, express, passenger, and local freight traffic. The one portion of the Erie's entire New York-Chicago route never to be double-tracked was the 26-mile segment from Shenango, through Greenville, to Meadville.

CREATING A RAILROAD FOR THE PITTSBURGH STEEL INDUSTRY
By Frederick Houser

The perennial financial problems of Atlantic & Great Western Railway in extending its main line into the Midwest led to the decision in early 1865 to organize a separate railroad to run to Pardoe. The Atlantic & Great Western turned over to the new Bear Creek Railroad all the surveys and property agreements it had already made. Interestingly, the Bear Creek was to be of standard gauge (not over 4 feet 10 inches), while its parent would continue to be broad gauge (6 feet) for another decade.

A large tract of land two miles south of Greenville was purchased in 1866 as the point for connections with the Erie Extension Canal and the Erie & Pittsburgh Railroad. The site soon became known as Shenango for the river that flowed alongside it. This junction point was acquired about the same time that all work on the Bear Creek line came to a halt because of a lack of funds. No further construction was done under the Bear Creek corporate name. The railroad's directors approved changing the name of the proposed line to Shenango & Allegheny Railroad in 1867, raised new capital, and resumed construction.

The Shenango & Allegheny's 20.5 mile railroad from Shenango to the Pardoe mine was completed and regular train service instituted in 1869. Mercer Mining and Manufacturing and other coal producers began to open mines further south, around Grove City, and then into northern Butler County. By 1872, the Shenango & Allegheny had been extended to Harrisville, which was originating not only coal, but also crude oil. By 1883, Shenango & Allegheny trains were running to Butler, where other railroad connections could be made to Pittsburgh.

A third rail was laid on the Atlantic & Great Western main line between Shenango and Greenville by 1872 so that Shenango & Allegheny trains could reach Greenville. The Panic of 1873 depressed the nation's economy for much of the remainder of that decade. This depression led to the closing of mines and a reduction in revenues for the Shenango & Allegheny and most other railroads. The Atlantic & Great Western operated the Shenango & Allegheny until early 1875 when the Shenango & Allegheny's trustees reclaimed their property and began independent operation. In 1883, Shenango & Allegheny began running into Greenville on its own track and to its own station. Also, in the early 1880s, expansion of pipelines had brought an end to the Shenango & Allegheny's crude oil traffic. In 1884, the insolvency of Shenango & Allegheny and its affiliated coal company was affirmed by a federal court. Ultimately, a bankruptcy sale led to reorganization as the Pittsburgh, Shenango & Lake Erie Railroad in 1888.

Meanwhile, the Erie & Pittsburgh had, by the mid-1880s, disposed of its Erie Extension Canal property north of Greenville. When the Erie, Shenango & Pittsburgh Railway was organized in 1887, it initially undertook construction on 3.5 miles of the canal towpath from Greenville north to Osgood to connect with the Lake Shore & Michigan Southern (which included the Jamestown & Franklin). The Erie, Shenango & Pittsburgh was merged into the Pittsburgh, Shenango & Lake Erie a few months later. The Erie, Shenango & Pittsburgh brought with it not only the new Osgood extension, but also a continuation of the canal right-of-way ownership north through Girard in Erie County and property for a railroad leading to the mouth of Conneaut Creek on Lake Erie in Ohio. The Pittsburgh, Shenango & Lake Erie went bankrupt at the very time it sought to extend its line north from Osgood to the Lake. It was able to resume construction in 1890, however, and reached Erie in 1891 and Conneaut, Ohio, about a year later. The Pittsburgh, Shenango & Lake Erie had, by this time, made arrangements with railroads south of Butler to handle its traffic through to the Pittsburgh area.

The first boatload of Minnesota iron ore arrived at Conneaut Harbor in November 1892, with the cargo then moving south over the Pittsburgh, Shenango & Lake Erie en route to Pittsburgh steel mills. The pattern for one of the nation's busiest and most successful railroads was emerging, although the Panic of 1893 intervened to cause new financial problems for Pittsburgh, Shenango & Lake Erie. This struggling western Pennsylvania short-line railroad, however, was about to become associated with the largest and most profitable steel business in the world.

Andrew Carnegie, with the onset of the depression of 1893, became obsessed with the need to contain costs and control all phases of the steel-making process. One of Carnegie's particular targets was the Pennsylvania Railroad, which he felt charged excessive rates on traffic so essential to the profitability of Carnegie Steel Company. His attention was soon directed to the Pittsburgh, Shenango & Lake Erie, which still terminated at Butler, however, far north of the Carnegie mills in the Monongahela River Valley. Carnegie entered into negotiations with the railroad's president Col. S. B. Dick in late 1895 to reorganize the nearly defunct railroad as part of Carnegie Steel and extend it from Butler to Bessemer on the Monongahela River, at a cost of $3 million. Col. Dick was superseded by Judge James H. Reed as president of the new Pittsburgh, Bessemer & Lake Erie by 1896. Within fifteen months, iron ore was able to move from Lake Erie at Conneaut to Carnegie's furnace and mills on his own railroad.

The Pittsburgh, Bessemer & Lake Erie's rolling stock was already becoming the wonder of the industry with the first fleet of all-steel freight cars and, soon, some of the largest steam locomotives that had been built to that time. The railroad's general offices moved from Greenville to Pittsburgh. The Pittsburgh, Bessemer & Lake Erie gave Carnegie a bargaining tool that enabled him to negotiate lower freight rates from competing railroads, particularly the Pennsylvania.

RAILROAD CONNECTION TO NEW CASTLE
By Frederick Houser

In addition to the Erie & Pittsburgh Railroad, the Pennsylvania Railroad's other Mercer County presence was its line across the eastern portion of the County from Stoneboro, through Jackson Center, Mercer, and Leesburg to New Castle. Two local coal branches also connected with this line within the county. Although a New Castle-Mercer route had been surveyed in 1853, not until 1864 was the New Castle & Franklin Railroad chartered. Financing for this road was such a problem that construction did not commence until 1872. The line was completed to Mercer in 1873 and connected with the Jamestown & Franklin Railroad at Stoneboro in late 1874. Arrangements were soon made to allow New Castle & Franklin trains to operate over the Jamestown & Franklin to Oil City. However, by 1878, New Castle & Franklin was in receivership. The line was sold in foreclosure in 1881 to the Buffalo, Pittsburgh & Western Railroad, which ran from Oil City through Titusville to Buffalo. The New Castle & Franklin was then renamed the New Castle & Oil City and, shortly thereafter, the Oil City & Chicago Railway.

Early in 1883, Buffalo, Pittsburgh & Western and its Oil City & Chicago subsidiary were acquired by the Buffalo, New York & Philadelphia Railway. The Buffalo, New York

& Philadelphia's six hundred mile system connected New Castle and Emporium, Pennsylvania, with Buffalo and Rochester, New York. Through trains of the Buffalo, New York & Philadelphia began to operate between Pittsburgh and Buffalo, using the Pittsburgh & Lake Erie Railroad from Pittsburgh to New Castle and then their own line through Stoneboro, Oil City, and Titusville. This activity took place at the same time the boom era in the Pennsylvania oil fields was ending, reducing traffic so crucial to this railroad's solvency. It was thus in receivership by 1885; it emerged from an 1887 reorganization as the Western New York & Pennsylvania Railway.

The Panic of 1893 precipitated yet another receivership. The reorganized company was barely able to pay its fixed charges until it was taken over by the Pennsylvania Railroad in August 1900. The Western New York & Pennsylvania then failed to earn its interest payments in any of the ensuing twenty-five years. In 1902, the Pennsylvania Railroad built a branch southeast from Leesburg along the southern boundary of Mercer County into Butler County to serve a cluster of coal mines. The line terminated at a mine at Redmond, near Slippery Rock. By 1928, five miles of this branch into Redmond were abandoned. The line was cut back to Leesburg in the following decades.

As had been the case elsewhere on the Western New York & Pennsylvania, the Pennsylvania Railroad made a number of physical improvements to the New Castle-Stoneboro line. Several bridges of greater capacity were built to permit the operation of heavier locomotives, thus improving the efficiency of the line. The line also hosted three passenger trains on weekdays between New Castle and Stoneboro, with one of these continuing on to Oil City. The final passenger run to Stoneboro was made in the summer of 1932. By the following year, freight traffic was also becoming very scarce: only one freight train per week operated over this line to Stoneboro. The Pennsylvania Railroad abandoned the line from Jackson Center to Stoneboro in 1938 but continued to serve coal mines southeast of Jackson Center. The spur that reached this mining area, and the remainder of the line to New Castle, lasted until the 1970s when all the track was lifted.

FRANK H. BUHL
By Mairy Jayn Woge

Frank H. Buhl was a grandson of Christian Buhl who left Bavaria in the late 1700s and settled in Zelienople, Butler County, in 1804. Frank's father, Christian H., was involved with other Buhls in operating the Detroit Copper and Brass Rolling Works in Michigan.

In 1835, Joel B. Curtis, a native of the Ohio Western Reserve and a previous resident of Mercer, bought 100 acres north of State Street from Isaac Patterson for $2,000 because veins of coal cropped out of fields on the Patterson property. Curtis and his brother-in-law, George Boyce, mined the coal. One mine extended from the Curtis land at the intersection of West State Street and North Irvine Avenue to the opening on the west side of the west hill in Brookfield Township, Ohio. The east side of the mine is now the location of the United Way. Curtis founded Sharon Iron Company in 1850. He used some of the coal he mined to melt ore at the industry. The firm failed after it was sold in 1855 to a partnership that sought to make steel from raw iron, but belonged to Curtis and some investors in 1860. Curtis died in 1862. The year before, he and partners had sold Sharon Iron to James Westerman and four other residents of Youngstown. In 1865, when two of the Youngstown residents disposed of their shares, Christian H. Buhl of Detroit filled one of the vacancies. The name of the company was changed to Westerman Iron. It sprawled over seven blocks in the flats east of the Shenango River, controlled a coal railroad, owned two mines, owned ten industrial buildings including a furnace and rolling mill and maintained red painted company houses occupied by employees of the iron company. Buhl and Westerman opened Home Coal Mine west of current Christy Road in Hermitage. Westerman and earlier partners developed 2,000-acre Big Drift Mine on Incline Hill in Brookfield Township. The mine employed 450 men.

In 1874, Westerman resigned from the iron company to become a banker. Christian H. Buhl and two Youngstown partners ran the firm. The partners [eventually] sold their shares and Buhl became the sole owner.

In 1887, Christian Buhl transferred the company to his son, Frank H. Buhl. The name was then changed to Buhl Company. The mine company store was on the north side of West State Street. Its customers were the fourteen hundred employees of the Buhl mill and mines.

Meanwhile, Shenango Iron Works had been established about 1863 on a three-acre tract off Clark Street in Hickory Township that Daniel Eagan and Samuel McClure had acquired. Frank H. Buhl was president. Two of his Buhl relatives from Detroit and Porter-Forker kin of his wife, Julia, had office jobs at Shenango Iron. Seven buildings were erected. An existing structure that had been a wool mill was converted to a machine and pattern shop.

Four years later, Frank H. Buhl was president; McClure, vice president; and Eagan, secretary and general manager of Sharon Steel Castings Company, the first steel mill in Mercer County. The firm's quarters were north of Shenango Avenue and in Hickory. The management purchased a 15-ton Siemans-Martin open hearth. Annual production of steel castings amounted to 10,000 tons.

Block coal was peculiar to the Shenango Valley area and a section of Alabama. It contained no sulfur and burned without leaving ashes. It was recognizable because it was laminated. Sharon block, as it was often called, was perfect for melting iron ore. It brought industries to the Valley. By 1900, the block coal that could be reached in shafts by the mining equipment available at the time was exhausted. Some mines were flooded. Miners were moving to eastern Mercer County where they dug coal slightly inferior to Sharon block. The coal was transported to the Shenango Valley by a spur of the Erie Railroad south of Greenville. The railroad sprouted numerous spurs. One of them extended to Mines No. 2 and No. 5 south of Grove City. The mines and mine towns were owned by Frank H. Buhl.

Frank H. Buhl built his mansion (pictured, in 2000) on East State Street in Sharon in 1896 for $60,000. Styled like a French castle, the fourteen-room home was decorated with furnishings from a French castle. While the gray sandstone mansion was being constructed, Buhl and his wife Julia stayed in the ten-room house on the property (now the caretaker's residence). (In 1939, after Julia died, her nephew inherited the mansion and converted it into apartments. Now owned and restored by James and Donna Winner, it is a bed and breakfast and houses one of the Winner Art Galleries.) (Photographer: Marilyn Dewald)

Now, houses and a pile of slack and "red dog" remain at No. 5. The Buhl Water Company is located there and adjoins the Prime Outlets of Grove City.

By 1897, the name of Frank H. Buhl was synonymous with iron and steel making. Towns and companies from all over the United States and some from Canada had invited him to build and operate mills for them.

In 1888, Buhl married Julia A. Forker who was among Sharon's elite. Julia was born in Mercer and a preschooler when her parents, Henry and Selina Porter Forker, moved to Sharon. Her social life blossomed on Sharon's East Hill. She was reluctant to live anywhere else.

The construction of their mansion took seven years. It was completed in 1898 and Julia was enjoying the lunches, concerts, and parties she held there. Since Julia was occupied, Buhl felt comfortable in turning his attention elsewhere. He became involved in irrigation, canals, railroads, and iron ore mining in Idaho and Minnesota. Towns in both states and in Alabama were named Buhl for him. He donated funds for a street railway in the Philippine Islands.

Frank H. Buhl was a contrast. As a capitalist, he charged the Erie Railroad Extension a nickel for every car traveling through Buhl Company (Sharon Iron) property that did not deliver or pick up merchandise from the mill. As a philanthropist, he supported the families of two coal miners who were killed on the job and provided food and milk for children from needy families. He socialized. On the Saturday nights when he did not attend elegant events with Julia, Buhl would walk from his mansion to Sharon bars where he drank beer with men who worked for him. And, he would get drunk. As a conservative, he insisted his wife not wear dresses with low cut necklines that were the style of the time. However, he did not object to the mounds of colored feathers on her hats. He gave generous sums to St. John's Episcopal Church in Sharon, but rarely attended services.

Soon after World War I started in Europe, Buhl pledged $2 million for victims of the conflict in Belgium and northern France. Frank H. Buhl died in 1918. After a number of years and the end of payments, a delegate for the beneficiaries traveled to Sharon and thanked the Buhl's widow for the gift. Julia Buhl died in 1936.

RUTH AFRICAN METHODIST EPISCOPAL CHURCH
By Roland Barksdale-Hall

Ruth African Methodist Episcopal (AME) Zion Church is recognized as the oldest existing African-American institution in Mercer County. During the late 1800s three prominent AME Zion churches existed in the community. In 1879, a church in Sharpsville was started, and in 1885, a Mercer church was established. The AME Zion movement reached Sharon in 1888 when a small group of African-Americans established a mission, now known as the Ruth AME Zion Church. Now, the Sharpsville and Mercer AME Zion churches no longer exist. Ruth AME Zion remains, the only reminder of the early development of the African-American church.

The early AME Zion church served as a cultural center. In its sanctuary the black community gathered to discuss vital issues of the day and to pursue intellectual pursuits. Mercer's Colored Literary Society met weekly at the Mercer AME Zion Church. Masons, Elks, Odd Fellows, and Knights of Pythias held memorial services at the church.

The AME Zion Church's membership rolls included some of the Shenango Valley's first African-American residents. John Fountain Reed, a barber, was one of the first coloreds permitted to live in Sharon; he operated barber shops, catering to all-white clientele, in Sharon and in Mercer where his family held church membership. Three colored fami-

Each ethnic community continues to make invaluable contributions in every field of endeavor, including medicine, education, law enforcement, sports, technology, and the arts. And through them Mercer County is blessed with ties to every continent.

MARY MCDOWELL VERMEIRE'S FAMILY IN THE 1800S
Written in 1980

"I'll start first with my mother, Nellie Eliza Dygert McDowell. The older I get the more I realize that a very wonderful person she was. Mother's parents were Joseph and Mary who lived on a large 400 acre farm they owned, about 4 miles from Sheakleyville. . . . Mother and her brothers walked every day to school, about 3 miles, a one room all grade school. Even in the cold snowy winter when they were six years old, the trip was made. Grandma Dygert would have hot baked potatoes to put in their pockets to be held to keep their hands warm. When lunch time came they were eaten. Mother's brothers all quit school to help on the farm at an early age. Mother finished her schooling in the country school, then attended Jamestown Institute for further education. She later taught for a year before she was married. Grandma D's parents were also farmers. Their last name was Goode. When Grandma and her sisters (she had several) were very young her Mother was driving the horses in the hay wagon as Great Grandfather walked along pitching the hay on the wagon. The horses were frightened and my Great Grandmother was pulled off the wagon and got tangled in the reins and was dragged to her death. The children were given out to friends or neighbors to raise. . . .

"I remember Mother telling us how much she enjoyed going with her Dad and brothers to the maple sugaring off She would ride on the big horse drawn sled through the woods to the sugar house. The buckets of sap would be taken, emptied in the drums, then the process of making maple syrup and sugar would begin. She enjoyed it when syrup was poured on dishes of snow and she would've a treat of maple 'ice cream.' . . .

The students of the Bower School (Delaware Township) in 1898 included (first row) Ralph Bower, Leslie Simmons, and Herman Gehser; (second row) Lawrence Simmons, George Anderson, Mabel Simmons, Lulu Bower; (third row, right of teacher) Ed Keen. The teacher was Mary Fruit Brown.

VISITING ETIQUETTE

Mairy Jayn Woge interviewed Olive Owen (Sharon) who remembers the demands of high society in the late 1800s and early 1900s. Women wore gloves when they went to a house to visit. They also carried cards on which their names were printed. On arrival at a house, a maid greeted a visitor with a tray. The name card was placed on it. If the woman of the house was not busy and at home, she advised the maid to bring the guest to the parlor or sitting room. If the housewife was unable to entertain company, the visitor was politely turned away.

Another recollection comes from Anna Black Bass, who was interviewed by Margo Letts in 1998. Born in 1908, Bass remembered from her youth that the ladies left cards when they went calling. "It was prestigious if your bowl was full of cards because it meant that you had many visitors." When Anna went with her mom, she had to sit next to her and not say a word. She liked to say that she had to "use the facilities" because she could go through the houses. Her mom had a case that held her calling cards.

"Now to go back to Grandma Wealtha. Her Mother, Emily Church Philips, also came from a distinguished family. Her father, Isaac, was a Justice of the Peace doing much legal work for the citizens in Sheakleyville. He was also an itinerate preacher, a great Baptist. In fact, many of my relatives though one would not go to Heaven unless they were Baptist and Republican. My grandmother was born in Sheakleyville [about 1830], and after receiving her education, taught school for a short time. A girl either taught school or got married in those days. I remember her saying she was paid $18.00 per month and boarded around her first term. That meant she stayed a week for meals and room with various pupils. Sometimes it was all right but many times one had to eat and sleep in undesirable homes. She was offered a raise of $25.00 per month the next time, but I guess she decided to get married. Grandma was a hard working talented lady. She taught a Sunday School class for many years and sang in the choir until she was 75 years old. . . . Grandma was always in demand as a practical nurse. Whenever there was a birth, she was always called on. Also when deaths were imminent she was present to help."

PASTIMES AND FASHION
From 1891–1893 diary of Sebastain Runser, transcribed by Margo Letts

"Our parties were not expensive but mostly a gain to those that held the party for we all had to work, both male and female. There generally was quilting or a family fall sewing or knitting for the little ones and then when night came on, our music did not cost as much for there were plenty of fiddlers that made music good enough for reels and french fours and if there were no fiddlers we took turns in singing for the dances and saved the expense of an orchestra. When the party broke up some of the young men had horses and would take their girls home behind them, and them that were on foot if they succeeded in being accepted and did not get the mitten as we called it, they would shoulder their axes and take the girls home on foot, sometimes three or four miles. This was hard work but it did not cost much and always found plenty to take the chances. Everything went merrily unless sometimes it happened that some fine young man got what we called the snack from some girl he had his eye on for a home trip, but this did not discourage him much for the next time there was another party or spelling school, he would offer his services again to the same girl and persevered on in the matter until he succeeded in capturing her or someone else.

"This whole affair was not costly or very expensive for our styles and fashions were nearly all home made and we were not waiting for the fashions to come from the slums of Paris or any foreign country with great expense, but they grew right among us and did not cost much, so we lived cheap and were mostly happy and contented. We did not wear long toed shoes nor late styled clothing. It is true that some kept a change for extra occasions. It usually consisted of a pigeon tailed coat, calf skin boots, and plug hat, and some had straps on the bottom of their best dress pants to keep them in good shape and they were not obliged to have them creased every time they wore them. But it was hard on the suspender buttons in climbing fences and they frequently met with accidents. The toes of their boots were short and they were not liable to meet with any trouble from them in going through the mud and climbing fences.

"I do not know when the style of long toed shoes will cease, but there is one thing sure they dare not make them much longer or finer pointed. The old dutch wooden shoe or the Indian moccasin looks no worse in my eyes than this late style of shoes. . . .

"I will now relate some of the matters took place from the time after we had plenty of fun in one way or another. We had full liberty to fish for the laws were not as strict as they are now, and fish were plenty and we could capture them in many ways, either by net or scoop net, or hook as we liked, and at anytime and some times succeeded in capturing some nice ones. In the summer-time we would go in swimming and hunting wild berries of which there were plenty and in the fall we gathered nuts for the winter, and in the winter did some skating on home made skates, hunted rabbits or any little game we could capture and when spring came, we knew nothing of football, baseball or golf, but played mostly town-ball, corner-ball and sock-ball. These were all innocent and easy games and were not liable to result in broken legs and heads as football is nowadays. In time some of the farmers became able to purchase buggies and those that had no horse would try to borrow from those that had and we would form strings of ten or a dozen and go somewhere which cost about 25 cents a dinner, horse feed was 10 cents and borrowed horses and buggies. This made a cheap good pleasure trip and was as satisfactory to us as a trip to the watering places of the present day. I remember of taking part in one myself, which cost me a little more than usual for I had bad luck in the end and cost me several dollars before I got all things made up again. It happened in this way, there was a party formed to take a drive to a Catholic church near Mercer and Greenville road, some few miles from Mercer, and I was invited to join and it was to be on Sunday, so I concluded to join them for it would not cost much for I had a friend that I knew would loan me a rig, who lived at Sharon Furnace, so Sunday morning came and I went after the rig which was a common open buggy with what we called panel body, set high on a pair of long springs and a buffalo robe in the seat for aquision [a cushion], and it looked quite tasty. But here is where my bad luck commenced, the horse he was to let me have become lame and was obliged to give me an old ebelusia [Appaloosa] or specold [speckled] mare which had a colt at her side. This was the best that could be done in the case, so I took the rig and made all haste to Sharpsville again. I left the colt at home for it would not look well to have a colt along in a Sunday party. When I got my girl I found the rest of the party had gone for some time, I started and lost the right road and got to Mercer and Church, it was about over when we got to the church and they were preparing to go to Delaware Grove to dinner at a popular place, kept by Flannagan Saterfield, who after some time moved to Sharon and many people remember him. Everything went nicely and satisfactorily until we were ready to start for home when the trouble commenced again. I drove up to a high perch in front of the hotel and as my girl stepped down into the buggy, the bottom of the buggy gave way and she was injured some. This delayed us some time while the others were on their way home merrily. After I got started I tried to catch up with them but this failed and when evening came on and became a little cooler I found the old mare had been foundered some way and became quite stiff, and it was hard work for me to make home with her. When we got to Sharpsville, my girl insisted on me to remain and have some supper for her sister had it all ready, she got home sooner than we did for she was not so unlucky as we were. I tied my horse to a tree that stood before the house and when I got busily engaged in eating my supper I heard a racket outside and I went to see what was up and found the old mare lying down and had the shafts of the buggy broken and this left me in bad. Some parties that were standing around said that she would die and this made me only a little angry and I made up my mind to do all I could for this poor creature and I succeeded in getting her up and I left the rig at Sharpsville and led beast to Sharon Furnace and got the services of an old teamster to assist me. He told me it was founder that ailed her. He gave her some medicine and told me to keep her walking as much as possible during the night, this kept me wake nicely and the next day we hitched her in a wagon with one other horse and did some light hauling small loads of native ore to the furnace and that evening she became fit to return to her home and the whole affair cost me $15.00 besides loss of time.

"This dwelt heavy on my mind and was a warning to me, it could not last long at the wages I was then receiving $40.00 a year, and so I adopted the old style and went on foot till some time after. We had lots of fun going to night school such as singing, geography, spelling, schools and sometimes had some hot debates, on some subjects but never mettled much in politics although I was a Democrat, was converted to that faith by an old lady of the name of Craig, who lived near state line in a log house, and she promised me a fine dinner if I would vote as she said when I became of age. I promised her I would do that act one Sunday morning, one of her sons came to Sharpsville and told me his Mother wanted me to come that day as they had killed a nice little pig a day or so ago, and wanted me to have some of it. So I looked up my Sunday suit and it was not hard to find for I had but one and it was in style for the styles did not change as often as they do nowadays. We wore the same hat the whole year, there was no change in spring or fall hats, one hat was all right for both seasons.

"My boots were also in style, were long enough for my feet and no longer and fit like a new kid glove, and gloves we did not use much, when the weather was cold we wore the good old home made mitt of glove knit by our Mothers or some other one, they were made of American wool or cotton to suit the season of the year."

A Century in Retrospect
From 1891–1893 diary of Sebastain Runser, transcribed by Margo Letts

"Our pleasures and festivities did not cost as much or take up as much time as it does now, yet there seemed to be as much satisfaction for we were nearly on a level with each other if not in this worlds goods, it was in the general feeling between us and I believe it was better for the poor man than it is now. Conceit and confidence has some what diminished and selfishness, pride and distrust have increased, so much doubt in one another. I have seen the time when you could get trusted for postage on a letter when we did not use stamps on envelopes and postage was from 6-1/4 to 25 cents, owing to the distance, the letter would be written on a large sheet of paper and nicely folded and a red wafer moistened with the tongue and the folds of the letter were fastened with a blunt thing or a stamp for the purpose, some had stamps with their initials on them. They were a little more advanced in wealth and could buy them.

"Times have changed considerable in the last fifty years, and it is hard to tell what the next half century will bring forth. Nowadays our letters go any distance and are delivered in our houses, and collected from mail boxes. The mail boxes being near our houses. At two cents this makes matters quite convenient, but the taxes are a little higher now than they were then. But wages are higher and postage lower so the young man can write oftener to his girl than I did for I never wrote after, I had a bad start. All went along smoothly till 1850, I concluded to get married and stop expense, and settle down for life, I thought I could keep a woman as cheap as to pay board, so I began to prepare for same, and commenced adding some things to my wardrobe.

"We cannot tell what the end of the next century will be if it improves as this one has so far. It has not been more than sixty years since I have taken notice to improvements and inventions, but in that time I could not enumerate all of them it seems the world was in the dark at the beginning of this century. I could go on and mention many of the improvements but I do not know where to commence or where to stop."

The structure known as the Boston Tavern was built in 1833 by John Crill outside Mercer on the Mercer-Slippery Rock Pike (now Route 258, Findley Township). With a distillery on his farm, Crill supplied spirits for the Saint Cloud Hotel in Mercer, which he ran. In 1845, Crill's daughter Christeena inherited the farm; and she and her husband Adam Boston converted the farmhouse into a tavern. Reportedly in the 1850s, a peddler with a carpetbag containing valuables stayed overnight at the tavern's inn. He mysteriously disappeared early the next morning before the arrival of the stagecoach, leaving blood stains on the floorboards. Later, bricks began to fall periodically from the wall above where the peddler had stayed. Claude Eckman, who has completely restored the inn, removed the paint that a former owner had applied over the stains, replaced the bricks, and has never been haunted by the peddler ghost. The home, still owned by the Eckman family, is now called Candlewood. (Photographer: Marilyn Dewald)

Timeline 1800—1810

A few facts to set the mood. The year is 1800. The Constitution has been in effect for 12 years and John Adams is the 2nd President. It takes 20 days for a letter to reach Savannah, Georgia, from Portland, Maine.

The World

- **1800** There are 16 states: Delaware, Pennsylvania, New Jersey, Georgia, Connecticut, Massachusetts, Maryland, South Carolina, New Hampshire, Virginia, New York, North Carolina, Rhode Island, Vermont, Kentucky and Tennessee; the construction of the White House is finished; the electric battery is invented by Alessandro Volta
- **1801** Thomas Jefferson becomes the 3rd president (first president inaugurated in Washington, DC); Kentucky outlaws dueling
- **1802** The establishment of the US Military Academy at West Point is authorized
- **1803** Ohio becomes the 17th state; the size of the United States more than doubles by buying all French territory west of the Mississippi from Napoleon Bonaparte
- **1804** Lithography is invented in Germany
- **1805** The British defeat the Spanish and French naval fleets at the Battle of Trafalgar
- **1806** Zebulon Pike sights a mountain that is later named Pikes Peak
- **1807** Congress bans slave trade
- **1809** James Madison becomes the 4th president (first president inaugurated in American-made clothes); the first US geology book is published

Mercer County

- **1800** Mercer County is created by an act of the General Assembly (with at least three churches already established: Old Salem United Methodist Church (Sugar Grove Township), established in 1798, and Fairfield (New Vernon Township) and Center (Pine Township) Presbyterian churches established in 1799)
- **1801** The four original townships are Neshannock, Salem, Sandy Lake and Cool Spring
- **1802** Wolf Creek and Pymatuning townships are created; Sandy Lake is dropped and Sandy Creek Township introduced; a grist and saw-mill is built on the Shenango River within the limits of Hickory Township
- **1803** Samuel Pew holds the first stake for survey of the county
- **1804** The jail building is ready for occupancy; the first budget for the county is estimated at $1,475
- **1805** West Salem, French Creek, Delaware, Sandy Lake, Shenango, Lackawannock, Mahoning, Springfield and Slippery Rock townships are added; the county establishes its own courts and board of commissioners
- **1806** A weekly mail route is established from Pittsburgh to Erie via Mercer
- **1807** A contract is signed to build the county's first courthouse for $7,116
- **1808** A strip of land on the county's north border is given to Crawford County
- **1809** Jonathan Cochran receives contract to move court bench and chairs from log structures to new building for $150

Timeline 1811—1820

The World

- 1812 Louisiana becomes the 18th state; the "War of 1812" begins
- 1813 The phrase "Don't give up the ship" becomes the slogan of the US Navy; the nickname "Uncle Sam" is born today in the *Troy Post* when a writer uses it as a symbolic reference to the United States
- 1814 The "Star-Spangled Banner" is sung for the first time
- 1816 Indiana becomes the 19th state
- 1817 For the first time, a street in an American city (Baltimore) is illuminated by gas lights; James Monroe becomes the 5th president; Mississippi becomes the 20th state
- 1818 Illinois becomes the 21st state; the carol "Silent Night" is sung for the first time
- 1819 In a treaty with Spain, Florida is ceded to the United States; Alabama becomes the 22nd state
- 1820 Maine becomes the 23rd state; Congress passes the Public Land Act, lowering the price of western lands to $1.25 an acre to promote settlement of the west; the first potatoes are planted in Hawaii

Mercer County

- 1811 The first school in the county is established by the State Legislature; the first newspaper in the county, the *Western Press*, begins publishing
- 1812 The *Western Press* reports an earthquake in Meadville, Pennsylvania
- 1813 Capt. James McCoy and all his men are ordered to Erie to defend the Shipworks
- 1814 Mercer incorporates as a Borough; Elias Jones builds a distillery in the Sharon area
- 1817 Heavy snowfall, 3 1/2 feet, keeps small pupils home for weeks
- 1818 Semiweekly postal routes begin; the Pittsburgh & Erie Turnpike opens for travel
- 1819 The second jail is erected

Timeline 1821—1830

The World

- 1821 Mexico gains independence from Spain; William Becknell leads a wagon train to New Mexico initiating the Santa Fe Trail; Missouri becomes the 24th state; sailors in New Orleans invent the game of poker; the first tuition-free public high school in the United States opens in Boston, Massachusetts
- 1822 The first patent for false teeth is issued to Charles Graham of New York; Congress combines East and West Florida into Florida Territory
- 1824 A Harrisburg, Pennsylvania newspaper publishes results of the first public opinion poll
- 1825 The Republic of Mexico is proclaimed; John Quincy Adams becomes the 6th president
- 1827 The first ballet group in the United States performs at the Bowery Theater in New York City; matches are invented by John Walker
- 1828 The first edition of *Webster's Dictionary* is published
- 1829 Andrew Jackson becomes the 7th president and an unruly crowd mobs the White House during the inaugural ball

Mercer County

- 1821 Dr. James Magoffin and family sail from Ireland for Mercer
- 1822 Georgetown (now Sheakleyville) is christened with considerable flare
- 1824 Tri-weekly postal routes begin; Gen. Lafayette visits the county and spends the night at the Hackney House; Mercer begins to organize a fire department after the burning of Union Church; during this winter almost no snow falls
- 1825 The first piano is brought to the county from Dublin, Ireland; John Bigler becomes an apprentice at the *Western Press*; a number of escaped slaves use the "underground railroad" to reach Sandy Lake and started a settlement known as Liberia (now Stoneboro)
- 1827 The first public movement in the direction of active temperance begins; ground breaking for the Beaver and Erie Canal occurs
- 1829 Clarksville is laid out
- 1830 The *Mercer Luminary* is published from the site of the Anderson Grocery Store in Fredonia

Timeline 1831—1840

The World

- 1831 The first steam locomotive makes its run between Albany and Schenectady, New York; the lawn mower is invented by Edwin Budding and John Ferrabee
- 1832 President Jackson vetoes a bill renewing the charter of the Bank of the United States
- 1833 The first US public library to be supported by municipal taxes is founded in Petersburgh, New Hampshire; the Boston Academy of Music is the first US music school established
- 1834 Refrigeration is invented by Jacob Perkins
- 1835 A crack appears in the Liberty Bell, the symbol of US freedom
- 1836 The Alamo falls after a 13-day siege; Arkansas becomes the 25th state; General Sam Houston is sworn in as the first president of the Republic of Texas
- 1837 Michigan becomes the 26th state; Martin Van Buren becomes the 8th president
- 1838 Samuel Morse gives the first public demonstration of his electric telegraph; 15,000 Mormons are driven out of Missouri
- 1839 France recognizes the Republic of Texas
- 1840 Antarctica is discovered by American Charles Wilkes

Mercer County

- 1831 A meeting is held at the courthouse over the hydrophobia issue; four rabid dogs are killed in Mercer
- 1832 Hickory Township is founded; the village of Jamestown is laid out; delegates from surrounding counties meet at the courthouse to petition for a canal from Erie to Pittsburgh
- 1834 A meeting is held in Georgetown (now Sheakleyville) to form a counter temperance society in the county; the disappearance or abduction of five-year-old Mary Ann Gamble occurs in Cool Spring Township
- 1835 Early in the year, coal is discovered in a hillside west of Sharon on land owned by Gen. Joel B. Curtis; townships are divided into school districts; hard frost kills the corn and seeds sell for $2 per bushel
- 1836 The Public School System is established in Pennsylvania; the town of West Middlesex is laid out
- 1838 Greenville is incorporated into a borough; the sale of lots begin in New Lebanon borough
- 1839 Deer Creek post office is established (later known as Milledgeville)
- 1840 Centertown's post office is established; the first effort towards organizing a fire department in Greenville begins

Timeline 1841—1850

The World

- 1841 William Henry Harrison, the 9th president, dies while in office and John Tyler becomes the 10th president; Oberlin College awards the first woman with a degree
- 1842 Ether is used as an anesthetic for the first time
- 1845 Edgar Allan Poe's "The Raven" is published in New York; Florida becomes the 27th state and Texas the 28th state; James Polk becomes the 11th president
- 1846 The first formal baseball game is played; the Smithsonian Institute in Washington is created; the sewing machine is patented; the planet Neptune is discovered; Iowa becomes the 29th state
- 1847 Brigham Young and his Mormon followers arrive at Great Salt Lake Valley in Utah
- 1848 Mexico signs a treaty agreeing to cede Texas, New Mexico, Arizona and California to the United States for $15 million; Wisconsin becomes the 30th state; "bloomers" become a radical change to women's clothing; President James Polk turns on the first gas light at the White House
- 1849 Walter Hunt of New York City patents the safety pin; Zachary Taylor becomes the 12th president; Mrs. Elizabeth Blackwell becomes the first female physician in the United States
- 1850 The US population reaches 23,191,876; California becomes the 31st state; Millard Fillmore becomes the 13th president; the paper bag begins to appear in stores

Mercer County

- 1841 Sharon is incorporated as a borough
- 1844 Greene Township is created; Mercer County Medical Society elects first officers; the construction of the Erie Canal is completed
- 1845 Clay Furnace is put into blast, named after Kentuckian Henry Clay
- 1846 Known as the "Locust Year"; six more blast furnaces are started to make pig iron; Wilmington Township is created; the first rolling mill in the Shenango Valley opens and establishes the valley as an iron and steel center; unofficial reports of the schools in the county showed 214 schools averaging five months and five days a year teaching (170 men and 145 women teachers); the New Hamburg log school burns
- 1847 Dysentery, or the bloody flux, kills 200+ people in the county; a meeting at the courthouse is held to study the idea of building a railroad from Big Bend, at the canal, to Mercer; the second Caldwell school is built on the site of Delaware Military Honor Roll
- 1848 Andrew Carnegie and his parents pass through Sharon on a canal boat; Clarksville is incorporated
- 1849 President Zachary Taylor and future president James Buchanan visit the county; the first canal boat from Greenville loaded with coal arrives in Erie; Findley, Worth, and Mill Creek townships are created; Mahoning, Slippery Rock, and Neshannock townships are given to Lawrence County
- 1850 The first nail mill opens in Sharon; the last issue of the *Mercer Luminary* is published; Fairview, Lake, and Jackson townships are created

Timeline 1851—1860

The World

- 1851 The city of San Francisco is almost entirely destroyed by fire; the first YMCA in America opens its doors in Boston
- 1852 A cartoon depicting "Uncle Sam" as the symbol for the United States appears for the first time; Harriet Beecher Stowe's "Uncle Tom's Cabin" is published
- 1853 Franklin Pierce becomes the 14th president
- 1854 The Republican Party is formed
- 1857 James Buchanan becomes the 15th president
- 1858 Minnesota becomes the 32nd state; the first transatlantic cable is completed stretching from Newfoundland to Ireland
- 1859 Oregon becomes the 33rd state; Acrobatic Frenchman Emile Blondin crosses Niagara Falls on a tightrope in just five minutes; the American oil industry begins when the first oil well is drilled by Edwin Drake near Titusville, Pennsylvania
- 1860 The first two Pony Express riders set out to deliver mail across the western United States

Mercer County

- 1851 Dr. McElrath charges $.25 for office calls and as high as $.50 for house calls; John and William Bigler become governors of California and Pennsylvania respectively at the same time; company houses in Sharon are built to accommodate workers; Dr. W. H. Axtell reports an epidemic of dysentery that is extensive and fatal in Sandy Creek and New Vernon townships; Liberty, Pine, Deer Creek, New Vernon, and Perry townships are created; Georgetown is incorporated as Sheakleyville
- 1852 Act of the Pennsylvania General Assembly authorizes the purchase of land for a "county farm"
- 1853 Ground is broken for the Erie Railroad; earliest known edition of the *Independent Democrat* is published
- 1854 The first election for the position of county superintendent of schools ($400/year) is held; Jamestown is incorporated
- 1855 Peoples Convention is held and creates the Republican party in the county; a very wet summer spoils the grain
- 1856 Residents of West Middlesex buy shares at $5 each to build a small frame house to serve as school and church; an act of the Pennsylvania General Assembly creates the Mercer School District; *West Greenville Times* newspaper publishes first issue; Hempfield and Sugar Grove townships are created
- 1858 A frost kills all the crops; flour soars to $18 a barrel the next winter
- 1859 Sandy Lake is incorporated

Timeline 1861—1870

The World

- 1861 Kansas becomes the 34th state; English Adm. Robert Fitzroy issues the first "weather forecast"; the first US paper money is issued; Abraham Lincoln becomes the 16th president
- 1862 The Homestead Act goes into effect; the Congressional Medal of Honor is authorized
- 1863 West Virginia becomes the 35th state; President Abraham Lincoln delivers the Gettysburg Address
- 1864 Use of the phrase "In God We Trust" on US coins is authorized by Congress; Nevada becomes the 36th state; the US Post Office introduces the money-order system
- 1865 President Lincoln is assassinated; the Salvation Army is founded in London, England; slavery is abolished in the United States with the adoption of the 13th Amendment to the Constitution
- 1867 Nebraska becomes the 37th state; the United States buys Alaska from Russia for $7 million; the first elevated railroad opens in New York City
- 1868 Impeachment proceedings are brought against President Andrew Jackson; the first "Type-Writer" is patented
- 1869 The first transcontinental railroad in America is completed; Ulysses S. Grant becomes the 18th president
- 1870 The population of the United States is 38,558,371; New York's first subway line is opened to the public; the US Department of Justice is created; the first boardwalk in the world is completed in the resort town of Atlantic City, New Jersey

Mercer County

- 1861 A lecture is given at the courthouse on "Our National Troubles"; Capt. James Wood plots out Wheatland; the first draft of the Civil War is held in Mercer
- 1863 The first freight train arrives in Sharon
- 1864 Brothers R. D. and James Frey publish the first edition of the *Sharon Herald* ($1.50/year in advance); the first locomotive crosses State Street in Sharon (the Atlantic & Great Western Railroad); the re-enlisting troop members of the 57th Pennsylvania receive a one-month furlough; West Middlesex is incorporated
- 1865 The first train leaves from Mercer Iron & Coal Company mine (near Stoneboro) with five cars
- 1866 Due to a faulty stove pipe fire destroys the courthouse; Stoneboro and New Lebanon are incorporated
- 1867 The second courthouse is erected for $98,000
- 1868 Mercer-born representative John A. Bingham is Judge Advocate General in the impeachment trail of President Jackson; the brick jail is erected for $67,000; an ordinance in Greenville prohibits wooden buildings on Main Street between the river and Penn Street; John L. Morrison buys the *Sharon Herald*

Timeline 1871—1880

The World

- 1871 The great fire of Chicago breaks out when Mrs. O'Leary's cow kicks over a lantern in her barn
- 1872 Nebraskans plant more than a million trees in celebration of the first Arbor Day; Susan B. Anthony is arrested while attempting to vote
- 1873 P. T. Barnum opens his Hippodrome in New York City, built to house the "Greatest Show on Earth" (covered five acres and accommodated 10,000 seated patrons at a time)
- 1875 The first Kentucky Derby is held
- 1876 Alexander Graham Bell invents the telephone; the first "no-hitter" in baseball history is pitched by George Washington Bradley; Colorado becomes the 38th state; Custer takes his "Last Stand"
- 1877 The first moon of Mars is discovered; Rutherford B. Hayes becomes the 19th president
- 1878 Thomas Edison patents the phonograph; the Mexican government is organizing an army corps to operate against the US troops on the Rio Grande; a law is passed fixing the weight of a ton of coal at 2,000 pounds goes into effect ($500 penalty)
- 1879 California outlaws the employment of Chinese workers; the electric light bulb is invented by Thomas Edison
- 1880 The population of the United States is 50,155,783; Broadway, New York's main thoroughfare, becomes the "Great White Way" as it is lit by electricity for the first time

Mercer County

- 1871 Laird's block on Main and Race streets burn in Greenville (losses amount to $44,000); the *Advance* newspaper is started in Greenville; the Erie Canal Extension closes (abandoned after the Elk Creek aqueduct collapsed)
- 1872 The cornerstone for "Greenville Hall" is erected (the first Thiel College building); Wheatland is created; railroad reaches Pine Grove (now Grove City); Bethel is incorporated
- 1873 An atlas of Mercer County is published; the "Chicago Fire" of Greenville engulfs 300 feet x 120 feet on the south and north sides of Main Street (35 buildings burn, total loss of $83,000)
- 1874 Sharpsville is incorporated; the *Sandy Lake News* newspaper is established; Fredonia Institute, originally for men only, allows women to attend
- 1875 The Woman's Christian Temperance Union of Mercer County forms at the courthouse
- 1876 Isacc Ketler opens "select school" in Pine Grove (now Grove City College); firebug burns several businesses in Greenville; the Mercer Iron & Coal Company has produced 629,158 tons of coal in 13 years
- 1877 A history of Mercer County is published
- 1878 A new game law is passed that any one catching a black bass less than six inches long will be fined $10; advertisements for Carters Liver Pills and land in Kansas for $2.50 to $5/acre appear
- 1879 The Academy Building, the structure of the forerunner of Grove City College, is built
- 1880 The county's population is 56,161; the *Sharon Times* ceases publication

Timeline 1881—1890

The World

- **1881** The American Red Cross is founded by Clara Barton; James A. Garfield becomes the 20th president; Chester A. Arthur becomes the 21st president when Garfield is assassinated
- **1883** The Brooklyn Bridge opens
- **1885** *Good Housekeeping* magazine makes its debut; Grover Cleveland, the first Democratic president since the Civil War, becomes the 22nd president
- **1886** Dr. John S. Pemberton sells the first Coca-Cola at Jacob's Pharmacy in Atlanta, Georgia; the Statue of Liberty is presented to America by France; Mark Twain publishes *The Adventures of Huckleberry Finn*
- **1888** *Casey at the Bat*, the immortal baseball classic, is published
- **1889** More than 2,000 lives are lost in the Johnstown, Pennsylvania flood; North Dakota and South Dakota become the 39th and 40th states; Montana and Washington become the 41st and 42nd states; Benjamin Harrison becomes the 23rd president; *Wall Street Journal* is first published
- **1890** The population of the United States is 62,622,250; the Daughters of the American Revolution is organized in New York City; Idaho and Wyoming become the 43rd and 44th states; the first Army-Navy football game is played

Mercer County

- **1881** Wheatland Bessemer Steel incorporates
- **1882** C.H. Buhl becomes sole owner of the Sharon Iron Company; Sharpsville Furnace opens a new and modern furnace; first issue of *Pine Grove Telephone* is published
- **1883** Greenville Water Company and the Sharon Water Works are incorporated; the Mercer Heat, Light & Power Company is chartered; Grove City is incorporated from Pine Grove; Samuel S. Mehard is appointed judge of Mercer County
- **1884** People are riding the first bicycles (the "hi-wheels")
- **1885** The *Evening Eagle* is sold and changes its name to the *Sharon Eagle*
- **1886** Protected Home Circle No. 1 is organized
- **1887** Miller & Gordon Opera House in Mercer burns destroying the *Mercer Dispatch*; Wheatland Iron incorporates; the Shenango Hook & Ladder Company reorganizes as the Sharon Fire Department; the Sharon Steel Casting Company make its first steel
- **1888** The number of dogs on the tax roles for the county is 4,843; a history of Mercer County is published; the first passenger train from the new station on Main Street leaves Greenville
- **1890** The county's population is 55,744; fire destroys much of North Broad Street in Grove City; the Shenango Valley Electric Light Company (now Penn Power) begins operating

Timeline 1891—1900

The World

- 1891 The zipper is invented by Whitcomb L. Judson
- 1892 The first basketball game is played in Springfield, Massachusetts
- 1893 Grover Cleveland becomes the 24th president
- 1896 Utah becomes the 45th state; the first demonstration of x-rays is given by German physicist Wilhelm Roentgen; gold is discovered in Klondike Creek in the Yukon Territory
- 1897 The body of Ulysses S. Grant is moved to a tomb, now a national monument; the editor of the *New York Sun* writes an editorial in response to an 8-year-olds question and answers, "Yes, Virginia, there is a Santa Claus"; William McKinley becomes the 25th president
- 1898 United States declares war against Spain; Theodore Roosevelt and the "Rough Riders" stage a victorious assault on San Juan Hill in Cuba; the first female telephone operator, Miss Emma Nutt, is employed in Boston
- 1899 The Literary Digest predicts a dim future for the "automobile", claiming it will never "come into as common use as the bicycle"
- 1900 The population of the United States is 76,094,000; the US Navy acquires its first submarine; the first National Automobile Show opens at New York's Madison Square Garden

Mercer County

- 1891 An ordinance for construction of a plant to furnish electricity to Greenville is approved
- 1892 The first paving ordinance occurs in Greenville; electric street lights are put up in Sharon; James S. Fruit applies for a charter for the Sharon-Sharpsville hospital; the daily *Sharon Telegraph* and the weekly *Sharon Star* begin publication
- 1893 Construction of sewers connect two lines in Greenville and in Sharon
- 1895 Bars have to close promptly at 10:00 p.m.
- 1896 The Mercer County Telephone & Telegraph is organized; the doors of the Christian H. Buhl Hospital open to the sick of Shenango Valley; the second courthouse has work completed to ensure the safety of county records from fire
- 1897 The Soldiers Monument in front of the courthouse is dedicated as "Mercer County's Tribute to Her Soldiers"; the last issue of the *Sharon Record* is published
- 1898 Dr. Fithian and John Carruthers start the Friction Clutch Factory (forerunner of Cooper-Bessemer); fire destroys much of South Broad Street in Grove City
- 1899 The dismantled, numbered pieces of the John Stevenson, Jr. mansion in New Castle are loaded onto railroad cars and reassembled in Sharon; an ordinance passes to curb and pave streets in Sharon from Sharon Rail Way on the east to Irvine Avenue on the west
- 1900 The county's population is 57,387; ground is broken for South Sharon; the Sharon Steel Hoop Company is incorporated

Clarksville was named after Samuel Clark (pictured on facing page). In 1802, Samuel Clark purchased a tract of two hundred acres and in 1804 established his wife and six children in a log cabin on his land. In 1806 the Clarks had a daughter, Susannah, who was the first white child born in the settlement. Samuel Clark's wife was Mary Custer Clark (pictured). (A descendant of her family was General George Custer, famous for his services in the Civil War and his death in the Sioux massacre.) Clark and his son, also named Samuel, built the first bridge that spanned the Shenango River at State Street in Sharon. The younger Clark was an early operator of boats on the Erie Extension Canal and delivered what was likely the first canal boat of Lake Superior ore to Shenango Valley industries. (Caption: Clyde Moffett)

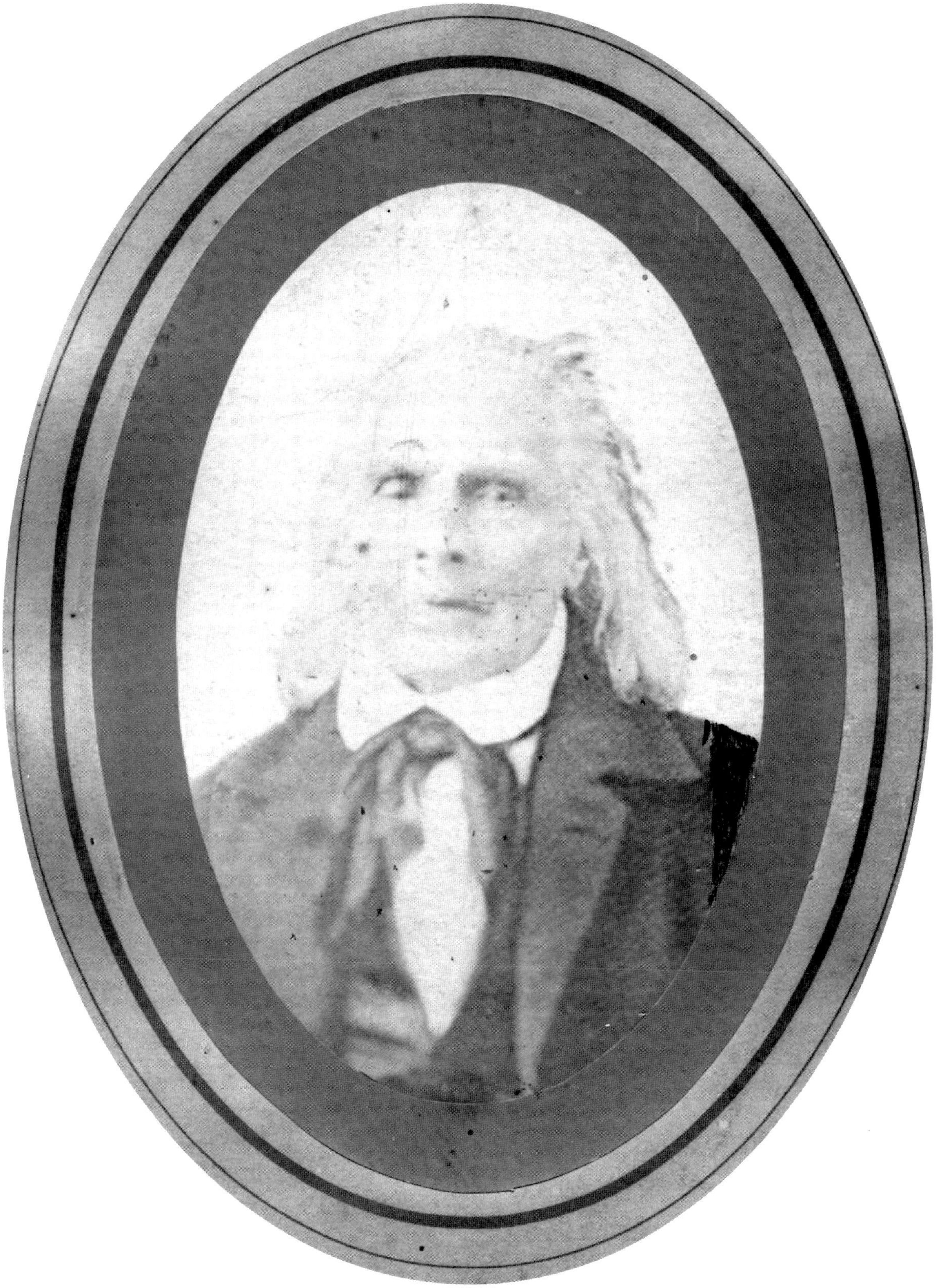

Johnston Tavern (pictured, in 2000) was built on the Pittsburgh-Mercer Road (now Route 19) in 1831 by Arthur Johnston, who managed the tavern until 1842 under the name New Lodge Inn. It served workmen from the Springfield iron furnace nearby. In 1836 the Springfield post office was opened in the building, with Johnston as the postmaster. (The post office was moved to Leesburg in 1845.) Restored by Charles M. Stotz under the direction of the Western Pennsylvania Conservancy, the building is administered by the Pennsylvania Historical and Museum Commission. The front entrance, with a fanlight above the door, has been reconstructed as it appeared originally, and the furnishings are from the Andrew Jackson period. (Photographer: Marilyn Dewald)

At the present-day site of O'Neill's Coffee Company (pictured, in 2000), a coffin factory was built and operated by the Gundy brothers in the early years of West Middlesex. A distillery was also operating there on the Shenango River at that time. The first industry in the town was a tannery. In 1836 West Middlesex was laid out by James McConnell and surveyed by James Gilkey. (Photographer: Marilyn Dewald; caption: James Campbell)

Number 10 lock of the Erie Extension Canal, a guard lock, is on the east end of Sharpsville off the Shenango River. The lock was built in the 1830s, and its wood gates on the ends were intact until the 1930s. Although the canal was officially closed in 1871, it had continued to be used in some sections for transportation through to the late 1920s. Over the years, much of the canal land was bought by individuals, including members of the prominent Pierce family of Sharpsville who had hoped to use it for a railroad spur. During the redevelopment project in Sharpsville in the early 1970s, Dean Alexander (Hermitage), who owned the lock (pictured, in 2000), gave it to the borough. (Photographer: Marilyn Dewald)

John A. Bingham was born in 1815 in a house on South Diamond Street in Mercer. Bingham presided as judge advocate at the trial of Mary Eugenia Surratt and other alleged conspirators in the assassination of Abraham Lincoln. Bingham, a Republican, was also U.S. minister to Japan and was counsel in the impeachment of U.S. President Andrew Johnson in 1868. The Bingham house is now the Mercer County Republican headquarters (pictured, before the current jail was built next door and in 2000). (Photographer in 2000: Marilyn Dewald)

The county jail system can be traced to 1803, when Mercer County separated its judiciary system from Crawford County. In 1804, a two-story log building, located on the north side of the Mercer public square, was ready to be used: the lower half as a jail and the upper half as the courthouse. No separation was made based on offenses or race because the jail had only a few cells. After the first jail, came the "Old Stone Jail," built in 1810 on West Venango Street (Mercer). Costing $3,000 to build, this jail was made of heavy stone and iron, was two stories, and had eighteen feet of stone fence built around it. The basement of the building was filled with large stones to prevent the prisoners from attempting to escape by digging. By the late 1860s, the building was no longer used. Eventually sold for $3,000, it was remodeled into a hotel. The building (pictured, in 2000) remains intact and is now configured as apartments. (Photographer: Vonda Minner; caption: Jimmy Gill)

Whatever else may befall, I trust in God that in this, as in every other American Court, the right of the whole people may be respected and that the Republic in this, its supreme hour of trial, will be true to itself and just to all, ready to protect the rights of the humblest, to redress every wrong, to avenge every crime, to vindicate the majesty of the law and to maintain inviolate the constitution, whether assailed secretly or openly, by hosts armed with gold or armed with steel.

Extract from Judge Advocate John A. Bingham's address made at the trial of the conspirators in the assassination of Abraham Lincoln mid–1860s

One of the largest landowners in early Otter Creek Township was Andrew Bush, an Ohioan who came to the region in 1845. He purchased nearly all the large valley lying southeast of Pleasantville, a village that was located at the intersection of Callahan and Donation Roads. Samuel Hendrickson built the village's first store, which also served as the post office, at this intersection in 1858. The Shannons now own this building, and its style remains the same (pictured, in 2000). (Contributor: Joyce Young)

Wales, Ulster, Ireland (including Scotch-Irish), France, and the German-speaking areas of Europe arrived. Many were motivated to leave their homelands to improve their economic situation, while others sought religious freedom.

Many of them found their way across the Allegheny Mountains and settled in Mercer County, where amid a wilderness, they established towns and farms, churches and schools, and businesses. Through their leadership, values, and vision, these hard-working men and women laid a strong foundation for the future.

In the latter decades of the 1800s and opening years of the 1900s, an influx arrived from eastern and southern Europe. Again, these people were drawn to America to improve their economic status.

Many of the newcomers found jobs in the mills, while others were employed in the coal mines, by the railroads, on farms, and in the construction trades. Some opened small businesses, such as grocery, jewelry, and furniture stores, and became successful entrepreneurs.

One of those enterprising newcomers was Jacob Traxler. Born in Hungary in 1841, he spent eight years in the Austrian Army and was slightly wounded at the Battle of Solferino on June 24, 1859.

[The Battle of Solferino was a major engagement in the Franco-Austrian War. The allied troops of France and the Kingdom of Sardinia (commanded by Emperor Napoleon III) and the Austrian Army (under Emperor Franz Josef I) fought at Solferino, a village in northern Italy. Appalled by the suffering of the wounded soldiers at the battlefield at Solferino, the Swiss philanthropist Jean Henri Dunant suggested in 1862 that neutral organizations should be established to provide relief to the victims of war and other disasters. An international conference held in Geneva, Switzerland, in 1863 and the Geneva Convention of 1864 established the International Red Cross.]

In 1865 Traxler left the Austrian Army on furlough and in 1866 immigrated to Cleveland, Ohio. In 1867 he relocated to Sharon and ten years later bought the L. Bash clothing store and became a prosperous merchant. While living in Cleveland, Traxler sent for Fannie Schiffer, a native of Hungary, to come to the United States. Following their marriage, the couple had six children, Joseph, Jennie, David, Aaron, Rose, and Bertha and reared them in the family's Jewish faith. Traxler didn't forget his roots. Through his membership in the Hungarian Aid Society of Cleveland, he helped provide aid and encouragement to other Hungarian immigrants.

The presence of immigrants with their diverse religious and cultural traditions wasn't always appreciated. Some of the local newspapers in the late 1890s published articles that discussed the belief held by a segment of American society that restrictions should be imposed on the numbers of immigrants permitted to enter this country.

Despite the challenges, the newcomers established churches and social and fraternal organizations, which provided not only valuable services and fellowship, but also helped to ease the transition into American society.

Between 1890 and 1924 approximately 500,000 Greeks immigrated to the United States. Those who located in the Shenango Valley found jobs and homes for their families and began holding Greek Orthodox worship services in various rented halls. In 1942, through the efforts and aid of the Greek American Progressive Association, the Greek Orthodox Church of the Annunciation, one of the county's architectural treasures, was built on Washington Avenue in Farrell.

Other ethnic groups that settled in the county include Slovaks, Poles, Serbians, Bulgarians, Czechs, Romanians, and Ukranians. In the latter years of the 1900s, people arrived from the Middle East, Asia, Africa, Mexico, Latin America, and the Caribbean.

lies, former members of the First Methodist Church of Sharon, joined Ruth AME Zion: the Hiram Wheeler family, William Hill family, and John and Sarah Houston.

Many of Ruth AME Zion's founders worked in private families, as people of color often did throughout western Pennsylvania. Other founders made their mark in other employment. George W. Burke, Sr., a window trimmer, was recognized as the "chief colored around Sharon." He decorated store windows up and down State Street. Charles Beard was born a slave in Virginia in 1830, migrated to Sharon, and worked as a janitor. Few opportunities outside of charwoman existed for Maria Chinn. Yet, she and her family earned a distinguished reputation. The Russell L. Chinn American Legion Post, named in honor of the first colored soldier killed in battle during World War I, was established in 1921. The church leaders established a visible presence in the African-American community in various ways.

As time passed, a cadre of black community leaders, ranging from civic and fraternal to labor and business leaders, arose from Ruth AME Zion's small congregation. Theodore L. Yarboro, MD, organized the Shenango Valley Urban League, Maceo Patterson Future Physician's Society, and a local African-American investment club. Edward Johnson served as director of the Carver Community Center and Sharon School Board director. When Clarence Hall, Sr. was elected the first African-American president of Union Local 1477 of the United Steelworkers of America, he served on the interracial leadership team as chairman of the Local's Grievance Committee. Thomas Dillard was a charter member of the local NAACP and its first treasurer. His daughter, Sara Dillard Austin, served as local president for the National Association for the Advancement of Colored People and Grand Worthy Matron for the Pennsylvania Order of Eastern Star. Clarence Mitchell, colored fraternal group leader, served as the exalted ruler of the local Elks. His son Gerald Mitchell, owner of Mitch's Laundromats, served as Sharon School Board director and carried on the tradition of service begun by his elders.

The Ruth AME Zion clergy, being well-educated, were equipped to assume leadership roles in the black community. In 1916, the Reverend Janifer D. Meade, then pastor of the Sharon AME Zion Church, organized Calumet Lodge No. 25 Free and Accepted Masons, Prince Hall Affiliation. The Lodge became a stronghold of Sharon's black intelligentsia. In Farrell, Prince Hall Masonry played an important role in the development of bourgeois values, as Prince Hall Masonry did across the country. During the Civil Rights Era, Reverend K. Melvin Taylor pushed for fair employment and opened the door for enrollment of the first black student nurses at the Sharon General Hospital of Nursing. The local affiliate of the National Black Nurses' Association later held its organizational meeting at Ruth AME Zion Church.

Ruth AME Zion Church has not only served as a community meeting site, but also a vital community agent. The Community Food Bank operated out of Ruth during the administration of Reverend Samuel Perry who served as its president.

Today, Ruth AME Zion Church continues a proud heritage of racial uplift and benevolence begun more than 120 years ago. After the urban renewal of the 1970s, the multi-ethnic community, known as the "flats," where the church is located was removed. Through the efforts of concerned community members, however, the church escaped destruction. As a result, Ruth AME Zion Church remains an important historical site in the African-American community, bridging the past and the present with the future.

A RICH MOSAIC OF ETHNIC COMMUNITIES
By Gail Habbyshaw

Mercer County encompasses a rich mosaic of ethnic communities from all parts of the world. In the opening years of the nineteenth century, immigrants from England, Scotland,

The first Catholic church in Mercer County was All Saints in Jefferson Township, about three miles north of Mercer. This church was organized about 1838. The red-brick building that replaced it in 1885 cost $12,000 and was described as "Commodious," ornamental, and substantial. The church served as parish for the first Catholic settlers at Sharon and other communities and for the large number of Catholics who came to the county to help build the Erie Extension Canal between 1835 and 1844. Missionary priests made regular trips along the canal to minister to these newcomers. Shortly before 1850, Catholic priests began to hold mass in houses of members in Hickory Township. Father John O'Keefe, first resident pastor of Sharon, held services in member homes until he built the present pastoral residence (south of where the current church is). A room there was used as a church until the mid-1860s when, at the corner of West State Street and Irvine Avenue, the congregation built Sacred Heart Church [pictured, in early 1900s (between the Baptist Church and the first church school) and in 2000]. It was the first Catholic church in Sharon. After several expansions, including the bell tower in 1867, the basement was used as a parochial school until a school building was completed in 1889 (later razed and now part of the church parking lot). The first religious teachers in the parish were the sisters of the Holy Humility of Mary. In 1892 the church purchased the Peter Kimberley mansion and the land surrounding it. The western portion of this parcel (now Logan Avenue and Nirnick Street) was sold as building lots for new homes, netting the church $10,000. The beautiful brown-brick rectory was built on Irvine Avenue in 1900. When the Kimberley estate was purchased, the Benedictine Sisters of Erie took charge of the school and occupied the mansion. In 1932, during the Great Depression, a $75,000 improvement program was announced for the church, including an extensive alteration to the church front and vestibule, new ceiling, new windows, new sanctuary and sacristy, and conversion of the basement into a social center with two dining halls, new kitchen, restrooms, and furnace room. The rectory was enlarged and completely remodeled. In 1935, Father James Murphy was appointed pastor of Sacred Heart Church and in 1947 named monsignor. In 1958, Murphy broke ground for a new $450,000 parochial school on the top portion of the former John Stevenson estate (North Irvine Avenue), which the church had bought, including the mansion, in 1944. The school opened for classes in 1959 with 550 students. In 1970, Murphy retired, Father Donald Scully was named pastor. Fire struck the church in 1977, but quick action by the Sharon Fire Department kept the damage to a minimum. Due to declining enrollment, Sacred Heart School closed in 1984. When fire struck and destroyed the neighboring First Methodist Church in 1987, the Methodists used the old Catholic school until they could build a new church. Father Daniel J. Kresinski has been serving the Sacred Heart congregation since 1995. (Photographer, in 2000: Vonda Minner; caption: Jean Thompson and William Cowan, Jr.)

Some of the most common offenses in 1850 included larceny, robbery, assault, fornication and bastardy, wagering and betting on Election Day, and illegal cutting and felling of timber. An example of a court case is when David Brown was sued by the Commonwealth of Pennsylvania in 1831. He was charged with assault and was fined $5. He also had to pay his attorney $3, the sheriff $1, the clerks $1.87, the justice $1.29, and finally Mercer County Court $6.15. Another example occurred in 1848, when Patrick Hagan was found guilty of murder of the second degree. He was fined $20 and had to serve ten years in prison. During the Civil War, the county prisoners provided a cheap method of labor when they were put to public work and farming. The number of offences and court cases increased as the county's population increased from 8,277 in 1810 to 49,977 in 1870. A new county jail was built in 1869 at a cost of $67,000. Located on the south side of the public square, it was an imposing, two-story structure with turrets (pictured in a postcard dated 1910). (Now, without turrets, the building (pictured, in 2000) provides additional office space for the courthouse. When the old jail was converted to the office space, the salvage fees collected for the old steel fixtures were $100,000. Also, pictured in 2000 in the basement are two cells and the blocked-off entrance to a tunnel that was used to transport prisoners from the jail to the courthouse under South Diamond Street.) (Photographer: Vonda Minner; caption: Jimmy Gill)

According to Richard Whenry, a retired correctional officer, an entrance door from the warden's residence to the old jail rotunda (built in the late 1860s) was made of boiler plate steel. The door (pictured, in 2000) is an example of all jail doors of that period and has been given to the Mercer County Historical Society. The murals on the door were painted by inmates in 1938. (Contributor: Vonda Minner)

One February Sunday morning in 1866, the courthouse caught fire. The fire's start has been attributed to stove pipes that had been rearranged the week before to accommodate cooking stoves brought into the building for a festival that used the courthouse. Apparently the pipes had not been returned to their original configuration; when the heating stove was lit to warm the building on Sunday for church services, the fire broke out. While the building burned, people rushed around and successfully saved the records and documents that had been stored in it. However, the building was lost, as was the borough's fire engine, which had been purchased after the destructive Union Church fire in 1824. According to one account, by 1866, the engine had been neglected to the point that it was unable to produce a stream of water. The engine was pushed into the fire and destroyed along with the courthouse. The county commissioners acted quickly after the fire to build a new courthouse in the same location. Work on this "second" courthouse commenced almost immediately (pictured above). (Caption: Robert Fuhrman)

N. W. Cor. Diamond, Mercer, Pa., 1866

Available histories reveal only fragmented details of the church known in its early years as Mt. Pleasant Methodist Episcopal Church at New Virginia (now part of Hermitage). The 1873 deed to the original church property states that Joel and Priscilla Frazier transferred title to Mt. Pleasant Episcopal Church for $100. (About 1826, Frazier had purchased and cleared 133 acres of land in the area known as New Virginia, and from this parcel he donated the land for the church and a school. In the early years, the nearest post office was at the crossroads, a half mile south and called "Five Points." New Virginia had one store, the Methodist church, a school, and a small cluster of dwellings; in fact, it was a continuation of Neshannock, situated one mile east. The residents were mostly engaged in coal mining.) It is not known now why the church was first called Mt. Pleasant, nor why the area was called New Virginia. Old maps show it as Virginia Station, a stop on the Sharpsville & Oakland Railroad, which ran between Sharpsville and New Wilmington and hauled locally produced coal to market. Virginia Road still exists, and, along with New Virginia Church, is all that remains of the village of New Virginia. The church was apparently on the preaching circuit with Clarksville, Charleston, Bethel, and Five Points. Records show that Reverend James Rollinson began preaching at New Virginia in 1865, gave two thousand sermons there, and died in 1909. As first constructed, the church was built close to the ground with no basement. Heating was provided by two barrel-shaped stoves. A clear-toned bell was purchased through the efforts of William Lydel in 1890. Lighting consisted of oil lamps hung from the walls on each side of the six large windows. About 1919, a remodeling program was begun. The building was raised four feet to sit upon a cement-block foundation. The basement was then excavated to provide space for a furnace room, kitchen, a large room for Sunday school, social activities, and a nursery. A brick chimney was built on the outside of the building. In 1938, a second remodeling program began, primarily to repair the sanctuary, and continued for about ten years. New stained glass windows were installed to brighten and beautify the sanctuary. More improvements were undertaken during the 1950s. In 1955, New Virginia Church had its own minister, the first in many years: Russell Babcock, as full-time lay pastor. In 1961, Reverend Reed Hurst was appointed as the first full-time pastor for New Virginia. In 1962, the congregation inaugurated the first part of a three-phrase building project: an education unit, (five large classrooms, library, parlor, and pastor's office) was consecrated in 1963. Because no kindergarten was offered in the public schools then, one was begun at the church. It was later replaced by a preschool, which is still being run. In 1966, the Hurst Chapel was completed. In 1973, the mortgage on the educational unit was burned, and a new sanctuary, consecrated. When the educational unit was remodeled in 1978, the original building was torn down. In 1980, the mortgage was burned on the new church (pictured, in 2000) and remodeling project. (Photographer: Vonda Minner; caption: Virginia Snyder)

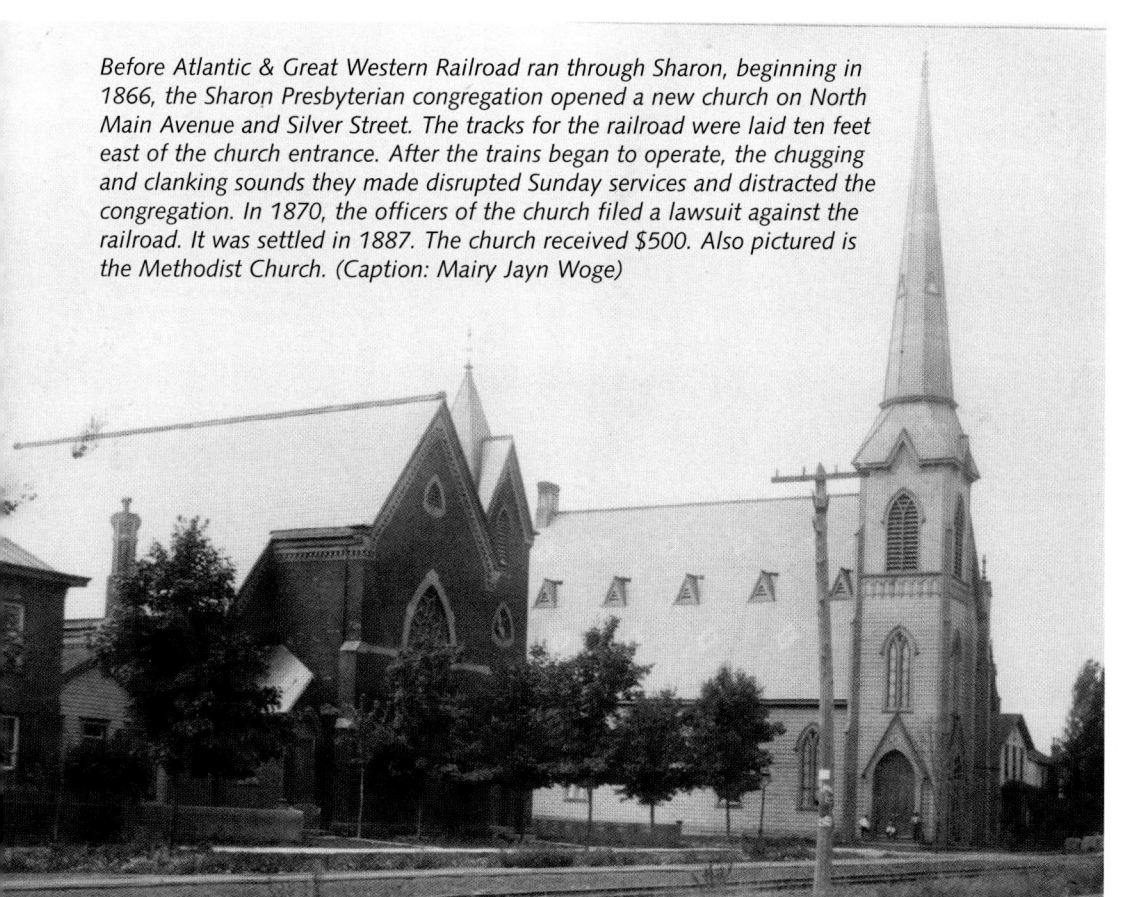

Before Atlantic & Great Western Railroad ran through Sharon, beginning in 1866, the Sharon Presbyterian congregation opened a new church on North Main Avenue and Silver Street. The tracks for the railroad were laid ten feet east of the church entrance. After the trains began to operate, the chugging and clanking sounds they made disrupted Sunday services and distracted the congregation. In 1870, the officers of the church filed a lawsuit against the railroad. It was settled in 1887. The church received $500. Also pictured is the Methodist Church. (Caption: Mairy Jayn Woge)

Mt. Hope United Methodist Church (pictured, in 2000) was built in 1878 in New Vernon Township. (Photographer: Marilyn Dewald)

Many of the first houses in the county were log cabins built near a source of water. The large, two-story house pictured was on a river, possibly the Shenango River, and has a mark on the front indicating the water level from a flood in 1883. (Photo: Vinson Skibo)

From the first signs of settlement, fire was always a major concern. Not only did the courthouse succumb to it, twice, but also many churches, businesses, barns, and homes have been burned over the years. For example, East Main Presbyterian Church in Grove City was lost to fire just nine years after its frame building was completed in 1883. The fire started from the sparks of a burning nearby store building. Within a few minutes, men from the college and townspeople formed a bucket brigade from Wolf Creek. For hours they passed the buckets from hand to hand. Finally in despair they watched the flames destroy the church. Bucket brigades were common until communities organized fire departments, usually volunteer, and started purchasing or engineering fire-fighting equipment. The Sharon Fire Department was organized in 1856. Borough council outfitted it with six ladders and six fire hooks on poles. In 1873, when the narrow brick municipal building (pictured) opened on Chestnut Avenue, the engines, hoses, hooks, and ladders were stored on the first floor. The fire horses were stabled outside in a barn. After 1892, it was easier for firemen to answer some calls: a contract was awarded to brick-pave three principal streets and add stone curbs. (In 1939, the brick streets were blacktopped.) Among the other fire departments in the county, volunteers in South Sharon (now Farrell) organized in 1902; Grove City, 1904; Stoneboro, 1928; Fredonia, 1934; Jamestown, 1938; Sheakleyville, 1947; Clarksville (now Clark), 1948; and Hempfield Township, 1962.

Seth Hoagland was born in Mercer County in 1822 and owned land in East Lackawannock Township. He introduced fertilizer to improve crop production, raised animals, and cultured bees. He also established the Hoagland post office in 1882, operated a general store (pictured here), and founded the Hoagland Cemetery, renamed Mount Pleasant Cemetery, where he was buried in 1890. The Village of Hoagland was located at the intersection of North Stonebase and Mercer-Pulaski roads. (Harold and Laverne Newton now own this property.) (Photo: Margaret Anderson; caption: Ruth Woods)

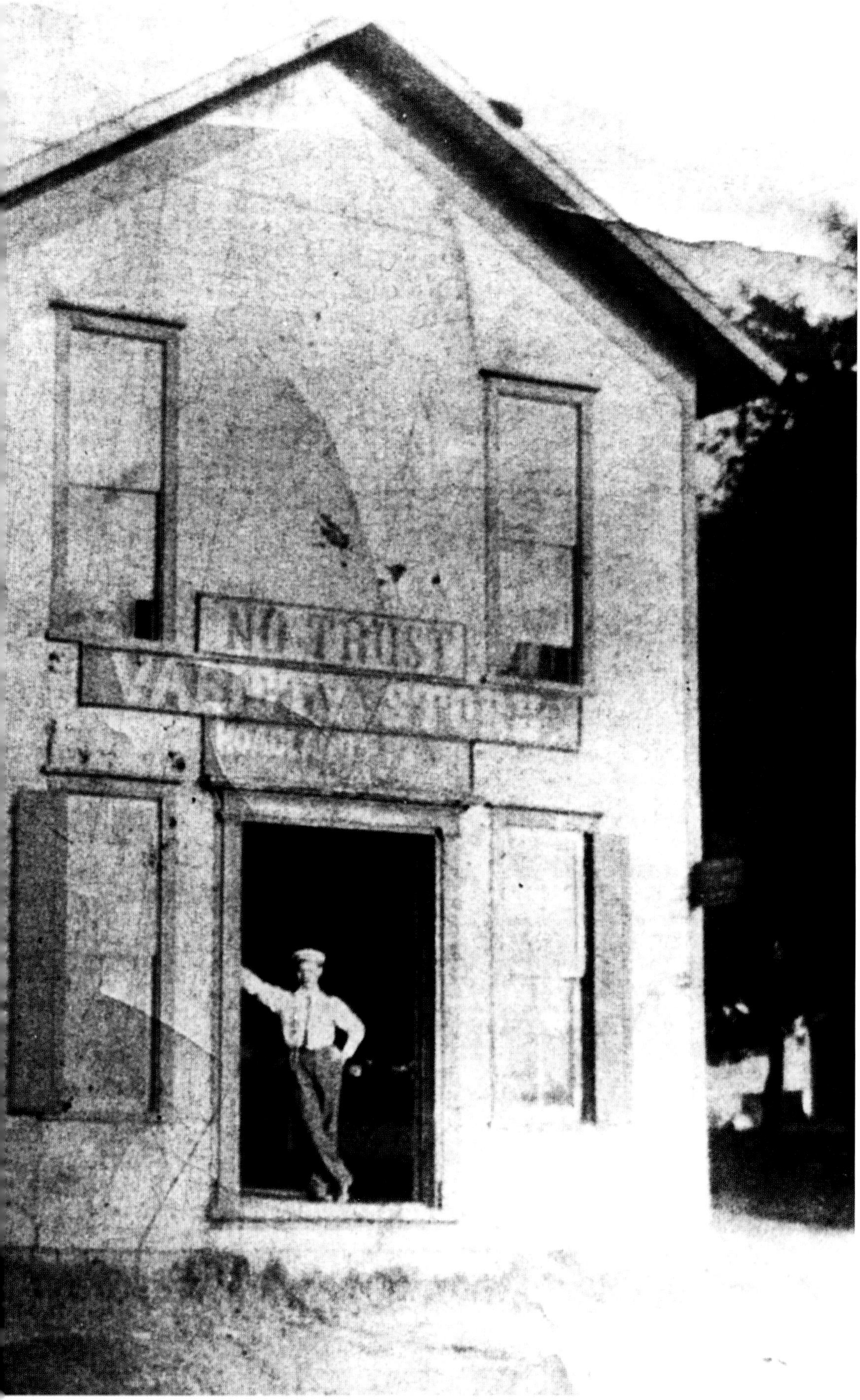
NO TRUST

Bridges have always been critical to a good transportation network and fascinating for photographers. Two early bridges in the Sharon area were over the Yankee Run (pictured, in 1886 with Dr. Heilman's horse and buggy) and the Budd Avenue bridge (pictured, in 1887).

In Sharon, the South Ward had a school, whose students are pictured in 1890.

Born in Blacktown in 1851, Luther Melanchthon Solomon John Nunamker Nelson was a musical genius with perfect pitch. He invented an organ (pictured) featuring an improved system of reed voicings and a contrivance that allowed a prompt response when the keys were touched. Nelson patented his innovations and was soon approached by a New York City organ manufacturer. The company wanted not only to use his improvements, but also to open a plant in Mercer under his management. The firm's representatives promised to erect a two-story iron building with machinery run by steam power. Nelson was instructed to hire forty to fifty employees. Acting on their word, he chartered the Centennial Organ Company in 1876. Although the New York firm made a huge profit from Nelson's improved organ, he never received a cent in royalties. Mercer offered to sue the firm for $75,000, which they judged the patents were worth. Nelson decided against such action. Instead, he produced at his own Mercer facility organs that were said to be instrumentally better than ones manufactured by larger companies. Nelson also tuned the pianos at Grove City College and the organs at many churches in the county. In the 1880s and 1890s, Nelson made a colorful figure at Christmas, when he wrapped old musical scores around his shoe tops to keep his stockings dry; strolled from one farmhouse to another; and told stories, sang carols, and tuned pianos and organs for free. (Photo: **The Herald***; caption: Gail Habbyshaw)*

Death of a Waterloo Veteran.

Mr. John George Lescher, a soldier of the great Napoleon, who fought under that leader at Waterloo, died at his home in Delaware township, on Sunday, Oct. 2nd, aged 89 years, 8 months and 5 days. He was born at Muhlivilie, in the kingdom of France, on the 26th day of January, 1792, and was the son of John Philip and Anna Catherine Lescher. He entered the French army at the age of twenty, as a private of 1st company, 142nd regiment of Grenadiers, Colonel Reny commanding. He belonged to the 132nd Corps, commanded by General Moss. He took part, under Napoleon, in the following battles: Ruttenbach, River Elbe, Hambuch Hill, Lowenbach, Katzebuch and Waterloo. At Katzebuch he escaped by swimming the river, being assisted by holding on to the tail of one of the horses. He also took part in the seven days' fight at Kotzebuch river. When General Waudun took Litzen, where the Saxons had rebelled, he was wounded in the leg above the knee. He was again wounded at Litzen, and crossed the bridge over the river Elbe an hour before it was blown up, when every man that was on it was killed or drowned, with the exception of one officer. It is said that the river was dammed back with the bodies of those who perished. Mr. Lescher emigrated to America in 1817. He was fourteen weeks crossing the ocean, and was shipwrecked, losing all his property and being obliged, after landing, to work out his passage money. Being assisted by friends, he was sold in Maryland for a term of three years, but after serving three months was helped to obtain his liberty. He was twice married, first in 1829 to Mary Detmer, by whom he had one son, who survives him. In 1836 he married a sister of his first wife, by whom he had eight children, six of whom are now alive. He had lived on the place where his death took place about forty-eight years. He retained his faculties up to the time of his death. Mrs G. W. Myers, of this place, is a daughter of Mr. Lescher.

(Source: unidentified local county newspaper, 1881)

Kitch and Mower Hardware (Sharpsville) went through several changes and showed signs of aging over the years. Notice, for example, the placement of the anvil and the deterioration of the paint.

111

Sharon teachers, 1890.

Shenango Valley Street Railway electric trolley car No. 1 is pictured at the end of the line in Sharpsville in 1892 with Pierce mansion at right. That company and its successors eventually connected Valley towns from Sharpsville through Sharon to West Middlesex. In 1901, an electric interurban was completed from Youngstown to Sharon, which ran until 1939 when remaining Shenango Valley local operations were also replaced by buses. Another Mercer County interurban was projected between Grove City and Slippery Rock. The company actually graded some of a right of way and acquired an electric freight car, but never went any further. (Photo: Vinson Skibo; caption: Frederick Houser)

The first hospital in the Shenango Valley was at the corner of Shenango Avenue and Vine Street. It was followed in 1893 by the Sharon and Sharpsville Charitable Hospital that was built on East State Street (where the Sharon Regional Health System is now) and cost $40,000 to erect. In 1896, the hospital's name was changed to Christian H. Buhl Hospital (pictured). (Postcard: Daniel Maurice; caption: Mairy Jayn Woge)

Identified by Marilyn McCutcheon Byerley are Clara Peirsol (front row, left) and Rexford Peirsol (front row, second from left) from the 1894 graduating class of Grove City High School. (Contributor: Marilyn McCutcheon Byerley)

Not only have girls played sports separately from boys throughout most of these two hundred years, in the 1800s and early 1900s, the girls had to play in dresses with most of the body covered in some way, as pictured in 1897. Marian McConkey (Grove City) attended Grove City College in the mid-1920s. She recalled, "We wore serge bloomers, a very coarse drill cloth, and you had to wear long stockings because you couldn't show your knees; and we wore middies. Girls that age just about lived in middy blouses until about World War II. In college we had to wear the same outfits. When I took lifesaving, we had to dive for a weight, and I had to dive in those heavy serge bloomers. It's a wonder I got myself up. Very shortly after that they became more liberal about what girls wore. If you lived in Colonial [girls dormitory], you had to put on a coat [over your gym clothes] before you went out to [gym] class." (Caption: **Reflections of Our Past**)

The students who attended the Stokely School in 1897 included (first row, sitting) Mont Uber, Don Lees, Leslie Cathers, Lottie Lees, Blanch McWhertor, and Less McKenna; (second row, sitting) Margaret Narlee, Dora Borthwick, Lester Bestwick, Mont Anderson, Frank Uber, Howe Lees, and Drayton Stokely; (third row) Will Huey, James McKenna, Ruby Maxwell, Maude Cook Fox, Zella Anderson, Maude Uber, Kate Bestwick, Ida Bentley, Minnie McKenna, John Pearson, Mont McMillan (teacher), John McKenna, Mont Maxwell, and Cliff North; (fourth row) Melvin Maxwell, Ray Lees, Riley Maxwell, Will Fox, George Fox, Bert Bestwick, Jay Boak, Lewis Worley, George Stokely, and Elmer Livermore.

The industrialist John Stevenson originally built his home in New Castle in 1891. Seven years later, finding more land in Sharon, he had the house dismantled, the sandstone hauled by rail, and a new mansion with twenty-two rooms built on Sharon's West Hill. Andrew Carnegie and President Taft were among the distinguished guests entertained in this mansion. The building (pictured, in 2000) was later used as a kindergarten and nursery, damaged by fire in 1961, but still stands now. (Photographer: Marilyn Dewald)

James H. Leyde married Barbara Ann Hollibaugh (pictured, late 1800s) and lived most of his life on Mill Street in West Middlesex. There he worked as a mill operator after starting and owning various mill businesses along the Shenango River and its tributaries. James and Barbara had four children, Francis, Samantha, Emma, and Joseph. After his children were born, James went on to enlist in Company M, Pennsylvania Heavy Artillery. He served until June 17, 1865, when the regiment was disbanded. Son Joseph (pictured, about 1900) spent most of his early life in West Middlesex with his family. He married Carrie Cuttings of Wauwauka, Indiana. Joseph owned the first bus route between Mercer and Sharon and sold it to purchase an automobile business with his son Frank and son-in-law George Cross. Leyde, Cross, and Leyde prospered, and Joseph worked there until his death in 1923. Shortly after that Cross was bought out and the name became Leyde Automotive Machine Company. (Contributor: Jane Leyde)

St. Hermengild's Church was founded in 1877 and dedicated in 1897 as St. Ethelridge's Catholic Church at Pardoe. (The name was changed in 1948.) Meetings in the homes of fellow Catholics had pulled together people of German, English, Austrian, French, Irish, Polish, Dutch, and Italian descent; and they eventually decided to build a real home for the congregation, a parish church. Each Catholic family generously donated to the cause for ten years, from 1867 to 1877. After raising enough money, the congregation, aided by Protestants of the area, worked together to build a box-type rustic church. Like the good St. Hermengild, men put in long hours and suffered many trials to create the little church. Priests came once a month by horse and buggy from All Saints Church of Mercer. In 1898, Reverend Dennis O'Mahony took charge of the Pardoe church, and his service to the church extended over about fifty years. During that time, St. Hermengild's not only increased the congregational size, but also added to the original building. O'Mahony held mass every Sunday rather than once a month. The service and love that he gave St. Hermengild's will long be remembered and appreciated by area Catholics. Money was collected from the parishioners monthly in the beginning years of the church. Donations are made weekly. Two members of the congregation were chosen to travel to homes of all parishioners and collect the monthly dues owed by each family, a total of sixty cents a month, per family. Also penny collections were held during Sunday mass. The money was given to support the priest and for any other expenses. (Photo: Rita Kreidle Holler; caption: Jean Thompson)

Andrew Shilling (pictured) was a farmer all his life in Mercer County. He served in the Volunteer Infantry (3rd Brigade of the 16th Division) as a first lieutenant in 1835. His wife, Salina Satterfield Shilling (pictured), was the mother of his six children. No longer farmland, the former Shilling property, now part of Sharpsville, is filled with residences and businesses. Their original house on Mercer Street still stands (pictured on facing page, in 1996), although updated through the years. It was reportedly built by Shilling and his father George, who was the first settler in the Wheatland area with his family in 1814. (Contributor: Marge Crompton)

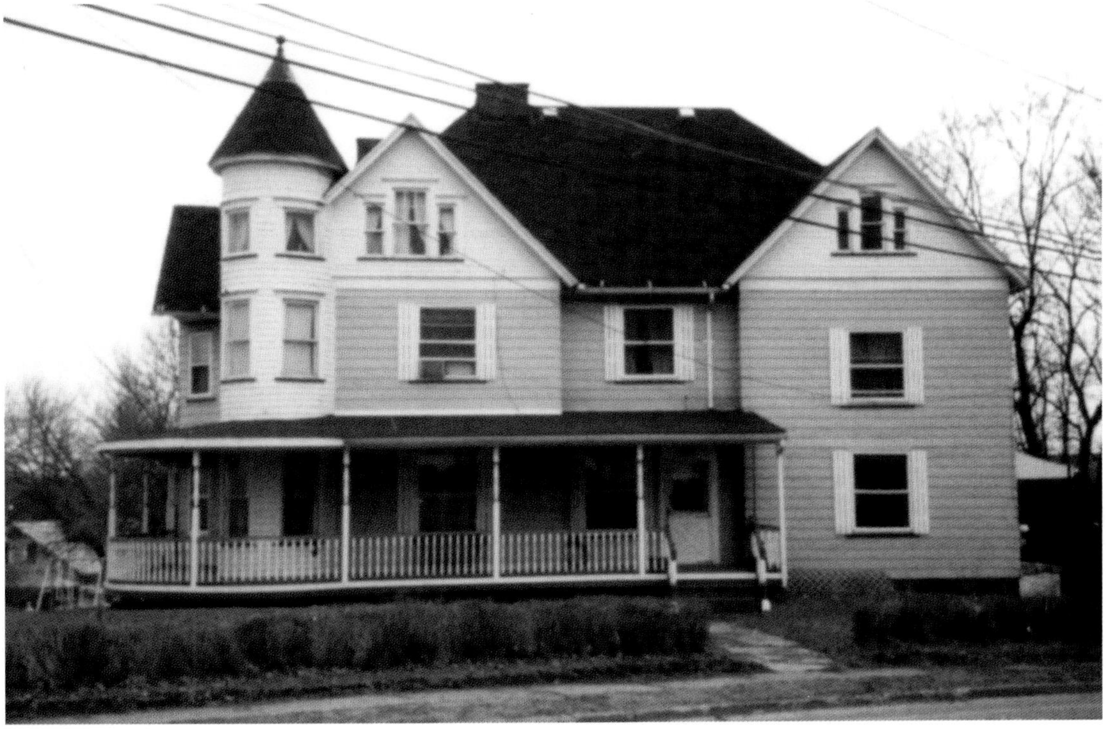

(Pages 120–127): As Main Streets developed in communities across the county, shopkeepers opened hardware, farm equipment, millinery, general and drug stores. T. A. Walker Hardware (Sharon), William Bell's store selling McCormick harvesting machines (West Middlesex), Miss Carrie Davenny Millinery (Stoneboro), Emma Neville's Shop (Sharpsville), Montgomery & Sons (Grove City), and Carter Brothers (Transfer) represent such retailers. Standing in front of Hazen pharmacy (Sharpsville) are owners Will Hazen (right) and Mr. Jewel (left). [Also pictured in the upstairs windows are Will's wife and son, Mary Elizabeth Logan Hazen and Eugene (right), and Agnes Logan Hull (left).] Hotels, banks, liveries, and blacksmiths were also opened. Sharon Exchange Hotel; Strawbridge Bank (West Middlesex); Harry Bowmers, blacksmith (Sandy Lake); and Gilkey's livery (West Middlesex) are examples of such establishments. As people came and left, so did businesses, such as Ashton's Grocery (Sharon), whose signs indicate the owner was selling all his stock in a "removal sale." In addition to the docks in Clarksville's glory days of the canal era in the mid-1800s, the town had two sawmills; two tanneries; a hardware store, drugstore, hotel, and livery stable. In Big Bend's canal heyday, it had warehouses; two wool and lumber mills; two grocers; and a hotel, blacksmith, and iron furnace. Later after the railroad opened up the mining industry around Pine Grove (now Grove City), the town had two grocers; two mills; five general stores; and a pottery, farm equipment dealer, bank, hotel, drugstore, planing and sash factory, carriage manufacturer, saddlery shop, and furniture maker. (Davenny millinery photo: Ila Ayre; Bowmers blacksmith: Idella McConnell and Lucille Eagles)

120

HARDWARE.
PAINTS

CARTER·BROS.
CARTER BROS.
CARTER'S CASH STORE

122

BANK
BANK

ASHTON'S
GROCERY
REMOVAL SALE
MY ENTIRE STOCK MUST BE CLOSED
OUT BY APRIL 1ST.
ASHTON'S

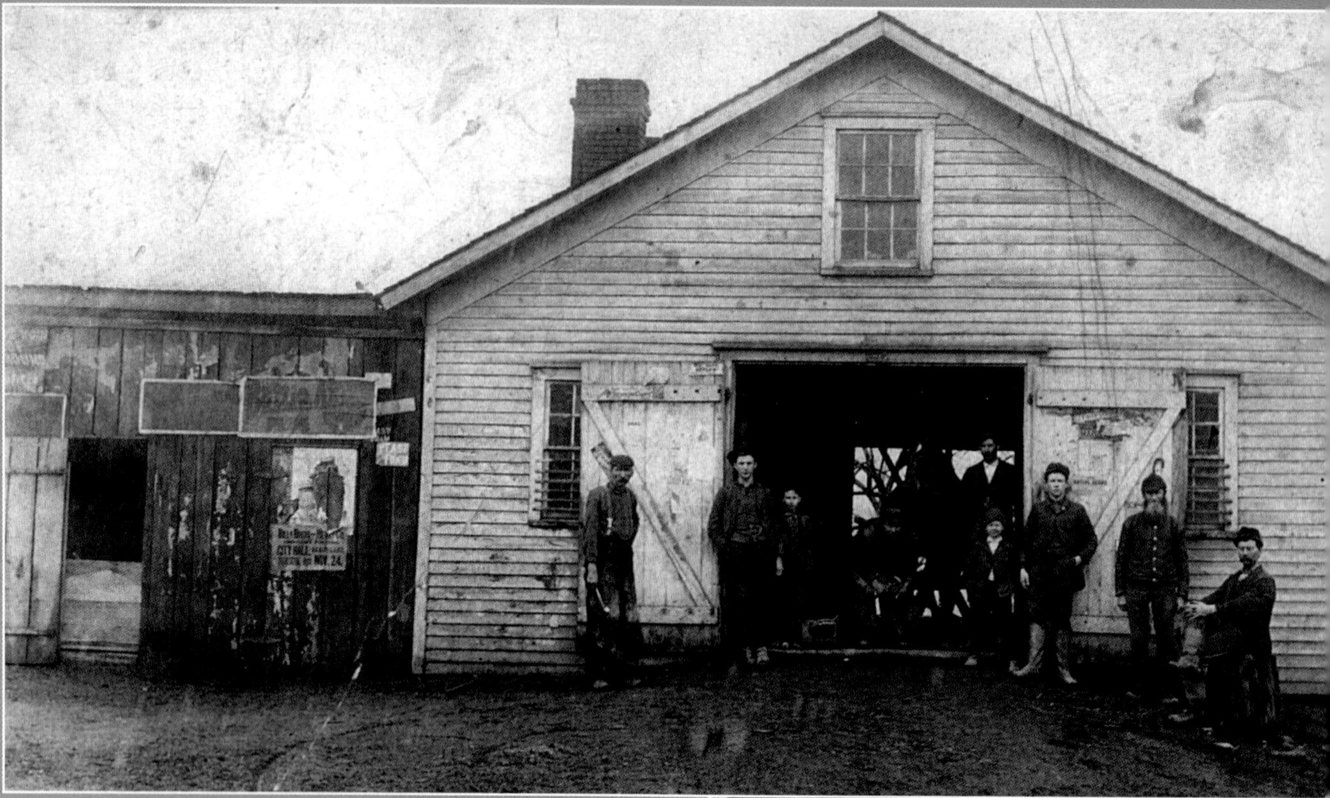
CITY HALL

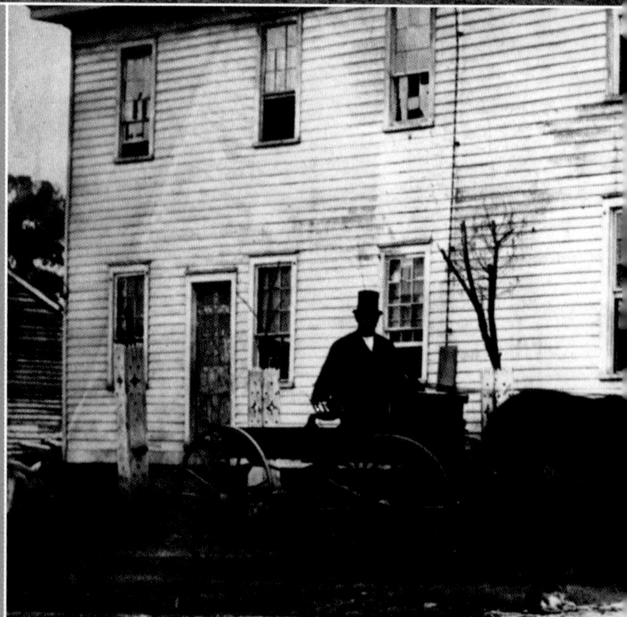

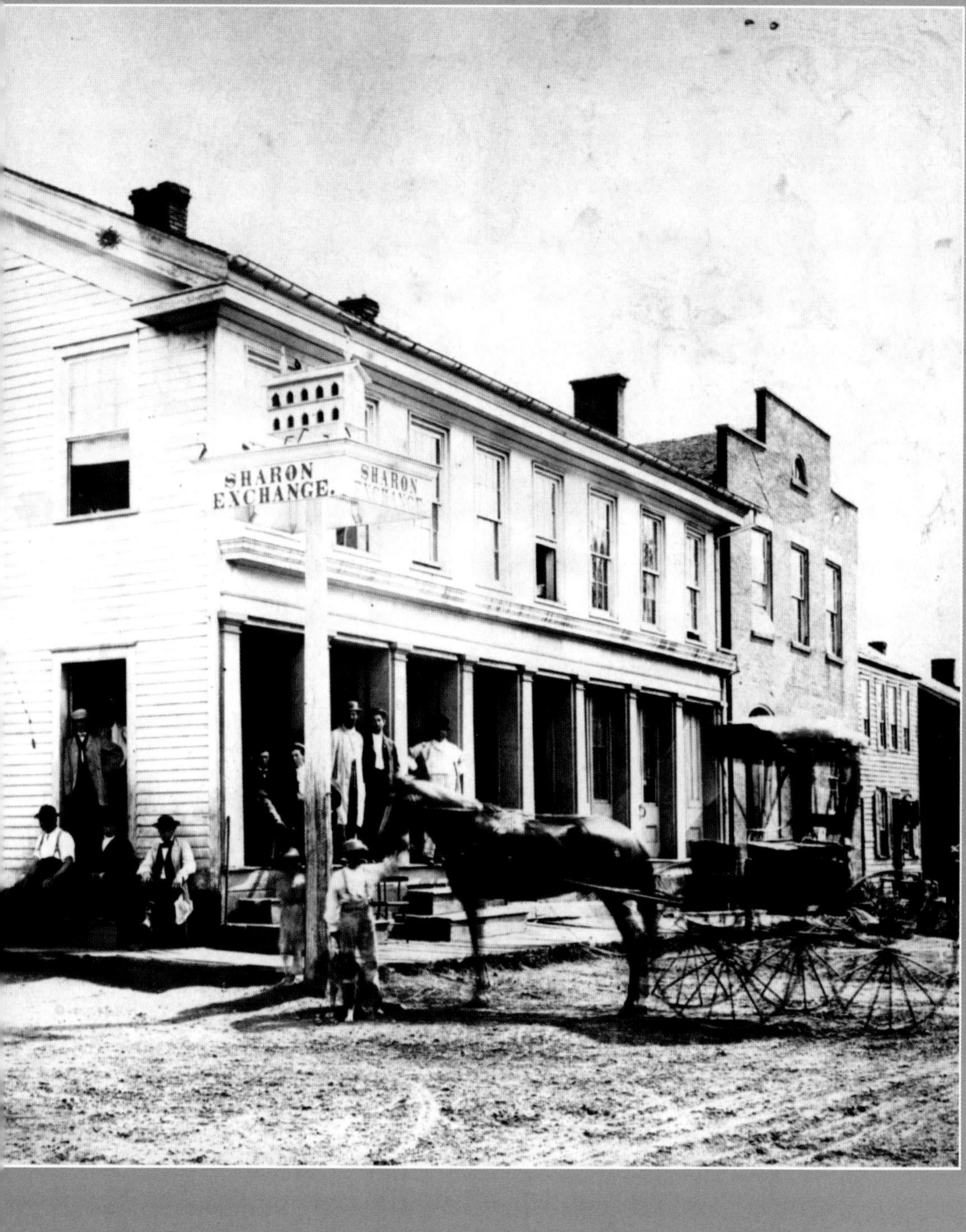
SHARON
EXCHANGE.
SHARON

126

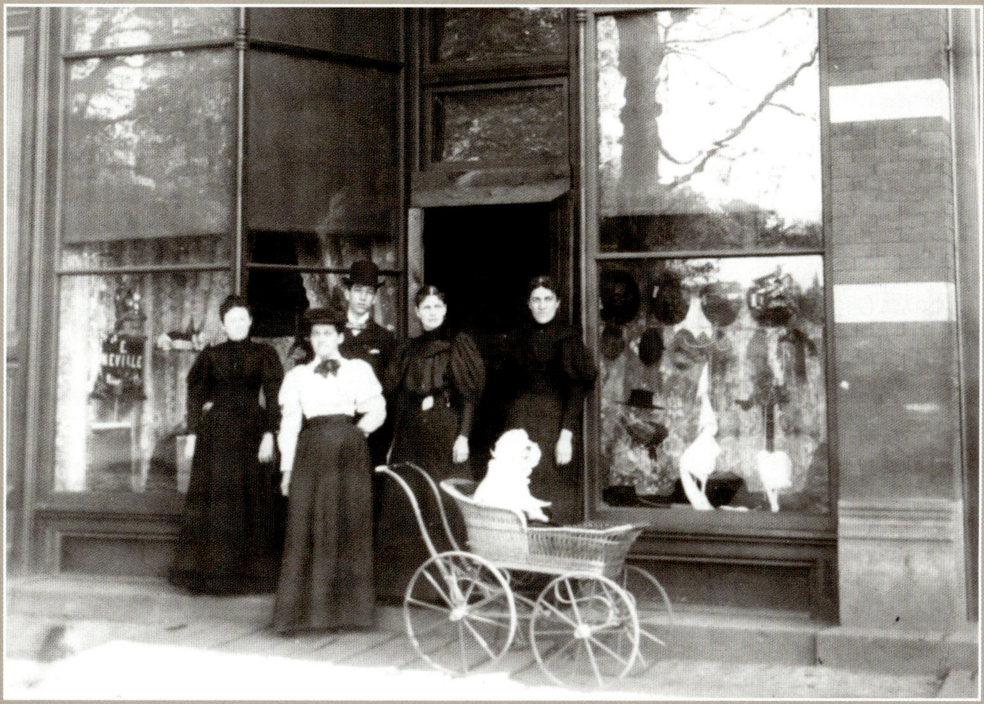

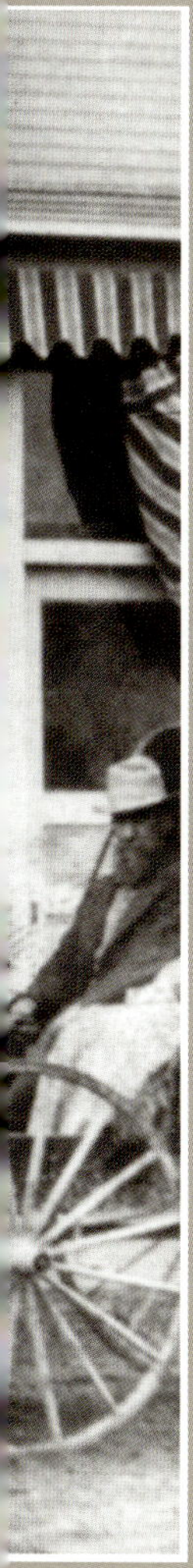

View of R.R. Station — Stoneboro Pa

Leesburg Sta. Pa.

As the railroads began to crisscross the county, stations were built in the communities along the tracks. After the Jamestown & Franklin Railroad reached the coal mines near Stoneboro in 1865, the fledgling borough built its railroad station. After the railroad came to Pine Grove (now Grove City) in 1872, its railroad station was built. (It operated until 1952, when the passenger service was discontinued. The station was dismantled in 1954.) Jamestown had the first station in the county. Leesburg (Springfield Township) was served by a small railroad station as pictured until 1902, when the Wolf Creek Branch of the Pennsylvania Railroad was built and altered the track layout at that point. Major stations, such as the Erie & Pittsburgh (Pennsylvania Railroad) building at Sharon (pictured, in 1900), were often the individual works of architects as contrasted with standardized buildings erected in smaller communities. Chimneys indicate fireplaces in waiting rooms plus a central heating system in the core of the building. Not surprisingly this passenger facility was on South Railroad Street, which was typical of almost every municipality that had a railroad. Baggage rooms and an express office usually were in such buildings; a freight station would be nearby. (Stoneboro photo: Ila Ayre; Grove City postcard: Rita Kreidle Holler; Jamestown postcard: Vinson Skibo; Sharon photo: Frederick Houser; caption: Frederick Houser)

Sharon

129

Gathering to celebrate the Fourth of July or the turn of the century.

Chapter 2: 1900–1910

TOWNSHIPS

In 1900, area roads were all dirt, requiring regular upkeep. A township resident was selected to serve as pathmaster who was given a book listing all taxpayers in his school district and the tax owed by each resident. The pathmaster would call the men to repair the district roads as needed, working for their road tax. Later, tax assessors were hired and tax was paid in cash.

In 1903, government laws granted the schools free books, required the teachers to be better educated, and changed the length of the school year to nine months.

Lackawannock Township, along with most other townships, was well organized by 1900. During the cold winter months, dirt roads were being covered with "red dog," which was hauled by teams of horses. Later, gravel was used. (Now, all roads in Lackawannock are black-topped, and most other township roads have also been improved.) Lackawannock Township had four mines, including the mysterious Buchanan Mine that operated in the late 1800s. Madge Mine was one mile south of Greenfield. When it closed, a large pile of coal remained. Later the coal was burned in a process that took several years to make "red dog" and used as a solid foundation for township roads. Pilgrim Mine operated over several years and closed in 1910. The fourth mine was near Pilgrim Mine and operated by Floyd Spears.

In 1900 the residents of *Wilmington Township* were almost entirely Scotch-Irish Presbyterian farmers. A few Amish families had settled there also. Farming was the primary occupation with traditional crops of corn, wheat, and alfalfa. Ice houses, gardens, and orchards were prevalent. Horses pulled the plows and livestock and chickens were also part of the farm scene. Grist mills were about the only kind of nonfarm activity in the township.

From *Worth Township*, two physicians are noteworthy from the first half of the 1900s. When it was still uncommon for females to become doctors, Rose Dunn graduated from Grove City College and Women's Medical College in Philadelphia in the late 1800s. Although Dr. Dunn lived and practiced medicine in Franklin for forty-two years, she spent the rest of her life, after retiring in 1941, at the Dunn homestead near Hendersonville (Worth Township). Her grandmother was a third-generation Henderson. Dr. David H. Smith and his wife, Ester G., moved to Millbrook in 1899 and were held in high regard. Dr. Smith practiced medicine in Venango, then Mercer County, for forty-seven years. His office was known for the bookshelves that lined the walls from the floor to the ceiling.

MUNICIPALITIES

In 1902, many citizens of **Fredonia** envisioned their town as a flourishing resort area because of the remarkable mineral springs located in their area of Mercer County. It was believed by doctors and chemists to have curative powers for gastric disturbances and rheumatic diseases.

In the early 1900s, **Greenville** grew in both size and stature. The town eventually evolved into a cultural center with the aid of the excellent Laird Opera House. Greenville's stop on the railways was conveniently equidistant from New York City to Chicago, providing an ideal stop for entertainment and rest.

By 1900, **Jamestown** had acquired one thousand residents and was considered to be a thriving railroad center. During this time, the community was busy improving its sidewalks and constructing brick roads. The town was set back a little when a tornado came through in 1902 and damaged, among other things, the United Presbyterian Church.

Stoneboro's first theater was the Coliseum, built in the early 1900s on Maple Street. The complex had facilities for lectures, plays, and eventually silent movies. High school graduations and basketball games were held there (with the chairs removed). (The theater burned down in 1925 and was never rebuilt.) The Allegheny Conference of the Wesleyan Methodist Church purchased land in Stoneboro in 1901 for a camp meeting ground where worshippers continue to come from a multistate area each summer, culminating in the

---

CLARANCE BOWSER (GREENVILLE)

By Woodrow S. Dixon (grandson)

Clarance Albert Bowser was old enough in 1910 to get a job at the Greenville Steel Car Company and later worked on the Empire automobile built there by Frank Fay. "As my grandfather told it, the cars were built in Greenville and shipped to Chicago where the coach work was installed. His job was in final assembly, part of which was installing the gas tank and a seat. The seat may have been temporary. Clarance also participated in the final quality testing. The bare car was gassed up and driven up the West Main Hill (hence the need for a seat). If it made it up, it passed, and was ready to ship!"

Clarance was born in 1891 in Parker, Pennsylvania. His father James worked for the Bessemer Railroad, and that job eventually brought the family [wife Anna Mae (Wesner) and two children Clarance and Mabel] to Greenville where James and Anna lived out the rest of their lives. James retired after forty-four years with the Bessemer & Lake Erie Railroad. (James's father Thomas and Anna's father, Marcus Wesner, had fought in the Civil War with Pennsylvania regiments, the former with the 62nd Regiment, Co. C, and the latter with the 142nd Regiment, Co. I.)

Clarance married Edith Florence Lever in 1911 and raised three children in Greenville: Alta Dorothy (Dixon), Margaret Mary (Arnold) of Greenville, and James William Bowser later of Pittsburgh. Clarance retired from Greenville Steel Car in 1957 with forty-six years of service as a machinist. He was a seventy-four-year, life-time member of the Moose and the Knights of Pythias. Edith died in 1985, and Clarance in 1990.

actual meeting itself each August. Since 1965 the site has been shared with the Stoneboro Wesleyan Methodist School.

South Sharon *(by Mairy Jayn Woge).* The 1900s began with Carnegie Steel, South Works, (formerly Sharon Steel Company) dominating the South Sharon (now Farrell) economy. Carnegie reported an output of 420,000 tons of steel annually, in part, because workers were on the job every day of the year but Labor Day.

Before 1904, three other industries were in South Sharon. All required manpower. Sharon Steel Hoop was on former Sharon Steel Company property. It opened in 1901 and produced billets, metal bars, hoops, bands, and cotton ties. In addition, the American Steel and Tin Plate Company and the American Steel and Wire Company, which were suppliers for Carnegie Steel, built plants in the vicinity of Carnegie. Earlier, the fledgling Sharon Steel Company had imported workers from Europe. Carnegie brought ore.

Timeline 1901—1910

The World

- 1901 Three car racers in Brooklyn speed over the Ocean Parkway at 60 mph, the first drivers to achieve such a record; first automobile law is passed (Connecticut) and sets speed limit at 12 mph; Theodore Roosevelt becomes the 26th president; the washing machine is invented
- 1902 America's first moving-picture theater opens in Los Angeles ($.10 for a one-hour show); Marie and Pierre Curie discover the atomic weight of radium; the American Automobile Association (AAA) is founded in Chicago
- 1903 The Wright brothers, Orville and Wilbur, make the first successful airplane flights in history; the windshield wiper is invented by Mary Anderson; Billy Sunday is ordained (famous big league baseball player who becomes famous as an evangelist)
- 1904 The Olympic Games are held in the United States (St. Louis) for the first time; the ice cream cone is invented; the first jail sentence for the crime of speeding in an automobile is handed down
- 1905 Las Vegas, Nevada, is founded
- 1907 Oklahoma becomes the 46th state
- 1909 American Robert Peary is first to discover the North Pole; William H. Taft becomes the 27th president
- 1910 The population of the United States is 92,407,000; the Boy Scouts of America is incorporated; the Pennsylvania Station in New York City is opened

Mercer County

- 1901 The first rural mail route occurs in the county from the Jamestown post office
- 1903 Wayside Inn is built in Grove City by Odd Fellow's (forerunner of Fellowship Manor)
- 1904 The first countywide individual mail routes begin (67 routes are laid out); Isaiah Jones is elected first Justice of the 4th District in Mercer; the volunteer fire department is organized in Grove City
- 1905 First medical hospital opens in Grove City
- 1906 The courthouse gets its first toll phone in the corridor
- 1907 The Sharon Herald Publishing Company is formed; the clock in the cupola of the courthouse is completed; a fire that started in the clock tower destroys the courthouse
- 1908 Billy Sunday holds weeklong revival; 18 architectural firms submit plans for the third courthouse; Greenville Cottage Hospital (one of forerunners to UPMC Horizon) opens
- 1909 Billy Whitla is kidnapped; James Boyle's trial for kidnapping Whitla is held at the temporary courthouse and lasted for less than a day; the *Sharon Herald* becomes a daily newspaper after 45 years as a weekly newspaper; the cornerstone is laid for the new courthouse; Dr. John Goodsell, later a Mercer County resident, accompanies Peary to discover the North Pole; a book covering the history of Mercer County is published; George Junior Republic opens in Grove City as a home for wayward boys and girls
- 1910 The county's population is 77,699; two coffins are discovered on Fourth Street in Sharon when workman are excavating to put in curbs

Betty Rose Broderick Gibbs wrote (in the Jubilee Book sponsored by the Farrell Chamber of Commerce in 1951) that immigrants flooded the town. Boarding houses were so crowded that rooms in them were used on a rotation basis. A mill hand who worked on the day shift slept in a room at night and a mill hand who worked on the night shift occupied the room during the day. There frequently were several tenants renting a room at a boarding house or at one of the four hotels in South Sharon. Men with families rented the company houses.

Gibbs wrote that because the Beechwood Improvement Company houses were too few and the boarding houses too infrequent to service the burgeoning town, realtors Mason and Miller sold numerous lots for houses. During the first decade of the 1900s, ten handsome brick houses were built on Darr Avenue. By 1905, the population of Farrell had reached five thousand, half the number of persons living in Sharon.

Some of the population of Sharon was composed of Farrell steelworkers who could not find housing close to the industries that employed them. After the depression in 1907 and 1908 that temporarily closed most Shenango Valley mills, a recovery was accompanied by high employment, good wages (an average of $1,500 a year), and construction of two-story, six-room-and-bath wooden houses that could be purchased for around $4,000 and painted on the exterior for $3.44. A blue steel stove for a kitchen was available for $29.97 and burned coal, wood, coke, or corn cobs.

Many of the eighteen congregations in Farrell in 1938 stemmed from a meeting at a local school in 1902. A bulletin containing the time the meeting was to begin was tacked to the door. A crowd of South Sharon residents attended to select the religious denominations they felt should be available to them in the new steel town. They had some guidance. Lots designated for church buildings were marked on the Beechwood Improvement Company map of South Sharon. A few disagreements arose during the three-hour session; but, on the whole, it was businesslike. Suggestions made by participants were treated with respect. When the input was exhausted, the group voted. Ballots, when opened, showed the majority were in favor of Methodist, Congregationalist, United Presbyterian, and Baptist congregations spreading the Word of God in South Sharon. A Catholic congregation had begun to build a church before the meeting. Nationality and Afro-American congregations came later. The nationality churches were most often Catholic and Orthodox, and their congregations were made up of emigrants.

During a speech delivered at the seventy-fifth anniversary observance of Saint George Serbian Orthodox Church, Slobodan Jovic, the priest, pointed out that the church had been a place for the Serbians who flocked to the burgeoning steel mills of South Sharon to find solace and companionship. In 1909, a group of Serbs purchased three lots at the corner of Union Street and Darr Avenue on which a church was built, in 1924, with loans from Saint George Lodge Number 64. (In 2000, the Serbian congregation meets at an imposing new church along South Keel Ridge Road.)

AFRICAN-AMERICANS
By Roland Barksdale-Hall

The unusual availability of steady work and good-paying, semi-skilled jobs in local mills contributed to the success of the Twin City Elks Lodge of Farrell, organized in 1914. Between 1909 and 1923 there were two waves of African-Americans, moving from the South to the industries of the North.

American Sheet and Tin Plate Company exploited racial antipathies in an attempt to break the union, Amalgamated Association of Iron and Steelworkers. When the union called a strike in 1909, local company officials employed African-Americans as skilled, nonunion workers. At that time few African-Americans in western Pennsylvania held semi-skilled positions in the hot mills. However, early in the 1909 strike, the African-American employees of American Sheet and Tin Plate experienced a brief period of upward mobility, as was common throughout the nation during strikes. One six-year veteran of the South Sharon plant, African-American Arthelia Jones profited from the strike, moving up from laborer to catcher. After the 1909 strike, another African-American, Joseph W. Young, assumed the highly skilled position of roller.

POSTAL SERVICE

According to a May 12, 1939, article in *The Mercer Dispatch and Republican*, "Rural free delivery was established in Mercer in 1901, five years after the first experiments were made. The first route opened on March 15, 1901, was out of the Jamestown post office and covered twenty-one miles. Rural service over the county was established on February 15, 1904, when sixty-seven routes were laid out. Ten of these radiated from the Mercer post office, each covering upwards of twenty-four miles. Only recently these have been reduced, by changed routing, to seven."

FARMING
By Vonda Minner

In 1900, Reed McFarland started the McFarland Dairy in Wilmington Township (and ran it until 1975). In 1904, the Alexander farm (Fairview Township) was already one hundred years old and, in 1908, so was the Paxton farm (Findley Township). In 1903, the Friendship Grange was started on Greenville-Jamestown Road (Route 58) with twenty-five charter members.

A canning factory was started in Sandy Lake in 1908, but was unsuccessful. It was subsequently taken over by Holly Rice and Milk Co. and so started the milk industry in Sandy Lake.

Campbell's Pioneer Dairy was started by Newton Campbell in 1910 in Pine Township near Grove City. [That land was later bought by the Independent Order of Odd Fellows (IOOF), who have developed the property, with adjacent former farm land, into the Fellowship Manor, a senior citizens home, and Orchard Manor, a nursing home.]

Thomas and Lucy Darby (pictured) arrived in Hickory Township (now Hermitage) in 1869 from the coal fields of England to start a new life. Their son David (pictured, mining) mined coal into the 1900s until it was no longer profitable and then took up farming the very same land. He later turned the farm over to his son William (pictured, with car), who raised four sons. The sons continue to live and work the family farm, and their children and grandchildren have remained in Mercer County into the 2000s. (Contributor: Tom Darby, fourth generation)

MINING

Mercer County had fifteen major coal mines in 1906. They yielded 884,184 tons of coal that year. Mehler Block Coal Mine, near Sharpsville, was in Hickory Township (and closed before 1920). The others were along the route of the Bessemer & Lake Erie Railroad in Sandy Lake, Stoneboro, Fredonia, Pardoe, and Grove City. Four of the mines were managed by Frank Filer (Hickory Township), a son of Enoch Filer, who opened the first shaft mine in the Shenango Valley during the 1850s. Another Filer son, Enoch L., opened and supervised two mines in Pardoe. The bulk of the fifteen mines were manned by English or German emigrants, the first miners in the area, and the descendants of those miners.

By 1906, Mercer Iron and Coal Company's No. 2 Mine near Stoneboro was closed, but its No. 3 Mine that year produced 88,011 tons with 130 miners. By that time a majority of Mercer Iron and Coal's output was from its operations south of the borough. The company was producing about 25 percent of the coal mined in Mercer County. (In 1924 because of labor and financial problems, operation of the large Mercer Iron and Coal mines abruptly terminated. Within a few years the company was liquidated. For a time, smaller, deep mines in the area continued to produce considerable quantities of coal. Then came stripping operations over much of the area where Mercer Iron and Coal had had mineral rights; these were concluded by the 1970s, and the coal era ended for Stoneboro.)

UTILITIES
By Mairy Jayn Woge

The electric light company and natural gas company operated as one unit until 1907. In 1908, United Natural Gas Company reported it was servicing 5,287 customers. (By 1939, 12,375 industries, commercial firms, and households in the Valley used fuel gas.)

Statements show that the electric lines along downtown streets in Sharon were costly. The city paid $12,000 for arc lights on State Street in 1908. The figure included the cost of electricity for the lights.

The availability of electricity was responsible for the beginning of telephone service in the Shenango Valley as well as streetcars.

The early Bell operators worked at a switchboard installed on the second floor of a drug store at the intersection of East State Street and Chestnut Avenue. During the 1913 flood, the operators who were on duty were trapped there. Later operators were quartered at the Bell offices on South Dock Street. The women who handled the long distance calls for Bell were often able to advise callers about where a recipient of a call had gone.

Bessemer No. 150, described when built in 1900 as the "heaviest and most powerful locomotive in the world," attracted a crowd in Grove City on what was probably one of the initial trips for this 125-ton Consolidation type engine. Possibly of greater significance was its train consisting of some of the world's first all-steel hopper cars, which had been built for the railroad a couple of years earlier. (Contributor: Frederick Houser)

Bessemer & Lake Erie Railroad
By Frederick Houser

The Bessemer & Lake Erie Railroad and its predecessors have been regarded as a hometown institution by Greenville citizens for well over a century. While virtually all other Mercer County rail lines became components of varying importance in the expansion of the major eastern trunk-line railroads, the Bessemer & Lake Erie has retained its regional character. Although incorporated in 1900, the events that led to the creation of the Bessemer & Lake Erie started in the early 1860s when stockholders of the Atlantic & Great Western Railway wanted a railroad to handle coal produced at the Mercer Mining and Manufacturing Company's first mine at Pardoe. Meanwhile, the Jamestown & Franklin Railroad was building track to Stoneboro to obtain coal from a new mine at Stoneboro owned by a subsidiary, the Mercer Iron and Coal Company.

The cost of ever-more-scarce wood that locomotives were then burning was escalating. The abundance of coal and the proven economy of converting locomotives to burn coal were major incentives for connecting railroads to coal mines.

By 1900, track had been laid to bring out the coal not only for the locomotives, but also for the burgeoning steel industry. The resulting Pittsburgh, Bessemer & Lake Erie Railroad stretched from Conneaut, Ohio, on Lake Erie to the Monongahela River Valley steel mills of the Carnegie Steel Company.

In time, well over half of the original 111 miles of the Pittsburgh, Bessemer & Lake Erie Railroad between Conneaut and Butler was bypassed or realigned to reduce grades and curvature so that some of the heaviest freight trains ever operated could become routine. Carnegie Steel took a further step on December 31, 1900, when it incorporated the Bessemer & Lake Erie Railroad to construct the Pittsburgh, Bessemer & Lake Erie's first bypass line in Mercer County. The new cut-off past Greenville eliminated heavy grades and expedited ore movements. Less than two months later, however, Andrew Carnegie suddenly sold Carnegie Steel and its subsidiaries (including the Bessemer & Lake Erie) to the newly formed U.S. Steel Corporation. The new owner continued to pursue the improvement of its western Pennsylvania ore hauler.

The Greenville bypass between Kremis and Osgood, named the K-O Line, opened in 1902. The 8.8-mile cut-off made it unnecessary for loaded trains to drop down into the Shenango Valley and climb back out of it with the assistance of expensive pusher locomotives between Shenango and Kremis. The next such bypass in the county was the Porter Cut-off, built from 1916 to 1928 between Filer, just north of Grove City, and Coolspring, south of Fredonia. The huge embankments required on this line consumed 79,000 carloads of fill and resulted in a new ten mile route with no highway crossings. The line's southbound ascending grade was reduced from almost 1 percent on the original alignment to just 0.3 percent.

The Bessemer & Lake Erie at times carried the heaviest freight traffic density in the United States—maybe the world. Part of the rail link between Lake Erie and the Monongahela River Valley, it handled over twenty-seven million tons of freight traffic in 1942 and over thirty-two million tons in 1966. Between these two traffic peaks, several technological advancements were introduced. Diesel-electric locomotives displaced the last steam engines in 1953. Centralized traffic control, installed by 1956 over its entire main line, made it possible to remove much of the second track that had once been a hallmark of the double-track Bessemer & Lake Erie main line and to abandon the original main line through Pardoe and the short branch into Mercer.

In 1903, Frank H. Buhl opened the F. H. Buhl Club for men and boys. It was and is at the intersection of East State Street and Pine Avenue. Buhl bought the building lot for the club from some of the Porters and Forcers. When it went into operation, it contained a gymnasium, bowling alleys, courts for squash and handball and a billiards and pool room. Buhl Library was on the first floor and a music room on the third. At the time, the library could be used only by members of the F. H. Buhl Club. Women bought memberships but did not participate in the sports and games. The library replaced some private book lending clubs that had operated in Sharon for a number of years. New books were stocked at Samuel McKay's literature and paper products store on West State Street. Eventually, library users were no longer required to belong to the Buhl Club. The library was the Buhl Library until it moved to a new building facing Sharpsville Avenue in 1971. George Henderson, who had been born in Sharon, was a financier in Pittsburgh and married into the Mellon family. He and his wife donated funds to the Buhl Library, other community organizations, the Boy Scout camp at Custaloga Town, and the Johnston Tavern, south of Mercer. The new library building was named Buhl-Henderson. Henderson died in 1978. Now, the library is named Shenango Valley Community Library. The community room on the basement level is dedicated to Frank Buhl and George Henderson. (Postcard: Daniel Maurice; caption: Mairy Jayn Woge)

SHARON STEEL COMPANY
By Mairy Jayn Woge

Sold to Frank H. Buhl to make way for his new Sharon Steel Company were wool, grist and flour mills along the Shenango River, an iron works equipped with a massive chimney and a cemetery. One of the casualties was Clark's Mill that was on former Dr. Mitchell's tree property south of Sharon and west of Wheatland. Other properties purchased had belonged to John J. Spearman and to the Stantons, Keaneys, Higgses, Hovers, Haywoods, Perkins, Conovers, Myers, Cooks, and an heir of Joel B. Curtis. He took control or provided rights of way for the Pittsburgh & Erie and Stewart railroads, the latter the line that hauled for Stewart Iron Company of Sharon. A small piece of land acquired for Sharon Steel was in Ohio, near Masury.

The initial officers of the proposed steel company were Buhl, president; D. W. Darr of Pittsburgh for whom Darr Avenue in Farrell would be named, vice president; James S. Fruit, a Pennsylvania legislator who lived next door to the Buhls in Sharon; and Henry P. Forker, Buhl's brother-in-law. Darr, Fruit, and Forker resigned when John Stevenson, Jr. of New Castle invested a large amount in Sharon Steel and became the vice president.

Stevenson and Victor Delamater, a son-in-law of Joseph Forker, filled two of the vacancies. Stevenson had been an industrialist in New Castle before he became involved in a dispute with some Lawrence County politicians. He subsequently bought a lot for $20,000 in Millionaires Row along North Irvine Avenue in Sharon and moved his mansion, stone by stone, from New Castle to the Sharon site on railroad gondola cars and had it built on the North Irvine property.

Buhl bought a large piece of land along the hill east of the proposed mill. In 1900, Buhl transferred the property to the Beechwood Improvement Company of Pittsburgh. The company, represented by Peter Shields, opened an office in the former John J. Spearman home at the corner of Broadway and Adams Street. Sharon contractors Wallis and Carley manufactured parts for a couple hundred prefabricated wood house that were assembled in South Sharon (now Farrell). (When Sharon Steel Company did not materialize, the houses were rented for $13.50 to $16.50 a month by employees of Sharon Steel Hoop Company that opened in 1901 on a tract belonging to the owners of Sharon Steel.)

In the fall of 1898, an official of Shifler Bridge Company of Pittsburgh, that had been awarded the contract to build Sharon Steel Company told a correspondent for *The Pittsburgh News* that ground for the industry would be broken in the spring of 1899 and that the company would manufacture pig iron and open hearth steel in competition with the consolidated iron and steel concerns. A blast furnace plant with one furnace at the beginning and the open hearth plant would be erected first, the Shifler official said.

William Tod or Todd of Youngstown received the contract for the engines. Tod said there would be two, each providing 1,000 horsepower. According to the Pittsburgh newspaper, the mill would open in March 1900. Buhl would employ twenty-four hundred workers.

The consolidated iron and steel interests referred to by the Shifler spokesman moved in. During 1899, the real estate of Sharon or Buhl Iron Company, was sold to National Iron and Steel Company of Chicago. In March 1899, the steel company bought eleven acres that included parts of the Shenango Valley Railroad (to Brookfield) and the right of way of the Erie Railroad north of the railway bridge on North Water Avenue, the rolling mill, sheet mill, boiler and engine buildings, offices, shops, a warehouse, and scales. Another tract containing 9.127 acres and containing a section of the Erie Railroad also was bought by the steel firm.

National Steel leveled the buildings on both pieces of land. Republic Steel of New Jersey obtained the tracts from National in May 1899. In August, they were absorbed by U.S. Steel Company (later Corporation). The U.S. Steel Works in the North River flats became Carnegie Steel Company, North Works.

MERCER VALLEY RAILROAD

By Frederick Houser

Another local common carrier was the Mercer Valley Railroad, which operated within the Carnegie Steel Company's Farrell mills. It connected these facilities with the Pennsylvania, Erie, and New York Central railroads. The Mercer Valley was incorporated in 1900, and ultimately had three miles of main line and thirty miles of sidings and yard tracks. By 1918, it was no longer anything but a private, in-plant switching carrier. The operation continued in that capacity for Sharon Steel Corporation, successor to Carnegie Steel, until the end of Sharon Steel's production in the 1990s.

These steelworkers from one of the Shenango Valley mills posed in front of stacks of pig iron, an inferior grade of iron that was not used to make steel. One of the many uses for pig iron was in the newspaper printing business. After the lines of type were created, they were moved to a metal casting mechanism for automatic spacing. Next, molten metal was forced into the faces in the matrixes, forming lines of metal letters. Compositors placed these lines on the galleys where they went into metal forms to be positioned on the press. This process was called "hot type." After the paper was printed, the metal type was melted again, placed in iron forms where it hardened into metal bars called "pigs," which were lowered into a pot of hot metal on the side of each linotype. As the pigs entered the metal that already was molten, they too melted, keeping the supply of molten metal adequate for the linotype operation. Since the linotype made its own type then remelted it for reuse, publishers had no further need for the long cases of type. The hot-type not only was faster, but was much less expensive to the publisher. (Caption: Teresa Spatara)

Little Hills of Saving Make Mountains of Fortune.

Do you realize how quickly little savings accumulate? Open an account with the Farmers and Mechanics National Bank and you will see how fast your regular deposits will grow at Compound Interest.

3% INTEREST PAID ON SAVINGS ACCOUNTS OF $1.00 AND UP.

Farmers and Mechanics National Bank,
Mercer, Pa.

CAPITAL, $80,000.00   PROFITS, $40,000.00

ATTENTION FARMERS.

We have for sale the best of fine hydrated lime for agricultural purposes. Just what you farmers need for your wheat ground. Also Universal Portland Cement, the same that is being used on Mercer County's new Court House, and what is good enough for that is good enough for anybody. None better. Have you ever tried the famous Badger Dairy Feed? It will produce more milk and butter for the money than any feed you can buy. Get some, try it and see for yourself.

Mercer Milling and Lumber Company, Ltd.

(Source: **Mercer Dispatch and Republican***, 1909)*

THOMAS D. WEST
By Mairy Jayn Woge

Foundryman and inventor Thomas D. West spent time at Alice Furnace experimenting with making ingot molds by "direct metal." The project was a success and in the late 1890s adopted by Illinois Steel Company and Carnegie Steel Works.

Later, West moved his headquarters to Sharpsville, built a large plant, and named it Thomas D. West Foundry Company. He introduced safety programs to protect mill workers and people on the streets from injuries and accidental deaths. West wrote the book *Accidents and Their Causes and Remedies* between 1901 and 1906 and later became president of the American Anti-Accident Association. His pamphlet dealing with safeguarding life and property sold for a quarter and was distributed throughout the United States and Canada.

In 1902, Andrew Carnegie sold his holdings in U.S. Steel for $480 million. His name remained on two mills in the Shenango Valley.

J. Pierpont Morgan, head of the Steel Trust had taken over many of the companies in the United States for his U.S. Steel Company (Corporation). He threatened Frank H. Buhl and John Stevenson with bankruptcy if they opened the just finished buildings and began operations at Sharon Steel Company in South Sharon. After hopeless maneuvering, the partnership sold out in 1902 for $13 million.

Shenango Iron Works and the Sharon Steel Casting Company both were sold by Buhl and other partners for a profit. In 1902, Steel Casting became a company operated by American Steel Foundries.

In 1890, the Sherman Antitrust Act was passed by Congress. Almost as soon as Theodore Roosevelt became president in 1901, he enforced it. He took actions against monopolies, concentrating on financier Morgan's U.S. Steel Corporation that had assets of $1.4 billion. Morgan was indicted in 1902. However, it was too late to retrieve Sharon Steel Company. Sharon Steel's new name was Carnegie Steel, South Works.

In compliance with antitrust laws, Carnegie Steel of U.S. Steel was split. In 1918, after a series of negotiations with the U.S. government, the Farrell plant became Carnegie Illinois. The Carnegie North Works had closed in 1915.

A DAY IN THE ONE-ROOM SCHOOLHOUSE
By Joannie Appleseed (4 July 1996)

Dear Aunt Mae,

I'm working on a graduate paper regarding the history of educational curriculum. If you could send some information about the curriculum, or how a typical day in the school might go, I would appreciate it. Thank you for your assistance and information.
Alice Simmons

Dear Alice,

An average day in a one-room school is at the mercy of the weather. In winter, the temperature in northwest Pennsylvania may drop to 10-20 degrees below zero; the snow may drift to all but close roads.

Country kids and teachers must face icy winds walking to school. The teacher arrives no later than 7 am to shovel paths to the wood-coal shed and toilets. When the pupils arrive, some have frost damage to their hands, feet, face and must be treated as needed by the teacher, who keeps working with the fire in the big stove to bring the temperature above freezing in the areas 10 feet from the stove.

By nine, the Bible is read and prayers and pledge over. Until 10:30 am, the attention is on numbers for grades 1 and 2, and real business in arithmetic for grades 3-8. Some students are at their desks, others are working out problems on the blackboard. (Many such "blackboards" were simply wide boards painted black; slate, if affordable, was introduced around 1910.)

Recess from 10:30-10:45 was a time for big boys to bring in coal and go for water—often a quarter mile away! Only a few schools had well or spring water on the grounds.

Spelling, daily penmanship and geography were heard from 10:45 until noon. Always the teacher is checking the fire to keep the school room as comfortable as possible.

Reading and English for every grade is heard from 1-2:30 pm. Seat work is a never-ending activity supervised by the teacher.

At 2:45 pm, History, Physiology, Health, more reading and miscellaneous unfinished helps for as many as 60 pupils must be completed. The teacher checks each pupil out for the cold walk home through a blinding blizzard at 4 pm or after. More coal, the cleaning, the checking may conclude the teacher's day by 5:30 pm, when she is ready to brave the weather for the walk home and get ready with every lesson for another day, another day of vigil. The teacher is in charge of whatever is needed. There is no helper other than the pupils themselves, who in a well-ordered school help each other as well as themselves.

One-room school kids are a family. In a one-room school, they have the advantage of learning from all the grades, regardless of age: a big plus!

The teacher, however, learns from the review of each grade's lesson, from every child's personality, from problems that must be faced and solved, one of which is the weather—be it cold or hurricane, mud or wind.

One-room teachers may know (the book); they go as their good sense dictates. Their students have been among the best leaders in any walk of life.

Sincerely,
Mae Little Beringer
Always a one-room teacher.

Courthouse Fire (1907)

From memories of Julia Stamm Hugo as recorded by her son Bill Hugo

"Yes, I remember when the new courthouse was built [in 1909]. I also remember the burning of the old one. [Julia would have been about 10 years old.] I think most of the town came to watch that, and among all of these were two women, wife and daughter of one of the county commissioners. These women were rare types. They appeared a bit late at the scene of the fire, clothed in complete evening dress!

"This was not really surprising, at least not to me, for had I not watched these two pass our house (they lived on our street) wearing long silk gowns and pushing a wheel barrow full of manure for their garden. But to take the time at two or three o'clock in the morning, with our courthouse afire, to bedeck themselves with finery?"

"The first courthouse cost $7,116 and the last one $324,000, but the transformation from the hand-hewn log building to the present Gothic temple of beauty [pictured, in the 1920s] was a bitter experience for the contractors. . . . The first courthouse was contracted for in 1807 and in 1840 was supplemented by a $1,300 addition. This burned to the ground in 1866 and the second courthouse, erected the following year, cost $98,000. On a Sunday night in 1907, this, too, was consumed by fire and, once more the county started to build a courthouse. This time, the structure was designed with dimensions double those of its predecessor. It was twice as high, twice as wide, twice as long. Its beautiful well-groomed park bears little resemblance to the ground which surrounded the former courthouse. A high iron fence bounded it, with four gates of entry from which cinder walks led to the building. The east end was kept in fair condition, but each year a hay crop was harvested from the west side." (Source: **The Sharon Herald**, *September 12, 1953*)

BILLY SUNDAY'S REVIVAL IN SHARON (1908)
By Margo Letts

Billy Sunday was an evangelist in the late 1800s and early 1900s. He was born in 1862, and a month later his father was killed in the Civil War. Sunday's first career was in baseball, playing for the Chicago White Sox and the Pittsburgh and Philadelphia teams. The fastest base runner of his time, he was the first man to run around the bases in fourteen seconds.

Sunday was converted to Christianity in 1887 and became a charismatic speaker.

In May 1908, Sunday arrived in Sharon to preach for six weeks. He set up his tabernacle on the corner of Vine and Silver Streets, and it could hold forty-three hundred people. The Baptist Boy's Brigade and the Buhl Independent Rifles escorted Sunday into the tabernacle for the first meeting. Reverend L. K. Peacock from the United Presbyterian Church led the group in prayer, and James Whitla introduced the evangelist. While in Sharon, Sunday stayed in the home of N. S. Lewis of Logan Avenue.

Sunday came to town to "clean up old Sharon" and wage the relentless war against the world, the flesh, and the devil. He preached the old-fashioned gospel of Hell fire and perdition for the sinners who refused to give up their wicked ways. He was a frank speaker, not at all nice in his language. His spirited sermons were contagious.

Never less than three thousand people attended Sunday's meetings, which were held twice a day except on Mondays, when he rested. On May 10, a record sixty-five hundred people came to Sharon to hear him preach, and thousands more were turned away because no provisions were made for an overflow of people. People came from New Castle (Lawrence County) and Warren, Niles, and Youngstown (Ohio). Special trains brought in people from Sharpsville and New Wilmington. Greenville and Jamestown sent delegations of hundreds that first week. Arrangements were made to bring hundreds from Grove City and Mercer.

Sunday or one of his workers would preach outdoors between the meetings. Noontime meetings were held at plants in Sharon, South Sharon (now Farrell), and Sharpsville. He also went to the public schools to preach to the children and their teachers. Businessmen were given the chance to hear him or one of his workers every noonday at the Protected Home Circle Building.

One Sunday morning, over sixteen thousand people flocked to Sharon to hear Sunday preach a patriotic sermon planned especially for the Grand Army of the Republic. Delegates from Mercer, West Middlesex, Grove City, and Sharpsville reinforced Sharon Post GAR No. 254 and the fife and drum corps. In addition, the Buhl Independent Rifles, Women's Relief Group, Spanish-American War Veterans, and Sons of Veterans showed up in strong force. That afternoon he spoke only to men and made a powerful plea for pure manhood, right living, and decency.

The "Greatest Revival in Pennsylvania" came to a close on June 7, 1908. Sunday's campaign in Sharon finished with 4,765 converts, 711 of whom came forward on the last day he preached. Sharon has not seen a revival that large since. Many people became Christians and gave up drink, amusements, cards, and dancing—their lives transformed by the preachings of Billy Sunday.

"Rev. Sunday's Tabernacle," Sharon, Pa.

On May 10, 1908, Billy Sunday held an evangelical session in Sharon in a temporary tabernacle, which could hold over four thousand people. The photo of the crowd returning from that session was taken in the afternoon about thirty feet north of Pitt Street facing north on Vine Street. (Postcard of tabernacle interior: Daniel Maurice)

145

THE KIDNAPPING OF BILLY WHITLA
By Mairy Jayn Woge

On March 18, 1909, the sky in the Shenango Valley was blanketed with smoke from local mills, and the temperature was cooler than expected for late winter. East Ward Elementary School was on First Avenue in Sharon, two blocks and a ravine away from the Whitla house on East State Street. Bella Whitla wondered why her eight-year-old son Billy had not come home for lunch, but was not worried. He had missed his noon meal numerous times before.

Five blocks away from East Ward School, James A. Boyle and his wife, Helene McDermott Boyle, had been staying with Boyle's mother since Thanksgiving 1908 because they were broke.

On the same March 18, Boyle announced to his mother that the couple was moving to Denver, Colorado. Instead, however, Boyle drove a buggy he had rented in Warren, Ohio, to East Ward School where he informed the janitor, Wesley Sloss, that Mr. Whitla wanted his son Billy to come to his law office right away. The unsuspecting janitor delivered the message to Anna Lewis, Billy's third grade teacher, and she bundled Billy in his warm coat.

By evening, Billy had not returned home, and Mrs. Whitla telephoned her husband who was in New Wilmington, working on a case. One of Billy's classmates, who had skipped school that day, had seen Billy drop a letter in a mailbox on the West Side of Sharon, less than a mile from the school. Billy had then gotten back into a buggy, the youth told police.

Meanwhile, after having returned the buggy to the livery stable, the Boyles, with Billy, had boarded a train for Cleveland. The note Billy had put in the mailbox arrived at the Whitla house the next day and demanded $10,000 in small bills. By the night of March 19, police all over the country were looking for Billy Whitla. He was described as being small for eight years, with gray eyes and yellow hair. When he was taken, he wore a gray coat trimmed with red.

James Whitla soon received a second note telling him to leave the ransom at a rock next to a cannon in Flatiron Park in Ashtabula, Ohio. Whitla traveled to Ashtabula and, when he reached the rock, found additional instructions. He was to leave a note at a local hotel in an envelope addressed to C. A. White. Whitla followed the orders. However, because the hotel clerk knew no C. A. White, he opened the letter, read it, and turned it over to police. Officers arrived at the hotel at 3 a.m. on March 20 and searched all over Flatiron Park to no avail.

Whitla recovered the money from the park and returned to Sharon for additional instructions. When he got off the train, numerous residents of the Shenango Valley and a brass band met him at the railway station. Other persons greeted him in front of his home. They thought he had brought Billy home.

The note Whitla expected arrived two days later. It instructed the father to go to Cleveland and find Dunbar's drugstore for further instructions.

A detective from Perkins Detective Agency in Pittsburgh suggested Whitla keep a record of the serial numbers on the bills he was leaving for the kidnappers. By this point, the ransom had been reduced to $5,000.

Whitla found the Cleveland drugstore where a note gave him further directions. He walked to a specified candy store and delivered an envelope containing the ransom money to a woman there, who in turn gave him another envelope with instructions. Whitla was

> ## COST OF LIVING
>
> *From memories of Julia Stamm Hugo as recorded by her son Bill Hugo*
>
> "I also remember my first trip to 'the nickelodium' to see my first motion picture, a well named place, for 5¢ admission. Later this became a regular theater with a restaurant next door which, with wide doors on the approaching corridor, was opened on show nights. One could get ice cream or oyster stew.
>
> "And mentioning oyster stew, just think of a quart of oysters for fifty cents, sixty if you wanted selects. Well, there was also the two cent stamp. And I well remember the reaction of the family when the price of milk went from six cents to seven cents a quart! And think of a loaf of bread, fresh baked, for five cents. As one is wont to say, 'those were the days.'"

told to go to the Hollenden Hotel (also in Cleveland) and engage a room. The boy would be returned in three hours. He waited in his hotel room for two hours and then moved to the lobby where he sat in a chair and fell asleep. He was exhausted.

A few hours later, Billy strolled into the lobby. His father jumped from the chair where he had been sleeping, ran to his son, and hugged him. People in the lobby cheered.

Billy and his father rode home to the Shenango Valley in a passenger car operated by the Pittsburgh and Erie Railroad. Two bands, the local militia, and a large crowd met the train.

Billy Whitla's picture was in newspapers all over the United States. On the night Billy and his father returned to Sharon, a man and woman appeared in Patrick O'Reilly's bar in Cleveland. They spent cash and treated other patrons to drinks. O'Reilly examined the serial number on one of their $5 bills. (The serial numbers on the money given the kidnappers had been circulated to northern Ohio businesses.) O'Reilly telephoned the Cleveland Police Department. When the police arrived, the Boyles were carrying $5,000 minus $40. The money was pinned on the inside of Mrs. Boyle's clothing.

Tried in Mercer County in May 1909 before Judge Alfred W. Williams, Boyle was sentenced to a life term and died in prison. Mrs. Boyle was fined and sentenced to twenty-five years in prison. She died two years after she was released.

Billy Whitla became a prominent lawyer in the Shenango Valley, but died at the early age of twenty-seven. His kidnapping had nothing to do with his father's reputation or income. Instead, it was over money the Boyles figured Frank H. Buhl, Billy's uncle by marriage, would put up for the boy's release. Buhl was a multimillionaire, having earned his wealth in the iron and steel business, and he and his wife had no children of their own.

EAST MAIN PRESBYTERIAN CHURCH (GROVE CITY)

In 1879, East Main United Presbyterian Church was born in the small community of Pine Grove (now Grove City). The community then had two churches, Methodist and Presbyterian. The nearest *United* Presbyterian churches were over four miles away, in Harmony, Scotch Hill, and Springfield. A handful of Pine Grove people with the strong Covenanter background felt the need for a church of their own denomination in their own town. Reverend William B. Barr from the Springfield church agreed to come to preach an occasional sermon if the group in Pine Grove could guarantee a payment of $100 a year. The small group raised subscriptions for $154.

Sheet music for a song that popularized the Billy Whitla kidnapping.

Billy Boy The Kidnapped Child

Words by
SAM BULLOCK.

Music by
Wm. E. KREPPER.
(PADDY)

And Con espressivo.

The sun was shin-ing bright-ly one morn in ear-ly spring A
A let-ter came to dad-dy it told the sto-ry old The

lit-tle school boy has-tened he heard the school bell ring The
kid-nap-pers were dream-ing of their ill-got-ten gold They

class was soon as-sem-bled no thought of dan-ger there The
car-ried Bil-ly with them on trol-ly car and train While

Copyright, MCMIX, by Sam Bullock & Wm. E. Krepper.
International Copyright secured

East Main Presbyterian Church in Grove City, in 2000. (Photographer: Vonda Minner)

The conception of the United Presbyterian Church was completed, but a suitable meeting place was hard to find. Because of capacity audiences, the fifty-year-old school used for the first two services was not safe as a meeting place. On warm days services were held in a pine grove along Wolf Creek where the Penn Grove Hotel now stands. Sometimes the group met in the vacant Presbyterian Meeting House, which stood on a hill now graded down on the corner of Broad and Poplar Streets. It was a building of outside walls and room, no floors or lining, just a protection from the elements.

Because these meetings encouraged the small band of faithful worshippers, a petition signed by twenty-one supporters was presented to Butler Presbytery to organize a church in Pine Grove. The petition was granted, and a new church was formed in 1879.

Then followed a long period when problems of the new church were many and difficult. Funds were slow in coming in, interest was aroused slowly, and often many were discouraged and advised that the church charter be returned to Presbytery. A few, however, held on persistently, and slowly the church advanced along all lines until numerically, financially, and spiritually the church's future was assured.

During this period, Barr continued to minister to a congregation scattered over fourteen miles. Barr's big wheeled bike or his mule could be seen on the streets of Pine Grove at all hours of the day. His enthusiasm, energy, and spiritual concern for every member of his church caused the congregation to continue to grow in Christ. By this time, the members were meeting in the chapel room of the Academic Building of Pine Grove Academy (now Grove City College). Later called Recitation Hall, this building was the second home for the congregation for three years. Always beside the young energetic minister was Mrs. Barr. Within three months after the founding of the congregation, she had helped organize and direct the Pine Grove Ladies Missionary Society, which solicited funds to build a church.

In 1883, the village of Pine Grove became the borough of Grove City, the Pine Grove United Presbyterian Church of Grove City became the First United Presbyterian Church of Grove City, the Pine Grove Ladies Missionary Society became the Women's Missionary Society of the First United Presbyterian Church, and the congregation completed its first church building. Bar remained as pastor of the congregation until 1885. After having several ministers, Reverend R. P. McClester became the minister in 1890.

Just nine years after the completion of the frame church, it was destroyed by fire. Within seventeen months, the group of about 150 people had a beautiful, red-brick church built on the site of the burned frame church. They sang praise to the Lord, with great happiness they rang the nine hundred pound recast bell from the original frame church. Then, the members set to work to pay off their $12,000 debt. The Women's Missionary society served dinners and quilted quilts to pay for the wallpaper they hung in the church and for the 340 yards of carpeting they sewed and laid in the new church. Sabbath School rooms were now available for young and old. Each Sabbath morning the hitching ground was filled with horses or mules and with buggies and surreys.

In 1903, Dr. W. E. Purvis became the leader of the congregation for the next twenty-one years. Working with him were dedicated laymen, such as the Calderwoods, Englishes, McClellands, and Smiths.

Within ten years after the brick church had been built, the church family had grown to 350 members with 170 in the Sabbath School. The ivy-covered church was no longer large enough for the congregation. A building committee was appointed in 1907. Three lots across the street from the church were purchased. The committee chose Old English Gothic as the style of architecture to be built in Hummelstone brown stone from near Harrisburg. In 1908, a contract was let for $32,000; a pipe organ purchased for $2,000; and furniture, carpeting, and other essentials costing $3,798 chosen, making the entire cost, including interest, $50,398. In 1909, the beautiful new church (pictured on page 150, in 2000) was dedicated.

New members continued to join. The membership was dealt with lovingly, but firmly, by the forefathers. (Some were dismissed because of failure to financially support the church, drunkenness, membership in secret orders or trade unions, fornication, and adultery.) Members participated in the town's civic projects and were leaders in the community's industrial growth. Some were noted educators at the college, like Dr. H. W. Harmon, nationally known in the field of radio transmission.

Following World War I, the New World Movement fund was instituted by the national United Presbyterian Church, and the Grove City United Presbyterian Church joined in this effort. Monies were sent to increase the number of missionaries on the field; build new churches, schools, and hospitals in India and Egypt; and help United Presbyterian churches and seminaries wipe out debt and erect new buildings.

In 1925, the pulpit was filled by Reverend D. Homer Robinson. Under his leadership, great emphasis was placed on evangelism within the church and the importance of young people working within the denomination, in the Presbytery, and in the national denomination. Groups of local young people often attended the national Young Peoples Christian Union (YPCU) conventions, held offices in the organization, and were winners in its national oratorical contests. Sabbath School attendance continued to rise. For forty-four years, R. E. English (1906–1950) was Sunday school superintendent. The classroom of the King's Daughter's Class, organized in 1904 overflowed with members; and the Dorcas Class (1906) and the P & A (1928) classes flourished. In competition with other classes in town and the Presbytery, the Men's Bible Class with Dr. Henderson as its teacher averaged three hundred men each Sabbath morning. The membership of the church reached almost one thousand.

In 1934 Dr. Henderson, then pastor, toured the Northwest and Pacific Coast territory as an evangelistic speaker for the United Presbyterian national board. In 1940, the congregation was honored in Buffalo, New York, at the General Assembly Meeting by having its minister chosen to the highest office in the denomination, that of Moderator of the General Assembly of the United Presbyterian Church of North America.

Following the retirement of Dr. Henderson in 1949, the steady growth of the congregation continued during the pastorate of Dr. Emerson Ray, who stressed the oneness of the church family through visitations by both minister and laymen. During the ten years of his ministry, the congregation continued to hold two worship services every Sabbath and midweek prayer service.

The Sabbath School department outgrew the educational facilities. In 1950, a building committee, consisting of John J. Campbell, Fred Holstein, Ralph Shellito, David Shelley, and E. N. Turner, was elected to study the possibility of a new educational wing. Elected to serve as a finance committee were H. C. Jones, Ed Burton, Emery Madenoff, Bob Neely, and Evert Swarts. In 1953, the new addition was completed. Soon, Nancy Lee (Paxton) was elected as youth director, and for twenty-three years, she capably guided the church's young people.

In 1958, the Presbyterian Church in USA and the United Presbyterian Church of North America in Pittsburgh formed one church, the United Presbyterian Church in USA. Because of this union, the area secretary office of the Board of National Missions became available. Dr. Emerson Ray was elected in 1959 to fill that office; consequently the pulpit was vacant. That same year, Dr. Gordon Boak became pastor of the church, which, within three months, because of the union, changed its name to East Main United Presbyterian Church. To assist Dr. Boak in the visitation of the members of the congregation, Dr. R. C. Sherrard and later Dr. J. Y. Jackson were elected Minister of Visitation.

September 1960 brought a change in the organization of the women's work within the church. The Women's Missionary Society (1880), Mable Campbell (1914), King's Daughters (1915), and Non Nobis Guild (1941) now joined to form an association with several circles forming the basis for the mission, spiritual, and fellowship work.

During this time the membership reached 1,315 with attendance at communion services reaching over 1,250. The sanctuary was not large enough. In 1961, David Shelley, Harvey Young, Raymond Turner, Evert Swarts, and Albert Chanadet prepared plans for remodeling and renovating the sanctuary costing $100,000. Plans were approved with a stipulation that payments equal to 10 percent of the cost of the alterations be made to mission giving. Five months later the sanctuary was dedicated. Permanent seating capacity was increased from 680 to 980 with an overflow capacity of 1,100. New carpeting, pews, lights, pulpit, and lectern were installed. At the rear of the choir loft was hung a red dossal cloth in the center of which hangs a Celtic cross edged in gold leaf that was made and donated to the church by Grover Baker.

In 1971, the pastor became Dr. William O. Dandoy, with Reverend Jack Dunlap assisting him. They, with strong laymen, guided the congregation in a thematic, in-depth Bible study program and in a new evangelistic program stressing Christ within each member, proclaiming Him within the church, and finally witnessing to these beliefs in the community. As of 1997, the church has grown to nine hundred members.

Groups that meet for study and fellowship include Mothers' Guild (for mothers of children from birth through grade 2), Presbyterian Women, Men's Association, Weigh Down Workshop, Crown Ministries (Christian family financial management), 50+ singles Ministry, Divorce Recovery Workshop, and Small Group Bible Studies. Also, the church has various groups that enjoy fellowship, such as quilting, basketball, golf, softball, and Scouts. A new project called Noah's Crew helps at-home elderly church members who have no relatives nearby. The project provides repairs, yard work, and rides.

East Main has a goal of giving 50 percent of income to missions. Each year it comes closer to reaching the goal. It supports many missionaries around the world and sends three mission teams on trips each summer to help build homes for people in Erie, South Carolina, and Mexico. In 1997 over one hundred adults and youth from East Main went on these mission trips. To support these trips and building expenses, East Main operates Shalom Cookie Company, a group of church volunteer bakers, and Feed My Sheep, a church volunteer catering group. East Main also supports local missions such as the Food Pantry, and Meals on Wheels, and an Angel Tree Project that provides Christmas gifts for children with a parent in prison.

As of 1998, the pastor was Don Hoagland and director of student ministries was Lori Rhoads.

Polar Expedition
By William Philson and Robert Olson

Robert E. Peary had made several arctic explorations; and, when the field surgeon from his 1905–1906 expedition was unavailable, plans were arranged for Dr. John

Stoneboro, on the banks of Sandy Lake.

Goodsell to be part of the 1907 foray. As the two corresponded, however, the planned expedition was postponed a year or so.

Goodsell first met Peary at a lecture in Pittsburgh concerning Peary's 1905–1906 Arctic travels. Goodsell later invited him back to his house where he "instinctively liked and admired" the Arctic explorer. The original plan called for Goodsell to remain behind on the boat and perform only medical assistance, but the doctor was later able to persuade Peary to let him join the actual expedition.

The *Roosevelt* left in early July 1908. Goodsell was eager and for the entire expedition was generally in good spirits as was his nature. The crew departed Eagle Island, and the goal on the first leg of the journey was Greenland. Minor expeditions were made to collect scientific specimens and make notes for journals. Goodsell conducted many observations, both scientifically and socially. (Of a special note were the Innuit Indians of the Smith Sound region. They remain a small population that covers millions of square miles. A census taken during the 1908–1909 expedition period showed a total of only 211. Generally isolated from the rest of the world, they are still much like the early American Indians in their hunting and migratory practices.)

As they proceeded toward the pole, more stops were made to forage for game (such as Walrus, Arctic hare, auk, seal, fox, and caribou), other food, and scientific notes. During the winter months, ice forming in the waters was a major consideration. A clear path had to be maintained through the ice until the winter resting place of the *Roosevelt* was found. Such travel took skill and luck.

Once the ship had reached its destination, a team of men proceeded on foot. Temperatures during March reached as low as -65° F. Gloves drying out over lanterns in the igloos were frequently covered over by frost. One advantage to such cold, according to Goodsell, however, is that "one felt the joy of living in areas where the air is free from dust and bacteria . . ., we were practically immune from colds and respiratory troubles."

As the team approached Peary's last expedition checkpoint, the farthest his team had reached in the past, Peary started sending men back to the ship. In his ultimate plan, he was to have only a few men go with him to the pole. Peary only took a few Eskimos and a black man with him in hopes of being the first white male to reach the pole. Goodsell was one of the men who were sent back to the ship. This return trip was no easy task, as supplies were getting low. Goodsell reached the ship weak, but with no major accident, and made many more scientific observations.

The dam at Sandy Lake in 1906. (Photo: Ila Ayre)

Goodsell lived in Sandy Lake for many years before his death in 1947. A prized collection of the Mercer County Historical Society is the Goodsell collection, which includes

Next to Sandy Lake sprang the towns of Stoneboro (pictured at top), with its icehouses and train near the lake, and Sandy Lake, with its churches and homes advancing into the nearby hills. (Photo, about 1905: Ila Ayre)

a variety of arctic artifacts and his unpublished manuscript on his adventures in the frozen north. Because of a dispute over publication rights with Peary, Goodsell was the only principal participant who did not publish a book on his experience. The society subsequently sponsored the publication of Goodsell's manuscript *On Polar Trails*.

Miss Josephine Noll was a grade school teacher in Mercer for many years. Born in 1885, she died in 1963.

Of the many medical professionals practicing in the county over the years, Dr. Hoyt, who practiced medicine in Sharon in 1900, is featured in this photo.

Settlers came gradually into Lackawannock Township. They generally gathered in homes, or under shade trees during the summer, to worship. Two Presbyterian churches had been built in northern Mercer County, namely, Fairfield in 1799 and Coolspring in 1800. In the early 1800s, Lackawannock settlers moved toward organizing another Presbyterian church in their area. By 1823, they had constructed a small log building on land owned by the father of James Blackstone (on the south side of present-day Route 318 several hundred feet across from the present township-municipal building). In 1832, the Unity Presbyterian Church was created. Reverend James Satterfield was the circuit pastor. Soon, a much more spacious church was needed. In 1837, a few acres were purchased from John Wilson across the road from the present church. However, the building never was completed. Therefore, in 1853, the congregation decided to try again. They built a new church across the road, where the present church stands. By 1900, the congregation had grown both spiritually and materially. The old building was sold to Stewart & Son in Charleston to be used as a blacksmith shop, and a new, "modern" church was built. Sixty shelters were also built, to the south of the church, to accommodate the teams and carriages. The first service was held on April 1, 1900. Three outstanding features were the slanting floor, tall steeple, and beautiful stained glass windows, all of which are still enjoyed by visitors and members now. Many additions and changes have taken place since, such as a large fellowship hall and stainless steel kitchen, several Sunday school class rooms, convenient bathrooms, a one-level chancel and chairlift, and most recently a "lift" plus two handicapped restrooms.

The congregation has been served by a number of ministers, each with his unique contribution. For example, the first resident pastor was Reverend D. C. Reed, who was installed in 1849 and served until 1882. Reverend T. D. Stewart was installed as pastor in 1884 and served twenty-two years, including chairing the building committee for the current church. Reverend W. C. Ferver was installed in 1922, celebrated the church's centennial in 1932, guided the congregation through the Great Depression, and served many years until retiring in 1944. In 1959, Reverend James E. Wigley came to Unity from Meadville and served until 1982. Now, Reverend Robert E. Dunkleberger is leading the church. Since the 1850s, Unity Church has actively participated in the Women's Home and Foreign Missionary Society. The Maude Ferver Auxiliary was organized. The southern Presbyterian women joined with Presbyterian ladies. Several changes were necessary, but a stronger mission effort has been the result. Shenango Presbyterian Women is an active organization, and Christian Endeavor has been active since 1895. Unity sent Dr. Watson Hayes and wife Margaret on their wedding day in 1882 to China, where they served until 1947. An active Sunday school operates the year around. Many qualified men and women serve as teachers. The vacation bible school is supported by the Sunday school. The music department is well organized by the Congregation Worship Committee under the supervision of Jane Bartholomew, who serves as organist and choir director. A monthly newsletter, "Unity Press," is sent to all members of the congregation.
(Photographer: Vonda Minner; caption: Genevieve Bartholomew)

One of the many blast furnaces around Sharpsville was the Mabel Furnace, where Bert Hayes (left) and Harry I. Kantner (right) worked.

Robert Coyer opened his first mine on his own farm in 1898 south of Grove City. Due to his family's honesty and fair dealings, the miners would load coal by the car instead of by the ton. This mine closed in 1963 due to the construction of Interstate 79. I. P. Coyer also had a mine south of Grove City. The coal from this mine, which had no sulfur and no "clinkers," would be brought north on Route 173 to the railroad in Grove City by horse-drawn wagons (pictured). (Source: **Reflections of Our Past***)*

Captain John W. Campbell was the commander of Company F, 15th Regiment, of the National Guard (Grove City area) from 1891 to 1900 (except during the Spanish-American War). (Caption: Richard Christner)

Below: At a reunion in the early 1900s (possibly at Shiloh, Stone River, or Chickamauga), members of Company E, 77th Regiment, Pennsylvania Volunteer Infantry, posed for the camera. The unit was recruited from Mercer County in late 1861 and early 1862 and mustered out in December 1865. (Caption: Richard Christner)

In 1900, Company F, 15th Regiment, of the National Guard from the Grove City area became Company M, 16th Regiment. Some of these soldiers posed for the camera (probably within a few years after that change) because their uniform style still reflects the Spanish-American War. In 1917, the unit was consolidated with Company M, 8th Regiment, to become Company M, 112th Regiment. (Caption: Richard Christner)

Company C (1901) and Company B (1902), 16th Regiment, of the National Guard.

The West Middlesex band joined the Fourth of July parade in Grove City in 1906.

The old Sharon High School (pictured, in the early 1900s) was on the banks of the Shenango River.

Fredonia baseball team, 1908.

The Gibson-Byers baseball team, apparently from the Sharon area, defeated the Lawyers team 11–0 at Conneaut Lake Park on August 6, 1908. The Gibson-Byers players included (first row) Fred Gibson, right fielder; F. P. Byers, second baseman; Charlie Gibson, catcher; Charlie Byers, center fielder; and Jim Gibson, shortstop; (second row) E. L. Byers, left fielder; G. W. Byers, first baseman; John Gibson, third baseman; and J. W. Byers, pitcher. The team's mascot was Paul Gibson, seated in front.

STRUTHERS & HANNAH,
ARCHITECTS,
Successors to W. S. Fraser,
Rooms 12-16, Jackson Building,
Penn Ave. and Sixth St.

PITTSBURGH, PA. May 12/02

Dr Isaac C Ketler,

Dr Sir:—

The following is list of bidders with amounts of their bids on Ladies Dorm Building,

The Constable Bros Co.	Erie Pa	$34,257—
Henry Shenk Co,	Pittsburgh	31,565—
Geo J Hollar	Allegheny	36,650—
T J Williams	Pittsburgh	30,800—
Geo Schenck	Butler	30,290—

Mr Jas Orr of Mercer had the plans but has not as yet sent in his bid.

Mr Pew is away at present & will not return until about Wednesday. Shall we take the matter of bids up with him? In regard to Science Hall it would be well to have one of your professors take measurements we could then work up your suggestions.

If you prefer however we can go out & talk matters over on the ground. Awaiting your further instructions We Remain Struthers & Hannah

Before the Colonial, a women's dormitory, was built for Grove City College, bids were received for the construction contract.

THE MATTHEWS SQUARING SHEAR GUIDES

Patented Aug. 22, 1916

FOR ALL TIN PLATE MILLS

Here are ten <u>real reasons</u> why these guides should be used <u>exclusively</u>.

1. The plates can be sheared more accurately than was ever known before.
2. They are convenient and will wear for years.
3. Close sizes can be sheared without the use of special or double guides.
4. They are a time-saver for the shearmen.
5. The guard-rod on back guides save the guides from wear, thus relieving the machine shops from constantly making guides.
6. Inexperienced shearmen can do 100 per cent better work with the use of these guides.
7. They are not an experiment, but tried and proven, and are now in use.
8. To advertise that you are using these guides will not only help me to do business, but will show to your customers and to the trade in general, that you are putting forth every effort to increase efficiency, and you will be able to compete along these lines with all others.
9. You can purchase a license to manufacture guides for your own use at a reasonable figure.
10. They will save time, material, and money.

For demonstration, write

J. E. MATTHEWS,

Box 311   Farrell, Pa.

An African-American who benefited from the brief upward mobility during the 1909 strike at American Sheet and Tin Plate Company was James E. Matthews, a six-year veteran at the company's South Sharon Works. Already denied promotion twice because of white union men's protests, he was offered a job as a shear foreman during the strike. Given the union's record of discrimination, the twenty-three-year-old Matthews accepted management's offer. Due to a lack of shearing experience, however, he requested a shearman's job, which he held for over eight years. During that time Matthews invented a shear guide, which was recognized as the work of a genius. (Contributor: Roland Barksdale-Hall)

This 1902 Grout Steam Runabout, purchased by John Fahnline, is believed to be the first car in Sharon to run. (Another family had a car earlier, but did not succeed in operating it.) The car remains in the purchaser's family—in a manner of speaking a "one-owner" car. In 1941, the car was towed in the Sharon Centennial parade, with a grandson of the purchaser as a passenger. More recently, James F. Warren, married to the granddaughter of the purchaser, put the car into running condition again. The car is now garaged with the Warrens in Fort Washington, Pennsylvania, and takes to the road on occasion. (Contributor: Richard H. Fahnline)

Mercer's Old Home and Fair Week in 1909 promoted the following poem:

Home

I want to go home to the dull old town,
With the shaded streets and the open square,
    And the hill,
    And the flat,
    And the house I love,
    And the paths I know.
    I want to go home!
If I can't go back to those happy days,
Yet I can live where their shadows lie
    Under the trees
    And over the grass;
I want to be there where their joy was once.
    Oh! I want to go home.
    I want to go home!

(Postcard, about 1909: Vinson Skibo)

Grace Methodist Episcopal Church originated in two camp meetings: one in 1830 near Albin's Corners (five miles north of Grove City); the other in 1832 on the George Taylor Farm (east of Grove City). Later, a class was formed in each neighborhood: one in a log house near Perry's Blacksmith Shop at Brisco Springs (north of Grove City); the other in a stone house 1.5 miles southeast of Grove City on Slippery Rock Road. These classes were named Wolf Creek and Pine Grove. In 1843, J. T. Hirst donated ground (now the Methodist Cemetery) on which the first church building was erected for $2,000 and dedicated in 1844. It was lighted by candles hung around the walls, later replaced by lamps with reflectors hung on the window casings. Membership was about forty. By 1880, the church was known as Pine Grove Methodist Episcopal Church. In 1884, a new, red-brick church was completed on the southwest corner of Grace and East Pine Streets. The cost was $9,700; seating capacity, 500; and membership, 325. The name was changed to Grace Methodist Episcopal Church, and the church was incorporated in 1885. Also in 1885, the 2,240-pound tower bell was donated by D. G. Courtney in memory of his sister, Anna Maria Courtney. In 1908, ground was broken for a new church at the southeast corner of Broad and East Pine Streets. The buff-brick building (pictured, in 2000) was completed and dedicated by Bishop Berry in 1909. By actual count, 2,240 persons assembled in this church in 1910 to hear Billy Sunday preach. In 1926, the Educational Building was added. When the Methodist Episcopal Church, Methodist Episcopal Church South, and Methodist Protestant Church nationally merged in 1939, the local church became the Grace Methodist Church. In 1947, the tower music system was dedicated in honor of the soldiers from the congregation and in memory of members who were killed in combat. After the union of the Methodist Church and Evangelical United Brethren Church in 1968, the church became the Grace United Methodist Church. Missionaries who have gone out from this church include Harry Rowe, Mary E. Williams, Martha Robinson, Ernest Robinson, Margaret Pierce Stewart, and John McMullen. Since 1834, fifty-three ministers have served the congregation. (Photographer: Vonda Minner; caption: Reverend John Jefferis and Jean Brown)

With S. D. Hum, treasurer, and Harry Watson, president, the Farmers and Merchants Trust Company of Greenville had $467,462.96 in deposits and $619,722.69 in assets (loans, bonds, real estate, cash, and reserves) on November 16, 1909. (Later, during the Great Depression, according to the September 1, 1933, Mercer Dispatch, the Farmers & Merchants National Bank reopened after closing due to bank failures. New capital stock totaling $60,000 was to be sold, and 45 percent of deposits were to be frozen for an indefinite period. The First National Bank of Sharon and Fredonia National Bank also reopened.)

James Sheakley, a prominent Greenville resident (at one time a U.S. senator, then territorial governor of Alaska, and finally burgess of Greenville), was honored by having the town of Sheakleyville officially named after him. However, the town came by this name in an interesting way. The first settler in the area was William Byers, who built his house in 1798. In 1803, Byers was appointed the first sheriff of Mercer County and moved to Mercer. He sold his five hundred acres to John Sheakley, who brought his wife, five sons, and three daughters to the property in 1804. After Sheakley died, he left his land to his surviving (only four) sons, William, Moses, George, and John. George apparently became well-known and respected. In 1818, he built a house and later a tavern. The town grew, and in 1820 it was christened Georgetown in Sheakley's honor. However, the town was also known as Culbertson (after another family of settlers) and Exchangeville, which was also the name of its post office. As the town awaited its charter as a borough, many merchants had signs painted with Exchangeville. However, when the charter arrived, the name of the new borough was Sheakleyville. The name caused quite a stir, enhanced because the honoree was not a local resident, but from Greenville. (Caption: Ethel Hildebran and Gwen Lininger)

The interior of a general store in Sharpsville, about 1907.

167

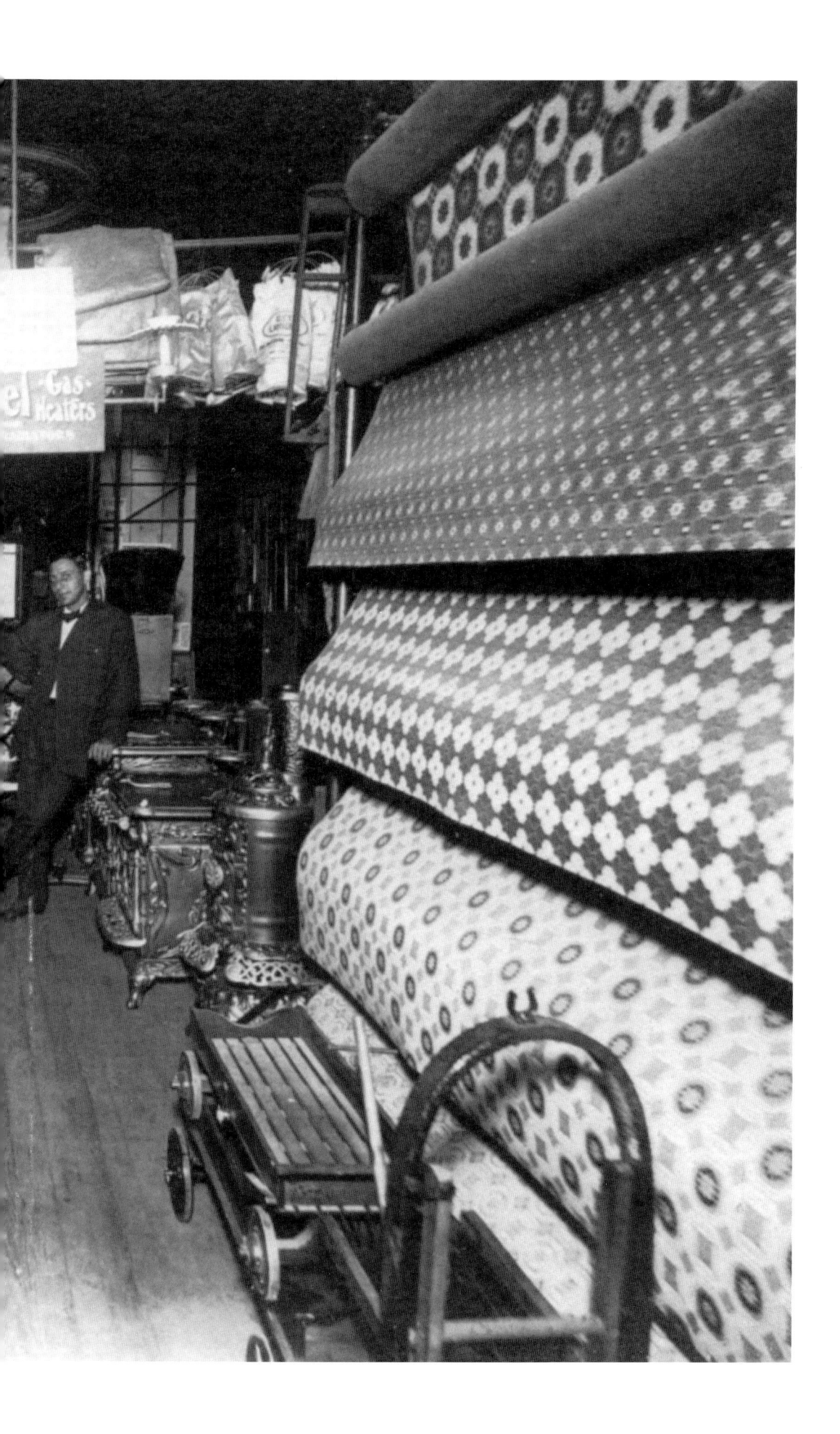

After John Stevenson Jr. received his cut for selling Sharon Steel Company in 1902, he bought Driggs-Seabury of Philadelphia and moved the company to Sharpsville Avenue in Hickory Township (building pictured, about 1909). Driggs-Seabury assembled the Ritz and Twombley automobiles, Vulcan trucks, and guns; the last gun the company built was shipped out in 1909 (pictured). At the time Stevenson was named a supervisor at Stewart Iron Company, he sold Driggs-Seabury to Savage Arms Company. Savage Arms produced guns and ammunition, some of which was used by the military during World War I. The products were tested at a sandbank on the Hoagland property west of the Shenango River. (The sandbank is a target range for police in 1999.) Savage Arms was a debtor of Westinghouse Electric Company, and Westinghouse collected that debt in 1922.

In 1905, Lincoln School (pictured, above left, about 1909) was built on Gilmore Avenue in Grove City. Eventually, its use as a school ende it was converted to apartments (pictured, above right, in 1997). (Postcard, 1909: Vinson Skibo; photographers in 1997: Nick and Kathy Po

In 1909, a parade in Greenville included a horse-drawn fire wagon (pictured, in front of the old Shenango Street station and borough building) complete with the firemen dressed as clowns. (Contributor: Gwen Lininger)

The Grand Army of the Republic was an organization of veterans from the Civil War. On February 12, 1910, the following men dined in honor, at least in part, of President Lincoln's birthday: C. W. Whistler, George Reznor, Robert Stranahan, J. E. Shipler, Charles Clawson, F. A. Filson, Thomas McKean, Johnson Grandle, George E. Hamilton, Robert Orr, William Taylor, T. J. Gillespie, J. M. Bell, John Clinefelter, P. M. Butler, H. A. Broadbent, Akin Thompson, G. W. Wright, J. B. Nickum, W. F. Gibson, W. A. McCormick, W. A. Eastlick, A. M. Clawson, G. W. Riddle, John Lytle, C. G. Byers, Alex Donaldson, J. M. Wingard, J. B. Bell, G. W. Bell, J. W. Nelson, John Eagleson, J. W. Anderson, and Crosby Richards. Erasmus Wilson (Pittsburgh) and A. W. Williams (Mercer) were honored guests.

"My grandfather, Isaac Jefferson Pizor, and my father, Ira Leigh Pizor, came to Mercer around 1910 from Grove City. Other members of the Pizor family had a feed mill in that community. My grandfather had two houses built on South Otter Street, and the house in which my parents later lived at 225 South Otter Street was remodeled. A feed mill was built at the end of one property at the corner of Plum and East streets. A large barn and warehouse were built on the property at 225 South Otter Street. These streets, although named by the borough, were called alleys at the time. The feed mill flourished. Local farmers brought their grain to be ground, and flour was made at the mill. The family dealt with Armstrong Grocery Company in Sharon and other grocery stores. On April 1, 1924, a windy spring night, the mill caught fire, probably from spontaneous combustion. My dad was in bed with a bad back—lumbago as it was called then—but through superhuman effort he got a truck and our car out of the barn and off to a safe distance. My grandmother, Zelda Magee Pizor, who was then in her late sixties, used a garden hose to spray her home and try to protect it. Families on South Pitt Street also had their garden hoses out, spraying their homes to protect them from flying debris. The fire took a garage owned by John Orr who lived on East Butler Street and seriously damaged the home and garage owned by Margaret McKenna and her mother. The firemen were able to save the barn on my parents' property. Because I was a toddler, my mother had to stay with me. I was told that I kept saying, 'Want to see,' but my mother refused to pick me up for fear of frightening me. The mill cellar remained as long as I lived in Mercer. We children were cautioned not to play there because of crumbling cement. It was such a fun place to play so we ignored that advice. After my father passed away, Mother was able to have the barn torn down. She always said she didn't fear man nor beast, but she had a terrible fear of fire. The mill cellar is now gone. Grass and flowers grow there, and it would be hard to imagine two large buildings standing at the corner of Plum and East streets." (Contributor: Margaret Pizor Bower)

Main Street, Greenville, around 1908.

State Street, Sharon, around 1910.

Eagle Street, Greenville, around 1904.

Osgood

The Lake Shore & Michigan Southern Railroad (LS&MS) station at Osgood (Sugar Grove Township) also served Bessemer & Lake Erie Railroad (B&LE) passengers. They descended a ramp to reach the B&LE trains, which ran under the LS&MS track along Little Shenango River at that point. The two railroads interchanged freight cars at Osgood. The LS&MS tower controlled the track crossing with the Erie Railroad east of Osgood at a point known as Amasa by the two railroads. Three-level railroading evolved at Osgood in 1902 when workers (pictured) finished the high-line bridge on the K-O line (between Kremis and Osgood) and the B&LE started using the new bridge under which ran both the LS&MS's Oil City line and the Erie Railroad's main line. The latter two tracks then crossed each other (pictured on pages 172–173, in 1957 aerial) just beyond the new bridge. The original B&LE line passed under the LS&MS truss bridge when passengers used the ramp to reach the track. (Photos: Richard Sherbondy; caption: Frederick Houser)

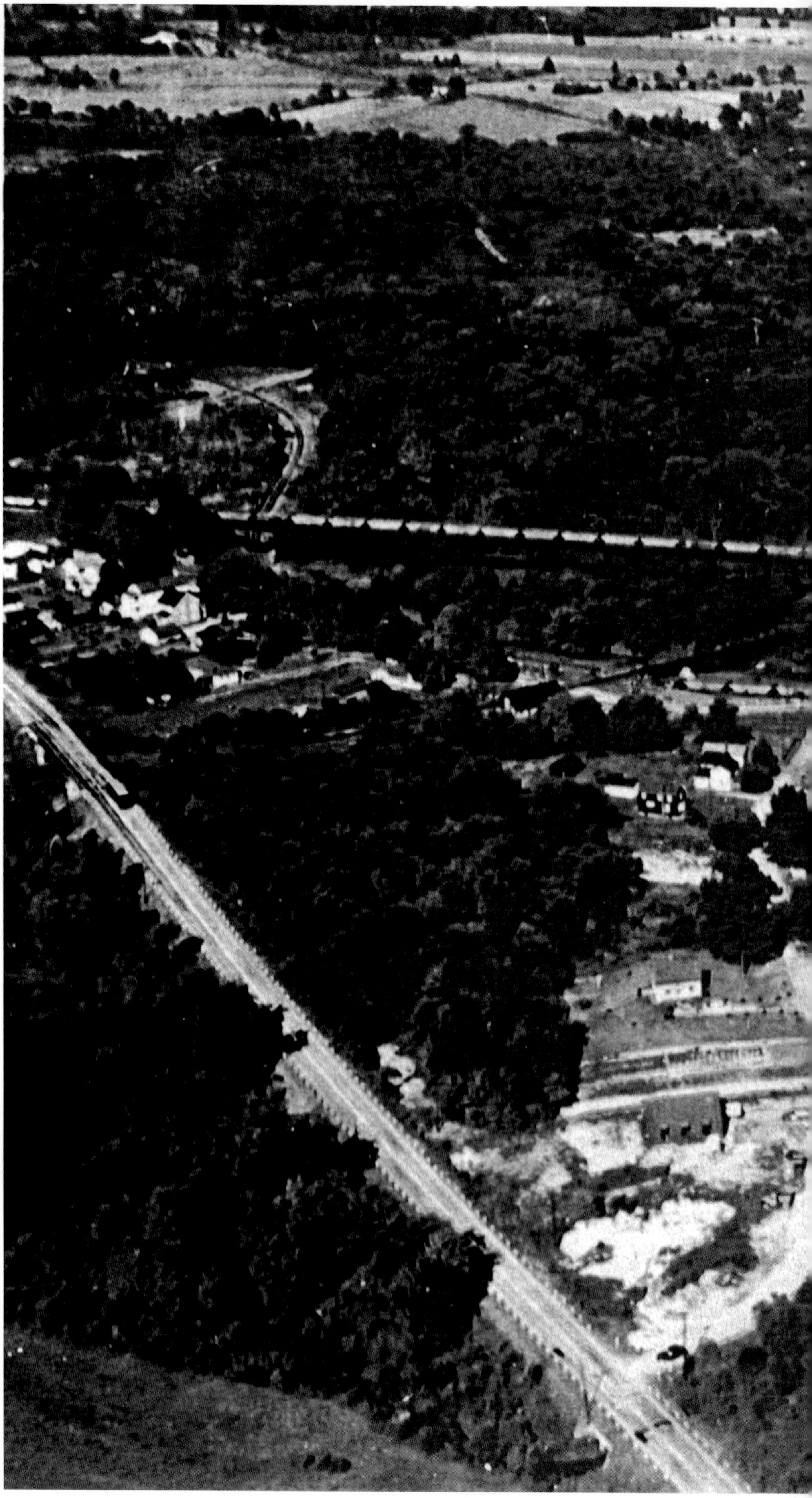

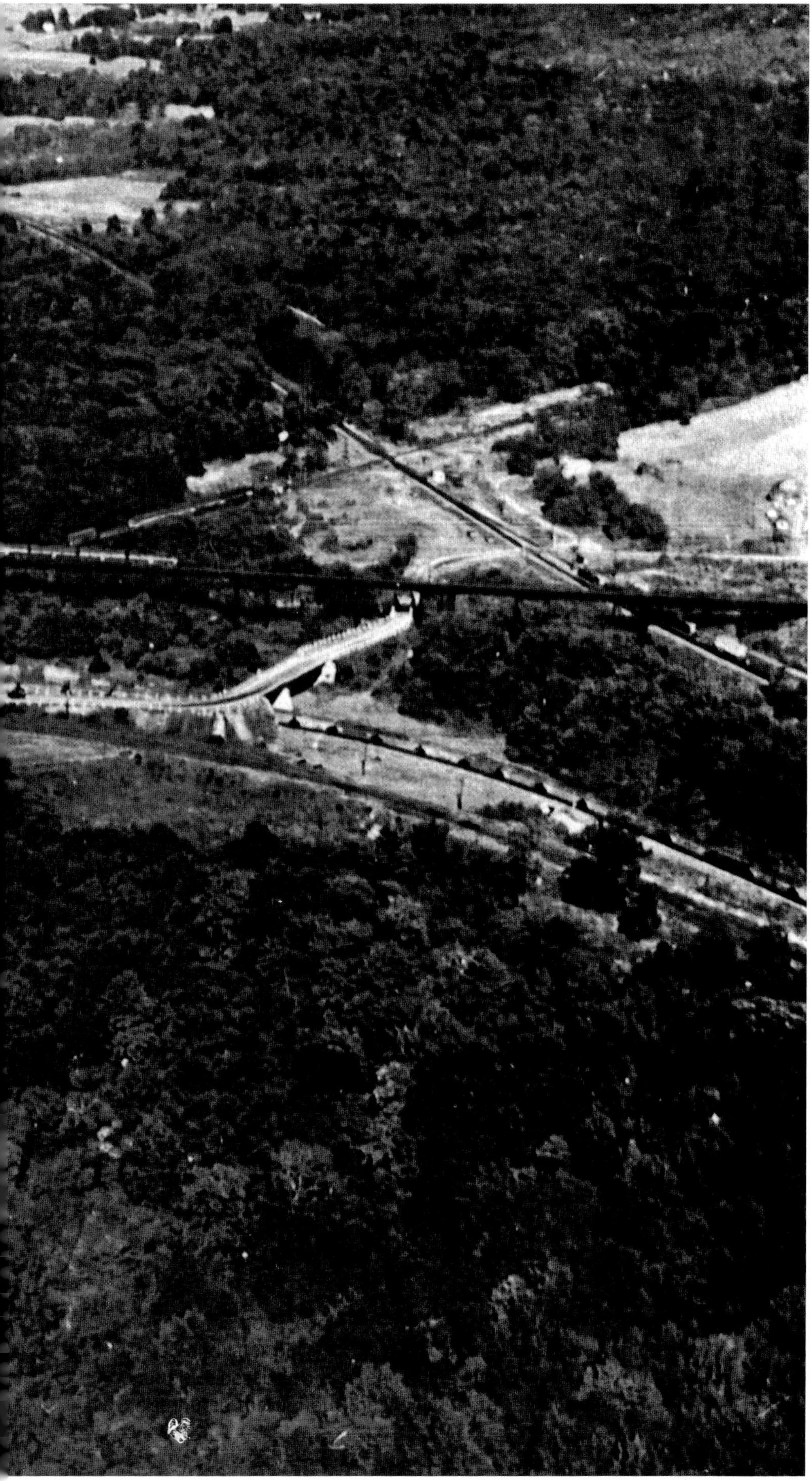

Tipple, Pardoe.

Company Store, Pardoe.

View from top of Tipple toward town, Pardoe.

The Pardoe Mine was opened by Enoch Filer in 1864 under the name of Mercer Coal and Manufacturing Company, which also operated Monkey Run Mine. Both mines were successful. Started in 1865 as the "Bear Creek" Railroad, construction of the Shenango & Allegheny Railroad's 20.5-mile line from the Shenango station to the mines at Pardoe was not completed until 1869. By the early 1900s, the village of Pardoe (Company store pictured, about 1908) was established and typical of other mining settlements in the county. Mules (pictured with drivers, about 1909) were used to transport the coal from the mines to the tipple over the railroad tracks. The tipple was extended across the main line so the locomotives could be fueled directly with newly mined coal. The view from the top of the tipple toward the railroad station includes the local church, and the view in the other direction shows the extent of the tracks and the village (tipple and views pictured, about 1907). One hazard of living close to the tracks was the risk of train wrecks, as evidenced by three photographs of the Frank Kreidle home after a 1909 derailment. (The mines closed in 1927.) (Caption and postcard of tipple with train: Frederick Houser; postcards of tipple with station and view of town from tipple and photos of Kreidle home: Rita Kreidle Holler)

View from top of Tipple toward station, Pardoe.

Pardoe, Pa

Frank Kreidle Home.

175

The following young men showed their cattle and sheep in Millbrook Park (Worth Township) in 1916, possibly for a 4-H or grange league event: Paul Jamisen, Fred Westlake, Harold Perrine, Fred Coleman, Carl Davidson, Homar Cochran, Kenneth Waldron, Lloyd Grace, Forrest Hollebaugh, Vernin Perrine, and Alvin Grace. (Contributor: Mary Wilson)

Chapter 3: 1911–1920

TOWNSHIPS

In 1916, Mount Pleasant Grange No. 1687 in ***East Lackawannock Township*** purchased the church building from the Prospect Free Methodist congregation after it disbanded. Over one hundred grangers had been meeting at the Mount Pleasant election building, adjacent to the Hoagland (Mount Pleasant) Cemetery on Stone Base Road. (Saturday night square dances during the 1940s and 1950s attracted a crowd of young and old; refreshments of homemade pie and ice cream with soft drinks were a hit during intermission. Annual chicken pie sales and pancake and sausage suppers continue to raise money for grange projects. About fifty members remain active and support the annual Mercer County Grange Fair held east of Mercer on Route 58.)

Built in the 1800s, the original structure for the Kennard United Presbyterian Church in ***Sugar Grove Township*** was completely destroyed by fire in 1919. As an Erie Railroad train passed by the fire, a thoughtful engineer blew the train's whistle to warn the people. The church was rebuilt by 1921 and is still used now.

The total population for ***Wilmington Township*** was 345 in 1920. Trucks and tractors were beginning to make an appearance throughout the farmland.

MUNICIPALITIES

City postal delivery service was established in ***Mercer*** in 1914 with two carriers employed.

By 1911, ***Jamestown***'s streets were lined with lights, and the town was enjoying new gas and water systems. Churches were developing during these years as well. Andrew Carnegie donated money to pay for half the cost of the United Methodist's new organ. Many Jamestown residents were celebrated for their service in World War I, including Hazen Kelly who was dubbed the "world's greatest bomb thrower."

After 1900, Franklin Manufacturing Company, which already operated two plants in Franklin, established its third plant in ***Stoneboro***. It had one of the first reinforced concrete multistory factory buildings in western Pennsylvania as its central structure. Output of the plant was described as "Magnesia Products" and was primarily insulating materials for steam boilers. While a major employer during this decade, the plant closed about 1920 just three or four years before Mercer Iron and Coal also shut down. A substantial number of the displaced workers then began to commute to new jobs that opened up elsewhere. For example, Westinghouse Electric Company was converting the former Salvage Arms plant in Sharon to manufacture transformers, and many of the Franklin Manufacturing workers went to work there. (As time went on, Stoneboro became increasingly a "bedroom" community—a role that it fills now.)

MERCER OPERA HOUSE
Sources: Mercer County Herald, June 11, 1920, and a week later

"Fire of unknown origin, which broke out in the opera house building at Mercer Wednesday night, caused one of the biggest damages by fire which the county seat has experienced for a number of years. The opera house was completely destroyed together with six other business houses included in the block, among which were the Star Theatre which is under the same management as the Strand Theatre at Grove City, the Western Press Newspaper Plant, the Ashe Confectionery Store, the Currier Meat Market, Byers Plumbing Shop and several other smaller losses. The loss is conservatively estimated at $100,000, partly covered by the insurance."

"A. L. McCartney is the only one of the unfortunate sufferers from last week's disastrous fire who has so far succeeded in finding new quarters in which to conduct his business. He has rented the basement of the Taylor restaurant where there was a full equipment and machinery for the manufacture of ice cream and is ready to commence business. He was without insurance on the plant which was destroyed. J. M. Currier & Son have a new storeroom in view and expect to reopen their meat market at the earliest opportunity. J. M. Byers is looking for a room for his plumbing establishment and in the meantime doing outside work. Several deals for the establishment of a moving picture house are rumored."

FARRELL
by Mairy Jayn Woge

Four laborers were killed and seven injured during a strike against the management at Carnegie Illinois steel company in Farrell in 1919. George J. Hostetter (Mercer) recalls that the strike occurred at both the North Sharon and Farrell Carnegie mills, but was bitter and violent in Farrell. State police were stationed at the Farrell mill and plant guards hit pickets with night sticks while circulating among them. Hostetter said the reason for the strike was wages. When no agreement was reached and the fighting did not stop, the steel company imported Afro-Americans from South Carolina in buses to break the strike. After a settlement was achieved, many of the Afro-Americans stayed in Farrell. The Ku Klux Klan, composed mostly of Anglo-Saxon Protestants, was already in the Shenango Valley, initially opposed to some of the nationality groups and Catholics who worked at Valley mills, and turned its attention to the Afro-Americans.

The business section of Farrell in 1920 contained two bakeries, two barber shops, the Lavine Hotel, a few auto repair garages, DeBrakeleer Grocery, the first food store in the community, loan companies, a newspaper, a meat market, an electric shop, two dry cleaners, two pharmacies, offices for three physicians, and an ornate opera house, the last on Hamilton Avenue. Street lists in the *Polk Directory* showed boarding houses "for foreigners" were on Haywood (later Roemer Boulevard), Staunton, and Idaho streets.

In 1918, the American Sheet and Tin Plate Company (AMSTP) contracted for the construction of one hundred houses at the east end of Farrell, off Shenango Boulevard and Buhl Terrace. They were covered with stucco and are in good condition in 2000. (In 1924, the company erected four new hot mills; in 1935, AMSTP was absorbed by Carnegie Illinois.)

Electric lights were installed in the business section of Farrell in 1918.

AFRICAN-AMERICANS
By Roland Barksdale-Hall

Racial antipathies existed in other northern industrial mill towns where the union, Amalgamated Association of Iron and Steelworkers, operated; and local American Sheet and Tin Plate Company officials moved to exploit these breaches. African-Americans Marshall and H. Russell Wayne, brothers who had worked as "tin men" in Little Washington, were offered jobs at the South Sharon Works. There, Marshall held the semi-skilled position of heater, while his younger brother worked as a rougher for $1.75 a day. In 1919, Russell worked his way up to the position of roller, the highest classified job in the American Sheet and Tin Plate mill. As a chief roller, Russell had six whites working for him, an exceptional circumstance for an African-American worker in western Pennsylvania.

Another African-American, Ernest Fields, had distinguished himself as a roller in the South Sharon plant as early as 1910. Eight years later, Bussell Long was working as a doubler, a job that required much skill and adaptability. Such attainments were remarkable in a time when African-American workers typically were relegated to unskilled positions in the steel industry. Most African-American newcomers to the area came from Pittsburgh and Little Washington and from Ohio, although they traced their family's roots to Virginia, West Virginia, Maryland, Tennessee, Alabama, and a few other border states in the upper South. The upward occupational mobility of these African-American made South Sharon an unusual community.

Before 1916, African-Americans found varying degrees of upward mobility at other mills in the Shenango Valley as well. Although the American Steel and Wire Company employed fewer of them than did American Sheet and Tin Plate's South Sharon Works,

Timeline 1911—1920

	The World		Mercer County
1911	Ronald Amundsen, a Norwegian explorer, discovers the South Pole; air conditioning is invented by Willis H. Carrier	1911	Thunderstorm hits Mercer and lightning strikes the new dome of the courthouse; the first marriage license is issued at the new courthouse around 3:00 p.m. to John W. Fier and Edna E. Cornelius; the new (third) courthouse is dedicated
1912	New Mexico and Arizona become the 47th and 48th states; China becomes a republic; the Titanic sinks at 2:27 a.m. after striking an iceberg in the North Atlantic; the first municipally owned street cars appear on the streets of San Francisco, California	1912	First osteopathic hospital opens in Grove City; South Sharon becomes Farrell
1913	Congress is empowered to levy income taxes by the 16th Amendment to the US Constitution; Woodrow Wilson becomes the 28th president	1913	Grove City witnesses the county's first plane crash; the Shenango River floods with 16.87 feet of water and causes an estimated damage of $200,000
1914	Henry Ford revolutionizes the manufacture of automobiles by inaugurating the "assembly line"; the first "Mother's Day" is observed; Archduke Franz Ferdinand and his wife are assassinated in Sarajevo, beginning WWI	1914	Stephan Banic (an immigrant coal miner who lived in Greenville) is granted a patent for the first workable parachute; South Pymatuning Township is created
		1915	The Grove City Creamery opens
1917	The Russian Revolution begins with street rioting in St. Petersburg; the most famous spy of WWI, code name "Mata Hari," is executed	1917	All single men between the ages of 21-30 are required to register for the draft; the county's first 800 soldiers leave to serve in WWI
1918	Woodrow Wilson becomes the first American president to visit a foreign country; the Spanish flu epidemic kills 600,000 Americans	1918	Heatless Mondays, Meatless Tuesdays and Wheatless Wednesdays are observed due to rationing; Frank Buhl dies at home and leaves $2,000,000 to war-torn Northern France and Belgium in his will; the Spanish flu epidemic hits the county
1920	The population of the United States is 106,461,000; American women receive the right to vote; the first play-by-play description of a football game is broadcasted over a radio station in Texas	1919	Sharon's Welcome Home Day for 1,000 soldiers is held at Buhl Farm (between 25,000-30,000 people were in the crowd); the steel strike suspends five blast furnaces, and other plants in the Valley become idle or part time
		1920	The county's population is 93,788; the night before Prohibition begins, Greenville ministers and the Women's Christian Temperance Union hold a symbolic funeral for "John Barleycorn"; switchmen on the eastern railroads go on strike

the wages of these who did work as wire drawers were considered high. Typically, these workers transferred to the Valley from American Steel and Wire mills in Cleveland and Lisbon, Ohio; they too were natives of the upper South and border states. At the Driggs-Seabury Gun Works in Sharon, a few African-American machinists, considered to be the most independent, skillful, and reliable workmen there, also received good wages. In contrast, African-Americans were generally excluded from good-paying industrial jobs at National Malleable Casting Company in Sharon. (Mills in Sharon generally employed fewer African-Americans in skilled positions that did the mills in South Sharon.) Despite Sharon's record, the relatively high number of African-Americans employed in semi-skilled jobs in the Shenango Valley as a whole distinguished this community from many other mill towns in western Pennsylvania.

African-American recruiters used promises of good-paying jobs to attract Southerners to the North, and within a few years of the first (1909) migration, the mass migration of African-Americans to the region began. In 1912, South Sharon, changed its name to Farrell, and four years later, Frank Wilson arrived in the town and found employment at the Sharon Steel Hoop. Through his activities in the Hoop mill, this African-American helped other South Carolina natives move to Pennsylvania, earning himself the reputation of a "big man" in the process. In 1917, M. S. Lennon came to Farrell to learn first-hand about the wages paid to colored people who had recently arrived from South Carolina. A native of North Carolina and a graduate of Shaw University, Lennon was hired as the African-American welfare official at the Farrell Carnegie Steel Works. One of his major responsibilities was recruiting African-American laborers from his home state.

During a 1919 strike, southern migrants were heavily recruited. Most came from the Carolinas, Georgia, and Alabama, with others migrating from Florida, Mississippi, Tennessee, and Kentucky. Between 1916 and 1930, the majority of these southern migrants to the Shenango Valley were hired as unskilled workers, as they were throughout western Pennsylvania. Still, the prevailing wage rate of sixty-four cents an hour for unskilled workers in the northern steel mills vastly exceeded average earnings possibilities in the South, so such work was viewed by African-Americans as an opportunity for economic advancement. Moreover, although most migrants were hired for unskilled jobs, in Farrell it was ability—not race or prior place of residence—that was considered the determining factor in upward occupational mobility. In 1918, American Sheet and Tin's Farrell Works employed a remarkable 187 skilled and semi-skilled colored workers who earned more than the average African-American in the Valley. Among their ranks were migrants from different regions of the South who worked as doublers, heaters, roughers, shearmen, and catchers.

FARMING
By Vonda Minner

In 1911, the Empire Milk Products Company began operation in Jamestown. On its first day, 10,000 pounds of milk were received. Empire also made powdered milk, cottage cheese, and butter. On the first day 800 pounds of butter were made. The company delivered to Greenville, Erie, and Pittsburgh.

In 1912, the Colonel Hunter Farm (West Salem Township) was one hundred years old. The farm is now owned by Mrs. Elizabeth Andrews.

In 1913, the first corn club was organized with the assistance of H. E. McConnell, superintendent of Mercer Schools.

The fifth annual poultry show was held in Greenville in 1914. About 900 birds were entered, and 20 silver cups and 100 merchandise prizes were awarded.

A contract between the Grove City Creamery and the U.S. Department of Agriculture was signed in 1914, and the creamery officially began in 1915. On the first day milk was received from 250 cows. By 1930 the creamery was delivering nine million pounds of cream and milk annually.

In 1915, the Shannon Farm (East Lackawannock Township) was one hundred years old as were the Rea Farm and Scott Farm (both in Shenango Township) in 1920. The Shannon home and barn were by William Shannon on donation land deeded to three Shannon brothers for military service during the Revolutionary War. (The farm was reduced by seven acres as Interstate 80 cut through the front yard in 1964. A further distinction for the Shannon family, Sandra, daughter of William Earl and Hallie Shannon, was named the 1957 Pennsylvania Miss Milkmaid. During her reign, she traveled throughout the country, representing the dairy industry.)

In 1916, the Stony Point Grange was started on Kremis Road. (In 1998, 105 members belonged to this grange.)

The Dairy Herd Improvement Association was started in 1917. The first average production in 1918 showed 225 pounds of butterfat and 5,093 pounds of milk. (The 1961 average was 422 pounds of butterfat and 10,809 pounds of milk.)

AVIATION
By Richard Christner

Some of Mercer County's first contacts with aviation involved attempts to build flying machines. In 1911, John Taflin of Sharon completed a home-built monoplane, but it never flew. Two mechanics from Greenville, the father-and-son team of August and Carl Rauschenberg, collaborated in 1916 to build a French-style Berliot. However, in its first flight on a farm near Sharon, the plane crashed and was totally demolished; and Carl was knocked unconscious, but not seriously injured. These pioneers were the forerunners of today's builders of experimental aircraft, represented in Mercer County by chapters of the Experimental Aircraft Association.

The Army Air Corps during World War I was relatively new to the U.S. Armed Services. As a result, only a small number of volunteers and draftees served in the air arm, often in the air sections of other Corps. Among the Mercer County men who served in the air arm were: Lt. Thomas H. Frankenberry, a flying officer with the 120th Air Squadron, who lived in Sharon after the war and worked in the Sales Department of the Westinghouse Electric plant; Arthur Myers of the 375th Aero Squadron; Arthur Moore and Karl W. Tait of the Aviation Section of the Signal Corps; Ensign Wilbur Ehrhart; Sgt. Robert L. Keck and Stuart Zahnizer of the Marine Aviation Division; and William T. Ward of the Naval Aviation Corps. Lt. Frankenberry's uniform is on display at the Mercer County Historical Society in Mercer.

BUHL INDEPENDENT RIFLES
By Richard Christner

On February 15, 1898, at a time when tensions between the United States and Spain were at their peak, the battleship *Maine* was sunk by an explosion in the harbor of Havana, Cuba, killing 266 officers and men of the ship's crew. Fueled by provocative newspaper reports and editorials about the incident and by the clamorings of politicians, a wave of war fever and patriotism swept the United States. When Spain failed to meet American demands, war was declared, and President McKinley issued a call for 125,000 volunteers. This call for volunteers and the departure in April of Company G (Sharon) of the 15th Regiment, Pennsylvania National Guard, led to the formation of a military and civic

Buhl Independent Rifles muster at the Buhl Armory in Sharon in 1911.

organization that served the residents of Sharon and surrounding municipalities for over forty years—the Buhl Independent Rifles (BIR).

Shortly after Company G left, Tom Price was walking to downtown Sharon from his home in Patagonia when he met his friend Alf Hoagland on a similar mission. Tom mentioned the possibility of forming a new military company to replace Company G and, if possible, to join in the war effort. Their discussion resulted in a meeting at Fitzgerald Hall attended by sixty-four men, who unanimously voted to form an independent company. In July, the BIR offered its services to the Secretary of War, but no action was taken in response to this offer. In September, twelve members were called to fill vacancies in Company G. At this time, Price was elected as captain, a position which he held for the next forty-three years. Assisting Price were Alf Hoagland as first lieutenant and Charles McCurdy as second lieutenant.

Thomas J. "Cap" Price was born in Wheatland in 1875 to David and Ellen Bailey Price. Educated locally, Price served as food administrator in Sharon during World War I and was Shenango Valley investigator for the Mercer County Home and Hospital in Mercer.

As an independent military and civic organization, raising funds for operations was a constant but necessary task. Donations were important, and Frank H. Buhl made the first donation, $50, to the fledgling organization and was a frequent contributor. Members had to buy their own uniforms and equipment. To assist in generating money, the Ladies Auxiliary was formed in 1900. Its continuing support by organizing fund-raising events was critical to the BIR's financial health. Also critical were the efforts of William S. Organ, who died in 1920, but helped to build the BIR's financial structure.

Military drills were held first in Grimm's Hall on West State Street. By 1900, the organization leased the Gibbons Building on Railroad Street. The chronic lack of suitable space, however, led to the appointment in 1903 of a Building Committee, which approved the construction of an armory. The BIR purchased a site from the Thomas J. Forker estate, and members did much of the preliminary work before contractors Albert E. Wales and the Wishart Company began constructing the main building. When funds ran low during construction, Frank Buhl loaned $6,000 to the BIR to complete the project. This debt was cancelled by Buhl in 1917. The Buhl Armory was dedicated in 1905, but the retaining wall on Lincoln Street was not completed until several years later. The Armory had three floors, with space for a kitchen and dining room, bowling alley, billiard hall, drill hall (which doubled as a dance and social hall), parlors, and lounge rooms.

The Armory more than satisfied the BIR's needs for weekly drills, social and civic events, annual banquets, and rentals to outside organizations for meetings, dances, and other social events. Such events were, of course, closely monitored by the BIR. Thus, a dance party for out-of-town debutantes led the directors to ban dances classified as "societal wiggle," such as the bunny hug, brulu drag, angleworm glide, Apache and Jellyfish wobble, the latter featuring "hootchie-cootchie" movements. The BIR's nonmilitary activities were handled by a separate group of civil officers. Its band, numbering as many as twenty-two pieces under the direction of members such as Aaron Trexler and Ferdinand Dalo, as well as the military company marched often in parades and performed at other civic events. The company's silent drill, often over one hundred movements without voice command, was a highlight of its public performances. The BIR supported charitable works, including providing a home for the Sharon chapter of the Sunshine Society and a meeting place for the Sharon chapter of the Grand Army of the Republic. It also sponsored a basketball team, which was active in local leagues.

In 1917, the BIR again offered to go to war. Assistant Secretary of War W. H. Ingraham noted in his reply that the BIR was the first independent company to volunteer as a unit. Although nothing came of the offer, 85 of the 125 members eventually joined the armed services, including five in the 15th Engineers, which was part of the first volunteer unit to reach France. Only one former member, Fred Pence, a Marine, was killed in action in France. His body was returned to the United States and buried in Clarksville Cemetery. During the flu epidemic at the end of World War I, the Armory was used as an emergency hospital, much as it had been used as a home for refugees during the Shenango Valley flood in 1913. Following the war, the BIR leased a site for a rifle range and maintained a hunting, fishing, and health camp in Centre County.

During the 1920s and early 1930s, the normal activities of the BIR continued, although with declining membership. About 1930, Buhl Trustees had converted the Armory to the Julia F. Buhl Girls Club. (After the club closed in 1987, girls and women joined the F. H. Buhl Club.) New quarters for the BIR were leased in the Weisen Building on East State Street. In 1941, Captain Price died. The membership elected Joseph Ingram as Captain, who had been a member since 1905 and held the positions of corporal, sergeant, and lieutenant. Despite Ingram's pledge to rejuvenate the BIR, the death of Captain Price sounded the death toll of the BIR, and it soon passed out of existence as an active organization.

1913 SHENANGO VALLEY FLOOD
By Wally Wachter

Some people still around may remember the area's first serious brush with flood waters. The flood started on Easter Sunday and hit its peak three days later, March 23, 1913, when the Shenango River crested at 18.6 feet.

A booklet, *Official Souvenir History of the Shenango Valley Flood*, was published a week after the waters had receded. It was prepared and written by C. B. Lartz, a reporter for the old *Sharon Telegraph* and later a copublisher of *The Herald*. The coauthor was an associate, Z. O. Hazen.

"Rumors of every sort were published in newspapers all over the country, giving the death list in Sharon and vicinity at from 500 down," the booklet said. Locally, the Sharon newspaper carried headlines that twenty-six had died in the deluge. However, the booklet finally substantiated that only one person, a woman who was being evacuated from her Vine Avenue home, fell victim to the flood waters. An autopsy later determined that her death was due to a heart attack.

Utter panic among residents in the low-lying areas was described in the booklet.

"Many of them [the residents] believed the whole town would go. There were reports of deaths coming in every hour, almost every moment.

"Men who had gone to business on Tuesday found they had no business to attend to, and when they attempted to return to their homes a few hours later they could not, so rapid was the rise of waters.

"Most of the telephone lines and other means of communication were not working. Wives and mothers alone in their homes, even though they knew there was no danger to them in the hill districts, were frantic. They did not know whether their husbands or sons were safe or had drowned in the now-raging Shenango. So garbled were the reports that spread like wildfire that their anxiety was further increased by news of death and disaster that reached them."

During the height of the flood, a fire at a four-story brick warehouse of A. Wishart and Sons on River Street, fanned by high winds, threatened to destroy the downtown area. Heroic work by firefighters kept the blaze from spreading to adjacent homes, storage places, and two lumberyards.

"It was at the height of the flood on the third day that the crash of falling buildings added further to the fear of the people," the booklet reported. "From Monday on, the surface of the Shenango was a mass of swiftly flowing debris. Houses, barns, pieces of roofs, dead animals and trees were being carried in sight of watchers on both sides of the river. But it was not until Wednesday that the realization of the flood destroying business blocks reached the people."

The falling of the "V Bridge" and the destruction of the *Sharon Herald* building on that day were called "the two worst wrecks of the flood." The newspaper was located on River Street at a point commonly was called "Herald Square" (the junction of River, Pitt, and Shenango Streets). It folded with a crash; and linotypes, presses, and other heavy equipment were seen floating down the river. The "V Bridge" was a massive steel structure connecting Silver Street with Boyce Street and Porter Way. The rising waters buoyed the northern spur connecting with Boyce Street sufficiently to allow the current to tear out the center pillar. With the center pier gone, the northern spur dropped into the river and was wrecked.

The official property damage figure was set at $2 million, including loss of buildings, damage to streets, railroads, industries, and lost wages. The many floods that followed before the construction of the Shenango River Dam in 1965 may have matched or exceeded the damage of this flood; but, due to improved means of communications, the Valley avoided repeating the intense uncertainty and panic the victims had experienced during the disastrous flood of 1913.

A. Wishart was a Sharon contractor and builder in the early 1900s. His warehouse was destroyed during the great Shenango Valley flood of 1913.

The "V Bridge" over the Shenango River in Sharon.

LOUIS (LUIGI) ELIA
By Rose Elizabeth Elia O'Hare

"My father, Louis (Luigi) Elia, was an outstanding citizen. He came from Europe when he was only 15 years of age, leaving his parents and siblings to come to this country, the land of opportunity. He didn't speak English but managed to go west to the state of Washington with his brother-in-law, who accompanied him to the United States. There he was a willing worker on the railroad, sometimes going as far as the Alaskan border. Later on he heard from a friend in Farrell, Pennsylvania, that a steel mill was hiring, so he left to go to Farrell. He boarded with kindly folks. He was employed by the Carnegie Steel Co. I believe his job was straw boss, whatever that meant. He enrolled in night school and learned to read, write, and speak the English language fluently. Later he helped friends and relatives get their citizenship papers. I believe at that time the office was in Pittsburgh, Pennsylvania.

The Shenango Valley flood of 1913 hit Greenville as well as Sharon. (Contributor: Ila Ayers)

Daring photographers caught the raging water of the Shenango Valley flood of 1913 on Chestnut, Railroad, and East State streets in Sharon.

187

"He was quite athletic and adventuresome. He learned to box, rode a motorcycle, lifted weights, and bowled.

"He looked for a good woman to marry; at age 23 he met my mom, Margaret, who was 17. He later became a foreman for the steel mills, walking to work each day, no matter what the weather. He worked for 47 years and retired at age 68. He had 110 men in his care at the Blooming Mill and Scrap Yard. He expected the men to do a day's work for a day's wages. During hard times (the Depression) he had three gardens, and if he was working 2 days a week he looked for other ways to support his wife and seven children: four daughters and three sons. He was an avid reader and ordered products to sell such as canning kits, kitchen stainless steel knives, and rubber aprons and took orders for shoes. My father walked from Farrell to Sharon and Masury. He wore suits and ties and was friendly and honest. We always had food on the table and gave away vegetables from our gardens.

"My father instilled in us the work habit. My two brothers served in World War II, and my younger brother served in the army in Korea. My father was proud of our country; he helped many others get jobs when work was available. He also shaved and cut hair for the elderly relatives every week and gave my brothers haircuts. Our house was the barber shop.

"My father was a friendly, likeable man and quite a talker. I was proud to be his eldest daughter."

BUHL FARM PARK
By Mairy Jayn Woge

In 1907, Frank H. Buhl announced he was going to accumulate land and put together a recreation site, later named Buhl Farm, for "the people of the Shenango Valley."

Once accomplished, Buhl Farm contained 312 acres bounded on the north by 10th through 15th Street in Sharpsville and Hazen Road, on the east by North Buhl Farm Drive (the Sharpsville-Wheatland Road), Woodlawn and Lillian Drives and Rockwell Avenue. On the south were and are Thornton Street, Putnam Drive and Yahres Road as well as the backyards along Highland Road, the last containing part of the Sharon Country Club golf course. On the west is a field off Bechtol Avenue, Hall Avenue, Furnace Road, and Deweyville. Forker Boulevard, where the office of the Buhl Trustees is now located,

BUHL DAY
By Mairy Jayn Woge

Buhl Day was first observed in September 1915, following the opening of Buhl Farm. Buhl had opposed naming Buhl Farm a "park" because it might be compared with the amusement parks of the time. (Now, it is called Buhl Farm Park or simply Buhl Park.) The largest parade in the history of the Shenango Valley, up until 1916, passed the Buhl mansion that September day. Participants included the Buhl Independent Rifles and their band and former employees of Buhl mills and mines.

The next Buhl Day was held in 1918. After that, there were Buhl Days annually until 1940. The observance resumed in 1980 and has continued. One of the highlights of Buhl Days in the 1930s was a large rectangular lighted sign that resembled a movie marquee and contained pictures of Frank H. and Julia Buhl.

extends from the southernmost end of the Farm and concludes at Martin Avenue in Sharpsville. The bulk of the Farm is in Hermitage.

Lake Julia was scooped out and the Casino built on the property purchased from James Milliken. Sand for the edges of the lake and ponds was brought from Lake Erie. Stones used for markers and borders were quarried in Buhl Farm. Trees and shrubs numbering 75,000 were planted. (Overhead lights were introduced to Buhl Farm in 1933.)

Most of the lots that compose Buhl Farm were obtained by Buhl himself or through his secretary, Frederick Koehler, between 1909 and 1915. Few of the buildings that were on the Farm when it first was developed still stand, but the cement steps to George McClintock's once elegant house still climb a small bank south of Thornton Street. The house was razed after 1975. Part of the McClintock barn is used as a storage area by maintenance persons for the Buhl golf course. This course, sometimes referred to as "Dum-Dum," is thought to be the only golf course in the United States that can be used by golfers for free.

The Sharon Country Club was built with funds furnished by Buhl in 1913 and the 18-hole golf course used by club members is partly on the McClintock land purchased for Buhl Farm.

Research by attorney Edward Madden showed the properties that constitute Buhl Farm can be traced back to donation lots given by Pennsylvania to veterans of the Revolutionary War. For example, part of the Thornton farm originally belonged to Beshara Hull, who with his brothers John and Daniel settled along the Shenango River east of the Ohio line in 1798. Dewey Park and Deweyville were named by George Heinz, who owned property at the location, for George Dewey, an admiral during the Spanish-American War. Dewey Park preceded Buhl Farm as a recreation area. Deweyville is in Hermitage and separates Sharon and Sharpsville. It consists of a ravine cut by Thornton Run and streets adjoining Hall Avenue and Furnace Road. In its prime, it was the location of Sharon Iron Furnace. Approximately a third to half the properties obtained for Buhl Farm were from Mary L. Stambaugh and Florence M. Freed, daughters of Jacob L. Miller. Miller, a farmer and realtor, purchased some of the pieces of land that became part of Buhl Farm at sheriff's sales. Land for Buhl Farm also came from the William Haggarty farm.

In 1915, the Buhls transferred Buhl Farm to the first F. H. Buhl Club Trustees: James P. Whitla, Thomas J. Forker, Simon Perkins, Peter L. Kimberly, Samuel McClure, John Carley, Alexander McCowell, John J. Spearman, and Norman Hall. Guidelines for future trustees, drawn up almost simultaneously with the appointments, specified that all trustees should be residents of Sharon. That requirement was overturned by Mercer County court. The Buhls deposited $500,000 into an account for the maintenance of Buhl Farm. The sum was invested and by 1999 had increased to $9 million. Only the interest from the total is used for upkeep and improvements for Buhl Farm. Current life trustees are Louis Epstein, James Feeney, Katie Ekker, Carlton Hutchison, Leslie Spaulding, and G. Leo Winger. As of 1999, three-year trustees were Judy Achre, Colin Applegate, Michael Cummings, Donald Hunter, Robert Jazwinski, Philip Marrie, George S. Warren III, and Richard Werner.

NEW YORK CENTRAL RAILROAD
By Frederick Houser

By 1915, the New York Central Railroad had absorbed the Lake Shore & Michigan Southern Railroad (including the Cleveland, Painesville & Ashtabula Railroad and the Sharon Branch) and the Jamestown, Franklin & Clearfield Railroad (which combined the Jamestown & Franklin, Jackson Coal, and Franklin & Clearfield railroads).

Back in 1862, the Jamestown & Franklin Railroad was chartered to build a line between those two municipalities. Several prominent Mercer County residents and the president of the Erie & Pittsburgh Railroad were on the railroad's first board of directors, which met in Sheakleyville. At that time, the Erie & Pittsburgh was the only railroad in the county, having reached Jamestown in 1859.

In 1864, the still unbuilt railroad was leased to the Cleveland, Painesville & Ashtabula Railroad, which was so interested in reaching the closest coal deposits (near Sandy Lake) that it advanced the funds to begin the Jamestown & Franklin's construction. The track was pushed through to Mine No. 1 of the Mercer Iron and Coal Company near the future town of Stoneboro. The new line carried its first coal cars in 1865. A mixed train (carrying both passengers and freight) was instituted later that year between Jamestown and the mine three days per week. The train ran on three other days each week over the Erie & Pittsburgh to take coal to Girard for delivery to the Cleveland, Painesville & Ashtabula. The parent company used much of this fuel to supplant the wood its locomotives had been burning.

In 1866, the Jamestown & Franklin began construction east from Stoneboro and reached Franklin in 1867. Almost immediately, scheduled passenger trains began operating daily except Sunday between Franklin and Jamestown. That August, the first carload of crude oil moved between those points en route to a refinery in Cleveland. In 1870, the Jamestown & Franklin was extended to Oil City and tapped still more crude oil traffic. Crude oil traffic became a major source of revenue for the Jamestown & Franklin until the mid-1870s when transport by pipelines between the Pennsylvania oil region and Cleveland started to dominate.

At that time, no direct connection existed between the Cleveland, Painesville & Ashtabula and its lessee, the Jamestown & Franklin. Traffic between the two moved via trackage rights over the Erie & Pittsburgh. Back in 1864, the Cleveland, Painesville & Ashtabula had let a contract for building a direct line between Ashtabula, Ohio, and Jamestown. Although considerable grading had been done initially, the work was suspended until 1871, when it resumed. This line was completed and placed in service in 1872. The Cleveland, Painesville & Ashtabula (along with the Jamestown & Franklin) had by then become part of the Lake Shore & Michigan Southern Railway.

The Buhl Club (foreground) and Casino (background) in Buhl Farm Park, Sharon. (Postcard: Daniel Maurice)

About 1917, a Pennsylvania Railroad train wreck destroyed the bridge over the Shenango River near Clarksville. The bridge was completely off its foundation at one end. Within about four days, however, crews had built a 580-foot temporary trestle so the railroad could continue to operate on this line.

In 1887, the Lake Shore & Michigan Southern built a short line, chartered as the Shenango Valley Railroad, to connect with its existing line north from Youngstown to Ashtabula. The Shenango Valley Railroad ran from just west of Hubbard, Ohio, and extended across the state line to the north side of Sharon. The original plan for this Sharon Branch was to extend it to Sharpsville and also branch south to West Middlesex. Instead, the Lake Shore & Michigan Southern acquired trackage rights over the Sharon Railway (later the Erie Railroad) into Sharpsville and also down river to West Middlesex. The Sharon Branch was later a key route for "hot metal runs," which transported molten iron in specially insulated "torpedo" cars between mills in the Mahoning and Shenango Valleys. (After the 1968 Penn Central merger, the Sharon Branch became redundant for access to the Shenango Valley for Penn Central, which had a more direct route via the former Erie & Pittsburgh Railroad. The portion of the Sharon Branch east of the state line was abandoned in 1972.)

Meanwhile, in 1883, the Jackson Coal Railroad was opened south from Stoneboro for five miles to a cluster of new coal mines in Lake and Jackson Townships. (This trackage was abandoned in 1924 after these mines closed.)

By 1900, the Lake Shore & Michigan Southern transferred the Jamestown & Franklin from a rural branch line to a main line operation. The Lake Shore & Michigan Southern acquired a significant financial interest in the Reading Company, which had a network of rail lines serving the anthracite coal mines in eastern Pennsylvania and had a main line from Philadelphia to Williamsport, Pennsylvania. The New York Central & Hudson River Railroad already had leased a railroad between Williamsport and Clearfield and to bituminous coal mines in Indiana County. These railroads then undertook the construction of a brand-new line that, in cooperation with the Reading, would enable them to compete directly with the Pennsylvania Railroad for freight moving from Chicago and Cleveland to Philadelphia.

The Franklin & Clearfield was chartered in 1902 to build a line from Franklin to Brookville—one of the last major railroad construction projects in Pennsylvania. The entire line was laid out to be double-tracked, although no second track was ever installed. The Jamestown & Franklin, however, was double-tracked between Polk Junction and Stoneboro, and an automatic block signal system was installed. In addition to anticipated growth of traffic over the new Clearfield Branch, numerous passenger and freight trains ran between Stoneboro and Oil City each day. Before the new line was formally opened in 1911, the Jamestown, Franklin & Clearfield Railroad was chartered to consolidate the original Jamestown & Franklin, the Jackson Coal Railroad, and the Franklin & Clearfield. The Jamestown, Franklin & Clearfield was absorbed into the New York Central Railroad in 1915, as had been the case with the Lake Shore & Michigan Southern the year before.

(While the Clearfield line had come into its own during World War I, it was during World War II that this route proved itself by handling tremendous freight traffic. By 1942, however, traffic was declining rapidly. Philadelphia-Chicago through trains ceased in 1951, and the final Clearfield-Stoneboro train ran in 1963. After that, freight service was only provided between Brookville and Ashtabula, and the predominant traffic was outbound coal from local mines and inbound sand for glass making. In 1988, the line was finally taken out of service, and contractors removed the line, including all of the track through Mercer County.)

MARY MCDOWELL VERMEIRE (BORN 1901) REMEMBERS
Written in 1980

"My grandparents had very white hair and my grandmother's hair was so long she could sit on it. She wore it in braids around her head. I always remember my grandfather with his long white beard. They were members of the Sheakleyville Baptist Church where he was a Deacon for many years. Each Sunday they drove in from the farm in their two-seated surrey. They always came after church to our place for dinner. It was always quite an occasion as that was the day we had beef to eat. Each Saturday the 'meat man' would arrive from Fredonia. He had a large box built on his horse-drawn vehicle. This was a covered box; inside was a scale hanging from the top amidst all the meat. We always bought a piece of boiling beef (it was the cheapest). If I remember correctly it was always less than a quarter. Of course, the 'meat man' always threw in a bone with a lot of meat on it. He sat up on the high seat of the wagon ringing a bell that was attached to the box. This alerted the housewife that the Saturday wagon was there. This meant we always had noodles for Sunday dinner. My Grandma McDowell could make the most delicious ones. . . .

"One of my uncles always plowed and prepared the ground for work on our large garden. They also owned several acres about a mile up the hill. This was planted in corn, onions, or potatoes. I can still see Mother pushing a wheelbarrow with tools going up to hoe and weed the vegetables. Down on the lots on the Franklin road, we would pasture our two cows. It was my brother Ed's and my job to take the cows there after milking them morning and evening. . . .

"The spring and summer was the only time Dad had work as he was a house painter. After all he was twenty years older than Mother. Dad was an avid reader and a very intelligent man, but not overly ambitious. He never wore glasses yet would read and smoke his pipe sitting by the stove for hours at a time in the winter. He was a good storyteller and always willing for us to jump on his lap, and his imagination would make up wonderful adventure stories. He sometimes illustrated these with fierce-looking animals; two of these, 'flim flam' and 'flub dub,' were his favorites. . . .

"We never knew what entertainment in the evening was, no TV's, radios, not even a Victrola. We read and as a special treat sometimes popped corn or even made fudge or taffy. I read all the Alger books with the Rags to Riches theme. I usually had a paperback

Mary McDowell (Vermeire). (Contributor: Al Vermeire)

hidden in the paper box (a box nailed on the wall with old sheets of the Sears catalog). This was in the corner of the 'privy' or closet or outhouse, whichever you wished to call it. It usually took me a long time when 'I had to go.' You may wonder where we got the books. There was no public library, but our Sunday School had a small one with used books. We exchanged with our friends and usually got some new ones at Christmas and holidays.

"Christmas was always a big event for us as children. We never had a tree when we were young. We each hung up our stocking on the chair that was designated as our special one. Many Christmas mornings we were up waking our parents as early as 4 a.m. It was very cold until Dad got the fire stirred up and going in the 'sitting room' stove. . . . Dad always saw that we had an orange and hard candy in our stocking. Our gifts usually consisted of books and games. . . .

"Two jobs I especially disliked were cleaning the lamps each morning and emptying the pots. I had to wash the glass chimney globes, fill the bottom with kerosene, and trim the wicks. I also had to empty the pots (chambers they were called in better society) each morning. These were carried to the privy, emptied, and rinsed out, then brought back in and placed under the beds. These were used in the night rather than make that long cold walk out in the dark. . . .

"Each of my brothers sold papers at various times, the Grit, (Dad always called it 'The Pennsylvania Liar'), Colliers, Country Gentlemen, and Ladies Home Journal, at least those are the ones I remember. Each week if any weren't sold, the covers were removed and returned for credit and we could keep the rest to read. . . .

"When I was about 12 years old I worked at the telephone office for 10 cents an hour. We had to remember everyone's number as they'd call and ask for 'H. M. Davis' residence. We'd also get calls as to the time of day. Most everyone was on a party line and when we'd ring a number, one could hear receivers clicking and the neighbors all listening to the news. . . .

"The early history of Sheakleyville, as I remember it, were the inches thick dusty roads in the summer, which turned into hub deep mud in the spring. It became a paved road around 1926. On Saturday nights several of the young blades would race their horse and buggies up and down through town.

"Many of the residents had wooden sidewalks. It was a big event when they installed oil burning lamps. At dusk a man would carry his step ladder and a box of matches going along lighting each lamp. . . .

"As I remember my youth, I never was underprivileged at all even though we were poor. Dad had bought us a lawn swing. We had a rope swing on the old apple tree and a croquet set we enjoyed in the summer. When Edwin and his friends needed an extra player in the baseball game, I was always available. My first love though was always my books. In the spring the girls always had their jacks and a jump rope, an old length of clothes line. In winter we played fox and geese and built snow forts for snow-ball battles.

"I never had any babysitting jobs as every family had a grandmother available. We never played cards—they were the work of the

William Steen, 1916.

devil—but we did enjoy Lotto, Parcheesi, and chess, which Dad taught us, and, of course, checkers and dominos. Holidays were special and on the 4th of July, Elsie Limber would often go on a picnic. Her specialty was marble cake in the picnic basket. In the afternoon we'd go wading in the creek. Often we'd go across the street to Herbert Davis's and he'd make ice cream. It was always a big treat. . . .

"John Adams had a hardware store near Martins. He also carried cough syrup and old-time medicine such as Lady Pinkums. I was always wanting perfume so one day Dad took me down and bought me a little bottle of wintergreen oil. I thought this was wonderful. When I was quite small, I once found a wallet. I took it home to Dad who opened it and found it belonged to Joe Adams. It had several hundred dollars in it. The owner was very generous and gave me 25 cents when I returned it.

"There were several early industries here or nearby, a lumber mill, grist mill, carriage shop, two livery stables, two blacksmith shops. We'd often watch the blacksmith shoe the horses; and, if he wasn't too busy, he'd take a horse shoe nail and shape it on the anvil into a ring for our fingers. We had two hotels, two undertakers, a cheese factory, and four churches (Baptist, U.P. [United Presbyterian], M.E. [Methodist Episcopal], and Presbyterian). We also had two doctors. The doctors charged $5.00 for a baby delivery, but the price had raised to $7.00 for Don since the local doctors were both away and Dr. Grace from Clarks Mills was called. . . .

"On Memorial Day everyone would pick their flowers and take them to the IOOF Hall. There several ladies would make small bouquets. There would later be a parade to the cemetery. The three Civil War vets would head the parade: Uncle John Clar, Mr. McCracken, and Saul Bell. Sometimes there would be a band. The children, each with their flowers, would follow, and all the soldiers' graves were decorated. After there would be several speeches, prayers, and songs. . . .

"Our house in Sheakleyville had no electricity, furnace, or indoor plumbing. We had a hand-operated pump for water in an enclosed room at the back of the house.

"It was a cold long walk in the winter to the outhouse located several rods from the house. I didn't mind the trip in nice weather as I usually had a forbidden paperback book hidden in the box under the very useful Montgomery Ward catalog. One of the favorite past times on Halloween of the young blades was to overturn the outhouse. Thank goodness we never had that experience.

"As a child I never heard of trick or treat. Most October 31s were just another day. I do remember several times when Mother filled a small tub with water and we went bobbing for apples. She would sometimes make taffy, depending on the sugar supply, and we'd have a taffy pull.

"May Day, the first of May, was always an exciting time. We had previously made small paper baskets, pasted on handles, and then filled them with any spring flowers available. We'd go to a neighbor's home, knock at the door, put down the basket, and run and hide. The first of May was also important as that was the day we started to go bare foot, except for Sunday. We were all waiting for that freedom.

"For a very short time our town boasted of wooden sidewalks from one end of the borough to the other. There were narrow boards laid close together. That didn't last too long as they were not replaced when one was broken. We were soon back on the worn paths.

"We also had kerosene street lamps for a short time. I remember as a child, following the man with a small ladder under his arm. His job was to light the lamps each evening as dusk fell. That period didn't last and we were again carrying our lanterns when we attended evening service on Sunday and the Wednesday night prayer meetings at the Baptist Church.

"I'll never forget my first automobile ride. Only one car was owned in the town and that by William Streit. One day at the post office waiting for the mail to come in, he asked several of us 'kids' if we'd like a ride. I imagine I was 10 or 12 at the time. He said to come up to his house that afternoon. Needless to say we were there. The car was a large touring car, ornate with brass. The top came down and there was a large horn along the side. We stepped on the running board and climbed in to wait for our driver. He soon appeared dressed as all good drivers did in those days. He had on a long gray-tan duster, which buttoned tightly from his neck to his ankles. He wore gauntlet gloves, a cap, and, of course, goggles. He took us for a short spin and a slow one as several signs in the town had been posted as to a 10-mile-per-hour speed limit. Nevertheless it was a wonderful event for all of us.

"The present younger generation often wonders what we did for entertainment. We had no gramophone, no radio, no TV, no telephone; and the nearest nickelodeon was miles away with no transportation or money. I remember one day when my girlfriends came to play we decided we'd be Indians. After raiding the chicken coop for feathers and the yard for sticks to be our weapons, we went to the flower bed where tiger lilies were in bloom. We pulled the brown centers from the petals and smeared it on our faces. After whooping, yelling, and chasing each other till we were tired out, we decided, with much parental urging, to wash. Low and behold it wouldn't come off. After rubbing on lard and many washings, it finally disappeared. We never tried that game again. . . .

"There were three general stores in our small town. I will write concerning one of them. It was a typical country store. In the center was the large pot-bellied stove. It was fueled with coal carried in by coal buckets from the coal pile outside the back of the store. There were several chairs and a bench around the stove and, of course, a number of spittoons. These places were usually occupied by local characters who came down daily to discuss gossip as well as national news. One side of the store had the glass-fronted mail boxes of all families living in the borough. Each had a number. Twice a day the appointed mailman drove to Hadley, about three miles, to pick up the mail from the nearest train to our village. One part of the store was used to display shoes and dry goods. Most everyone did their own sewing. It was a very special occasion when one would order a 'ready-made' dress from the Ward or Sears catalog. The store sold some canned goods, flour, coffee, tea, sugar, and salt. When empty, we always use the bags the flour, sugar, and salt came in. The larger ones were made into towels, the others into handkerchiefs. (Tissues were unknown.) On Saturdays the farmers from the outlying districts would bring in their butter and eggs for trading. They paid for any store articles in this way. No counter was seen with fresh fruit or vegetables since everyone had their own garden. My family had two cows and we had several milk customers in town. I would deliver the milk in a tin pail, a quart a day to these families for 10 cents a quart."

TEMPERANCE, PROHIBITION, AND WOMEN'S ISSUES
By Mairy Jayn Woge

The Women's Christian Temperance Union (WCTU) had started meeting in Sharon in 1874. The Anti-Saloon League was formed later. Membership in the WCTU during the 1870s in Sharon totaled 120 women and 11 men out of a population of about 900. Committees were appointed to visit places where liquor was sold, approach the proprietors, caution them about their sinful ways and offer prayers. The WCTU met once a day. The *1888 History of Mercer County* states, "The temperance crusade worked up to a white heat and members of the WCTU were so persistent, people in Sharon divided into factions."

A large and vigorous WCTU in Sharpsville included a number of members of the General James Pierce family. A small WCTU formed in West Middlesex. A Mercer County Temperance Union had started as early as 1827. A number of counter groups existed, too, the most active one in Sheakleyville.

Tippling and tipplers were frequent in the Shenango Valley from its early settlement. Elias Jones, who opened the first dry goods store, grocery, and hotel on the site of Sharon and was the first Sharon postmaster, erected a distillery on land abutting current Sacred Heart Catholic Church. He served liquor at his hotel in the 1820s when tending bar was a violation. Daniel Budd, a brother of William Budd, the second settler on the site of Sharon, and Achsah Quinby, the wife of Samuel Quinby, a pioneer, put up $1,500 in bond for the release of Jones from Mercer County jail after he was arrested for selling whiskey.

The 18th Amendment to the Constitution of the United States, Prohibition, was approved by Congress in 1917, but was not ratified by all states until 1920. Nonetheless, it was considered unpatriotic to buy or sell liquor during World War I because of the amount of grain involved in making it. (Since the prohibition amendment failed to fulfill its purpose, however, it was repealed in 1933.)

Also in 1920, the 19th Amendment, Woman Suffrage, was passed by Congress. Movements for voting rights for women started in the mid-1800s. Opposition to extending the franchise to females was based on the belief that women did not understand government and were do-gooders who lacked judgment. In 1920, a number of immigrant women who had taken Valley Chamber of Commerce classes where they learned American history and the English language had become citizens. They accompanied the teachers, housewives, nurses, and secretaries to the polls. They ignored hecklers who tried to discourage them. The number of women who voted on November 2, 1920, in the Shenango Valley was a small proportion of Valley women who were over twenty-one; but the ballots cast by them may have contributed substantially to the 60.2 percent of the votes for Warren G. Harding who became the twenty-ninth president of the United States. KDKA radio in Pittsburgh, owned by Westinghouse Electric Company, was on the air for the first time on November 2, 1920, and that broadcast included news about the election and the ladies who voted. Despite accomplishing that franchise, women were not elected to school boards or city and borough councils in the Valley until the 1960s. The League of Women Voters prompted more interest in participating in government among women.

INFLUENZA EPIDEMIC (1918)
By Margo Letts

Named the "Spanish" influenza because the King of Spain was the first known person to get it, this flu hit the United States in March 1918 in Kansas. It was also reported in Russia, Great Britain, North Africa, and India. October 1918 was the deadliest month for the flu: in all, it killed 195,000 Americans. That month, the Spanish influenza hit Mercer County and showed no mercy.

On October 4, 1918, the Pennsylvania health commissioner ordered that all public places be closed due to the flu. On October 5, the Sharon Board of Health closed all poolrooms, bowling alleys, and clubs. In Sharpsville, pastors were asked to tell their sick parishioners to stay home, funerals were private, and churches were forbidden to be used for funerals. Mercer closed everything except the schools (which were not closed until October 25). Greenville closed all public buildings.

Also on October 5, Farrell closed its theaters, but kept the poolrooms, clubs, and schools open. Farrell Board of Health did not expect the epidemic to be bad. They would later regret this stand, as Farrell was badly hit by the epidemic.

On October 7, reported cases of the flu numbered 400 to 500 in the Shenango Valley. Bethel (Lackawannock Township) reported fifty cases. Health officials were cautioning about panic and fear.

Buhl Hospital allowed no visitors until after the epidemic ended. Effective October 9, the hospital took no patients other than accident victims. Buhl Hospital opened an emergency hospital at the Buhl Armory for flu and pneumonia patients. Schools and churches in Farrell were closed, but Sharon did not close them until October 14. Once the schools were closed, teachers were asked to volunteer at the hospitals.

Dr. P. P. Fisher was placed in charge of the epidemic in Sharon. Once he took over, all schools, churches, soda fountains, and public diners were closed. Also no public meetings, banquets, or public gatherings were allowed anywhere in the county. By this time, the flu was so widespread that officials were trying to make everyone stay home regardless of whether they were sick.

The Red Cross was already short of volunteers due to World War I, but sought throughout the county for volunteers to help fight the epidemic. The flu, however, made it even harder to get volunteers, as many people were sick. Even doctors and nurses were sick.

By mid-October, five homes in Sharpsville were quarantined, and Farrell had seventy-five homes on the list. October 17 through 28 was the worst period for Mercer County. Many people died, and the hospitals and Red Cross desperately needed volunteers. Eleven deaths were reported in Farrell, Sharon, and Sharpsville in a 24-hour period.

The government put restrictions on coffins. No oak coffins were to be made: only plain ones were allowed. Because coffins were scarce, the orders were handled in the order in which the factories received them. Some places dug trenches and buried the bodies in the trenches.

Patients who were treated under canvas tents seemed to be less severe. Therefore, physicians were told to open the windows in sick patients' rooms. Carnegie Steel, Savage Arms, Bessemer & Lake Erie, and Cottage Hospital offered free inoculations. Employees and families took advantage of this offer, and over four hundred people were inoculated.

Schools in the Shenango Valley were reopened on October 30, 1918. However, Mercer schools were closing as the Valley schools were opening back up. Not many tricks were reported on Halloween because of the quarantines. In Farrell, 148 houses were quarantined on October 28. Only one church held services on November 1.

Finally on November 8, 1918, Pennsylvania lifted the ban on public places. People were allowed to hold meetings, and churches were once again opened for services.

The official report for Sharon from October 1 through November 5 was 2,000 cases and 49 deaths. The C. A. Black Funeral Home in Grove City reported that 26 deaths out of 70 were due to the flu and pneumonia for the months of October through December. The *Mercer Dispatch* reported that the flu was not bad in the Borough of Mercer with only 77 cases and 2 deaths. However, on November 1, every family at Mine Number 5 of the Sharon & Limestone Company had one or more family members sick with the flu; and eventually six deaths occurred at Mine Number 5 from the flu.

Well into November, Farrell was still being hit hard with the flu. By November 19, the city had had 50 deaths, and 34 were due to the flu or pneumonia. In December Pardoe was hit by three deaths in three days.

Greenville Advance Argus and the *Mercer Dispatch* did not report on the flu as in depth as the *Sharon Herald* did. The newspapers reported that the epidemic was not bad in Greenville, Mercer, Fredonia, and Sandy Lake and did not report on the more rural parts of the county. We do not know how many were sick or died in Hickory Township, Jamestown, West Middlesex, Wilmington Township, or other parts of the county.

One-hundred-year-old Sylvia Jarrett recalled the flu epidemic to her daughter Marge Crompton. A week after visiting a sick little girl, Mrs. Jarrett's mother contracted the flu and died. According to Mrs. Jarrett, the doctors did not know what to do for the sick people. The doctors believed that the lungs quickly filled up with fluid and that those who died did not suffer in pain. She said her mother appeared to suffer no pain. The funeral services had to be outside at the gravesite and had to be private. These restrictions were so the epidemic would not spread further. Mrs. Jarrett remembers the horse and carriage taking them to the cemetery. Her father also became sick, but thankfully lived. She said that people were discouraged from traveling by train so that the epidemic would not spread.

Dr. Montrose Magoffin of Mercer was stationed at the Base Hospital in Camp Hancock in Augusta, Georgia, during the epidemic. In his letters home he talked about how the flu was affecting the army. In October they had twenty-five deaths a day. He also told his mother not to travel, especially on trains.

Although no formal records exist of the number of deaths and cases of the flu in Mercer County, we can ascertain some details from newspaper accounts and personal recollections. Even with only this snapshot view of how the flu affected residents of the county, it is amazing how the whole county was brought down by the epidemic particularly for two weeks in October. By the end of 1918, nationwide, 600,000 Americans had died from the Spanish influenza.

FALL ACTIVITIES
By Mary McDowell Vermeire

"It was always a busy time when fall came around. Some things were canned, tomatoes and fruit mainly. Corn was cut from the cob and dried in the sun, or on the back of the stove, or large tin pans. This was stirred several times a day until it was thoroughly dry. It was then placed in clean white bags that had formerly held salt or sugar. They tied strings around the filled bags and hung them from the wall in the pantry, a room off the kitchen that held the pots, pans, and dishes. The same process was carried out with the apples. They were peeled, cored, and sliced as for pie. When either corn or apples are to be used, we would soak them in water for several hours, and then they were used as fresh.

"We had no cellar at our house [Sheakleyville] so after everything was pulled up in the garden (turnips, cabbage, carrots, potatoes and even some apples), a pit was dug below the frost level. The vegetables were buried and covered with straw, leaves, and dirt. It then looked like a small tent out in the garden. During the winter, when things left inside were used up, the pit was opened and some more vegetables were taken out. Beans of several varieties were pulled up in the fall.

"Each fall, near Thanksgiving, my uncles would come in and butcher the two pigs we'd bought as shoats in the spring. When purchased, they cost around $5 each and by fall weighed in a nice amount. The hams and shoulders were usually smoked in the neighbor's (Dave's) smokehouse. Sausage was ground, cooked in patties, and placed in large crocks. These were left in the pantry where it was really cold in the wintertime.

"Mother and Grandma would 'fly out' the fat and place the resulting lard in containers for future use in frying or even an occasional pie. Meat from the heads was made into headcheese; the liver into liverwurst; the feet skinned, cooked, and pickled. The bladder, when a string was tied around the open end, made a good balloon. We had to buy sugar and flour, and the homemade bread was always so delicious. All our butter was churned in the kitchen in the old-fashioned churn. It took hours, raising and lowering the dasher, to turn the yellow sour cream into butter and delicious buttermilk, not of this synthetic kind we have today.

"The calves that usually arrived in the spring were kept a couple of months and then sold. The few dollars were used for shoes . . . or some other useful item. Many of our clothes were 'hand-me-downs' made over from things sent by our Greenville or Meadville relatives. I never knew my father to have a new suit. Both Mother and Grandmother sewed on the foot-propelled Singer machine. Mother even made Ed's suits from someone else's that had been given to us. It was a wonderful occasion when there was money to pick out a new coat or garment from the Sears or Montgomery Ward catalog. . . .

"I've just remembered another highlight of my young years, the annual Chicken Pie Supper sponsored by the Baptist Church. This was always held in October after the fall crops were harvested. For weeks before this event all the 'rigs' (horses and buggies) were hired ahead from the nearby towns livery stables, Stoneboro, Sandy Lake and even as far as Greenville. None of the members were wealthy, but all furnished till it hurt for this supper. I remember my mother killing, dressing, cooking, and deboning a dozen chickens the day before. She'd also bake cakes, shred cabbage, etc. The menu was chicken pie (1/4 pie), gravy, mashed potatoes, slaw, homemade rolls, pickles, jelly, coffee, and cake. For many years the cost was 25 cents and they later raised the price to 35 cents each. My grandma McDowell was one of the chief pie bakers.

"They had two wood-burning stoves in the church basement. They started to bake very early in the morning and kept it up all day and night. For many years they served customers who had filled the upper part of the church until 4 a.m. All the food was donated, and the four or five hundred dollars made went for paying the preacher's salary. I don't remember when the last supper was held, but it became too hard for the women so it was decided that the members should give more in their weekly contributions and save the women this hard work."

DRESSING FOR WINTER
By Mary McDowell Vermeire

"We never seemed to mind the winter snow drifts we waded through on the way to school. If my grandchildren could see how we dressed for the winter, they would really have a good laugh. First we had our heavy, I mean really heavy, long-legged and long-sleeve underwear. The young ladies would put on a camisole, I didn't know what a bra was. Then came at least two petticoats and finally our skirt, waist or sweater, or dress. On our legs, over the long-leg undies, we pulled up black, ribbed heavy stockings, then heavy buttoned leggins. These were held up by a garter belt or rubber, elastic bands. My shoes were high laces ones. On top of these were worn rubbers or arctic boots. We arrived at school, needless to say the smell of wet clothes was with us all day. At recess and before school we enjoyed ourselves in the winter snow balling, making forts, and playing fox and geese. . . . Both Caroline and I had our feet frozen when we were very young. . . . Each winter the chill caused us much discomfort. Many times when my feet would burn or itch, I would take off my shoes and stockings and run out in the snow. I was bothered each winter until I got into high school then I seemed to outgrow it."

A military draft began in June 1917. Among volunteer groups were the Buhl Independent Rifles and forty members of the Young Men's Slovak Association of Farrell who served as a group. Neighbors and friends signed up together and were placed in the same units. At home, people who were from Germany and other enemy countries and not U.S. citizens were questioned and watched. Several county industries converted their machinery so that products that were manufactured contributed to the war effort. Guns, anchor chains, tank parts, fencing, and other equipment were fabricated. Farmers were encouraged to plant more crops than normal. Unless women were nurses, they infrequently were sent overseas. They worked in the fields. The government took control of prices for farm goods and their distribution. Americans at home experienced Heatless Mondays (to save coal), Meatless Tuesdays, and Wheatless Wednesdays. Red Cross volunteers knitted and sewed for servicemen at the Buhl Independent Rifles Armory. Propaganda was used extensively and successfully to sell Liberty Bonds. In four separate Bond drives, the government raised $21 million, about 65 percent of the cost of the war. (Ad: unidentified local county paper; caption: Mairy Jayn Woge)

If You Were "Over There"

If instead of being comfortable at home, you were "over there" in the trenches, what would you think of the man who refused to buy a LIBERTY BOND?

Wouldn't you think it was un-American for him not to do everthing in his power to help you when he knows that you are risking your life at the front to protect him and all that he possesses.

Thousands of American soldiers at the front today must wonder whether it is possible for such a person to exist as a man who does not buy LIBERTY BONDS to provide the government with the money needed to furnish the necessary supplies.

Many of these men may come back invalided this fall. How will you feel if you have to say "No" when one of them asks you if you bought LIBERTY BONDS?

Don't take any chances. Don't run any risk of being left out. Buy your LIBERTY BONDS TODAY so that whatever happens in the future you can look everyone straight in the face and say "I did my share."

BUY LIBERTY BONDS
AND BUY THEM FREELY
FROM ANY BANK

This LIBERTY LOAN ADVERTISEMENT has been contributed by

THE SHARPSVILLE FURNACE CO.

as a patriotic contribution towards winning the war

Teachers Institute, 1912, gathered on the west lawn of the courthouse. (Photo: Autumn Buxton)

Ralph Bower (Delaware Township), about 1915. (Photo: Autumn Buxton)

In the early 1900s, snow (pictured, in Mercer) brought out the horse-drawn sleighs since automobiles were still so new.

After London School, at the intersection of Routes 208 and 258 (Springfield Township), was abandoned, its bell was donated to the Caldwell One-Room School Museum (Delaware Township). During subsequent restoration, the bell from Stokely School (Coolspring Township) was purchased from an antique shop and now hangs in the London tower. The building is now a gift shop. (Source: Mae Beringer)

A popular recreation spot mentioned several times in submissions for this publication, but with little detail, is Idlewild Park in Sharon (pictured, about 1911).

The Stoneboro Strawberry Association are loading strawberries in 1911 at the Stoneboro and Chautauqua Lake Ice Company icehouse onto refrigerator railroad cars. (Contributor: Jennifer Reinhart)

Busch Cemetery is on Donation Road, just north of Busch Road, in Otter Creek Township. The cemetery's earliest stone is dated 1858 and the latest 1931. A historical marker in the cemetery commemorates the Emmanuel Evangelical Lutheran Church, also known as Busch Church because Andrew Busch donated land for the original log church in 1842. In 1855, it was replaced by a frame building. After the congregation disbanded, the building was offered to the Grove City Lutherans. Men and women traveled by train from Grove City to carefully save the lumber, which they hauled by horse and wagon to North Center Street where they built their church in 1912. (In 1954, Grove City's current Holy Trinity Lutheran Church was built at Columbia Avenue and Spring Street.) (Contributors: Joyce Young and Vonda Minner)

Early Mercer County contacts included flying exhibitions at local public events. Perhaps the most publicized of the early exhibitions were the demonstrations by Lewis Earle Sandt at the Grove City June Festival in 1913. Sandt, born in 1888 in Brookville, Pennsylvania, moved to Erie in 1908 and opened an automobile repair shop. Fascinated by airplanes, Sandt learned to fly with the help of Glen Curtiss. In February 1912, with one crash under his belt, Sandt made the first flight across a frozen Lake Erie, crashing on the return trip five miles from the Pennsylvania shore. He walked over the ice to the small town of Harborcreek and took a late evening trolley home to Erie. On June 12, 1913, during the early evening of the second day of the June festival and after take-off from Grove City College's athletic field, a strong wind caused Sandt's biplane to dip downwards. Its bicycle wheel struck the roof of a garage at 146 East Pine Street, and the plane crashed into the backyard. Sandt suffered a broken leg and arm. Unfortunately, Sandt developed tetanus while in the Grove City Hospital and died on June 22; a supply of serum arrived too late to save his life. (Contributor: Richard Christner)

During the second decade of the 1900s, the Fannie Furnace (West Middlesex) was served by the Erie Railroad (pictured) and by the Erie & Pittsburgh Railroad. In fact, the Erie & Pittsburgh bridged the Shenango River just to serve Fannie Furnace.
(Caption: Frederick Houser)

As president of U.S. Steel, Carnegie Steel, American Steel and Tin Plate, American Steel and Wire, Central Furnace, and the Bessemer & Lake Erie Railroad, J. A. Farrell (center, holding umbrella) was a prominent man in the Shenango Valley. The other men pictured with Farrell when South Sharon was changed to the borough of Farrell in 1912 were officials of either the steel company or the new borough. (The borough was changed to a city in the 1930s.) Not only was the borough named after him, but also an ore-carrying ship on Lake Erie bore the name "JA Farrell," according to George Hostetter (Mercer). According to Mairy Jayn Woge, South Sharon almost did not happen. It was governed by Hickory Township in 1901 when Sharon began distributing petitions to annex it. The first set of petitions, however, did not have enough signatures. Before more Sharon residents signed the petitions, the population of South Sharon signed their own petitions requesting that the community be independent. A meeting of the two sides resulted in an agreement that made South Sharon a separate community. (The organization of South Sharon crimped the growth of Sharon on the south side, but did not stop it. Sharon annexed from Hickory the properties north of South Sharon from the Ohio line to the fairgrounds east of Stambaugh Avenue.)

The entrance to the Farrell Works, 1913.

These houses, built by the Farrell Works for its employees, were located on First Avenue, north of Highland Avenue, and in 1913 rented for $12.50 per month. They each had six rooms, a hall, bath, and cellar, and hot and cold water. The water bill was paid by the company, and the tenants paid for heat, either gas or coal. Other houses were available for $13.50 and included a finished attic. A seven-room house without a finished attic could be rented for $16.50. Similar houses were located on Fruit, Wallis, and Spearman avenues.

Steel mills used pouring cranes like this one at the Farrell Works, 1913. Safety doors would be closed when the crane was operating.

209

Working in the steel mills was dangerous. Farrell Works, for one, had an emergency hospital where nurses could attend to injuries quickly, here, in 1913.

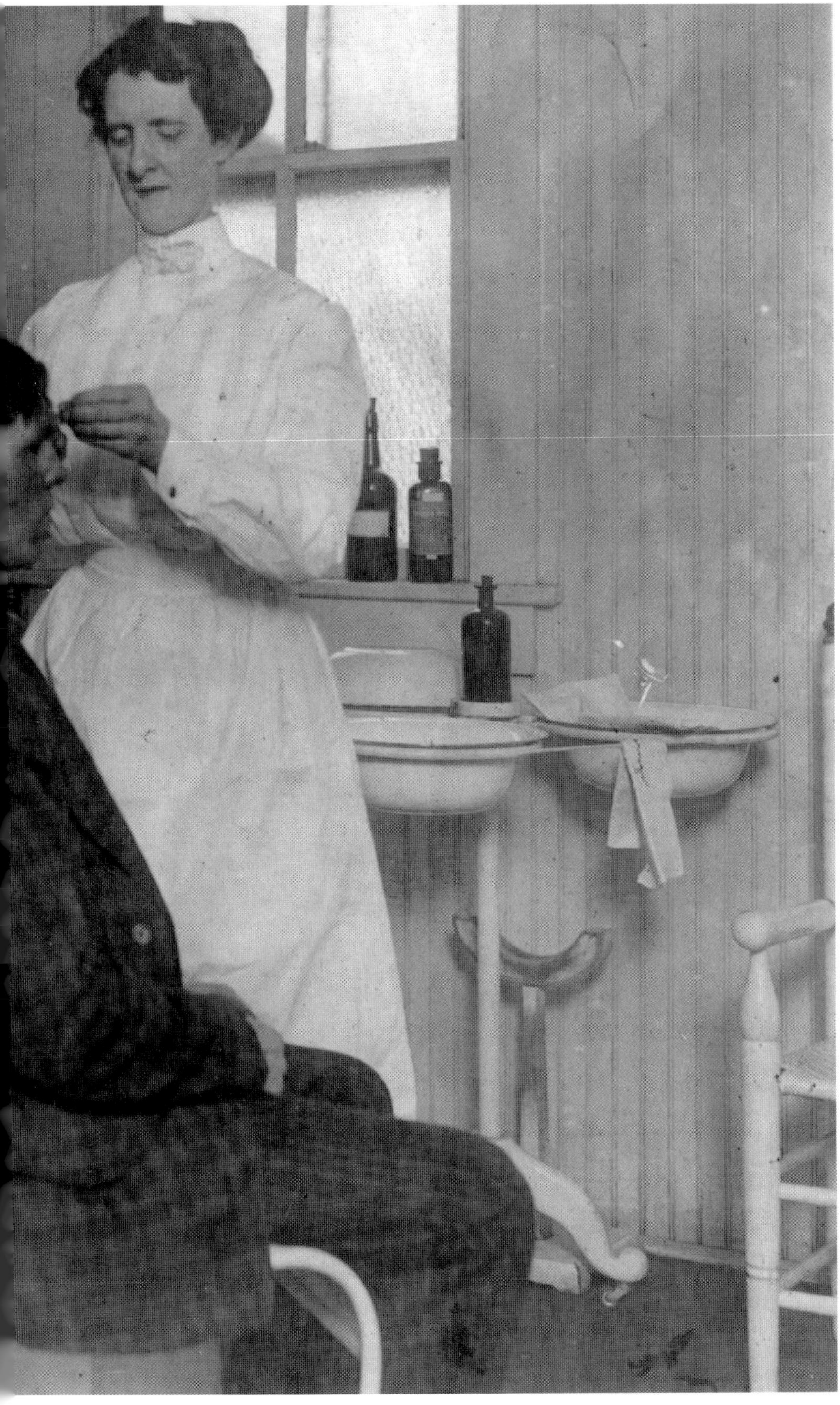

At Camp Corn Tassel (near New Hamburg), the Four Leaf Clover Club, a predecessor of the Future Farmers of America, held activities such as the pictured 1915 gathering. (Photo: Autumn Buxton)

Lulu Bower, friend Carrie, and Myrtle Bower (Patterson) on the old Hamburg bridge near the Hamburg dam on the Shenango River (Delaware Township), about 1915. (Contributor: Autumn Buxton)

First National Bank, interior, with Dan Zahniser, W. V. Anderson, Ted Craig, and C. G. Williams, 1915.

Carnegie Steel Company, North Works, Sharon, early 1900s. The plant was closed in 1921. (Contributor: George Hostetter)

Through the years, the communities in the county have held parades, such as the Stoneboro Industrial Parade (pictured at right, 1913). (Photo: Rita Kreidle Holler)

Above: Crowds lined the street for the Industrial Parade during Greenville's Old Home Week in 1913.

In the early 1900s, State Street in downtown Sharon was brick and filled with the clanging of streetcars (pictured, about 1914) until about 1939, when the streetcars stopped running, the tracks taken out, and the streets paved.

One of Stoneboro's biggest traditions, the Stoneboro Fair was started in 1868. Organized as the Mercer County Agricultural and Manufacturing Society of Stoneboro, the group purchased land from the Mercer Iron Coal Company and Jeremiah Bonner for its first fairground between the Jamestown & Franklin Railroad tracks and the south shore of Sandy Lake and held its first exhibition, all in 1868. Original officers were local businessmen: J. P. Kerr, president; R. J. McClure, vice president; Samuel Hines, secretary; and H. B. Blood, treasurer. (The officers have continued to be local and area residents.) Early fairgoers (pictured, about 1907) saw displays of livestock, agricultural products, and farm machinery. They also attended horse races, stage presentations, carnival attractions, and animal judging contests (pictured, lower left, in 1914). (1907 Postcard: Rita Kreidle Holler; caption: Frederick Houser)

215

Perrine School (pictured, in 1914) was a white frame building on Rou 173 near Perrine Corners (Worth Township). (Contributor: Idella McConnell and Lucille Eagles)

Identified only as the East End Fire Department Basketball Team of Mercer, these players posed with what appears to be a Mercer High School ball dated 1915.

In 1914, Grove City's Commercial Club (the forerunner of the borough's Chamber of Commerce) started a creamery that was leased to the U.S. Department of Agriculture for dairy experiments. Operating from 1915 until 1948, the Grove City Creamery established dairy routes, sold to local stores, and catered to walk-in customers. Its products included butter; Swiss, Roquefort, Camembert, cottage, and club cheeses; bulk condensed milk; cream; buttermilk; and ice cream. Pictured in 1919 are Mrs. Phillips in the laundry room, Tib Hill in the condenser room, and employees posed outside the main building (on the ground from left, D. White, A. Ghost, Filson, Mathieson, Whittenhall, Lester Mallot, Paul Latshaw, Mr. Voss, Bill White, Joslin, Mrs. Gilderslieve, L. Perry, Mable Coulter, Agnes Spears, Mae Turk, Mable McCoy, Ollie Heylep, and M. Phillips; on the wall, Shaw, H. Ghost, Matthews, Cubbison, Dahlburg, Jordan, H. Garner, Cecil Gills, and unidentified). In 1925, the operation expanded to include a hatchery with a 7,000-egg incubator to hatch chicks for patrons. (By 1934, the government moved its experimental operation to Maryland, and the creamery was sold to Borden Company, which ran the facility for a number of years. In 1941, Lewis Dairies took over; but, by 1948, it sold the creamery's assets to other companies, and the creamery closed.) Thomas F. Ritchey, Jr. was in charge of the creamery's hatchery. When the government discontinued the hatchery experiments, Ritchey bought the equipment, added to it and opened his own, private hatchery on Mercer Road outside Grove City in 1927. Not only did Ritchey eventually build the largest accredited hatchery in Pennsylvania, but he also earned additional respect by mastering the Japanese technique of determining the sex of the chicks. Ritchey's Poultry Farm closed in 1951. (Sources: **Reflections of Our Past** and an unidentified newspaper article)

The class of 1916 was the last to graduate from the Fredonia Institute. Their yearbook, the **Fredonian**, was the first one published in the Fredonia school district. The Fredonia Institute opened in 1874, and the red-brick building (pictured) was constructed in 1890. From an account of an unidentified former student, "We could take up the common branches and review to prepare to teach them and also High School work and college work at Fredonia Institute. It was a very fine school. The tuition was $10.00 a semester or term and there was a fall term, winter term and spring or summer term. I earned my tuition by doing janitor work for a year for $30.00 which paid my tuition. Some students taught school in winter and went to school in the summer to gain their education and had to take examinations under the Co. Superintendent and pass in order to teach each year." In the same year the Institute closed, the Fredonia Vocational School, otherwise known as "Fruits Valuable Scholars," was founded by Frank A. Fruit. It made use of the Institute building and other new additions. (The last year of classes held at the Vocational School was 1942. During that year, the Fredonia-Delaware High School was built through the efforts of the Works Progress Administration. This high school closed in 1960 when Fredonia students started going to the newly consolidated Reynolds High School.)

West Middlesex graduating class, about 1915.

The dam and state fishway at Greenville, about 1916.

In 1909, George Junior Republic (Pine Township) was founded by William R. George to create a community where youth with troubled backgrounds would be guided to become self-sufficient and productive citizens of a democratic society. The special school was originally for boys and girls (pictured, in 1916, with teacher Nancy M. Corbett, back row with black hat). The school still operates, however, only for boys. (Now, over 450 boys live on or near the 400-acre campus (pictured, in 2000), which is one of the largest residential facilities in the United States. The youth live in small-group homes with families who have been specially trained in counseling, attend a fully accredited educational program, and participate in a wide variety of therapeutic activities.)
(Aerial: **The Herald;** caption: **Reflections of Our Past**)

Steam engines like "Bob" (pictured with, from left, Ralph and Frank Minner, about 1918) were used by many farmers in the county to power their farm equipment. (Contributor: Vonda Minner)

220

Ladies of the World War I Red Cross, in front of the First National Bank of Mercer, about 1918.

The trestle spanning Thornton Hollow between Sharon and Sharpsville, pictured here about 1920, was replaced by a viaduct in 1926. (Contributor: Julia Swaelon)

In 1918, the U.S. Secretary of War established Student Army Training Corps on the campus of Grove City College to provide military training. The young men who enrolled under the plan were considered privates in the Army; housed, clothed, and fed at the expense of the federal government; and received a private's pay of $30 a month. The Corps existed only during the fall term of 1918. (Photo: Grove City College; caption: **'Mid the Pines**)

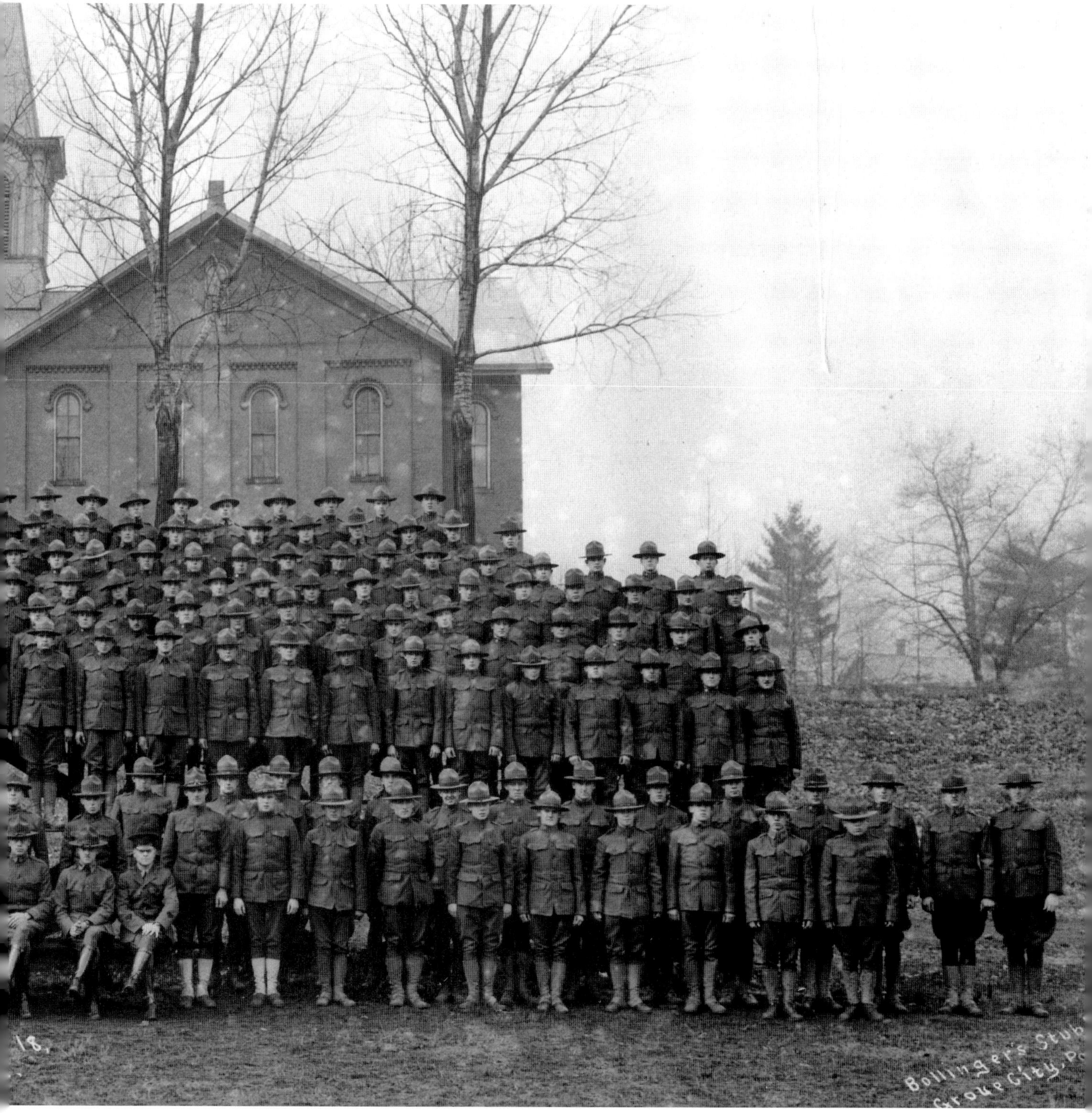
18,
Bollinger's Stu
Grove City, P

Myron W. Jones served during World War I and was the mayor of Sharon for eighteen years. He also served as Mercer County Recorder for four years.

During World War I, John C. Kuhn (West Middlesex) was a private in Company A, 313th Machinegun Battalion, 80th Division (pictured, in 1918).

An airplane in a field near Stoneboro drew lots of attention in 1913.

With the coming of World War I, a new era in aviation began. While public exhibitions, barnstorming, and air races would continue to be popular attractions into the late 1930s, the airplane as a utilitarian machine began to develop quickly. In the case of the Great War, the purpose was to create an instrument of potential destruction. Related developments were also in motion, for example, an invention of Greenville resident Stefan Banic, born in 1870 in Hungary. At age thirty-seven, he immigrated to the United States, settling in Greenville where he worked in the nearby coal mines and as a stone mason. In 1914, Banic patented the parachute, personally demonstrating it by jumping off a tall building and then from a moving airplane. Banic donated his patent to the Army Air Corps which, at the time, was experimenting with military observation from dirigibles. (Banic retired to Czechoslovakia in 1921, where he died in 1941. In 1989, the post office offered a commemorative cachet about Banic's invention.) (Caption: Richard Christner)

The Bessemer & Lake Erie Railroad's time table gave the schedule for the main line and its branches, effective September 26 1920. (Contributer: Richard Sherbondy)

BESSEMER & LAKE RAILROAD COMPANY

MAIN LINE AND BRANCHES

TIME TABLE No. 54

TAKES EFFECT

SUNDAY, SEPT. 26th, 1920

At 10:00 O'clock P. M.

EASTERN STANDARD TIME

E. H. UTLEY, General Manager
J. S. MATSON, General Superintendent
A. D. CHITTENDEN, Supt. of Transportation
W. M. JOHNSON, Superintendent
C. L. PASHO, Assistant Superinten...
F. W. SMITH, Assistant

TO ERIE / NORTHWARD — BUTLER TO ERIE

FIRST CLASS

STATIONS	Distances from East Pittsburg Via Old Line	Distances Between Stations	12 Daily Ex Sunday Pass'ger	202 Daily Ex Sunday Pass'ger	14 Daily Pass'ger	114 Daily Ex Sunday Pass'ger	10 Daily Pass'ger	206 Daily Ex Sunday Pass'ger	2 Daily Ex Sunday Pass'ger
(B.& O. STATION) PITTSBURGH					A.M. 7 45		P.M. 12 50		P.M. 4 00
			A.M.	A.M.	A.M.	P.M.	P.M.	P.M.	P.M.
BUTLER (B & O STA)	41.1	40.1	4 45		9 55		2 45		6 00
ALVIN	43.3	2.2	4 52		10 02		2 52		6 07
ONEIDA	46.0	2.7	F 4 57		F10 07		F 2 57		S 6 12
JAMISONVILLE	49.2	3.2			S10 13		*		S 6 18
QUEEN JUNCTION	51.0	1.8	F 5 05		S10 22		S 3 07		S 6 26
Y TOWER	51.2	.2	5 06		10 23		3 08		6 27
EUCLID	52.7	1.5	F 5 09		S10 27		S 3 13		S 6 31
LAYTONIA	55.4	2.7	F 5 13		S10 32		S 3 18		S 6 36
ALLSTON	56.8	1.4			*		*		F 6 40
T TOWER	57.6	.8	5 16		10 36		3 22		6 41
ISTERS	59.8	2.2	F 5 20		F10 41		F 3 27		S 6 46
BRANCHTON	61.7	1.9	S 5 26		S10 53		S 3 35		S 6 55
HARRISVILLE	64.4	2.7	S 5 32		S10 59		S 3 41		S 7 00
K TOWER	64.5	.1	5 33		11 00		3 42		7 01
GROVE CITY	70.8	6.3	S 5 50		S11 17		S 3 54		S 7 16
TOWER	71.7	.9	5 52		11 19		3 56		7 18
ARDOE	75.7	4.0	S 5 59		S11 26		S 4 03		S 7 24
HOUSTON JUNC	80.1	4.4							F 7 32
MERCER JUNCTION	80.7	.6	6 09		11 36		4 13		7 34
MERCER	81.6	.9	S 6 15		S11 42		S 4 19		S 7 40
MERCER JUNCTION	80.7	.9	6 17		11 44		4 21		7 42
COOLSPRING	84.8	4.1	F 6 23		*		*		S 7 49
LEDONIA	87.3	2.5	S 6 29		S11 55		S 4 31		S 7 55
BEMIS	91.0	3.7	S 6 35		*12 01		S 4 37		S 8 01
TOWER	91.8	.8	6 37		12 02		4 39		8 03
TOWER	98.9	7.1							
SHENANGO	96.1	4.3	{6 44 / S 6 51		{12 09 / S12 17		{4 46 / S 4 55		{8 10 / S 8 15
GREENVILLE	98.0	1.9	{6 56 / S 7 00		12 22 / S12 26		5 00 / S 5 04		8 20
W TOWER	101.1	3.1	7 05		12 31		5 09		
GOOD	101.6	.5	S 7 07		S12 33		S 5 11		
JUNCTION	103.9	2.3	7 12		12 37		5 15		
AMSVILLE	106.6	2.7	S 7 17		S12 41		S 5 20		
ARTSTOWN	109.4	2.8	S 7 23		S12 47		S 5 26		
GERMANSVILLE	114.8	5.4	S 7 32	S 8 18	F		S 5 35	S 6 33	
MEADVILLE JUNC	116.3	1.5	S 7 36	S 8 22	S12 57		S 5 38	S 6 37	
PENN'T LAKE PK	118.8	2.5							
MEADVILLE JUNC	116.3	2.5	S 7 41	S 8 40	S 1 05		S 5 43	S 6 55	
HARMONSBURG	118.3	2.0	S 7 46		S 1 08		S 5 47		
JACKSONBURG	121.3	3.0	S 7 52		F 1 13		S 5 52		
CONNEAUTVILLE	125.4	4.1	S 8 02		S 1 21		S 6 01		
SPRINGBORO	128.4	3.0	S 8 10		S 1 28		S 6 09		
SHADELAND	129.6	1.2	S 8 13		*		F 6 12		
INNSIDE	132.3	2.7	S 8 18		*		S 6 17		
SHEEPVILLE	133.7	1.4	S 8 21				S 6 20		
K TOWER	135.8	2.1	8 25		1 37	1 44	6 24		
ALBION	136.1	.3	S 8 30		S 1 40	S 1 46	S 6 31		
CRANESVILLE	137.1	1.0	S 8 36		S 1 43	S 1 51	S 6 35		
A TOWER	137.4	.3	8 37		1 44	1 52	6 36		
ATEA	3.1	3.1	S 8 44		S 1 51		S 6 42		
K CREEK	6.2	3.1	8 49		1 56		6 47		
GIRARD	7.9	1.7	S 8 54		S 2 02		S 6 52		
LACE JUNC	9.1	1.2	8 59		2 07		6 57		
DE	21.3	12.2	9 21		2 27		7 19		
	23.5	2.2	9 32		2 38		7 30		
			A.M.	A.M.	P.M.	P.M.	P.M.	P.M.	P.M.
			12	202	14	114	10	206	2

227

In 1922 the Randolph Young Men's Bible class of the Methodist Episcopal Church set a record for attendance—280—the largest body of men ever gathered together in Mercer for a Sunday School class.

Chapter 4: 1921–1930

Townships

According to the April 4, 1930, *Mercer Dispatch*, Mercer County had 202 one-room schools in 1920, and by 1929 that number had dropped to 166.

Robert Osborn (**Salem Township**) recalled that James Henry took ice out of the Little Shenango Creek during the winter and stored it in a cement block building. He sold it in the summertime. Osborn also remembered "Milt Hill bought his land from William Freeland and built a home and recreational park by the Little Shenango. It was called Sycamore Park and was a very popular spot for reunions and camping. It had a large pavilion, swimming, and ball park. Hill worked for the Bessemer. He lost a leg and most of his money in the 1929 stock market crash. The 1929 crash did not cause the loss of his leg, as he had diabetes; but it was during this time of panic that he also suffered that loss."

In 1925, **Sugar Grove Township** started closing its schoolhouses due to a decrease in the number of enrolled children. When Riley School and Lyon's School closed, the children had to attend other schools.

In **Worth Township**, Anna Westlake was the operator of the telephone switchboard in her home in 1926. Anna was a widow and continued to operate the switchboard until it was moved across the street to the home of Roy and Sara Shipton, where it remained until it was moved to Wesley in Venango County. The Worth Township R. R. Wright Education Fund was established in 1925. R. R. Wright placed $12,000 of 7 percent preferred stock of the Crucible Steel Company in control of the First National Bank of Mercer. For the next thirty years, income from this stock was to be paid to the Worth Township School District and used to assist young people in their education beyond high school. The first person to receive money from this fund was Elise Nystrom. Now, trustees are responsible for administering the fund. Over the years it is estimated that over one hundred students from Worth Township have benefited from Wright's generosity.

Municipalities

In the 1920s and 1930s, entertainment in **Greenville** was enhanced by the Sunnybrook Orchestra, which performed in New York City for eight months.

Sharon (by Mairy Jayn Woge) All but the last two months of the 1920s were economic boom times for the Shenango Valley. Sharon was the largest community among the five Valley towns. According to the 1920 census, it was home to 21,747. The blocks along State Street between the east bank of the Shenango River and Sharpsville and Walnut Avenues, half of the city's downtown, contained ninety-eight businesses and offices. Among those facing State Street were two banks, two hotels, headquarters for two railroads, a school for barbers, a couple of five-and-tens, two tea houses, three restaurants, a candy store, a pharmacy, a large hardware establishment, a furniture store, a clothier's, a storefront that was the office of a labor union, an insurance company, a newspaper dis-

Acquired in 1940 by Meadville Telephone Company, the Cochranton Telephone Company had been organized by the owner of a Cochranton hardware store (Crawford County) in 1901 and had quickly expanded to serve northeastern Mercer County. Each community had its own telephone exchange, or "central" switchboard, which required the attention of full-time operators around the clock. Local phone businesses were among the first to have all-female staffs. (Soon after World War II, Meadville Telephone's entire system was converted to dial operation, and the need for local operators was eliminated. Meadville Telephone went through several mergers and is now called Alltel Pennsylvania, Inc. The use of party lines in the rural areas of the county continued into the 1960s. In the Shenango Valley, the handling of long distance calls by operators continued until 1969.) (Pictured, operator Eva Butler at Blacktown telephone switchboard; caption: Frederick Houser and Mairy Jayn Woge)

tributor's and a cigar sales outlet. Six lawyers and seven physicians practiced in the four blocks. One of the four hotels in the red brick business district burned down in 1928. The estimated loss from the fire was $350,000. The water in the lines connected to the hydrants was insufficient to extinguish the blaze even though the part of Sharon between the East Hill and West Hill and the low areas of Wheatland were flooded by the Shenango River on the average of once every three years.

The first tube mill in the Shenango Valley opened in Sharon in 1929. It was along North Water Avenue and Ellsworth Street, where the former Sharon Boiler Works had been operated by William McGilvray and Frank H. Buhl beginning in 1878. Meyer Yanowitz was the manager of Sharon Tube, which manufactured small-diameter pipe, including airplane steering columns, airplane accessories, and electrically welded pipe. By 1949, Sharon Tube had moved to Mill Street in Sharon, buying property and buildings that previously were part of the Westerman Iron Company.

In 1929, the population of Sharon was 30,211. Farrell had 21,000 residents, and Sharpsville a little over 5,000. Rollers at Valley industries were paid $160 a month. Riveters earned 65 to 72 cents an hour and welders, 65 cents hourly.

RAILROADS
By Frederick Houser

The venerable Baltimore & Ohio Railroad gained a toe-hold in Mercer County when it obtained a controlling interest in the Sharpsville Railroad in 1884. The B&O may have intended this line between Sharpsville and New Wilmington to one day provide entry into the Shenango Valley, but no direct track connection was ever built between New Wilmington and the Baltimore & Ohio main line through New Castle. This orphan line of the Baltimore & Ohio ceased operations in 1930. Some yard trackage at Sharpsville was conveyed to the Pennsylvania Railroad, but the rest of the line became the county's first lengthy common carrier railroad abandonment.

FARMING
By Vonda Minner

In 1921, the Bethel-New Wilmington Road (Shenango, Lackawannock, and Wilmington Townships) became a public road. The diary of Thurman Hover recorded, "Material was hauled for three weeks to build the new road. No steam shovels were used—mostly done with mules and wheel scrapers. About 200 men scattered in gangs from Wilmington to Sharon—grading and building bridges and various other jobs and they have some of the gosh darnest biggest concrete mixers I ever saw. They haul the stuff in two cylinder auto car trucks. They have 36 x 7 pneumatic tires and run like the devil. They are short coupled and will turn shorter than a Ford. They have two hoppers side by side and that stand up. The hoppers hold 11/4 each and they fill the hoppers with sand and gravel and throw 10 bags of cement on the platform making a 3-ton load and each hopper makes a charge for the mixer, which takes one minute to mix."

Timeline 1921—1930

The World

- 1921 Warren Harding becomes the 29th president; Albert Einstein gives lectures in New York on his new theory of relativity
- 1922 Insulin is first administered to a diabetic patient
- 1923 *TIME* magazine is published for the first time; Calvin Coolidge becomes the 30th president; magician Harry Houdini struggles free from a straightjacket hanging head-down 40 feet above the ground; first nonstop transcontinental flight is made
- 1924 Frozen packaged food is invented by Clarence Birdseye
- 1925 School teacher John Scopes is found guilty of teaching evolution in a public school
- 1926 Gertrude Ederle becomes first American woman to swim across the English Channel
- 1927 The first successful long distance transmission of television is demonstrated; Ford discontinues production of the Model T
- 1928 The first color motion picture is demonstrated by George Eastman
- 1929 The first "talking" movie filmed in color, "On With the Show" is released; the stock market crashes beginning the Great Depression; Guy Lombardo and his Royal Canadians play "Auld Lang Syne" as a New Year's Eve song for the first time
- 1930 The population of the United States is 123,076,741; the planet Pluto is discovered by American astronomer Clyde W. Tombaugh

Mercer County

- 1922 67 of 119 cases tried in the county courts are for liquor violations; Westinghouse Electric & Manufacturing acquires Savage Arms Corp (an ordinance firm employing 300 people) and becomes one of the world's largest transformer manufacturing facilities; no expense is spared at the formal opening of the Columbia Theatre in Sharon
- 1923 Thomas Edison and his wife pass through the county enroute to New York; the Sharon Public Library opens at the Buhl Club; record-making transcontinental flight is made by Grove City pilot Oakley Kelly
- 1924 S. F. Stambaugh's estate gives Sharon land; the *Telegraph* and the *Farrell News* merge
- 1925 Earthquake tremors startle basketball fans at West Middlesex
- 1926 Porter Smith is injured in a 38 feet fall from scaffolding erected under the south portico of the courthouse
- 1927 Pardoe Mines close
- 1928 The last cattle show is held in Grove City's Memorial Park; the Stoneboro Fire Department is organized
- 1929 A "vivid and vicious bolt of lightning" strikes the courthouse tower (several people felt the shock, and County Treasurer McQuiston received a "rude jolt" while using the telephone); an earthquake rocks Sharon; Cooper-Bessemer is formed
- 1930 The county's population is 99,246; a bright flash of meteor at 5:30 a.m. alarms many residents of Sharon

The Aiken Farm (Shenango Township) was one hundred years old in 1922; the North Farm, in 1923; two Courtney Farms and the McClelland Homestead (all in Findlay Township), in 1925; the Forbes Farm (New Vernon Township), in 1927; and the Hazen Farm (Fairview Township) and the Jennings Farm (Jefferson Township), in 1930.

The Vengold Dairy was started in 1922 on the main street in Sandy Lake. (In 1939, robbers blew open the company's safe and stole $500 in cash and checks. The dairy business was eventually sold to Meadowgold Dairy in 1957. In 1971, the old Vengold building became a bowling alley, and today it houses a doctor's office and home health care offices.)

In 1924, all herds in the county were tested for tuberculosis and were accredited disease-free. Mercer County was the first county to be accredited in Pennsylvania.

"MASTER FARMER" DESIGNATION

The "Master Farmer" designation is given to farmers who demonstrate long-term financial progress. They are sharp in business and marketing. Their operations are efficient. Their good stewardship extends far beyond their souls and their livestock. A Master Farmer takes time to live, love, and do for others.

In 1926, Howard C. Thompson opened for business at the Mt. Hickory Dairy Farm on Keel Ridge Road in Hermitage and signed a contract with International Harvester Company to sell International and Farmall tractors. In 1928, he formed a partnership with his brother Francis, and the company become known as Thompson Brothers. (After the death of Francis in 1944, the name changed to Thompson's Farm Equipment, and in 1947 Howard's son Delmont joined the business. In 1953, D. R. Thompson Farm Supply opened on the Hadley Road east of Greenville, but closed in 1997, ending over seventy years of the Thompson farm equipment business.)

In 1929, John and Andrew McDowell were named "Master Farmers." (The next time anyone in Mercer County received this honor was not until 1998.)

The Horvath Dairy was started in 1930 in Lackawannock Township.

AVIATION
By Richard Christner

In the early days of aviation, aircraft often used farmers' fields to take off and land. Sometimes, there was no choice in the face of an emergency. The unevenness or wetness of the ground, however, could cause damage to the plane. Such was the case in June 1924 when two airmail service planes were wrecked because of saturated ground. John Johnson, a pilot on the New York-Cleveland run, landed in a meadow on the farm of Nels Olsen near Stoneboro after he was forced to turn back because of fog west of Clarion. His plane became mired in soft soil, breaking a propeller. A relief plane sent from Cleveland landed on a nearby field on H. P. McMichael's farm. Johnson transferred the mailbags to the relief plane and attempted to take off. However, soft ground slowed the plane down, and it hit a tree just as the plane left the ground. Somersaulting two times, the plane came to a stop upside down. Unhurt, Johnson was rescued by spectators.

ARMISTICE DAY
By Wally Wachter

(Editor's note: In this chapter, this section and the other pieces written by Wachter about his childhood in the 1920s and 1930s were originally published in 1983 or 1984 in **The Herald.**)

November 11, now called Veterans Day: "The holiday originally was Armistice Day. It was on that date in 1918 that the Armistice was signed ending all hostilities on European battlefields and giving America and its allies an important victory in World War I.

"President Woodrow Wilson proclaimed the holiday in 1919. Several conflicts late, Congress in 1954 changed it to Veterans Day to honor all US servicemen.

"Unlike Memorial Day, which was set aside to honor the many who had given their lives to preserve America, Armistice Day was intended as a celebration of missions accomplished.

"And that's how it was observed in its early days.

BRIGADIER GENERAL NORMAN J. MAXWELL

A carriage maker by trade, Norman J. Maxwell served during the Civil War and rose through the ranks from sergeant to colonel, with command of a regiment, the 100th Pennsylvania Volunteers (known as the Roundheads). The brevet rank of brigadier general was awarded to Maxwell for his gallantry at the Battle of Fort Steadman outside Petersburg. Postwar Maxwell served as burgess (mayor) of Grove City and owned a retail establishment there for many years. He also served as adjutant and later commandant of the Erie Soldiers and Sailors Home. Maxwell died in 1929 at age ninety-four.

"When we were young tykes in school, I recall, every Armistice Day at the stroke of 11 a.m. we were asked to stand next to our desks and face eastward (the direction of the European war). We observed a minute of silence in tribute. Then there came a speech by a judge, or another prominent resident in the community, or a veteran who had experienced the horrors of the big war.

"The rest of the day was a school holiday.

"In the afternoon or evening, the community generally staged a huge parade and program. The parade usually was dominated by marching units from the American Legion and Veterans of Foreign Wars, including many who had served their country overseas. It generally was augmented by the high school band and strings of city fire trucks.

"Riding in open cars and drawing a lot of attention were a few of the still-living veterans of the Civil War, most of them in their 80s and 90s. Then there were some more sprightly participants of the Spanish-American War that rode in the procession.

"Following the program, which again featured speakers emphasizing the importance of democracy and recitations of patriotic poems by students, there was a display of fireworks.

"All of this was against the backdrop of patriotism that emanated from each household in the community. Every porch along the parade route as well as many other places in town displayed a large American flag. Sidewalks were lined with crowds of spectators, some small children waiving tiny flags.

"Most of us were too young to understand the messages that the speakers were trying to convey, but we did absorb a sense of patriotism from the events that lasted through the years.

"As youngsters we were in awe of our young school buddies who fathers, uncles or other relatives had served in the war. It was exciting to visit their homes, to touch and feel some of the war souvenirs that had been brought home—a German helmet, or a rifle, or a bayonet—or even to wrap our legs with the bandage-type leggings that the American doughboys wore.

"Little did we realize what the future held for us. Some day we would be bringing back the war souvenirs. We would be among the honored veterans marching in the Veterans Day parade. We would be making the speeches on democracy that today's youngsters don't quite understand. . . .

"One eminent US statesman once said: 'Peace is an ideal situation. It is even worth fighting for.'"

The Columbia Theater (shown at right, in 1991) opened on West State Street in Sharon in 1922. The interior was decorated in a Spanish motif, and a huge chandelier hung over the first floor. The balcony was the hangout for youths. Rose DeSantis (Sharon) recalls that the Columbia had been too expensive for her as a youth. Admission was 10 cents and candy a nickel. She earned money by gathering pieces of metal along the railroad tracks and selling them to a trash dealer. In 1927, silent movies were replaced by movies with sound. Colored movies were introduced at the end of a Shirley Temple film in the 1930s. In 1939, "Gone With the Wind" that starred Clark Gable was filmed in color. The appearance of Walt Disney cartoon figures on screens began in 1933. (The Columbia was almost totally destroyed by a fire that began in a photographer's shop adjoining it in 1980. Now, it is being rebuilt with public and private funds.) (Caption: Mairy Jayn Woge)

THEATERS
By Wally Wachter

"In the pre-television days, movie houses abounded in the Valley. Most of them catered to their own particular clients. Movies were the chief entertainment in those days. And pictures would change every three days. You could go to a different theater each day of the week and never run out of films to see.

"A typical date in those days was a good movie, a bit of hand-holding in the balcony and an ice cream sundae or banana split in the confectionery store that always was found next door to the theater.

"Parents had little worry over what type of movies their youngsters were seeing. Yes, there was sex and violence in those days. But the violence happened only to the bad guys. The 'sex' amounted to a five-second sisterly kiss on the lips.

"There was none of the foul language that flourishes in today's productions. There were plenty of suggestive innuendoes cleverly disguised in well-written dialogue that only the sharp minds (or gutter minds) could extract.

"Today's movie makers must resort to the spectacular to compete. Such films as 'Star Wars,' 'E.T.' and 'Return of the Jedi' have set box office records not because of their outstanding stories, superb acting or clever dialogue, but because of the public's fascination of the unknown.

"Except for the old westerns and comedies, most of the old-time movies had a good plot and good dialogue. The story and the acting made the hit. When movie critics talk about the classics, they go back to such films as 'Gone With the Wind,' 'Casablanca,' 'It Happened One Night,' 'The Jazz Singer,' 'A Star is Born,' etc.

"At one time four movie houses flourished in Sharon, four in Farrell and one in Sharpsville. Each had a different attraction playing.

"The Columbia Theater on West State Street, victim of a destructive fire several years ago, was the showplace theater of the Valley. It generally offered first-run films. On weekends, it was not unusual to see its long entrance foyer jammed with people waiting for the previous show to end.

"The Columbia prided itself on presenting, in addition to films, top-rated stage shows. Each Thursday evening featured a famous big band or variety show with noted film stars or entertainers. Among the ones that I remember the best were the Ted Weems Orchestra that featured Perry Como on the vocals and the Vincent Lopez band that introduced Betty Hutton.

"A step down in class, but nevertheless providing good film fare, were the Nuluna Theater, also on State Street near the bridge, and the Liberty Theater on Shenango Avenue, now [law offices]. . . .

During the Depression, movie-goers could pay a potato for admission to the Gable Theater, which opened on South Railroad Street in Sharon in 1906. The Gable's specialty was cowboy movies. Frequently called "the rat house," the Gable was managed by Charles E. Gable whose family lived on Gable Hill near West Middlesex. He and his wife, Florence, lived on South Oakland Avenue in one of the large wood mansions that adjoined the viaduct. Gable also managed the Ritz Theater in Sharpsville. (Gable was reportedly the uncle of the movie star Clark Gable.) The Gable Hotel (pictured, about 1906) abutted the movie house. (Postcard: Vinson Skibo; caption: Mairy Jayn Woge)

Built in 1927 on Broad Street in Grove City, the Guthrie Theater (pictured, in 1997) first showed silent movies to the accompaniment of a pipe organ. Now, it continues to operate as one of only a few remaining independent, single-screen movie houses in the area with a bargain ticket price of $3. The current owner, James N. Ahonen, is restoring the theater with fixtures and antiques from other old theaters scheduled for demolition. (Photographers: Nick and Kathy Pompa; caption: **Reflections of Our Past***)*

"In Farrell was the old Strand Theater, located on Broadway between Roemer Boulevard (then Haywood Street) and Federal Street. It specialized in weekend double features, complete with comedy, cartoon and exciting serials which tested the endurance and fortitude of the heroes and the anxiety of the movie fans for sometimes 12 to 15 weeks.

"The oldest theater in Farrell was the Rex, located at the northwest corner of Idaho Street and Market Avenue. The movie house went out of existence long before talking pictures made their debut. I remember seeing old Jackie Coogan films there when I was a toddler.

"The Capitol and Colonial theaters, within a block of each other on Idaho Street, were the first-run shows in Farrell. The two theaters hold many memories.

"Each Wednesday night was Amateur Night at the Capitol. All local talent who wanted to compete for the weekly prize of $5 did their thing on the stage. The winner was selected by applause from the audience as the master of ceremonies held his hand over the head of each performer.

"During the Depression days [the 1930s], the Capital or Colonial would feature a special 'potato show' on Saturday mornings. Admission to the show, which included a feature film, comedy, cartoon and short subject, was one potato. The spuds would be turned over by the management to the welfare society for distribution to needy families.

"Sharpsville had its Ritz Theater at Main Street and Second Avenue, generally featuring regular films during the week and westerns on the weekends.

"For those with transportation, the Jordan Theater in Greenville and the Guthrie in Grove City offered good fare. . . . And then came television."

Henrietta Crosman, actress of the stage and screen, was usually cast in grande-dame roles. A slim, petite, dark-haired woman, she made a striking presence. Her career began during the silent film era with "The Unwelcome Mrs. Hatch" in 1914 and continued over two decades. Her last film was "Personal Property" in 1937. Her portrayal of Rosalind in "As You Like It" made that Shakespearean character a living and vital figure to her generation. Crosman was born in 1861 in West Virginia, a daughter of George Hamilton Crosman, Jr. and Mary Wick Crosman and a granddaughter of General George Hamilton Crosman and Hannah Blair Foster Crosman. In addition to her acting career, Crosman married twice and had two sons. She died in 1944. Crosman's paternal great-grandfather Foster had a brother Samuel, who in turn married Elizabeth Donnell and had six children. One daughter, Caroline, married Mercer attorney Samuel Griffith, who owned the home that housed the **Western Press** *before becoming the site of the present-day post office. Crosman's paternal grandmother, Hannah Blair Foster Crosman, had monuments erected in Old Mercer Graveyard in "tender remembrance" of her own father Alexander William Foster (died in Mercer in 1848) and grandmother Hannah Blair Foster (died in 1810). Samuel and Elizabeth Foster are also interred in Old Mercer Graveyard. (Photo: www.perspicacity.com; caption: Gail Habbyshaw)*

GYPSIES

By Mairy Jayn Woge

Gypsies visited the Shenango Valley and peddled services, repairing roofs, for instance, almost every spring or summer. They hoisted tents in vacant fields near woods. The men performed daring tricks on horseback and the women danced barefooted while wearing long, colorful dresses. Music from string instruments accompanied the performances. Traveling with the gypsies were cows, pigs, dogs, and bears. The bears wore ruffs around their necks.

Suspicion about the gypsies and their bears caused a Valley newspaper editor to dispatch a reporter to a gypsy camp near West Middlesex with instructions to determine if the bears were eating children. After investigating, the reporter wrote, "The bears are too skinny to have eaten children."

In May 1921, Lena Miller, the queen of Russian gypsies, became ill while telling fortunes in a tent belonging to the Wallace Brothers Carnival that was leasing a lot on Sharpsville Avenue. Dr. Harry W. Milliken diagnosed her ailment as severe pneumonia. Frank Miller, the Russian gypsy king, and the couples' six children gave the queen the medicine that was prescribed, but she was too sick to survive and died in the family tent on May 10. The funeral service was delayed until the queen's parents, Louis and Mary Granch Mitchell, arrived from St. Louis. The Mitchells had moved to Russia from Egypt where they were born and emigrated to the United States because of discrimination against gypsies in Europe. Mitchell had amassed a $3 million fortune. During the parade that preceded the queen's funeral service, she was placed on a slab and wrapped in a silk robe made by the Russian gypsies. The queen's body was carried along Valley streets in a colorful parade in which local dignitaries, bands, and clowns participated. Her tribe had purchased a lot at Oakwood Cemetery and ordered a tombstone with only her name and the date of her death on it. The priest of the Greek Orthodox Church in Farrell presided at the funeral and the priest of the Romanian Orthodox Church of Farrell led the prayers at the burial ground.

OAKLEY G. KELLY
By Richard Christner

After World War I, airplane manufacturers and pilots strove to set new records in speed, endurance, and maneuverability. During this period, Mercer County's most famous aviator came to national prominence. As a young boy, Oakley G. Kelly moved with his parents, Wallace J. and Nettie M. Kelly, to Grove City in the 1890s where his father owned and operated a feed store. Young Kelly was educated in the Grove City schools and spent three years at Grove City College before enlisting in the Army Air Corps, becoming a flying cadet, and being commissioned in 1918 as a second lieutenant in the Aviation Section of the Signal Corps Reserves. In 1920, he received a commission in the Regular Army. As an armament officer and test pilot at McCook Air Force Base, Kelly established two world records in 1922: the endurance record of 35 hours and 18 minutes and the record for non-stop flight of 2,060 miles. Kelly's most famous exploit occurred in May 1923: Kelly and Lt. John McCready flew a Fokker T-2 Transport from New York to San Diego, the first nonstop, transcontinental flight, completing the 2,600 mile journey in 26 hours, 50 minutes, and 38.4 seconds. In subsequent years, Kelly served in the Phillipines, graduated from the Air Corps Tactical School, participated in ceremonies honoring Charles Lindbergh's 1927 flight from New York to Paris, visited his parents in Grove City (often landing in nearby fields or farms or at the old Grove City Airport), and participating in Grove City's Golden Jubilee in 1933. During World War II, Kelly served in England, North Africa, and the Mediterranean. He retired in 1948 as a full colonel and died in 1966. Kelly's official awards included the Mackay Trophy, Distinguished Flying Cross, and numerous prestigious medals. He was rated a command pilot, combat observer, and technical observer and had over five thousand hours of official flying time. Locally, the Grove City Airport, located on Oakley Kelly Drive, has a commemorative plaque in his honor.

TWIN CITY ELKS LODGE
By Roland Barksdale-Hall

For African-American migrants, adjustment to life in the North was not always smooth. Before 1908, the Shenango Valley's small African-American population worshipped at the AME Zion Church of Sharon, the First Baptist Church of South Sharon (later Farrell), and South Sharon's Triumph Church of the New Age. However, southern migrants found some African-American churches less than hospitable. Between 1908 and

During the late 1920s and 1930s, a number of prominent and not-so-famous aviators visited Mercer County, often unexpectantly. On March 4, 1928, two French trans-Atlantic fliers, Dieudonne Costes and Joseph Lebrix, were forced down on a farm near Sharpsville while flying from New York to Detroit. A month earlier, a small airplane carrying W. F. Piper, a businessman from Chicago, and the pilot Elmer O. Beardsley, crashed after taking off from the farm of Paul Hefius just east of Sharpsville. Both were hurt, but survived. On August 25, 1929, an open-cockpit Gypsy Moth landed on the grass strip of a small airport along Route 18 near Transfer. The plane was occupied by Charles Lindbergh and his wife, Anne Morrow Lindbergh. The airport owner, Frank Bowers, met the Lindberghs and, at their request, pumped ten gallons of gas into the plane's gas tank. The Lindberghs took off after a twenty-minute stay during which Charles signed the airport's registration book (now at the Greenville Historical Society). The Lindberghs flew on to Cleveland to complete their flight from New York. (The airport closed in 1931.) (Caption: Richard Christner)

1944, African-American newcomers to the Shenango Valley organized ten Baptist churches; three holiness churches; and a Catholic, a Colored Methodist Episcopal, and an African Methodist Episcopal church. Factors in selecting a church included class, worship styles, and the desire for autonomy. As might be expected, this proliferation of churches, rather than minimizing factional strife, actually contributed to the fragmentation of the community.

The existence of two local civil rights organizations further discouraged unity within the African-American community. In western Pennsylvania, competition existed between Marcus Garvey's Universal Negro Improvement Association (UNIA) and the National Association for the Advancement of Colored People (NAACP), as it did throughout the nation. Given the relatively small attendance at Mercer County NAACP meetings and the lapse of its chapter during the 1920s, its position in the community was not as strong as the influence of more tenuous than the local UNIA branch, which was under the capable direction of Michael S. Askerneese in its early years. African-American millworkers typically found Garvey's social and economic platform more in line with their concerns, and his organization had greater mass appeal among black steelworkers in western Pennsylvania.

During the prosperous 1920s, elitist fraternal groups also worked against African-American unity by promoting classism. The African-American Knights of Pythias Lodge was not only the richest fraternal group in the nation, it was also recognized as one of the

One of several private orchestras that often performed at public events in Farrell in the early 1900s was Miller's Band, here in 1927 at the Knights of Pythias memorial service. (Contributor: Roland Barksdale-Hall)

best organizations nationally. In Farrell, however, the Knights' Golden Rule Lodge and its female auxiliary, the Lily of the Valley, Court of Calanthe, lacked mass appeal; membership in the latter never exceeded forty. Their rich endowment attracted semi-skilled African-American workers, but their exorbitant fees, exclusionary practices, and accusations of financial mismanagement worked against them in the long run.

In Farrell, Prince Hall Masonry played an important role in the development of "Bourgeois" values, as it did nationally. Yet during the 1920s, it was no less susceptible to factional strife. Locally, Calumet Lodge, organized in 1917, became a stronghold of black intelligentsia: in 1920 its forty-one members reflected Farrell's middle-class African-American community. Among its ranks were four chefs, three clergymen, two barbers, two proprietors, two chauffeurs, two teamsters, a postal employee, a policeman, a mechanic, and a messenger. Three years later, a challenge to the status quo erupted when a group of African-American men moved to establish another Masonic Lodge in Farrell. Appeals for unity thwarted this drive, yet a rift among the wives of those involved led to two female auxiliaries until 1929, when attrition forced a merger.

In contrast, Farrell's Twin City Elks Lodge, organized in 1914, gave African-American steelworkers an opportunity to participate in their own institutions. Unlike other fraternal groups, the Elks accepted people into membership regardless of family background, socioeconomic status, or moral character; a policy that contributed to its popularity among southern migrants throughout western Pennsylvania. As a result, the Twin City Lodge, with members from Sharon and Farrell, flourished. Membership (which included unskilled southern workers as well as the elite of the community and everyone in between) peaked at over seven hundred, and all managed to coexist peacefully. It was recognized as the largest Elks lodge in Pennsylvania for almost twenty years. During these peak years, the membership of its female auxiliary, Zylphia Temple, reached three hundred.

The Twin City Lodge sponsored beneficial activities for young people, including basketball, roller-skating, a drum and bugle corps, majorettes, a marching band, and a youth council. During the Christmas season, the Elks provided treats for children and spent as much as $300 on charitable works in the African-American community. They also spon-

AFRICAN-AMERICANS IN MERCER
By Margaret Pizor Bower

"Mercer was an underground slave station as has been told many times, often by Hal Johnson. Some of the runaway slaves remained in Mercer, and their descendants lived there. Mr. and Mrs. Crosby Richards lived across from our barn on East Street with their sons, Roy and Roxy. Both young men worked for my grandfather and my dad [at Pizor Feed Mill].

"After the fire at the mill, Roxy went to Sharon to work for the Roux Feed Company. He married and had a family. On warm Sunday afternoons he would come over to see his mother and Roy. He would always stop beside our front porch and call a greeting to my dad.

"Roy never married and became a handyman to families in town who could afford such a service. When I was a preschooler, Roy would walk home for lunch, and I would watch for him as he came back up Plum Street. I remember running out to walk up to the corner with Roy. It was probably a little girl's chatter to a quiet older black man; but we would say 'Good-bye' at the street crossing.

"One day while I was over at my grandparents' home, my grandmother, Zelda Magee Pizor, said Mrs. Richards hadn't been well, and grandmother was taking a tray of food to her. (Welfare and Social Security didn't exist then.) I went with her and sat in the living room. The outside of the house was black from lack of paint, but the inside was neat and clean with some of the furniture covered with handmade quilts. Grandmother and Mrs. Richards sat together and chatted about their families.

"The black folks in Mercer were able to have a church and manse at the very end of South Otter Street and supported their own minister. On humid Sunday evenings in the summer, they would bring their chairs outside for service. I would stand in the middle of South Otter Street and listen to them sing.

"As the depression deepened, the members of the church moved away to look for better employment. The church and manse stood unused and were later sold for lumber. Today a housing project stands near where the church stood."

sored a softball team for adults; arranged field trips to Pittsburgh and Cleveland; and had raffles, picnics, and cabarets. The Lodge's club held floor shows and attracted such celebrities as Duke Ellington, Ray Charles, Peg Leg Bates, and Jesse Owens. Availability of steady work and decent wages enabled the community to support these Elks-sponsored activities. A national lodge dignitary, the dynamic J. Finley Wilson, traveled across the country telling people, "If your want to see somebody with money, go to Farrell, Pa."

The Elks lodges were considered by many politicians to be a strategic approach to the African-American community. In the aftermath of the Great Migration (roughly 1916 through 1930), it was the only national secret society to increase its membership nationally. Between 1922 and 1946, under Wilson's leadership, the organization grew from

32,000 to 500,000 members in 1,000 lodges. The phenomenal growth of the Twin City Lodge reflected this national trend. Small wonder then, that in addition to the national Elks leader Wilson, special guests at the 1926 Elks burning-of-the-mortgage ceremony and banquet included Sharon mayor Frank Gilbert and Farrell burgess J. H. Moody.

In Farrell—and across the country—African-American professionals participated in Elks activities to broaden their exposure to the varied lodge membership. Dr. Harry A. Whyte, for example, migrated to Farrell in 1918. Nine years later he was treasurer of the Twin City Elks and president of a local colored political-action committee. That same year he ran for a seat on the Farrell council, losing by a mere thirteen votes; his strong showing reflected the support of working-class lodge members. Between 1927 and 1935, he became exalted ruler and was recognized as a political boss; white and Negro politicians sought his endorsement. Another doctor with political ambitions was John H. Ingram. In 1927, Dr. Ingram was chaplain of the Twin City Lodge and a member of the board of trustees. Two years later he ran an unsuccessful campaign for Farrell tax collector.

Despite these two defeats, members of the Twin City Lodge did play an influential role in borough affairs. The first two African-American office holders elected in Farrell were Elks: In 1928 Charles S. Butler and John Edmunds served as register assessor and constable, respectively. Butler joined the Twin City Lodge in 1920. A doubler at the Farrell Works of the American Steel and Tin Plate Company (AMSTP), Butler joined the Elks band and by 1924 was exalted ruler. During his administration, the lodge held vigorous membership campaigns. Butler was also active in the Masons, but Edmunds belonged only to the Twin City Lodge. Edmunds also worked at AMSTP in Farrell; later he was hired as the Shenango Valley's first Negro insurance agent. In 1930, a charter member of Twin City Lodge, Joseph Young, succeeded Butler as the elected register assessor. Young had served as the lodge's treasurer from 1921 to 1926; and his wife, Cora, had held several offices in the Lodge's female auxiliary. Farrell's first elected African-American councilman, James Renshaw served a term concurrent with Young's. While little is known about Renshaw, family members were in the local Elks.

The fact that three out of four of these African-Americans elected to major public offices in Farrell were Elks is proof of the organization's high visibility in the borough. However, although African-American Elks were seen as leaders, their position in the larger community that determined their electability. Farrell was an unusual community because, with its short history, it had no significant white Anglo-Saxon Protestant presence, a circumstance that contributed to good race relations in the borough. Before World War II, African-American families in Farrell lived in mixed neighborhoods where neither they, nor any of the borough's numerous white ethnic populations, were able to maintain a majority. Under these circumstances, a degree of social mixing took place, and African-American migrants and European immigrants participated in local politics.

As early as 1915, political meetings were being held by ethnic club committees of the Italian, Jewish, Croatian, and African-American communities to endorse candidates. By 1928, elements from among the Croatian community encouraged John Edmunds to run for office and supported his candidacy. Similarly, James Renshaw received support from African-American Elks and from Italian and Jewish voters. Since African-Americans represented less than 12 percent of Farrell's total population in 1930, coalitions with ethnic whites were necessary to elect them to public office.

This period of judicious mixing soon ended, in 1931, as a result of plans by white ethnic businessmen to reclassify Farrell from a borough to a third-class city. Since African-Americans in Farrell had not developed enterprises comparable to those of ethnic whites, their political influence diminished during the change. Joseph Franek, a Slovak businessman, was the first mayor of the new city; and the city council was controlled by white ethnic business interests, with no representation from the African-American community.

The change from district to city-wide elections in Farrell did favor people with broad-based community connections, however. Therefore, Twin City Lodge's exalted ruler remained an influential person because of the organization's large membership. As spokesperson for Farrell's largest community-based African-American organization, the council of Elks leader Charles Vactor was sought between 1938 and 1951. Nevertheless, African-Americans were left as odd man out, as the Americanization of second-generation ethnic whites further encouraged conformity. Then, too, as the different ethnic groups began to marry within their communities, they formed even stronger voting blocks. As a result, by the end of World War II, African-American Elks were dismayed by the deterioration of race relations and subsequently turned inward to strengthen their own institutions.

Helping to meet the aspirations of African-American migrants—those from northern industrial communities as well as those from the rural South—Farrell's Twin City Elks Lodge touched the lives of many people. Its community-based programs and activities had wide appeal. During a period of major social discord, Twin City Lodge's open-door membership policy and ability to contain factional strife stimulated growth, while the unusual availability of steady work and good-paying jobs meant large numbers of African-Americans could afford the luxury of membership. A rallying point for the community and an advocate of black self-help, Twin City Elks Lodge was vital to the welfare of the community it served.

ELECTRICITY AND THE HOUSEWIFE
By Wally Wachter

"Without electricity, our mothers' chores bordered on slavery. They had to overcome the lack of today's conveniences by working from sunup to sundown, with little time for her own diversions or interests.

"Most of the average homes in my pre-school years had no electricity. Very few had in-house plumbing, attaching an important and urgent significance to the little shanty in the backyard.

"Thank goodness that most of the homes had natural gas in those days. It was used to cook, heat water for clothes-washing and baths, and to provide lighting. Gas was not used extensively for home-heating.

"Monday was always wash day. The only access to water was from a hand-operated pump that was located at the kitchen sink. It drew water from an outside well.

"For washing clothes, the housewife generally had a large oval-shaped copper tub in which she boiled all the clothes on the burners of a large cast-iron oven range. Most of the stoves were fired with gas, others with wood. Boiled with the clothes were chips off bars of homemade soap concocted from a recipe of lard and lye. After the boiling, the clothes were all hand-washed on a ridged washing board.

"The washing equipment also included one or two regular tubs used for rinsing. On one of them was fastened a wringer which had to be turned by hand, the clothes passing through hard rubber rolls. The process extracted much, but not all, of the water.

"Clothes were hung to dry in available spaces. In the summer they were hung outside in the sunshine. On inclement days, it was generally the kitchen, with makeshift lines strung every which way. Steam from the pots cooking the day's supper retarded the drying process. In the winter, large drying racks were placed in the dining room around a wood or coal stove that served to heat the whole house.

"Tuesday was ironing day. Ironing always was done in the kitchen where the women had easy access to the stove burners that were used to heat the heavy irons used for pressing. Most housewives had two or three of the irons, using one to press with while the others were heating.

"On Saturdays, the kitchen took on a new dimension, with the use of the same equipment. It was bath day. The washtub became a bathtub. The copper tub heated the water. The homemade soap was used only by those whose skin could condone it. The makeshift drying lines, draped with sheets, provided the privacy.

"A frequent disruption to the washing and bathing routines came in the bitter wintertime when the frigid weather froze the outside waterlines from the well to the pump. It took a hot fire from wood or coal above or beyond the pipes to thaw the lines.

"There was little time for diversion for our mothers after the long, hard day. There was no television and no radio. A few of the homes had phonographs which had to be cranked by hand to maintain the playing speed, then recranked when the tempo ran down.

"Some women resorted to crocheting, mending clothes and quilting. This had to be done under the dim illumination of a gas light.

"The gas fixtures each had cloth web-like 'mantles' which retained the gas and burned, casting off the light. The mantles were very light and delicate and broke with the slightest jar or bump. The light then was useless until the right-sized replacement could be bought. In most cases there was only one light fixture in each room. The wise homemakers always carried spare mantles for the important kitchen lights.

"I was about six years old when our family moved into a home with electricity. It was like taking a rocket trip to the moon. I spent several days just flicking switches, watching the lights go off and on at my command.

"It was just the beginning of a new way of life."

The woman, identified as "Molly," probably wondered why someone would want to photograph her as she cleaned laundry by hand on ridged washboard. Mary McDowell Vermeire remembers washday at her home in the early 1900s: "Wash day was always a very busy time. The previous day, water was pumped, carried into the kitchen range and poured into the reservoir attached to the side of the stove. With no washer or dryer, the following were needed: two large zinc tubs and stools, a washboard, a boiler for the top of the stove, and, of course, a strong back and arms. After being soaped with a cake of Naphtha Soap, each piece of clothing was rubbed on the board, doused in tub #1, and wrung out by hand. The white clothes were then placed in the boiler for some time. They were lifted out with an old broom stick and placed in tub #2 with the rinse water. After being wrung from the tub, they were carried to the yard and hung on the clothes lines. Summer wasn't too bad; they soon dried in the wind and sunshine. In winter one would often see the long undies frozen stiff on the line, the arms and legs grotesquely pointing in the air. In order to be truly dry, the clothes later were hung on the lines in the kitchen near the stove."

THE DEATH PENALTY
By Margo Letts

In the two hundred-year-old history of Mercer County, only four death penalty verdicts have been given. Two young men were put to death in 1925. The other verdicts came later in the 1900s, and those sentences were eventually commuted to life in prison.

On March 1, 1924, William Z. Turner of West Middlesex was killed during a robbery at his gas station. Michael Weiss and John Girsch (both of Farrell) were accused of the heinous crime. After being caught in Cleveland, Weiss and Girsch confessed to the crime. Girsch gave details of the murder to the police in his confession and said he did not fire his gun. However, Weiss confessed that Turner shot first, then Girsch, and then Weiss. They both said the other was the murderer. They had already robbed Turner's Gas Station once in January. After the March robbery and murder, they went to Farrell, robbed a tailor, and fled to Cleveland where they ran out of money and were captured. The defense alleged that the confessions were coerced. Girsch denied his confession, and Weiss denied killing Turner.

However, the jury did not believe them and, after deliberating nine hours, found them guilty. The average person attending the trial thought that Girsch was lying when he testified and did not believe that he was abused by the police officers. These two men were the first to be sentenced to death in Mercer County. The Pennsylvania Board of Pardons denied that the sentences be changed to life in prison. In the end, Girsch took all the blame for the crime, trying to spare Weiss's life. Although Weiss said he was ready to die, he still professed his innocence. Both tried to escape from the Mercer County Jail before they were transferred to Rockview Penitentiary (Center County), where they were executed on October 29, 1925.

On the night of February 18, 1938, Edward Williams, a barber in Jamestown, walked into a tavern in Greenville and shot Nick Floros, the owner. The shooting occurred a few days after the two men had had an argument. Williams had insulted Mrs. Floros, and the police told him to leave town. Williams had gone into the restaurant and immediately opened fire on Floros. After one gun was empty, he pulled another and began firing.

A Mr. Johnson was Williams's lawyer, and the trial was his first jury case since he had passed the bar. He fainted a few minutes after beginning his summation, so the case was delayed a few hours. Williams's defense was that he had been drunk for weeks consuming a quart or more of whiskey a day. He denied any memory of arming himself and entering the restaurant. He had no knowledge of what happened until he saw Floros on the floor.

The jury deliberated seven hours before coming to a verdict. Johnson asked for a new trial, but the motion was denied. In December 1938, the Pennsylvania Board of Pardons commuted Williams's sentence to life in prison. The *Mercer Dispatch* reported that sparing his life would only encourage contempt for the laws which the courts must administer.

John Martin (Farrell) was convicted September 20, 1952, of killing his wife Susan in their home. Martin had come home drunk on August 16 and stabbed his wife. He claimed he did not remember doing anything to her after he picked up his knife. However, his nine-year-old stepdaughter saw him enter the bedroom and beat her mother. The couple had been married for only two months, and Martin was on parole for another stabbing at the time of his wife's murder. The trial lasted five days, and the jury was out for 4.5 hours. He was sentenced to die, but in 1970 his sentence was changed to life in prison.

HOME BREW
By Wally Wachter

"From the time the 18th [Amendment (Prohibition)] was enacted in 1917 and ratified in 1919, until its repeal it was illegal to manufacture or sell alcoholic beverages in the United States.

"Many with a palate for the potent refreshments took matters in their own hands, defying the law and the revenuers. They turned the seclusion of their cold cellars (most homes had unheated potions of their basements where potatoes, apples and home-canned fruits and vegetables were stored) into their own alcohol labs. Most of the time the results were costly, and in some cases disastrous.

"Winemaking was an art. There were those who brought their expertise with them from the old country. They chose the right seasoned barrels. They selected the best grapes. They knew how much sugar to add. They knew how many days and thunderstorms it took to properly ferment the grapes. And when to tap the keg and bottle their concoctions.

"The homes of these experts generally were the gathering places for neighborhood men and ethnic brothers to sip, to taste, to gulp the fine vintage while the maker beamed with pride over his achievement.

"But these experts were few. Some of their friends thought they knew better ways to enhance the recipes and took up the hobby on their own. They washed out old pickle barrels and bought the cheapest grapes. They ignored the fine points in speeding the fermentation process.

"They found out that instead of rare vintage wine they had discovered a new process for making vinegar. When tolerable, it ended up on salads or made a good hair rinse for the ladies of the house. Most of the time it was poured into the sewer before their friends could hear of it or sample it.

"Home brew often was the beer that made the brewers infamous.

"Almost every household had a braumeister. A large earthenware crock generally was the vat. In it was mixed the water, the malt, the hops, the yeast in amounts that varied with the different experimenters.

"It always was puzzling to me as a youth how grocery stores could sell cases upon cases of canned malt and hops without raising the suspicions of the prohibition enforcers. I have never heard of those products being used for anything but home brew.

"When the time was ripe, or thought to be ripe, the beer was siphoned through a small corrugated rubber hose into bottles, generally dark brown. The bottles were capped with a gadget that resembled a water pump, the handle forcing the cap onto the opening of the bottle.

"On many occasions the time was not ripe. Or the bottled brew was stored in a place that was too warm. This triggered explosions that often happened in the middle of the night, waking everybody from a deep sleep. One exploding bottle often set off a chain reaction, sometimes shattering most of the bottles. Despite scrubbing and scouring in cleaning the mess that was left, the family had to endure the yeasty odor for days.

"The beer that was left varied in taste. Some tasted like hops. Some tasted like malt. Some tasted like yeast. But all of it appeared to be potent, much more potent than the beer that is sold over the bars today. Despite how it tasted, every home braumeister bragged that his beer was the best.

"The temperate households had the same experiences with root beer. But it was legal. A root beer extract was available in little brown bottles which was mixed in the crocks with water and yeast. It produced a fizz that when bottled prematurely had the same explosive qualities as home brew."

Keeping Cool
By Wally Wachter

"Air conditioners were a thing of the future. Refrigerators were boxes with square insets on the top to fit blocks of ice. Ice cubes were what you could chip from the ice block, but if you chipped too much away, you jeopardized the food inside of the box that you were trying to preserve. Ceiling fans were found only in grocery stores and restaurants. Milk would seldom get cold. Taking a dip meant walking or hitchhiking miles in the hot sun to Shenango River swimming holes at Purple Cow and Fruit's Mills or a trek to the infamous B. A. beach in Wheatland, near the old Carnegie cinder dump. And then the walk back home in the blistering sun.

"Crude refrigeration that we considered a convenience in those day, nevertheless was a problem.

"Every morning the iceman would make his rounds. Families who were fortunate enough to have ice boxes would make their daily ice needs known to the vendor by means of a four-cornered card which they hung on their front porches. The corners were numbered 25, 50, 75 and 100. Whichever corner was up was the size of the block that the iceman would chip and carry by iron tongs to the ice boxes.

"Neighborhood children would gather at the rear of the ice wagon, and while the man was making his delivery, would pick up the small bits of ice that flaked off the blocks and refresh themselves with them. Ice supplies would last from two to three days. Home-delivered milk with thick cream at the top of the bottle (milk was not homogenized in those days) was generally delivered before the iceman cometh. It would last three days at most without souring. Butter would be rancid in less than a week, but it was only 19 cents a pound. There was no such thing as freezing leftovers.

"Neighborhood grocery stores in the pre-supermarket days also felt the inadequacies of refrigeration. They had larger ice boxes where they kept the perishables such as milk, cream and cheeses. But their produce was wilted at the end of the day and most of what was left ended on the garbage pile.

"My first job after graduating from high school [in the mid-1930s] was as a clerk for Kroger Grocery and Baking Co. at a store in Farrell. A suggestion I made five days after starting on the job won me a $50 bonus and the opportunity to attend their managers' school. It was just a simple idea of placing the leftover produce in layers in a large barrel, with chipped ice between the layers. The next day, the fruits and vegetables were as fresh-looking as they had been the day before. All of the stores in the Kroger chain adopted the idea.

"Children, in those days, awaited the iceball man. He was an enterprising young man who fashioned a two-wheeled cart, topped with an oil cloth roof, which he pushed through town selling iceballs. His cart contained a large block of ice and bottles of various fruit flavors. He shaved ice from the block into paper cups and saturated them with the flavor of the youngsters' choice. These were iceballs. You could buy one-cent, two-cent or five-cent quantities.

(Source: *Mercer Dispatch and Republican*, December 5, 1930)

Sandy Lake's clear waters brought another industry into Stoneboro. From the 1880s to the 1920s many people were employed during the winter months as ice cutters. The firms that operated the two huge frame icehouses (pictured) on the south shore were based in Oil City and Pittsburgh: Stoneboro and Chautauqua Lake Ice Company and the Consolidated Ice Company. Each firm could store up to 40,000 tons of ice cakes, which were packed in sawdust for delivery. As the weather turned warmer, ice was shipped in refrigerated railcars to western Pennsylvania cities. Of course, ice-skating and ice boating were also popular pastimes on Sandy Lake. A large dance hall (see long white building between the two ice operations) was opened by Lake Recreation on the south shore of Sandy Lake. The hall was opened just after World War I and hosted many famous entertainers such as Cab Caloway, Doris Day, Guy Lombardo, and Lawrence Welk. (In its declining years, the hall functioned as a roller skating rink. It burned to the ground on New Year's Day, 1946.) (Contributor: Frederick Houser)

"Many prominent valley residents, including several doctors, earned their college money in the iceball business.

"Another hot summer refresher was giant towering ice cream cones that you could buy for a nickel at Isaly stores which had several locations in the valley [and elsewhere in Mercer County].

"On exceptionally hot days, congenial firemen in the various communities would provide a treat for the kiddies. They would attach fire hoses to hydrants and spray water on the bathing suit-clad youngsters, a refreshing relief from the heat."

FUNERALS
By Wally Wachter

"When death came to a member of the family it put an extra heavy burden on the household. Undertakers, as they were called then, had only embalming facilities. They had no quarters for displaying the bodies. Consequently the caskets were taken to the family homes where constant visiting hours were held for three days before the funeral.

"The open caskets were displayed in the living room, draped with floral tributes from relatives, neighbors and friends. The adjoining dining room had a buffet table set with casseroles and cold cuts brought in by neighbors. The kitchen was a barroom stocked with whiskey and beer.

"Friends who came to pay their last respects generally stayed for hours in the crowded house, partaking of the food and drink.

"In order to allow the family to get some rest, several close friends were designated to stay up and guard the body all night. It never quite worked that way. A whole houseful generally stayed, nibbling and sipping, and the family, obligated to their considerate friends, stayed up, too, and never did get their rest.

"The wake generally lasted three nights until the funeral.

"Large floral wreaths or bouquets were mounted on or near the front door of the deceased, indicating a death in the household.

"On the day of the funeral, the casket was taken to church in a white hearse, with a padded brocade interior, for the funeral rites. Neighborhood children, curious over the mysteries of death, would line the sidewalks in front of the house and church to get a glimpse of the coffin.

"The memories of loved ones, suffering in illness and lying cold in the grayish-white casket in the living room, gave an eerie feeling that was hard to erase from the minds of youngsters. They lived with those visions for years. Today's method of displaying the deceased in a funeral parlor, with limited calling hours, has eased pressures on family members and allows them to remember their departed loved ones as they were alive in their homes.

"One of the chilling memories in my early school years was the death of a neighborhood playmate from diphtheria. When I worked up enough nerve to pay my last respects, I found that his body had been laid out behind the porch window and could be viewed only from the porch through the glass. No one could enter the house because of the communicable disease that had taken his life.

"The weeks and months after the funeral brought more grief for the bereaved. By tradition set by customs of their forebears, there was a long mourning period. It varied anywhere from six months to a year, generally depending on nationality customs.

"If a widow was seen in public wearing other than a black dress, or a widower without his black arm bank, it would set tongues wagging. Family members of the deceased were bound to refrain from attending any social functions during the mourning period or they were doomed to be looked on as disrespectful to the dead.

"Although a few still observe them, some of these strict customs have vanished but are still imprinted in our memories."

"Extras" Brought Excitement of News
By Wally Wachter

"Newspapers always have been the chief source of providing the news. Particularly in the days before radio and television.

"They were exciting times when the shouts of 'Extra! Extra! Read all about it!' shattered the stillness of the evening or the night, heralding some major news event that occurred after the afternoon editions were off the press.

"People would flock out of their homes either to hear the vendors scream out the headlines or to shell out their three cents for a copy of the hot issue.

"Two competing papers in the area—the *Herald* and the *News Telegraph* which later merged into today's *Herald*—were both alert to the happenings and tried to beat each other on the street with the big scoop.

"The first 'extra' I remember was on the death of President Warren G. Harding and his succession in the White House by Calvin Coolidge. Although the news event held little significance for a four-year-old, the household excitement generated by the headline left an indelible impression on me.

"A later 'extra' shocked the area over the brutal slaying of a young girl in another part of the country by a man who later became widely known as the 'gorilla man.' While he was a fugitive, a fear spread over the entire nation. There were many reports and rumors that he had been seen in this area and local police picked up several suspects which they later had to release.

"Parents kept their doors locked, escorted their children to school and never allowed the youngsters to play outside the homes. The 'gorilla man' eventually was captured, tried and executed. His exploits were a ripe target for the 'extras.'

"Sporting events in the late evening always were good subjects for the 'extras.' Sports fans would wait with bated breath for the midnight shouts of newspaper vendors after a major prizefight or sporting event. I distinctly recall the stunning news of a fancy virtually unknown by the name of Gene Tunney defeating the great Jack Dempsey for the world's heavyweight championship.

"One of the most surprising items heralded by the special editions was about a young airmail pilot named Charles A. Lindbergh who flew a mono-plane non-stop from New York to Paris.

"Radio began coming into its own in the late part of the 1920s, but offered no threat to the newspapers' way of breaking the outstanding news happenings.

"Most radio receivers were battery-operated sets with earphones that allowed only one person at a time to listen. Even when radio became more sophisticated, stations were located only in large cities and were unable to adequately supply the news. Therefore it did not concentrate on it. It wasn't until the networks formed and smaller communities began to start their own radio stations that some of the gloss was removed from the 'extra' editions.

"However, the 'extra' cry continued through the early 1930s. It heralded the 1929 St. Valentine's Day Massacre in Chicago, the stock market crash that set off the Great Depression that same year, the untimely death of Notre Dame football coach Knute Rockne in an airplane crash in 1931, the kidnapping of Charles Lindbergh's son in 1932, and the almost nightly episodes of bank robber John Dillinger in early 1934 which included 'visits' to area banks in Volant and Farrell, and eventually his being gunned down in July of that year.

"These were the 'extras' I remember. When they broke the silence of the night they brought surprise, or shock, or fear, or good news, or sadness. Their way of breaking the news seemed to have a more exciting impact than today's 'special news bulletins' on radio or television."

HOSPITALS

By Wally Wachter

"Hospitals in those years were dedicated mostly to surgery patients and afforded only by a scarce few. There was no hospitalization insurance then. But those in dire need of the institutions' facilities could arrange to pay a little at a time.

"Most of the seriously ill people remained in their homes and were treated there. The family doctor would make daily visits to provide medication from his little black satchel, a catchall for stethoscope, hypodermic needles that came in little wooden boxes, and tiny round phials of colorful pills.

"When medical help was futile, most of the hopelessly ill died in their own beds. Many of them wanted this because they believed it was pre-destined. Others simply could not afford the luxuries of a hospital.

"Most babies, in those days, were born at home, many delivered by the neighborhood midwives who were well-trained in the delivery process of normal births, but knew little of what to do when complications presented themselves. The incidence of childbirth deaths and stillborns, which is practically nil today, was excessively high.

"Even in hospitals, which lacked today's sophisticated equipment, any type of surgery presented a big risk. Today's operations like appendectomies, tonsillectomies and even gallbladder removal, routine and safe, were touch-and-go in those days."

St. Anthony's Croatian Roman Catholic Church (Sharon)
By Helen Marenchin

The Croatian people began settling in the Shenango Valley in the late 1800s. It has been estimated that between 1892 and 1894, at least thirty-five Croatian families resided in the Valley. In later years, as these numbers increased, the Croatian immigrants realized the need for a Croatian church. Although Catholic churches existed in the area, the language barrier proved to be increasingly difficult.

Finally in 1924, after many years of struggle and disappointments, Bishop Gannon of the Erie Diocese appointed Reverend Leo J. Medic, a Croatian Franciscan, pastor for the Croatian people in this area. Because they had no church, Medic conducted mass at the Hungarian Holy Trinity Church on Fruit Avenue in Farrell. In the meantime, property was purchased on Idaho Street and Sherman Avenue in Sharon with the intention of some day building a church. Almost two years later a new church was erected on this site.

In 1926, a beautiful, engraved bell and an organ were purchased. Catechism classes were initiated, and twenty-seven children received their first holy communion in 1927. Just as the church was progressing, however, disaster struck when the building was completely destroyed by fire. The congregation once again returned to Holy Trinity Church to celebrate mass.

Meanwhile, an "independent" Croatian church on Market Street was heavily in debt. Barko Bakmaz purchased the mortgage to the church and the cemetery on New Castle Road and transferred it to the supported Croatian church with Medic as pastor. The first mass was celebrated in 1929; the cemetery was consecrated and named Mt. Carmel Cemetery.

Six months later Medic was reassigned to another parish, and another Franciscan priest, Reverend Spiro Andrijanic, was named as his replacement. Andrijanic was a kind and spiritual leader. Under his pastorship, church membership increased, and the small building on Market Street could no longer accommodate the large number of parishioners. Fundraising efforts began for a new church on the property on Idaho Street.

A singing society and a tamburitza group were formed to present plays, concerts, and dances. These events were held in the Croatian Hall, and all proceeds set aside for the new church.

The St. Joseph Ladies Society was organized to help raise funds. They catered dinners and special banquets and took care of the altars and the rectory. Karolina Anjelic was the first president and continued in that capacity for many years. Under her leadership, they raised enough money to purchase the altar for the new church that would eventually be built. The young, unmarried parishioners also wanted to participate so they established their own group, the Youth of St. Anthony, with Frank Klecic, Katherine Stefanak, and Marco Pendel as its leaders.

Andrijanic was transferred to Chicago before the new church was finished. Another kind, caring, and dynamic priest arrived in 1931: Reverend Anselm Sliskovich. With his encouragement, the men formed the Sacred Heart of Jesus Society, later renamed the Holy Name Society, with Frank Jereb as its first president. A new church committee was appointed with Anton Pintar as its leader.

In spite of Great Depression, Sliskovich continued plans for constructing a new church, and in 1934 the cornerstone was dedicated. Everyone helped in the building of the church. The men and their sons did the actual physical labor, the youngsters ran errands, and the ladies of St. Joseph Society prepared the food that was donated by the parishioners who owned farms. Sliskovich not only supervised the work, but he also labored as hard as the men, working with them to get the building completed. After many interruptions in building due to lack of funds, bad weather, and material shortages, the building was completed in 1938. The rectory was added in 1939, and the church was complete.

In 1940, the St. Theresa Altar Society was organized with Mary Phillips as president. They helped with banquets, took care of the altar, and most especially managed the children's religious education. The ladies of St. Theresa approached the nuns from Sacred Heart, who initially agreed to teach catechism every Saturday at St. Anthony's. The society's goal then became to have nuns stay at St. Anthony's. They realized this undertaking was enormous, as the nuns would need a convent, which was almost unthinkable at that time. After the Sacred Heart nuns stopped teaching at St. Anthony's, Sliskovich taught religious classes with the help of volunteers. Over the years, the ladies of St. Theresa's never lost sight of their goal, and eventually it was accomplished.

In 1947, Sliskovich was transferred, and Fr. Francis Cuturic was assigned as his replacement. When St. Theresa's ladies informed him of their desire and the church's need for its own sisters, Cuturic not only supported the idea, but also was instrumental in helping them reach this pinnacle. He arranged to have three nuns assigned to St. Anthony's and encouraged St. Theresa's with ideas on how to secure funds to build a convent to house the sisters. With their confidence and tenacity intact, these ladies approached the American Croatian Citizens Society at their monthly meeting and asked for their monetary contribution. The group immediately voted unanimously to donate the huge sum to pay for the cost of the building. With the support of the parishioners, St. Theresa's also held fundraisers and contributed to the project.

In 1947, Sr. M. Anne, Sr. M. Bernadette, and Superior Sr. M. Paula, from the Daughters of Divine Charity Order, arrived at St. Anthony's new convent. With the addition of the nuns, the parish improved. They organized the young people; taught them catechism; trained the altar boys; taught music, piano, and choir; and organized the young ladies Sodality and annual May Crowning of our Blessed Mother. The sisters cleaned and decorated the altar, and a form of order and respect was instilled in the parish. The interior of the church was redecorated, and new pews and steam heating system installed. The young and the old were involved in parish life and the church flourished.

In 1949, Cuturic was replaced by the former Franciscan Commisar, the Very Rev. Dr. David Zrno. Loved and respected by the people, Zrno was an inspiration to the parish. He first thought that St. Anthony's should have its own school. However, being conservative, he realized this goal was not possible until repairs and renovations of the church were completed. Much work was done, including installing beautiful stained glass windows. Zrno purchased the Tellers pipe organ from St. Anthony's Italian Church in Farrell and had it completely rebuilt. It is still in use today.

St. Anthony's Church in Sharon, in 2000. (Photographer: Vonda Minner)

To begin saving money for the school he hoped to build, Zrno started bingo games in the antonium and helped institute the famous "Noodle Brigade" by purchasing the equipment St. Theresa's requested. Zrno's greatest legacy to St. Anthony's Church is the many people he helped through Catholic Charities. People sent here from Croatia found refuge through him and the church. He assisted these people until they could adjust to this new life and become self-supporting. He helped them find jobs, homes, and new friends and acquaintances. Most became faithful members, assimilating and contributing innovative ideas to help the church.

As the church continued to grow it became apparent that an assistant pastor was needed. In the ensuing years, several priests served in this capacity. One, Fr. Roko, helped organize a successful tamburitza group involving children and parents. Under the direction of William Prezgay, they presented concerts and Kolo dances. For a money-raising project, the strudel sales were started with parents and parishioners baking and selling the delicious pastries.

When Zrno was reassigned in 1958, he left St. Anthony's a hefty bank account to be used towards the school he dreamed of building. Fr. Zoran Ostojich soon arrived and remained until 1972. He and his assistants continued supporting the Kolo groups and were involved with the new parishioners from Croatia. In 1959 the rectory was again remodeled and enlarged. But his largest task was still before him: a parish school.

Fr. Zoran was aware of the need for a school. He personally approached the Archbishop with the plan and was granted permission to proceed with the building. Ground was broken in May 1960, and classes were held in September in the yet unfinished school. Initially four grades were staffed by three nuns. Each year another grade was added and by 1965, the first class was graduated. Ground adjacent to the school had been purchased earlier for a playground area and parking lot, which were completed in 1962. The antonium hall was refurbished for the children's use, and basketball nets installed. The school basketball teams were competitive with the other parochial schools in the Valley. Many students gained experience and went on to play basketball in high school. The parents organized the Parent Teacher Organization to assist the school. To raise money, card parties, fashion shows, calendar teas, and other social functions became a mainstay of the school. Parents assisted in the classrooms as homeroom mothers, planning holiday and birthday parties, and chaperoning various student activities.

During Fr. Zoran's tenure, changes in the Catholic Church were instituted by the Ecumenical Council under Pope John XXIII. The Latin mass was replaced by the English mass; the priest now celebrated mass facing the people from a table in front of the altar. Fr. Zoran complied with these changes and had the old white altar removed and replaced with the new ecumenical requirements. Another change requested by the Bishop was the selection of a church council to serve as a consultative board to the parish priest. Ray Matta served as first council president.

After fifteen years of faithful service, Fr. Zoran was transferred to Beaver Falls in 1972. Fr. Bruno Raspudic became the new pastor only to be transferred a year later. During his short stay, however, he succeeded in revamping the CCD program and purchased new buses for the school and a car for the sisters.

Fr. Jerome Kucan followed immediately after Fr. Bruno's departure. More repairs were made and new items donated to the church to prepare it for its fiftieth anniversary celebration. Parishioners Lena Sulich, Emma Sulich, and Evelyn and Bernard Wlodarski donated the "Risen Christ," which was placed above the tabernacle, and a processional crucifix and statues of St. Anthony and St. Francis, all in memory of their beloved deceased. Special cloths for the altars and a new mass missal were donated by Gloria Parcetich in thanksgiving. In memory of deceased pioneer members Joseph and Helen

Ference, Joseph and Anita Ference and Gibbs Flower Shoppe decorated the altars. Truly, this celebration was a glorious reminder of the many accomplishments incurred since that small church on Market Street served as the house of worship for the Croatian people in the Shenango Valley.

The years between 1976, when Fr. Jerome left, and 1989 were years of struggle. The Valley was in the throes of economic decline due to the crisis in the steel industry. Most of the mills in the area had ceased operations leaving abandoned factories, unemployed workers, and demoralization of the communities. Women were not going to work and not available for volunteering their services; the youth were leaving the area to seek employment or just moving to escape the dismal, distressed environment. The church was directly impacted by these circumstances. Church membership slowly decreased, contributing to the decline in school enrollment. With only eighty students enrolled and mounting debt, the school was no longer self-sustaining. The burden on the church became unbearable. During these years, the pastors each in their turn tried to keep the school and the church intact. Eventually, the church council had to close the school to save the church. The school building was sold to the Blind Association and the CCD program was expanded to accommodate the children affected. Mary Ann Bonani agreed to act as coordinator to keep the program operating.

In 1983, Fr. Ilija Puljic founded the St. Leopold Mandic Kolo Group to teach the children to read and write Croatian and to learn about the culture of the Croatian people. Vinko Pujic helped in the organization, and he and Ann Mesin assumed the difficult job of teaching the children. The group traveled throughout the United States and Canada presenting traditional songs and dances of Croatia. They held fund-raisers and clothing drives for humanitarian aid during the Croatian war for independence and to raise money for the needs of the Church.

New fund-raising projects were instituted and prior ones continued: catering banquets; selling strudels, nutrolls, and noodles; and the most extensive project, baking French bread and various pastries and rolls. Initially, the food was sold at the Shenango Valley Mall. For five days, twice a year the products were made at the church and transported to the mall. When this was no longer feasible, monthly sales were held in the antonium. Many men and women worked hard to make this a success, giving unselfishly of their time and labor. Even the sisters and students participated with a unique idea; they collected pennies from all over the community, with the help of the local newspaper. All this work did not rescue the school, but did help in other causes.

At this time, Fr. Galinac approached Fred Hughes to accept the position of finance manager. The debts were astronomical and someone was needed to control expenditures and income and attempt to balance the budget and pay the bills. Fred Hughes set up a system where nothing was purchased without his prior approval and that was only granted if there were cash to pay for it. He kept in communication with Erie to slowly begin paying the accumulated debt owed them. To finance needed repairs to the church, campaigns were held for each project. The parishioners, with new hope, became motivated to save the church. They rallied behind every campaign and project and were most generous in their donations. When Fr. Vincent Cvikovic replaced Fr. Galinac in 1989, he continued with these plans and also gained the support of the parishioners.

In 1991 the council, after years of discussions regarding building a cemetery chapel, decided to launch a campaign to raise funds. People were asked to donate to a chapel fund for memorials, remembrances, anniversaries, etc. The response was overwhelming. When Fr. Dan Kresinski replaced Fr. Vince as pastor in 1991, not only was the goal surpassed, but the people again more than supported the project with volunteer work, materials, and furnishings for the interior. The dedication and dinner celebration was held in 1995 just as Fr. Dan was assigned to Sacred Heart Parish in Sharon. The twenty-five-member choir, with renewed spirit and under the direction of organist and choirmaster Christopher Novak, became more aware of their importance as an integral part of the liturgy. They began, and continue, to sing at every funeral mass and during services at the cemetery chapel to bring comfort and closure to the bereaved. Faithfully attending rehearsals they learned to combine the new hymns with the traditional Croatian, appropriate for holidays and all special occasions.

When Fr. Matt Ruyechan arrived in Sharon, the church was thriving, but much was still to be accomplished. Fr. Matt, a young spiritual but "common" priest, made an immediate impression on the people. His friendliness and caring nature, his concern for all, was the catalyst to inspire the people both spiritually and sociably. The church membership continues to increase as well as attendance at mass. A general feeling of hope and confidence and a keen desire to cooperate together in sustaining St. Anthony's Church prevail.

Stoneboro Fire Department
By Frederick Houser

Stoneboro's first firefighting equipment, purchased by the borough council in 1888, was a hand-pulled, two-wheeled mixing tank. Water was supplied by a bucket brigade, and pressure for this water developed from the chemical reaction of soda and water in the mixing tank. Not until 1928, however, was a Stoneboro Volunteer Fire Company organized, with twenty-two volunteers and a used fire truck the borough had bought for $200.

Hydrants were installed as the borough water system was put in soon after 1900. A new hand truck, pulled by volunteers, carried a 2.5-inch fire hose. This system ended firefighting by "bucket brigades and snowballs." A fire bell, installed in the tower of the original borough building on Beech Street, summoned firemen to duty. A secondary alarm system was provided by railroaders working in the yard and on the shop track who would blow the whistles of the steam locomotives to alert the town if they spotted a fire while at work. "Anyone who ever heard the train whistles blowing in the middle of the night to summon volunteers will never forget it," one observer noted at that time. In 1930 the original fire bell was replaced by a large siren on the old borough building, and this alarm was subsequently moved to the nearby fire hall on Linden Street.

(Between 1951 and 1976, Stoneboro's firemen responded to 375 alarms—a few of these were false, others involved vehicle accidents, and many others were responses to out-of-town fires alone or jointly with other area fire companies. Since the inception of the 9-1-1 countywide system in 1995, the number of alarms has increased substantially. Firemen are alerted routinely when any type of ambulance activity takes place. The company has consistently put in service new equipment as technology has advanced. It now has five different emergency vehicles; the newest is a 1998 high-capacity pumper costing $300,000. It is a far cry from that 1888 mixing tank.)

Teaching in a One-Room School
By Mary McDowell Vermeire

"I finished high school in Sheakleyville and then went to Edinboro Normal College for a summer term of six weeks. I then taught a year in the country school receiving $60 a month. When I went to my first school, I rode the four miles back and forth each day on an old swayback horse we bought for $25. It was a 'tuff' thing to do, traveling that way and building the fire in the large pot bellied stove. I also had the cleaning and sweeping to do each day.

"Even when I was in grade school, I never had any idea that I'd be anything but a teacher. Whether it was because there were many teachers in my family or that my folks always encouraged me to be at the top of my class, I don't know. I never questioned where the money would come from, I knew I must go to Normal School. In those days one could teach a country school by attending a six-week course at Normal after graduating from a four-year high school. My first year teaching was a country school, all eight grades, in Deer Creek Township. Even though I rode the horse to school, I never missed a day. It was over country roads, feet deep in the winter with snow and in the spring with mud. I had to keep the horse in a nearby farmer's barn during the day. The school was located in a large field with many trees. At noon we'd sit on the grass and eat our lunch. In back of the school was a house in which the coal and wood was kept. Also there were the two outhouses, one for the boys and one for the girls.

"Inside were rows of screwed-down desks, a large pot-bellied stove, and nails along the walls where our coats were hung. Of course I had to get there early enough in the morning to build the fire and have the room warm. I stayed after school to sweep the floor and get the kindling ready for the fire next day. For my $60 a month, I had to teach [children in grades 1 through 8]. I taught Reading, Spelling, Writing, English, Arithmetic, Geography, and History to grades 3 to 8 inclusive. In the first two grades only Reading, Spelling, Arithmetic, and Writing were taught.

"After the first term was over, I returned to Edinboro for one year and several summer terms. I waited on tables in the dining room to help with the cost and also delivered mail in the dorms.... After receiving my diploma, I got a school in Farrell. I taught there steady with only time off when [my two children] were born. After [they were] in school, I went back to teaching and continued until I retired in 1966."

KIDS' PLAY

By Wally Wachter

"The closest thing to [the arcade games of the 1990s] were nickel pinball machines, not as sophisticated as today's variety. But those were found mainly in pool parlors where kids under 18 were forbidden to tread.

"You could spot youngsters with a keen interest in major league baseball by the imprint of screen on their noses. They crowded around the front doors of the pool halls, noses to the screen, to glimpse the large scoreboards and check scores on games they were interested in. All the scores were delivered via a glass-domed Western Union ticker which all pool halls had.

"One corner of some of the giant scoreboards had a special block to chalk in the day's 'bug' number—illegal in those days but still very popular.

"With a lack of today's electronic fun, kids back then had to make their own good times. Most of their time was spent in backyard and alley games which had been passed on or were made up as they went along.

"Almost every alley telephone pole had an old open-ended coffee can mounted on it. It was here that the youngsters learned their basketball, trying to shoot a grapefruit-size rubber ball through the tiny coffee-can opening.

"Pickup games in cinder-based alleys generally ended with scraped knees, black eyes or bloody palms.

"There were many other improvised alley games that kept kids out of the house and busy all day.

"One was caddy. A three-inch cut from an old broomstick was whittled into a point at each end. A paddle was fashioned from a flat board. It was similar to the one used by teachers to discipline their naughty students.

"From a home base, a player would strike the pointed end of the 'caddy,' flipping it into the air, and while it was airborne, would see how far he could swat it with the flat end of the paddle. The winner was determined by the number of paddle-lengths the caddy ended up from the home base.

"Another popular game in those days was 'durkee on the tincan.' A tincan was set up in the middle of the alley. A large rock was stationed on top of it. One player, determined as 'it,' would be a guard of the rock. Other players fortified themselves with large rocks of their choice and from about 20 yards away would roll their rocks at the tincan. When the can was upset, players who had missed the can could rush and retrieve their rocks while the guard set up the can and its rock again. If he tagged anyone before they escaped from the 'home' zone, the captured player became 'it' and the game continued.

"For the rough and more aggressive youngsters, there was 'shinny.' This was hockey on tincans. Instead of ice skates, players would imbed each foot into the side of a small tincan. Another can was crumpled into a small ball and served as a puck. The hockey sticks were clubs or poles of the players' choice—no regulations on size or weight.

"Then the free-for-all began. Everybody tried to hit the little can. Mostly they hit the other players' legs. The name 'shinny' probably emanated from the numerous bruised shins that resulted from the pastime.

"The more placid youths spent their time flipping baseball cards, playing a baseball game with dice, or joining the girls in a fast game of jacks or a rope-flipping round of 'I went downtown to meet Miss Brown.'"

From another article, Wachter continues, "while the boys were occupying the alleys with their sports, the fronts of the houses and sidewalks were generally buzzing with girls' activities.

"Most homes back then had front porches. During the lazy summer vacation days it was a familiar sight to see rings of girls on each porch working on their 'twosies or threesies' in a hot game of jacks. Meanwhile, on the sidewalks in front of the homes, others chalked squares for 'hopscotch,' a game that tested balance while hopping on one leg and bending over to pick up a slate or rock. Sometimes, in the lack of chalk, slate was used to draw the lines on the walk.

"In the front yard, or another part of the sidewalk, a game of 'High Water, Low Water' generally was in progress. This was a rope exercise in which two girls holding the ends of the rope would continue to raise its level as the third would attempt jump over it. The winner was determined by whomever could jump the highest.

"Rope-jumping was a great girls' pastime, with many games and music-chiming rhymes associated with it.

"In the streets, girls played a game of 'Kick the Can,' a little tamer version of the 'shinny' the boys were playing in the back alley. They would set a can in the middle of the street and then scramble to see who could kick it. There were few interruptions from passing cars in those days.

"Probably the most popular games for the fairer sex were playing 'House' and 'School.'

Horses drew early milk "trucks," used to deliver milk products from the local dairy farms to the homes in towns.

Bertha Batman (Wise) was the teacher for the West Middlesex third- and fourth-grade class about 1921.

"Most girls had dolls and many of them owned small doll buggies. They would pretend they were mothers, dressing their dolls and treating them to the love, and often punishment, that was bestowed on them.

"Many of the girls aspired to become teachers and would coerce the younger kids in the neighborhood to become pupils in their game of 'School.' Those with an early interest in the medical profession would also use the younger neighborhood kids as their patients in their game of 'Nurse.'

"Backyard plays and amateur shows also were a big rage, with crudely erected stages draped with old curtains and sometimes even remnants of old rugs.

"Playing with paper dolls and dressing them with cut-out clothes was another favorite pastime, generally more popular on rainy days.

"Some girls used their spare time more educationally. They would sit at their mothers' feet during sewing circles or learn the cross-stitch. Some became so adept that they made their own doll clothes.

"The more aggressive joined the boys in their games of 'Cops and Robbers,' 'Kick the Can,' and even baseball.

"The evening hours after supper called for less active fare. The activities generally wound down with 'Mother, May I?,' 'Red Rover,' 'Tag,' 'Hide and Seek,' and 'Simon Says.' Evening darkness called for renewed gatherings on front porches to tell stories or sing songs until bedtime.

"The start of school, generally the day after Labor Day, signaled the end to most of these activities until the next summer."

Yearnings

By Esther Shaffer

There are many things young folks have missed
So I thought that I'd just make a list.

They've never seen the open spaces
Where years ago, we ran our races
The fields and meadows where wild flowers bloomed
Until man's push said they were doomed.
They've never heard the raucous horn
Of the fish man on a Friday morn
Or the fruit truck coming down the road
We all ran out to check his load
Or chase the ice man down the street
He always gave us ice to eat.

They've never seen the old ravine
Where all our games were played, unseen
Wild Indians stalked their victims there
While cowboy yells rang through the air.
We'd choose up teams to play our games
The biggest kids would call the names
And sometimes, if your luck ran true
Both sides would argue over you.

Jingle bells on a hot summer day
Meant the buttermilk man was on the way.
They will never see the old gray horse
Who pulled the ice cream cart, of course.
When we heard the dinging of the bell
We'd grab our money and run pell-mell.
The ball games played in our back yard
The circus, where we worked so hard
To show our parents all our acts
We charged two cents without a tax.

In summertime when it was hot
Dad sprayed the hose
It helped a lot.
The brook that chuckled on its way
The frogs and minnows caught each day
The endless games of Run, Sheep, Run
Suppertime when the day was done.
Rainy days were best of all
When attic treasures gave their call
We'd play dress up or gone to sea
And ate our lunch on gram's settee.

When winter came, with ice and snow
What fun it was for us to go
Down the hill upon our sled
Till it was time to go to bed.
We'd never heard of the TV
But we had books for company.

Progress, of course, must have its day
But the kids lost out along the way.

The poem "Yearnings" was written in 1978 by Esther A. Shaffer, age eighty-one, for Mr. Duncan's creative writing class at Mercer High School.

Recreation at Sandy Lake has always included swimming (Photos: Autumn Buxton)

The Mercer Avenue School in Sharpsville was renamed "Deeter School" in honor of Miss Emma Deeter who taught grade one there for fifty years. From 1922 until 1948, Hosack H. Hedglin was principal of the school. These photographs were undated, but appear to be from the 1920s, 1930s, and 1940s, respectively.

Center Presbyterian Church had its start in the late 1790s. By 1801, it was requesting that a minister be installed, to be shared with a Plain Grove church. The first building was on Cranberry Road and made of logs with a thatched roof. A second building was reportedly located near where the swimming pool in Grove City's Memorial Park is now. The present church was built on Center Church Road in 1836 for $1,800. The 50-foot-by-50-foot building was made of locally made clay brick and hewn timbers. It had four doors and four stoves, and the location was chosen because of a good spring nearby. The building (pictured, in 1921) was considered one of the best churches in the county. From 1925 until 1967, several additions and renovations have been made, and about 1973 the original building was gutted out down to the dirt basement and completely refurbished. Now, the complex includes the sanctuary (in the original church) plus a Christian education building, picnic and recreation area, outdoor chapel, and fellowship wing. (Source: **Reflections of Our Past**)

In the early 1920s, after the lead engine of a train had reached the Clarksville Bridge over the Shenango River, a trailing coal car jumped the track before the bridge. The pusher engine kept pushing, however. As a result, several train cars were shoved into the river, and the bridge was destroyed. A large crane had to be brought on site to lift the damaged train cars out of the water.

(Source: **Mercer Dispatch and Republican**, April 25, 1930)

Although John McDowell bought his first tractor in 1921 for $800, he still used horses for many tasks throughout the 1920s, including spraying potatoes and harvesting wheat. (Potatoes continued to be one of the major crops grown in Mercer County throughout the 1900s.) Like many farmers, McDowell also took advantage of developments in fertilizer to increase yield and quality. (Source: Vonda Minner)

The Mercer County Home (pictured) opened in 1883 and replaced the Mercer Poor House established in 1853. The County Home was about 2.5 miles north of Mercer on Route 58 and about 1,600 feet south of the old poor house, which was later torn down. The Home had 270 beds; and between 1906 and 1921, about 2,400 individuals were admitted. T. C. White was the steward for many years and was assisted by his wife Belle Chalfant White, who also served as president for the Children's Aid Society of Western Pennsylvania. Similar to the old poor house, the County Home served men and women, old and young, lame and blind, sane and insane, and people of all nationalities. However, the conditions of the first institution were deplorable, the grounds were not maintained, and the inmates did not work. The consensus was that the poor house was an eyesore for a prosperous county. Therefore, many changes came with the County Home. Inmates were on a more nutritious, although modest, diet and worked to maintain the Home's grand edifice and grounds, including the farm. The Home's farm eventually became known as one of the finest and most up-to-date in Mercer County. (The grand edifice was razed and replaced by newer buildings as the Mercer County Home evolved into a modern nursing home. It was bought by a private company in the late 1990s and is now known as Woodland Place.)

263

T. C. White (pictured in the hayfield in the 1920s) was elected steward in 1906 of the Mercer County Home. The County Home's 316-acre farm produced corn, oats, hay, potatoes, tomatoes, and cabbage. Farm labor was done by the inmates and under supervision of the steward and the State Department of Agriculture.

St. John's Lutheran and German Reformed Societies in 1836 built a log church known as the Haas Church, one mile east of New Hamburg (Delaware Township). In 1846, use of the log structure was discontinued when a two-story edifice (pictured) was built across the road. When the second building became too small, it was moved aside to the parking lot so a new church could be constructed in its place. In 1921, the congregations dedicated the substantial $50,000 red-brick building (inset picture, in 2000), then known as St. John's United Church of Christ. The old building was torn down in 1924. The church changed its affiliation in the late 1990s and joined the Conservative Congregational Christian Conference. As a result, the church is now known as "Christ Community Church, A Bible Believing People Worshipping at St. John's." Caldwell One-Room School Museum is across from the church on Route 58. (Photographer, in 2000: Marilyn Dewald; caption: Dr. K. Joshua Christiansen)

Church of God camp meetings in West Middlesex gave southern migrants an opportunity to maintain a rural tradition. (Contributor: National Association of the Church of God)

Charter executive board of the Mercer Chamber of Commerce, organized in 1922, included (first row, from left) S. S. Smith, George Drenning, Russell Forbes (executive secretary, whose salary was $3,000 a year), Lillian Jamison, Norris Huey, William Hagar, and C. R. Langdon; (second row) James W. Byers, M. K. Hefling, L. H. Crill, George Rummell, Harvey Ebbert, and A. "Spike" L. Myers; (third row) H. A. Black, Frank Leisher, Charles Dillon, John Logan, Charles Kline, Harry Filson, and Jack Ellis; (fourth row) Elliott "Alec" Armstrong, Wilbur Cramer, John Amy, and Earl M. Hogue.

Wallis & Carley Company was listed in the **1922 City Directory** as general contractors on South Dock and Bank streets in Sharon. (To the right of the Dollar Title and Trust building is the old armory, first used by the Buhl Independent Rifles until about 1930 when it became the Julia F. Buhl Girls Club, which closed in 1987.)

Marian McConkey (Grove City) recalled "the swimming pool in which I was pleased to dispart myself along with almost all of the junior Grove Citizens on hot summer afternoons" in a park that was closed when the Penn Grove Hotel (pictured, in 1997) was scheduled to be built in 1924 on the same land. To the adults at the time, however, the hotel was a fine addition to the prosperous town. McConkey also recalled that during World War II, "groups of British Navy officers were sent to observe at the Cooper Bessemer who was making diesel engines for the war effort. They were entertained at the Penn Grove." The Grove City College "Class of 1926, my class, was the second class to hold their Junior Spring Banquet at the Penn Grove. It was not a prom. No dancing. We were socially inept. . . . Some of the girls went with boys. They were mostly the girls who had store-bought dresses for the occasion. The rest of us went in 'home-made.' It was the era of the long waist and uneven hemline. We were a group of the dowdiest damsels who ever defaced the earth. . . . Most of us were home by 8:00. Fifty years later the Class of '26 held its reunion. In the same room. Those of us who had grandchildren talked about them; those of us who didn't, listened. There was very little talk about the days we spent in school. The Penn Grove was the social center for the town. All four service clubs lunched there. Clubs met there. College and town social events were also at the Penn Grove. One year when the girls dorms [at the college] were overcrowded, the overflow lived on the second floor of the hotel for an entire year." The hotel is now a retirement home, but continues to offer a public restaurant and private dining rooms where service clubs continue to meet. (Photographers: Nick and Kathy Pompa; source: **Reflections of Our Past**)

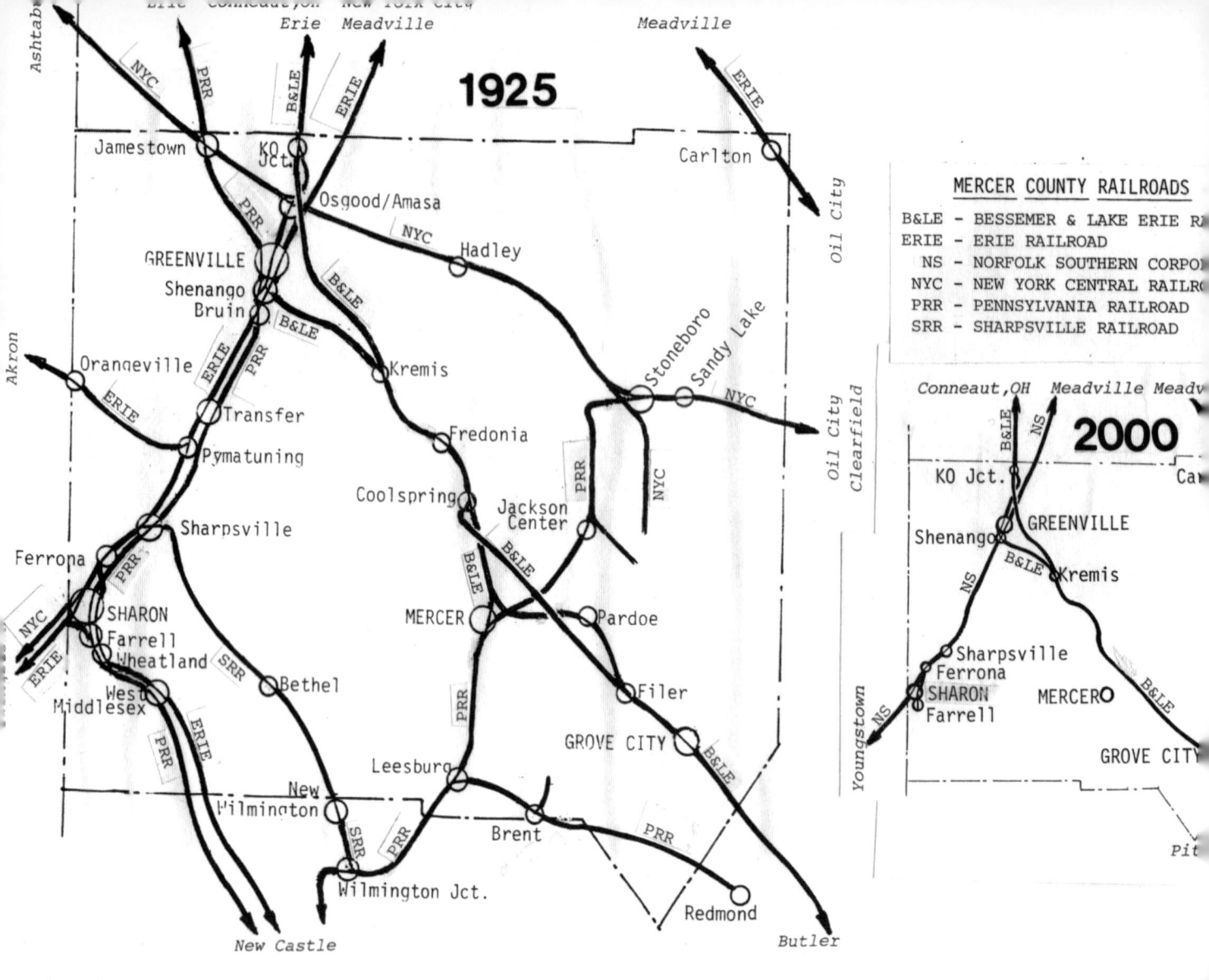

Through railroad company mergers and the decline of the mining industry, most of the trackage in Mercer County that was built up from the first point at Jamestown in 1859 to the height of railroad activity in 1925 has now been abandoned. (Contributor: Frederick Houser)

MERCER COUNTY RAILROADS

- B&LE – BESSEMER & LAKE ERIE R
- ERIE – ERIE RAILROAD
- NS – NORFOLK SOUTHERN CORPO
- NYC – NEW YORK CENTRAL RAILR
- PRR – PENNSYLVANIA RAILROAD
- SRR – SHARPSVILLE RAILROAD

Before the school district consolidation that created the Lakeview School District, Sandy Lake had its own high school (pictured, behind the sophomore class of 1924).

The Grove City Accredited Dairy Cattle Show and Sale Organization was organized, bought land for show barns, and held annual shows and sales throughout most of the 1920s. [The land is now Memorial Park, and the show barns have been converted into picnic shelters (pictured, in 1997.)] (Photographers: Nick and Kathy Pompa)

268

In 1926, the teacher for the Pardoe School (Findley Township) was Frank McCullough.

Members of the Mercer High School Orchestra, probably 1925, included (front row, from left) Alma Weber and Marguarite "Toots" Jamison (violins); (middle row) Jim Vone and Don Miller (saxophones), Dave Lewis (alto horn), Clayton Swickard (tenor horn), Stan Smith (tuba), and Kenny Redmond (drums); (back row) Harry Black (cornet), Don McCracken (trombone), Guy Ringer (clarinet), Mary (Stewart) Glenn (piano), Mary McLaughry (director), Walter Anderson, Orval Anderson (cornet), and Wade Patterson (clarinet).

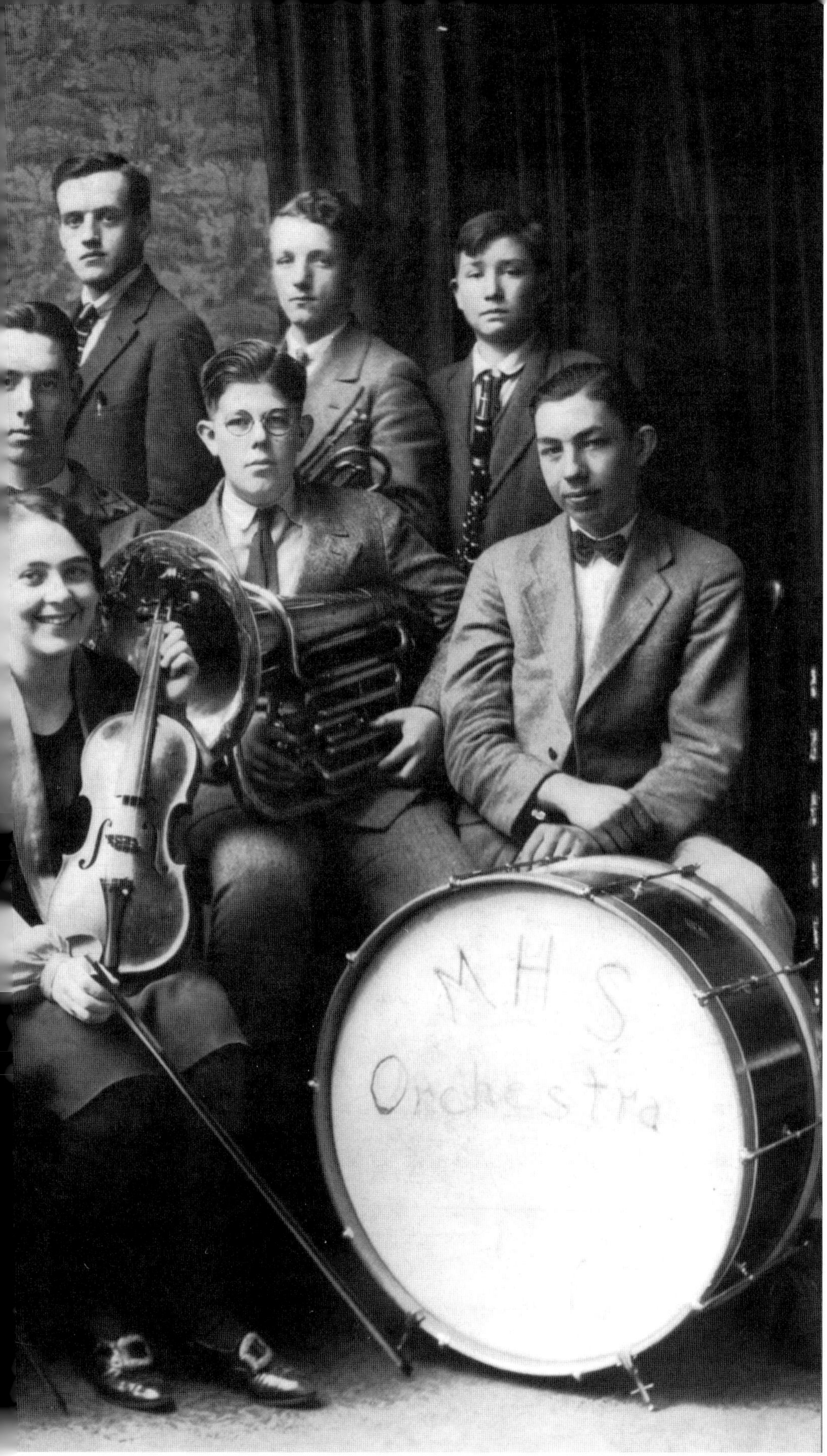
MHS
Orchestra

A December 1, 1926, newspaper article tells about Samuel Clendenin, who retired on pension that year after over forty-three years of active service. Clendenin went to work for the Pennsylvania Railroad as trackman in 1883 and was assigned to crossing watchman in 1910. For fifteen years he worked at the crossing at Walnut Street, Sharpsville, during which time only one accident occurred on the crossing while he was in charge. (In 1911, a seventy-three-year-old man attempted to cross ahead of a train. After flagging him, Clendenin called to him and narrowly escaped injury while trying to rescue the man.) Clendenin was well liked. For example, for a long time, three small boys have called on him every morning to see if he had anything for them to do. After sending them to fetch some water in his glass jug, he usually tipped them a penny or nickel. He nicknamed the boys Joe, Tony, and Mike Penny. When Joe was hurt and taken to the hospital, Clendenin visited him there. Later, one day when Clendenin became ill while on duty at the crossing, one of the Penny boys helped him find a relief man and escorted Clendenin home. (Contributor: Pete Joyce)

>   ***************************************
>   Now in the year of 1872 , two years later on this property above
> NOAH & Catherine ZOOK'S five children all died at once , with in
>   five weeks from deptheria. After Noah and Catherind Zook were in
>   old age , living alone on this farm and had no children anymore,
>   They was wanting a young married couple to live in with them till
>   the die, then they will receive the farm, Some young couples tryed
>   it, but they did not hold out, Then Jacob H. Byler born Aug. 12, 1865
>   An Amish Boy, Married   Jan. 3, 1927 to Sadie A. Turner, An English
>   girl, daughder of John and Ella (Chamberlain) Turner. In Sharon, Pa. .
>   She was an orphan, and had the liking of Jacob, So she joint the
>   Amish Church, To get married to Jacob H. Byler.
>   So this young couple Jacob H. & Sadie(Turner) Bylers moved in with
>   Noah Zooks, and stayed there till   Noah and Catherine both died,
>   And inherited the farm.

(Caption: Eli J. Byler, Lackawannock Township)

*An academy was built on North Erie Street (Mercer) in 1857 for $15,000, which was a large sum for a building then. The Mercer Academy had seven rooms and a chapel with a large stage. During the 1880s, the chapel was converted into three rooms, and an eighth grade and a high school were added. It became known as one of the most complete public school buildings in the county. After a new Mercer High School was built, the building was sold to the stockholders of the Mercer Academy and School of Music. The music school struggled along for several years and then closed. When the courthouse burned in 1907, the old Academy building was used as temporary quarters until the new courthouse was built. Then, the Academy fell into disrepair. In 1924, it was sold at a sheriff's sale for $2,650 to Mathias Adams (Mercer). The building was torn down about 1928, and a gas station and several tourist cabins were built on the property. In about the 1940s, the cabins were torn down. Now, the Subway Sandwich Shop stands in place of the gas station. (Source: several **Mercer Dispatch** articles)*

In 1927, members of the New Castle Christian Assembly conducted evangelical services in various homes in Farrell. Later that year, Reverend Peter Bonafiglia was invited to serve as pastor. So successful was the ministry of "Brother Pete," that the enthusiastic group first rented, then bought, the Polish Falcons Hall on Emerson Avenue, which they used until 1959. By that time, the church was too small. Meanwhile, Bonafiglia had resigned in 1956, and Reverend Guy Bongiovanni had succeeded him. From 1927 until 1956, many of the services were preached solely in Italian, the heritage of most of the congregation's members. However, Bongiovanni started using English for the regular Sunday and Wednesday services while offering a Friday Italian-only service and a Sunday school class, which was taught in Italian. By the end of 1959, the growing congregation had moved into a new edifice at 1825 Roemer Boulevard. As part of the Christian Church of North America, the church was called Farrell Christian Assembly. A building on Idaho Street was donated by the Chido brothers and remodeled for use as a Youth Center, and many youth programs were begun. Other programs were started by other segments of the congregation. After seventeen years as pastor of the church, Bongiovanni accepted the position of Missions Director with the Christian Churches of North America. After several ministers, Reverend Gene Carver became pastor in 1980. During Carver's tenure, missions giving continued to increase; and he was able to make several trips to Africa, where the congregation helped monetarily to build spartan, but much needed, local churches. At Carver's resignation in 1990, Reverend Larry Haynes moved from youth minister to senior pastor. Since the Farrell Building had become too small for the congregation, services were begun in 1995 in a new church (pictured above, in 2000) on North Keel Ridge Road in Hermitage. Other new things were initiated. The congregation became affiliated with the Assemblies of God. The structure of the worship services changed. New classes were added to the Sunday school and Wednesday night services. A more detailed and inclusive children's program was in full swing. Since Haynes resigned in 1997, Reverend Ken Martin, with the help of his wife Marlene, has been leading the church. (Photographer: Vonda Minner; caption: Pat Leali)

Mary Vanatta O'Mahoney was crowned Miss Mercer in the 1928 Old Home Week celebration, which included a parade.

274

Many communities and businesses organized bands that played at public functions and parades, including employees of the Bessemer & Lake Erie Railroad in Greenville (pictured, in 1928).

The faculty of (back row, from left) Neil Homer, Mary Clauson, and Wendell McConnell taught at the high school in Transfer (Pymatuning Township) in 1929. Their students included (first row, from left) Wade Frampton, Donnell Thompson, Stanley Durst, LeRoy Heile, Pete Bassick, Frank Cooper, Owen Lininger, and Jerald Uber; (second row) Robert Zuschlag, John McKnight, Walter Scott, John Morrison, Emerson Heile, Charles Thompson, and Maynard Durst; (third row) Mary Carroll, Eileen Artherholt, Rose Hogue, Vista Mowry, Nellie Chestnut, Eva Kolbrick, Marian McKnight, Eva Schweiss, Mae Taylor, Virginia Van Harlinger, Mayme Morrison, Helen Larson, Mildred Burnett, Rachel Bundy, Irene Young, Frances Green, Gwendolyn Morrison, and Lucinda Defendifer; (fourth row) Mary Reimold, Margaret McKnight, Augusta Reimold, Dorothy Heile, Gayle Reimold, Hilda Zuschlag, Pauline Morrison, Sara Zuschlag, Bernice Smith, and Lillian Lininger.

In midsummer 1927, a small group of local music students gathered on Mrs. Brown's front porch on North High Street in Greenville. They had been invited by Paul Moss, a local businessman and viola student who loved classical music. Moss was convinced that Greenville needed and would support a symphony orchestra. The hometown musicians were students of John Bebbington and Dwight Reese, music faculty at Thiel College. During the next year they practiced on the porch and in the N. N. Moss store. Moss, aware that they needed an oboe, a bassoon, trumpets, and trombones, knew a young man named Vesper, from Greenville, who was by then the business manager of the Cleveland Symphony Orchestra. Moss explained his plight, and Vesper is quoted as saying, "I have a big Maxwell car and I'll load up as many 'horns' as I can and we will help you put on your concert in Greenville." In the autumn of 1929 they were ready for their first concert, which was played in old Penn High School to a full house. Reese was the conductor until the onset of World War II, when the orchestra became dormant. After the War, the orchestra was reactivated, again by Moss, and now provides a three-concert series annually, plus yearly school concerts. In February 2000, a Mercer County Bicentennial Salute completed the seventy-second year of the symphony. Some names remembered: Dwight Reese, conductor; Paul Moss, viola; Jacob Huebert, H. Gruwer, cellos; Ficocelli brothers, Isabel Ghost, Grace Martin, Russell Smith, Bertram Adams, violins; William McMillen, trombone; and Joseph Mulvey, tympani. (Contributor: Gwen Lininger)

After the Erie Extension Canal closed in 1871, the trains flourished as a means of bringing raw material and goods from Mercer County to the port at Erie. By the 1920s, great barges transported iron ore and other materials on Lake Erie to many destinations. (Photo: Jean Fleet)

Sharon Savings & Loan was located at the corner of State and Chestnut Streets in Sharon (pictured, early 1920s).

Two trust companies that were heavy dealers in building lots, other real estate, and trades opened in the early 1900s: Colonial Trust in South Sharon in 1902 and Dollar Title and Trust at East State Street and Dock Avenue in Sharon. One of the officers of Colonial Trust was John Stevenson Jr., the former partner of Frank H. Buhl in Sharon Steel Company. Stevenson liked to point out that Colonial Trust had a burglar-proof safe within a heavy chrome and steel vault protected by the latest in burglar alarm systems in 1929. Valley residents could obtain loans at low interest rates. Few had paid off what they owed before 1928. [Until the 1960s, the massive Dollar Title and Trust Company building (pictured, in the 1920s when the Penn-Ohio four-wheel trolley would come north from West Middlesex on Dock Street and turn west on State Street) survived from the rental of offices on its upper floors. A restaurant and paint store occupied the first floor for a time. The building was torn down in 1970. A structure that replaced some of it accommodated lawyers' offices.]
(Caption: Mairy Jayn Woge and Frederick Houser)

Below: The industries that contributed to the transportation saga of Greenville were the early steel mills, which have come and gone: the Kimberly Rolling Mills, Greenville Iron Company, and Carnegie Steel, manufacturing steel rails for railroad tracks. Another large business, Chicago Bridge and Iron, fabricated, among other things, large, standing water tanks in the Greenville plant, which were vital to transportation and to municipal and industrial sites in a world market. In 1909 or 1910, the Greenville Steel Car was founded, making various railway cars and, still in business, employs as a general rule about one thousand men. It has operated under the company, Ampeo, and, now, Trinity Industries. Early in the company's history, it assembled passenger cars—the "Empire" car in particular. One Empire car is displayed at Greenville's Railroad Park and Museum. Officers and friends of the Greenville Steel Car Company dined in the 1920s at the Duquesne Club in Pittsburgh: (clockwise around the table) Wells Fay, John Brennan, K. C. Gardener, George Rowley, Ed Hodge, Frank Fay, Edwin Templeton, Ralph Zimmerman, William Dietrich, and A. J. Rose. (Photo: George Hardy Rowley; caption: Gwen Lininger)

Interior of a barber shop, 1928.

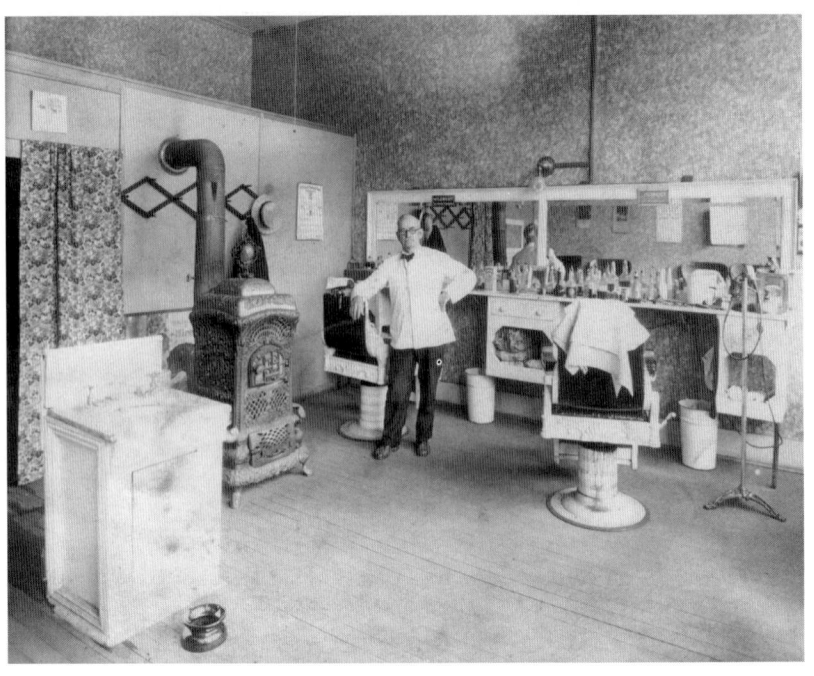

Before the opening of Perry Highway (Route 19) in 1930, people from Mercer County who wanted to go to Pittsburgh traveled on the Butler Pike (Route 258), went through Youngstown, or took the train. Taking its name from Commodore Perry who, along this route, led wagon trains carrying supplies, powder, and cannon for his fleet to defend the Great Lakes during the War of 1812, Perry Highway continued as a major artery of commerce and travel between Pittsburgh and Erie before Interstate 79 was built in the mid-1960s. During the 1940s, 1950s, and 1960s, traffic jams on Route 19 were a fact of life during the summer. People would leave Pittsburgh on Friday night, heading to Lake Erie, the Pymatuning Reservoir, or other points north; and a five-mile line of cars was not unusual south of Mercer. On Sunday nights, the same cars would return to Pittsburgh—causing a line of cars to form north of Mercer. This bottleneck was a boon to local business, and many small stands sprang up on the side of the road. Interstate 79 took this traffic on a different route. Now, although many travelers use Perry Highway to traverse Mercer County leisurely, the interstate carries the bulk of the fast-paced, Pittsburgh-Erie traffic. (Picture: **Mercer Dispatch***, October 3, 1930; caption: William Philson)*

THE PERRY HIGHWAY PARADE

The great outdoor feature of the celebration of the opening of the Perry Highway in Mercer Wednesday was the pageant and parade, carried on depite inclement weather and in the face of almost insurmountable difficulties. Three hours of steady rain failed to dampen the ardor of those who participated, or to discourage the committee in charge. With but few omissions, the features listed below were all in line, braving the drizzle that prevailed and following the line of march up the Perry Highway and about the Diamond and adjoining streets with bands playing, colors flying, old uniforms and costumes flaunting, young girls and youths smiling and everyone doing his best to carry out the program planned:

Marquis de Lafayette, John P. Orr
General Hugh Mercer, Will Courtney
Buffalo Bill, W. W. McCullough
Daniel Boone, Joseph Thompson
Pioneer, Jack Thorn
Captain John Junkin, Joseph Junkin
Aids—Harry Filson, Roy Weller, Harry C. Hunter, J. W. Byers, John Barnes

Numbers Correspond with Features

1—Bessemer Railroad Band of Greenville.
2—Indians—"Chief Hathegig," Will Tait, and tribe.
3—Covered Wagon, with pioneer family.
4—Indian Tribes.
5—Pioneer Scouts.
6—Spirit of '76.
7—Squad of Soldiers of 1776.
8—Circuit Rider.
9—Family Doctor.
10—Marines of 1812.
11—Flagship "Niagara" manned by Commodore Perry, Officers and Sailors.
12—Powder Wagon, accompanied by a guard of soliders of 1812.
13—Stage Coach.
14—Huidekoper carriage, built in 1812, been in the Huidekoper family since 1813, and at present owned by Mrs. Winthrop Bates Perry of Meadville.
15—Man and Woman on Horse Back.
16—Old Bier.
17—Fredonia—"Passing of Old Road."
18—U. S. Mail—Three different periods of transportation.
19—Tin Wagon driven by John Campbell, last of the tin peddlers.
20—Horse drawn vehicles of different
21—Millburn Grange—"Harvest."
22—Meadville Pike—Float.
23—Gay Nineties.
24—Tally-ho.
25—High Wheel Bicycle. Sharon High School Band.
26—Columbia.
27—Town Council.
28—Mercer Civil War Veterans—Thomas P. Munnell, A. M. Clawson, Samuel Landis, Geo. E. Hamilton.
29—Style Period—Puritan, 1776, 1812, 1830, 1865, 1880, Flapper.
30—Stoneboro, Fife and Drum Corps, with the oldest fifer in the United States, "Uncle Jake" Roberts, 97, Leesburg.
31—Apple Butter Making.
32—Shingle Making.
33—Nos. 2 and 5 Mines and Union Supply Company Division.
34—Boy Scouts.
35—Zelienople Division.
36—World War Firing Squad.
37—"Spirit of Progress."
38—Farrell Floats and Band.
39—East End Fire Department and East End.
40—Children's Home.
41—"Amos an Andy" in Person.
42—Old Automobiles.

278

Mercer Dispatch Tidbits
(Researched by Shirley Minshull)

January 24, 1930: Superintendent of Mercer County schools, H. E. McConnell, retired after serving a record five consecutive terms. McConnell was born and reared in Mercer County and was a graduate of Thiel College.

March 21, 1930: Line of idle men gathered at entrance of Liberty Theatre hoping for borough or county road work, making it apparent that Mercer County is facing an unemployment situation.

April 11, 1930: School directors elected W. M. Johnston (Mercer) to be Superintendent of Mercer County Schools. Johnston was educated in the rural schools of Mercer County and was a graduate of Grove City College.

April 13, 1930: The census showed Stoneboro with decrease in population from 1,405 in 1920 to 1,187 in 1930. Sugar Grove showed increase to 530 in 1930 as opposed to 510 in 1920.

June 6, 1930: Four Civil War veterans of Mercer County honored at Memorial Day program: George E. Hamilton, M. Clawson, Samuel Landis, and Thomas P. Munnell.

July 4, 1930: Sampling of food prices: Puffed Wheat Cereal, two packages for 25 cents; Lorna Doone Cookies, 10 cents a package; bananas, 6 pounds for 25 cents; bacon, 29 cents a pound; and rice, 2 pounds for 15 cents.

July 25, 1930: Mercer County is ranked high in agriculture among the counties in Pennsylvania: third in number of sheep raised; third in wool production; third in amount of lime used; and fifth in farm-made butter.

August 8, 1930: The summer's drought menaced crops. It was compared to the dry summer of 1854. The lack of water suspended construction work on Perry Highway (Route 19) in Fairview Township. The 120th anniversary of founding of Old Springfield "Seceder" Church, which was established in 1810, was celebrated. The first minister of the congregation was Rev. John Walker.

August 29, 1930: Lamont Hughes, son of John and Mary Hughes, was elected president of Carnegie Steel. Hughes was born and attended public school in Mercer.

September 5, 1930: The annual Grove City Dairy Cattle Show was held at Memorial Park. The type of cattle shown were Holstein, Guernsey, and Jersey. The judges were experts from State College.

October 10, 1930: Despite bad weather, the opening of Perry Highway (Route 19) was observed in fitting way. The highway runs from Pittsburgh to the northern border of Mercer County. The celebration and dedication, including a large parade and a noon dinner, were held in Mercer and arranged by Mercer citizens.

November 14, 1930: Fire razes Willis Garage in Sharon. The early morning blaze destroyed 47 automobiles and a large quantity of shop equipment. The loss was estimated at $75,000.

The Fairview School was built at a stagecoach stop on Route 19, known now as the village of Fairview. The original building in the mid-1800s was stone. Later, frame structures were built, twice, and the second one has been used for other purposes after the school closed about 1950 with the formation of the Lakeview School District. The 1930 reunion of Fairview School alumni (pictured) appears to have been held at the Fredonia Institute. (Sources: Mae Beringer and Patricia Jones)

"I believe that the whole neighborhood of boys [in Mercer] learned to swim in Neshannock Creek [during the late 1930s and early 1940s]. We would build a dam a few hundred yards below the Grove City road [now Route 58]. We used rocks that we gathered from the stream bottom and when we managed to raise the water level adequately, we would commence with doggie paddling or whatever system we had adopted and progressed to a point where we could actually swim with some degree of competence. The neighborhood girls learned that we were swimming without suits so they were always trying to sneak up on us. None of us really cared and often, when someone detected them, some of the boys would lift others out of the water so they would be in full view. The girls would scream and run away, thus allowing us to retain the dam as our own private swimming hole." (Photo: a less rambunctious, coed group of unidentified swimmers; caption: Joseph Hood)

Chapter 5: 1931–1940

TOWNSHIPS

The Fairview Friendship Club was formed in 1934 by a group of *Fairview Township* women who gathered to do quilting while their husbands cut firewood for their family homes. (It continues as a social organization and quilting group in that township now.)

First broadcasting in 1938, WPIC radio had its buff brick broadcasting studio, offices, and tower along Pine Hollow Boulevard in **Hickory Township**. The boulevard was formerly called Strawbridge Avenue, named for the Strawbridge coalmines in the fields north of it. (In 1925, it was called Dutch Lane.) One of the popular announcers heard on WPIC was Johnny Pepe. Pepe was sports editor of *The Sharon Herald* (now *The Herald*), but once or twice a day, he entered a small booth on the west end of the newspaper's newsroom and broadcast scores of local basketball and football games played on Valley school fields. Pepe's voice was transmitted to the radio station by a telephone wire. Sometimes the telephone conversations of residents who lived along the route of the wire from Sharon to Mercer Avenue were broadcast rather than the ball scores. Later newscasts from the newspaper office were broadcast by WPIC. The radio station was owned by John Fahnline of Sharon before it was taken over by another and larger broadcasting company.

In the 1930s, during the trip to the grocery store one would hand the proprietor your list and in record time your food was bagged, boxed, and out the door. Some merchants delivered goods such as the Watkins (Rawleigh) man in **Worth Township**. He was well known and sometimes considered an old friend, talking about the happening news, someone to share politics, planting, and plowing. Everything a housewife needed to keep her home running smoothly was within reach. Another person that came around each month was the milk tester. This person came before milling in the evening, ate supper, tested evening milk, spent the night, and tested the morning milk. During World War II, the milk tester was a "conscientious objector" and was permitted to stay out of the Army and do this job. Electricity came to Worth Township in 1938 and 1939 and gradually changed everyone's way of life—from overhead lights and ironing clothes to a furnace and indoor plumbing. Even telephone wires were strung for a telephone on the wall giving access to the "party line."

Salem Township (by Robert Osborn). "Edwin Freeland was born and raised on the John Freeland farm in Salem Township. Five acres of this farm lay south of the Little Shenango, fronting on Route 358. By the time he finished going to Thiel College, he had worked up quite a business in livestock and butchering. The butchering was conducted in a small building on the Freeland farm. After his marriage, his father gave him one acre along Route 358. This would be in 1938 or 1939. On this land, he built a house. A short

THE GREAT DEPRESSION
By Wally Wachter, written for this publication

The Great Depression struck in 1929. The nation was panic-stricken on the "Black Tuesday" that followed Wall Street's "Monday Massacre," in which stocks took their biggest plunge in history. However, the small mill towns in Mercer County did not feel the effects of the calamity until the aftershocks. Steel orders began to dwindle until eventually plants were forced to shut completely. Some local banks were forced to close their doors and leave depositors at a loss about what was to become of their savings.

The biggest local concern was what would become of the mills, the lifeblood of the communities. Layoffs faced fathers and older brothers. No unemployment compensation existed at that time. The welfare program was virtually nil. The worry was that most families would face bleak futures without any means of income at all. Few families had savings or investments. It took all their work earnings to support families, many with ten or more children.

Only the rich who had extra money to invest—mostly steel officials and businessmen—dabbled in the stock market. In Mercer County communities, when the crash came, those who had been poor were still poor. Many wealthy investors, however, were wiped out and joined the ranks of debtors.

During the Depression, pessimists vented their frustrations and anger at Herbert Hoover who was just unfortunate enough to have been president of the United States at that time. Optimists raised an oft-repeated war cry: "Prosperity is just around the corner." The corner must have been miles away because it was an entire decade and World War II before the full impact of the Great Depression was wiped away.

Matching the effects of the financial failures on private lives were the millions dollars in property damage inflicted by frequent floods that ravaged the lowlands of the county. Every time torrential rains hit the area, the Shenango River swelled over flood stage, inundating the entire business area of downtown Sharon and other communities downstream. It was thought that the erection of the Pymatuning Dam near Jamestown in the 1930s would ease the problem. (The problem was not solved, however, until the construction of the Shenango River Dam was completed in 1965.)

time later, he also built a larger slaughterhouse. His business expanded and prospered to the extent that cattle had to be shipped from Chicago. At the highest point, eighteen carloads each week were shipped. This, on top of local supply. Then a large addition was built onto the slaughterhouse. More help was added. (By this time, World War II was on, and Edwin was drafted into the Army. He had injured his back a couple of years prior to this while unloading meat. After several months of Army training, he was having trouble getting up and down. He was then given a medical discharge and sent home. Shortly after this, he built the Friendly Tavern. He did not operate it, himself, but sold it to Joe Stampha and a fellow by the name of Nicklin. I believe it was Homer Nicklin."

"Life as it was during the 1930s in Salem Township.... The depression, which began in 1929 and was at its worst in the early 1930s to late 1930s, had a devastating effect on

The Shenango River had a long history of flooding. The channel of the Shenango had been moved west in 1832 to prevent the river's overflowing into the planned Beaver and Lake Erie Canal even though the bed of the canal would be slightly higher than the natural riverbed. Buildings close to the rerouted Shenango often were elevated on stilts high enough to avoid floodwater. The Protestant Methodist Church, which had opened about 1835, held services in two connected frame buildings on South Main Street. The stilts that supported the church provided sufficient space for the pigs that roamed in the city to wander under the structure and snort and squeal during Sunday services. Norman S. Powell, a civil engineer for Carnegie Steel Company South Works in Farrell, proposed draining the Pymatuning Swamp near Jamestown and constructing a dam and reservoir there to prevent floods like the disastrous one in 1913 and to increase water in the river for industries during summers. Powell was joined by representatives of four other large Valley companies and executives in Lawrence and Beaver counties and called the group the Pymatuning Land Company. They were instrumental in obtaining the funding to build the dam (pictured, in 1999).
(Aerial: **The Herald***; caption: Mairy Jayn Woge)*

Salem. To begin with, there were only a couple of families who could be called 'well-off.' Some were more-or-less in the middle—but very few. Farming, sawmill work, and road work were the occupations of 95% of the population. Very few farmers sold milk. They sold cream and fed the skim milk to hogs and calves.

"In the case of my Granddad Osborn, cream, wool, and lambs were his only sources of income. His wife taught school and took in summer boarders from Pittsburgh.

"The cream was picked up by Littles of Kennard. Littles operated a general store and sold everything, including groceries, clothing, and hardware. You called in by a certain time of the week and gave them your grocery order. Then they would the deliver groceries when the cream and eggs were picked up. Whether your produce paid for your needs was a question. If not, it went on your bill. My parents did not farm but did sell eggs and had groceries delivered from Littles.

"For entertainment, it was pretty much centered around church. Two congregations were in Salem: Methodists and Baptists. There were a few Amish, and one Catholic family. In the case of the Methodists, of which my family were members, there was some kind of activity almost every evening. People took turns hosting Sunday school class parties. These included food and games. In summer, there was baseball almost every night.

"There were some good baseball players, and every little burg had a team. Some of the better players from Salem were Ralph Riley (pitcher), Max Donnell, Paul Donnell, Elmer Snyder, Ralph Snyder, Charles Osborn, and James Osborn. There were others, such as Lawrence Stevenson, who was an outstanding pitcher, who could not play on Sunday afternoons, because the Baptists would not allow playing on Sundays. His brother, Harold,

In May 1931, Governor Gifford Pinchot (pictured) signed a bill, known as the Stevenson Bill, to fund the building of Pymatuning Dam. Five months later, Governor Pinchot dug the first shovelful of soil for the dam and reservoir and announced, "The reservoir will stop the floods, help industries, furnish sufficient water for the area and be a place for recreation." The construction of the dam and the reservoir it created was completed over three years and provided numerous jobs. The reservoir was cleared of large trees and other obstacles before it began filling with water in 1934. Before digging commenced, the depth of Pymatuning Swamp and some adjoining bogs was to be measured by engineers who reported the bottoms of some of the deep, wet places could not be reached. Quicksand was also a problem occasionally. The dam and reservoir did everything Governor Pinchot said it would other than stop flooding along the lower Shenango River in the Valley. (Caption: Mairy Jayn Woge)

Long-time business owners in Grove City, James and Mary Karfes (pictured, in 1980) recalled memories of the Depression and better times in the 1920s in a May 17, 1980, article in **The Herald**. "When the Great Depression struck, Karfes was in a position to help others. 'I couldn't charge my tenants rent,' Karfes said, 'so I let them live in my building without charge until times got better.' He said people dug coal in what is now Grove City Community Park [now Memorial Park] and the borough paid to have it delivered to their homes by truck. That took care of their fuel. 'Fortunately,' he added, "the borough had its own electric plant at the time and didn't turn off the electricity for residents who couldn't make their monthly payments. Two or three families would move into a home together and pool whatever resources they had. Government flour and sugar would be sent by train to a warehouse behind what is now Five Filer Brothers. A grocery company from Butler had a wholesale house there and owned the building. Roger Ormond distributed the goods to needy families. We all pitched in and helped each other,' Karfes said of those lean years. Mrs. Karfes' father, George Linderman, owned a confectionary and ice cream parlor in Grove City for four years [in the 1920s] before moving to Youngstown. 'The ice cream parlors were really elegant,' she said. 'The stores were adorned with mirrors all around the walls. There were marble-topped tables with wire legs and chairs with round seats and wire legs. I remember Tiffany chandeliers and bowls of fresh fruit that sat in the center of the tables. The ice cream was made of real milk, cream and eggs and the sundaes were topped with real whipped cream, fresh fruit and walnuts.'" (Contributor: Theo Karfes)

was also an excellent player. Most of these men worked at Steel Car or Bessemer shops and hurried home, did their chores, had their meals, and played ball until dark.

"During the early 1930s, preachers visited residents often, usually around mealtime. During these times, I never saw a skinny Methodist preacher! On one such occasion, the preacher was at my Granddad Osborn's eating supper when a bad thunderstorm came on. The Baptist church was in plain view of where we were seated at the table. It was only about 1/4 mile up Osborn Road when a terrible bolt of lightning struck, hitting the church. In a short time, it was burned to the ground.

"The Methodists offered the Baptists use of the basement of their church to hold services, but some of their congregation were against accepting because we held supper, etc. in the basement; however, they did use it, and I think to appease some of the dissenters, used the upstairs by holding services in the afternoon. Soon after this catastrophe, they bought a church in Otter Creek and moved it on rollers, pulling it with horses to the site of the fire.

"During this period, there was s split among the congregation. Part of them bought an empty church at Sheakleyville (presently the Nazarene Church). Many who made this move were Osborns (Claud, Chester, and others). The ones who stayed (Stevensons, Chesses, etc.) changed their church name to Wesleyan Methodist. It remains that to this day.

"During the early 1930s, a government work program called CWA was put into effect. Most of the farmers worked on this. It included road building. Salem Township roads were nothing but mud, and this program was a great benefit, not only for the added income, but in helping to get out of the mud. This program did not last very long.

"About this time, work was started on building Pymatuning Dam. This provided work for many men of the area. My dad worked at the dam, and we have pictures of him and

Timeline 1931—1940

The World

- **1931** "The Star-Spangled Banner" is designated by an act of Congress to be "the national anthem of the United States of America"; the Empire State Building is dedicated
- **1932** Mrs. Hattie W. Caraway becomes the first woman to be elected to the US Senate
- **1933** The famous radio western, "The Lone Ranger", is heard for the first time; Franklin D. Roosevelt becomes the 32nd president
- **1934** Babe Ruth makes his final appearance as a regular player with the New York Yankees
- **1936** The Hoover Dam is completed; the first issue of *Life* magazine is published
- **1937** Connecticut becomes the first state to issue permanent license plates for cars; the first Blood Bank is established; the Golden Gate Bridge opens; Amelia Earhart disappears over the Pacific
- **1938** Orson Welles causes a national panic with a radio dramatization of "The War of the Worlds," a story of an alien invasion
- **1939** The first televised football game (Fordham vs. Waynesboro College) airs; the US Supreme Court outlaws "sit-down strikes"
- **1940** The population of the United States is 132,122,446; the Germans begin the Battle of France; the climax and turning point in WWII's Battle of Britain takes place when the British destroy 185 German aircraft

Mercer County

- **1931** The *Farrell Tribune* publishes its first issue; ground is broken near Jamestown for the Pymatuning Dam; the first buildings are erected on Grove City College's upper campus
- **1932** Wendell August moves his aluminum forge to Grove City
- **1933** The county votes to repeal Prohibition; the first public playground opens at Buhl Farm (more than 1,000 children attend); the first no-direct-contact continuous process is placed into operation at the Sharon Steel Hoop Corporation
- **1934** Police search for infamous bank robber, John Dillinger, who may have robbed the Sol J. Gully bank in Farrell; the Pymatuning Reservoir is dedicated
- **1935** The Farrell Public Library board formally opens library and arts center; a merger of the *News Telegraph* with the *Sharon Herald* leaves the new *Sharon Herald* as the Shenango Valley's only daily paper; the Better Housing Campaign begins
- **1936** The Sharon Steel Hoop Corporation changes its name to Sharon Steel; the "Human Fly" attempts to scale the courthouse; GOP candidate for US President, Alf Landon, delivers his opening address to 10,000 people on the Tam O' Shanter Golf Course
- **1938** Flood Control Act authorizes the Shenango River Reservoir project; first air mail is flown out from Mercer Airport
- **1939** The last trolley car is removed from the runs in Farrell
- **1940** The county's population is 101,039; the Home Economic building at the Fredonia-Delaware High School is destroyed by fire; the Sawhill Manufacturing Company announces it will establish a plant in Wheatland; the Federal Food Stamps Program is established in the county

Clint Powell of Hadley sawing down a tree with a 10' crosscut saw with very few inches of the ends of the saw sticking out each side.

"Later, the WPA program was started. This provided work on roads, parks, etc. Many skilled men worked on this program. The pay was $52.00 a month, and you were eligible for articles of clothing, beans, etc. You had to work to get it.

"In 1936, electricity came to Salem Township. This was an exciting time for young and old. Gone were the old ice boxes, spring housecoolers, cook stoves, washboards, oil lamps, hand pumps. A few at this time put in bathrooms—but not many. Later, some said that you made kraut in the house and went outside to the toilet, but now you made kraut outside and went to the toilet inside. Also about this time, the state took over many of the roads. This got a lot of us out of the mud.

"Then around 1939, war clouds hung over Europe and this created demand for our farm products."

MUNICIPALITIES

Fredonia. The Works Progress Administration (WPA) program implemented many projects for Fredonia workers in 1933. "City" water was made available to the town through underground water lines, rather than from springs and wells. Program workers were also involved in street work and constructing new buildings.

During the spring of 1933, the Fredonia National Bank was robbed of more than $5000.00 by two armed men. The police eventually captured the "bad guys" and a portion of the stolen money.

In 1934, the Fredonia Volunteer Fire Department and Relief Association was formed under the direction of Jack Bear. It was deemed necessary for the community after a fire broke out on Second Street. Although the community did own a Model T Ford with a chemical tank, it would not start the night of the fire. Following this incident, volunteers banded together to build their first fire truck and the association was born.

Farrell (by Mairy Jayn Woge). Carver Center in Farrell was a learning and recreation facility for Afro-Americans. It was financed by the Buhl Trustees and continued to receive financial help from the Trustees after it became an agency of the Community Chest (now the United Way) in 1948. Carver Center operated through 1960. Its duties were then transferred to the F. H. Buhl Club and Julia Buhl Girls Club. Carver Center was the first local organization of its kind.

Farrell became a third-class city in the late 1930s.

Jamestown (by Norma Leary). In 1932, C. T. Houck began publishing his weekly newspaper, *Jamestown Journal*, which he continued until 1995.

Jamestown became known as "The Gateway to Pymatuning" in 1934, when Pymatuning State Park opened and Gable Glen and Hollow, a local playground and picnic area, shut down. Mike Sutherland (Jamestown) built and ran the first ice boat on Pymatuning Lake. He also had the first radio in Jamestown and invented a part that is on all record players.

The community banded together throughout the Great Depression. The United Methodist Church served "Penny Dinners" weekly to all community members. They also helped those who were traveling through town without money, food, or jobs. Many houses provided these vagabonds with meals or a place to stay for the night. Such wanderers were regular occurrences in many towns, particularly along the railroad lines. Some of them would notch the sidewalk in front of houses where housewives were both generous and good cooks. By doing so, the next traveler who came along could tell where was a good place to stop.

Sharon *(by Mairy Jayn Woge)*. Many Mercer County residents lost houses and cars. Businesses closed. Churches were crowded. Only a few members or worshipers tithed. Most prayed for financial help. A small amount of steel was manufactured in the Shenango Valley. Only one of every four persons who had a job before 1930 kept it. Services by local governments were trimmed. Some bank and trust companies closed before the edict by President Franklin D. Roosevelt that closed banks in 1933. The S. J. Gully Bank in Farrell and McDowell Bank and the First National Bank in Sharon continued operating up to that time.

Bread lines formed. The Sunshine Society on Walnut Avenue in Sharon fed and clothed the poor and found places where they could live at the behest of Julia Buhl and other wealthy and some not so rich people. Charitable acts were the acceptable thing of the time. Children took piano lessons at no cost. Food stores spiced up orders with treats. Physicians treated patients and delivered babies at no cost. There was an unprecedented amount of hunger and numerous beggars. Diphtheria was the scourge of the early 1930s. The inadequacies were most difficult for people who had come from post World War I in Europe to work in the United States.

Boy Scout Troop 17 was founded by the Optimist Club of Sharon with the goal to assist needy families by supplying jobs for their teenage male children. Scouts cut grass at the homes of Club members two or three times a week in summers to earn money and tips.

Sharpsville *(by Mairy Jayn Woge)*. The "Old Sharpsville Railroad," started in 1881, made its last run from New Castle to Sharpsville in 1931.

Sharpsville is unique in that it is home to 22 Santa Clauses. In 1934, George F. Mahaney, who owned a clothing store at a prime corner in the borough, arranged for a Santa Claus suit to be made for a Sharpsville man who, on Christmas Eve of that year, traveled to the homes of Sharpsville children. A signal that a child was in a house was a glowing porch light. (The Sharpsville Service Club adopted the project, and by 1953, Sharpsville had 21 Santas and 21 helpers. Each participating Service Club member provided his own Santa suit. The "Santa Claus Project" continues even now.)

Stoneboro *(by Frederick Houser)*. Route 845 was paved through Stoneboro in the 1930s, and Route 62 about ten years earlier. A federally assisted program of the 1930s saw most of the borough's secondary streets also paved. (Now, the borough maintains 6.34 miles of streets and roads; the Pennsylvania Department of Transportation is responsible for another 5 miles.)

One could purchase *two* scoops of ice cream for a dime.

A new, fireproof, 400-seat auditorium was built in 1939 in Stoneboro along with the Borough office building. (The theatre was only used for twenty-five years before the competition of television proved overwhelming.)

Wheatland *(by Betsy Cooper and Mairy Jayn Woge)*. In 1931, the hall of the Knights of Pythian burned down. (Organized in 1873, they had met in the Weaver House until they had built their own hall.) After the fire, they met in the upstairs of the old school on Second Street. During the meetings, social events (such as birthday parties, dances, and wrestling matches) took place in the lower level. Later, the Knights moved to the new booster building in the playground below the railroad station. Dances were held there. For a dime, one would be admitted if dressed nicely, and popcorn and a movie on an outdoor screen were available for another nickel.

The growing season of 1939 was perfect for crops. Corn, winter wheat, rye, oats, buckwheat, potatoes, apples, and peaches beat the records of previous years in size and taste. When potatoes were dug up in the fall, some were large enough to feed a small family. Farmers were on the look out for a hobo who was a member of a prominent Shenango Valley family, but lived in a cave near Wheatland when he was not traveling in boxcars. The roof of the cave was close enough to the soil where crops were grown that he could reach up and pull carrots and other vegetables down by the roots to eat them. A newspaper advertisement asked the public to capture the thief; the farmers were tired of the empty holes where their crops had been. The Shilling family of Wheatland was the most frequent victim.

FARMING
By Vonda Minner

In the 1930s, the Agriculture Stabilization and Conservation Office was formed as an agency of the U.S. Department of Agriculture. Its purpose was to promote conservation in the aftermath of the Dust Bowl in the West. Farmers were helped with financing new fences and adding lime to their fields. The farmers were taught to put something back into the land.

The Canon Farm (Shenango Township) was one hundred years old in 1931; the Rhodes Farm (Salem Township), in 1933; the Masson Farm (Findley Township), in 1934; the McDougall Farm (Pine Township), in 1935; the Lackey Farm (Perry Township, now owned by Steve and Kathy), in 1935; the Straub Farm (Otter Creek Township), in 1937; and the McDowell Farm (Pine Township), in 1938.

In 1934, the Fruit Growers Association was started.

Arleigh and Glenn Artherholt started selling J. I. Case Farm Equipment (Pymatuning Township) in 1935.

MERCER AIRPORT
By Richard Christner

Mercer Airport's beginnings can be traced to World War I. It quickly developed as an auxiliary landing strip for the U.S. Air Service, principally on the New York-Cleveland run. In 1928, it was expanded with government support to accommodate all types of small aircraft, with a lighted field, electrified tower beacon (originally battery-powered), and supporting buildings. The main north-south runway was supplemented by a smaller east-west grass strip. The airport was located on the Tait Farm off Airport Road (formerly Old State Road) in Coolspring Township, a few miles northeast of Mercer.

(For many years, it was managed by William Tait, son of owners Samuel F. and Margaret Tait. Later, the land was leased to Louise Skelton, who managed the airport with her son Billy until 1949 or 1950, when the airport closed. The last user was Rocky Filer, who turned down an offer to sell the airport.)

(The only buildings now standing are the well-weathered and empty maintenance shop and office building. A hanger next to the maintenance shop fell down and was removed a number of years ago. A storage barn across the road burned down when an airmail plane accidentally dropped a flare on it while trying to land at night. The beacon is now part of the New Castle Airport. The property is still in the Tait family, presently Nancy Tait and Festus Tait.)

A footnote: According to LeRoy Haag, as recorded by Joyce Young, a P-38 was running out of gas or maybe lost and had to make an emergency landing. The pilot landed the plane safely at Mercer Airport; however, he could not fly it out because the runway was too short. People had to dismantle the plane and cart it out on a truck.

The commercial use of aviation for airmail service developed in the late 1920s and 1930s. In the early years, special stamps were required for airmail delivery. Other means of transporting mail were used if normal (and supposedly longer) deliveries were to be made. By the late 1900s, airmail stamps were no longer in use, since a significant amount of mail and packages are normally transported via regularly scheduled airline and by special air carriers such as Federal Express and Emory. As early as the 1920s, the Mercer Airport was an auxiliary airfield for the Cleveland/New York airmail route. During National Air Mail Week in 1938, Greenville pilot Warren B. Skelton (accompanied by Greenville postmaster Fred W. Moser) flew from Greenville to Mercer to pick up air mail from southern Mercer County communities, then back to Greenville to pick up airmail from the northern communities, and then to Meadville where the mail was transferred to a regular airmail plane. The mail consisted of 2,300 letters and packages weighing sixty-nine pounds. Postal officials from all parts of the county attended brief ceremonies at the Mercer and Greenville airports. Ironically, a few days later, Skelton's light monoplane crashed on the farm of U. S. Artman three miles northwest of Greenville. Skelton and a passenger were slightly injured. Continual landings at interim stopping points were time-consuming, and new procedures were developed which enabled planes to pick-up mail sacks while in flight. In 1939, a 465-mile regular airmail route between Pittsburgh and Philadelphia with intermediate points including Grove City was inaugurated by All-American Aviation. The first pickup at Grove City occurred on May 14, 1939, and was witnessed by a crowd estimated at 6,000 to 7,000. The pick-up point was at the Grove City's Memorial Park, near the present ball field. (The outbound mail pouch was hung on a rope strung between two poles; the plane would swoop down, drop an inbound mail pouch, and grab the hanging outbound mail pouch with a grappling hook.) A second route from Pittsburgh to Buffalo with intermediate stops including Grove City was approved by the Civil Aeronautics Board in 1940. All-American used a Stinson SR-10C Reliant, with a 260-horsepower Lycoming engine, for the pickups, which were accomplished by a hook on the bottom of the tail. (Photo: Grove City Community Library; caption: Richard Christner)

AN EYEWITNESS ACCOUNT . . .
*By Nick Sicilian (Source: **Area Friends Remember When: A Collection of Nostalgic Memories of Times Gone By**)*

"I was born in Number 2 Mine in 1921, and so I was nine years old in 1930 when Marco Demifonte committed his mass murder. Everybody was a coal miner in Number 2 Mine. Everybody was related and knew each other. Marco was a very nice gentleman. He used to shoot blackbirds and we as children used to go and pick them up for him. He was a barber as well as a coal miner, and he used to cut our hair for us. The mine itself was half a mile below the town, and the company store was the brick building on the corner. . . .

"Mr. Demifonte was a sociable man, a nice man. There was no hint of his being mentally unbalanced. He used to come over to our house to play cards. . . .

"Mr. Demifonte lived at the west or lower end of the street. On the fateful morning, he was supposed to go to work and was having coffee waiting for the mine whistle to call him to work. His sister-in-law, who lived at the east end of the street, had come over and was having coffee with his wife.

"He went upstairs and got his shotgun and came down and shot both women. Thirteen children were made orphans in an instant. Then he started walking east to the street. The next door neighbor, Mrs. Iacella, was out hanging clothes. He shot her in the head and killed her. The undertaker told me later that all three women had been shot in the head. I was playing with my wagon in front of my house half way up the road. I had not heard the earlier gunshots. When I saw his shotgun, I thought he was going blackbird hunting, so I called to him, 'Going hunting, Marco?' But when he pointed the shotgun at me, I turned and ran. He shot me twice in the back and knocked me over. The doctor later worked for four hours to get the pellets out of me. I still have pellets in my lungs and shoulder. When he first raised his gun, I was about 15 feet away from him, and by the time he fired at me running away from him, I was far enough away that the pellets were dispersed. Each time he hit me, it knocked me down, but I was able to get up both times and run for the house. The expression on his face was blank, but I knew he meant to kill me, and I ran the instant he raised his gun.

On July 23, 1931, George W. Masters, thirty-eight-year-old manager of the Union Supply Company store at Number Two Mine (Springfield Township) was suddenly called to the aid of his neighbors when a miner, suddenly and without warning, began a murderous rampage through the quiet community. When called to help, Masters armed himself with a shotgun and sought out Demfonti. Upon finding the assailant, who tried to shoot him, Masters wounded Demfonti in the legs and helped subdue him until the arrival of the state police. For his brave actions—that risked his life and doubtless saved others—the Carnegie Hero Fund Commission awarded Masters a silver Carnegie Medal. Masters, according to newspaper accounts, used the monetary portion of the award for a college education for his son, Charles. A commission in lunacy examined Marco Demfonti and adjudged him insane. He was confined for the rest of his life at the Pennsylvania Institute for the Criminally Insane at Farview.

"My mother had heard the shots and came running out of the house. . . . My mother came and picked me up and carried me into the house and locked the doors. In his demented state, he apparently had to kill anyone who crossed his path, because he smashed a window and came into the house after me. My mother tried to protect me. She went and got a pistol called a 'lemon squeezer' because there was a safety on the back of the handle, [and] if you did not squeeze it in your grip, [the gun] would not fire. She tried to shoot him, but the gun wouldn't fire because she didn't know about the safety. Marco then shot her in the side with his shotgun and mortally wounded her. I was lying on the floor and watched everything. She fell on the floor and he began to hit her with the gun. He didn't say anything, he just made grunting noises as he hit her. I can remember it as plain as though it were today. . . . I tried to run up the stairs. I was terrorized and couldn't help yelling as I ran, 'He killed my mom; he killed my mom!' He heard me and shot me again, this time in the leg. I lost consciousness and I suppose that he thought I was dead. I must have been covered with blood.

"Marco then . . . started down the street again, and shoemaker came along. He was a good friend of Marco's. The shoemaker said, 'Marco, what are you doing?' And Marco turned and blew part of his head off. . . .

"By now someone had run up to the company store to call the police, and so George Masters, the 40-year-old store manager, heard about what was happening. He grabbed a shotgun and ran the hundred yards to the residential street of Number 2 Mine. Just as Marco shot the shoemaker, George Masters came down over the hill.

"George Masters told Marco to stop where he was. Marco whipped up his shotgun and pulled the trigger, but the gun was empty! Marco began to reload. George Masters raised his shotgun and fired. . . . Marco fell, hit in the legs, into a puddle of water. A bunch of guys rushed out and held him down. Then they threw him into the back of the truck and the police took him to the county jail.

"The police thought I was dead, so they asked Mr. Cunningham, the funeral director from Leesburg, to take me, too, along with the other dead bodies. But Dr. David Vogan said not to, that I wasn't dead. . . .

"I was in the hospital for 43 days. My father visited Marco in jail and asked him why he had killed my mother. He said that he had only wanted to kill his wife and sister-in-law because they were plotting against him, and after that he was crazy. . . .

"The families all rallied around to raise the children. None of us was ever sent to an orphanage."

MAJOR GENERAL C. BLAINE SMATHERS

According to his obituary in the November 1, 1940, *Mercer Dispatch*, Major General C. Blaine Smathers (Grove City) graduated from Grove City College in 1902. He remained at the College as head of the cadet corps until 1905 when he was elected supervising principal of the Grove City schools. After World War I, Smathers was made superintendent of the State Soldiers Orphans School in Scotland, Pennsylvania. He held that post until his death at age sixty-three.

Smathers had an active military career of forty-two years. He enlisted in Company F, 15th Regiment, of the National Guard and held every rank from private to major general. He served on the Mexican border and in France; for the last four years had commanded the 56th Brigade of the National Guard; and only a month before his death received his final promotion.

BACKYARD GARDENS
By Wally Wachter

(*Editor's note: In this chapter, this section and the other pieces written by Wachter about his childhood in the 1920s and 1930s were originally published in 1983 or 1984 in* **The Herald**.)

"When I was a youngster, there was scarcely a home that didn't have a backyard garden.

"The alleyways between street blocks used to be the best baseball fields. But one had to learn to hit the ball to straight centerfield. To left field or right field the ball was sure to land in someone's garden—and that meant goodbye baseball. Only the most congenial neighbors allowed you to retrieve it.

"Many of the old-time gardeners brought their agricultural know-how from their homelands. They knew what to plant and when to plant it. They knew nothing of today's sophisticated scientific plant foods and fertilizer. All they knew was to fertilize generously with cow or sheep manure or sludge they promoted from the sewage disposal plant.

"The results were amazing. Tomatoes were round and juicy. The corn was tender and sweet. The salads were scrumptious.

"Back in the throes of the Great Depression, when work at the old US Steel Corp. and Carnegie-Illinois Steel plants in Farrell was virtually at a shutdown, the companies took steps to help their willing employees.

"They divided a large tract of land at the rear of Wheatland Tube Co. in Wheatland into large garden plots. They donated the use of these plots to any of their workers interested in growing their own food to help ease the burden of the work shortage. The land was fertile. Most of those who accepted the offer were expert gardeners and all of the plots were lush and productive.

"I recall how with great reluctance and under heavy parental pressure my brothers and I hauled small wagonsful of the repulsive 'plant food' for more than a mile to the Wheatland plot. It paid dividends at the end of the summer when the return trips from the garden were wagonsful of fresh, tasty vegetables."

Henry A. Roemer
By Mairy Jayn Woge

In 1930, Henry A. Roemer made arrangements to buy Sharon Steel Hoop Company in Farrell. At the time, the thirty-year-old industry was on the brink of bankruptcy. The buildings and equipment were run down, and it had become increasingly difficult to meet the payroll.

Roemer was an experienced steel maker. He had quit school while he was fourteen to become a water boy at Anna Blast Furnace in Struthers, Ohio, and continued to work in the steel industry. (Later, as superintendent of the Canton Sheet and Steel Mill, Roemer was one of the founders of the Canton Bull Dogs, the first professional football team in the United States.) By 1930, he was president of Continental Steel Company of Indiana in Lowellville, Ohio, and had earned the reputation of being a savior of sick steel companies.

Before taking over Sharon Steel Hoop, Roemer relinquished the presidency of Continental Steel and turned down an offer to become president and chairman of the board of Pittsburgh Steel Company. One of Roemer's early undertakings at Sharon Steel Hoop was to assign an employee named Scott to make certain food, clothing, and medical care were available for the men who had been laid off by the company and their families.

Roemer upgraded Sharon Steel Hoop. In 1931, it earned $10 million and five times more employees were working than in 1930. In 1936, Roemer changed the name of Sharon Steel Hoop, Farrell, to Sharon Steel Corporation.

In 1915, U.S. Steel closed its North Carnegie Works in the north Shenango River Flats in Sharon. Rose DeSantis (Sharon) recalled that children in that neighborhood in the 1930s crawled onto the roof of the building where the stack had been and counted the number of tramps who were sleeping on the floor.

During the late 1930s and early 1940s, management of Carnegie Illinois was abandoning others of its older steel mills, among them the South Works in Farrell. Hundreds of local jobs were jeopardized. Carroll D. Kearns, superintendent of Farrell schools and later a congressman, and Farrell mayor Lewis Levine decided to do something about the crisis. They approached Roemer and persuaded him to take over the Carnegie mill. He purchased the plant in 1945. It involved ninety-two acres, about seven in Ohio, two blast furnaces, a blooming mill, twelve stands of steel bars, and hot-strip mills and equipment for cold rolling, pickling, and galvanizing.

Some of the buildings were erected between 1898 and 1901 for the Sharon Steel Company. Most of the early U.S. Steel buildings were on the site. Henry Roemer named the layout Sharon Steel Corporation, Roemer Works.

Street Rovers
By Wally Wachter

"'Rags! Rags! Any rags today?' was the Saturday morning cry that emanated from the broken-down truck that canvassed all of the alleys in the city.

"It sent youngsters scampering about collecting old clothes and pieces of cloth that had been stashed away for the occasion.

"The rag man, whose attire matched the shabby appearance of his vehicle, was making a good living while providing spending money to the contributors of torn shorts and worn-out dresses.

"For the rags he paid top price of three cents a pound. He got much more for them from brokers who then peddled the old garments to paper mills to use in making paper. The accuracy of the rag man's ancient scale was always in doubt because it was hard to pile the bulk rags on the little round disc that served as a base for the old produce-type weigher.

Sharon Steel Hoop Works. (Postcard: Daniel Maurice)

"The rag man generally won the disputes when someone contested that the rags were hanging over the sides and touching the truck, therefore were not being weighed fairly. For the more vehement arguers, he threw in an extra penny or two to cut off further hassling.

"Rags were just the most common item in his business. He also collected iron, copper, brass and old junk. The nickel-a-pound price on iron, the 10-cent offering on a pound of copper and the 12 cents he paid for brass made it worthwhile for many youngsters, and some elders, to scour the city dumps looking for saleable metals or junk items.

"Some of the old junk pieces for which he sometimes paid as high as a quarter would bring a small fortune at today's flea markets and garage sales.

"During the Big Depression years, many needy families turned into scavengers and depended on the rag man to provide them the meager funds they needed for existence.

"The rag man was not the only one in those days who provided home service for the people, most of whom did not have automobile transportation.

"The umbrella man was another who wandered from neighborhood to neighborhood offering his services. He made regular rounds, straightening or replacing bent spokes on the bumbershoots, or sewing or patching the silk canopies. The fascinating manner in which he went about his work always attracted a curious audience.

"Sometimes the umbrella man had a side business of sharpening scissors and knives.

*(Source: **Mercer Dispatch and Republican**, August 31, 1934)*

Howard McCartney (O. H. McCartney's son) still lives on the family farm and remembers when Route 19 was a dirt road that was oiled to keep the dust down. He remembers the paving of the road in the early 1930s. It took all summer to pave the road starting at Camp Perry and continuing south toward Mercer. Pictured are scenes from when Route 18 was paved south into Clarksville. (Photos: Jean Fleet; caption: Patricia Jones)

But generally it was another craftsman who made the rounds providing that service. A large emery wheel strapped on his back identified the sharpening man.

"The umbrella man, like the rag man, used his bellowing voice to attract attention during his trek through the city—'Umbrellas! Any umbrellas to fix today?' His familiar cry inspired a popular song which became a hit in the early 1930s.

"The sharpener, on the other hand, made his presence known with a clanging cow bell.

"Both were usually followed down the streets by an entourage of young children.

"Many fathers who prided themselves as expert barbers or who wanted to save the two bits it cost for professional haircuts, would avail themselves of the services of the knife sharpeners. They would have their scissors and hand clippers tuned up for a piddling sum, readying them for an assault on the thick overgrowth of their protesting children's hair.

"Either the emery wheel was faulty or the parents' expertise was lacking. The scissors and clippers tugged, pulled and ripped, leaving a finished hairstyle dangling strands and steps which almost always had to be righted anyway by a professional barber.

"Then there was the ice cream man whose tingling bells attracted kids from all over town to his truck. He followed a schedule you could almost set your clock by. It generally was just in time to spoil the kids' lunches or evening meals.

"And there was the organ grinder who went from corner to corner grinding his music box while his monkey did all kinds of crazy tricks to amuse the audience which responded by flipping a coin or two into his tin cup.

"Some of the organ grinders had popcorn and peanut stands. Some sold hotdogs with ketchup and mustard.

"These street rovers, whether they bought rags, sharpened knives, fixed parasols or provided a monkey show, were all shrewd businessmen who drew on their own individual talents to provide a living for themselves in an era where survival was rough. They also provided an impressive chapter in the saga of our growing up."

WALTER KITCH'S SHIRT
By Joyce Young

"In reviewing old minutes of Otter Creek Township's supervisor meetings, I found a yellowed sheet of tablet paper with a list of expenditures for 1933 and 1934. The last entry was for a shirt for Walter Kitch, costing 45 cents. As the township's secretary, I received a telephone call from Robert W. Kitch (Stoneboro) following a 1989 article in *The Sharon Herald* about the township's newsletters that mentioned the expenditure. Robert said he vividly remembers the day his father Walter came home bruised from armpits to stomach, and he shared the details of the incident with me.

"Walter grew oats, wheat, and other produce and raised cattle on his farm in Otter Creek Township. He also worked at the Greenville Steel Car plant. In addition, Robert and his father spent many summer evenings huckstering strawberries (at six quarts for a quarter) and his mother's homemade pies and cookies door to door in Greenville.

"But during the Depression, even money from two jobs and evening peddling was not enough to feed Walter's family. So, he signed on with the Works Progress Administration and would occasionally get called to help maintain the township's roads, which were all gravel then. For example, sometimes he used his team of horses to drag the roads.

"One time, Walter and some other workers were at the township's gravel site near the Little Shenango River. They were shoveling the stones on to a conveyor belt, which dropped the stones into a truck or more likely a wagon. Walter got too close to the belt. His shirt got caught in the gears of the motor that powered the belt and pulled him in.

"'The wind could have caught the shirt,' Robert speculated. 'But then my dad was a horse of a worker. He could have just been too eager and got too close.'

"The other workers managed to stop the belt, but not until after Walter's midsection took a good beating from the gears. They had to cut him loose from the machine. The resulting bruises took three or four weeks to heal.

"'I don't know if he went to a doctor,' Robert said. 'Probably not, we had all kinds of home remedies then. And he probably couldn't afford it.'

"But the township could afford to pay for a new shirt. While Robert wasn't aware that the township had reimbursed his father for the shirt, he figured there couldn't have been another Walter Kitch needing a shirt from Otter Creek Township when Robert was 12 years old."

EARLY GROVE CITY BUSINESSMEN
By unidentified interview transcript, 1990s

"Jack McCune and Dr. Fithian and Mr. Carruthers were the founders of the Bessemer Gas Engine Company in Grove City [in 1898] and Jack McCune was a mechanic essentially (he wasn't an educated man) and he was the inventor of the one lung diesel engine. The one lung diesel engine became sort of a fixture in the industry, especially the oil industry. Eventually around 1928 they decided to sell the Bessemer Gas Engine Company and they sold it to a company from Ohio. The price for it was $1 million each and this was to be paid in cash. At the time the transaction was to be made, three suitcases were brought in and each, Mr. Caruthers and Dr. Fithian, and Jack McCune were given 1 million dollars each in the suitcases. They then left and each one of them built a very elaborate house. The Carruthers house was later the residence of Dr. Weir Ketler and currently the residence of Dr. Ketler's son George. The Fithian house is now down but it was on the boulevard and its present site holds apartment structures off Woodland Avenue and the boulevard. At the time Fithian was done living in it, the house was sold to the Bashlines and it became the core facility for the Bashline Osteopathic Hospital which had to be moved from the corner of Pine and North Center Street. Jack McCune built his house along Woodland Avenue in a circle that was called The Knoll. His house had all plate glass in it. It was a magnificent house. All three were magnificent houses. Jack brought over Italian stonemasons to build it. That set off a building craze at the time. Shortly after that, Ed Harshaw built a house on Lincoln on the 600 block that was to rival the houses of the three founders of the Bessemer Gas Engine Company and those houses with the exception of the Fithian property are still being utilized.

"Jack McCune then ascertained that something had to be done about the Catholic community. The original Catholic Church was out in Hallville. It was apparently run down or not an edifice of any importance, so Jack with his own money, built the Church of the Beloved Disciple in Grove City which still stands. As Jack had been a business man, Jack wanted a business priest to run the place. So he contacted the Bishop and the Bishop sent Father Andrew Quirk [in 1935] who had been a business man in Brooklyn and had taken no vow of poverty and undertook the development of the Catholic Church in Grove City. At the time he took over there was $17 in the till and he began to build the congregation. Father Quirk had some concerns because the dominant churches in Grove City were the United Presbyterian Church, the Presbyterian Church, and the Methodist Church. The Catholic community at that time, Father Quirk felt was marginalized. He felt that the first thing to do was to get the Catholic Church into the mainstream of the Grove City community, so he did. Jack McCune was his most prominent parishioner and was the first Secretary of Welfare in the commonwealth of Pennsylvania. I believe he became the Secretary of Welfare (he was a democrat) shortly after the election of Franklin Roosevelt. Father Quirk proceeded with the idea to mainstream the Catholic community and he took a very conservative position in the community. Basically, his motto was that when the Baptists agree to it, he will too. For example, the Knights of Columbus were never allowed to hold any types of bingo or anything of that nature. If there was a wet/dry issue, you never saw the Catholic church taking a position, nor any prominent Catholic layperson. Sunday movies or opening the swimming pool all were things which he felt would bring his parishioners into conflict with the mainstream of Grove City. He never took a public position or even a private position that any of these changes should be undertaken.

"Father Quirk was also opposed to Catholic schools in Grove City. He felt that the basic complaint that Catholics had in general was that the public schools were Protestant schools and he felt that eventually this had to end. However, he felt that a Catholic parochial school was a tremendous economical undertaking. Understanding that he was a business man, I think he felt that the business plan was bad. He felt that the schools would be less and less involved in religion and the market for this particular type of service would dry up. . . . Many years later in the 1960s . . . there was no prayer in the schools, there was no substantial market for this in Grove City, and the Catholics were thoroughly integrated into the town, so a school was never built. . . .

"Occasionally there would be an upheaval. I grew up in an all Catholic neighborhood, though I am not Catholic. In the 1940s when I would go to school with all of my little friends school would open and they would want to bring their Bible. They'd bring the Dewey Bible and they'd be sent home because the only acceptable version of the Bible was the King James Version of it. So they couldn't bring their Bibles or they had to go get one. The Lord's Prayer had a different ending for them as well. When I started school, we would open in the morning with the Lord's Prayer which would be the Protestant version. Then it would be followed by the Bible verse which had to be memorized because on Fridays you were going to have Bible school. That, of course, was a Protestant thing. Then you'd have a hymn. We'd use a Protestant hymn and that would take the first fifteen minutes. Then on Friday afternoon, Miss Huskin and Miss Peyser from the WCTU [Women's Christian Temperance Union] and Methodist Church would arrive and from 1:30-3:00 we would have to recite our Bible verses and the things we had learned during the week. During that time, the Catholic children (all my friends) were shipped down to the nurse's office. This didn't sit well with them. I think the last upheaval we had that I was aware of had to do with the hiring (to be schoolteachers) of two girls, eminently qualified, who were found not to be qualified because they smoked. They were a couple of my neighbor girls. They had come back to town and were looking for jobs and they weren't hired because they smoked. In any event, now the church is pretty well integrated into the community and I would suspect that half of the community leadership today in Grove City is Roman Catholic. I don't think anybody worries much about that anymore.

"[Over about 40 years,] Father Quirk . . . built the church and set it in this unique foundation which I don't think exists in many other communities. As I said, he had been a Brooklyn business man, a practical man. In retrospect, this was the only way to do it. We have not had a lot of religious friction basically because there was no way to pin the tail of a vice or the supporting of vice on the Catholic church in Grove City. To this day I think this is one of the reasons the neighborhoods were all easily integrated and no one really thought about anyone's religion very much. . . .

"This brings us back to Jack McCune, Secretary of Welfare. . . . Jack at one time was in charge of the Department of Public Assistance and things were very hard in Grove City all through the depression. Things were not easy. In my neighborhood, a lot of people I knew had just gotten off relief. What caused people to get off relief was the war. That's what brought the jobs. In any event, the municipal park was built by WPA [Works Progress Administration] money that Jack McCune funneled into the town. He had a little bit of a problem because much of the community's leadership were rockbed Republicans and didn't want anything to do with Roosevelt money. The best example of that has to do with education. Grove City in about 1934 or 1935 with T. C. Cochran as congressman was chosen to receive funding for a brand new public school. The funding for the new public school, the Grove City High School, was to be funded by WPA money. The community leadership said they didn't want any of the Roosevelt money so the money was taken from Grove City and that's what built Farrell High School. Even Farrell High School's design was the design that was going to be Grove City High School's. . . .

"Roger [Ormond, son of Grove City College president Alexander T. Ormond] went to Europe for his degree. Roger spoke good German as was expected. At this time the First

World War broke out. Roger joined the National Guard and there was a famous story of Roger. He was a machine gunner. He got separated and after about four days he showed up again naked with a German helmet carrying a broken German rifle. Everybody figured Roger must have been in a hell of a fight cause Roger never remembered what had happened but he always had a tick after that in his face. Roger was a man of considerable principle. He married Jack McCune's daughter Grace. She had a degree from Trinity University. Roger had very little truck with hypocrisy. For example, Grove City had a rule against the municipal swimming pool opening on Sunday. Roger thought it was sheer hypocrisy cause he knew that the people who could afford it took their kids up to Sandy Lake and let them swim. One Sunday, Roger appeared at the swimming pool, cut through the fence. When the police arrived, there was Roger swimming in the municipal swimming pool. . . . Roger came back every Sunday until the pool was opened. Another time, at the country club you couldn't play golf on Sunday mornings. One Sunday morning, Roger (who couldn't even play golf) would show up at the Grove City Country Club with his golf clubs. . . .

"Dr. O. O. Bashline . . . and Dr. Rossman opened the Bashline Rossman Osteopathic Clinic in Grove City [about 1923]. For a number of years the Bashline Rossman Osteopathic Hospital was a medical school and Dr. Bashline was a professor of medicine there. Of course, this scandalized the MDs and the town was just polarized on the issue of who went to the osteopaths and who went to the MDs. The MDs and the DOs was where there was real friction. It got really bad. There was a fellow from Erie who was injured on Route 19 and was brought into the Bashline Hospital. Dr. Bashline operated and put pins in there. So Dr. Hammond [MD] went to him and said he was in the hands of the real butcher. So the family took him to Hammond and the thing got infected and he lost his leg. He sued him for malpractice. The defense was basically that they had caused the problem by hauling this guy out and causing the wounds to open. It had nothing to do with the treatment. It was one of the original cases in the United States where it gets the school of the physician. You cannot testify as an MD as to good osteopathic practices so they couldn't get any witnesses. So the case was won. Dr. Bashline then went on for a number of years and he had three children. Wayne was a straight DO. Then the other two boys, Woody and Don, were MDs and had honorary DOs. Dr. Bashline actually saw that there was a real problem with this DO business so he just sent his kids off to medical school and they could practice. So the hospital was divided between the two factions. One of the more interesting things about the DOs was that if you went to an osteopathic hospital for surgery they used chloroform and if you went to the MDs they used ether. That seemed to be what divided the medical practice. If you were a woman and had a baby in the osteopathic hospital, the silver tea set was brought out and you were served. But they were around long before the hospital over in the valley. Later on, it ceased being a medical school and became a regular hospital."

Michael Ristvey
By Wally Wachter

Among the pioneers who paved the way for better living in Mercer County during the 1900s was a Sharon man whose interest in electronics provided both service and entertainment to a growing community. A self-made man, with a flair for electronics, Ristvey's life was one of perseverance and hard work, not unlike that of many who had to make their mark during the Depression years.

He was born in 1911 in Cambria County. His immigrant parents, John and Susan Sheftic Ristvey, had come to the United States from what is now the Republic of Slovakia.

Ristvey's mother was a housewife, and his father worked in the coal mines in Cambria County. Disturbances in the coalmines led his father in 1928 to move the family to Mercer County.

Before moving to Sharon, Ristvey had held a series of odd jobs as a youngster, which kept him out of the coal mines. On arrival in the Shenango Valley, with only an eighth-grade education, young Ristvey went to work in the Valley's steel mills.

When the Depression hit in 1929, mill work slowed to one day per two weeks. Ristvey decided he had to find some other type of income for himself and his young family. He enrolled in a radio correspondence course. Upon finishing the course, he set himself up in business, doing several things with radio at that time.

He was also employed by the Capitol and Colonial theaters. During that time is when he rigged up his sound truck and hired out to anyone who wanted commercials or announcements broadcast over the speakers. Farrell, the melting pot of various ethnic groups, had many people who could hardly speak or understand the English language. They could not read newspapers. They became the targets of his travels through the streets announcing various commercial activities and advertising the movies that were playing at the Capitol and Colonial. Ristvey played music over the sound system, made announcements for local merchants, and even aired political announcements during election campaigns. The side of the truck sported a large billboard, which also provided additional income for him.

Taking the correspondence course involved Ristvey in radio in its infancy. He opened a radio repair shop near the corner of Sharpsville Avenue and State Street, where the present Shenango Valley Library is located. The first high school football game to have a public address system announce the games was in Sharpsville, set up by Ristvey.

With the threat of World War II, Ristvey became a part of the U.S. Navy. Because of his electrical background in radio, he was assigned to the Sharon Westinghouse plant to inspect all transformers and to approve them for shipment for use in various Navy construction projects. He also tested equipment in the torpedo tube components that were manufactured at the local Westinghouse plant.

At the end of World War II, he was discharged from the Navy and started a business as an electrical contractor and wired new houses. He then opened a shop, under the name of Ristvey Radio and Electric, on Thorton Street in Sharon around the bend from the old Westinghouse plant.

Later, when television was being introduced, Ristvey was the first in the area with the new medium. Recognizing the future of television, still in the experimental and development stages, he decided to expand his field. In March of 1948, the first set in the area appeared in his little radio sales and repair shop on Thornton Street. Monstrous compared to today's sleek models, the first set was a 15-inch TCA (Television Corporation of America) unit. Channel 5 in Cleveland was the only television station in the area then. It had gone on the air only three months earlier, in December of 1947.

Public acceptance of the new fad was spontaneous. Ristvey's son, Michael Jr., now an attorney in Hermitage, recalled how people would jam the shop in the evenings to watch the novelty. Test patterns would appear most of the day, and telecasts were only during several hours in the evening. "When special events, like boxing matches, were on the air, we had a full showroom. Of course, 1948 was the year the Cleveland Indians won the pennant and were in the World Series. This, too, brought the crowds," he remembered.

In 1970, Ristvey closed his little shop and a chapter on the early days of radio and television in the Shenango Valley. He continued to repair radios in his home on Bechtol Avenue, Sharon. The basement of the home was full of radios, equipment, and parts.

Ristvey died in 1972 and was survived by his wife, Anna, and three sons, Michael Jr., John Daniel, and Thomas, along with seven grandchildren.

THE RADIO FOR ENTERTAINMENT
By Wally Wachter

"'Good evening, everybody!' and 'So long until tomorrow!'

"That was the patented sign-on and sign-off of newscaster Lowell Thomas back in the days when stay-at-home entertainment was only the radio. There was no TV, but some of the top network radio shows excelled today's television offerings.

"Grownups could hardly wait until 6:45 p.m. when Thomas came on. They had just finished reading the daily paper of what had happened the night before and looked forward to hearing of new developments from their favorite news announcer. They gathered around their radios, some large clumsy rounded sets that set on shelves or end tables or equally awkward floor models that had phonographs that swung out from the lower half.

"Those who had no particular interest in Lowell Thomas or the news turned him on anyway, because they knew that at the end of his 15 minutes he would be followed by their favorites, Amos and Andy. The extremely funny comedy half-hour which featured the antics and humorous situations of two lodge-going buddies and their friends, the Kingfish in particular, delighted the elders.

"Radio offered a wide variety of entertainment in those days—comedy, drama, mystery and suspense, children's fare, pleasing music, and yes, even soap operas.

"Housewives took a respite from their chores at mid-morning or early afternoon to lend an ear to The Goldbergs, Jake and Molly, or to Stella Dallas or other popular afternoon serials. Then, like Molly Goldberg did with her neighbor Mrs. Bloom, they'd compare notes with the neighbor ladies, either over the backyard fence or on the telephone. This was not unlike what TV fans do after an episode of 'Knot's Landing,' 'Dynasty,' 'Falcon Crest' or one of the afternoon soaps.

"Later afternoon belonged to the kids. It featured the old wrangler relating stories about popular cowboy Tom Mix, or the antics of 'Skippy,' or the heroic adventures of 'Jack Armstrong, the All-American Boy.' It was as hard to pull the youngsters to the dinner tables as it is now difficult to prod the elders away from their late-afternoon money movies on TV. I wish I had a nickel for every cereal boxtop I sent to Checkerboard Square, St. Louis, Mo.

"Comedy was king. It was little wonder, though, with the caliber of comedians who reigned in those days, many of them continuing their popularity when television took over.

"Sunday nights belonged to Jack Benny. The violin-playing comic gave a memorable variety program which also featured his wife, Mary Livingston; his chauffer, Rochester; tenors Kenny Baker and Dennis Day; and his butt-of-jokes announcer, the rotund Don Wilson.

"Bob Hope was generally a Thursday night attraction. The master comedian, with his quick wit and comic satire, was assisted by his falsetto-voiced friend Jerry Colonna. Other nights of the week were occupied by such laugh experts as Fred Allen; Bob Burns and his Ozark-yarn spinning which featured Bus Bazooka; George Burns and Gracie Allen in a family comedy; Fibber McGee and Molly which created the still famous line, 'T'aint funny, McGee'; and the popular Georgie Jessel.

"The creaking door that accompanied the sign-on of 'Inner Sanctum' provided many chills and sometimes sleepless nights for the mystery fans. Other hair-raising and nail-biting suspense shows were 'Enu Crime Clues,' 'The Green Hornet,' and 'Mr. Chameleon,' the latter the experiences of a police inspector with many disguises he used in solving crimes.

"For good music there were such offerings as 'Rubinoff and His Violin,' the Phil Spitalny all-girl orchestra, and interludes of music by the popular bands of the day interspersed with the morning and afternoon featured programs. But the popular show was Saturday night's 'Hit Parade.' It highlighted the 10 top tunes in the nation performed by outstanding singers and musicians.

"Sponsored by a tobacco company, the Hit Parade at one time offered a carton of cigarettes to anyone who guessed what the top 10 would be for the following week in the right order. A featured singer for a long time on the program was Jeff Clark, nee Dave Harbin, a former Westminster College student who got his start in radio as an announcer for Sharon's station WPIC. Illness forced him to leave the program.

"The most memorable drama program was Friday night's 'Little Theater Off Times Square,' which was emceed by Don Ameche who also starred in many of the presentations.

"Sunday afternoon was the time for Major Bowes' popular amateur hour where budding young entertainers were given a chance to compete for prizes. It opened the door for many to become radio stars on their own.

"Later years which brought more local stations to compete with the networks also brought regional favorites.

"Among those best remembered in this area were Gene and Glenn, a song team emanating from Cleveland, who opened the day with a smile and added spice to their act by portraying the comic characters, 'Jake and Lena.'

"There also came a wealth of hillbilly talent, including Pie Plant Pete whom I remember most for playing a harmonica to the accompaniment of his own guitar."

UNIONS
By Mairy Jayn Woge

One of the early labor unions in the Shenango Valley, the Amalgamated Association of Iron, Steel and Tin Plate Workers lost most of its contracts locally in 1901 and the remaining ones, in the sheet and tin mills in 1909.

Then in the 1930s, after organizing coal miners, John L. Lewis turned his attention to U.S. Steel. He visited mills, interviewed workers, and learned some of the laborers in the steel industry earned but $359 annually. In 1936, Lewis and his associates engineered the founding of the Steel Worker Organizing Committee (SWOC). The SWOC affiliated with the Congress of Industrial Organizations (CIO). During the Little Steel Strike in 1937, John Grajciar (Sharon), an organizer for the SWOC, was shot through the hat during a gunfight at a Valley industry. Partially as the result of the strike, a number of Shenango Valley industries agreed to the SWOC-CIO's representing workers in their mills. Those participating were Carnegie Illinois Steel Company, Sharon Steel Corporation, National Malleable and Steel Castings Company, Sharon and Mercer Tube companies, General American Transportation Corporation, Petroleum Iron Works, Sharpsville Boiler Company, Inc., and Sharpsville Penn Mold Company. The United Steel Workers (USW) was organized in 1936. Grajciar was named a director of District 20 of the USW of America, in 1941. In 1955, the CIO merged with the American Federation of Labor (AFL), and the USW became part of the AFL-CIO.

Strikes over the amount workers were paid closed thirteen Shenango Valley industries for up to ten weeks in 1946 and 1949. In 1950, the USW was bargaining agent for seventeen Valley industries.

During the 1990s, Steelworker locals in the Valley have been reorganized and amalgamated so that five super locals represent workers at approximately twenty work sites, according to Richard Miller (Greenville), who is executive director of the county labor-management organization.

ALF LANDON AND THE ELECTION OF 1936
By David Miller and Aaron Jarvinen

Alfred Mossman Landon was born in 1887 in his grandfather's parsonage in West Middlesex. As a boy, he attended Marietta Academy in Ohio, where he was active in football. However, he was only an average student, and he rarely, if ever, read a book outside of the classroom. *Harper's* observed, "He has a good mind, but no one ever accused him of being intellectual. His friends say that he gets most of his information by questioning those he comes in contact with, particularly those from outside his own intimate circle."

In 1904, Landon moved with his family to Kansas where he was considered a rich man's son because his father was successful in oil. He shortened his name to Alf and attended Kansas University, making the best fraternity. After graduating from the Kansas University Law School, however, Landon took a job in a bank and invested part of his earnings into oil-drilling ventures. These investments enabled him to quit his job after only three years and go to the oil fields as a wildcatter. Landon was a real go-getter and known to scramble for leases and constantly trade and barter. His hard work boosted his oil fortune to something just short of $1 million by 1929.

Landon was not satisfied with his wealth in the oil fields. He decided to be more active in politics. He started by managing the successful campaign of Clyde Reed for governor in 1928. He enjoyed this work and in 1931 decided to run for governor himself.

Landon was a terrible campaign speaker. His voice was a monotone; and he stuttered, stammered, paused, backtracked, and tied himself in knots. But, after a speech, he would stay at least an hour to shake hands and talk with the audience. The people of Kansas did not seem to want a fancy talker, but rather a businessman. In 1932 when the country went Democratic, Alf was the only Republican governor elected west of the Mississippi.

While in office, Landon gave the people of Kansas the kind of administration they had asked of him: sound, economical, and business-like. Landon proved to be a high-minded

On the Tam O'Shanter Golf Course (pictured, in 1999), over 110,000 people listened to West Middlesex-born Alf Landon announce his candidacy for U.S. president in 1936. Built in 1929 by T. Wade Walker and designed by Emil Leoffler, this golf course has seen such golf professionals as Bob Toski, Lew Worsham, Dutch Harrison, Betsy Rawls, Betty Hicks, and Patty Berg. A bronze plaque by the first tee commemorates Sam Snead's record score of 65 in his 1949 exhibition. Located in Hermitage, the 18-hole course is now owned by John and Rick Kerins.

and hardworking administrator. Even people who had not voted for him began to praise him for his tact, honesty, and governing ability. Landon became even better known when he was the only Republican governor to be re-elected in 1934.

Landon began to think seriously about the U.S. presidency in the summer of 1935 and was supported by many members of the Republican Party. After he announced his candidacy, the news spawned excitement in Mercer County, particularly West Middlesex. Landon won the Republican nomination easily. His running mate was Colonel Frank Knox, who finished second in the primary election. Their political philosophy was basically conservative. They believed that many of the new governmental functions should be taken up by the state governments and had complaints about the wasteful and inefficient deficit spending that was at hand with Roosevelt's New Deal.

Landon announced that he would kick off his campaign in the town where he was born. This announcement put West Middlesex in the spotlight, and the residents planned for a rally and the expected influx of approximately 100,000 people. Landon's speech was set for August 22, 1936, to be delivered at the Tam O'Shanter Golf Course. The speech was a success, and Landon stayed around the Valley a while to visit some of the scenes of his boyhood. Then, he hit the nationwide campaign trail.

The fall campaign was mainly a two-party contest between Roosevelt and Landon. It was bitter because both sides stirred up class hatred even though both candidates deplored such tactics. Landon maintained his basic themes during the campaign and had reason to believe that he was doing well. The Gallup Poll taken among church members in October showed 51.3 percent of the voters were for Roosevelt, while 48.7 percent were for Landon. However, the outcome did not turn out to be this close at all. The final returns gave the Democrats every state but Maine and Vermont.

The Democrats made great showings in the urban areas. The Shenango Valley mirrored this trend when Sharon and Farrell returned solid Democratic majorities. The rural areas of Mercer County went for Landon as he generally had a better appeal for rural areas. Had it not been for Sharon and Farrell, Mercer County's votes would have gone to Landon.

AMELIA EARHART
By Richard Christner

Amelia Earhart, the pioneering female aviator who disappeared during a round-the-world flight in 1937, played an interesting role in Thiel College history. Earhart's grandfather, the Reverend David Earhart, was one of the founders in 1845 of the Pittsburgh Synod of the Evangelical Lutheran Church, which twenty-one years later established Thiel Hall, the forerunner to Thiel College. Her father, Edwin S. Earhart, graduated from Thiel College in 1886. In December 1932, Amelia Earhart visited Thiel, where she received an honorary Doctor of Science degree.

Shortly before her disappearance, Earhart met with the President of Thiel and expressed a desire to assist young women in furthering their education. A year later, the College established the Amelia Earhart Foundation in her memory. The fund-raising phase, with a goal of $500,000, officially began at a White House luncheon in February 1938, with Eleanor Roosevelt presiding. Objectives included postgraduate scholarships for women, an Amelia Earhart Hall for women students, an annual memorial lecture, and an Amelia Earhart chair of science. Unfortunately, the fund-raising effort failed, but the Earhart name remains a part of Thiel history.

An interesting footnote to Amelia Earhart's relationship with Mercer County is the first Akron Funk airplane owned by Clarence "Buzz" Winder of Grove City. Built in 1934 by Joseph and Howard Funk of Akron, Ohio, the airplane was flown by Earhart in 1935 at the Akron Airport. Winder, a veteran flyer and a member of Chapter 161 of the Experimental Aircraft Association, acquired the airplane in 1972. Several years later, it was damaged in an accident at the Slippery Rock Airport. In 1980, Winder was approaching Slippery Rock Airport's landing strip when the plane lost power and crashed into some trees. In both cases, Winder repaired the airplane, and it is now the oldest plane based at the Grove City Municipal Airport.

STREETCARS IN THE SHENANGO VALLEY
By Mairy Jayn Woge

Streetcars went out of business by 1939. However, they had been running through the Shenango Valley for nearly fifty years. Electricity for traction was available after an ordinance was passed by Sharon government that permitted streetcars in the borough in 1888, but the group that made the request for the franchise did not follow through. Construction of the Shenango Valley Railway started in 1892. The first streetcar line was built on State Street in downtown Sharon and connected to lines on Sharpsville and South Irvine Avenues. A few years later, a connection was made with West Middlesex by a line that crossed the swamp south of current Broadway Avenue. (Broadway was not cut until the World War II period. A bridge that spanned the most perilous stretch of the swamp stands in 2000.) The swamp was attributed to the Beaver and Lake Erie Canal. When Samuel Satterfield sold five acres of Satterfield land south of current Broadway, he did not charge the buyer for "an acre and a half flooded by the canal," according to the Satterfield deed.

The streetcar line to Wheatland was not finished until 1900. The streetcars were short and almost square.

Because of the scarcity of connections, residents of the Valley often found it necessary to use other transportation to ride them to and from streetcar stops. The late Clyde "Ike" Fleet, a son of Samuel Fleet who lived along the Sharpsville-Mercer Road (now Lamar Road), told about driving his father in a horse-drawn buggy to the streetcar stop at Dock and State Streets where the elder Fleet boarded a streetcar that took him to the mills in Farrell and Wheatland where he worked. After Samuel Fleet finished his shift, one of his sons was waiting in the rig at Dock Street to pick him up.

Corwin Hoelzle (Hermitage) was a resident of Patagonia in 1940 while he was employed by a tin mill in Wheatland. He was afraid to ride the streetcar on the Broadway-Dock line "because the motorman drove too fast" and "drove his flivver to and from work when he knew the dangerous motorman would be on duty." Hoelzle added that the line to West Middlesex was almost as frightening because "there was no base or bottom to the swamp that was under the track."

Mary Hull (Sharpsville) recalls that during the summers, the tops of the streetcars were removed, an early form of air conditioning. While the lids were off and the streetcars were traveling over the ravine at Deweyville, she sat on the part of the wicker seats that was closest to the aisle because, she said, "the edge of the tracks were too close to the edge of the hollow and that scared me." Hull said the motorman did not need a roundhouse to change the direction he was going to travel. At the end of the line, he simply moved the pole with the fare box on it to the controls at the other end of the streetcar.

Hoelzle noted the East Hill line was built after 1918 and, before then, the streetcars were not able to climb or safely descend the steep hill. Instead, the streetcars traveled through a hollow behind the Whitla and Porter houses and the F. H. Buhl Club, which paralleled Silver Street. During summers, the hollow was beautified with pink and white hollyhocks. Hoelzle described the route east from downtown Sharon and connections with Sharpsville, Wheatland, and West Middlesex as "following the ravine then turning onto

State Street at Oakland Avenue where the streetcars headed east to Stambaugh Avenue with their horns continually clanging at auto traffic." The streetcars turned south onto Stambaugh Avenue. The hill that starts in the first block of Stambaugh was just as treacherous as the East Hill but shorter. From the bottom of the hill where the Shenango Valley Freeway now crosses Stambaugh, the streetcars proceeded southerly to King Street. They headed west on King then turned south again on Spruce Avenue from where they traveled to Farrell.

A spur terminated at Carley Avenue off Highland Road from where passengers could walk to Buhl Farm.

By the late 1930s, the streetcars were succeeded by buses. When the rails were removed, the brick streets in Sharon were paved. The buses, called "interurbans," connected the Shenango Valley, Youngstown, and some other communities. Hoelzle said the interurbans were four times larger than the streetcars. They parked in a lot east of St. John's Episcopal Church in Sharon.

Neighborhood Groceries
By Wally Wachter

"Food shopping then generally was on a day-to-day basis. One reason was that people bought only what they could carry from store to home. Only the more affluent had cars in those days. Another reason was that lack of refrigeration made it safer to buy meat, butter, cheeses and other perishables a day at a time.

"You entered a grocery store with a list. You read it off to a clerk. He would scurry around the store, picking things off shelves, weighing produce, sugar, salt, etc., and piling things on the counter until the entire list had been filled. He then tallied the prices with a pencil on some white butcher paper. He rang up your money on an old cash register, then bagged your groceries.

"Customers had to wait their turns to be waited on. Sometimes it was between 20 minutes and an hour. During busy peak periods, some of the bigger stores had two or three clerks.

"Most stores had the same personalities.

"Cookies came loose in large square cartons which fit in a large rack, which covered each carton with a glass lid. You picked out the cookies you wanted and put them into a small bag. Most popular were fig bars which were about two pounds for a quarter, or ginger snaps that sold for about a nickel a pound. Other favorites were chocolate-covered marshmallow mounds and rectangular-striped coconut macaroons, but at about 19 cents a pound, they sold only on paydays.

"Oranges and lemons came wrapped individually in colorful tissue paper in wooden crates. The crates and tissue were almost as popular with some customers as the citrus treasures they contained. The crates made good storage boxes. The tissues, well, it's not hard to imagine.

"Sugar, salt, rice, dry beans and other such items came in bulk. They were displayed in sacks or small barrels, each with its small metal scoop which you used to fill your paper bags.

"Washing detergent was unheard of then. Housewives used soap chips which also came in bulk drums.

"Potatoes were generally weighed in advance in peck-size bags. Most apples also were preweighed. Bananas hung from big stalks in the produce department. With a large knife, the clerk would cut off as many as you wanted.

"Canned goods, cereals and other boxed commodities were neatly stacked on floor-to-ceiling shelves behind the counter. To reach the upper shelves, clerks used long poles

The Henderson Clover Farm Store was owned and operated by Roy Henderson and his sister Rhoda Henderson. They were fifth-generation Hendersons. This store sold all the necessary groceries and home needs, such as hardware items, thread, fabric, and other items. The lodge men met at the store on Monday nights. On Tuesday mornings, the kids would search the Popsicle sticks left on the ground by the men for the "free" stick, which in turn gave the finder a free Popsicle. (Caption: Idella McConnell and Lucille Eagles)

In 1927, "the Drennan & Phipps Drygoods store, catering especially to women's and children's needs, was established by Miss Elizabeth Drennan and Miss Maud A. Phipps, former clerks in the T. A. Houston store. They opened business on the North Diamond. Three years later, following the death of Miss Drennan, Miss Phipps took over the business under her own name and carries it on today. The store is truly one where 'every woman likes to shop' with up-to-date stock, well chosen and well displayed. The store has weathered the Depression and its future promises well." (Ad: **Mercer Dispatch and Republican,** *February 14, 1930; caption: same paper, June 30, 1939)*

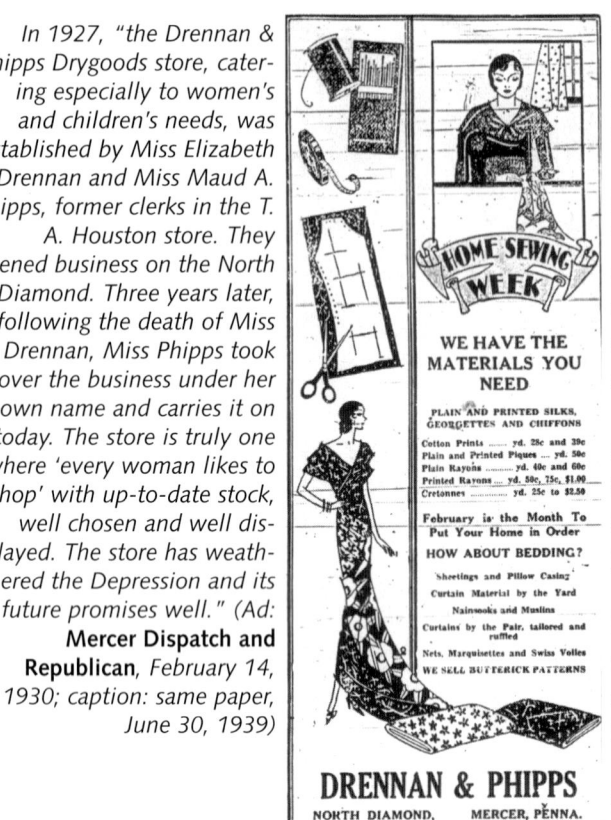

with finger-like prongs on the end that were manipulated by a lever that was grip-high. After removing the item from the shelf, the clerk generally moved the one behind it to the front to make it appear that the shelf was completely stocked.

"The big cereals in those days were corn flakes, Shredded Wheat, and the cooked cereals such as Cream of Wheat, Mothers' Oats and farina. Shredded Wheat was a big seller because of its attractive box that had a colorful picture of Niagara Falls, and because in between layers of the biscuits were picture cards to be colored that kept kiddies busy and out of their mothers' hair for hours.

"People who had more to buy than they could carry usually had their groceries delivered by their neighbor boys in a small wagon for a nickel or a dime. Some stores provided a service whereby you could telephone your order and have your groceries delivered.

"Saturdays were generally the big shopping days, because of the weekends. Farmers would come into town and stock up on foodstuffs for the entire week, sometimes carting off $100 orders in the back of their trucks. A hundred dollars in those days bought almost a truckful.

"The neighborhood groceries were a boon to their customers, because most of them did a credit business. Customers could charge their purchases and pay for them on payday. During the lean Depression years, many of the stores carried their prime customers on the books until they were able to pay. Many stores went broke for this reason."

Mercer in the Late 1930s
By Joseph Hood, written in 1998

"In the late summer of 1939, when I was 13 years of age, we moved to Mercer and lived in a small two-story house at 515 East Market street. Mother had obtained a job at the Mercer Sanitarium serving as a nurse. She had received her Nurses training, in part, at the Sanitarium and also at the Sharon Hospital. I assume that the pittance we had been receiving because of Father's disability and death, was not enough to support growing children, so Mother's training allowed her to obtain additional income to better support our needs.

"Mercer was and is, a town of around 2,500 people, and is the Mercer County seat. A great courthouse is in the center of town, and in those days, it was surrounded by many business places. Except for the courthouse, Mercer was typical small town USA. So that you can get a feel of the times, here are the business places to be found on or adjacent to the town square.

"PITT STREET—Willis Chevrolette, Mercer Bowling Alley, Vath's Meat Market, Braden and Rigby's Grocery Store, Miller's Furniture Store, Isaly's Restaurant, Grill's Hardware, Murphy's five & ten, Weaver's Drug Store, Dillon's Stationery, Scott's Men's Store, Redic's Barber Shop, Jamison's Photo Studio (2nd floor), Emery's Drug Store, Fry's Barber Shop (East Market), Olive McClure's Beauty Shop (East Market), Pennzoil Gasoline Station, Dr. Howe's (MD) office, Dr. Coombe's (dentist) office, and Parker's Ford Garage.

"NORTH DIAMOND STREET—1st National Bank, Mercer Gas and Water, Mercer Library (2nd floor), Montgomery's Drug Store (A special note is required here.

FISHING

By Joseph Hood, written in 1998

"When we first moved to Mercer [in 1939], we [brothers] allied with each other, while slowly reaching out to the neighborhood kids. As a result, Okkie and I spent a lot of time together. We fished mostly. I can't recall catching too many fish, but the attempt certainly kept us busy and out of trouble. Neshannock Creek, in those days, held many varieties of fish, and most were extremely large. Even the suckers were unusually big. I remember one time seeing a fisherman carrying his catch home and the largest sucker appeared to be several feet long. We did not have any fancy fishing equipment, but we managed to improve our equipment by purchasing a 10-foot-long bamboo pole that was available at the hardware store for about one dollar. We would rig it to accept string, and after we purchased the line and sinkers along with the necessary hooks, we had a pretty good outfit and managed to catch a few fish.

"The house in which we lived was rather small, but most adequate. I recall there being a hand pump outside, near the rear door, and it actually pumped water from a deep well. It had a wooden trough which directed the unused water away from the well head. Okkie and I found it convenient to block the end and use this as a place to keep fish we had caught in one of the several creeks within short walking distances from our house. I remember a large catfish that we managed to keep for several days. Eventually, we received orders to cease and desist. (I'm sure the orders came from on high—MOM.) . . .

"Okkie and I, during the spring of the year, built a lean-to along Neshannock Creek, where we could fish in the rain and not get wet and also could build a fire to provide warmth. We managed to borrow materials from the old mill nearby. The building standing there was 'Adam's mill.' Burt Adams sold fertilizer and other farm supplies. I believe that it also included a grist mill operated by Adams. At any rate, there were a lot of materials strewn here and there which made it possible for us to construct quite an elaborate fishing place. They never complained or asked us to leave so during the spring of the year, we could spend a lot of time fishing, mostly for suckers."

Montgomery's store included a pot-bellied stove at the rear of the sales area. In the winter, men would sit around this stove smoking, chewing and spinning tales.), Sine's Grocery, Page's Restaurant, Dr. Hope's (MD) office, Soda Shop, Hoon and Stewart Appliances, Anderson's Barber Shop (basement), Dr. T. W. King (dentist) (2nd floor), Heilig's Bakery, A&P Grocery Store, Langdon's Department Store, Hogue's Shoe Store, Phipp's Dry Goods, Ginader's Candy Store, Liberty Theatre, Farmers Bank, and *Mercer Dispatch* Building on Pitt Street.

"SOUTH DIAMOND STREET—Thompson's Grocery Store, Diamond Restaurant, Ben Lemon's Shoe Repair, Mongiello Apartments, Tom McClain's Print Shop and Notary Public, State Police Barracks, County Jail, Guilar's Restaurant, McCartney's Ice Cream Plant (basement), Bus Station, Clark's Barber Shop and Beauty Shop, Liquor Store, and Guitar's Service Station (Erie Street).

TRAPPING

By Joseph Hood, written in 1998

"While living at 535 East Market [in Mercer], I worked in the fall and early winter for Jimmy Jackal. His house was on the street behind us where he had a large garage that he converted into a fur dealing business. I used to get 5 cents per hide for skinning the animals that he bought. Most of the catches were muskrat, but there were also possums, coons, and skunks. He also bought mink, but Jimmy skinned them himself. He wasn't about to let us kids mess with something that valuable. Sometimes I would go to work and Jim would show me a pile of carcasses to get started on. Then sometimes there were burlap sacks laying on or near the pile with additional animals inside. When I would untie the sack, out would walk a possum. This was supposed to be a joke because it was always a possum. You know, possums are supposed to feign sleeping or unconsciousness so the trapper got some kind of kick out of this rather gruesome joke.

"Jimmy had a terrific fur business. We would work for him during the trapping season. He alone would stretch the furs and allow them to cure. Then he would sell them to buyers who came by periodically.

"After several years, Jimmy moved to a new home on the Clark Road about a half mile from the edge of Mercer. Ironically enough, when my son Joe was a teenager, he too worked for Jimmy, skinning animals as I had done 25 years before. . . .

"Okkie [Joseph's brother] and I took up trapping and after a fairly long learning curve, became fairly adept at capturing muskrat and skunks. I remember one time, however, that we had snared a skunk under a small barn near the center of town. The set was a little short so our method of dispatch was hindered by the fact that the skunk was under the edge of the building. I found a clothesline pole and from the corner of the building, I pried on the chain until the skunk had been moved out where Okkie could strike it in the head. He did. The wind was coming my way and I got nailed in the face with the whole spray. By the time we had completed the sordid episode, both of us were reeking of skunk. This all occurred in the morning before school so when we arrived for classes, we were summarily removed from the school and told not to return until the smell was gone. I don't remember how long we were off, but it must have been several days before we were rid of the odor. It didn't take long for us to lose the urge to catch any more skunks."

"ERIE STREET—Humes Hotel and Restaurant, Sterling Gasoline Station, Drenning's Grocery Store, Penn Power Office, and Cumming's Garage.

"As I continue writing, this last day of 1998, I cannot resist comparing today's 'Uptown' with that of my youth. First of all, a good number of the buildings are gone, some removed by fire and others to make room for county buildings. On Pitt Street, Willis's Garage is now Bissett's Garage. All of the other business places are gone. On North Diamond Street, the 1st National Bank (now Mellon) and Page's Restaurant remain.

The Reznor Manufacturing Company was founded in 1888 by George Reznor. "The Reznor plant... was pretty much family owned. They manufactured heating units for both residential [pictured] and commercial/industrial use. During World War II, they manufactured clips that were used to join individual grate-like metal mats. These mats were designed to be used in the construction of temporary landing fields, mostly in the Pacific area. They also manufactured flair tanks, which were fastened to aircraft and housed aerial flares used for signaling. When I was at Barin Field, outlying field of Pensacola, I was more than surprised when one day I walked into the post office on the base and there, hanging from the ceiling was a heater with a name plate, identifying it as made by Reznor of Mercer Pa. After the War, I took employment at Reznor. My beginning pay was 60 cents an hour." Pictured are (front row) Tom McCann, Filson, Sam Bell, Fred Gibson, Poxberry, Weldon Ringer, Floyd Ringer, Charles Sleingrave, and Milt Adams; (back row, order unclear) Frank Vansitta, Hughie McCann, Ralph Ayers, Wheat, Bill Broad, Ben J., Bill Graham, Muggs McLain, Frank Larry, John Kilner, and unidentified. (Photo: Joyce Young; caption: Joseph Hood)

On South Diamond, the Thompson Grocery Store remains but mostly as a butcher shop. The owners also created a coffee house that doubles as a church group meeting place. The county jail has been rebuilt on land that originally was the Mongiello property. The old county jail now functions as a county office building. The only business that remains on Erie Street is the Penn Power office.

"Most of the remaining buildings are in use. There is one sandwich shop and a number of antique and curio shops. There are now three banks, all with drive-in service. A large hardware store replaces the Cumming's garage. The four gasoline stations that once were located within the town's borders have all disappeared. They have been replaced by new companies, in totally new locations. A small shopping plaza is at the edge of town and includes a supermarket, drugstore, liquor store and pizza shop with restaurant. The Hotel has been replaced by several bed and breakfast establishments.

"Interesting to note, I found employment in several of the businesses that existed back in the 1930s. I worked at the Emery's Corner Drug Store making sodas and milk shakes and filling in as a clerk. I was an usher at the Liberty Theatre where Paul Mulhern was manager and I did all the signs and changed the marquee each time the show changed. I pumped gasoline at the Pennzoil Station that was owned and operated by Pete Mellon, and worked as a dishwasher and waiter at Guitar's Restaurant. For a long time, I set pins at the Mercer Bowling Alley. So you can see that I remained quite busy and was able to earn money with regularity. I was able to buy much of my own clothing and never worried about spending money. . . .

"Because Mom found it difficult to take care of our needs such as food and the other requirements of housekeeping, while at the same time trying to earn the needed income, she arranged to have a housekeeper. Mother usually came home from work, but there were times when her hours prevented this. Sometimes she would stay at the nurses quarters at the Sanitarium. Our housekeeper was a young woman, Josephine Brunner. She had been a patient at the Sanitarium and after being released to go home, Mom had arranged, through her parents, that she could stay with us and tend to some of our needs. Her parents lived at the George Junior Republic where her father was the superintendent.

Josephine was old enough to know what was best for us and yet young enough to be a little like we were. So we got along pretty well. The only problem I ever had with her was I really did not care for the same lunch every day. It consisted of cheese sandwiches and root-beer-flavored cool aide. It didn't matter what we may have desired or if the weather was hot or cold, lunch was always the same.

"We made several visits to the Brunner residence and stayed overnight. The Brunners seemed happy to have us and we in turn enjoyed going there. George Junior Republic was then, and is now, a place for wayward youth and in some cases, wards of the state. Therefore, we were expected to avoid these boys and spend our time at or nearby the Brunner home. [My brother] Okkie apparently could not abide by their wishes and ultimately found his way into one of the dormitories. When we were sitting at dinner that evening, he divulged a planned breakout he had overheard while in the dorm. Mr. Brunner admonished him for going there but took him at his word about the breakout. It did happen and the juveniles were soon apprehended. They received appropriate punishment. We, on the other hand, were no longer allowed the freedom of going where we wished, so our ensuing visits to the Brunners were more closely monitored. . . .

"Our neighborhood included a large number of youth so it wasn't difficult to get neighborhood games started. Most games were team oriented, with team members selected by chance and not by preference. We played, KICK THE CAN, RUN SHEEPIE RUN when it was dark, and STICK BALL when it was daylight. Also, Choog George had a basketball hoop where we played basketball, but most of the time we played HORSE, a shooting game of follow the leader where when if you missed five times, you were out.

"The games played after dark were similar in nature. They included a jail usually under a street light, where anyone captured was held. To be captured simply meant that someone from the other team touched you as you tried to evade capture. These prisoners could be released from jail if one of their team members, still at large, could sneak in and either kick the can that was located at the jail or loudly declare RUN SHEEPIE RUN, without themselves being tagged and consequently put in jail. The game ended when all of one team was incarcerated or when the jailers conceded. Concession was completed by loudly yelling OLLIE OLLIE OUTS IN FREE. At this time, the teams reversed roles and the game was on again.

"Stick ball was played in the alley behind our house. We usually used a sponge ball that was pitched as in baseball, to a batter who was armed with an old broom handle. Once the batter struck the ball, he headed to base just as in the game of baseball. This, as you might discern, was the poor man's version of the national pastime. . . .

"At the time we moved to Mercer, the town was sprinkled with grocery stores. Our neighborhood included two within about two blocks. Bowman's store was located further down the hill from our house and another store that was almost directly across the street from our house was owned and operated by Ralph Blair. For some reason, we dealt primarily with Bowman's. Mother would always call and order what was needed and one of us kids ran there to pick it up. I believe that most everyone bought on credit and paid at the end of the month. This method of doing business prevailed rather universally, no matter where you dealt. The important thing was to faithfully pay up on schedule to maintain your good status. It wasn't until the advent of the super markets and shopping malls that pay-as-you-go went into practice. . . .

"The Reznor plant was just a few blocks from our home so naturally we would visit there, especially where they deposited their scrap. . . . When they punched holes in the sheet metal, metal slugs of all sizes were generated in great quantities. With the workers' permission, we would gather these slugs in appropriate sizes to use in our slingshots, which were homemade from pieces of old inner tubes and select sections of tree limbs. One of the spots we chose to train our sights was the unused manufacturing building where Mercer Forge is now located. We could break the windows with our sling shots. We also practiced on blackbirds which seemed to overrun the area.

"I remember one time we were planning to do a little shooting and as we approached the area we heard a commotion in the woods behind the unused factory building. We went to check it out and discovered that a bunch of the town men were conducting rooster fights. They had dug a pit into which they placed the roosters where they fought to the death. The men thought that we should leave and told us so. We were reluctant, but were finally persuaded to leave."

From One-Room School to Spacecraft
By Donald Lewis

"I would like to tell you about a journey that started in a one-room school and eventually involved helping to launch our spacecraft. Back then, no one could have conceived that trip could have happened. Looking back, I can only say that fate has many turns. In 1926 we moved to Coolspring Township and I was enrolled in first grade. As a new kid, it was rough for they teased me as being 'tough' being from Pittsburgh. I took it for a while then cleaned out the school room with a stove poker. From then on, I was part of Stokely School. During the next eight years, a number of teachers all contributed to my education. They drilled me in the basics and gave me the tools I needed in life. We never ceased to be an individual and from the many games of 'Andy over,' 'tag,' and 'fox and geese' in the snow we learned to be competitive. From there in 1935, I went to Mercer High and graduated in 1940 with a huge debt of thanks to Joannie Appleseed for making it possible. [Editor's note: During these school years, Lewis frequently walked to the Mercer Library and eventually borrowed and read every book in its collection.]

"Having no marketable trades and seeing a war coming, I enlisted in the Army and served five years, three of them in India, going from working in the Signal Corps to running a projector repair shop and film depot in Calcutta for the Overseas Motion Picture Service. After getting out of the Army, I went to Carnegie Tech in Pittsburgh and graduated with a bachelor of science degree in electrical education. At one of our socials, Hezel Fox, dressed up as a gipsy woman, told my fortune. She said that I would be an engineer. But I think she meant I would be on the railroad. I worked for IBM for eight years and, not getting up the ladder, quit. I then went to Electro Data in Pasadena. When they went belly up, I took a job with Jet Propulsion Laboratory and stayed there for 29 years, retiring in 1988.

"My first job there was the installation of a data system at their rocket test base at Edwards Air Force Base. When that was up and running, my job was done and I was sent back to Pasadena. There I volunteered to be the instrumentation engineer of a spacecraft in vacuum and solar radiation to test response. After several data systems, I ended up with a computerized system recording spacecraft and environmental data. The spacecraft we worked on included Ranger 1 through 9, Mariner, Mars, Viking, Galileo, and Voyager.
"And it all started in a crude one-room school."

DR. EDITH MacBRIDE-DEXTER
Secretary of Health

DR EDITH MacBRIDE-DEXTER was born at Grove City, Mercer County, May 3, 1887, the daughter of Robert and Ellen (Bigler) MacBride. She received her early education in the public schools, graduated from Grove City College in 1906 with the degree of Bachelor of Science, and from the Women's Medical College of Pennsylvania in 1910 with the degree of Doctor of Medicine. Her education includes also special laboratory work at the University of Pittsburgh in 1916, post graduate work at the New York Eye and Ear Infirmary in 1917, special work in eye and ear surgery in London and Vienna in 1925 and 1927, and later in Philadelphia and Boston.

She engaged in the general practice of medicine in Grove City until 1917, during which time she was physician for girls at Grove City College, instructor of nurses at Grove City Hospital, and medical inspector of schools in the district. She left Grove City in 1917 to become Chief Resident Physician at St. Vincent's Hospital, Erie, and take charge of the practice of Dr. G. W. Schlindwinis during his absence at a Base Hospital during the World War. She returned to Mercer County in 1919, and from then until January 1935 engaged in the practice of Ophthalmology in Sharon, being also a member of the staff and Training School Committee of Christian H. Buhl Hospital and ophthalmologist to the Sharon plant of the Westinghouse Electric and Manufacturing Company.

Member of Mercer County Medical Society, Medical Society of the State of Pennsylvania (Past Vice-President), American Medical Association, State and Provincial Health Authorities Association of North America, and the American Public Health Association.

Married in 1929 to Allen T. Dexter and resides at 2114 Bellevue Road, Harrisburg, and 894 Linden Street, Sharon.

Appointed Secretary of Health by Governor George H. Earle, January 15, 1935.

Edith MacBride–Dexter(Source: **Biographical Sketches of State Officials**)

Mercer Dispatch Tidbits
(Researched by Shirley Minshull)

October 9, 1931: Ground is broken for the construction of Pymatuning Dam. Govenor Pinchot turned the first shovel of earth, while the world's largest dirigible, the Navy ship *Akron*, soared above the ceremony.

October 8, 1931: Grove City College dedicated two new structures on campus: the Hall of Science and Harbison Chapel.

January 1, 1932: About 1,200 idle men from Mercer County obtained work on road jobs in Mercer County.

January 29, 1932: Mercer Sanitarium's Jersey cow herd was judged "Best in the State" at the Harrisburg Farm Show.

August 5, 1932: The Mercer Silk Mill worked day and night to fill rush orders for raw silk, rayon, and burial robes.

September 2, 1932: The 50th anniversary of the Mercer Fair was celebrated.

January 27, 1933: Mercer County dairymen formed an organization to control prices of milk.

August 4, 1933: The businessmen of Mercer gave their full cooperation to the Recovery Program (President Roosevelt's plan to restore employment).

August 25, 1933: Mercer County coal operators fix wages and hours.

September 29, 1933: The "Miners Holiday," also known as a coal strike, extended to Mercer County. Mines No. 2 and No. 5 closed.

January 12, 1934: The American Legion Emergency Corps formed in the county to assist during fires, riots, and all disasters. The new organization was the first of its kind in western Pennsylvania.

April 6, 1934: Schaeffer Woolen Mill, a county landmark near Sandy Lake, was burned to the ground on April 2. It was built in 1823 by Enos Sanford and his son Joel.

June 1, 1934: The gates of Pymatuning Dam were opened for the first time on May 29 to increase the water supply for mills in the Shenango Valley.

July 26, 1935: Mercer County received over $2 million for relief work, making employment available for 2,826 men for one year under the Work Progress Administration (WPA) program.

September 27, 1935: A strike paralyzed soft coal industry. Mine operations were seriously affected in Mercer County with about 1,000 diggers idle.

March 27, 1936: The Pymatuning Dam saved the Shenango Valley from a bad flood.

April 24, 1936: Fire swept through the Sharon business district with a loss estimated at $1,000,000.

September 25, 1936: Fire in McCurdy Mine in Jackson Township causes 100 men to be out of work for many weeks.

January 29, 1937: Mercer County suffered its worst flood since 1913.

February 12, 1937: Grove City Flour Mill is Mercer County's oldest mill. Located on Wolf Creek, at North Street, the date 1807 is engraved in the massive millstone still in use. It was formerly known as Shaw's Mill.

July 2, 1937: Pymatuning Lake opened for fishing. Daily limit was set at 30 fish of combined species.

February 24, 1939: About 700 county farmers protested reduction of milk prices.

March 17, 1939: Liberty Theater, erected in 1921 on North Diamond Street in Mercer, was destroyed by fire in the early hours of March 11. This disaster was the first major fire in Mercer since the First Presbyterian Church on North Erie Street was burned to the ground on New Year's Day 1928.

Local passenger trains, such as this Bessemer No. 1 bound from Greenville to East Pittsburgh, arrived in Grove City in the 1930s with the community's morning mail and express, which the station agent and helper unloaded. By this time, only a few passengers were still using such trains. For decades, however, such service had been essential for Mercer County towns and villages, until a paved highway network was established. (Contributor: Frederick Houser)

What began as a little blacksmith shop in Brockway, Pennsylvania, in 1923, by Wendell August has now become a nationally known forge (pictured, in 1997) in Grove City, where August moved his operation in 1932. Working with aluminum, bronze, and pewter, the metalwork is still handcrafted by highly trained artisans using hammers and anvils: no two pieces are alike. The focus of the creations has evolved from predominantly architectural items for banks, churches, and private homes to giftware that includes presentation and award items, ornaments, platters, coasters, and serving dishes. The company's first catalog was a three-fold sheet of paper in black and white. Over the years, its marketing strategy has grown to include a showroom and museum for walk-in customers, multiple catalogs and mailers, a teleservice center to process telephone orders, and an electronic direct marketing site on the World Wide Web that reaches people all over the world. The company helps Mercer County communities through fundraising programs, such as recently producing and selling an Easter Egg ornament designed by a local elementary student. Two pieces from the Forge are on display in the National Museum of American History of the Smithsonian Institution. (Photographers: Nick and Kathy Pompa; caption: Brian Krall)

Included in the surprisingly long list of houses that have been moved over the years in Mercer County is the McConkey home in Grove City. When the borough wanted to build its first governmental post office on the north side of East Pine Street in the early 1930s, authorities picked the lot where the McConkey house stood, on the west bank of Wolf Creek. (Also on the north side of the same street, the Penn Grove Hotel had been built recently, but on the east bank of the creek.) Mrs. McConkey sold her land, but wanted to keep her house (pictured, in 1997). She bought the vacant lot across the street from the Penn Grove, and movers carefully rolled the house over the Pine Street Bridge to its new foundation without disturbing any pictures on the walls or spilling anything. (Photographers: Nick and Kathy Pompa; caption: 1997 interview with Marian McConkey, Mrs. McConkey's daughter)

Frogtown School, a frame building (pictured, with the 1931–32 class), was built in 1870 on a hill in the northwest corner of Lackawannock Township for $1,000. The name "Frogtown" was given to this coal-mining village because of the frog "music" emanating from the local ponds. (Photo: Genevieve Bartholomew; caption: Mae Beringer)

The Borchert Store was located just a quarter mile south of Perrine Corners and owned by Jim and Mary Borchert. The store was the only place to draw water to supply Perrine School. The teacher assigned different students each day to walk to the store to carry water by bucket. According to their daughter, Judy Borchert Randell, in 1933, the Borcherts bought property from Jack and Florence Osborne and built a combination country store, gas station, and home (pictured). The Borchert family lived in the upstairs apartment. In the spring of 1946, the house and store caught fire and burned to the ground. The Borcherts decided not to rebuild and sold the property back to the Osbornes who in turn built on the same location another store, known to all the Worth Township residents as "Jack's." After the fire, the Borcherts bought a grocery store in Eau Claire and lived there for two years. In 1948, they moved back to the Millbrook area and bought the Sterling Gas Station and Garage from Clyde Atwell. (Contributors: Idella McConnell and Lucille Eagles)

NEW McCORMICK-DEERING

YEARS from now it will look just as glossy and beautiful when you wipe it clean. That's because it is Japanned, by the high-temperature and long-baking process which provides one of the most durable metal finishes known.

We are demonstrating that the new McCormick-Deering is just as far ahead in every other way as it is in appearance. Come in and see the complete ball-bearing equipment and any number of other fine improvements. We have all six sizes, hand, belted, and electric, with capacities 350 to 1500 pounds of milk per hour, and we will give you up to a year to pay.

J. H. McWHIRTER

Phone 335-J   Mercer, Pa

(Source: **Mercer Dispatch and Republican**, May 8, 1931)

Members of the Greenville Sea Scout Troop at the Sea Base in Riverside Park about 1938 included (seated) Ed Hildebrand, scoutmaster, and (standing from left) John Cullen, Robert Campbell, James Lewis, (unidentified), George Welch, George Rowley, (unidentified), William Best, William Linn, and Charles Peterson. (Contributor: George Rowley)

Built in 1934 as a Works Progress Administration project, the Sea Scout Base was on the Shenango River in Riverside Park in Greenville. A troop of Sea Scouts met in the building and held their sailing and water skills classes there. Later, the building was rented for birthday parties, teenage dances, and Thiel College events. (Contributor: Ed Loreno)

From 1922 to 1935, the front part of the home named Whispering Pines (Hermitage) was operated as a teahouse by the Jesse Wilsons. Built in 1855 by Robert Stewart who named the estate, the house has fourteen rooms and a tower originally with a cupola. Stewart was a dealer in sheep and lumber. Also known as the Stewart House and Locust Grove, the house had been a residence until recently, and the Hermitage Historical Society began leasing it in 1998 for its headquarters. The house (pictured, in 2000) has been used for meetings by the Boy Scouts, Hermitage Recreation, sewer authority, recreation and parks authority, and for dinners by the local Rotary club, commissioners, and school board. The historical society plans to open the house to visitors on a regular basis. (Photographer: Marilyn Dewald)

The Sharpsville Presbyterian Church was organized in 1870. Worship services were held in a hall over the Pierce & Son Store and later in the Baptist church until the congregation built a church in 1882 on the corner of Main and First Streets for $4,000. The congregation continued to grow, and in 1928 under the pastorate of the Reverend Harry E. Woods, the foundation for the present building (pictured, in 2000) was laid at Ridge Avenue and Sixth Street. (Woods served the congregation for fourteen years, from 1923 to 1937.) The congregation had to overcome many obstacles during this construction project, in particular the Great Depression. After determining the exact center of Sharpsville was a house and lot owned by a McCracken family (equal-distant from Buhl Farm, viaduct, West Side, and East End), the church bought the property, which was on a steep rise in the street. The house and six thousand cubic yards of dirt had to be moved. The foundation was dug out by pick and shovel, wheelbarrow, and horses pulling a drag. Selling the dirt at about $1 per cubic yard covered the cost of the excavation. Native gray sandstone from the Blaney Farm east of the borough was used for the outside of the building. The wood came from the Woods Farm on Route 846. The hard oak was cut and tongue-and-grooved for the floors right on the farm. The wood and stones were hauled to the site on a Model T Ford. Due to the Depression, money was scarce; fundraising efforts, difficult; and most of the church's construction work, done by volunteers. Although the congregation moved into the building in 1935, it was not finished. They built it over a total of twenty-three years. The dedication of the present sanctuary was not until 1950, during the pastorate of Reverend W. S. Blair. Much of the work in the educational wing was completed during the pastorate of Dr. Edwin G. Sloan, who served for twenty-one years until 1972. (Photographer: Vonda Minner; caption: Mrs. W. S. Blair)

When snowstorms like the one pictured in 1936 occurred, children took advantage of the conditions. "Sled riding was permitted [in Mercer] on the full length of Beaver Street, from Otter Street to Route 58. Cinders were thrown on the surface over the last 50 to 75 yards to aid in stopping the sleds. Gene Adams had a really long bobsled on which as many as eight or 10 kids could ride. When this behemoth got going, it was impossible to stop until it either reached the cinders or hit something. One night it hit a telephone pole. Luckily it occurred near the top rather than near the bottom so the bumps and bruises were just that, except I recall that someone at the front lost a few teeth in the collision. I had one of the longest Flexible Flyers that could be bought and it also was able to descend that hill with great speed. We all would begin the trip down the hill with a long run, carrying the sled, and then dive along with the sled, onto the slippery surface. This gave us a really good start at the top and guaranteed a hair-raising descent. Problem always was that the sled had to be dragged all the way back up the hill if you wanted another ride. I remember the ride down, not the walk back up." (Caption: Joseph Hood)

"John Baskin (Jack) Thorne, 53, nationally known legitimate stage and movie actor, is dead at his boyhood home in Mercer. He was the son of the late William and Lillian Baskin Thorne, both members of the pioneer families of Mercer. He was born in the village of Leesburg, where the Thornes were pioneer merchants. Later his parents came to Mercer. He was orphaned when a child and was reared by his aunt, Mrs. Emma Thorne Alexander. He graduated from the Mercer High School. The stage had always held an attraction for him, and he appeared in numerous home-talent performances. His first 'break' on the legitimate stage came in Pittsburgh. From there he went to New York, where his talent was recognized and he soon was engaged with some of the best theatrical companies in the metropolis. He appeared in juvenile roles and was featured in 'The Little Shepherd.' He later appeared in 'The Clinging Vine,' 'The Vagabond King,' 'Experience,' and others of the best productions of the legitimate stage. It was while playing in 'The Vagabond King' (pictured on facing page) that he achieved his greatest success, and became one of the outstanding actors at a time when the motion pictures were overshadowing stage productions. Some of his friends who had deserted the stage for the silver screen induced him to enter motion pictures. He appeared in several silent pictures, but later returned to the stage. He attained the ambition of all actors when he became a member of the New York Theater Guild." (Source: 1935 article in a Pittsburgh newspaper; also pictured, a program from Mercer's Liberty Theater when Thorne was acting there)

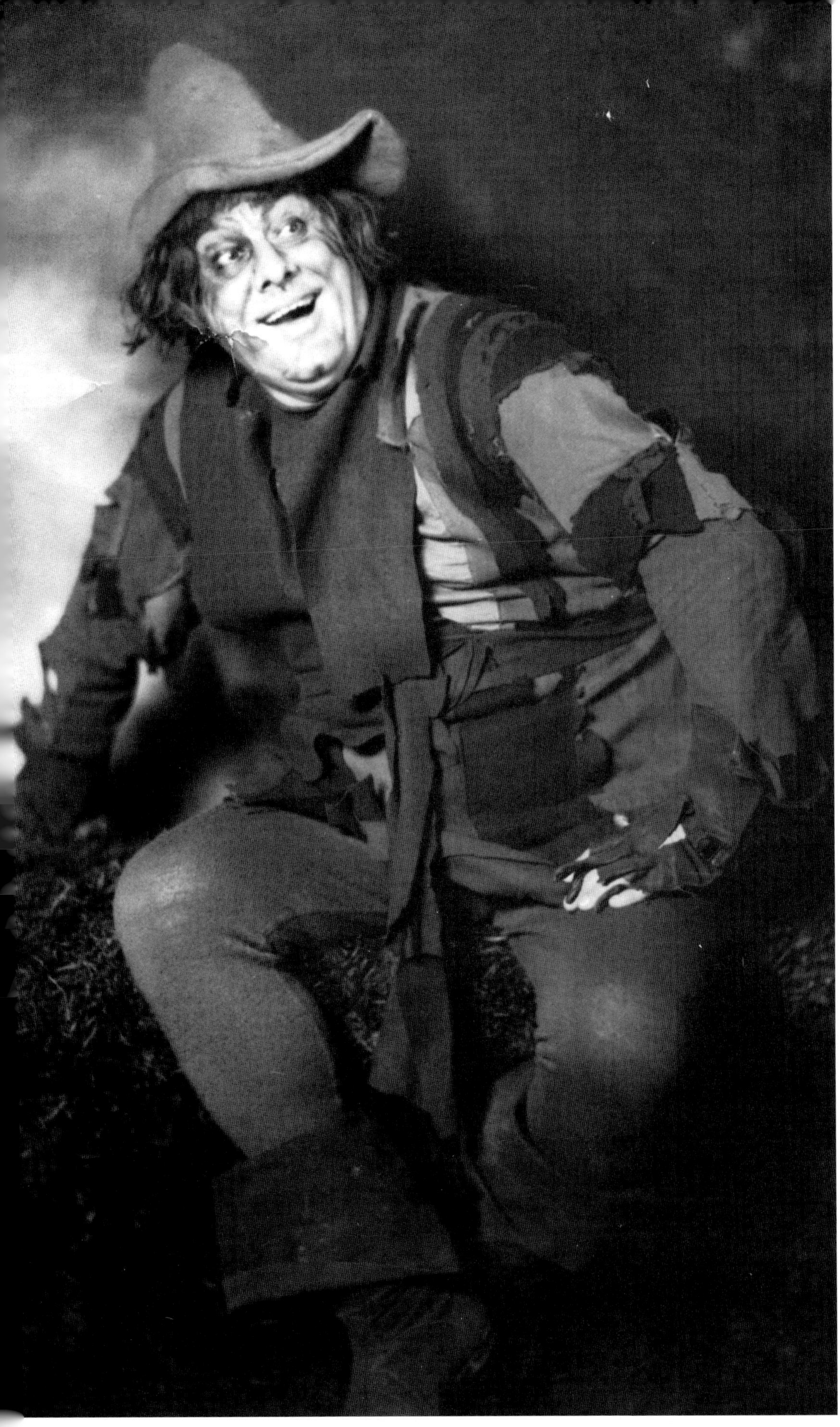

The State Street Bridge over the Shenango River has always been a vital element in downtown Sharon and a favorite subject for photographers. After a covered bridge was used, the second bridge had no cover, but had a separate walk on at least one side (pictured above, about 1865, with Bell's store on the east end of the bridge). In the early 1900s, an iron bridge spanned the river (pictured, below left, with the First National Bank building on West State Street). A later bridge had separate walks and trolley tracks [pictured below right, in the early 1930s, with the national headquarters of the Protected Home Circle, a life and health insurance company, on the right. The Protected Home Circle (PHC) had been founded in 1888 and by 1909 had 1,860 members, including women. One of the worst of fires in Sharon involved the PHC building and occurred in 1936. On the evening of April 22, at a large meeting in the PHC building, members were told the stone building would be modernized. However, at 1 a.m., April 23, an alarm bell sounded because the building was on fire. All of the PHC records were destroyed; and, before the west wall collapsed into the river at 6:20 that morning, five adjoining businesses in the Smith and Cohen block were damaged. Rain wet roofs and saved other nearby structures. The PHC building was replaced, and the Protected Home Mutual Life Insurance Company is still in business.] (Caption: Mairy Jayn Woge)

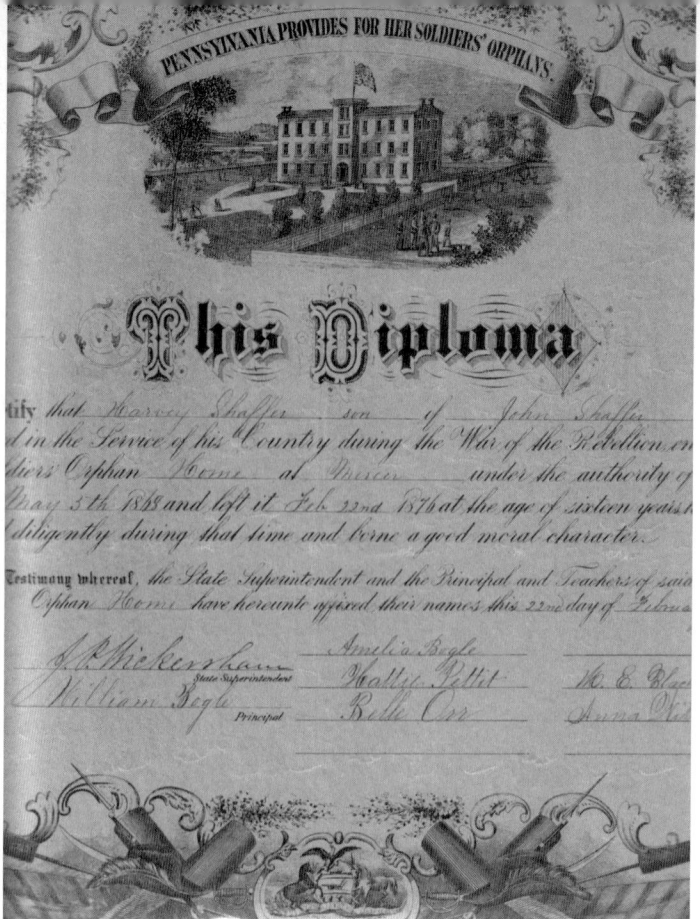

According to the Golden Jubilee program of the Sixteeners Association, celebrated in 1938 at the Hotel Humes in Mercer, the Mercer Soldiers Orphans School was opened in 1868 and closed in 1889. It had been maintained by Pennsylvania and operated by local teachers and staff to provide a home and education for the children of the soldiers and sailors who were killed during the Civil War. After the school closed, many former students banded together to form the Sixteeners Association, and its first reunion held at the old school in 1888. Reunions were held almost annually in Mercer (with exception of one in Pittsburgh and one in Grove City) at least until 1963. In 1926, a bronze tablet in memory of the school was placed at the left of the north entrance of the courthouse.

The construction of a new viaduct over the Shenango River in West Middlesex was budgeted by the Pennsylvania Department of Highways and began in 1940. The viaduct was opened in 1941. An estimated six thousand people came to the opening ceremony and watched the Girl Scouts cut the ribbon.

Built in 1939 when J. W. Byers was postmaster, Mercer's post office on the corner of East Venango and North Pitt Streets was the first building constructed by the federal government in the county seat. The structure (pictured, in 2000, with a spirit face carved on a front lawn tree by local artist Clyde Daugherty) occupies the site and replaced a home used for the same purpose one hundred years earlier by Postmaster William Garvin. Established soon after 1800, the post office was usually located in the home or business of each postmaster. When Garvin was appointed postmaster of Mercer in 1837, he leased a brick house on the same corner as the current post office, but facing North Pitt Street, and there established the post office in the front room and the printing press of the Western Press, which he edited, in the back room. The house was reportedly built in 1822 by Epaphroditus Cossitt, the first physician of note to locate in Mercer County. Samuel Griffith bought the house in 1848, and it remained in that family for ninety years. Griffith married Caroline Foster. A cousin who visited Caroline Foster Griffith said, "Caroline Griffith lived in the old home in Mercer for many years. She did not marry again and was living alone when I remember visiting her with Father and Mother on one of our eastern auto trips in the 1920s. She was an interesting, talkative person. The Mercer Post Office now stands where her home used to be." (Photographer: Marilyn Dewald; source: **Mercer Dispatch and Republican**, May 12, 1939, and Gail Habbyshaw).

The Mercer Silk Mill was about half way down East Market Street on the northside (upper left, long white building, in picture at right). According to recollections written by Joseph Hood (Mercer), the mill (interior pictured) was operated by the Zwikert family and made silk liners for coffins.

"The Mercer School building was located about four or five blocks from home at the top of East Butler Street hill so the walk to school was a pretty good climb. The building, while built in sections, housed all grades, from 1 to 12. Some of the district's students in grades 1 through 6 went to country schools and then came into town for grades 7 through 12. Therefore, the Jr-Sr high school was physically larger than the elementary school. There was a combination gym and auditorium. Basketball games were played on the stage, and a large net was suspended across the front of the stage to protect the audience from wayward basketballs and to restrain any exuberant players from falling into the seats. There was one chemistry room and absolutely no cafeteria. Everyone carried a lunch if they planned to eat. I believe, if memory serves me correctly, there was government-supplied milk available and it was served in small half-pint containers. The school actually had three floors; the bottom one was the basement where rest rooms and janitorial and maintenance materials and equipment were stored. I believe the chemistry lab could also be found in the basement. All other classrooms were on the first or second floor. All health classes were taught in the auditorium by the gym instructor, Mr. McTaggert. We did have gym classes, which often were held outdoors if the weather permitted. Gym included basketball, volleyball, and flying rings. . . . Only the top six grades changed rooms at the end of each class. There was no bussing in those days, so many of the country kids lived in town with friends and relatives during the school months. There were very few who commuted in and out of town, the numbers being limited by whether there was an automobile or not. There was only one student who owned a car and he drove it to school each day. His name was Earl Chadderton and he lived on a farm about four or five miles out of town." (Caption: Joseph Hood)

"Since I had several gloves, one of which was a catchers mitt, I was as well equipped for the game as anyone else in the neighborhood. In addition to the gloves, I also had a catcher's face mask. This made me the number one candidate to be catcher. [About 1940,] we constructed a diamond beyond what we called the flats, a group of homes that stretched for about 1/8th mile beyond Otter Creek on Scrubgrass Road [pictured, (Findley Township) looking toward Mercer]. The field was just beyond the last house and adjacent to the road leading to Oakland Junction. This is where we spent many summer hours playing the national pastime. Because all I had was the face mask for protection, I took a pretty bad beating behind the plate, suffering bruises of the shins and a few stove fingers. Problem was, I seemed to always be stuck with catching. One day the Redic boys asked me if they could use the equipment, whereupon I agreed. I never saw that equipment again. I didn't miss it to be honest, so I never pressed them to return it." (Caption: Joseph Hood)

"On [Route 58, south Mercer] was a bar and restaurant called Buckham's [pictured]. Behind the building someone had created a fine concrete dam that could be filled in the summer and emptied in the winter. The filling was always delayed until there was confidence that the flood season had subsided. Until this swimming area was ready, we resorted to the rock dam [on Neshannock Creek across the road]. [During the late 1930s and early 1940s], we swam at Buckham's Dam, primarily because there was a diving board. [Hood's sister] Isobel was a fairly accomplished swimmer and so she was paid to be a lifeguard through the summer months. I remember one time, after I had become a fairly good swimmer in my own right, I filled in for her while she ran home for something. Ironically, a young girl had slipped down the sloping dam wall and was in real trouble. I dove in and literally pushed her to safety, because I didn't have the slightest idea how to rescue anyone. Fortunately, my style of rescue worked. At night, us fellows would sneak across the wooded area that bordered the dam and swim naked. When Mr. Buckham realized we were there, he would flood the area with lights to drive us away. We would leave but would return, once the lights were turned off. One night, while I was diving from the board in the dark, one of the fellows threw an empty five-gallon oil can into the water and I landed on it, cracking three ribs. This was a very unpleasant injury that took weeks to heal. I never did find out who threw the can." (Caption: Joseph Hood)

As of 1939, "Ninety-six years of uninterrupted service to the community with 66 years of management by the one Barton family is the record of the **Mercer Dispatch and Republican,** the one surviving paper of many that have sprung up, lived and died in Mercer. . . . Its one real rival, **The Western Press** (Democratic), . . . was burned out in 1920 after 109 years' existence, leaving the field to the **Dispatch**. In January, 1930, the old paper and print shop 'stepped out' into an attractive new home [pictured], erected by the owner, Dunham Barton, and his wife, who, over the signature, J. B. Barton, had been editing and managing the paper and plant while the former served the Mercer Community as postmaster. The building was the first erected in Mercer County specifically to house a newspaper plant. The building stands on North Pitt Street . . . [and] is heated with natural gas, a fuel of which Mercer has had an apparently inexhaustible supply for more than 50 years. The type of heater is the Reznor gas fired heating and ventilating unit, a recently perfected product of the Reznor Manufacturing Company, which has been Mercer's chief industry. It consists of a large gas radiator with forced circulation, the whole being thermostatically controlled. Three of these units have been installed, one in the front office and two in the composing room. They give a uniform and adequate temperature at all times. In name the **Dispatch and Republican** is only 52 years old, though actually the paper . . . [dates] back to the establishment of the **Mercer Whig** on June 15, 1844. Some historians have claimed that it springs from the **Mercer Luminary**, established in 1830. This, we believe, cannot be supported, but from the **Whig** in 1844 to the present the record is clearly marked and indisputable."

The **Mercer Dispatch** began in 1857 when the wing of the Whig party, now Republican, was pro-slavery. The Whig's paper, **The Whig**, had been started in 1844 because the **Luminary** (established in 1830 by William and James Moorhead) refused to support Henry Clay as the Whig candidate for president. Prominent Whigs from all over the county were determined to have their own paper and established the **Mercer Whig**. They bought the equipment in Pittsburgh and shipped it to Mercer by the river and canal to Big Bend. From there an ox team took it to Mercer. In 1864, the two rival papers, the **Whig** and **Dispatch**, merged and became known as the **Whig and Dispatch**. Eventually becoming known as the **Mercer Dispatch**. In 1881, a group of reformist Republicans established the **Mercer Republican**. When the **Dispatch**'s complete operation was destroyed by fire in 1887, the **Mercer Republican** was declaring heavy dividends. Therefore, the proprietors of the **Dispatch** bought the **Republican** and called the merged papers the **Dispatch and Republican**.

The 1939 article goes on to say, "The **Dispatch and Republican** changed hands in 1898, the late Hon. B. J. Haywood purchasing the interests of all its owners and retaining the late D. L. Barton as manager of the property. [Barton had become part owner in 1881 after serving several years as local editor and foreman.] The latter continued in charge until June 1910, when he and his son formed the Mercer Dispatch Printing Company . . . and purchased the paper from Mr. Haywood's widow. After 29 years, Dunham Barton is still the publisher and managing editor and Mrs. Barton is his associate. D. L. Barton who for so many years guided the destinies of the **Dispatch** was an old-school printer and a man of outstanding character and force. . . . He came from Cleveland . . . in 1873 and from that time until his death just 50 years later he dominated the business and political policies of the paper. . . Its political policy has been unequivocally Republican."

In the early years of newspapers, job printing was important as it provided quite a bit of the capital needed to run a newspaper. Job shops of newspapers printed stationery, business cards, programs, posters and dozens of other items. The **Mercer Dispatch** had a huge job printing business in Mercer until the late 1970s although the newspaper was eventually purchased by Edgar "Ted" Hassler and consolidated with three other area newspapers, now known as the **Allied News**. (Caption: Teresa Spatara and June 30, 1939, **Mercer Dispatch and Republican** article)

The first two Farrell schools were subsidized by Hickory Township. It took ten days to raise the money to build the first South Sharon (as Farrell was called then) school. The school was at the corner of Fruit Avenue and Kishon Street. It was paid for with money raised at a box social. The first high school was occupied in 1908. It was a brick building and cost $8,000. Between 1922 and 1933, the school was enlarged to twenty-six classrooms. The Works Progress Administration (WPA) built the second Farrell High School (pictured) along Haywood, later Roemer Boulevard, in 1929 and 1940. (Caption: Mairy Jayn Woge)

During the 1930s, pictures were taken of several "grade crossings" for the various railroad lines that traversed the county, for example, (from top) Pennsylvania Railroad crossing Route 43061 in 1933 (road and track) and crossing the Route 238 spur (road and track) in West Middlesex in 1936; the Erie Railroad crossing the Route 238 spur in West Middlesex in 1936; and the Bessemer & Lake Erie Railroad crossing Route 213 south of Fredonia in Coolspring and Fairview Townships in 1930.

327

GROVE CITY COLLEGE
By Jennifer L. Mahurin

In 1930, Grove City College embarked upon a long-range program of campus expansion on what is called the Upper Campus [pictured, about 1937, before Crawford Hall was built; *notice in the distance in one photo the town of Grove City, including the Cooper Bessemer plant, the post office, McKay Works, and the armory; and in the other photo, looking east, the homes that lined East Main Street*].

From 1930 to 1956, when Weir C. Ketler retired as president of the college, nine buildings plus several additions were built. The enrollment grew from approximately 800 students in 1916 to 1,200 students in 1956.

Ketler was just the third president the college had known since it was founded in 1876 by his father, Isaac. Actually, as early as 1858, Richard M. Thompson had provided instruction in college preparatory subjects, conducting classes in a room of William A. Young's house on Liberty Street in Pine Grove (now Grove City). For ten years, beginning in 1864, the Reverend William T. Dickson and his wife Harriet had taught business and college preparatory courses for the young people of that community. Then, in 1874, the school directors of Pine Grove built a two-room common school and raised funds by public subscription to add a second-story room to house a "Select School." Isaac C. Ketler furnished this room, and, on April 11, 1876, opened his school with thirteen students.

Pine Grove Normal Academy, chartered in 1879, grew rapidly, and once again the local people supported the school by financing the construction of an academy building. The two-year course of study of the nascent academy was divided into four departments: College Preparatory, Music, Normal, and Primary.

In 1884, the academy was rechartered as Grove City College, taking the new name of the community, which had just incorporated the year before. The sale of $10 shares of stock continued to financially underwrite the college. The residents of Grove City had contributed almost $100,000 toward the establishment of the institution by 1894.

J. Newton Pew joined the Board of Trustees in 1894, on the condition that the college became rechartered as a nonprofit institution supported by philanthropists. Accordingly, the board of trustees of fifteen local members was doubled in size to include leading businessmen and ministers from outside the Grove City area. The revised charter provided that the college should be Christian and evangelical in character.

By 1900, the enrollment had climbed to 660 students, the faculty had been enlarged to twenty members, and the campus had increased in size to forty acres (later known as Lower Campus) with four substantial buildings [pictured, from right, the Academy Building (also known as Recitation Hall), the Colonial (the women's dormitory), Ivy Chapel, and Carnegie Building]. The curriculum had been expanded to include courses of study leading to a bachelor's degree in arts, science, or philosophy; master's degree in arts; doctor's degree in philosophy; teacher's diploma; or certificate in music and art.

Pew, president of the board of trustees since 1895, died in 1912 and was succeeded by Frederick R. Babcock. Less than a year later, Ketler, the college president, also died, and Dr. Alexander T. Ormond of Princeton University was elected his successor. Under Ormond's direction, the faculty was enlarged, the curriculum underwent a major revision in which the faculty spelled out specific courses of study leading to the following degrees: bachelor of arts, bachelor of literature, bachelor of science, master of arts, and doctor of philosophy.

When Ormond died suddenly in 1915, Weir C. Ketler was appointed acting president. In 1916, he was elected president, an office he held for forty years. During his administration, the curriculum underwent several changes: the doctor of philosophy degree was discontinued in 1916, the bachelor of commercial science degree was started in 1919, the master of arts degree was discontinued in 1929, and the bachelor of literature degree was discontinued in 1930. Meanwhile, in 1922, the college became accredited.

William L. Clause succeeded Babcock as president of the board of trustees in 1928 and served until his death in 1931. Then, J. Howard Pew, son of J. Newton, was elected president—a position he held until his death in 1971. (Following the elder Pew's death, the family had selected J. Howard to succeed his father as president of Sun Oil Company, a position he held for thirty-five years. During that period, Sun Oil expanded into shipbuilding, supporting American forces through two world wars, and built national and international enterprises.)

The college not only survived the Depression, but also served her country well through the two world wars. During World War I, the college organized a military training program for the government, but the armistice was declared before the program really operated efficiently. Students called into active duty were granted credit for the remainder of that semester and were guaranteed admittance after the war. During World War II, the enrollment dropped from 1,020 students in 1940 to 481 students in the fall of 1943. During this time, the college operated several defense-training programs for the government, including a Naval Training School, Pilot Training Program for the Air Corps, and several civilian defense programs.

From 1956 to 1971, J. Stanley Harker was president of his alma mater. During his administration, the student body grew from 1,200 to 2,050, and the faculty increased from about 80 to 120 members. The curriculum and academic phases of the school underwent extensive revision. The bachelor of science degree in commerce was discontinued in 1959 and, since then, graduates in business administration and secretarial studies have received a bachelor of arts degree. The number of books in the library was more than doubled to over 115,000 volumes. Eight buildings and several more additions were built. Homecoming, May Day-Parent's Day, and the sports program were expanded; and greater emphasis was placed on alumni and public relations.

Dr. Charles MacKenzie joined the college as its president in 1971. MacKenzie, a Presbyterian minister, ushered in a new emphasis in religious life on campus. He saw the completion of three new buildings (Mary Ethel Pew Dormitory, J. Howard Pew Fine Arts Center and the Weir C. Ketler Technology Center). Perhaps the most significant change was the introduction of the Keystone Curriculum, which consisted of four courses required of all students, giving them a common grounding in the liberal arts tradition.

Grove City College landed in the national spotlight with the 1984 Supreme Court case *Grove City College v. Bell, Secretary U.S. Department of Education*. Title IX, which prohibits an institution that operates programs or activities receiving federal financial assistance from discriminating in those programs, became the battle ground between the government and the college. The college refused to sign the assurance of compliance form because it contended that it did not receive federal financial assistance and signing the form would obligate the college to abide by regulations that controlled nearly all aspects of the college's life. The Supreme Court ruled the college was subject to Title IX regulations because some of its students received Pell Grants to help pay for their education. As a result, Grove City College

GROVE CITY COLLEGE *continued*

now refuses all federal assistance programs, including Pell Grants and Stafford/PLUS loans, offers its own financial assistance programs, and maintains its freedom from federal regulations.

When MacKenzie retired in 1991, Dr. Jerry H. Combee was promoted to president from vice president of academic affairs. Combee was instrumental in moving the college into a position of national recognition and prominence through a greatly expanded marketing and public relations program. Additionally, the academic program was strengthened and an emphasis placed on improved relationships between the college and the Grove City community.

Dr. John H. Moore assumed the presidency in 1996. (Moore had served as a member of the faculty and administration at George Mason University in Virginia. U.S. President Ronald Reagan had appointed him deputy director of the National Science Foundation in 1985.) The campus now extends to the corner of Madison Avenue and Pine Street. Moore is leading the college through its first major capital campaign to continue to provide students with superb facilities and minimal debt.

Now, Grove City College has a student body of 2,300, a faculty of 153, and the employer of 250 members of the greater community. The college offers nineteen bachelor of science majors, eleven bachelor of arts majors, and four bachelor of music majors. Additionally, the college offers degrees in electrical and mechanical engineering and the master of science in accounting. To the public, the college provides cultural enrichment through cultural events, various speakers, and guest artists. Students can be found actively involved in local churches, community service projects, and volunteer work. From the Grace Food Pantry to the YMCA, Grove City College impacts the lives of many residents of Mercer County and beyond. (1937 aerials: Grove City College; lower campus postcard: Rita Kreidle Holler)

1937 aerial looking east

1937 aerial looking northwest

Lower campus

Spectators lined the street as representatives of the armed forces marched by in Sandy Lake's Centennial Parade in 1949. (Contributor: Lois Blake)

Chapter 6: 1941–1950

TOWNSHIPS

Penicillin was developed in 1927, but was not available for civilian use until after World War II. Vaccines for mumps, chicken pox, whooping cough, measles, diphtheria, hepatitis, and other communicable diseases were developed and used after the 1930s. Poliomyelitis was the scourge of the late 1940s and early 1950s. Dr. Jonas Salk of Pittsburgh produced a vaccine in 1955 that provided immunity from polio.

Thomas and Myrtle Durisko (***East Lackawannock Township***) started their Durisko Egg Production in 1947. (In cooperation with their son Thomas and his wife Donna, they now claim the largest work force in the township: 25,012 employees, "who" produce two thousand dozen eggs per day.)

Fairview Township had four one-room schools: White, Fairview, Godfrey, and Orrs. They were closed in 1948 with the formation of the Lakeview School District. (Now, Dorothy Campbell Krem is the only living school teacher from the country schools.) James Winner, a well-known Sharon Businessman, attended White School for several years. The township bought the White School and used it for an election hall until the township building was built in 1992.

In 1947, Ed and Alice Gilliland started a prosperous trucking company in ***Lackawannock Township***. With as many as fifteen drivers, Gilliland trucks have hauled steel from coast to coast and, in the late 1960s hauled material to help build Interstate 79. (The company was passed on to the Gilliland's three sons in 1984 and is still operating in 2000.)

In 1949, the Osgood School in ***Sugar Grove Township*** was discontinued, and the children taken by bus in Greenville.

Township supervisors were largely occupied with maintaining township roads. In 1945 ***Wilmington Township*** supervisors decided to acquire a few acres on Auction Road to keep their road grader and snowplow. They have since built a garage and gradually added more facilities. Electricity was extended to the far reaches of Wilmington Township by 1940 and opened the way for milking machines, bulk tanks, and specialized dairy farms. By 1950, various small businesses were appearing. The most important for the area was probably the New Wilmington Livestock Auction started by Sandy and Doris Sommerville in a barn built with Amish labor in 1946 on the Mercer Road. The auction proved to be a instant success. (It was later owned by Richard and Zana Skelton and is now owned by Tom and Amy Skelton.) After 1940, two sawmills began operation in the township.

Salem Township *(by Robert Osborn)*. "In the early 1940s, the USA went to war. I was a sophomore at Penn High School—in class—when the news was announced. Some of the

Timeline 1941—1950

The World

1941	The United Service Organization (USO) is founded to serve the social and educational needs of men and women in the US Armed Forces; Japan bombs Pearl Harbor and the United States officially enters WWII
1942	The Atomic Age is born when a self-sustaining nuclear reaction is demonstrated for the first time
1943	Congress passes a law authorizing employers to withhold income tax from paychecks
1944	The US troops liberate Paris in WWII
1945	The Americans invade Okinawa; the first test of the atomic bomb takes place in New Mexico; Japan surrenders after the bombing of Hiroshima and Nagasaki, ending WWII; Congress officially recognizes the "Pledge of Allegiance" to the American flag
1946	The Cold War begins as an "iron curtain" descends across Europe
1947	The microwave oven is invented by Percy L. Spencer
1948	Velcro is invented by Georges de Mestral
1950	The population of the United States is 152,271,417; the Korean Conflict begins

Mercer County

1942	Westinghouse accepts a US navy contract to produce the "Wakeless Torpedo," delivering more than 10,000 torpedoes and credited with sinking almost 400 enemy ships; US engineers survey Pymatuning Township to build an army base
1943	The county's most gruesome murder takes place (3 people killed at the Wilson farm in Lackawannock Township)
1944	Camp Reynolds Prisoner Of War (POW) Camp is established; POWs are working at Meadville Iron Works and National Radiator Company; troops and operators are transferred to Fort Indian Town Gap
1945	The US War Department designates Camp Reynolds an "inactive installation"; Greenville and Buhl Club USOs close, Greenville's USO entertained 812,530 servicemen and Buhl's entertained 475,000 soldiers
1946	A meeting is held at the courthouse and reorganizes the Mercer County Historical Society
1947	Tornado rips through the county and 14 are killed
1948	The Grove City Creamery closes
1950	The county's population is 111,954; Buhl Hospital changes its name to Sharon General Hospital; the county is buried by a snowstorm that measures just over four feet (damage in Sharon is estimated at $110,000)

older people were happy about it because of the money that could be made. Most people, though, were aware of the suffering the lay ahead.

"As things progressed, the draft was started. All sorts of things were in short supply, such as gas, tires, tools, sugar, coffee, soap, tobacco, butter, etc. Price controls were imposed. Men were being drafted, and women were taking their places in the mills.

"In Crawford county, the army bought thousands of acres of land to build the Keystone Ordinance and began hiring men and buying equipment. A bus ran from Greenville on Route 358, hauling men to work.

"Then, they began building Camp Reynolds. When I was 17, during Xmas vacation from Penn High School, Kenneth Beatty and I hired on at Reynolds. He was a sophomore, and I was a junior. The government had lowered the age of work in 17, with parental consent. The year before I had tried for a job, but was too young.

"Harve McKean's son, Roy, was head of the employment office. Harve McKean was head of the welfare office for many years. His home was in Sheakleyville. When I was 16, he told me he could put me on as office boy. Kenneth and I were hired at age 17—after passing our physicals.

"Our first day, we were put in a covered truck and hauled to our worksite. It was terribly cold, and the snow was deep. We were put with a gang of alien workers from Mexico and Polish workers who had worked in the mining regions of Pottsville, PA. Few could talk English. Beatty and I were scared and were put to work by the boss carrying mud in a bucket from a pit. The bucket was handed up to us from the pit, and we were to carry it outside and dump it. We both hopped right to it and were soon told to slow down or take a break.

"We were all required to join the union. I could have been a carpenter, as well as a laborer. The only difference was the union dues. I saw several cattle dealers who never drove nails in their lives working as union carpenters. If I had hired on as a carpenter, I could have gotten a union card for life.

"At the end of two weeks vacation, Beatty went back to school, but I got a working permit and stayed on. The pay for labor was $.82 per hour, for 10- to 12-hour days. A bus ran from Oil City to Camp Reynolds.

"After Kenneth Beatty went back to school, his Uncle Rutherford Beatty hired out. I would walk up to Beattys on Route 358 and catch the bus with him. On occasion, I would drive my 1934 Ford. This did not happen very often, as my gas stamps were only good for 3 gallons.

"In the spring of 1943, I asked the superintendent if I could quit. He said the only way he would let me go was to fire me. I told him that if that was the only way, then he should go ahead and fire me. I wanted to have some time at home, since I had collected some livestock and a team of horses and knew for sure I would be called for service.

"Before I left work at the camp, which was in the disposal area, the first waste came through. A great cheer went up. Most of the soldiers who came were from the south and were not dressed for the cold. The barracks were long and on stilts. They were heated with pot-bellied army stoves. I saw soldiers picking up coal with their fingers and putting it into buckets for their stoves.

"From Camp Reynolds, they were shipped overseas. Greenville was filled with soldiers. Military police were everywhere, and the saloons of Greenville were overwhelmed. Many of the workmen at the camp were renting in Greenville. I sold produce and meat to some of the men with whom I worked. Most of them were from the eastern coal mines of Pennsylvania. Many were shipped here on cattle cars.

"By 1946, when I returned from service, both the Keystone Ordinance and Camp Reynolds were finished and within one year were being torn down.

"During the war years and after, Salem Township prospered. Some people had tractors, and new hybrid seed became available. At first, home-built tractors from old cars and trucks were the rage. My dad bought one from Charles Donnell. I used it in my farming operation and thank God for my horses! I cranked until my hands were raw and when I got it going, the radiator boiled! In other words, it was easier to use horses than a home-built tractor.

"In 1947–1948, many farmers in Salem began selling milk, including myself. None of my family ever sold whole milk before. The thing that induced me to do this was that I could see that those who did were more prosperous than those who did not.

"At this time, I was going to farm training under the GI Bill. I received $92.00 per month. Dairy farming was not for me!"

MUNICIPALITIES

In 1944, William Munnell developed a progressively prosperous trucking company in **Fredonia**. He began by delivering coal to local houses and schools with only one dump truck. Eventually, he obtained more trucks and called the business William C. Munnell and Sons. The business is still intact more than fifty years later and is operated by his widow and son. In 1945, J. C. Moore also started his own business, J. C. Moore Industries. It featured a product that he invented, which sharpened the teeth on pipe wrenches. His grandson Gary A. Rhodes inherited the business in 1967. Rhodes focused his work on the production of antique fire apparatus and flat beds. Some of these trucks are displayed in three European museums and have been sold to famous people throughout the world. In 1944, a tornado swept through Fredonia and Fairview and Coolspring Townships and damaged Sam Weld's home, for one, and destroyed his barn. Utility service was disrupted, many trees were blown down, and many roofs were damaged in these areas.

Many **Jamestown** residents helped in various ways throughout the years of World War II, for example, as block wardens and as workers at Camp Reynolds. George Emerson (Jamestown) served as the director for Civil Defense. In honor of Jamestown residents who served in World War II, the Blue and Gold Star Mothers, Chapter 5, constructed a War Roll Memorial in 1942. It was replaced with a brick memorial in 1949. Jamestown's high school was built in 1943, and the gymnasium was added later. The Jamestown Community Fair Association was established in 1944. The annual fair includes a parade, a queen, a Homecoming assembly, and many concessions sold by local business establishments.

Temple Beth Israel moved from downtown **Sharon** to Highland Road in Sharon in 1950. A synagogue had been located in Sharon's North River Flats as early as 1885.

FARMING
By Vonda Minner

During the 1940s, five 4-H dairy clubs were organized.

The Babcock Farm (Delaware Township) was one hundred years old in 1941; the Slater Farm (New Vernon Township), in 1941; the Lackey Farm (Perry Township; now owned by Norman and Janice), in 1943; the Nutt Farm (Pine Township), in 1944; and the Slater Farm (Fairview Township) and the Hover Farm (Wilmington Township), in 1950.

The Carey Dairy began in Clarks Mills in 1944 (and was closed in 1962).

Also in 1946, artificial breeding was started, and seventeen hundred cows were bred that year. (In 1962, ten thousand cows were bred.)

Thurman Hoover wrote in his diary for June 4, 1947: "Cyclone that passed through Sharon left a track about 1/4 mile wide that looked like a German city after the war. 300 houses damaged or ruined, 2 persons killed and 40 or more pretty badly mussed up."

Also in 1947, Hoover wrote: "Corn & oats were poor, but wheat, hay and potatoes were good. Apples about 1/2 of crop. All livestock was high. Veal calf 10 weeks for $58.00, another for $64.00. Eggs were 70 cents a dozen. On one Saturday 34 school boys picked 500 bushel of potatoes and the next Saturday picked 600 bushel. In September, 1947 potatoes were selling at $2.50 per bushel, but later dropped in $2.10. A neighbor, Fred Hilton was working at Westinghouse and making $12.52 a day."

The Veg Acres Farm started near Stoneboro in 1948 (and was moved in 1953 to Greene Township as the Commercial Vegetable farm). Goods were sold at the farm and to wholesale chain markets and food processors, such as H. J. Heinz Company in Pittsburgh.

AVIATION
By Richard Christner

Mercer County's fascination with aviation is apparent from the large number of its men and women who served their country during World War II, Korea, Vietnam, Desert Storm, and interim periods of relative peace. None achieved higher rank than the son of a Mercer County pastor. Frederick R. Dent, Jr. was born in Pittsburgh in 1908. His parents, Reverend Frederick R. and Jennie Hoon Dent, moved to the Hoon homestead in Coolspring Township in 1930. Reverend Dent was the pastor of several Presbyterian churches in the area, including the Sandy Lake, Lebanon, Fairfield, and Jackson Center churches. Fred, Jr. graduated from the U.S. Military Academy at West Point in 1929 and received a BA summa cum laude from St. Mary's University, San Antonio, in 1930 and an MS in aeronautical engineering from MIT in 1938. He also graduated from the Harvard Business School in 1947 and successfully completed programs at the Primary and Advanced Flight Schools, the First Command Course at Fort Leavenworth, Kansas, and the Air Corps Engineering School at Wright Field, Dayton, Ohio.

Dent was more than a book soldier. He received his flight training at Brooks and Kelly fields, Texas, and became an instructor in four-engined aircraft. From 1941 to 1943, he pioneered the Air Corps glider program, including a stint as the first glider pilot. In 1943, Dent was ordered overseas, initially as an Air Observer and then as Chief of the Air Technical Section, Army Air Forces, London. Dent served as a Combat Wing Executive Officer and later as Group Commander of the 95th Heavy Bombardment Group, Eighth Air Force. In his eleventh mission in June 1944, Dent's B-24 Liberator was hit by flak, wounding him in several places. After recovering from his wounds, Dent returned to the

United States, having flown one hundred combat hours. He finished the war and served afterwards in various command positions, lastly as Commanding General of the Wright Air Development Center, directing the Air Research and Development Program in the Dayton area. Promoted to Major General in 1951, Dent retired, soon moved into the civilian sector as vice president, Electronics Controls Corporation, and died in 1969. Among his numerous military decorations was the Silver Star.

Mercer County's two colleges—Thiel and Grove City—played an important part in World War II-era aviation. From October 1939 to June 1942, Thiel offered the Civil Aeronautic Administration's Pilot Training Program, coordinated by Professor Guy Bradshaw with Warren B. Skelton as flight instructor. Under this program, sixty-nine pilots were trained and certified including twenty-seven residents of Greenville. In September 1942, the U.S. Army took over the program, and the Army Reserve Corps began operating a program to train Air Force Reserve college personnel during eight-week training periods. Each group of fifty to one hundred received 35 hours of flight training and 240 hours of classroom instruction. In charge of the program were Lt. Paul W. Russell, a Thiel alumnus, Bradshaw as coordinator, and three other instructors—John B. Stoeber, Janet Ward, and Mary Mowry (also alumni). In all, sixteen programs were completed with a combined enrollment of 367. The program was discontinued by the government in 1944.

Grove City College also participated in the Civilian Pilot Training Program from 1939 to 1942. Flight instruction was given at the New Castle Airport or at the old Grove City airport. Beginning in February 1942, the College operated a U.S. Army Corps School for pre-flight training. The program focused primarily on the social sciences rather than technical subjects. It was discontinued in 1944, having trained almost one thousand pilots, navigators, and bombardiers.

MERCER IN THE EARLY 1940S
By Joseph Hood, written in 1998

"The most unforgettable game of stick ball occurred on Sunday, December 7, 1941. One of the kids came to join the game and told us about some woman named Pearl Harbor who was attacked by a bunch of Japanese. Conjecture about the incident was rampant until we were told what actually happened. We were still pretty young to grasp the situation but in due time, we realized that we were at war and there was a good possibility that some or all of us would be involved in one way or another. We heard by radio the sobering declaration of war made by President Roosevelt. Soon, recruiting stations were doing a land office business. I was 16 at the time and would not be going into the service for about a year and a half. Some of my friends volunteered when they were old enough. Lefty (Elmer) Livermore was one. There were three of my class that died in the military. George Rowbottom was one. . . . Then there was Bob Bestwock and Ronnie Grill, both of whom died in the European theatre of operation. Considering there were 30 males in our graduating class, a 10% loss of life due to the war seems low when you consider the enormous losses suffered by the entire military.

"During winter months, we gradually acquired such things as ice skates and sleds and joined others in those activities. Ice Skating was done wherever we could find ice. Neshannock Creek would often freeze over to the extent that we could skate for literally miles if we dared. Then there was Robinson's pond that was located right smack in the middle of what is now, Plantation Park camping area. There, we would ice skate when the creek was not adequately frozen. . . .

"There was an annual Mercer Fair at the fairgrounds. We would gain entrance to the fair by helping set up the vendors on the midway. We could earn tickets by being gofer's

"During the summers when I was 16 and 17 years old [about 1941 and 1942], I lived at the Wilson Dairy Farm, which was around four miles from Mercer on the Pulaski Road. I was paid 15 dollars a month and was given room and board on top of this. The farm chores were no different than other farms. Milk twice a day. Clean out the stalls twice a day. Feed and water the cattle. Help with milk delivery. Hoe the garden. Hoe the corn. Put up hay. Harvest the oats. Harness the horses. Muck their stalls. And the worst job of all was cleaning out the calf pen, which was two to three feet deep with manure, straw, and hay. Harvest time was busy. We usually had a lot of help with the oats and the hay. All the harvest was put into the barn. There was a day of threshing when tables were set out on the lawn and at meal time, all would be treated to a 'thresherman's dinner.' So many hands were needed during this time because we did not have the equipment that is available today. Hay was cut with horse-drawn cutter and left to dry in the sun. A horse-drawn rake was then used to turn the hay over for additional drying. It was then raked into a narrow row which was eventually picked up and lifted onto a flat hay wagon by a loader that was trailed along behind the hay wagon. Men on the wagon would adjust the loading for equal distribution. The wagon was then taken to the barn where a hay fork was used to pick the hay up and hoist it to the peak of the barn where it traveled a short rail system to the spot it would be released. People in the barn would direct its release and then would try to make sure that all was even. Hand-loading of shocks of oats onto a wagon required the wearing of a stout, long-sleeved shirt. The oats whiskers would make your arms raw in short order. I learned this the hard way. No one would tell you. I guess they figured if you made your arms raw, you would never forget to wear a long-sleeved shirt the next time. A thresher was brought in to harvest the oats and also to provide straw to the barn for bedding cattle and horses. The threshing machine was located just outside the barn and had a discharge nozzle that extended into the barn. The thresher was driven from a power takeoff on a tractor. One occasion, I was given the job of directing the nozzle inside the barn. I was to make sure the straw was distributed evenly by moving the nozzle as required for the purpose. This was one of the easiest jobs I ever had on the farm. But isn't there always a price to pay? That evening, I got my bike and called the herd dog to bring in the milk cows. In order to get to the pasture, I had to peddle up a short hill. By the time I got to the gate, I nearly collapsed for lack of air. My lungs were obviously full of straw particles and dust. It took several days to get back to normal. Most of it I guess I coughed up. I never looked forward to that job again. Thank goodness the next harvest time I was in a new line of work. . . . The Wilson folks were pretty nice to me, especially Mrs. Wilson. Her elderly mother lived there also and she was another nice lady. Everet, on the other hand, wasn't so nice, but we got along. [Later when] I was in the Navy at boot camp, Mother had arranged for me to get the local paper. One day as I unfolded the paper, huge headlines exploded in my face. Mrs. Wilson, her mother, and a hired hand had all been murdered. The culprits allegedly were two other hands, one male and one female. Everet Wilson had been in Canada on a fishing trip. He may have been spared the same fate. All of this was a severe shock to me. . . . I personally was never convinced about the outcome of the trials. Somehow I felt there were others involved but I guess we will never know." (Caption: Joseph Hood)

and doing other menial tasks like driving stakes and carrying equipment. Once I gained entrance, I spent most of my time watching the harness races. Ed Moon was a local who at one time was the county district attorney. He always had good horses and won very often. Moving starting gates are used now, but back then the drivers were required to direct their horses in the opposite direction and upon command, all would turn 180° and approach the start finish line. The judge would observe that all were in the correct

EDIE ADAMS

By Gail Habbyshaw

Edie Adams was born Edith Elizabeth Enke in Kensington, Pennsylvania, to Sheldon Alonzo and Ada Dorothy Adams Enke. Her parents married in Wilkes-Barre in 1921 and the following year had a son, Sheldon Adams Enke. His sister, Edie, arrived in 1932.

When Edie was seven, her family moved to Nanticoke, Pennsylvania; and a few years later, when she was in fourth grade, they relocated to Grove City about 1941.

In her autobiography *Sing a Pretty Song*, Edie described Grove City as a "college town full of Presbyterian gothic architecture. Life was structured. . . . Lots and lots of church and music, music, music, that's what I did to fill the time."

In late 1989 Edie was presented with Slippery Rock University's Award of Achievement. While she was in the area, she made a return trip to Grove City and, among other places, visited Tower Presbyterian Church, which she attended as a child.

When Edie was eight or nine, some relatives took her to New York City, where she had the opportunity to see a Broadway play. For a child who had never been allowed to go to a movie, this experience was thrilling. And it changed her life. From that moment on she aspired for a career in show business.

Edie attended Juilliard School of Music and John Robert Powers School of Modeling in New York City and began getting stage roles, such as the leading character in "Junior Miss" and the ghostly first wife in Noel Coward's "Blithe Spirit."

---

location and if so, would yell 'Go!' Two circles of the track were made to complete the one-mile event. To me it was all pretty exciting.

"Mercer Sanitarium had a huge front lawn so we used this area to play tackle football. One day when we had one of our games going, and after a play, someone noticed that John Strosser's arm was bending the wrong way at the elbow. As I recall, he didn't feel any particular pain but did agree that he was unable to continue since he could no longer move that particular arm. After a committee meeting, we all decided to escort him to the hospital that was only a few hundred yards away. We arrived and summoned a nurse who immediately recognized a dislocated elbow when she saw one. Being told that John would be fine, we finally were persuaded to leave, whereupon we returned to the game and suffered no more serious medical traumas.

"Sye Adams junk yard sometimes was a real blessing. Sye bought metals of all sorts, so when we accumulated enough junk to make it worth our while, we would load up a wagon and off we would go to Sye's to pedal our wares. It was exciting to see just how much we would receive. . . . So in our travels if we spotted something of that nature that did not appear to have a specific owner, we would carry it home and save it for Sye. To locate Sye's place, it was almost directly behind the silk mill and was on an alley that was an extension of Grant Street. . . .

"At the foot of east Market Street, stood a hotel. It was called the Waverly and was put there long before to accommodate travelers who may have used the train station that was nearby. When we moved to town in 1939, the Mercer railway station existed, but I don't believe it was in use any longer. This rendered the Waverly almost useless as a hotel, so the owner converted it into apartments. As I write this [in 1998], the hotel no longer exists, but there is a lot with some playground equipment located there. The railway station has long departed the scene, and all of the tracks have been torn up. For a long time, however, some of the tracks were used to bring boxcars to the Reznor plant, where products were loaded and sent on their way all over the United States and Canada. The tracks routed through New Castle. Gradually, the shipping was converted from rail to trucks and this meant the demise of the railroad in Mercer. The last boxcars left Mercer at least 25 or 30 years ago, with the rails leaving shortly thereafter. The old bed is now used as a hiking and ATV trail. . . .

"It was along about this time that I began to work for Vic Adams. We built chimneys and I was the one who carried the mortar and bricks up the ladder. Believe me, as that chimney became taller, my work became exponentially tougher. But we built a number of chimneys in and around Mercer. Vic was really good at masonry. His home on McKinley Avenue was constructed of stone and it still stands today. Vic and I also moved a house while I was in his employ. As I think back on it, the work was really hard, but I was driven by curiosity and the disbelief that we were actually going to move that house. One day during the move, Vic captured a snake and demonstrated how you are supposed to kill them. He had it by the tail and he cracked it like a whip. This sent some of the contents flying, some of which struck me in the face. Vic thought this was extremely funny, but I sure didn't. We got the house moved onto a foundation and basement that was already in place. I think the move took about 10 days and to me, was a small miracle. Just Vic and I and Vic's truck, along with a ton of house jacks and heavy timbers. Vic told me that there was a cup of coffee sitting on the kitchen table during the move, and we didn't spill one drop. . . .

"Crill's Hardware sold model airplane kits and in order to drum up business, they always had a contest where the best models received ribbons. All the models were displayed in their front windows. I remember getting second place one time with a Piper Cub having water floats. Bill Pollard always won first place. His models were the envy of everyone. Bill eventually became a commercial pilot who flew for TWA and became their chief instructor during his later tenure there.

"Speaking of Bill Pollard, we were good friends and classmates. Bill owned a small plane that he kept at the Mercer Airport in Coolspring township. He had his license and would take me along for rides. He used to buzz his girlfriend's house which was located on the Butler Pike. Her name was Ruth Weinet and her parents owned a farm near where the state prison is now located. . . .

"This was when I worked at the Liberty Theater, the bowling alley, and Perska's garage. I was an usher at the theater and also was responsible for the message on the marquee and the new pictures that were always displayed throughout the entrance, which advertised coming attractions. I remember the real excitement when 'Gone With The Wind' appeared in Mercer. As I recall, the school literally closed one day so that most of the students could go to the matinee. You have to remember that this movie, in addition to being quite a drama, was also the first major picture done in color. As an usher, I saw the picture a number of times.

"At the bowling alley, I set pins and received something like 6 cents a line for ten pins and about 4 cents a line for duck pins. Each setter was responsible for two adjacent alleys.

There was a pit behind the alley that caught the pins as they were knocked down. In the pit was a foot treadle that had to be stepped on by the setter. This treadle, when stepped on, raised metal rods about a 1/4 inch in diameter, up out of the alley where the pins were to be located. Each pin had a hole in the center of the bottom. The setter simply set each pin on one of those rods. An efficient setter would grab 3 or 4 pins in each hand and rapidly locate them on the rods. When done, the treadle was released, the rods retracted into the floor and the bowler could go ahead and deliver the next ball. There were two bowlers which I hated to see preparing to bowl on my alley's. One was a fellow by the name of Ted Craig and the other was Ralph Rhodes. They threw the ball so hard that it was really dangerous being in the pit. We would sit at the rear of the pit and hold our feet in front of us to ward off flying pins. For the most part, this worked quite well but there were times when my feet actually hurt from stopping pins that these two guys had sent flying. After the bowling stopped, the setters would proceed to the billiard room and shoot Keno or eight ball until either they were broke or the place closed.

"I worked at Perska's along with Gene Adams. We pumped gas and clerked the small candy and pop business at the front of the establishment. Gene had purchased a 1934 Ford sedan and so we spent a good many hours acting like mechanics on this car. . . .

"John Nickum paid me to tend the furnace that heated the apartment house [where Hood's family had moved]. It was a commercial size furnace and had an automatic coal feeder. My job was twofold. First, I had to make sure the hopper always had coal in it, and second, I had to remove the clinkers from the fire box. I managed to handle this quite well by visiting the site at least twice each day in the heating season. I don't remember what my pay way, but I believe it was 10 or 15 dollars a month. Removing the clinkers, sometimes, was testy because the clinkers would often take the shape of a donut and when I tried to break it up for removal, I often got too close to the door and got a strong whiff of sulfur. This would nearly incapacitate me for several minutes because it burned my throat and lungs and literally took my breath away."

THE MURDERS AT THE WILSON FARM
By John Moser

On October 7, 1943, Helen Minner made a shocking discovery when she went to visit her neighbor's farmhouse. Originally built in 1896, the house, part of a 160-acre dairy farm, stood near the Pulaski Road, about two miles west of Mercer. Receiving no response to her knocks, she entered the house to find the bodies of Catherine Hoagland Wilson, age 78, and Robert McKay, age 61. Both were dead of gunshot wounds, the former on the living room floor, the latter on the landing at the top of the stairs. The apparent murder weapon, a 12-gauge shotgun with a still-warm barrel, lay nearby, as did the telephone, which had been ripped from the wall. A few hours later a man delivering hay to the barn found a third body—that of Helen Crawford Wilson, age 48, on the barn floor. She was tied up and appeared to have been strangled.

Thus begins one of the most horrifying, bizarre, fascinating, and newsworthy incidents of Mercer County history. Soldiers and sailors from the county, stationed far from home, recall reading about the grotesque crime in newspapers as far away as California. For a brief moment, Mercer County made national news.

The victims were all connected to the owner of the farm, Everett Wilson, a prominent citizen of Mercer County, prosperous dairy farmer, and an officer of the Pymatuning Insurance Company. Helen was his wife; Catherine his mother; McKay, a hired hand and itinerant Salvation Army preacher. Wilson, however, had been out of town for about a week when the murders took place—on a fishing trip to Canada with his friend William DeMine.

Although the police could find no usable fingerprints on the apparent murder weapon or the telephone, it did not take them long to formulate a theory about the killings. Missing from the household were its two youngest members, nineteen-year-old farmhand William Morrell and twenty-one-year-old servant Janice Graham. Suspicion immediately fell on Morrell. An orphan since the age of fifteen, he had spent several years in George Junior Republic, the state home in Grove City for delinquent youths, and had been placed in the county jail early in 1943 for having forged a check. The Wilsons, like most farm families, had been experiencing a shortage of labor due to World War II and had arranged to have Morrell released into their custody provided he worked on the farm. With a history of petty crime, no more than a fourth-grade education, and a physical disability that caused his arms to hang out menacingly in front of his body, Morrell was an easy target for blame.

It would be difficult to imagine two young people more different than Morrell and Graham. Graham, a timid graduate of Mercer High School, had come from a respected family and once worked as a librarian. Nevertheless, a rumor existed that she and Morrell had been dating.

First, Morrell was considered the murderer. Once the young couple was apprehended, Morrell was put on trial. However, in spite of his several confessions, the jury could not convict him of the three murders based on the evidence presented at the trial. They convicted him only of the manslaughter of one of the victims, and suspicion shifted toward Graham.

Graham was originally going to be tried as an accomplice. However, after Morrell's trial concluded, the charges against Graham were changed to murder.

Meanwhile, Everett Wilson was evasive and apparently disinterested in the proceedings. Police finally found him in Texas and brought him back to Mercer County, but he offered no help in solving the mysteries of the murders and was eventually dismissed.

The evidence presented at Graham's trial turned the tide again, and the jury acquitted her. Without really solving the crime, the courts decided not to pursue the mystery any more. It did not take long for the murders to fade from popular memory. The names of Janice Graham, William Morrell, and Everett Wilson, which had been front-page news in the county on and off for two years, were eventually forgotten.

Graham and Wilson went on to lead fairly normal lives. Graham eventually married, raise a family, and died in 1992 at age sixty-nine. Wilson served in the U.S. Navy's construction battalion (the fabled Seabees) during the final months of the War. Then, he moved to Florida, remarried, and died in 1988, having lived to be ninety-two.

Morrell served the full twelve years of his sentence and was released in 1955. He returned to Mercer County and moved in with his younger sister and her family, who lived in Sandy Lake. He found a job and appeared to get his life in order. But within a few months, he was arrested again, this time charged with assault and attempted rape. As the alleged victim was his own sister, he was committed to the state mental hospital in Warren for observation. After a couple of months, however, he was released and fled the county. He was never heard from again.

The infamous house and barn still stand today; however, the dairy farm is no more. The house has largely been remodeled, and the barn used for storage.

More than fifty years later, the Wilson murders and subsequent trials continue to offer more questions than answers. Were the crimes the act of one disturbed young man? Did Janice Graham escape her fair share of the blame for what happened at the farm that day? And what role did Everett Wilson play? Is it possible that he had known in advance what was going to happen, or perhaps even put Morrell (or, for that matter, Graham) up to it? With the death of the principal players, it is unlikely that any of these questions will ever be answered.

HOME DURING THE WAR
*By Wally Wachter (published in 1984 in **The Herald**)*

"When President Franklin D. Roosevelt remarked back in 1941 that 'War is hell' it must have been because he was back on the home front.

"Those of us who were called to the colors or who volunteered to fight knew of the rigors that awaited us and were prepared for them, whether it was on the battlefields of Guadalcanal or Anzio, in the dog fights over Germany or Wake Island, in the torpedo-laden waters of the Coral Sea, in the plush office in Honolulu or the bistros of Paris.

"Few of us were aware of the 'hell' that was created back home by scarcities of food, materials and other items that were channeled into the war effort.

"I never knew rationing and all I know about it was learned from those who had experienced it. I do recall that when war clouds gathered over Europe, long before the bombing of Pearl Harbor which brought our country into the world conflict, we were beginning to prepare for the eventuality. The Selective Service System was installed and draft boards were set up to begin inducting young men into the service. A drive was on for aluminum foil which generally was piled in fire stations until it was picked up and taken to a central location for remelting and reuse. There was talk of rationing and the establishment of rationing boards to implement it.

"Then the war erupted, we were gone, and we never knew until we came back about the battle on the home front.

"Aluminum foil had been used extensively to wrap candy bars, individual sticks of chewing gum and many other everyday items. But it gave way to light waxed paper as aluminum went to war. It was used to make airplanes.

"The demise of the domestic use of aluminum foil was the start of the rationing movement. It became worse as the war progressed, reaching to food, gasoline, shoes, wearing

The Pennsylvania Department of Highways put up victory speed signs along state highways, including in Mercer County, to inform motorists that thirty-five miles an hour was the maximum speed for the war period.

MASANOBU MORISUYE
By Mairy Jayn Woge

Masanobu Morisuye lived along Buhl Court in Sharon with his wife and daughters, Jean and Eleanore, on December 7, 1941, the day Pearl Harbor was bombed by Japan. Jean heard about the attack while she and friends were listening to a speech about Russia in the Sharon High School auditorium that Sunday afternoon. Her father was an engineer at Westinghouse in Sharon, a member of the First Methodist Church, and active in numerous civic organizations. He was born in Japan before his parents moved to California. Since Japanese residents of the United States were barred from becoming American citizens until the mid-1960s, Morisuye was an alien. His brother was born in the United States and worked for the Federal Bureau of Investigation before coming to Sharon.

After the U.S. Congress declared war against Japan, the Morisuye home was searched; and cameras, rubber boots, and other items were seized by the government representatives. Westinghouse officials intervened when they learned Morisuye was to be sent with other Japanese residents of the United States in an encampment in California. Morisuye was permitted to stay in the Shenango Valley, but under surveillance.

ERIE RAILROAD

By Frederick Houser

In 1906, the Erie Railroad acquired trackage rights via the Bessemer & Lake Erie Railroad's nearby route between Shenango and Meadville by way of Hartstown. These rights, along with an early installation of centralized traffic control that allowed remote operation of signals and track switches from a central location, made it unnecessary for the Erie to add a second track. This important segment near the midpoint of the Erie system was able to safely and routinely handle nearly seventy trains per day in both directions during World War II. The Erie also introduced its first diesel-electric road freight locomotives over this route during the early 1940s, which also improved the capacity of the line by allowing the railroad to handle more tonnage with fewer trains.

The post-War years were not happy ones, however, for what was often referred to as the "Weary Erie." A final reorganization, which ended in 1941, was followed by resumption of the payment of common stock dividends in 1942, the first time in seventy-six years.

---

apparel, rubber products and practically every other daily necessity. Artificial chocolate and rubber-like gum were among the only confections available.

"Families were issued ration coupons for the various commodities, based on the number in the family and the degree of necessity of the items. Strict limits were placed on the purchase of such food items as meat, butter, coffee, cheese. When the coupons were gone, families did without until the next month's allotment.

"The clamp on gasoline use was probably the cause of the greatest inconvenience. Stickers on car windshields showed the owners were allowed just so much a month, the amount based on the extent the car was needed to provide transportation to work.

"All rubber was turned over to the war effort. That meant no replacement for worn out auto and bicycle tires. Elastic in clothing vanished and was replaced by buttons. Electrical plugs and fixtures gave way to synthetic substances.

"The women were the biggest losers. No more silk underthings or sexy sheer hose. The silk were to factories to make parachutes for US paratroopers. The only available hose were made of the new synthetic, rayon, with the sheerness determined by denier (the number and thickness of threads).

"By the waning years of the war, even cotton goods became hard to come by. Rumors reached us that men had to resort to wearing women's panties for shorts. Even these became scarce.

"On my homeward trip across the Pacific by troopship, I recall my luggage included a barracks bag full of undershorts and jerseys, most of them olive-drab colored which I vowed I would never wear again. To lighten my load, I dumped the whole bag overboard. When I arrived home, I had trouble finding men's underwear and would have settled for even the olive-drab ones. If I had been wise I could have kept them, retailed them and made a small fortune.

"Many times during my nearly four war years in Hawaii, my family and friends sent me food packages of cheeses, salami and crackers which I later found they were sacrificing their ration stamps to buy. Any of these items I could have bought there without ration restrictions.

"The start of the war triggered a rebounding of the economy which had just begun to weather the Depression years. Money again was plentiful, but thanks to rationing, there was nothing around to buy with it.

"And while rigors of war touched most of us who were called or volunteered to participate, we sometimes forget to remember that it was hardly a picnic at home, either."

THE OLD ORDER AMISH OF MERCER COUNTY
By Norma Fischer Furey

One group of Old Order Amish from the Atlantic settlement in southern Crawford County formed a community in 1942 near Jackson Center and in Fairview Township. In 1998, a new group of Old Order Amish families came to Delaware Township, west of Route 19, from a community in Kentucky. These people are of a totally different group that the groups east of Route 19 in Fairview Township. The movement of families in and out of established Amish communities continues to take place regularly for various reasons: a new area proves to have potential for future growth, land is cheaper, differences of opinion emerge among the members of the church concerning the code of conduct and rituals, or people simply want to be nearer to other family members.

All of the relative newcomers to the northern sections of Mercer County are Old Order Amish and share the strict beliefs of their neighbors to the south, who came to this region as early as 1841.

The Old Order Amish have maintained their nineteenth century rural lifestyle while industry and technology have gone beyond our imagination. The Amish can trace their roots to the Anabaptist movement in Switzerland during the early 1400s. Persecuted from the beginning, the Anabaptists continued their teaching and migrated from place to place within Switzerland, Germany, and France seeking religious tolerance. One major Anabaptist group journeyed to the Netherlands in the mid-1500s and became known as the Mennonites.

The Mennonite sect observed strict rules of conduct as outlines in two documents developed in Europe during the 1500s and 1600s. However, eventually, a Mennonite bishop, Jakob Ammann, became concerned that the members of the church were straying too far from the stringent and literal translation of the Bible that formed the foundation of the Anabaptist movement. He traveled from congregation and congregation to persuade other Mennonites to join with him and espouse his stricter beliefs. These visits continued for several years, and a serious conflict resulted. Eventually, in the late 1600s, Ammann and his faithful followers broke away from the Mennonites and became known as *Ammansch* and, eventually, the Amish.

Meanwhile, William Penn had acquired a large tract of land in the New World as a debt repayment. A Quaker, Penn understood religious persecution and invited the Ammansch to become part of his "Holy Experiment." In Pennsylvania, the General Assembly had, in 1682, enacted its first statute, a law that guaranteed religious freedom for all. Thus, in 1727, the first Amish immigrants set sail for a new life.

The original community of Amish was northeast of Lancaster in Berks County. But, because of the settlement's proximity to the Indian frontier, the settlers moved west to Lancaster County, away from the mountains and danger from Indian raids. They were accomplished farmers and stewards of the land. They survived, prospered, and for the first time in their long history had the freedom to live and worship without fear of prosecution and death. Immigration continued, and before 1800, the number of Amish is estimated to have been around five hundred.

Some Amish continued west, however. Besides being tempted by the general American migration westward, these Amish began to move away from the Lancaster area

Amish farmer plowing his fields and a group of buggies parked for a social or religious gathering, both in the 1990s. (Photographer: Marilyn Dewald)

due to disagreements that were festering between church leaders concerning the doctrines and rules to be followed by members. The most conservation groups were mainly either to Somerset County or to Juniata and Mifflin Counties as early as 1791. They continued to live apart from the other religious groups, cleared land, planted crops, and established new communities.

New differences between the factions in the Juniata-Mifflin settlement caused an undercurrent that, again, eventually brought about a schism within the Amish community. The groups split away from each other and about 1841, the first of the extremely traditional group migrated to an area near the western border of Pennsylvania to what is now Lawrence County. At the time of the migration, however, the area was part of Mercer County. (Lawrence County was formed from portions of Mercer, Butler, and Beaver Counties in 1849.)

The Amish who settled in the Mercer-Lawrence Townships of Neshannock, Pulaski, Hickory, Washington, Shenango, and Wilmington in the mid-1800s are ancestors of the many Amish who still live here. Over the years they have expanded to the north and to the south. Now, the communities straddle the Mercer-Lawrence County border, and New

Wilmington is the commercial center of the settlement. The southern Mercer County group of Old Order Amish has continued to grow and prosper and has maintained the rigid code of conduct of their forefathers, which is based on the Bible.

In contrast, New Order Amish have origins identical to those of the more exacting Old Order Amish, but their leaders have chosen to interpret the teachings more liberally. For example, the New Order Amish erect buildings specifically for worship, while the Old Order Amish continue to meet for services in each other's homes. New Order Amish are permitted to have electricity in homes and barns; Old Order Amish are not. New Order Amish use tractors in the fields, and Old Order Amish can use only stationary gasoline engines to power farm equipment in the fields. New Order Amish are allowed to own automobiles, and Old Order Amish continue to use horse-drawn buggies for transportation.

Generally speaking, the Old Order Amish are the only ones who migrated to Mercer County in any significant numbers. The bishop of each church district is the final authority on every facet of the members' lives. These men are chosen by lot and serve for life. They take seriously the responsibility thrust upon them and strive for harmony and unity among their congregations. They do make minute changes occasionally, but they keep the traditions of previous generations whenever possible. Thus, even among communities with similar customs and beliefs, subtle differences may exist. Among the Mercer County Amish, the most obvious difference to a non-Amish, or "English," observer is the color of the buggy tops. The group in southern Mercer County has brown tops, while the others have all black buggies. The women from the southern part of the county wear brown bonnets, but their counterparts to the north wear black bonnets. The women's clothing is similar, but varies in skirt length, pleating near the hem, style of the "cape" which covers the bodice, and adornment at the back of the waistband. The white organdy caps worn by all Amish women is nearly identical to those worn by their ancestors in Switzerland, but have slight differences in width of the band and number and width of pleats in the back. Men, too, have strict rules concerning their appearance. Length of hair and beards, width of hat brims, style (or absence) of suspenders are all determined by the bishop and are not open for discussion. When Amish people move into a new community, they will begin immediately to adapt the clothing and hair styles to conform with the rules set down in the congregation. Amish from one area can immediately recognize and identify where the strangers in their midst come from, just by observing their physical appearance.

The Amish mode of dress is little different from that of centuries ago, and their way of life is still simple and based on agriculture, even in the face of technology, tourism, and temptation. These temperate people, who have persevered through hundreds of years of adversity and suffering in the name of faith, are more prosperous and productive than ever. Their example stands as a model for people of all races and creeds. Their faith has never wavered. Steadfast and modest, they continue to live according to the Scriptures and to make only the changes necessary for them to endure.

BETTY HARTER SPENCE

Betty Harter Spence, a Greenville native and a graduate of Thiel College, enrolled in the College's Civilian Pilot Training Program in 1940. She was one of the few women to participate in the program. After receiving her pilot's license, Spence joined the 99's, a national flying organization for women pilots. During World War II, Spence joined a government-sponsored course in meteorology at UCLA, but shortly transferred to a course in air traffic control, receiving her controller's license in 1942. She was later assigned to the San Diego Information Center for aircraft identification, but resigned to take a position in the engineering department of Ryan Aircraft. After the war, Spence returned to Greenville where she married and had two children.

In Spence's own words, "During World War II, a great many ordinary American citizens gave hours of their time when they volunteered to be stationed at a designated location to search the sky for any plane overhead and immediately report information on that plane to the area Information Center. The towns, country fields, even lonely mountain tops were covered as loyal patriots helped the war effort with the talent they had.

"The Information Center for southwestern United States was located in San Diego, the place to which I was now assigned.

"Arriving at the Information Center, I was ushered upstairs to a large windowless room on a balcony overlooking an even larger room below, in the center of which was an extra large table manned by two Army sergeants. Jack, the current CAA representative was seated on the balcony at the table across which was a constantly moving tape with the flight plans of every plane allowed to fly in that section of the United States. Below, when the sergeants received a report of a plane spotted, that information (direction of flight, location spotted, altitude, number of engines, etc.) was placed atop a pip at the proper site

CIVILIAN PLANE SPOTTERS

During World War II, Joseph Hood (Mercer) recalls, "airplane lookout stations were scattered throughout the United States and I supposed Canada also. Mercer had one that was manned by teenagers and people that were too old to be in the service. The lookout was a small building, elevated off the ground a few feet and containing a small porch or deck from which to visually and audibly identify aircraft which entered the area. We became adept at identifying whether the plane was single or multiple engine. Since this, in my case, was done at night, there was no opportunity to provide any further identification. A telephone was at the site and it was tied in to a network that apparently was used for aircraft tracking to be certain that no unforeseen incident would befall the country.

"One night, Gene Adams and I worked the lookout, some time after midnight until daylight. The weather was bitter cold, but luckily we had a pot bellied stove with which to keep warm. We had driven there in the Adams family car. The lookout was located just out of Mercer, on the road to New Wilmington. Precisely, it was beyond Paterson's woods on the east side of the road and at the very top of the long hill, for which I have no name.

"When daylight arrived, Gene and I proceeded to the car and Gene attempted to start it. It was frozen solid, and the battery could move nothing. It was because of this possibility that Gene had parked the car facing down the hill so we could at least start it by popping the clutch after allowing the car to drift for a ways. The car was so cold we could barely move it, but we finally got it in motion. After it proceeded down the hill some distance, the speed, while still quite slow, was enough to pop the clutch and it actually started. As I recall, we had to allow the engine to warm up real good, so there was adequate power to climb the hill toward town. We volunteered for this work many times but had no further problem with the cold weather."

on the oversized table. Jack, and later I, was to identify that plane from seeing its flight plan cross before us. We then called out to the sergeants below ('Army,' 'Navy,' etc.) who then took it off the board as friendly and nonthreatening. We had to identify the plane by the third sighting or we would call out the Fighter Command—P-38s—to shoot a shot across its bow ordering it to land. Theoretically, if that plane then didn't land, it would be shot down. There were so many aircraft factories in the area that a hit by an enemy plane would be disastrous to our war effort.

"After observing Jack calling so many single engine planes 'Navy,' thus removing them from the table below, I protested to Jack that I had not seen the flight plans of those planes. Jack's reply: 'There are so many young trainees flying Navy planes from the local North Island base to the Salton Sea and back each day, and these kids like to sightsee to places not on their plan, we are not going to shoot them down.' But, he added, 'never identify a plane, without a flight plan, coming in from the Pacific Ocean or from outside our borders, like Mexico, especially those with four engines as they would likely be bombers.'

"After some time, on this my first day, Jack asked me to take over while he left for a smoke. I was still protesting as he left the room. All went well for awhile until we got a report of a four-engine plane in Mexico and headed for our southern border. As I had no flight plan for it, I would not identify it. First, one report, then a second report of the same plane heading closer to our southern border. Tension filled the entire area and all eyes

"Nearly 57 years later I can still remember it like it happened yesterday," says William Young (Otter Creek Township) (pictured pointing to the crash site, in 2000). As a child, Young lived with his grandparents, Robert and Martha Young, on a small, rented farm (Coolspring Township). On that fateful day in 1943, Young, age twelve (pictured), was mowing a hay field on the Norris Rodgers property while his cousin John Robert Robinson, age fourteen, (now, of California) was riding the mower. They saw and heard a plane overhead. The small Piper Cub training plane, which had taken off from the Mercer Airport, was having problems. The motor had quit, and the boys immediately moved the equipment from the field and began to wave the pilot into landing. The plane was low enough that they could see the pilot and his passenger. All of a sudden the motor caught, and the plane began to climb. Shortly later they heard the motor quit again, and looking eastward they could see the plane heading for the ground, nose first. It crashed about 7 p.m. in a pasture on the R. J. Bums farm about two miles south of Fredonia. The boys ran toward the plane and were the first on the scene. They knew right away that the passenger was dead. The pilot was conscious, but badly hurt. With the boys' help, he managed to get out of the plane and lie under a crumpled wing. Robinson recalls, "the sound of the crash was awesome. . . . the conditions were really intimidating. There wasn't much we could do." Van Miller Ambulance (Fredonia) transported the pilot to Mercer Cottage Hospital where he soon died. The pilot was E. Joel "Brownie" Brown, who had become a resident of Meadville the year before and renewed his flying instructors certification. He had taken a leave of absence from the J. C. Penney stores to participate in an activity he felt valuable to the war effort. He gave flying lessons from Mercer and was well-liked by his students. The passenger, Robert Martin Daugherty, was a Grove City native, married and father of two, employed at Cooper-Bessemer, popular in community sports and business circles, and just thirty-one years old when he died. The plane was owned by a group of Cooper-Bessemer men who had formed the C-B X Club. (Contributor: Joyce Young)

focused on me waiting for me to identify it. Just as the third sighting was placed on the table below, Jack returned, while I wilted. 'Oh,' he said, 'I forgot to tell you that a regularly scheduled airlines comes up from Guadalajara at the same time every day and their flight plan is kept on file.' As my toes began to uncurl and my racing heart began to slowly return to its normal beat, over Jack's protest, I vowed aloud to resign."

DUSTY RHODES
*From **Our Naval Views and Comments**, April 1, 1942*

"Just before dawn a few weeks ago, not far off Cape May, N.J., a thundering explosion shook the USS *Jacob Jones* and a few minutes later she sank with a loss of more than a hundred lives. Although full details were lacking as this was written it was evident that the torpedo or torpedoes made a shambles of the destroyer and that she sank quickly. Under such conditions there would naturally be confusion both topside and below decks.

"In the Philadelphia Naval Hospital one of the few enlisted men who lived to tell of the USS *Jacob Jones* end, Adolph R. Storm, said:

"'If ever a guy should be given a plug it's Dusty Rhodes. He got order on the ship and stood by giving directions. The last I saw of him he was still standing there telling others to jump.'

"Wilbur (Dusty) Rhodes was one of the seamen who went to his death on the stricken destroyer.

"'Dusty Rhodes had taken command,' Storm said. 'He was just a seaman but someone had to restore order and he did it. When I finally left the ship I saw Rhodes on the deck, telling the men what to do.'

"This is only one of many stories of heroism by enlisted in this war and there will be many more of them. But it seemed to illustrate something about this Navy of ours. It is not only the officers who must be fit to command. There is always the chance that the moment will come when an enlisted man may have to take charge. It is typical of the United States Navy that its enlisted men learn and understand that this is so. It has already been demonstrated time and time again that enlisted men, when that time comes, are ready. . . .

"Dusty Rhodes died, yes. So have many other enlisted heroes. They gave their lives for their country. But perhaps they did something else for their shipmates throughout the naval service. Perhaps then and the other heroes who will follow them in the days to come are proving to the ranking officers of our Navy that many enlisted men are well fitted for command."

DRAFTED INTO THE NAVY
By Joseph Hood, written in 1998

"Sometime, shortly after my 18th birthday, I received my draft notice. I was sent to Erie for a physical and assignment. After a full day of all kinds of checks and tests and questions, I was asked what branch of the military I preferred. I hadn't given much thought to my preference, but the fellow asking me the question had a Navy uniform on, so I immediately said Navy. He said I made a good choice and that I should go to a certain place within the facility. There I was directed to return home and I would receive my orders my mail. I was not required to do anything until sometime in September. This was 1943 and the war had been going on for about a year and a half. The Allies were turning things around, but there was still a lot of work to do.

"I went through boot camp at Great Lakes Naval Training Station. Upon completion of this training, I was sent to Aviation Machinist Mate School at Navy Pier in Chicago.

Around April of 1944 I was shipped to Pensacola, Florida, where I spent the remainder of the war. All my attempts to get a billet aboard an aircraft carrier bore no fruit. The only time I could have got my wishes was when the war had ended and most military people were heading home. Then they wanted me. But I no longer wanted them. So I got discharged from the Navy and in 1946 became a civilian again.

"It isn't that my stint in the Navy was wasted; believe me, none of us were wasted. We worked lone hours in the day-to-day work of training pilots for the Navy and Marines. We mustered every day at 7 a.m. and with a short break for lunch, worked the squadron until around 5 p.m. All aircraft were secured and tied down. There was about an hour break for dinner and then we returned to the squadron, untied the aircraft, and commenced night flying. This often lasted until after midnight. The next morning it was back to the daylight schedule. This day we would secure at 5 p.m., have dinner, and get the night off. Next day we would again commence daylight activities, securing at 5 p.m. and breaking for dinner. Then we would have four hours of guard duty sometime through the night and commence the next day's activities at 7 a.m. So you can see we remained very busy.

"I did manage to get in a lot of hours in the air. I was even allowed to fly the plane on many occasions. Further, we didn't mind the long hours, but once in a while we would

The National Malleable and Steel Castings Company acquired an electric furnace for producing steel in 1910. That addition was a milestone in Shenango Valley industry. The Malleable had started business there in 1900 by purchasing the stock of Aschman Steel Castings Company. It bought the property between the Graff Stove Works and Sharon Boiler Company on Budd Street and Dock Avenue. Some of one tract was in Hickory Township, but most of the site of the Malleable buildings were on land Sharon annexed from Hickory. Two railroads crossed the property. During World War I, the Malleable sold parts for ships and railroad cars to the government. After the war, it continued to manufacture anchors, anchor chains, bolsters, side frames, couplers, and wheels. In 1939, it employed between twelve and fourteen hundred. During World War II, Joseph Hood recalled, "After graduation [from Mercer High School in the early 1940s] and before going to the service, I worked at the National Malleable Casting Company. I rode to work with three other fellows from Mercer. We all worked a swing shift, meaning each week we would go to work for a different eight-hour shift. First shift was 7 to 3, second shift was 3 to 11 and third shift was 11 to 7. The work was hard, dirty, hot, and dangerous. We manufactured frames for tanks and anchor chains. There was one blast furnace and two or three electric furnaces. A lot of the work was preparing molds to receive the molten steel. The dangerous part was made vivid to me on at least two occasions. First, I was nearly hit by a huge tray of castings that was being moved by an overhead crane. I challenged the crane operator to come down where I could show him how mad I was. He never showed up. The next occasion, I was working under one of the blast furnace ladles, when the man operating the lever to release the molten steel, got ahead of the crane operator and pulled the handle at the wrong time. The molten steel missed the clay funnel and struck a flat place on the mold. A great spray of the hot steel resulted. A number of us in the area were splashed with molten steel. I had a glob of steel fall into my shirt pocket and burn its way down the front of my body, terminating at the end of my private part. I invented the 'watootsie' that day. My burns were treatable with a little burn salve, but one of the other fellows had to be taken to the hospital for extensive treatment and therapy. So it was a rough place to work and going into the service would be like a vacation to me." (Postcard: Daniel Maurice; caption: Mairy Jayn Woge and Joseph Hood)

pull liberty and go into town for a little hell-raising. And occasionally, the Navy would treat us to a beer party at Gulf Shores. The closest we ever got to the enemy was talking to the members of Germany's Africa Corp who were prisoners or war and were sent to our base to provide manual labor. They patched runways, cut grass, dug ditches and the like, and were never a problem. Most were blond-haired and heavily tanned. Some could speak English while others just made had signals. Most smiled a lot. I think they were glad to be out of the war.

"An interesting note about military pay. As a boot in basic training, my pay was $21 a month. Once I had completed boot camp, I became a second-class seaman and got an increase of about $5. Then upon completing Aviation Machinist Mate training, I became a first class seaman. Shortly, I was able to get my third class petty officer pay and, along with flight pay, I drew about $60 per month. Granted, I didn't need a whole lot of money because most of my needs were taken care of by the Navy. But if you compare this with current military pay, it almost makes you laugh. The only real responsibility we had was for our clothing and shoes after our initial allotment of same."

DEVELOPING THE ATOMIC BOMB
By Frederick Houser

"One of the tragedies of the 1900s was that its major scientific triumph, unlocking the secrets of the atom, led first to military applications—destruction of the Japanese cities of Hiroshima and Nagasaki—in the summer of 1945. To their credit, those two atomic bombs brought an immediate and premature end to World War II and avoided tremendous casualties on both sides, which were anticipated with the scheduled invasion of Japan. To mankind's credit, in the course of wars fought through the remainder of the 1900s, no nation ever again resorted to this form of mass destruction.

"After graduating from Stoneboro High School, I went at Carnegie Tech, from which I was drafted. After going through Army basic training, I was assigned to the Army Specialized Training Program (ASTP, irreverently known as 'All Safe Until Peace') at Oregon State College. ASTP was intended to prepare technicians, taking advantage of their previous college training. I eventually arrived in the company of a couple dozen other enlisted men at the Army's top-secret laboratory, 40 miles northwest of Santa Fe,

OLD GREENVILLE AIRPORT
By Richard Christner

A small airfield was located on the east side of the Sharon-Greenville Road about four miles south of Greenville. Built in the late 1920s, the airfield was operated by Frank Bowers, assisted by flight instructor Merle Wilkinson. The field had two landing strips (each about 1,500 feet long), a hanger, gas pump, wind-sock, and one (later two) Waco biplane with an OX-5 engine. The facilities were destroyed by fire in 1931, and the airfield was relocated to West Main Hill about two miles from Greenville. The new field, with a north-south runway 1,200 feet long, was operated by J. P. Dart and Silas Moss. Closed from the beginning of World War II until 1943, it was sold in 1946 to Mickey Klenovich and Rudy Zarecky. The airfield closed for good in 1950 when serious discussions for a new Greenville Municipal Airport began.

New Mexico. 'American and foreign-born physicists, chemists, metallurgists and engineers, as well as military technical personnel, came together at Los Alamos to devise a weapon with a power hitherto unmatched by man,' write Vincent C. Jones in the US Army history of the Manhattan District, code name for this massive effort. The New Mexico program started in 1943 and culminated on July 16, 1945, with the world's first detonation of an atomic bomb in a test conducted in a New Mexico desert.

"Manhattan District facilities at Oak Ridge, Tennessee, and at Hanford, Washington, produced the uranium isotopes and other metallic derivatives, which composed the nuclear cores of the forthcoming weapons. The bomb dropped on Hiroshima was fundamentally different from the one dropped on Nagasaki. Hiroshima was destroyed by a 'gun-type' weapon with a uranium isotope core; Nagasaki, by an 'implosion' bomb with a plutonium core. Uncertainties about the potential of the implosion type led to the decision to test it before its use in combat; no uncertainty existed about the uranium bomb so the first one was used on Hiroshima on August 6, 1945.

"I was involved in producing the conventional high-explosive lenses, which squeezed (imploded) the hemispheres of plutonium at the center into a critical mass in milliseconds and, as a result, produced an explosion equivalent to 20,000 tons of TNT. The successful and experimental firing of this design on July 16, 1945, in the New Mexico desert was actually the world's first atomic explosion. The second plutonium bomb was then dropped at Nagasaki three days after the bomb on Hiroshima. Surrender of the Japanese armed forces occurred a week later and brought a close to World War II."

USING THE ATOMIC BOMB
By Jerry Johnson

"When I look back 50+ years, World War II seems to be a dream. It was not. It is real in my mind and a major event in world history.

"My outfit, the 9th Photo Technical Squadron, was headquartered on Guam in the Mariana Island Group in the western Pacific. I was a photographer. I processed film and eventually became a lab chief. The 9th was created to process and interpret aerial photos taken by the 20th Air Force in the Pacific theater of operation. As a part of many sorties (flights by varied aircraft, including B29s), the photos concentrated on several cities, including Hiroshima and Nagasaki. It is my understanding these two cities were chosen because of good weather conditions on two particular days, the 6th and 13th of August 1945—talk about bad luck. They, of course, were the sites of the atomic bomb blasts.

Trinity Site, where the world's first nuclear detonation took place in 1945, was finally visited by Frederick Houser (Stoneboro) in 1993. Although working on the same type of plutonium bomb (albeit 250 miles away at Los Alamos, New Mexico) at the same time, Houser needed a veterans' reunion forty-eight years later to gain access to this historic marker, which is still barred to the public most of the time. (Contributor: Frederick Houser)

"The 9th Photo Tech processed hundreds of photos of these two cities. The pre-strike, strike, and post-strike were all well documented. For the pre-strike and post-strike photos, automatic cameras having 24-inch-or-more focal lengths made many aerial passes over these cities. Hundreds of 9-x-9-inch photos were taken of each city. The result was a large photo picture (mosaic), depicting the cities before, during, and after the atomic bombing. Only 45 sets of these original pictures were made. One set went to President Truman, and others went to government or military leaders. Unfortunately for posterity, we were ordered to destroy the negatives.

"At the time these events took place, I had no concept of the historical impact of the atomic bombs. The overall impact will continue to be a matter of conjecture for years to come. In my opinion, President Truman was right in authorizing the use of the 'bomb.' Why? It saved millions of lives—not just American, but the lives of our Allies and the Japanese. I personally saw a hospital for 50,000 being built on Guam. It was a half-mile from my billet and was to be used for soldiers who would be wounded in the planned invasion of Japan. I am glad it was never used for its original purpose.

"During my tour of duty in World War II, the world changed forever. We went from guns and traditional bombs to atomic bombs. Looking back, perhaps the atomic bomb with Hiroshima and Nagasaki would be considered the major turning point in our history—and the history of the entire world. I witnessed—and in an extremely inconsequential way played a role—in that change. As I have continued my life back in Mercer, I often think of those days and wonder."

WAR MEMORIES FROM EAST LACKAWANNOCK TOWNSHIP
By Ruth Woods

Zella Garrett Cooper vividly recalls the day the war ended, November 11, 1918. At 11 a.m. at the Number 8 community, the excitement was electrifying: bells began to ring from every church and school belfry, and horns could be heard blowing all across the countryside. A phone call soon declared the celebration: "The war is over!"

The students at Number 8 school hurried to ring their school bell, too. The older boys commandeered the bell rope first and yanked so hard on the rope that it flipped the bell in the belfry, snapping the rope up through the ceiling. Zella, nine years old then, remembers that she never got a turn to ring the bell.

"The pride and patriotism of Americans was much stronger then than it is today," recalls Earl Shaffer, who was eighteen in 1942 when he enlisted in the Navy. He went to Pittsburgh and stood in line a block long at the old post office building on Grant Street. Boot camp at Sampson, New York, was brutally cold. After training at the Great Lakes Naval Training Station, Wisconsin, Shaffer was sent to Seattle, Washington, to board the *USS Enterprise*, an aircraft carrier. In 1943, they sailed to Pearl Harbor, and from there on, they were actively involved in every battle in the Pacific. Of all U.S. aircraft carriers in the war, the *USS Enterprise* was the only survivor of Japanese attacks. Their record was exemplary: 981 Japanese plane shot down and 70 enemy ships sunk. Following the war, they transported American servicemen home from Africa, England, and France. Their crew was honored in the huge tickertape parade in New York City. Shaffer returned on Amtrak to Pittsburgh in 1946. In 1999, he again traveled Amtrak, this time with his wife Mae to Rockland, Nevada, for a reunion of the crew from the *USS Enterprise*.

William "Bill" Black, who lived on Rodgers Road, was eighteen when he was called in the first Pennsylvania draft in 1943. Following basic training at Fort McClelland, Alabama, Bill was shipped out from Newport News, Virginia, on the *West Point*, a luxury liner converted to a troop ship that carried approximately 10,000 Army servicemen. It

Attending Hunter School (West Salem Township) in 1945 were (front row, from left) Philip Cook, Buster Matter, Robert Brest, Joyce Fenton, Joyce Brumbaugh, Margaret Vaughn, Robert Matter, Beverly Fenton, and William Brest; (back row) Richard Cook, Dorothy Gravatte, Eleanor Pinkle, Clyde Moyer, Donald Matter, Betty Cook, Nancy Cook, James Vaughn, Violet Moyer, [teacher Lillie Moreland (Jamestown)], and Norman Riley. (Contributor: Joyce Brumbaugh Young)

was so crowded, one had to stay in quarters. There was no room to lounge around. The kitchen crew had to serve meals twenty-four hours per day just to feed everyone. Letters from home were a treasure. The ship docked on Mother's Day, 1943 at Casablanca, Morocco, a major Allied base. Transferred to Naples, Italy, he served in a military police unit with the FBI. They were successful in shutting down a railroad battalion which was operating a million dollar black market trade. Although Bill's unit had an interpreter, he could speak fluent Italian when he was discharged in December 1945. Of his company, 75 percent had received the purple heart by the time they came home, so intense was the action they had experienced.

Ralph Kyle, Route 158 machinery dealer, served in the Army from December 1944 until fall of 1947. He was in the Philippines when the atom bomb was dropped on Hiroshima. He was transferred to Sapporo, Japan, where he served with the Army of Occupation. He recalls that the Japanese people were respectful and helpful.

Seldom were fathers drafted, especially if they were farmers. However, Mildred Swartz relates that in 1944, her husband Walter was drafted, leaving her, a "city gal," to run their dairy farm and care for three young children. At one point of desperation, Swartz was allowed to come home and help out with chores when all three children had the whooping cough. When he was discharged in 1946, Swartz had chilling tales to tell. En route to Germany, his convoy of ships was bombed repeatedly, and some were sunk by German torpedoes. While in Germany, Swartz saw the Nazi death camps with their gas chambers and ovens where thousands of Jews were killed. Swartz served with a company of engineers whose task it was to provide purified water for the troops in the field. His company later was assigned to keep order to German towns after the war. Snipers would frequently shoot at the Americans. A government check arrived each month that Swartz was gone, which helped to provide for necessities, but shortages still occurred of many things, which everyone had difficulty finding, including sugar, gasoline, coffee, and shoes.

Michael "Mike" Heini volunteered for active duty in the Army in 1949. He had basic training at Fort Knox, Kentucky, and additional training at Fort Bragg, North Carolina, with the 8th Army, where he drove and repaired trucks. When Americans became involved in the Korean War in 1950, Heini was sent to South Korea. He participated in the Inchon

> # GUS KEFURT
> *Source: Medal of Honor commendation*
>
> Staff Sergeant Gus Kefurt (Greenville) served in the U.S. Army, Company K, 15th Infantry, 3d Infantry Division, and "distinguished himself by conspicuous gallantry and intrepidity above and beyond the call of duty" on December 23 and 24, 1944, near Bennwihr, France. Early in the attack, Kefurt was confronted by about fifteen Germans and opened fire, killing ten and capturing the others. While under small arms fire, he disabled an enemy tank. When night fell, he maintained a three-man outpost in the town's center in the middle of the German positions and successfully fought off hostile patrols. Assuming command of his platoon the following morning, he led it in hand-to-hand fighting through town until blocked by another tank. Using rifle grenades, he forced the tank crew and some supporting infantry to surrender. He then continued his attack from house to house against heavy fire. Advancing against a strongpoint that was holding up the company, his platoon was subjected to a strong counterattack and infiltration to its rear. Suffering heavy casualties in their exposed position, the men remained there due to Kefurt's personal example of bravery, determination, and leadership. Although severely wounded in the leg, he refused first aid and resumed fighting. When the forces to his rear were pushed back, he refused to be evacuated. Under intense fire, he stiffened his platoon's resistance by encouraging individual men and by his own fire until he was killed (December 25); and the position was maintained. Kefurt, a 1935 graduate from Greenville's Penn High School, has been the only local man to win the nation's highest military decoration, the Medal of Honor issued by Congress, which he received posthumously. The Kefurt Army Reserve Training Center at Youngstown is named in his honor.

Landing, where the Allies captured Seoul. Working in a transportation division, Heini helped to haul North Korean prisoners to South Korean camps. He recalls living on canned rations. Whenever possible, as he was trucking supplies, he would just happen to arrive at an Air Force base at meal time because they had the best mess halls. Mike was discharged in December 1951.

ERIE & PITTSBURGH RAILROAD
By Frederick Houser

In 1870, the Pennsylvania Railroad leased the Erie & Pittsburgh Railroad for 999 years. The next decade, however, was not a profitable one for the new Pennsylvania Railroad subsidiary. In the wake of the Panic of 1873, Pennsylvania Railroad reported that 1874 saw nearly half of the blast furnaces along the Erie & Pittsburgh line shut down; deficits continued for this subsidiary for the remainder of that decade.

The Shenango and Mahoning river valleys had coal and limestone within short distances and, with the development of the railroads, had access to high-grade iron ore for steel making. This ore came from Minnesota by boat to the Port of Erie, where it was loaded to rail cars. The Pennsylvania Railroad hauled it south over the Erie & Pittsburgh to Shenango Valley mills at Greenville, Sharpsville, Sharon, South Sharon (now Farrell), and West Middlesex. The locally mined raw materials were moved by the common carrier railroads in Mercer County and by several private tramways.

Over the next few decades, traffic on the Erie & Pittsburgh grew, and the line again became profitable. By the World War I era, Erie & Pittsburgh operated five passenger trains daily in both directions through Mercer County. To handle the passenger volume and the heavy freight traffic which it by then enjoyed, the line was double-tracked from Sharpsville south to New Castle. Passenger traffic peaked about 1920. Then, as automobile ownership grew and improved roads were built, the erosion of passenger train ridership forced nearly all railroads to reduce frequency of service. The only interruption in this decline was during World War II, when there was a dramatic upturn in travel by train. In the Erie & Pittsburgh's case, patronage was further increased when the U.S. Army established Camp Reynolds near Transfer. A new station, named "Victory," was built to serve the many troop and prisoner-of-war trains that terminated or originated at the camp and to serve the scheduled passenger trains. The final Erie-Pittsburgh passenger round trip was discontinued in 1948, and the last Sharon-Pittsburgh local came off four years later.

THE SNOW OF 1950
By Wally Wachter

November 26, 1950, was a memorable date in the history of Mercer County. Despite previous incidents of flooding, tornadoes, and other emergencies, that day was the only time that life in the entire county stood still. It was the day always remembered as "the big snow."

The snow began with late afternoon flurries on Thursday, Thanksgiving Day. By noon Friday about three inches lay on the ground. The forecast was for only two or three more inches to fall Friday night with severe cold weather.

At five o'clock Friday, the Wheatland-West Middlesex bypass highway was opened with official ceremonies. Pennsylvania highways secretary, Ray Smock, cut the ribbon giving new status to the old Swamp Road. Municipal and county officials took part in the program. It was during that ceremony that the large snowflakes began to descend. The barrage continued throughout the night. More than twenty-eight inches of the white stuff fell, surprising residents who woke that Saturday morning and found themselves marooned in their homes.

Traffic was at a standstill as roads and streets were clogged by mounting drifts. Most stores and businesses were closed as employees were unable to get to work. City buses could run on the snow-piled streets. Automobiles were either marooned in their garages or buried in their drifts in parking places in front of homes. The few neighborhood stores that managed to open after a mammoth hand-shoveling job had a run on bread and milk as frantic customers plodded through heavy drifts to stock up for what they thought would be a long crisis.

Industries were hard-hit. Many employees who had worked the night shifts found themselves snowbound in the morning and worked double shifts because their replacements were unable to get to their jobs. It took more than a week for plants to resume their normal schedules.

Hospital care became a problem. Sharon General Hospital issued an emergency call for nurses because only one-third of its staff were able to report at the scheduled time. The Red Cross, veterans groups, radio stations, volunteer organizations, and individuals with heavy vehicles worked diligently to get medicines and food to the needy and perform other errands of mercy.

The weight of the snow on flat roofs took its toll and posed a difficult shoveling job for the owners. The snow caused three-fourths of the arched roofs and two walls to collapse at Swirl Arena on the Sharon-Mercer Road. It also collapsed the hangar roof at the old Chadderton Airport off Christy Road in Hermitage, damaging several planes inside.

The crisis had an even more personal affect as several funerals and weddings had to be postponed.

The day of the snow barrage was the day for the scheduled opening of the new Shenango Inn in Sharon. An open house had been planned for the public. It had to be postponed. For a week before, *The Herald* staff had been preparing a special Shenango Inn edition, which was to appear that Saturday in connection with the Inn's opening.

On Saturday morning the few of us who were able to fight our way through the drifts did double duty in putting out the day's edition. Many *Herald* carriers responded to an emergency call to get the edition to as many readers as possible. About fifteen hundred papers were given out free at *The Herald* office to readers who braved the weather to receive them.

The Shenango Inn opened the following Wednesday while snow in the parking lot was still piled high. Also dedicated a few days later amid major snow piles was the new Temple Beth Israel in Sharon and a new Sharon High School gymnasium.

The big snow became an emergency because it came as a surprise. No community, nor even the state highway department, had the proper equipment to cope with it. It took days to open the highways and main streets. It was more than a week before all streets were clear and life was back to normal. Only those who remember know how a Winter Wonderland can be turned into a nightmare.

AN INDUSTRIAL SITE FOR MAIN STREET, U.S.A.

GREENVILLE - REYNOLDS INDUSTRIAL DEVELOPMENT

This completely zoned and restricted industrial development offers industrial sites with in-place utilities and free land when jobs are produced. 100% financing is also available. For complete data write or phone (see address below).

VIRGINIA FREEWAY
INTERSTATE ROUTE 79

PITTSBURGH-WEST
ERIE

KEYSTONE SHORTWAY
INTERSTATE ROUTE 80

BEAVER VALLEY EXPRESSWAY

During the early stages of World War II, the federal government transformed about 3,300 acres of farmland in Pymatuning Township into one of the nation's two military replacement depots. In a matter of months, Mercer County had the largest Army installation in the state. First known as the Shenango Personnel Replacement Depot and later as Camp Reynolds, the sprawling military facility housed as many as 75,000 war-bound soldiers and officers at one time. In 1947, the former Greenville Businessmen's Association bought the Camp Reynolds site for development into a residential area and industrial park (pictured, in 1999). By 1988, almost two thousand people lived in the development, which also had nearly forty industries and businesses employing over one thousand. (Aerial: **The Herald***; map:* **The Sharon Herald***, December 2, 1967; caption:* **Greenville Sesquicentennial History***)*

Three feet of snow in November 1950 stalled most transportation in Mercer County, but a plow-equipped Bessemer locomotive opened the railroad's main lines so both passenger and freight trains were soon operating again. In many cases, highways were blocked for several days. (Contributor: Frederick Houser)

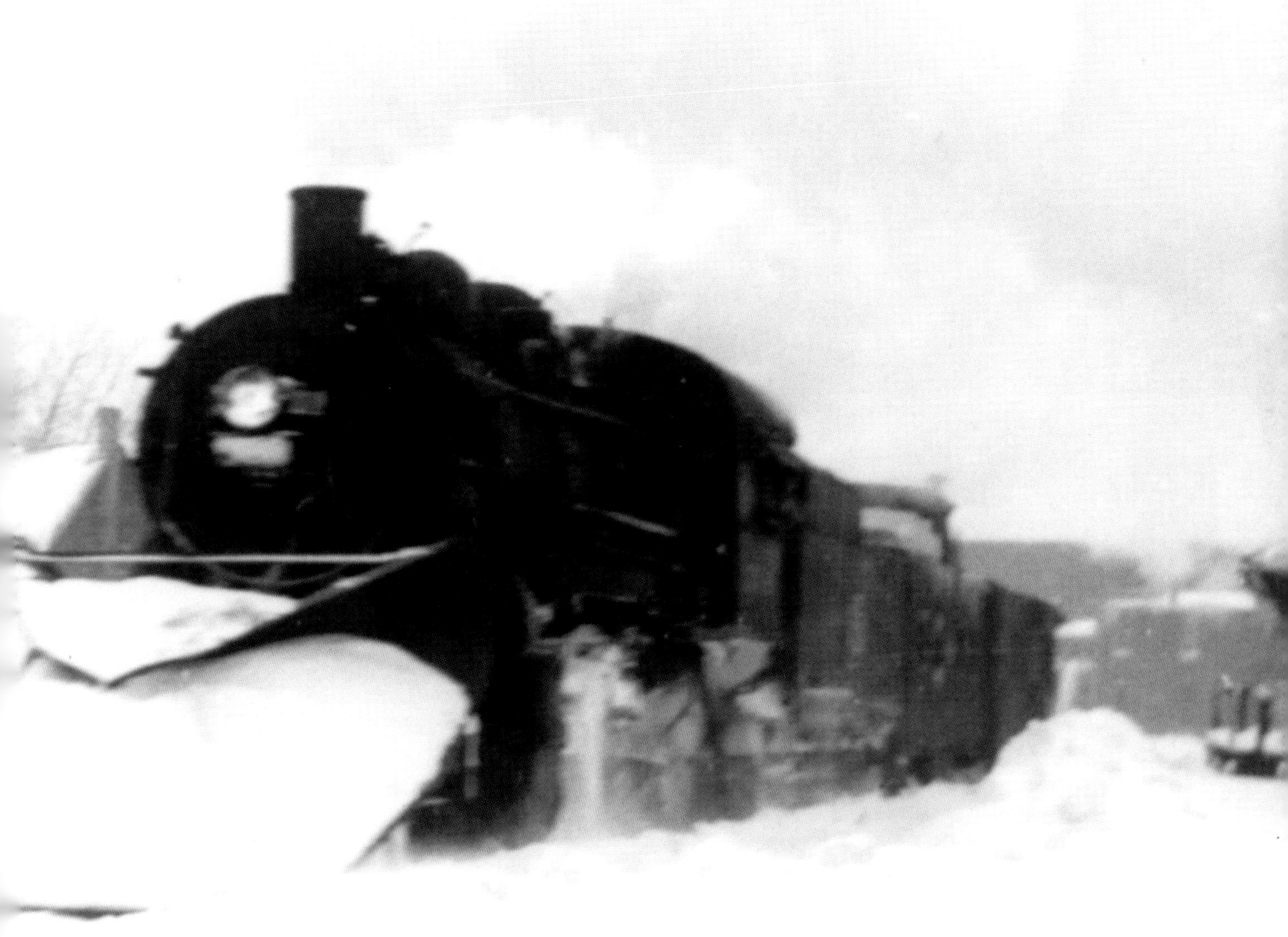

Persch Garage, Mercer

362

The Tornado of 1947

By Wally Wachter

Anyone less than fifty-three years old in 2000 will not remember it. But their elders probably have told them about the first deadly tornado ever to strike Mercer County.

The date was June 7, 1947. It was a lazy warm Saturday afternoon. *The Herald*'s weekend edition had gone to press with this weather report: "Cloudy and cooler with showers today, tonight and Sunday." Another story on Page 1, referring to storms and floods in the Midwest and a few wind gusts in this area, was headlined: "County escapes worst of storm."

Scarcely an hour before the paper hit the streets, the deadly twister struck with hell-like fury to belie both the forecast and the headline. The twister swept in from Ohio where it injured four people. It cut a six hundred-foot swath across the West Hill of Sharon, and then blasted through the heart of the city, elevating after splintering upper East Side residences and rising and dipping along the way as it extended its damage to Mercer before petering out.

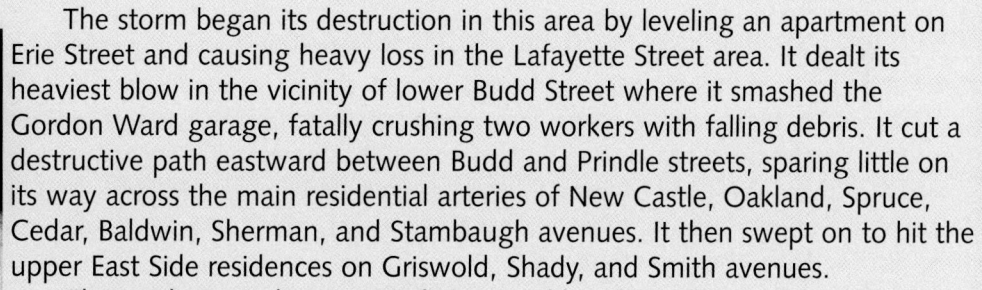

The storm began its destruction in this area by leveling an apartment on Erie Street and causing heavy loss in the Lafayette Street area. It dealt its heaviest blow in the vicinity of lower Budd Street where it smashed the Gordon Ward garage, fatally crushing two workers with falling debris. It cut a destructive path eastward between Budd and Prindle streets, sparing little on its way across the main residential arteries of New Castle, Oakland, Spruce, Cedar, Baldwin, Sherman, and Stambaugh avenues. It then swept on to hit the upper East Side residences on Griswold, Shady, and Smith avenues.

The swirling winds, estimated at several hundred miles an hour and traveling about seventy-five miles per hour, ripped off roofs, leveled garages, collapsed porches and canopies, uprooted trees, shaved off sides of buildings and home, and downed power and telephone lines. They blew wedding cakes, household items, and furniture to yards six or seven blocks away.

More than one thousand homes suffered some form of damage. Most of the buildings had power blackouts and were out of electricity for most of the weekend, some until the middle of the following week. Most of the telephone lines were out in the area and no means of communication with outside communities existed until two days later.

The entire damaged area was roped off and strictly policed by Sharon police, assisted by state patrolman, as a measure to keep the curious out of the disaster zone. There was some looting, but police did a creditable job in keeping it to a minimum. The American Red Cross sprang into immediate action to aid the victims of the storm. *The Herald* staff, called back after the regular Saturday edition, worked around the clock to cover the event. Some reporters worked all night, all day Sunday, and through the regular edition on Monday by canvassing the destruction area and reporting the plight of the victims.

The miracle of the tornado was that only two had been killed and only a few other injured seriously. Most of the injured victims treated at Sharon General Hospital had only minor wounds. The total damage wrought by the twister was estimated at more than $1 million. (First six photos, Sharon including the basketball hoop at Prospect Heights School, and the last photo, Persch Garage in Mercer)

THE WININSKY FAMILY
By Daniel Wininsky

The Wininsky family history in Mercer County begins with Michael and Katherine Wininsky. Michael was born in Poland in 1882. The southeastern part of Poland, his home, was occupied by Austria in the 1800s and early 1900s. The rest of Poland was occupied by Germany and Russia. By 1910 Michael had been conscripted into the Austrian Army for several years. His elderly father knew a big war was brewing and devised a plan to get Michael and his wife to the United States.

First, the Polish Underground arranged for Michael to leave Poland disguised as a German citizen seeking business in the United States. He was supplied with a false identity, travel papers, and a suitcase filled with German money. The suitcase of money made his phony identity all the more convincing when his baggage was checked. The plan worked. When Michael arrived in America, he sent the suitcase of money back to Poland so the Polish Underground could use it to help someone else escape.

Michael's wife Katherine soon followed. For their first few years in America they lived in Buffalo, New York, and had three children, one of whom died as an infant. Michael was a skilled carpenter and found work at the Curtis Wright Airplane Factory.

By 1919, Michael wanted to leave Buffalo, so he and a friend hopped a freight train. The train ended its run in Sharon, and the two men decided to stay. Michael soon found work and moved his family to the North Flats of Sharon in a house close to the Shenango River. Shortly after the move, Mike and Katherine bought an acre in Patagonia (Hickory Township) not far from the West Hill of Sharon. This area was largely newly subdivided farm property. When Mike began building their home, the area was mostly big fields with few houses and only dirt roads for the few streets.

The Wininsky family home in its original 1920 form was a four-room European cottage-style house. It was one story with an unfinished upstairs formed by the steep roof and a small one-room cellar with a dirt floor. By the later 1920s, the house had front and back porches and dormers for upstairs bedrooms. During the 1920s the Wininsky family had four more children, all of whom were born in the family's house. (Sadly, the little girl Florence died at age five in 1933.)

1930s

Mike worked as a carpenter, often self-employed, and built or worked on numerous houses in the area. Some of these houses were also in Patagonia, but much of his work was in the Shenango Valley and the surrounding communities and farms. Having never learned to drive, he was often seen walking to his job sites carrying his tool box that was said to look like a huge suitcase made out of wood. The people he worked for did not always pay him cash for his services. Among the items he received for pay were a Model T Ford and a milk cow. Although Mike never drove the Model T, his son Joe learned to drive it when he was a young teenager.

Having a cow enabled them to have milk, cream, cheese, and butter. They raised chickens and pigs for eggs and fresh meat. They grew vegetable gardens and fruit trees for fresh and canned food. With fruit from their various grape vines, they made wine. Katherine baked bread and cooked on her wood-and-coal-burning stove. This effort to be as self sufficient as possible on their acre of land required much hard work. With this family effort and Mike's working as a carpenter, the 1920s were good; although not affluent, they were able to provide for their basic needs.

The Depression era, however, was hard for the Wininsky family, as it was for many Americans. During that time the older children, Joe and Rose, worked jobs to help their family. Their father, of course, worked as much as he could doing carpentry. But because of the economic times, the jobs were not steady, nor were they well paying.

The situation was similar for other families in Patagonia. Many of these families were immigrants who also tried to be self-sufficient, work jobs when they could, and struggled to keep their families fed. Many families helped each other with food for supper. The women in the neighborhood would visit each other and find out what they were cooking that day and who may need parts or all of a supper. The women would then share food items or pots of stew and try to ensure that families did not go hungry.

For the rest of the 1930s the Wininsky family consisted of Mike and Katherine with their two sons and three daughters in their cottage-style house on an acre of land. This was their home, and like many of the European immigrants in their neighborhood, they worked hard to keep their home and provide for their family.

1940s

About 1940, when the American economy improved, the Wininsky family began to prosper. Mike still worked as a carpenter; and some of the children, who were out of school and still living at home, were working. For example, Joe, an electrician, worked at the U.S. Steel plant in Farrell. As a result of the family's new prosperity, they decided to remodel their home.

Joe

The cottage-style house built in 1920 was made bigger, renovated, and modernized. All of the renovating work was done by family members and by hand. The front porch was closed in to make a windowed sun room. The back porch was closed in to make a new kitchen with modern appliances, new handmade cabinets, and a separate breakfast room. A modern indoor bathroom was built upstairs. Hardwood floors were added, and sets of French doors were built by hand for the living and dining rooms. A separate library was built with an arched opening to the living room. All of the woodwork was hand-molded. New hot-water heating and electrical systems were installed. A fireplace was built in the living room. To replace the small cellar, a full basement was built by jacking up the outside walls of the house and building foundation walls to support the house. The new basement had a high ceiling and concrete floor. Excavating the new basement and sewage system and mixing the concrete were done by hand. A large garage-workshop was also added to the side of the house. In all, the remodeling project was a combined family effort that made the Wininsky family home spacious, modern, and beautiful.

By 1942 America had entered World War II and the two Wininsky sons entered the military. Ed went first, into the Army Air Corp, after high school. He was an airplane mechanic stationed in the States. Joe, while working in the mill and remodeling the family home, was drafted in 1942. He asked for a six-month deferment because he was the only son at home, his family house was under construction, and he was needed to finish some of the major work, as his father was about sixty years old by then. The deferment was granted. Joe finished up remodeling and went into the Army in 1943. He served as a radar technician with the U.S. troops that invaded Sicily, Italy, France, and Germany.

Most of the immigrant families in Patagonia were like the Wininsky family and had sons in the War. One family, the Bulicks, had five sons that were in the military during the War. (The Bulick boys' father was Mike's friend who had hopped a train with him from Buffalo to Sharon in 1919.) Many Patagonia families had origins in Eastern Europe where countries suffered from Nazi invasions. It was, therefore, a proud experience for these people to have sons serve as American soldiers. Mike would say to people, as he stood tall and dignified, swollen with pride, "I have TWO sons in the War."

During the War years, the Wininsky house was often a gathering place for the neighborhood men because Mike was multilingual, able to speak and read several Eastern European languages. Neighbors would listen to radio reports about war activity in Europe, and Mike would translate for friends whose English was not yet good. They would also talk about the war news in the ethnic newspapers. These newspapers would often report more details about particular cities and villages in Europe than the American news.

Katherine and Mike

The Wininsky family survived World War II without any personal tragedy. Joe returned to his job at U.S. Steel and had a career there as an electrician. Ed pursued a career as an automotive electrician and mechanic. Rose worked many years as a nurse. Jennie worked for several years as a secretary for Hickory High School. All of the Wininsky children were married in the 1940s and early 1950s. All of the grandchildren were Baby Boomers, born between World War II and the early 1960s.

Mike and Katherine lived in Patagonia for their remaining years. The family home was then passed on to Joe, the oldest son. He had been living on a farm near Mercer, moved his family to Patagonia, and saw another generation grow up in the old family home. Joe died in 1976, and the family home was passed on to Dan, his oldest son. Dan held onto the house and eventually moved his family there in 1993.

During the 1990s, Dan and his wife Tina and their children have undertaken major remodeling projects on the old family house. Rooms have been added; floor plans changed; and plumbing, heating, and electrical systems renovated. The cottage-style architecture has been preserved even though the house is now much larger than the original. All of the work for the remodeling, including the carpentry, plumbing, and electrical, has been done by Dan, his wife, and children. These children are the fourth generation to fill the home started by Mike and Katherine Wininsky.

1990s

Roy C. Gregory, a colonel in the Engineer Corps, commanded an engineer regiment in France on VE day.

James Alexander Stranahan III (Mercer) was a first lieutenant in the Marine Corps and wounded in action on the Island of Saipan on June 15, 1944. He received the Silver Star, Navy Cross, and Purple Heart.

David Barbour Barton, son of Mr. and Mrs. Dunham Barton (Mercer), was a lieutenant colonel in the Signal Corps. He was killed in action near Velletri, Italy, on June 3, 1944, and buried in the American Military Cemetery in Nettuno, Italy.

At left: First Lieutenant Thomas A. Sampson (Mercer) served in the 381st Bombardment Group of the U.S. Air Corps. He piloted a B-17 Flying Fortress in thirty-five missions over Germany and received an Air Medal with three oak leaf clusters.

Bruce Johnson, son of H. Clay Johnson, served in the T/4, 351st Infantry Regiment, 88th Division, 5th Army in Europe. He was killed in action and buried in Italy in 1944. His body was returned in Findley Township and buried in New Findley Cemetery in 1948.

The derailment of a northbound Bessemer & Lake Erie freight train at Coolspring interlocking beside Route 19 in the 1940s was cleared by the railroad's 250-ton capacity wrecking crane, which was acquired with the railroad's fleet of 100-ton cars and 500,000-pound steam locomotives. (Caption: Frederick Houser)

Super-railroad concepts of Andrew Carnegie had reached a high state of development by the 1940s when the Bessemer & Lake Erie Railroad had forty-seven locomotives like the No. 611 (pictured, at the K-O Junction) running over 155-pound (to the yard) rail and hauling trains of up to 16,000 tons mostly made up of 90-ton capacity hopper cars and dispatched by a centralized traffic control system. (Contributor: Frederick Houser)

FAMILY LEAVE HICKAM FIELD AND BOMBINGS FOR JACKSON CENTER

Cared For By Red Cross Before and During Long Trip To Mercer.

The first refugees to reach Mercer community from stricken Hickam Field, Hawaiian Islands, are Mrs. Arthur Fahrner, wife of Master Sergeant Fahrner, and their five children, who, on Monday, reached Jackson Center, joining Mr. and Mrs. George Fahrner at the home of the latter's mother, Mrs. Allen Clark. They left Honolulu on Christmas morning, with an hour's notice in which to prepare for their long trip and with permission to bring two suitcases only for the party of six.

Local Red Cross representatives are trying to outfit the family with sweaters, shoes, stockings and other warm clothing and to find blankets and household necessities and furniture with which to set them up in a small home or apartment. Four of the children have entered school. Their furniture, clothing and all belongings had to be left behind and transportation space cannot be spared to bring them to the states for an indefinite time; perhaps for the period of the war. An appeal has been made to the local American Legion to aid where the Red Cross assistance ends.

Mrs. Fahrner had a harrowing experience. The Japanese bombing attack started Sunday morning before the family had breakfast, but Sergeant Fahrner was at his duties in the mess hall at Hickam Field, a building destroyed by the bombs. A sleeve of his jacket was found in the wreckage and he was reported to his wife as killed. Two days later he found where his family was located and called her. He had stepped out of the mess hall on an errand just before the bomb struck.

Their home was only a block from the hangars burned and bombs fell within 100 feet of it, shaking the house. The children, Robert 13, Ruth 11, Theodore 10, Patricia 8 and a little fellow of six, first ran out to watch the bombs, then when machine gun bullets began to whine about and clip the branches from the trees, the mother gathered them in, wrapped them in blankets, padded them with pillows and tucked them under a large steel table on which she piled mattresses. They were there from 8:00 to 10:30 a.m., when they took advantage of a lull to pile into their car and, with neighbors, fled to the hills.

About 4:30 they were all rounded up by the Red Cross taken to the University of Hawaii and given their first meal of the day—hot coffee and sandwiches about 5:00 o'clock. School houses that had cafeterias were turned over to the ousted families who were not permitted for fear of further bombing to return to their homes until the 18th, by which time bomb shelters had been prepared. In the meantime they were provided blankets but had to sleep on the school house floors. They were fed by the Red Cross, which also provided water for the first two days when it was feared the army water supply might be poisoned.

Mrs. Fahrner had made the acquaintance of Mercer boys from the Jackson Center district and, before the disaster, had entertained them many times in her home. She mentioned Henry King, Carl Painter and Samuel McCurdy, with a fourth whose name she could not remember.

The five days' ocean voyage, starting Christmas, was another trying experience with 850 women and children on board and 85 wounded. Part of a convoy which traveled in complete blackout every night, every passenger was ordered to keep a life preserver constantly in his hand, while the ship zigzagged its way in reply to directions conveyed by shots.

The family was cared for by the Red Cross on landing in San Francisco and until they left that city New Year's night. Changing trains at Chicago they again were looked after by Red Cross and speak most gratefully of the kindness shown and service given them.

Their experience is a fine example of what is being done with the funds already raised or being raised in every community by the emergency Red Cross Drive. There were the other 845 women and children on this one ship to be cared for and other refugees arriving constantly to be helped by just this one phase of the work. Compare their lot with that of the herded and uprooted families in German hands, driven hither and yon at the bayonet point.

(Source: **Mercer Dispatch**, January 9, 1942)

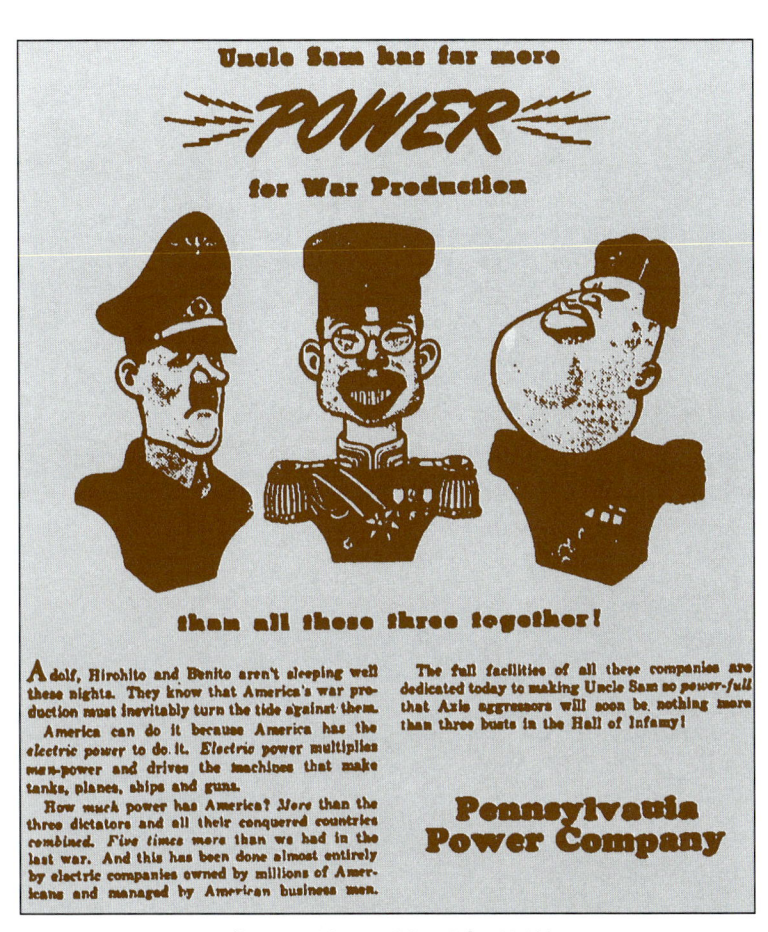

*(Source: **Mercer Dispatch**, 1942)*

Early settlers from Ireland and the Italian Tyrol were organized as a Roman Catholic mission in Stoneboro as early as 1865. By 1868 a barn was remodeled as Stoneboro's first church building. It continued in use until 1874 when a new frame church overlooking the town went up on Franklin Street. It functioned as a mission until 1887 when it was established as a parish, St. Columbkille's Roman Catholic Church. The building was enlarged and improved during ensuing decades until it was destroyed by fire after Sunday service on December 7, 1941, the same day the Japanese attacked Pearl Harbor. Despite shortages of materials and equipment during the war years, the new St. Columbkille's was dedicated in 1944.
(Photographer: Vonda Minner; caption: Frederick Houser)

Class from 1942 at Pardoe School (Findley Township)

In 1950, southbound over the K-O line (between Kremis and Osgood) at the Main Street overpass on Greenv east side was this Bessemer & Lake Erie (B&LE) four-unit, 6,000-horsepower diesel electric locomotive with a freight train. By that time, the Erie Railroad had been operating diesel power through Greenville for nearly se years. (By 1952, all B&LE steam locomotives were idled due to the increasing use of the more powerful diese engines.) (Contributor: Frederick Houser)

The 1943 freshman class at Sheakleyville High School reflected mixed emotions. Mary McDowell Vermiere remembers that high school when she attended it about 1915 through 1918 or so: "It was a large, wooden two-story building. In the downstairs, one large room housed the eight grades and one teacher. She taught all grades in all subjects from first to eighth. There were around 40 in these grades. We had large double desks; and our books, tablets, pencils and slates were furnished. When it was time to recite, each grade would occupy the front seats. Some years there would be anywhere from two to eight in a grade. The large stove was surrounded by a zinc shield so no one would be burned. There was a water pump outside the room, also an outhouse. At recess we'd play tag, fox and geese, and crack the whip. In the winter we enjoyed making snow forts, choosing sides, and having snowball fights. When we had finished the eighth grade, the county superintendent would send in a test we all had to take. This was given of a Saturday and one had to pass each subject with 75% or more in order to go on to high school the next term. It was literally high school as it was on the second floor of the school. Perhaps this is how the name of 'high school' came about. There were two rooms, the Freshmen and Sophomores in one and the Juniors and Seniors in the other. We had two teachers, and pupils from outlying county schools would attend the high school. By the end of four years, a number had dropped out. Four to 16 might be in the graduating class. We had no sports program, but once in a while we'd enjoy a candy or pie social. The girls would bring the boxes of candy or pie, and the boys would bid on each box. The highest bidder would sit with the girl and they'd eat together. . . . The last Friday of each month we had out Literary Society perform at school. This was quite an event as it was held upstairs in the evening at our old high school. The wall lamps would be lighted and we'd entertain. The program would consist of songs (there was an old organ in the room), a skit, essay, and recitations. I learned many of the recitations. Once when one of the acts couldn't go on, the teacher excused me at noon so I could go home and learn a new piece."

"A family dinner in honor of George S. Humes, Pennsylvania's oldest hotel manager, will celebrate his 90th birthday and also mark the end of his career after 52 years of activity in the county seat. Mr. Humes, whose well-known 'Humes Hotel' has offered lodging to many famous guests, will turn over the business to his son-in-law and daughter, Mr. and Mrs. Charles Rader, former residents of Indianapolis, Ind., who will continue the Humes tradition. Mr. Humes was born in Youngstown, O., in 1854 but early in life moved to the Bradford oil fields where he became a driller. W. W. Humes, a brother, leased the St. Cloud Hotel in Mercer and persuaded George to join him in the business. Later Mr. Humes purchased the Whistler House which was originally known as the Hackney Tavern, built in 1817 on the first three lots to be laid out in Mercer. This building held the famous 'room 12' which numbered among its noted guests Marquise de Lafayette, who stopped in Mercer while on a journey from Pittsburgh to Erie. The same room was given to president Zachary Taylor, who stopped on his way from Washington to the lakes and also to president James Buchanan. The Whistler House was completely destroyed by fire in 1916 and Mr. Humes purchased the present structure on the corner of W. Market and South Erie streets. Mr. and Mrs. Humes (the former Nancy Moon) celebrated their golden wedding anniversary on September 19, 1931. They have four daughters. . . ." (Source: **Mercer Dispatch and Republican**, April 21, 1944)

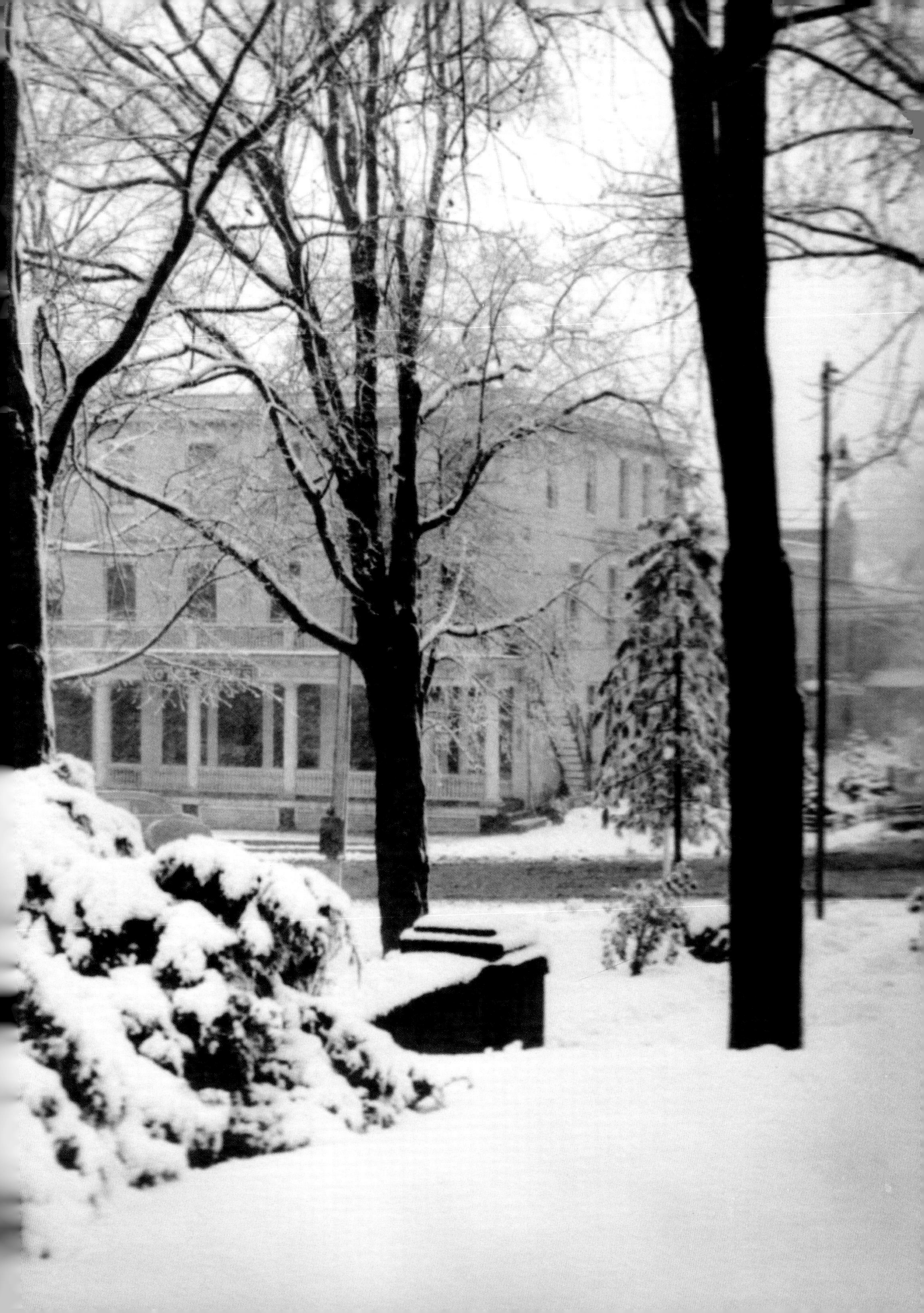

The Valley Baptist Church in Wheatland grew during the Great Migration under the leadership of Reverend Delane (front center, with choir members, circa 1944). (Photo: Dorothy Malloy; caption: Roland Barksdale-Hall)

Otter Creek Township old-timers recall coming every Saturday night for years to dances in the Rhodes house (pictured, in 1945), which was built in 1911. The area was first settled by J. Zook. Before the Rhodes House was built, three cabins were on this property: one in place of the house (pictured again, in 1999, and owned by William and Joyce Young since in 1960s), the second behind the house off Mack Road, and the third across the road from the house in the woods. Near each of these cabins was a natural spring, and the one off Mack Road runs the year around. (In 1975, the Youngs created a pond there.) A quarry on the property furnished the house's foundation stones. At one time all the steps coming into the house were stone, carved from this quarry. As the house has been remodeled, these stones have been moved to border a flowerbed. (Contributor: Joyce Young)

1945

1999

By 1944, the Twin City Elks Lodge, the largest African-American fraternal organization in the Mercer County (and for many years, in Pennsylvania), owned a meeting facility and a bus and had won the National Elks Basketball Championship in New York. (The Elks national commissioner of athletics organized twenty-eight lodges and temples into the Elks Athletic Committee of Western Pennsylvania and sponsored the National Basketball Tournament in 1942.) The completion of a $75,000 gymnasium eight years later was considered a great advancement and equated with racial pride. The Twin City Lodge is on Staunton Street in Farrell (pictured, in 1993). The building to the left is the gymnasium. (Contributor: Roland Barksdale-Hall)

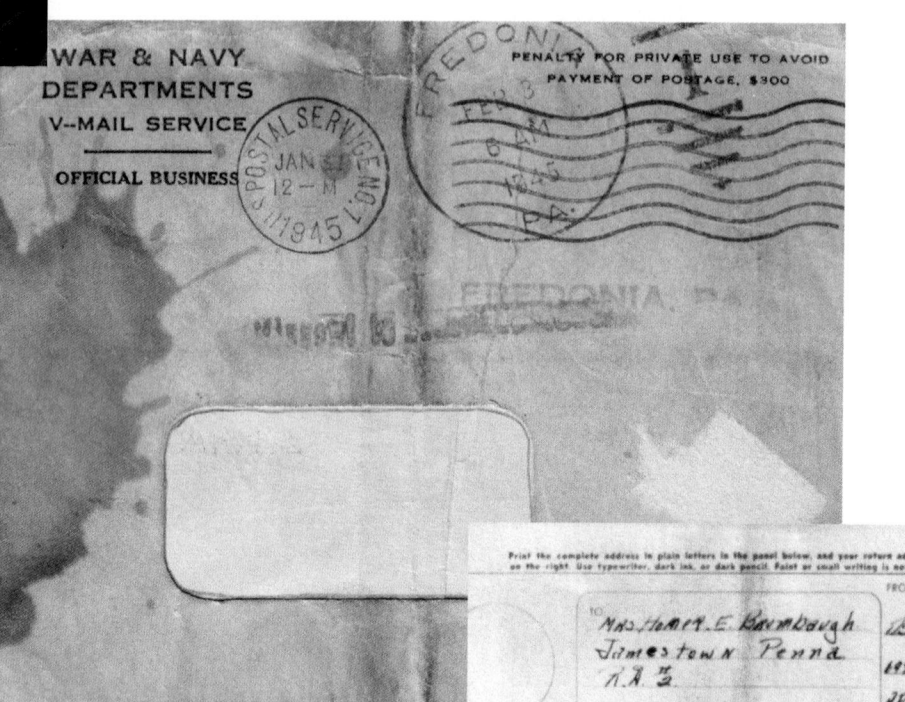

During World War II, soldiers were issued compact stationery on which to write letters home, as seen by this 1945 letter and envelope (full size) from Forrest Brumbaugh to his family (West Salem Township). (Contributor: Joyce Brumbaugh Young)

378

The M. L. Beach Store (Worth Township) started as a blacksmith shop and was owned and operated by Oliver Beach. It later became the post office with Martin Luther Beach as postmaster. It developed into a general store with merchandise ranging from horse collars to candy and groceries. A gas pump was out in front of the store. Customers had to turn the handle to bring up the gas from the tank. The gas was measured in the glass container on top of the tank, one to five gallons. The oil dispenser was one complete stroke of the handle to get a quart of oil. Reportedly, when the first bananas came to this area, no one knew how to eat them, so they ate them skin and all. In the early 1940s, Coca-Cola put in a pop case, which needed ice to cool the pop. The pop sold for five cents a bottle. The store closed in 1945 and was torn down in 1999. (Contributors: Idella McConnell and Lucille Eagles)

*As a first lieutenant in the Army Air Corps, Milford L. "Miff" McBride, Jr. (Grove City, pictured in 1945) was a meteorologist in the Pacific theater of operation during World War II. When he was released to report home in 1946, he sailed for twenty-one days from Saipan to San Francisco, where his ship docked alongside the **S.S. Grove City Victory**! McBride took a picture of the ship and vowed to find out whether it was connected to his hometown. Not until years later, after many inquiries by McBride and his wife Madeleine, did the McBrides learn the story behind this ship from research done by Mayes Mathews, husband of Grove City College graduate Cheryl Maria Hess, Class of 1966: A Victory class ship, the **Grover** is one of about eight hundred "alma mater ships," which were built toward the end of World War II. (Many were named for colleges and universities.) She could cruise at speeds over fifteen knots and weighed 10,800 tons. After serving her country in World War II, she went onto serve in the Korean Conflict and Vietnam War and now awaits her next assignment while docked with the Suisun Bay Reserve Fleet. (Contributors: the McBrides)*

Razed in 1947, the Henderson Hotel in Hendersonville had a long history. It had been used for a stopover for the stagecoaches that ran from Pittsburgh to Erie. Roy Henderson purchased it from Lowrie Henderson in the late 1930s. Many of the hand-hewed beams and the vertical planking from the hotel were used to make the framework for a new house for Roy's son, James and his wife Nancy. Their house stands on the exact spot where the hotel once stood. The hotel's hand-dug well, estimated to be over two hundred years old, is still being used for the Henderson's home. (Contributors: Idella McConnell and Lucille Eagles)

Reverend Cressy Hunt was the minister at Ebenezer Church when this bible school class picture was taken in 1948. The church was in Centertown (Wolf Creek Township). That building burned in 1958, and the present Ebenezer Church was built on Scrubgrass Road in 1959. (Contributor: Mary Rearick Wilson)

Ruth Filer was the teacher for the 1949 Sharon High School band.

*In 1948, Grove City celebrated the 150th birthday of its founding as a settlement on Wolf Creek. The Sesqui-Centennial festivities included a parade in which William Nicklin (left) was honored as the oldest resident of Mercer County. Olive McCoy (right) was Grove City's postmistress at the time and, life many revelers, dressed in period costume. (An obituary in a 1953 **Mercer Dispatch** disclosed that Nicklin died at age 103.) (Contributor: Grove City Community Library)*

381

Sharon General Hospital

Kimberly Memorial Nurses Home

In 1949, the Christian H. Buhl Hospital became Sharon General Hospital. The hospital was expanded and included the Kimberley Memorial Nurses Home. In 1990, it became the Sharon Regional Health System (aerial, in 1999). It is affiliated with Allegheny General Hospital and associated with Children's Hospital, both in Pittsburgh. (Top two pictures: Daniel Maurice; aerial: **The Herald**; caption: Mairy Jayn Woge)

At times during the late 1800s, Hickory Township had twenty-one one- or two-room schools. Maple Drive High School at East State Street and Maple Drive opened in 1909. Classes were later moved to a new brick high school (pictured, 1949, across Route 18 from Brookfield Dairy) and an extension added to that building in 1936. All the small schools were closed before 1947, and pupils were moved to three elementary buildings north of Route 62 after World War II. The current Hickory High School was built in 1958 (north of the old one on Route 18) and is now being remodeled. The old high school is now the junior high. Maple Drive School has been razed. [By 1963, Brookfield Dairy and the Strawbridge house, occupied by the George McConnell family, were torn down to make space for the Shenango Valley Mall (pictured, in 1999)]. (1949 aerial: Vonda Minner; 1999 aerial: **The Herald***; caption: Mairy Jayn Woge)*

THE SHARON (PA.) HERALD, SATURDAY, MAY 6, 1950

FOR SAFETY'S SAKE—East and west bound traffic halts at the Hermitage intersection in Hickory Township, east of Sharon, where an overhead light went into service for the first time yesterday. The signal is expected to put a stop to the increasing number of traffic accidents, several of them serious, which have happened at the junction of U. S. Route 62 and State Route 18, since the first of the year. It operates on a 50-second cycle, which means the signal requires that amount of time to go from green through amber (caution) and red stages and back to green again. The state Highway Department approved installation of the equ

Much development has occurred around the intersection of Routes 62 and 18 since the first traffic light was installed there in 1950. In the aerial taken in 1999, not only has Route 62 been rerouted away from State Street and the highways widened, but residences and farmland have been replaced by (clockwise from top) Walmart, Lowe's Home Improvement Center, the old Hickory High School, and the Shenango Valley Mall, among other businesses. (1950 article: Hermitage Historical Society; aerial: **The Herald***)*

Mrs. Mary Sewall was the teacher at Whittaker School (Pine Township) in 1950 and 1951. Her students included Bobby Dickson, Charles Wilson, Bob Wanger, David Bollinger, Jim Mahoney, Jim Rodgers, Dennis Micheals, Carol Feare, Katherine Collier, Roberta Wilson, Stanley Covert, John Law, Terry Robinson, Lewie Hart, Dick Battey, Alice Kalfman, Linda Fleming, Janet Sidney, Libby Zenobi, Jane McKnight, Frances Dumbroski, Evelyn Dikeman, Leora Parquette, Kathy McFadden, and Judy Lynn Horam.

Millbrook School, in the village of Millbrook, was the first school built in Worth Township, in 1834, under the Free School Law. In 1884, a two-story, red-brick building replaced the original plank structure. A boulder still projects out of the ground in front of the school (pictured, in 1950 with Arlene Thompson straddling it and, in 2000, with Scott and Kelly Magargee perched on it). Mary Rearick Wilson recalls that, from about 1945 until 1955, students would parade from the school to the Rearick Store (pictured) to show off their Halloween costumes (pictured, in 1948) and collect candy. Mrs. Williamson and Mrs. Harrison (pictured) were the teachers who started the tradition with the help of Mrs. Rearick. Mrs. Stevens was the teacher at Millbrook School in 1950. Her students (pictured above) included Mary Rearick, Ruth Cochran, Doris Frantz, Louise Hordisty, Laura Garlic, Penny Little, Carl Jack, Marcia Little, Jerry Amon, Bill Strouss, Sue Sopher, Norman Cochran, Ronnie Minor, Pat Montgomery, Ruth Ann Strouss, Charles Grace, Ginny Thompson, Erie Jameson, Andy Hardesty, Bob Minor, John Westlake, Bill Burchert, Gary Minor, and Tom Sopher. Gladys Harrison (Stoneboro) was the teacher when the school closed in December 1954. The students started at the new Lakeview School District in January 1955. Still standing, the old Millbrook School is now owned by Scott Blaine. (Contributors: Idella McConnell, Lucille Eagles, and Mary Wilson)

In the 1940s, constables were elected to protect the peace in Hickory Township. A military policeman in World War II, Ralph Kilgore (top, center) was one such constable, assuming his duties in 1949. In 1950, Kilgore was named Hickory Township's first police officer, a position created due to the township's increased population and traffic, and he was quickly promoted to chief of police. He later served as Hickory's justice of the peace for eighteen years. Kilgore holds another record in Mercer County history as the first private detective. In 1962, he established the Kilgore Detective Agency at 2800 East State Street where now his daughter, Barbara Kilgore Hunter, carries on the family's detective legacy. Other members of the Kilgore family (pictured, about 1936) including (clockwise from Ralph) Howard, Ellsworth, Myrtle (Bartholomew) (mother), Domer (father), and Grant. Howard and Grant were co-owners of Kilgore Sales and Service, and Ellsworth was a long-time employee at Westinghouse. Domer's father established the Kilgore Homestead in 1908. The fifty-seven acres reached from what is now Maple Drive to Kilgore Drive on East State Street and south to Morefield Road. Domer and his brothers George and Roy were the second generation to live in the house. In 1946, part of the Kilgore farm was sold to the Lambroses who opened and operated the Hickory Drive-In Theater there in the 1950s. Later the Hermitage Hills Plaza was built on the site. George and his wife Helen sold the house in 1976, and it was burned down to make way for the Sambo Restaurant. Later, the Shenango Valley Freeway cut the land into sections. Now, Lowe's Home Improvement and Ames stand on the old Kilgore property. (Contributor: the Kilgores)

387

(Source: **The Sharon Herald**,
December 2, 1967)

Chapter 7: 1951–1970

Townships

In 1954, the ***East Lackawannock Township*** machinery dealership started by Orville D. Anderson in 1912 was sold to Ed Ramsey and Ralph Kyle. (Anderson, son of Harry and Ethel Fyffe Anderson, grew up on a dairy farm now owned by Otto Ammer. In 1942, he established the Case machinery dealership on Route 19, adjacent to the present Interstate 80 East exit ramp. He and his wife Dortha also owned and operated school buses and lime trucks. Anderson's first coach bus was purchased for $13,000. Neighbors said he would never recover his investment; but the Andersons moved to Greenville and in 1948 established their successful Anderson Coach and Tour.) In 1966, Ralph W. Kyle, Inc. bought out Ed Ramsey and relocated to Route 158. Selling Case and New Idea machinery and tractors, Kyle also sells utility equipment. Son, Timothy, is also active in the Kyle machinery business.

A little racetrack in ***Fairview Township*** where they raced Micro Midgets and gocarts was founded in the 1950s and owned by Glenn Clark. They raced there until the early 1960s. A flood dam was built in 1970 on Small Road in the northeast corner of Fairview Township, the first of five dams to control flooding of Greenville.

The ***Hempfield Township*** Volunteer Fire Department was started in 1962. The department now has fifty-four members including officers, administration, support personnel, and firefighters. Some of the members are emergency medical technicians (EMTs). The department's equipment includes two Class A pumpers and a Class A pumper tanker, Class A pumper snorkel, 1,500-gallon tanker, rescue unit, utility cascade unit, brush truck, Hazmat trailer, 25,000-power light trailer, and a car for the chief.

Hickory Township was subject to several annexation over the years. The final annexation by Sharpsville was a large piece of land that included the former Joseph Troutman farm east of the Sharpsville-Wheatland Road (now Mercer Avenue) in 1950. As the result of that action and others like it, Hickory Township stopped annexations of its land by becoming a first-class township in January 1955. [An annexation by Wheatland before 1900 and numerous annexations by Sharon, South Sharon, and Sharpsville (all of which were part of Hickory before they were organized) reduced the size of Hickory to 27.1 square miles before it became a first-class township. Sharpsville took land from Hickory Township through a total of five annexations. In 1856, before Sharpsville was organized, some of its residents acquired a dozen houses that were clustered around an iron furnace. In 1909, landowners in a section of Hickory Township east of Sharpsville along Route 518 asked the borough to annex that neighborhood, called Irishtown for the Irish railroad builders who lived there. Peter Joyce (Sharpsville) said a section of Ridge and Ashtona

LIEUTENANT BARNES, JET PILOT AND HERO
*From **The Mercer Dispatch**, March 22, 1956*

"Services Saturday afternoon were held for Lt. (j.g.) John (Jack) Robert Barnes, 138 West Market St., Mercer, son of Mr. and Mrs. John H. Barnes, who died heroically Wednesday as he piloted his burning jet plane away from crowded Miami, Fla., instead of bailing out. The craft exploded and crashed over the Everglades.

"Born Oct. 12, 1930, in Mercer, he had enlisted in the Navy Feb. 23, 1951, spending 18 months at the Great Lakes Naval Station. He served on board the U.S.S. Darby and then transferred to the Air Naval Cadet School at Pensacola, Fla., where he was commissioned as an ensign in March of last year. In 1955 he was promoted to Lt. (j.g).

"For the past two years he had been stationed at Cecil Field, Jacksonville, Fla.

"Jack had attended Mercer schools, graduating from High School in the class of 1948. He had also attended Grove City College for two years.

"Besides his parents, he is survived by two sisters and a brother—Howard Barnes, high school teacher at Zelienople; Mary, wife of Robert Burgess, Chicago, and Jean, wife of A. H. Burnett, Harmony.

"Arrangements were by the Miller and Sons Funeral Home and burial was in the Pleasant Hill Cemetery. Officiating minister was the Rev. George Wilson."

---

avenues north of Deweyville was appended to Sharpsville through an annexation in 1919 and the hill district to Hazen Road, in 1925. In 2000, Sharpsville is composed of 1.4 square miles.]

In 1967, Exit 33 on Interstate 79 at Route 62 in ***Jackson Township*** was opened. A fifty-foot cornhusk ribbon was made by the Junior Girl Scouts and used for the ribbon cutting ceremony.

Lackawannock Township gradually closed its schools and began busing students to West Middlesex. In 1953, a new high school was completed in that borough for the consolidated districts of West Middlesex, Shenango Township, and Lackawannock Township. The West Middlesex borough council then took over the old high school for office space, a firehouse, and a community center. The 1960s saw the end and beginning of long terms of service by certain supervisors in Lackawannock Township. James Campbell served as township supervisor from 1934 until 1964 and as township secretary from 1964 until 1968. Emil Horvath served as supervisor from 1966 until 1987.

Up until about 1960, industry and farm products in ***Salem Township*** prospered. In the early 1960s, demand from overseas declined sharply. There were ups and downs until the early 1990s.

In 1951, the two remaining schools in ***Sugar Grove Township***, Kennard and Leech's Corner, were closed; and the children were taken by bus to Greenville. In this township, the village of Osgood had a general store operated by Mr. Black. Another well-known store in the township was the Leech's Corner Store, built in the late 1800s and owned by Guy Richards for many years. Later it became a tax collection office for the township.

> # BUILDING INTERSTATE 79
> *Source: **The Sharon Herald**, December 2, 1967*
>
> The *Sharon Herald* published more than 150 stories covering Interstate 79's progress from a paper to a concrete highway. The interstate "started coming to life after the federal government, with much prodding from such area highway boosters as Robert S. Bates, Meadville newspaper editor and publisher; G. A. Harshman, president and editor of *The Herald*; Gordon Ward, Sharon businessman, and a number of other supporters, announced in 1956 that is was considering the proposed relocation of US Route 19, between Pittsburgh and Erie, to connect with the Keystone Shortway [Interstate 80]."
>
> In 1957, the government announced that the proposed highway would be included in the Interstate system. Therefore, the federal aid portion would be 90 percent and the state's part, 10 percent. However, various delays, including cutbacks in federal funds, postponed the project. In 1960, public hearings at Mercer and Zelienople were held on proposed key sections for the highway. Construction eventually started and proceeded in sections. The first section of Interstate 79 in Mercer County, connecting London with Portersville, was opened in 1965. The interchange near Jackson Center at Route 62 was opened in 1966. Also in 1966, a contract was awarded to build 6.4 miles of the interstate between Stoneboro and Route 285, the last section of Mercer County's portion of Interstate 79 to be constructed.

Now, it is a gun shop. The Kennard General Store, like the Leech's Corner Store, initially was a Clover Farm Store. It was built in the 1800s and was owned by the Littles until 1946 where it was bought by Ray First. The store served as a post office, too. During the 1950s, Virginia Mitchell Sherbondy would set the mail out for the Erie-bound train to catch. Later, Richard Stevens owned it until it closed. The newest church in Sugar Grove Township is the Country Chapel. It was built in 1958 and founded by Glen Chess, Gail Stevenson, Glen Stevenson, and Lawrence Dodds.

MUNICIPALITIES

Confusion has always existed over the names associated with ***Clarksville***. Since another Clarksville is in Greene County, Pennsylvania, the post office seems always to have been Clark. The railroad station had been called Clark's station and later Clarksboro, and the Civil War volunteers were listed as living in Clark's Town. In 1968, the name of the new town was changed to Clark. Thus ended the confusion over having too many Clarksvilles in Pennsylvania.

Farrell had thirty churches in 1951. Most were nationality churches. WFAR, a radio station that dealt with matters of interest of Farrell, opened on Hoelzle Road in Hickory Township in 1955. After the original owner died leaving unpaid taxes, WFAR was financed by some local physicians and businessmen and transmitted programs from the second floor of the Phillips Oldsmobile garage (Dodge City in 2000). (WFAR closed in 1982.)

In 1952, Dr. Kelly established the geographical center of Mercer County by cementing a brass cylinder into the sidewalk near William Simmons' old country store, which had once been the center of ***Fredonia*** activity. After eighty-six years of continuous railway

Timeline 1951—1960

The World

- 1952 Microbiologist Jonas Salk develops a vaccine for polio (poliomyelitis)
- 1953 The Federal Highway Act authorize the construction of the interstate highway system, 42,500 miles of freeway from coast to coast; Fidel Castro begins a revolution against the Cuban government; Dwight D. Eisenhower becomes the 34th president
- 1954 The *USS Nautilus*, the world's first nuclear submarine, is launched; RCA begins production of the first color television sets
- 1955 Mrs. Rosa Parks is arrested when she refuses to give up her front-section bus seat to a white man; the first radio facsimile transmission is sent across the continent
- 1956 The US Supreme Court rules that segregation of the races on public buses is unconstitutional
- 1957 The Russians launch Sputnik I, the first man-made space satellite
- 1959 Alaska and Hawaii become the 49th and 50th states; the Barbie Doll is born; Fidel Castro, leader of the Cuban Revolution, is sworn in as that country's premier
- 1960 The population of the United States is 180,671,158; USSR agrees to stop nuclear testing; an American U-2 spy plane is shot down over the USSR

Mercer County

- 1951 The Magoffin House is officially dedicated to the Mercer County Historical Society; the Robert Jamieson & Sons Mill in Fredonia ships 75,000 bushels of buckwheat; Lakeview consolidated school district is formed
- 1952 The Shenango Valley Concert Band originates; the *Tales of the Mahoning and Shenango Valley*, a series of radio dramatizations, are presented; Fairview Cheese Company is started; the last steam powered passenger train leaves Fredonia (86 years of regular service)
- 1953 Amish purchase the Zuver school, the oldest school in continuous use in the county
- 1955 A production strike at Westinghouse idles 5,550 workers locally and at 29 plants nationwide
- 1958 The Grove City Community Library opens; the Shenango Valley Osteopathic Hospitals opens in Farrell (one of the forerunners of UPMC Horizon)
- 1959 The "frozen flood" is created when five inches of snow plus three inches of rain swell the Shenango River and flood most of Wheatland and downtown Sharon causing $6 million of damage; one of the newest application of electricity is in residential house heating and 27 homes install electric space heating
- 1960 The county's population is 127,519; statistics released by the Pittsburgh office of Dun & Bradstreet, Inc., reflect 132 businesses exist in the county; drag racing is banned on Pennsylvania highways; Miracle Whip costs $.49/qt. jar and pork chops cost $.59/lb; the average residential customer of Penn Power is using 3,960 kilowatt hours (average price is 2.53 cents/Kilowatt-hour); the last one-room schoolhouses in the county close; Reynolds consolidated school district forms

---

service, the last passenger train rode out of Fredonia on May 17, 1952. Richard L. Buchanan established his Kitchen & Bath store in 1969. He was the first dealer of his trade to develop a relationship with DuPont Company. The store is still in existence now, as well as the relationship between companies.

While cable television has been a relatively recent phenomenon in many communities, it was an early necessity for **Stoneboro** and **Sandy Lake** because of local terrain and the distance from broadcast stations. The pioneer cable system of James Reynolds was installed in the 1950s in the two towns. (The enlarged system and expanded coverage are now the property of Cablevision Communications supplying a wide range of satellite channels along with the regional broadcast stations.)

Jamestown (by Norma Leary). In 1965, Jamestown installed an up-to-date sewage treatment plant; however, it has since been covered up.

Jim Leary formed the Jamestown Area Recreation Board (JARB) in 1967, which worked together with the borough council and the school system. Eventually, the JARB became the manager for Jamestown Little League.

Also in 1967, Dr. Robert Amy (Jamestown) made the news for his work on the National Aeronautics and Space Administration's biosatellite projects.

In 1970, Jamestown Mayor Russell Owen, at the suggestion of Edrie Yoho, initiated the Arts Festival that ran for three years. The Festival ran for three days each year and included art displays, choir music, and contests for essays and poetry.

RAILROADS

By Frederick Houser

The process of railroad consolidations that affected Mercer County lines during the 1800s resumed in earnest during the latter half of the 1900s. Tremendous volumes of traffic during World War II had physically and financially drained many of the U.S. rail carriers. Heavy federal economic regulation under the Interstate Commerce Commission also contributed to a stifling drag on the ability of many U.S. railroads to compete effectively for freight traffic and revenue with a new foe: semitrailers. The trucking industry grew rapidly in the period following World War II, especially once interstate highway construction commenced in the late 1950s. While the railroads' major competitors benefited from the massive influx of public monies to build superhighways, many rail carriers struggled just to generate the private capital needed to maintain track and signals, repair or acquire locomotives and cars, and meet payroll.

A survival tactic from the early days of railroading was soon to be reemployed: rail companies would merge and shed duplicate personnel, track, and other facilities. With this aim for increased efficiencies, the Erie Railroad merged on October 17, 1960, with the Delaware, Lackawanna & Western Railroad. The two companies ran roughly parallel between New Jersey and Buffalo. The resulting Erie Lackawanna Railroad was thus the product of the first of the large railroad consolidations that continued through the end of the 1900s. Although the Erie Lackawanna merger led to considerable changes in the states of New Jersey and New York, operations on the former Erie Railroad main line through Mercer County to Chicago remained largely unchanged, but for new colors for the locomotives and rolling stock.

The 1960s also witnessed the merging of the Pennsylvania and New York Central Railroads. The 1968 creation of the Penn Central Transportation Company was supposed to be a partial salvation for a declining northeast rail industry, but the colossus created from two former archrivals was doomed to failure by, among other things, management infighting, Interstate Commerce Commission regulations, outdated labor rules, and incompatible computer systems. The struggling Penn Central declared bankruptcy in 1970, in what was, and would be for many years, the largest corporate bankruptcy in the nation's history.

ERIE RAILROAD

By Frederick Houser

Burdened by excessive state taxes and enormous commuter train losses in New Jersey and New York, the Erie Railroad's fortunes steadily declined as freight traffic dropped in the 1950s. Seeking to stem these losses, the Erie and its adjacent competitor in New York and New Jersey (the Delaware, Lackawanna & Western Railroad) merged to create the Erie Lackawanna Railroad in 1960. This union permitted the abandonment of certain parallel trackage and duplicate facilities, primarily those formerly belonging to the Delaware, Lackawanna & Western in New York state. The Erie paid its last stock dividend in 1957; the Erie Lackawanna merger never yielded income that permitted the resumption of dividends. The decline of heavy industry throughout the territory Erie Lackawanna served reduced its traffic base, despite efforts to diversify. In an attempt to broaden its sources of freight revenue, the Erie Lackawanna was the first eastern railroad to develop substantial intermodal traffic, whereby semitrailers and marine containers are carried long distances on railroad flat cars. The profit margins on this line of business were thin, however, and insufficient to arrest the Erie Lackawanna's financial decline. Meanwhile, railroad passenger service in Mercer County ended on January 5, 1970, when Erie Lackawanna discontinued its last passenger train operating between New York and Chicago.

The creation of the Shenango River Reservoir north of Sharpsville in the early 1960s required significant relocations of two Erie Railroad main lines and the Pennsylvania Railroad's Erie & Pittsburgh Branch.

Farming
By Vonda Minner

In the 1950s and 1960s, more and more farms attained the Century Farm designation. The Bishop Farm (Sandy Creek Township) was one hundred years old in 1951; the Bush Farm (Green Township) and the Gruber Farm (Hempfield Township), in 1952; the Hoffacker Farm (Perry Township), in 1953; the Burrows Farm (New Vernon Township), in 1954; the Saul Farm (Delaware Township), in 1955; the Baker Farm (Springfield Township), in 1956; the Jamieson Farm (Wolf Creek Township), in 1958; the McCurdy Farm, in 1960; the McCracken Farm (Springfield Township), in 1962; the Enterline Farm (Green Township), in 1964; the Kegel Farm (Mill Creek Township), in 1964; the Buchanan Farm (French Creek Township), in 1965; the Fritz Farm (Salem Township), the Osborn Farm (Delaware Township), and the Weygandt Farm (West Salem Township), in 1966; the Stamm Farm (Delaware Township) and the Hassel Farm (Jefferson Township; now owned by Joseph Paul and Gloria A. Trepasso), in 1967; the Barber Farm (Liberty Township) and the McFarland Farm (Wilmington Township), in 1968; and the Taylor Farm (Fairview Township), in 1970.

In 1957, Sandra Shannon, having been crowned Dairy Princess for Mercer County, went on to win the title of Pennsylvania Milk Maid, the only Dairy Princess to date who has won this honor. Crowned in Pittsburgh by Guy Lombardo, she served as an ambassador for the 350th anniversary celebration at Williamsburg, Virginia, of the three sailing ships that brought about one hundred people from England in 1607 to the first permanent English colony in America.

The Beverly Farms Dairy was started in Greenville in 1961 (and delivered milk until 1972).

Aviation
By Richard Christner

At the end of the World War II, the Grove City College applied for and the government approved an Air Force Reserve Officer Training Corps (ROTC) unit. The program began in 1951 under the leadership of Lt. Col. Roger H. Page, with compulsory military training in male students' first two years and optional advanced courses in the last two years. The College was the last in the northeastern states to have a compulsory ROTC, the program becoming fully voluntary in 1970. The program was discontinued in 1989, having commissioned over 900 Air Force officers during its existence. For many years, an Air Force jet stood as a memorial on the College's campus. It was eventually removed, bringing to an end the military presence at Grove City College.

Lakeview School District
By Serena Ghering, Jerry Drew, John Hamelly

Eleven subdistricts were combined to form the Lakeview School District: Jackson, Lake, Mill Creek, New Vernon, Worth, Sandy Lake, and Fairview Townships and Jackson Center, New Lebanon, Sandy Lake, and Stoneboro. The consolidation created the largest school district in area in Mercer County and the second largest in area in Pennsylvania, covering 146 square miles. (Together, the area now boasts a population of about 8,600 people with 1,412 students enrolled in kindergarten through grade twelve, supported by ninety-four faculty members. The district comprises three schools: Oakview Elementary School, Lakeview Middle School, and Lakeview High School.)

GREENVILLE AIRPORT

By Richard Christner

Greenville purchased a 137-acre site three miles north of town on the east side of Route 58 for the new Greenville Municipal Airport, which began operation in 1954 with two grass strips and an administrative building financed by local merchants. First leased to Forney Arc Welders, Inc., the airport was subsequently leased to Carl Thompson in 1962.

In 1965, the Greenville Airport Commission took action to improve the facility by adding a paved, lighted runway (2,700 feet long and 75 feet wide); a five-unit storage hanger; an apron; gasoline tanks; and a full-time daylight attendant. The formal dedication for the expanded airport was held on June 15, 1968.

The lease was taken over in 1973 by Motivation Air, Inc. (MAI), the present operator, managed by John and Bernice Julian. MAI has continually expanded and improved the facility, now comprising the paved runway (suitable for single- and double-engined aircraft), a 2,450-feet-long grass airstrip, the storage and maintenance hanger, thirty additional hanger units for storing small airplanes, and the administration building (which was expanded in 1988 and 1989). MAI provides flight instruction, aircraft rental, maintenance and repair, fueling, and general aviation services. The airport hosts an annual fly-in event for small planes, with breakfast provided by the Greenville Moose.

This consolidation began in 1949 when representatives of the Stoneboro and Sandy Lake school boards went to Harrisburg. The state Department of Public Instruction told the respective school board members that the facilities both boards had been seeking could better be accomplished by combining the two areas. This idea was at first rejected because of the strong rivalry between the two schools. It took nearly two years before either school board fully realized the implications of such a merger and acted upon what they had been told.

However, when they finally did act, they did so in grand style. Not only did Sandy Lake and Stoneboro school boards meet, but they also invited eight other local school boards to join in the consolidation. In 1951, the ten school boards formed the new Lakeview Joint Consolidated School Board, elected Lauren C. Jewell board president, selected Thayer Company Architects to design a new school building, and awarded Brusca Brothers Inc. (Pittsburgh) the general construction contract.

Ground was broken in 1953; Jackson Center joined the effort in 1954; the high school was completed on January 19, 1955; and students began attending classes there at the end of that January.

Lakeview Joint Consolidated Schools and its board officially became a school district in 1964. This development reduced the number of school board members from fifty-five to twelve, and the Joint Consolidated Schools were officially renamed Lakeview School District.

Many people played a notable role in the education of the students of Lakeview School District. One of Lakeview's first superintendents, Leroy A. Nutt, served the district for eighteen years. Another important figure was the district's first high school principal, John Hilkirk.

Audley Olson's legacy stretched out over five decades and is still felt now when he occasionally steps in to substitute for an absent teacher. A former Army soldier, Olson became known as a strong, disciplined, and dedicated mathematics teacher at Lakeview High School. He remembers many details of the early history of the school, such as the segregation of the male and female teachers' lounges, the busing of all students to school (none drove or walked), and, of course, his own form of disciplining students. "The Loving Touch," as he fondly remembers, was the refined method of paddling students. Olson also spent time as the high school principal.

Another important personality at Lakeview was Edith Myers. As a member of the Stoneboro faculty preceding the consolidation, Myers was included in the staff of the new consolidated district. During her years at Lakeview, Myers oversaw the cafeteria, the art department, and home economics which, she says, was much more than just sewing and cooking. Girls in the home economics program were taught many things, including how to deliver a baby. Myers was also deeply involved in the drama program. Every year she wrote a three-act play for the senior high and a one-act play for the junior high, making sure to include a part for every student. Because of her love of photography, Myers always had a camera ready to capture images of important events and became affectionately known as the school historian. Myers recalls that education was much more respected by the students and that few students ever skipped school. The only major problem that arose was smoking in the bathrooms, and all restroom doors were removed to curb this problem. After thirty-eight years of teaching, Myers retired in 1984. She stays actively involved in the community through her work with the Golden Age Program.

D. Lee and Ruth Mohney taught for many years in the Lakeview District. Their influence on students in the district continued for many years after their retirements through the presence of their daughter, Sherry Reynolds.

From its first year, students at Lakeview have found ways to express their personalities and interests through the clubs and activities that the school offered. Both the yearbook staff and *Lakeviewer*, the school newspaper, were hard at work in 1955 keeping the student body informed and becoming better writers. In 1959, the Quill and Scroll club joined them in their mission. Farming was extremely important to the families of the area, and clubs like Future Farmers of America (FFA) and its junior division stressed this importance. The male club, Tri-Hi, and its female counterpart, Tri-Hi-Y, existed "To create, maintain, and extend throughout the home, school, and community high standards of Christian character." Library workers went through several aliases in the 1950s, from the Bookworms to the Library Club. The National Honor Society has long been rewarding students for their academics, service, leadership, and character, even before the consolidation. Other clubs recorded in the school's first decade included the Projectionists Club, Business Club, Latin Club, Future Teachers of America, Future Homemakers of America, and Junior Historians. It was also during this time that the Student Council was formed.

The most notable music teacher in the early years of the school was Neil C. Fisher, the band director who taught from the consolidation and dedication ceremonies for the new high school, through many concerts, and into the early 1960s.

In the beginning, Lakeview sports consisted of three varsity sports: a boys' basketball team, their cheerleaders (male and female), and a baseball team. Before the consolidation, a great basketball rivalry had existed between the Sandy Lake and Stoneboro high schools. More often than not, Stoneboro had the better team. After the consolidation, many townspeople were concerned about who would get to play. Speculation at the time encouraged that, of the five starting players, two *had* to be from Sandy Lake, two *had* to be from Stoneboro, and the fifth player could be from either school. In 1958, with the cheering and support of the newly formed Sailorettes, the basketball team won the Tri-County Championship. The 1959 season followed with another Tri-County Championship. Also, the wrestling team made its first appearance that year.

In the spring of 1956, one year after the school was built, a tornado swept through the area, hit the back end of the auditorium, and tore off the back wall and part of the roof. Luckily, the damage was minimal. The auditorium was repaired to look as it had previously. However, the graduating class of 1956 held their commencement in the gym, being only one of three classes in the history of the school so far that did not graduate from the auditorium.

The 1960s were the beginning of a new chapter in Lakeview School District's history. They included continued growth for the district with a new elementary school, Oakview Elementary School in 1962; expanded athletic programs; additional faculty; and additions to the music department.

Oakview Elementary contained only ten classrooms at the time to accommodate grades one through six, with no kindergarten. Only 261 students attended Oakview in its first year; and David Alexander, the principal of the two existing elementary schools in Sandy Lake and Stoneboro, assumed the added responsibility of the new school. In addition to the classrooms themselves, Oakview contained an all-purpose room, a music room, health room, a cafeteria, and a material center along with the secretary's office and the principal's office.

The 1960s saw many athletic firsts at Lakeview. In 1965 the first sailor football team was established with thirteen players. And although the team played no official varsity games, they did scrimmage with the junior varsity teams of nearby schools. The 1966 season saw the first varsity football team in their brand new stadium. In 1970, the football team won its first Tri-County Championship.

In 1965 the first tennis team came along, and Joe Chalmers became the first Lakeview boys basketball player to break the thousand-point mark with 1,016 career points. The wrestling team won the Tri-County Championship, and the baseball team became Mercer County Champions in 1966. And in 1969 before the first man landed on the moon, a boys' track team landed at Lakeview. In 1970, the baseball team won its second consecutive Mercer County title.

A unique athletic phenomenon in the 1960s was the formation of Tingley's Raiders. In 1964, under the leadership of guidance counselor Floyd Tingley, a group of faculty formed a basketball team: Charles Kuhn, James Ploski, Freeland McMullen, Donald Deramo, Cecil Neely, Edward P. Carlson, Michael Roth, and, of course, Tingley. In their first season, Tingley's Raiders played only one game, which was with the Harlem Diplomats. The team was disbanded after 1965.

The 1960s were the beginning of a legacy for the Lakeview music program with the hiring of Ray McCallister. Throughout his many years at Lakeview, he was known to have a strict temperament. McCallister always demanded the best and received what he demanded. Under his direction, Lakeview turned out many of the finest instrumental and vocal performances, musicians, and bands the area has ever seen.

BRENNEMAN'S MOVE TO MERCER COUNTY
By Gail Habbyshaw

When Cloyd E. "Gene" Brenneman, an eighteen-year-old Clarion County native, stopped at the traffic light at the top of East Market Street in Mercer one morning in 1952, the courthouse and its spacious, tree-shaded grounds spread out before him. Brenneman

Cloyd E. "Gene" Brenneman, 1952.

had no way of realizing where the decisions he was making and the insights he was gaining would lead.

"I came through that light with $40 in my pocket and my clothes in a cardboard box in the back seat of my eleven-year-old car," Brenneman recalled, pictured here with that car in 1952. "I wanted a future. I was looking for a good job, to make a life for myself."

After high school and a short time of hauling coal for his father's trucking business, Brenneman decided to get a better paying job in a steel mill in Youngstown. He and Roy Whitmer, then twenty-one, packed up their possessions and drove west to Sharon. From there, they had expected to cross the Pennsylvania line into Ohio's Mahoning Valley. Instead, however, they decided to seek jobs in the Shenango Valley.

In the early 1950s, mills generally hired every day, and that very afternoon the two youths were hired by Sharon Steel. The foreman's assistant arranged for them to get physical examinations at the company's infirmary. Learning that they didn't have steel-toed shoes or hot mill gloves, the assistant issued them vouchers to go to Book's and Schwelling's, two stores in Farrell, to buy the safety equipment and work clothes they needed for employment in a mill. She also arranged for them to get identification cards and metal badges and recommended a boarding house on Jefferson Avenue in Sharon. When Brenneman and Whittner arrived at the boarding house, the landlady gave them directions to Walter's Delicatessen. It was located just a few blocks away on East State Street, opposite Buhl Hospital (now Sharon Regional Health System). After all these arrangements, they reported to work at 11 p.m.

Brenneman, Whitmer, and the rest of the men who showed up for work gathered together in a spot in the cold roll department. The foreman directed some of them to certain machines and others to the labor gang. Brenneman found himself working as a second helper on a tandem rolling mill, a position that required particularly hard work. Brenneman proved himself capable and conscientious, and on the next two nights he was assigned to the same work. On the third night, the foreman gave him a chance to bid on the position: Brenneman did and got the job. By working hard and demonstrating his productivity, he had earned not only his base pay, but also a bonus, bringing his pay to $10 more per day than a laborer's.

As a new employee, Brenneman had to work three weeks before receiving his first paycheck. The company took the money for the clothes and shoes from his pay, and he paid the landlady $24 for three weeks' rent. During his first month at Sharon Steel, Brenneman lived on tomato soup and toasted cheese sandwiches and hot roast

The Millbrook Grange No. 1601 was organized in 1914 under the direction of State Deputy Frank Troop (Crawford County) and Whitefield Burns (New Lebanon), a Mercer County deputy. With sixty-three charter members, C. M. Davidson was elected master; Eva Montgomery, lecturer; and Minnie Smith, secretary. Meetings were originally held on the second floor of the Millbrook School. Since members were from both Millbrook and Centertown, it was decided the name would be Centerbrook Grange. In June of 1914, the Union Hall in Millbrook was secured for the grange meeting place for an annual rent of $50. In 1920, the name was changed to Millbrook Grange. (Clipping, dated 1991, and caption: Idella McConnell and Lucille Eagles)

Honored grangers
Members of Millbrook Grange were honored for their many years of membership.
Front: Stella Amon, 55 year member; Nellie Amon, 65 year member; Kermit Bowmer, 75 year member; Velma Bowmer, 65 year member; Sara Bindas, 55 year member.
Middle: William Little, 55 year member; Vera Jamison, 50 year member; Ellsworth Jamison, 50 year member; Louise Jamison, 50 year member; Raymond Jamison, 50 year member; Carl Hoffman, 50 year member.
Back: Bert Montgomery, 55 year member; Gladys Bengs, 25 year member; Alfred Little, 55 year member; Jim Jack, 25 year member. Absent from photo: Frank Amon, 55 year member; and Betty Bowmer, 25 year member. (Allied News photo by Mary Jane Egger)

beef and gravy sandwiches, nourishing meals that were served up for a quarter each at Walter's Delicatessen.

Brenneman had grown up in the country, helping to care for his family's garden and livestock. He also saw both of his parents working hard every day, so tackling a physically demanding job was not outside his experience. He expected not only to work hard, but also to excel at any job he had. Thus began the career that helped put Brenneman on a path leading, forty-three years later, to his election to the Mercer County Board of Commissioners and to an office in an imposing structure, the courthouse he first encountered in 1952.

GRANGES
By Frances Steese and Vonda Minner

The most recently organized grange that is still active in Mercer County is the Shenango Township Grange No. 2057, started in 1952. This grange and the other "subordinate" granges in the county are part of the Mercer County "Pomona" Grange, which helps form the Pennsylvania State Grange, which in turn is part of the National Grange.

In 1867, Oliver Hudson Kelley conceived of the Grange idea to aid agriculture and to improve the farmer's opportunities. The name "Grange" came from a term used in Europe for "farmstead." The National Grange was the first organization for farmers in the nation and remains the only fraternal farm organization. It is a nonprofit, rural/farm fraternity dedicated, through family-oriented activities, to improving the quality of rural life through educational, social, and legislative activity; to advancing the cause of agriculture; to developing rural leadership; and to acting as a voice in public affairs. The Grange has also expanded to cover other concerns for rural and urban America, including health care, education, local roads and bridges, and the environment.

By 1876, Mercer County had thirty-one subordinate granges, and they banded together to form the county grange. The Mercer County Pomona Grange has a long record of introducing resolutions to the State Grange, many of which have become laws of

Pennsylvania. In 1948, the county presented more resolutions to the State Grange than any other county in the commonwealth.

Mercer County now has only eleven active subordinate granges. In addition to the Shenango Township Grange, New Vernon No. 608 (New Vernon Township) was organized in 1875; Friendship No. 1232 (Greene Township), organized in 1903; London No. 1492 (Springfield Township), 1911; Jackson No. 1506 (Jackson Township), 1912; Millbrook No. 1601 (Worth Township) and West Salem No. 1607 (West Salem Township), 1914; Pleasant Valley No. 1643 (Findley Township), 1915; Mt. Pleasant No. 1687 (East Lackawannock Township), 1916; Stony Point No. 1694 (Delaware Township), 1916; and Kennard No. 2040 (Sugar Grove Township), 1948.

UNITED METHODIST CHURCH (WEST MIDDLESEX)
Source: the church's sesquicentennial booklet, 1837–1987

Much of the history of the West Middlesex community and its Methodist church is sketchy, at best. Information is based upon brief and sometimes conflicting records and the hearsay of descendents. However, one thing is certain: one of the primary concerns of the early settlers in the county was meeting the spiritual needs of their families. Records show that as early as 1833, Methodists were meeting and organizing in the West Middlesex area. They usually met in homes and sometimes in a school and always welcomed itinerant preachers when they passed through town.

As the local economy developed and population grew, the haphazard visitations of the itinerate preachers was replaced by "circuits," where Methodist clergy served a specific number of churches on an established schedule. From 1838 until 1841, the West Middlesex Methodist Episcopal Church became a stop on the New Castle circuit that included churches in Mercer and Wilmington.

In 1842, for unexplained reasons, the West Middlesex Methodist shared, at times, the facilities of the Veach Methodist Church with the Methodist congregation from Hubbard. Located midway between the two towns, the building was near what is now Deer Creek Golf Course and was part of a five-church circuit, which included West Middlesex, Hubbard, and Niles. At least seventeen riders serviced the circuit during the fifteen years of its operation. (Much later, from 1936 to 1954, the West Middlesex Church shared its minister with the New Virginia Methodist Church in a more modern version of the circuit rider.)

In 1842 "Miller's prophecy" was circulated in the village. The prophecy stated that the world would be burned in 1843 and destroy the world. William Miller, a New York farmer, had been converted to the Baptist Church and after long meditation of the Bible prophecies became convinced that Christ would return in 1843 and destroy the world. Ernest disciples spread his views, apparently even to the West Middlesex area. Revivals of considerable intensity occurred in both the Methodist and Presbyterian churches, and membership increased to the point where both groups were forced to erect buildings to hold the new converts. When the first date passed without event, Miller rechecked his data and set the date in 1844. This year also came and went and Miller's followers, shunned by most churches, eventually evolved into the Adventists church. Nevertheless, the furor and the fervor caused a positive impact, both spiritually and physically, upon the community and church.

The two-story wood-frame structure built on North Street on property purchased from George McBride (now, the site of the borough fire/police department) was completed in 1846 and dedicated in 1848 as the first Methodist Episcopal Church in West Middlesex. It would serve the community for more than a century. By day the building served as a school. At night, prayer meetings were conducted in the second-floor hall. Sunday services filled the building from morning till evening and occasionally the building was shared on Sundays with the Presbyterians. Later this building was sold for $800 to the newly forming United Presbyterian congregation, and they in turn gave the building to the borough for use as a town hall, fire station, and jail in 1968.

The first Methodist preacher to serve this new independent charge on a full-time basis was Joseph Uncles starting in 1856.

By the early 1860s the trustees envisioned a grander edifice for worship, one more visibly and centrally located within the community to meet the needs of a growing membership. Land was purchased on Main Street, from E. F. and Susan Everhart, for $250. Ground was broken and construction started immediately. Steve and Allen Cameron were the contractors. The very first bricks were delivered to the site in July 1861 by Hiram Veach. The brick had been molded and fired at his kiln located just north of town, above the old mill. The carpentry work was performed by the Gundy men. By fall, work was far enough along that rough plank flooring covered the first-floor ceiling joists and a thatched roof with a wigwam structure allowed smoke to escape from a log fire.

As near as can be determined, the first service held in the present building was conducted on Thanksgiving Day 1861 by Reverend Philip P. Pinney.

Cold weather and the scarcity of available materials due to the outbreak of the Civil War slowed construction. Services were not held on a regular basis until a permanent roof was installed in 1862. Both the war and construction dragged on, and not until 1864 did dedication services take place.

Although commonly accepted today, the idea of Sabbath school was not widely held as being good in the mid-1800s. In fact, when two Methodist ministers initiated a movement to organize a Sabbath school for the village, their efforts were met with considerable opposition. Many thought that such an activity would most certainly lead to a desecration of the Sabbath. However, objections were finally overcome and the Methodists joined with the Presbyterians in establishing the school in the home of David Bradford on Main Street, opposite the St. Charles Hotel. Combined meetings were held for some time, but eventually the two separated and met in their respective churches. The first recorded account of Sunday school classes being held in the present building is April 14, 1872.

After more than fifty years, the plain glass windows in the sanctuary were completely replaced with magnificent leaded, stained glass designs. Installed in 1917, few churches regardless of size or wealth contain finer examples of the stained glass art.

The most recent remodeling of the West Middlesex United Methodist Church was initiated in 1956 and included a much needed expansion of facilities. Not only was the sanctuary totally redecorated, but it was also completely reversed. Even more impressive was the two-story brick addition containing eleven classrooms, rest rooms on each floor, and new entrance foyer and stairwell.

The first instrument used to lead the congregation in spiritual singing was simply the tuning fork. At some point, the church purchased a pump organ; and, as the name implies, power was supplied by pumping the instrument with someone's feet. The first member to be elected to the position of "pumper" for worship services was J. M. Finsthwaite. About 1908, a pipe organ was purchased with the help of a donation from philanthropist Andrew Carnegie. By 1956, however, natural wear and the high cost of pipe organ maintenance prompted the decision to purchase a Baldwin electronic organ as part of the overall remodeling of the sanctuary. The Methodist Youth Fellowship, through chili suppers, bake sales, and other moneymakers, raised $500 of the $800 needed for the organ. Fleming Music Store of New Castle contributed the chimes.

United Methodist Church of West Middlesex, in 2000. (Photographer: Vonda Minner)

No recounting of West Middlesex Methodist Church music would be complete without mention of William "Cappy" Ellison, whose remarkable keyboard touch moved all who heard it. A piano in the lounge was given to the church in his memory, and the piano in the sanctuary is a gift in honor of Mary Hoffman.

Over forty-five ministers have served this congregation, averaging about two or three years at a time until the late 1960s, when the assignments started lasting longer. John Kees accepted the pulpit in 1986 and is still with the church now.

As of 1987, the jubilee members and date they joined the church included Grace Davis 1918, Russell Garrett 1920, Ward Waldorf 1922, Mary Boal 1923, Raymond Genger 1926, Lucy M. Beck 1927, Eleanor Harry 1928, Leona Vaughn 1928, Aldene Garrett 1930, Helen Hill 1930, Laurence Metz 1930, Blanche McWhirter 1931, Sara E. Erb 1933, Wilma Genger 1933, Gertrude Schmidt 1933, Myrtle Canon 1935, Janet Garrett 1935, Edna Gilliland 1935, Sara Grundy 1935, Hilda Sweesy 1935, and Mildred Vannoy 1935.

Members who have pursued full-time Christian service include John Stevenson, James Erb, James Webb, Gerald Schmidt, Pam Summerville, and Nancy Thomas Foltz.

Record-Argus
By Teresa Spatara

John Morrison, editor-owner-publisher of the *Record-Argus*, died in 1957, one year after turning the editor's post over to C. Earl Miller, who had been a member of the news staff continuously since 1932. Miller became only the third editor in the paper's history and the title was retired with him in 1977, following a forty-five-year *Record-Argus* career.

After Morrison died, his widow, Daisy Thorne Morrison, became owner and publisher. She died in 1962 and was succeeded by her niece, Helen Thorne Frampton, who died in 1968 and, in turn, was succeeded by her husband, Frank E. Frampton. Frampton continued as owner-publisher until 1973 when he sold the paper to the Thomson newspaper chain, headquartered in Toronto, Canada. Thomson owned about 145 papers then in the United States, Canada, and the Caribbean area.

[Robert M. Bracey (a native of Michigan) was named by Thomson as publisher of the *Record-Argus* in 1987 and moved to Greenville. From 1989 until 1997, when a new press was installed at Greenville, the *Record-Argus* was printed on the presses of a sister publication, the *Meadville Tribune*. The *Record* was converted to a morning publication during that period. Bracey and Harvey K. Childs, both of Greenville, acquired the *Record-Argus* from the Thomson chain in 1992. Bracey continues as publisher and general manager of the *Record-Argus*. Childs remains as a nonactive partner and devotes his full time as chairman of the board of directors of the Greenville-based Bail USA bonding company which is the largest operation of its kind in the United States. Childs and Mrs. Cheryl Burns, president and chief executive officer of Bail USA, are directors on the board for the *Record-Argus*.]

The *Record-Argus* owes its origins to a number of newspapers that came and went in Greenville, each leaving its mark on the present-day publication.

J. W. Mason started the *Weekly Express* in 1848. Mason later enlarged the *Weekly Express* to a seven-column sheet and renamed it the *Express*, operating it in 1852 as independent in politics. The Reverend William Orvis, a Congregational minister, then bought it and changed its name to *Independent Press*, dropping the unpopular antislavery tag.

James C. Brown bought the *Independent Press* from Orvis in 1853 and ran it under the same name for a while. A year later, Jacob L. Weir became interested in the newspaper field and became publisher under the firm of Brown and Weir. After a short time,

Brown was elected county superintendent and continued only as editor; William S. Finch and Weir handled the business.

Before Brown completed his term of office, John S. Fairman bought the paper and called it the *West Greenville Times*, beginning a new series on November 22, 1856. Printing it as a six-column folio, he used the motto, "Independent not Neutral," and charged $1 a year for the paper, in advance.

On December 1, 1856, A. M. Campbell, a local druggist, joined Fairman; and they operated under the firm name of Fairman and Campbell. In April 1857, H. A. Bowman bought Fairman's interest and Bowman and Campbell ran the *Times* until the following October when Bowman retired. Campbell published the paper until 1859 when Allen Turner bought it for his sister, Mrs. Orpha Hammond. She edited the paper for nearly a year and was succeeded by W. F. Chalfant. After the Civil War broke out, James Brown traded to Turner a piece of land in Crawford County and again owned the paper, keeping the title and management until 1862.

Chalfant then bought the paper and changed its name to *Rural Argus*. But he sold it a short time later and went into the Army. In 1867, William Henry Harrison Dumars became a partner with F. H. Braggins and after a year sold it back to Braggins and returned to Erie.

In 1869, Braggins sold his interest to Jacob Miller and went to Mercer to become a manager of the *Mercer Dispatch*. Miller owned the paper a short time, then sold it to Chalfant, who became proprietor and editor again. This arrangement lasted only until October 1871 when he sold it to Harry Watson.

Watson changed the name to the *Shenango Valley Argus* and in the fall of 1875 sold the paper to George Morgan who ran it until November 1877.

Meanwhile, the *Advance* had been started in 1871 by Dumars, Amos A. Yeakel, and W. F. Harpst as an eight-column folio at $2 a year. It was published in the Goodwin block in downtown Greenville. The following April, Yeakel and Harpst sold their interest to James Brown, and the paper was published under the firm name of Dumars and Co. A few months later, Dumars sold his interest to Brown who became the sole proprietor until November 18 when E. W. Lightner bought the newspaper, complete with equipment, good will, and all. He ran the paper until January 25, 1873, when Brown bought it again and ran it for four more years.

Then, Brown bought the *Shenango Valley Argus* again and consolidated it with the *Advance*, which was strongly Republican and supported the platform and candidates of that party. The consolidated paper was called the *Greenville Advance Argus*.

Brown ran the paper until 1878 when Leech and Beachler became publishers and Brown, editor. In 1889, Brown sold a fourth interest to Beachler and the firm name became Brown and Beachler with Brown as editor-in-chief. Five years later, Brown bought back Beachler's interest and sold half of it to L. Hippee. Brown continued as editor and Hippee as business manager.

Meanwhile, the first Democratic newspaper in Greenville was the *Union Democrat*, a six-column folio that sold for $1.50 a year. William P. Hanna, who lived in Greenville from 1833 until his death in 1888, established the paper in 1861 after serving as postmaster. After three years he sold it to Braggins of the *Argus* who used the material in his paper.

In 1898, Levi Morrison (Sheakleyville) became sole owner of the *Advance Argus*. The following year, he started a daily edition called the *Evening Record*. At the same time he continued to publish the weekly *Advance Argus*. These papers were printed in the Morrison Building on Main Street. (It later housed the Friedman and Keller ladies' apparel stores.)

In 1907, Morrison moved his quarters to 236 Main Street, which it occupied until the present building was opened in 1969 at 10 Penn Avenue.

After the death of Levi Morrison in 1917, his son, John L. Morrison, took over the newspaper. In 1924, he merged the *Evening Record*, the *Advance Argus*, the *Jamestown World*, and the *Stoneboro Citizen* under the name of the new afternoon daily, the *Record-Argus*.

Westinghouse needed space for buildings other than those that had belonged to its predecessor, Savage Arms. Therefore, in 1923, Charles Flower helped Westinghouse acquire land belonging to Wiesens and related families that was located north of A. Wishart and Sons Lumber Company on now Dayton Way in Sharon. The property contained a piece of the Erie Railroad and a section of the Erie Extension Canal. Also purchased for Westinghouse through Flower was a piece of land along Clark Street from James Davis, a Congressman and one-time U.S. Secretary of Labor. In 1923, Samuel B. Clark and other grandchildren of Samuel Clark, for whom Clarksville (now Clark) was named, transferred 5.1 acres on the north side of Clark Street in Hickory Township to Westinghouse (pictured, in the 1960s). In a grand ceremony (pictured on facing page) in 1957, Westinghouse donated one of its few original transformers to the Mercer County Historical Society, where it is on display now. (Aerial: Vinson Skibo)

WESTINGHOUSE ELECTRIC COMPANY
By Mairy Jayn Woge

In 1922, Westinghouse Electric Company collected a debt owed to it by Savage Arms by assuming the ownership of Savage Arms property along Sharpsville Avenue in Sharon. A Westinghouse management team was transferred from Allegheny County to Sharon in 1922 and 1923. For about sixty years in Sharon, Westinghouse produced transformers, tanks, and electronic torpedoes, the latter two for the Navy near the end of World War II, at a growing cluster of specialty buildings. Shortly after Westinghouse opened, it employed two thousand. In the period that included World War II, the industry had a work force of ten thousand. To retain employees, Westinghouse acquired land for construction of company houses through Charles Flower, Michael Bobby, and the Interboro Improvement Company. Flower was said to have built the bulk of the houses, including seventy-five on the East Hill of Sharon.

Some land for houses was acquired in Sharpsville, but most was in Sharon on properties belonging to the Leslies, Stambaughs, Morrisons, Porters, Forkers, and Carvers. W. O. Leslie, a hardware merchant, owned land that included South Oakland Avenue (then Leslie Avenue) in the early 1900s. Current Leslie Street in Sharon is named for a Flower grandson. The Morrison land on the hill west of Stambaugh Avenue was referred to as Prospect Heights, and numerous houses for Westinghouse employees were built there. In 1938, after Westinghouse employees began buying the former company houses, Interboro was liquidated. William Zook, a Westinghouse employee, lived on Meek Street. In 1940, he paid Westinghouse $4,750 for the house.

ZION REFORMED CHURCH (GREENVILLE)
By Gwen Lininger and Janet Hills

The earliest settlers in the Greenville area were German. Seeking new homes in the West, they took up land on the banks of the Shenango River and in what is now West Salem Township. Lutheran and German Reformed circuit-riding preachers visited periodically, and in 1825, the first Reformed congregation was organized.

In 1861, the Zion's German Reformed Church of West Greenville was organized by Reverend Dr. Henry Hartman, a missionary, an astute businessman, and one founder of the First National Bank. He arranged the purchase and repair of a 1843 church building formerly used by Congregationalists, and the members of Zion's worshipped there, in German, until 1886. Reverend C. R. Dieffenbacher became the pastor in 1865. During his thirteen-year ministry, the membership increased to two hundred.

In 1884, the lot for a new church was purchased from James Law at 260 Main Street and considerable money raised. The contractors on the new building were members of the church. Giving freely of their time, they kept the total construction cost to $16,000. The church was dedicated in 1886. The membership increased to seven hundred in Reverend A. M. Keifer's ten-year ministry around 1900. A pipe organ costing $2,500 was purchased in 1903 with the help of a $1,250 donation from Andrew Carnegie. The same year a steam heating plant was installed.

Adult bible classes and a Community Leadership Training School were organized in 1917. Some of the leaders at this time were William Loch, J. Fred Christman, Carl Rosenberg, Mrs. H. A. Beachler, Mrs. D. H. Mathay, Mrs. James Grimm, and Maude Smoyer. Reverend Dr. Paul Dundore arrived in 1921, and during the 1920s many improvements were made to the church. The first Director of Religious Education, Miss Elsie Ashe, was hired, and a Mothers Guild was organized to strengthen the relation of the church to the home.

Stanley J. Seiple served the church as organist and choir director from 1906 to 1937, when he left to join the faculty of Grove City College. Since that time, organists and choir directors have included Marian E. Gerberich, Mr. and Mrs. William Loesel, Geraldine Kleffel, Betty Cooper Young, and Frank B. Stearns.

Always concerned with missions, the Women's Missionary Society was organized in 1878, followed by the Mission Band, Orphans' Home Club (because of the church's asso-

Zion Reformed Church in Greenville, in 2000. (Photographer: Vonda Minner)

ciation with St. Paul Orphans' Home, founded for orphans of the Civil War), teacher training department, Cradle Roll, Christian Endeavor, Campfire Girls, and Boy Scouts. Times and organizational interest have changed, but Zion's congregation remains active both in local and greater church community.

Due to a merger in national churches in 1934, the church became Zion's Evangelical and Reformed Church. By 1938, Zion's communicant membership had reached 1,500. Reverend Paul Shumaker became the new pastor in 1943 and served for nineteen years. The year 1956 saw a new education building added to the church on the east side and continuing improvements and growth.

Keifer's grandson, Reverend Robert K. Nace was installed as pastor in 1963. During his twenty-eight-year tenure, the congregational life of Zion's was characterized by democratization. The president of consistory became an elected layperson instead of a pastor as it had been for a hundred years. In 1963, another national merger brought the local church into the United Church of Christ, the largest denomination (in numbers) in the world. The church's functions were further democratized. Women were encouraged for the first time to become elders and deacons and take an equal role in the organizational life of the church. The first women installed as deacons were Jean Stamm, Joan Wentling, and Lucille Williams. By 1964, the church staff was enlarged to include a second clergy.

Also in 1964, Zion's voted to become a "teaching parish" and established a clinical pastoral education program with other local churches. A total of seventy-six interim pastors spent one-year living and working at these churches over the course of the program.

In 1979 Zion's bought the site of the former Penn High School and negotiated with Crossgates Inc. to construct a federally funded apartment building for senior citizens. The resultant nine-story "Greenville House" was dedicated in 1982. Also in the 1980s, Zion's took on the challenge of a million-dollar update and remodeling of the physical plant while preserving historic integrity.

The church opened its doors to the community at large and began to host many events and services, such as Scouts, a senior center, AlAnon. Several members have served in the larger church, for example, Betty Lou Artman, Frank B. Stearns, and Dr. Bruce Wolff. Lay members regularly serve on the board of St. Paul Homes, and the church maintains a certified preschool for children of the community.

After Nace's retirement, the church had several pastors until Reverend Philip Garner joined the congregation in 1994. Now, Zion's has a communicant membership of 820, a church school, and an preschool. The staff includes the senior pastor, parish associate, music minister, thirty-voice choir, office manager/program coordinator, preschool director, and sexton. The governing body is a large consistory with a lay person as president.

THE VIETNAM WAR AT THIEL COLLEGE
By Monica Copley

Between 1963 and 1973, the United States faced many of the greatest conflicts and toils in its history. One of the events that stood out was the Vietnam War. This conflict had an impact on the nation as a whole, including Thiel College (Greenville). The students at Thiel may not have reacted as strongly as students in other colleges, yet the decade-long conflict had an influence that was shown throughout the campus.

The Thielensian, Thiel's student newspaper, showed the evolving war throughout its pages. Major events were covered in articles distributed to colleges nationally and in articles written by Thiel students. The draft was covered repeatedly, starting late in 1964 with an anticipation that military service would become voluntary. An increased demand for troops in late 1965 caused many students to become nervous. The draft quotas in October and November were the highest of the war so far, leading people to speculate that students with borderline grades would lose their deferments. "With the escalating pressures in Viet Nam, the best insurance is an escalating grade point."

Thiel was a relatively quiet campus during most of the war, which was a point noted by many professors teaching during this time. Thiel was in a period of rapid growth and expansion, being matched by an enrollment of over one thousand. Yet the students generally were moderates or conservatives, with a small group of students and faculty members voicing opposition to the war. These people faced problems with an administration, and especially a president, which was not responsive to students who took a stand. Student freedom was supported by the Academic Dean, who even marched in Washington, D.C., for civil rights; and a few trustees were sympathetic. The divisions caused by the many issues in this era were few, yet they lasted a long time. The students did not often focus on the Vietnam War as a point of protest, choosing instead to concentrate on ways to gain freedoms on campus. This trend helped to create a "surreal, isolated situation" on campus.

But even in this relatively calm situation were students who openly criticized the war and the nation at large. One of the most vocal critics at Thiel was David Cuttler, who wrote editorials for *The Thielensian*. He began his writings on the subject of Vietnam by criticizing student protests in October 1965. He believed that college students were turning their backs on Vietnam, demoralizing American troops. "Yet one must wonder how it feels to be an American Marine, 18 years old, fighting in Vietnam, who has to listen to the propaganda spread by countrymen his own age who are fortunate enough not to be fighting in the jungles." The thoughts and questions running through the minds of his peers fighting in Vietnam were often addressed in Cuttler's editorials.

Cuttler's editorials reached their peak during the 1966–1967 academic year, when he wrote a column called "The World Outside" to speak out on issues affecting the nation and world at large. Vietnam was not his only topic, but it came out frequently. He criticized the Johnson administration. In one instance, he questioned the proposed bombing break of North Vietnam on Christmas of 1966. "Does Death take a Holiday? Hope the Viet Cong see it the same way." He would also criticize President Johnson openly by noting that his words often did not match his actions. For example, President Johnson's saying that he would not escalate the war meant instead large-scale troop movements, a new series of bombings, or a new draft call.

Cuttler would later write on proposed changes to the draft plan, questioning how they would affect the young people in this country. He felt that students might lose the

Carl James "Jimmy" Forrester was the first casualty of the Vietnam War from Mercer County. His mother, Emma Forrester, donated his uniform to the Mercer County Historical Society. The Forrester family in Mercer County dates back to about 1845 and includes such relatives as Jacob and Elizabeth Hassell (Jefferson Township), John Garvin and his son David, John McWhirter, and the Bridgets. Two of the Bridget sons served in Company G, 76th Pennsylvania Infantry, during the Civil War: Thomas, who left the service as a sergeant, and William, who died while serving. (Contributor: Kelly Elizabeth Hedglin)

motivation to achieve in areas such as math and science if they could be drafted while in college. The results could lead to another *Sputnik* episode in which the United States would show itself to be behind the Communist powers of the world.

The article with the greatest impact on the reader was the one that Cuttler wrote on December 9, 1966. In this editorial, he focused on the value of death. He began by speaking on the battle of Pearl Harbor, noting the deaths there. He then addressed the progress in the United States since then, questioning how a GI in Vietnam would view it. "He was pulled from this land, which is at 'peace' with the world; he had no reason to believe that he would die a young and violent death." This powerful article was written by a Thiel student who was trying to deal with the many questions and changes he saw around him.

Other students at Thiel used many methods to answer the questions they had during this changing time. The campus sponsored events, including speakers and debates, through the chapel and the student government to address these points. *The Thielensian* also had articles about events on other campuses throughout the area and national events in which students and faculty took part. One such event was a peace march in New York City in 1967. Three professors, two students, and a member of the Greenville clergy attended this event. Each had different reasons for attending, ranging from opposition to the war to political and economic motives. All participants noted the diversity of the group, the spirit of brotherhood, and the lack of problems with the police. Six other students attended a peace march on the Pentagon that year. They noted less diversity in this group: the majority of the participants were draft-age males. Some people, who may have been paid inciters, were encouraging violence, but the march and demonstration continued peacefully.

Nixon's time as U.S. president led to increased calls for troop withdrawal. Before his election, Choice '68 sponsored a collegiate presidential primary. The majority of the students who voted favored reduced military involvement in Vietnam. Views on bombing North Vietnam were more divided, with about 30 percent favoring suspension of bombing and the same amount favoring intensification of bombing. This result was a change from December 1967, when students favored escalation in a poll conducted by the Thiel Young Republicans. The changing opinions of the students were reflecting the increasingly critical views toward the war nationwide.

The voices for peace at Thiel would get louder as the war continued, climaxing on October 15, 1969. On this day, Thiel participated in the national moratorium in protest of the war. The "Victory Bell" rang throughout the day as a constant reminder of the Americans who had died in Vietnam. A morning discussion was attended by approximately 300 people, and about 450 attended the afternoon teach-in. Bands performed on campus, and a petition was circulated supporting McGovern's withdrawal proposal. Students brought the moratorium into the community by speaking at local schools and canvassing Greenville to discuss the war with residents.

Although the October moratorium was a success, little interest was shown in a second one in November. Thiel did have some activities on this day, but student interest in the war was waning again. It remained this way on campus until the death of four students at Kent State University on May 4, 1970. This national incident shocked everyone and showed the clear divisions that had erupted in society. Everyone could identify with this event because it could have happened anywhere. One professor, David Miller, heard the news on television while returning from getting computer equipment for *The Thielensian*. He was eating lunch with a student and another professor when the story broke. They were all speechless from the shock of the event. Miller was especially affected because he had been attending Kent as part of his postgraduate studies. He knew the locations mentioned from personal experience. Student response to this event included an editorial asking to remove the honorary degree that Thiel College had bestowed on Richard Nixon eleven years before the Kent shooting. This removal would not happen, but it did show the displeasure some members of the Thiel community had toward President Nixon.

One year later, the Thiel community would gather in a moratorium on May 5 to remember those killed at Kent and to call for an end to a war that had already lasted much too long for most Americans. Although the level of apathy at Thiel had risen and doubts existed about whether a moratorium could be successful, many activities were planned and well publicized. These strategies were successful, and hundreds of students turned out for the speakers and concerts designed to expose students to the different sides of the Vietnam question. This day was viewed as largely successful by the campus. Unfortunately, not much commitment resulted from any consciousness gained. From that time on, the Thiel students generally slipped back into their own lives and interests, leaving national affairs in the background.

Thiel may have seemed untouched by the tragic deaths of American soldiers during the war, but it was not. Professors from that time recall many students who went to war and some who never returned. Ronald Pivovar was outraged by the death of Merle Higgins, the son of a groundskeeper at Thiel. He felt the injustice of the fact that sons of the upper class could find ways to avoid the war, while sons of a lower status had to go and die in battle. Alvin Dunkle also noticed that the sons of workers were the ones that were fighting. Two maintenance workers had sons who were killed in action, and a carpenter had a son who served. However, both the president of the college and the academic dean had sons who were of draft age who did not have to fight.

Dr. James Bloomfield remembered when a good number of students and faculty members attended the funeral of a former student who lived in Pittsburgh. He also remembered some instances where students committed to join the armed service wore their uniforms to graduation. One or two students would be in uniform for a few years. Many students either enlisted or were drafted after graduation.

David Miller recalled one student, David Brugennan, who had attended classes at Point Park Junior College when Miller taught there. Miller then had this student for the same class after Brugennan transferred to Thiel. This coincidence was a joke between the two that helped to develop a good student-professor relationship. After graduating in the mid-1960s, Brugennan was drafted and sent to Vietnam where he was killed. A stained glass window in the Passavant Center was installed as a memorial to him. Keith Harmond was another student who was drafted. He knew he was practically guaranteed to go to Vietnam. He did and was killed in action. Paul Bush was an accounting major who graduated with honors before becoming a second lieutenant in the Marines. He was a Greenville native who was fighting in the Khe Sahn area. His death was the first that Greenville faced in the war, saddening both the community and the college. Miller noted that the Thiel graduates who were killed in action were all highly intelligent young men with bright futures ahead of them. "They were our finest. What a waste."

Even in the midst of these deaths were students who survived the war, leading to some humorous incidents. One of these young men, Verne Petz, was a short and stocky prankster. He was drafted and told that he was going into the Marines. He was one of the least likely candidates for the Marines, leading to many jokes about that assignment before he left and after he returned. Another incident concerned a student who left school for a while. He was drafted and sent to Vietnam, where he served his tour of duty. He then returned to Thiel, where he faced a strange reaction from the other students. Nothing had changed on campus, and it was almost like he had only been on a vacation instead of fighting in Vietnam. People would say when they saw him, "Hey Jordan, long time no see." This bizarre situation showed how relatively protected and untouched Thiel really was at that time.

> # WILLIAM D. PORT
> *From the Pittsburgh Post-Gazette, April 2000*
>
> According to an article highlighting Medal of Honor winners from the Vietnam War, "US Army rifleman Pfc. William D. Port and his platoon were moving to cut off reported enemy movement in the Que Son Valley on Jan. 12, 1968 when they came under heavy fire.
> "As the platoon withdrew, Port, 26, of Petersburg, Mercer County, was wounded in the hand. He ignored his injury and enemy fire to help a hurt comrade back to the platoon's perimeter.
> "The assault continued. Port and three fellow soldiers were behind an embankment when a grenade landed among them. Port shouted a warning and dove toward the grenade, shielding his comrades from the explosion."

The Vietnam War was one of the defining moments for the Baby Boom generation and changed the direction of the United States forever. Thiel may not have been one of the major sites of student protest and activism in the nation. In fact, it was not even close. But the events that were disrupting such schools as Berkley did have an impact on the mainly conservative, white, middle to upper class community of Thiel and the surrounding area. Students were realizing that they did have a voice in affairs of their schools, communities, nation, and world. Many students at Thiel focused on using this voice to make the campus a better place for them. Some students did not stop there. They wanted to make the world better for everyone. These students helped organize and attended the speeches and debates throughout this era. They were also involved in campus publications that allowed the student body to hear various viewpoints on the important issues of the day.

Even the students who sat back and tried to stay out of the conflicts were affected by the Vietnam War and other events of this decade. They heard their peers speak out for increased freedoms and decreased involvement in an unpopular war. They saw fellow students leave to fight in a foreign land, and they grieved when these young people did not return. They may not have understood all that was happening around them, but no one really did. This time of confusion, chaos, and change touched people all across the nation and made a lasting impact on Thiel College and the people who were there then.

THE BEATLES COME CLOSE TO MERCER COUNTY
*By Wally Wachter (published in 1983 or 1984 in **The Herald**)*

"'The Beatles are coming to Cleveland! Please, Dad, can you get tickets for me and my girlfriend?'

"This is how my 15-year-old daughter, caught up in the Beatlemania that was sweeping the country's teen-agers, greeted me when I got home from work one evening in late spring 1966. . . .

"Having been a frequenter of Cleveland Stadium for baseball and football games, I knew that the ballpark seated 80,000 people and there was no way they were ever going to fill it unless the Beatles were going to play the New York Yankees.

"I played it cool for about a week, bribing my daughter to do household tasks that she would never tackle before. Finally I succumbed to [her] prodding and pleading.

"I called a friend at the Cleveland station. 'Sure, we can fix you up. I'll send two tickets in the mail,' he said.

"'We're having a press conference with the Beatles before the performance. Would you like me to make reservations for you?' he almost begged me.

"I declined the invitation, figuring that these invaders from Britain were not my cup of tea. How many times since I wish I hadn't.

"The day of the concert arrived. I had taken the day off because I had promised to drive the two young fans to Cleveland. When I awakened about 8 a.m., my starry-eyed daughter and her friend already were dressed and waiting.

"'What time is the concert,' I asked.

"'It's at 7 o'clock tonight, but we want to get close to the gate so we can be the first ones in,' was the reply.

"To appease them, I figured we would take a leisurely drive, stop somewhere for brunch and kill some time before I took them to the stadium. I asked my 12-year-old son, Skip, along to help me spend the hours I had to kill until the concert was over.

"We stopped to eat. They all ordered heavy, but ate nothing. Finally I yielded to their urgency and took the two girls to the stadium where the crowds had already gathered.

"What to do the next 10 hours before we were to pick up the girls? We went to Cleveland-Hopkins Airport to watch the planes come in and take off. My son appeared uninterested. We returned to downtown Cleveland and had dinner. I suggested a movie. My son wasn't interested.

"Then like a bolt of lightning it hit me: This kid was a Beatle fan, too.

"'Did you want to see the Beatles, too?' I asked.

"'I would, but I think it's too late,' he confessed.

"'Let's go,' I said, and we drove down toward the stadium. I had to park in a garage on Third Street, about seven or eight city blocks away. It was about a half-hour before concert time and the crowds were still around the ticket booths.

"It wasn't too long a wait before I had our tickets. The seats were even better ones than I had procured for my daughter two months earlier. The stadium then was less than half-filled.

"The stage was about at second base. A high white fence had been erected around the field to keep the fans penned in their seats.

"I sat through an hour of about the most boring entertainment I ever experienced, while others around me were screaming with delight. A couple or three bouncing rock groups, with names like 'Red Rubber Ball' and other nonsensical nomenclatures took turns performing to set the stage for the Beatles.

"Finally they took the stage—Ringo Starr, Paul McCartney, George Harrison and John Lennon. The screams, the stomping, the yelling from the youngsters around us was deafening. Young girls were moaning and sobbing. The crowd appeared to be in a trance.

"It didn't take the Beatles long to convince me that they were top-rate entertainers. They were master showmen. Their instrumental prowess and stage presence far exceeded that of the groups that preceded them on stage. Their own musical compositions bordered on genius. The Beatles had made an admirer of me.

"Suddenly, as the concert was drawing to a close, an unexpected surge converged from the stands like flood waters rushing over a dam. The high fence around the field was trampled to splinters by the thousands of teen-agers rushing onto the field and toward the stage. Police were frantic trying to stop the stampede, but without success....

"My first impulse was to glance at the seat where my daughter had been sitting. She was gone. My son and I joined the stampede, not to mob the Beatles, but to find her and make sure she was safe.

"The Beatles were escorted off stage to safety. We found the girls at stageside, glassy-eyed and in a state of confusion, still reaching and pledging their love of Paul McCartney to an empty stage.

"My daughter had lost a shoe. We waited until the mob had cleared and then asked an attendant if anyone had found a shoe.

"He took us to a part of the stage and said, 'Take your pick.' There were hundreds of shoes there. We looked through all of them and couldn't find the missing one. . . .

"[Kathy] didn't care. She had seen the Beatles. It was a night that she and Skip have never forgotten."

In 1910, Samuel and Margaretta Meyer moved with their three children to Mercer County from the Pittsburgh area. They brought their household goods and all their farm animals and equipment by train and settled on a farm on Route 58 in Delaware Township. On the property was an oven (pictured at bottom of facing page), which the family used to bake bread, pies, and cakes until the mid-1950s (using the utensils pictured with grandchildren of the Meyers, Frank Meyer, Naomi Meyer Derr, and Lloyd Meyer). The oven was outside because it would be too hot in the summer to use inside. It was heated with wood and used at least twice a week. The oven is now at the Caldwell School Museum. (Contributors: the Meyer children)

During the early 1950s, "The Singing Sisters" (Nancy and Sally Hoffman) entertained before the featured movie at the Reynolds Drive-In Theatre. In payment for their show, they received $5 and free food and movie. Opened in the late 1940s by Carl McKnight, the theater is now owned by Rod Loomis and is the only drive-in still operating in the county. (Contributor: Vonda Minner)

In 1951, the Mercer County Historical Society acquired Magoffin House Museum as a permanent home. A gift from Miss Henrietta Magoffin, the house at 119 South Pitt Street, Mercer, opened to the public in 1953 with an addition of a fireproof vault for storing particularly valuable items. This complex (pictured, in 2000), also known as Henderson Historical Area, is the center for society holdings and activities and contains a wealth of materials from Mercer County's past—furniture, clothing, tools, books, documents, newspapers, and photos. The society library is also actively used by people studying the county's past. Census reports and cemetery records attract many genealogical researchers, and the museum staff devotes much time to answering queries of this nature. (Photographer: Marilyn Dewald; caption: Robert Olson)

Students from many schools, including Vosler School (Salem Township) according to Marilyn McCutcheon Byerley, collected metal for the war effort during the early 1940s. They also collected milkweed pods, which were used as fill in life vests, according to Mrs. Byerley. The teacher for the 1953 Vosler class pictured was Thelma Barrows McCutcheon (Contributor: Marilyn McCutcheon Byerley)

Hospital, Mercer, Pa.

*The Cottage Hospital (Mercer): "Dr. David E. Vogan has performed more than 27,000 operations in the 29 years since he purchased the hospital. Although a native of Sandy Lake, the young physician had been practicing in Kane in 1924 when he decided to return to Mercer County and settle in the county seat. An off-repeated tale of his skill is related about a local patient in a Pittsburgh hospital who was awaiting the arrival of a famous surgeon to perform a difficult operation. When the surgeon came, the patient was astonished and relieved to find he was Dr. Vogan. The modern hospital commands a magnificent view from its high hill just outside the borough limits in Findley Township. The property includes some 450 acres, five of which are in beautiful lawns surrounding the building, the nursing home and surgeon's family quarters. The rest is used for farming to help supply food for the trays. The hospital has 37 beds, a newly remodeled nursery, pillow radios and an important recent addition—X-ray machines equipped for deep therapy." (Source: **The Sharon Herald**, September 12, 1953)*

The Mother Church

The History of:
St. Elizabeth Church
St. Anthony de Padua
Our Lady of Fatima Church

William Lombardo

Our Lady of Fatima is the result of a merger between two churches: St. Elizabeth's and St. Anthony de Padua's. The former was started in South Sharon (now Farrell) in 1902. A church building was constructed on Haywood Street (now Roemer Boulevard) and Wallis Avenue, and in 1909, it was dedicated. The latter church was established in 1905 primarily to minister to the Italian immigrants in the Shenango Valley. A frame church was built in 1905 on Spearman Avenue and enlarged in 1929 and in 1939. St. Anthony's bought land on Indiana Avenue in 1951 for a larger building; however, with the merger with St. Elizabeth's, the land was used for a joint recreational and educational center instead. After the merger, extensive repairs were made to the St. Elizabeth structure; and in 1952, it was dedicated as the Church of Our Lady of Fatima. (Source: **The Mother Church**)

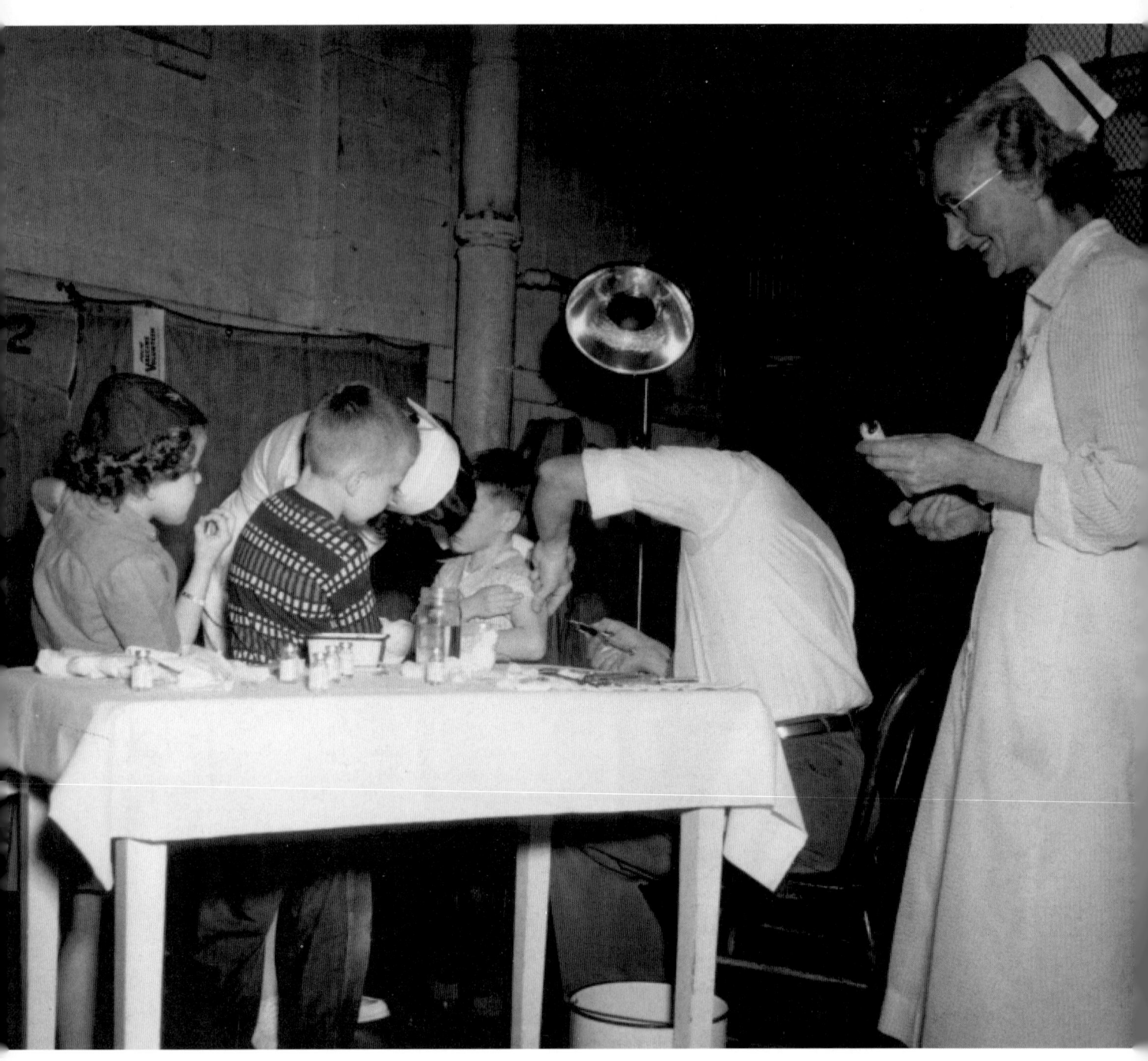

Polio shots being administered in the 1950s, probably at Mercer East Elementary School.

ECHOES OF THE PAST

Howard Mitchell was appointed postmaster of West Middlesex in 1962, the youngest in that borough's history. He had served in the Army during World War II and as a Shenango Township supervisor for eight years before his postmaster appointment. Howard was not the only Mitchell to make news, however. His brother Donald (originally, from Shenango Township) worked at Johns Hopkins University's Applied Physic Laboratory and during the 1970s helped develop a navigation set that used signals from Navy satellites to improve the accuracy of determining the positions of ships at sea. The father of these two brothers, LeRoy (pictured), was a blast furnace foreman at Sharon Steel Corporation. One of LeRoy's brothers, Coydon, had received a Carnegie Hero Fund medal in 1935 for helping to carry out two fellow workers from a gas-filled blast furnace at a Farrell plant, then owned by the Carnegie Steel Company.
(Contributors: Mary and Howard Mitchell)

Norman Rockwell, world-famous artist and illustrator whose works appeared regularly on the cover of Saturday Evening Post, gets the lowdown on Sharon Steel Corp. during a tour back in April 1966. Rockwell, right, is shown with LeRoy F. Mitchell, blast furnace foreman, at left, and J. Edwin Sowers, center, advertising and public relations manager for the corporation. Sharon Steel had commissioned Rockwell for a series of drawings for a newspaper advertising program the company had planned. Rockwell's wife, Molly, accompanied the artist here and photographed various steelworkers at their jobs. The pictures were referred to by her husband while he put the images onto canvas at his Stockbridge, Mass., studio. The photo was submitted by Howard F. Mitchell, son of LeRoy, and Edwin Sowers, son of J. Edwin, both of West Middlesex.

A group of employees celebrated their five-year anniversary with the Reznor Company (Mercer) in 1954: (front row, from left) James Dunn, Paul Forrest, Quincy Hause, Walter Miller, and Charles Black; (back row) Melvin Ryder, William Young, Robert Rowe, William Kerr, Frank Reeher, Paul Weinel, John Peters, and Walter Livermore. (Contributor: Joyce Young)

Before the 1950s, only a few Catholics were in West Middlesex, although many more were in the surrounding Shenango Township. No Catholic church was within miles, nor was a priest in town. To practice their faith, these isolated Catholics traveled to other communities to attend mass. Their children could not be baptized, receive holy communion or confirmation, or get married in their home town. Despite this void, no organized effort to form a parish was started in the borough until 1955. After organizing about forty-five families into the Catholic Action Committee, arranging with the borough for the use of the old high school auditorium (where the Sister of St. Scholastica Convent in Sharon had been conducting religious vacation school for local children), and approaching the Diocese in Erie, the group finally received approval. Auxiliary Bishop Edward McManaman and Msgr. John Gannon, Chancellor of the Diocese, traveled from Erie to West Middlesex to inspect the proposed building site for the church and to draw up the parish boundaries, which included West Middlesex, New Wilmington, and Shenango and Lackawannock Townships. The first pastor, Father Salvatore P. Mitchell soon arrived and remained until 1991. Less than a year after celebrating the parish's first mass in the old high school (with Stephen Fister and Richard Jazwinski as acolytes), ground was broken for the first permanent building of the parish, a social hall and all-purpose building. Mass was celebrated in this building until the church was completed in 1966. The building (pictured, in 2000) was the first circular church in the area. Under the capable leadership of its second pastor, Msgr. Richard Mayer, who arrived in 1991, the church was refurbished and brought up-to-date with the latest liturgical requirements, in time for its rededication by Bishop Donald Troutman in 1996. (Photographer: Vonda Minner; caption: Henrietta Jazwinski)

The Twin City Elks Lodge had a softball team in the mid-1950s. Cly Steverson (standing, second from left) was the pitcher. (Contributor: Roland Barksdale-Hall)

ALUMNI PROFILE:

NORA LYNCH KEARNS

THE WIFE OF A CONGRESSMAN, THIS THIEL ALUMNA IS ACTIVE IN WASHINGTON AFFAIRS AND SERVES AS A CONSULTANT TO THE POSTMASTER GENERAL OF THE UNITED STATES.

Historical records show that women have held positions in American Postal Affairs since 1754. Few women, however, have held a position of such high esteem as Mrs. Carroll D. Kearns (Nora Lynch) who, this spring, was named one of two special consultants to Postmaster General Arthur E. Summerfield.

In this capacity, she is assisting in the Post Office De-

(Source: unidentified Thiel College publication)

scene material directed at corrupting the morals of American youth.

Since her appointment as a post office official in March, Mrs. Kearns has traveled through many states of the Union to deliver addresses, participate in television and radio programs, and to conduct interviews in an effort to stamp out obscenity in the United States mails, a racket which has grown to become a $500,000,000 a year business.

"Mrs. Kearns' wide experience and background in working with youth groups, such as Junior Red Cross and Girls Scouts, and her active participation in many other civic activities will bring a wealth of knowledge to the postal service in our fight to smash the obscenity racket," Mr. Summerfield noted when she joined his staff.

A native of Greenville, Nora attended Greenville public schools and was graduated from Thiel in 1923. The Endymion of that year describes her as "an all-around girl . . . She has the distinction of completing her college career in three years. To her quick wit, resoluteness of purpose and optimistic attitude toward life may be attributed her great popularity."

Very much an athlete in those days, Nora won many trophies for diving, boating and swimming, and was the first woman to swim around Conneaut Lake, a distance of about ten miles.

After receiving a master of arts degree in history at the University of Pittsburgh, she studied at the American Academy of Dramatic Arts in New York. Returning to Greenville, she joined the faculty of Penn High School as a teacher of history and drama. Her strong interest in drama is evidenced by the fact that she is the author of several plays and has produced several historical pageants. When Greenville observed its centennial in 1938, Nora wrote and directed a dramatization of local history in which several hundred persons participated. An active member of the local little theatre group, she once played the title role in Ibsen's "Hedda Gabbler."

While she was a teacher at Penn High School, she met and married Carroll D. _____ who se____ d as music director in the same school syste_. _____r resigned to become professor of music at Slipp_____ _ck State Teachers College, and was superintendent of Farrell schools when he was elected to serve as congressman from the 24th district of Pennsylvania. At the present time, he is completing his seventh term of office.

As the wife of a congressman, Nora has led a very busy life. A past president of the National Federation of Republican Women, she has been most active in the Congressional Club and has served two terms as president of the League of Republican Women of the District of Columbia, 1949-53. She also has served the National Federation as program chairman and as a member of the editorial staff of its "Washington Newsletter."

She is a member of the Board of Management of the Washington Home for Incurables and of the Board of Directors of the Arthritis and Rheumatism Foundation, and is serving her second term as a member of the Thiel Board of Trustees.

Among her club affiliations are the Business and Professional Women's Clubs, Quota International, College Clubs and Historical Societies, International Neighbors Club II, the National Society of Arts and Letters, the American Newspaper Women's Club and the Congressional Club. She is a member of the Lutheran Church and the Congressional Wives Prayer group.

The same resoluteness of purpose, optimistic attitude toward life and interest in a wide variety of activities which she demonstrated in College have been characteristic of Nora throughout her life. This is evidenced by the fact that she has earned for herself a national reputation as a leader in the fields of public service and civic and women's activities.

In addition to the 1913 flood, considered the worst in the 1900s, the Shenango River flooded on a grand scale in 1936, 1937, 1942, 1946, 1950, 1952, 1954, 1958 (pictured, on State Street in Sharon), and 1959 (pictured, at the Sharon post office and in an aerial of downtown Sharon). The flooding was finally controlled by building the Shenango Dam in the mid-1960s in Sharpsville.

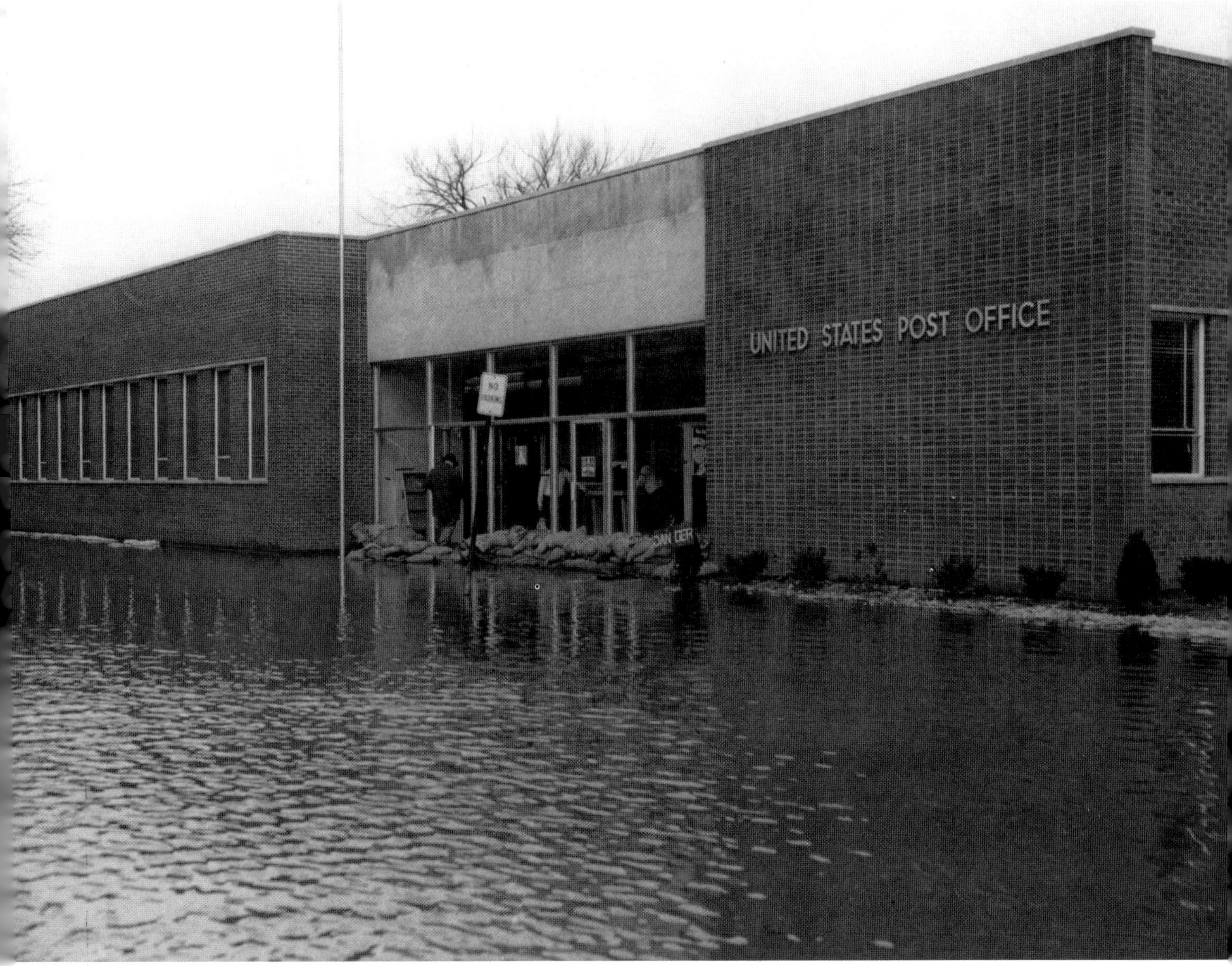
UNITED STATES POST OFFICE

Over the years, twenty pastors and several supply pastors have ministered to the spiritual needs of the Holy Trinity Evangelical Lutheran (Grove City) congregation. J. G. Butz was pastor when the present building (pictured, in 2000) was dedicated. Pastor Kranz served twice for a total of twenty years. Pastor Melcher served for thirty consecutive years from 1921 to 1951. The former Trinity Congregation of Grove City was an offshoot of Emmanuel's Church of Blacktown (or Balm, as it was known until recently). The same pastor served both congregations for over forty years. The church building in Blacktown no longer exists; however, the church cemetery is still there and maintained by the members of Holy Trinity. In 1954, the Emmanuel congregation merged with Trinity and formed Holy Trinity Evangelical Lutheran Church. In 1957, the building for the newly merged church was dedicated. Since 1988, Reverend James M. Seely has been leading the congregation. Esther Snyder's ancestors were charter members of Holy Trinity. Her grandparents lived in Blacktown, and her father told tales of how he would walk to Sunday school carrying his shoes so they wouldn't get dirty on the way. Esther's father and family moved to Grove City later. Esther remembered when the church raised money by collecting old newspapers and magazines, sorting and tying them into bundles, and putting them on the train, presumably to be sold for recycling. Another way they raised considerable money for the new building at Columbia Avenue was making Easter eggs and selling them to the community. Another woman remembered going by bus from her school to the Lutheran Church for a tour of the Easter egg productions. This tradition was repeated, although modified. When the youth needed funds to go to church gatherings, they made and sold, not Easter eggs, but Easter candy. (Photographer: Vonda Minner; caption: Holy Trinity Evangelical Lutheran Church)

The 1958 graduating class of Grove City College posed on the lower campus.

Timeline 1961—1970

The World

1961 John F. Kennedy becomes the 35th president; the Peace Corps is established
1962 John Glenn is the first American to orbit the earth
1963 President John F. Kennedy is assassinated in Dallas, Texas
1964 Cigarette manufacturers are required to print warnings on their packages; Rev. Martin Luther King, Jr. is awarded the Nobel Peace Prize
1965 The Beatles begin filming "Help"
1966 Lyndon B. Johnson becomes the 36th president; the National Organization of Women (NOW) is founded
1967 The first Super Bowl is held; Jimmy Hoffa is arrested and sentenced to eight years in prison; Twiggy is the image of the year
1968 Martin Luther King and Robert F. Kennedy are assassinated
1969 Neil Armstrong becomes the first man to step on the moon; Woodstock is held; Sesame Street airs first show; the cash machine (ATM) is invented by Don Wetzela; Richard M. Nixon becomes 37th president
1970 The population of the United States is 205,052,174; the first Earth Day is held; the Kent State riot occurs; the food processor is invented by Pierre Verdon

Mercer County

1962 The Little Red Schoolhouse Museum is dedicated to represent all former one-room school houses in the county (now known as the Caldwell One-Room School), owned by the Mercer County Historical Society; the county's Cooperative Extension office is erected north of Mercer; the Hempfield Volunteer Fire Department is formed
1964 The county's 4-H park opens next to the county's Cooperative Extension office; the Shenango Valley Mall is built
1965 The flood control dam in Sharpsville is dedicated; the Penn State University's board of directors in State College approve opening the Penn State Shenango Campus; *The Herald* acquires the *Allied* newspaper in Grove City; police raid several local gambling clubs in Sharon
1966 The county's Head Start program begins as one of 800 national summer pilot programs
1967 Lake Latonka is started as a residential development; Interstate 80 opens
1968 The new, relocated Clarksville is officially renamed Clark (relocated in the early 1960s due to the creation of the Shenango Reservoir)
1970 The county's population is 127,175; the January draft affects 47 county men; Westinghouse employees walk out due to disciplinary action against a draftsman; the post office cuts mail delivery from twice to once a day; the Erie Lackawanna Railroad discontinues its passenger service in the county

The rural tranquility of Clarksville was shattered with the announcement that the U.S. Army Corps of Engineers had decided, with funds provided by Congress, that a dam must be built to serve as flood control for the entire Shenango Valley. Rumors of a proposed dam on the Shenango River at Sharpsville had been circulated for many years. Devastating floods in the late 1950s on top of earlier floods increased pressure to build the project. Since the town of Clarksville was in the path of the area to be flooded, the entire village had to be moved to higher ground. In 1960, Clarksville annexed land from South Pymatuning Township south of the town. The Hoover, Newton, and Gibson farm lands were laid out in lots. Those who wished to remain in the new town purchased these lots. Others took up residence elsewhere. Power and fuel lines were completed, the community was literally placed on wheels, and the moving of houses began. Helen Hall wrote, "It was an exciting but sad sight. They [the houses being moved by the moving contractors] looked naked and unfamiliar, shorn of their grass skirts, unadorned by their graceful shrubs and protecting trees. They were dragged precariously over streets and fields and settled without incident in the mud of their new foundations. Time has taken care of the ugliness and old has blended gracefully with the new." Of Clarksville's two churches, one relocated within the new town. The Methodist congregation built a handsome edifice and parsonage on Gibson land. (The pastor now is the Reverend Fay Barca.) The Presbyterians decided to merge with Hickory Township Presbyterians to build a new church on Route 18 a mile south of town. The new town thus consisted of the new Methodist church and parsonage on the hill, a new post office at the foot of the hill on Charles Street, some homes that were moved from the old town, and many new homes. One of the largest buildings moved is another Clarksville landmark, the "Clark House." This present-day tavern has a history of its own, having been a general store for many years. One of the proprietors was William Douglas. The new Shenango Dam was started in March 1963 and completed in July 1965. The dam created a large lake called Shenango Reservoir with the new town of Clark situated on the south shore along and east of Route 18. (Aerial: **The Herald***; caption: Clyde Moffett)*

The Mercer Livestock Auction (pictured, in 2000) started in 1960. (Contributor: Vonda Minner)

Owned from 1887 until 1960 by the Reformed Presbyterian Church, a frame building was constructed on West Market Street in Mercer in 1852 by a Congregational congregation. After the Presbyterians used it, Baptist and Covenant groups used it and eventually sold it as a private residence (pictured, in 2000). (Photographer: Marilyn Dewald)

The Sharon-Greenfield Railroad line picked up coal at the Home Mine west of Christy Road and delivered it to Sharon Iron Company. The engineers who laid out the rail line arranged for a route that went only through properties that were on the tops of hills. It crossed Pine Hollow Boulevard at Smith Avenue and traveled on the course now used by the Shenango Valley Freeway through Pine Hollow and along Pine Run to the switch at the canal pond that turned the train north to take the coal to Sharon Iron Company for unloading. The train ran until the late 1800s. Replacement of the Oakland Avenue viaduct began in 1937 (bridge pictured, in the 1960s). Below the viaduct was Pine Hollow, a run and woods that were the favorite recreation site for children from Sharon's East Hill. Occasionally they would find a rail from the Sharon-Greenfield Railroad; however, most of the ties were gathered during the Depression and taken home to burn for heat. The railroad's right of way on land adjoining it lasted one hundred years until 1974. (Postcard: Vinson Skibo; caption: Mairy Jayn Woge)

Isaly's Dairy Products had deli restaurants in a number of towns in the county, including Grove City, Mercer, and Wheatland (pictured, in the 1960s on Broadway Street). During the 1960s, local men started a coffee club at the Wheatland Isaly's where they met to chat and eventually organized to help needy children. The building that housed the Variety and News Center still stands now. (Photo: Vinson Skibo; caption: Carolyn Phillips)

Christian Science Society is a branch of the First Church of Christ, Scientist, in Boston, Massachusetts. The religion was founded in 1879 by Mary Baker Eddy, the New England woman who organized the church "to commemorate the word and works of our Master, which should reinstate primitive Christianity and its lost element of healing." The Grove City society adheres to that purpose as do Christian Science branch churches and societies throughout the world. All of these branches have as their pastor two books: the King James Version of the Bible and the Christian Science textbook, Science and Health with Key to the Scriptures, *written by Eddy. Sunday services center around the reading of the weekly lesson-sermon, which are prepared in Boston by the Bible Lesson Committee. On any given Sunday, the same lesson is used throughout the world. In addition to Sunday services, the society holds Wednesday evening testimony meetings, where members of the congregation share testimonies of healings they have experienced through Christian Science prayer. The society maintains a public reading room, located in the church edifice, that provides a quiet atmosphere for study. Visitors may read, borrow, or purchase the Bible, Bible references and commentaries, Bible storybooks for children, the Christian Science textbook, and other books furnished by the Christian Science Publishing Society. Also available are the Christian Science Monitor, a nationally acclaimed daily international newspaper, and Christian Science periodicals, which present inspiring solutions to the many perplexing problems facing people today. Christian Science Society was started in Grove City in 1947, when a group of students of Christian Science began to meet in various homes to hold services. About ten years later, they moved their church services to the basement of First Seneca Bank and Trust Company of Grove City (now City National Bank). By the end of 1966, they officially organized and began constructing the church building at its present location at 855 North Broad Street Extension. After the building was under roof, the members and friends personally furnished both labor and materials to finish the interior, provide proper entrances, paint the building, complete the parking lot, and landscape the property. On May 21, 1967, the first service was held in the new church building (pictured, in 2000). (Photographer: Vonda Minner; caption: Eileen Hendrickson)*

The First Baptist Church in Grove City now has a membership of 165. Started in 1909, when a small group of believers, who had been meeting for prayer and preaching services for several months, voted to organize a Baptist church with seventeen charter members. The congregation first met in the Alliance Hall, which later became the Bashline-Rossman Hospital. Other meeting places included the Grand Army of the Republic Hall above the post office in the Rhodes & Redmond Building and Ivy Chapel of Grove City College. Eventually, an abandoned church building, owned by the Reformed Society of Amsterdam, was purchased, dismantled carefully, and moved to Grove City. From those materials, a church building was erected on the corner of West Main and Center Streets (now Henrick's BP gas station). The building was dedicated during in 1910. Building expansions and improvements were made over the years until 1959, when the church purchased the McBride estate on Cranberry Road. Groundbreaking for the present building (pictured, in 2000) was held in 1962. The congregation started a school, known as First Baptist Christian Academy, in 1973, but closed it at the end of the 1985 school year. During the church's ninety-year history, it has had fifteen pastors. While one pastor served as brief a time as three months, the present pastor, Reverend David L. Johnson, has served the longest, nearly twelve years. (Photographer: Vonda Minner; caption: First Baptist Church)

The Twin City Elks Lodge sponsored outstanding basketball. The lodge's last basketball team played (pictured in 1962) played under the direction of Coach Bobby Rapper (front, left) and Assistant Coach Samuel "Bo" Satterwhite (back, left). (Contributor: Roland Barksdale-Hall)

1999

1959

430

1966

In West Middlesex, William Barris built a Dairy Queen (pictured, in 1959, 1966, and 1999); and in 1963, it became the first in Pennsylvania to serve hot food in addition to the traditional soft-serve ice cream. (Contributor: Vonda Minner)

The United Presbyterian Church of West Middlesex started in 1964, by the merger of the First Presbyterian and Trinity United Presbyterian churches of that borough. Neither of the churches had a pastor at that time; therefore, it was an opportune time to unite. The First Presbyterian Church dates back to 1837, with eleven charter members who came from churches in Hopewell, Neshannock, and Moorfield. Reverend James Satterfield was the organizing pastor. The church met in various homes and occasionally in the school. A white frame church was built on two acres of land purchased from Thomas Miles in 1861. It stood behind the present church. A brick structure was built in 1877; and a basement was added in 1921 and education wing, in 1956. The Trinity United Presbyterian Church traces its roots to the Associate Presbyterian Church of Deer Creek, south of New Bedford. Families living a distance from this site requested that Reverend James Ramsey, who was pastor at Deer Creek, preach in the village part-time. The Deer Creek congregation was unwilling for him to do so. Reverend Douthett of the Cross Roads Church near Clarksville preached a few times in West Middlesex. The Deer Creek congregation protested that their territory was being invaded, and Douthett was ordered to confine services to his Cross Roads Church. Eventually, supply pastors were sent to West Middlesex. Services were held in the Wilson School and Gundy's barn around 1840. In 1841, two acres of land were purchased two miles south of West Middlesex, a tent was erected for worship, and Turkey Run Church began. When a spacious building was erected a year later, the name of the congregation was changed to the Beulah Church. After 1858, part of the congregation moved into the borough and were known as United Presbyterian Church of West Middlesex. The Old Methodist Episcopal building was purchased for a place to worship. (The Beulah Church continued as a Reformed Presbyterian Church and eventually disbanded around 1911.) The United Presbyterian Church of West Middlesex was served by several pastors over the years. Reverend John Armstrong of the Beulah Church served until 1868. Other long tenures included Reverend W. J. Snodgrass, from 1869 to 1909, and Reverend R. B. Harsha, 1922 to 1940. After the merger of the United Presbyterian Church of North America and the Presbyterian Church USA, the United Presbyterian Church of West Middlesex became known as the Trinity United Presbyterian Church. After the local churches merged, the First Presbyterian church building from 1877 was razed. The Trinity church building was deeded to the borough for use as offices, and a former borough building (on property adjoining the present church) was transferred to the merged church. (The building had been a gymnasium of the old West Middlesex High School and is now attached to the new church building.) The current church (pictured, in 2000) was built in 1968 and 1969. Many members have continued their upbringing in the church and become ministers and missionaries. (Photographer: Vonda Minner; caption: Janis Clarke)

In addition to the large public school system in Mercer County, several private schools operate. The largest network of private schools is run by the Erie Diocese with four Catholic schools feeding into Kennedy Christian High School (pictured), which opened in 1964. The first school year (1965–1966), it had 340 students and has had as many as 565 students in one year. The 2001–2002 school year enrollment is projected to be 400. Serving western Pennsylvania and eastern Ohio, Kennedy Christian has always been open to students of all faiths, and about 17 percent of its student body is non-Catholic. Since 1986, the boys basketball team has won its state championship five times. (Contributor: Peter Iacino)

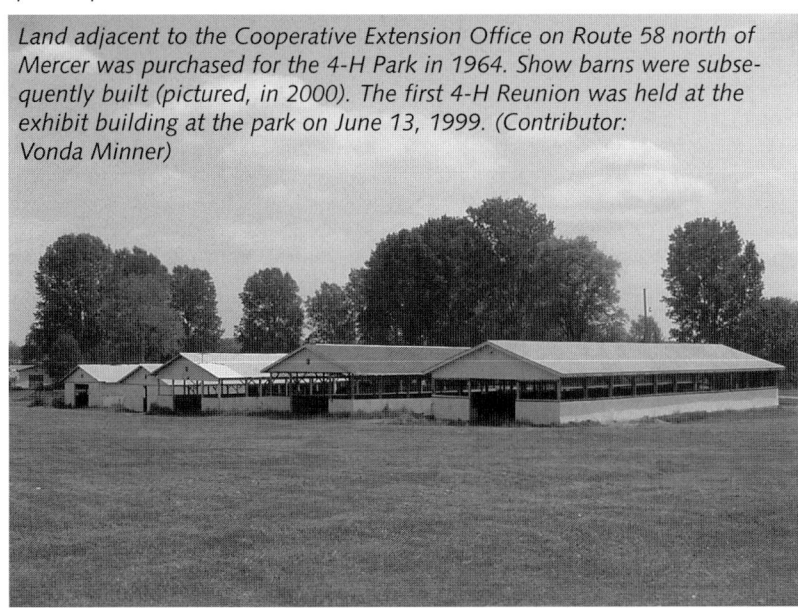

Land adjacent to the Cooperative Extension Office on Route 58 north of Mercer was purchased for the 4-H Park in 1964. Show barns were subsequently built (pictured, in 2000). The first 4-H Reunion was held at the exhibit building at the park on June 13, 1999. (Contributor: Vonda Minner)

One of the earlier airports was located off Airport Road southeast of Grove City, a half-mile east of Route 173 South. In operation in the early 1940s, it was used principally by the Cooper-Bessemer Corporation and other local businesses as well as individuals who enjoyed flying as a hobby. One paved runway ran east-west for about 1,500 feet, and the other, north-south for about 2,500 feet. The line of flight for the latter went directly over the screen of the Larkfield Drive-In Theater. Also on site were the main hanger, a smaller frame hanger, and, at one point in the 1940s, fourteen Piper Cubs used for training. For many years, the fixed base operator was Wilson Aviation, owned by Finley Wilson, which also operated the New Castle Airport. Later, it was leased to Cooper-Bessemer and was known as the Bessemer Airport. In the 1960s and early 1970s, as corporate use fell off, the airport became known as the August-Menzies-Monroe Airport after three of its most heavy users—Robert August, Dr. William Menzies, and George Monroe. Among the female pilots from Mercer County is Jane Menzies, who for many years alternated controls with her husband Dr. William Menzies (both pictured with their Cherokee Arrow plane in late 1960s at the old Bessemer airstrip near Grove City). A high point of Jane Menzies' flying career was her successful participation in the 2,916-mile twenty-ninth Annual All-Woman Transcontinental Air Race from Sacramento, California, to Wilmington, Delaware, from July 9 to 12, 1976 (the last Powder Puff Derby to be held). Other frequent users were Dr. Don Bashline, Raymond "Rocky" Filer, and Buzz Winder. The airport closed after the new Grove City Airport opened in the mid-1970s; the last user (in the early 1980s) was Buzz Winder. After the airport closed, the property was used for strip-mining coal, and traces of the paved runways and one shed are all that remain. (Photo: William Menzies; caption: Richard Christner)

In 1965, a train derailed at the Osgood high bridge (Sugar Grove Township). (Contributor: Richard Sherbondy)

434

Bus on South Diamond Street in Mercer, possibly in the 1960s, but probably as early as in the 1940s.

Faith United Presbyterian Church is both old and young. Overtures for the starting the church may have begun in 1836 or earlier, but the official beginning of the Presbyterian Church of Clarksville came in 1837. No mention of the church building is made until 1840, most likely the building on Line Street, which was abandoned in 1869. The growth of the membership was slow and steady. Then, in 1848, the minister left the church, taking thirty-eight members with him, to form a new church, the Free Church. Some bitterness is evident in church records; however, by 1869, the two churches had reunited and began worshiping in a new building. Over the years the church has had many ministers, in particular, Reverend VanEman who served for twenty-six years, until 1914. The Christian Endeavor Society was organized in the early 1900s, but was allowed to languish until 1934, when it was reorganized under the leadership of Genevieve Bartholomew. Since then, it has played a significant part in the life of the church. In 1960 the name of the church changed to Clarksville United Presbyterian Church, and shortly afterward, discussions centered on having to move the church. By 1964 the Shenango Dam above Sharpsville was becoming a reality. The church property was condemned, and church officials eventually accepted the government's offer of $65,000. Rather than relocate with the town of Clarksville, however, they chose to join with Presbyterians in Hickory Township (now Hermitage). In 1966, the united congregation dedicated a new church (pictured, in 2000) on Route 18 under the name, Faith United Presbyterian Church. The bell, dated 1867, from the former building was preserved and added to the new church. (Photographer: Vonda Minner; caption: Helen Hall and T. D. Stewart)

435

In 1851 the Associate Reformed congregation called Dr. George C. Vincent as pastor. The first elders were David Sample, George Allen, and John Gilkey. Most of the families lived in the southern portion of Lackawannock Township. Vincent served for eighteen years. He left no one in doubt as to where he stood on the great question of moral reform: slavery. In 1852, a small frame building was erected west of the village of Greenfield. During evangelist Billy Sunday's services in Shenango Valley in 1908, many people were converted, and the church grew. The church became known as the Lebanon United Presbyterian Church. In 1915 the church burned to the ground, cause unknown. A new church was soon built for $6,000. Several ministers served the church during the next few years. In 1936, Reverend Thomas Patton was called and served twelve years. Two Westminster College professors followed his pastorate: Dr. Wayne Christy and Dr. Joseph Hopkins. The first church organ was purchased about 1957 and a choir organized. In 1960 the pulpit was vacant in Unity Church (one mile east of Greenfield) as well as Lebanon's pulpit. Shenango Presbytery suggested a merger between the two churches. After prayerful consideration, the decision was to continue separately. In 1967 the Reverend Donald P. Wilson was called. He was finishing his work at seminary and was ordained that year in Lebanon. Under his leadership, this growing congregation has made several necessary additions with much voluntary help from elders, deacons, and trustees: an educational wing, brick siding on the white clapboard building, expansion of the sanctuary and basement foyer, and a new kitchen and office. The Women's Association actively supports mission work at home and abroad. Helen Artman Burrows gave her life in India as a missionary. Several other members served on the mission field in various places. The Sunday school has ten classes from nursery to adult. It helps to support the vacation Bible school and summer camp. Two youth groups meet regularly for Bible study and fellowship and are active in the community. The choir continues to sing for regular worship services, and visiting concert groups add to the music. A monthly newsletter goes out to all members of the congregation, and the church is now in cyberspace: Lebanon United Presbyterian Church has its own World Wide Web site, thanks to Bill Spangler. (Photographer: Vonda Minner; caption: Genevieve Bartholomew)

In 1967, Coolspring Township established a zoning ordinance when a private development was started. Lake Latonka, a successful residential development, is half in Coolspring Township and half in Jackson Township. The 270-acre lake is four miles from Mercer along Route 62. Although in the 1990s, many landowners live year round on the lake, in the 1960s, many had only cottages and vacationed there from the Pittsburgh and Youngstown areas. One morning in 1966, the dam that created the lake broke suddenly and caused millions of gallons of water to rush downstream through a fifty-foot-wide break. According to an October 21 article soon after the flood, the water dropped about twelve to fourteen feet in the lake, which is thirty-seven feet deep at most. The lake is wider at various points than the 1,900-foot-wide dam and is two miles long. The high water closed three roads in the Mercer area: Route 62 near the lake for about 1.5 hours, Route 58 for about 4.5 hours, and Scrubgrass Road for about 6.5 hours. Westrac Company, manufacturer of steel tracks and rulers for heavy equipment, sent its one hundred employees home early that day because of the rising waters. However, Reznor Division of ITT and Mercer Milling Company were not affected by the flood. Originally reported drowned because they were seen tumbling in the swift current, ten cows were returned to the Plummer McCullough farm, near the lake, later in the day. They were treated for pneumonia and jaundice. The worst of the flash flooding was over by late afternoon as the water rushed from the lake into Pine and Otter creeks, along to Neshannock Creek, and on to the Shenango River at New Castle. (Contributor: **The Herald***)*

(Source: **The Sharon Herald**, December 2, 1967)

"The Shenango Valley Chamber of Commerce takes this opportunity to pay tribute to Gordon Ward, 'Mr. Highway' in the Shenango Valley, Mercer County, Trumbull County and Mahoning County. Gordon has been active in the Keystone Shortway Association since its beginning in 1954. He has also worked untiringly, and often at his own expense, for the Erie-Pittsburgh-West Virginia Freeway (Interstate 79), the Beaver Valley Expressway and the Valley Expressway which currently is in the early stages, plus many other highway projects in our area. Gordon is Chairman of the Shenango Valley Chamber of Commerce Highway Committee, President of the Mercer County Turnpike Association, member of the Greater Youngstown Chamber of Commerce Highway Committee and a Vice-President of the Keystone Shortway Association. For your devoted efforts to better highways for our valley . . . Gordon, we hereby give a tip of the official 'Chamber hat' in grateful appreciation for a job well done." Exit 1 on I-80 (pictured, late 1960s) is known as the Gordon Ward interchange. (Postcard: Vinson Skibo; ad: **The Sharon Herald***, December 2, 1967)*

439

The farm known as the House on the Hill (pictured, in 2000) is on Route 318 in East Lackawannock Township. It was purchased by John Kerins in 1967. The barn burned in 1977, but the old silo remains. John's son Richard began renovating the home (into apartments) and found the history of the house intriguing. In the stone basement, Kerins discovered an 1840 newspaper Freemen's Monitor *among other antislavery publications from that period. During the early 1840s, the house was reportedly used as a refuge for runaway slaves. The farmhouse was built by Thomas Rogers in 1832 on two hundred acres of land, which had been deeded to Samuel Clendemn in 1809 for his service as a private in the Revolutionary War. Frank J. McCain owned the home from 1899 to 1910 and is famous for building the first Ferris Wheel at the World's Fair in Chicago in 1893. He also helped build the first steel skyscraper in Chicago. In 1908, McCain remodeled the house to make it more modern. He acquired stone steps from the burned-out courthouse that he had also helped build. (These stone steps still lead to the back porch.) In 1911, Alvah and Elizabeth Sharlow from Pittsburgh bought the farm. Alvah was known as a kindly and helpful neighbor. He raised crops, horses, and was a helpful member at Mount Pleasant Grange. He would purchase farm supplies in bulk, have them delivered by railroad, and pass on the savings to fellow grange members. (Contributor: Ruth Woods)*

In 1969, participants and spectators had fun in the Fredonia Pet Parade. (Notice the simple building to the right of the post office; it was known as Mother Black's Boarding House. When the Fredonia Institute was operating, Mother Black took in boarders and cooked for 50 cents a week per student. Each student also paid 7 cents per meal and had plenty to eat.)

The Farm Bureau was organized in Greenville in 1912, and the first county agent was C. G. McBride. Eventually, known as the Mercer County Cooperative Extension, Penn State, the group built an office in 1962 (pictured, in 2000) just north of Mercer on Route 19. The building is now named the Leslie N. Firth Learning Center. (Contributor: Vonda Minner)

During his two-week vacation from his job at Reznor Manufacturing Company (Mercer), William Young, also a grain farmer, had 146 acres of corn to shell, dry, and put in the bins. On October 23, 1970, one son, Tom, age twelve, was helping Young out in the field. Young's wife, Joyce, recalls, "I asked our oldest son Bob to run up to the field and see how soon they would be in for supper. My dad Homer Brumbaugh and my uncle Raymond Emerson were watching the grain dryer. Suddenly, my dad came into the house and said that something must have happened to Tom. They had seen Bob turn down Mack Road, and Bill was coming fast with the tractor. We watched as he jumped off the tractor, ran to the car, and headed to Greenville. When my dad and uncle reached the tractor, they found a bloody tennis shoe. Later I heard the details of the accident. When grain is wet, it sticks to the sides of the bin, which holds 50 bushels. For years, someone has crawled into the bin, holding onto the sides, and pushed the grain down with his feet. The auger is in the center of the opening and covered with a metal plate, leaving a three-inch opening on both sides for the grain to go in. When Tom got in that day, the bin was full and he slipped. His feet, toes first, went into an air pocket over the auger. He was pinned for about three minutes while Bill struggled to stop the auger and back it off by hand. He put Tom on the platform of the combine and ran to get the tractor. As Bill was coming back through the field, Tom was trying to walk through the corn stubble to him. We were later told that bringing him in on the tractor fender with the wind whipping at his feet probably helped to clot the blood, but it was amazing that Tom hadn't gone into shock. Dr. Thomas, a wonderful surgeon, was on call, and Tom underwent surgery 45 minutes after he arrived at the hospital. After the surgery, Dr. Thomas said, 'Tom will walk with a limp, but he WILL walk.' The first thing Tom said to us was, 'I'll be okay. You go home and get some rest.'

As a result of the accident, Tom lost his right 'foot,' but he has the heel. (I learned the medical term for 'foot' is the front part where the toes are.) His left foot was badly mangled and required corrective surgery. (As his feet grew, he had three more surgeries.) Ten days after the accident we laid my dad to rest. The doctor let Tom go to the funeral home, but only for a short time. The day of the funeral, Tom underwent his first skin graft, one of the last surgeries Dr. Thomas performed before he retired. Dr. Baker, also a skillful surgeon, performed all of Tom's other surgeries. For a month, I never missed a day at his hospital bedside. Neighbors volunteered to watch our toddler daughter. The nurses accused Tom of having a national fan club because he received so many cards, many with a dollar or two in them. He was always buying something from the volunteers' cart for other young patients on his floor. Many people who had faced similar experiences stopped by or wrote to encourage him: in farming, more accidents occur than in other businesses in the world."

Bandaged up and at home (pictured), "he used a wheel chair at first, but shortly before Christmas he was using crutches. On December 29, he put away the crutches and walked on his own. He even went back to school after the holidays. The following summer Tom played Little League, and that fall he shot his first four-point buck. Since 1977, Tom has been employed at Reznor, now a unit of Thomas & Betts. In 1979, he married Terri Walter [Grove City] and has two lovely daughters, Amanda [student at Grove City College] and Virginia [2000 graduate of Grove City High School]. As a mother, I had a hard time during this ordeal, but like all things in life, time helps and heals." (Contributor: Joyce Young)

After James Campbell settled in 1798 in what is now Jamestown and built a mill, more settlers were drawn to the Jamestown area. One such newcomer from New York, in 1836, was William Gibson, an entrepreneur and doctor. Gibson brought many developments to Jamestown, such as an opera house, the first bank, and the charter for the Jamestown Seminary. In 1856, the doctor and his wife, Susan Beatty Gibson, built a home (pictured, in 1999). The mansion was reportedly part of the Underground Railroad in the pre–Civil War era and, according to local lore, is haunted by the ghost of a young woman killed in a buggy accident on her way to her wedding, which was to be at the Gibson house. Willed to William McMaster in 1905, it later became the home of Riley and Esther McMaster Clarke. In 1955, it was sold to Harold Paxton and Baird Gibson (not related) (Greenville) and became "Mark Twain Restaurant." This Gibson claimed to have met the writer and once entertained him here. From 1969 to 1992, ownership of the restaurant changed several times until Dr. John and Helen Steele bought it and now use the building for offices. Gone are the fountains that flanked the front grounds and the large statue of a dog guarding the entrance. (Contributor: Norma Leary)

The borough of Sandy Lake, 1970.

Hickory Homecoming Parade, 1972.

Chapter 8: 1971–1990

Townships

Voters changed the name of *Hickory Township* to Hermitage in 1974. Al Wolgast (Hermitage) launched the campaign to name the township for U.S. President Andrew Jackson's plantation in Tennessee named Hermitage rather than continuing to call the community Hickory Township for Jackson's nickname "Old Hickory." (Jackson had been president when Hickory Township was formed in 1832.) Hermitage became a third-class city in 1984.

The *Lackawannock Township* Civic League was organized in 1975 with Rebecca Watson Humes as the first president. Many community events have been sponsored by this civil league, such as auctions, picnics, dinner parties, pancake and sausage suppers, "Clean Sweep Days" (flea market, recycling dropoff, and bake sale, including Amish-made raised donuts), and programs of recognition for township residents. The profits of these events benefited many other aspects of the community: coal for Amish schools, kitchen equipment, and scholarships for township college-bound seniors. One of the league's recent highlights is its "Citizens of the Year" award, honoring model citizens of Lackawannock. In 1974, the township supervisors purchased nineteen acres from Woodrow Wasson for $19,000 for a township-municipal building, which opened in 1981. The civic league has met in that building ever since. (The president of the civic league now is Richard Schuller. He has also served as supervisor since 1986 and is now the president of the board of supervisors.) In 1977 the township census declared 2,489 residents; in 1990, 2,675 residents and 937 housing units. The first gas wells in Lackawannock Township were tapped in 1984 on the Nych Farm and in 1985 on the Bartholomew Farm on Greenfield-Charleston Road. (Now, the township has 120 gas wells.)

In *Wilmington Township* during 1974, the Amish completely separated themselves from the public school system. In 1981, another educational institution came to the township: Rema Christian Academy, sponsored by the Living Word Church and located on Cowden Road. As the school grew, it added grades until it reached grade twelve. The Living Word Church, nondenominational, was the second church in Wilmington and came in 1974. Wilmington's steady population growth reached 1,177 in 1990.

Municipalities

Top Notch Products in *Fredonia* has been in business since 1976. This was the first company to thermoform Corian into objects such as ice buckets and other canisters. Although the company is relatively small, it is still servicing over one hundred businesses around the world.

CHADDERTON AIRPORT

By Richard Christner

A small airfield was located off Christy Road a few miles southeast of Sharon. Known as the Sharon Airport, it was also called Chadderton Airport for Edward Chadderton, who operated an over-the-road transportation company, but also used the field for charter flights, shipping air cargo, and flight instruction. Chadderton acquired the airfield in 1946, paving and extending the main runway to 3,200 feet; adding two grass airstrips; building an office, large hanger, and ten T-hangers for small planes; and installing ground lights for night operations. His air cargo operations used twin-engine Beechcraft and Cessna airplanes piloted at times by Robert Blatz and Joe Buckwalter, who doubled as flight instructors. Some of the small aircraft based at the airport were flown by Bruce Campbell, Don Hunter, and Dave Fuller.

Chadderton sold the airport in 1981, but a planned office park development never materialized. The site is now vacant, overgrown land.

A footnote about Ed Chadderton: According to LeRoy Haag, as recorded by Joyce Young, Chadderton once wrecked his plane by flying into a lightning rod on his parents' house. The plane smashed into the pigpen. Chadderton was not hurt, but his father was mad because the plane killed a new litter of piglets.

From 1971 through 1974, federal housing loans and grants totaling $2.7 million were used to redevelop the central area of **Sharpsville**. Up to ninety-two houses and fifty-two business buildings were torn down. Twenty-one businesses were relocated. The houses that were destroyed were, for the most part, company houses of the former Sharpsville Boiler Works. Out of this came the Sharpsville Plaza and abutting improvements. Dean Alexander, a Hermitage contractor, acquired some of the remaining General Pierce properties including the section of the Erie Extension Canal from Sugar Grove Township at the Crawford County line to a lock south of West Middlesex in Lawrence County.

Wheatland has set several records in the political arena. Most recently, Helen M. Duby was the first woman elected to a borough council in Mercer County. She served in that capacity from 1972 through 1976. In 1978, she was elected as the borough's mayor, again the first woman in that office, and served until 1990. [Earlier in the century, Benjamin Jarrett served a burgess (now, mayor) from 1903 through 1906. At twenty-one years old, he is the youngest person in the state to have been elected burgess. He went on to serve in the state senate. Also, Carl Marstellar, who served as Wheatland burgess from 1922 through 1926, was one of the youngest assemblemen in Harrisburg when he served.]

Clark *(by Clyde Moffett)*. Perhaps because of the turmoil of the 1960s, the town came together and community spirit prevailed. In 1976 land was dedicated for the use of a recreation area named the Henderson-Taylor Park, in honor of major benefactors. During the 1970s and 1980s, many fund raisers were held to secure money to develop the park and construct a fire house and social hall. Organizations sponsoring these benefits included the Clark Volunteer Fire Department, the Ladies Auxiliary, and the Clark Community League. Ground was broken for the new building and it was dedicated in 1976, during Clark's national Bicentennial celebration.

On May 31, 1985, a devastating tornado ripped through Wheatland. News of its devastation made headlines as far away as St. Louis, Las Vegas, Amarillo, and Phoenix. Yourga Trucking was in center of the storm. Seventy-five pieces of equipment were destroyed, including new trucks and tractor trailers. Part of Sawhill Tubular Division was destroyed and the rest of it heavily damaged. Wheatland Tube was one of the most heavily damaged industries in town. The Hotel Shenango (at the corner of Main and Rosedale streets) and the Valley Baptist Church were also destroyed. Although homes still existed south of Broadway, that area had been zoned industrial in 1957; homes that were more than halfway destroyed by the tornado could not be rebuilt. U.S. Vice President Bush toured the disaster area with Pennsylvania Governor Dick Thornburgh. Most crushing of all was the death of six people, including Michael Thomas Kurpe who was killed as he stood in the doorway of the Hotel Shenango. At the corner of Main and Clinton streets, Sawhill built a monument in honor of these fatalities. Wheatland's chief executive officer, Jack O'Donnell, pledged $100,000 to the borough for reconstruction. (Yourga, Sawhill, and Wheatland Tube stayed in Wheatland and subsequently rebuilt their operations. The Hotel was not rebuilt, and the Valley Baptist Church, in Wheatland since 1914, moved to Farrell to rebuild with the help of a $50,000 donation from Wheatland Tube.) (1999 aerial: **The Herald**; photos, in 2000: Marilyn Dewald; caption: Carolyn Phillips)

447

*Jamestown's downtown, in 1973 and in 1999. (1973 aerial: Norma Leary; 1999 aerial: **The Herald**)*

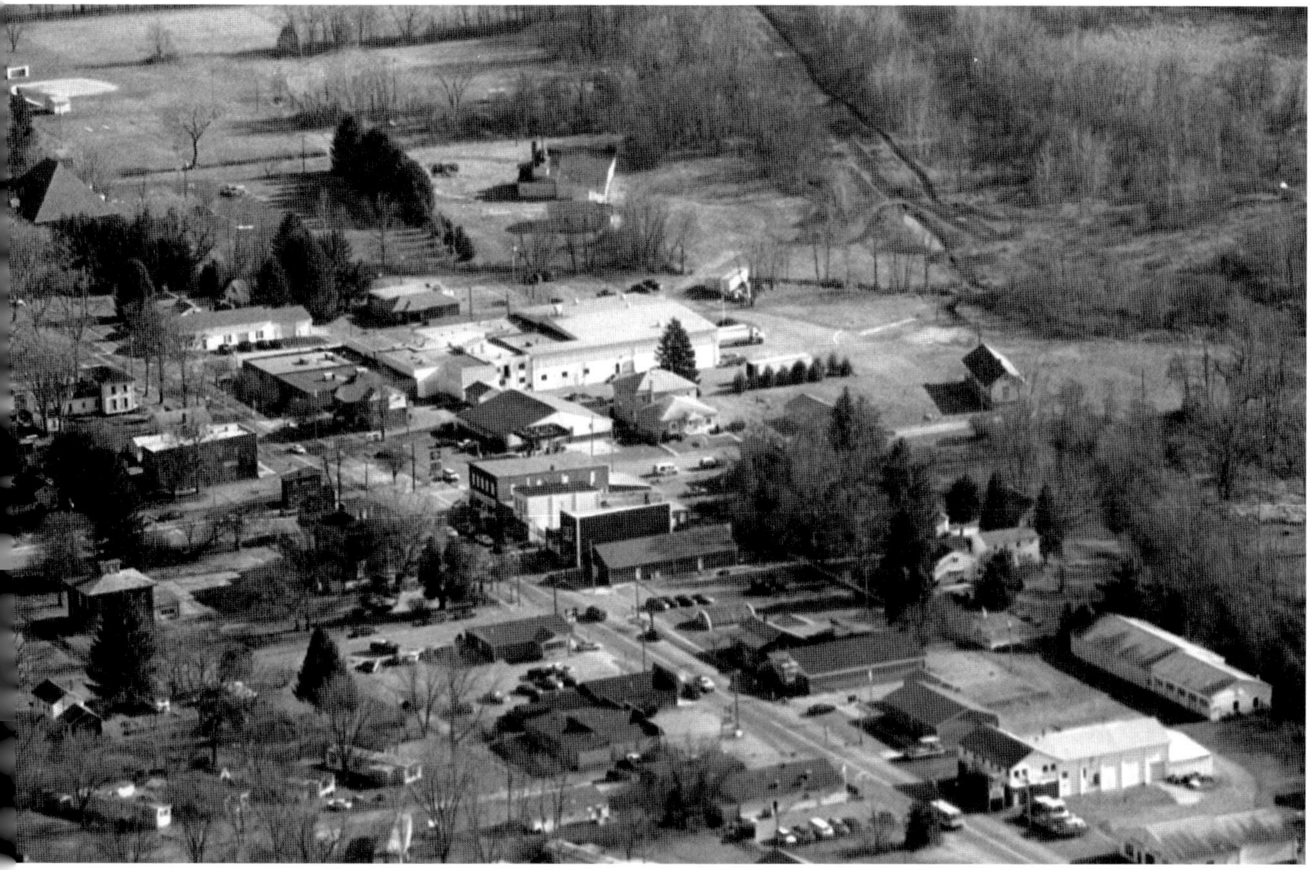

The park has been the site of many community activities, including the annual ox roast, the Firemen's Christmas parties and game dinners, Bingo, Halloween parties and Easter egg hunts. Private parties have also rented the building and park for family reunions, graduation celebrations, and wedding functions. Visitors flock to the lake for water activities and camping.

Jamestown *(by Norma Leary)*. In 1972, Daryl Pinney started a Ham Radio Club.

James McHale became the Pennsylvania Secretary of Agriculture in 1974.

A celebration took place in 1978 for Jamestown's 125th anniversary. Activities included the burial of a time capsule and a Recognition Day for the older residents.

A proposal for the zoning of Jamestown by the Jamestown Planning Commission was turned down in 1980 at a public meeting.

Lloyd Leary was inducted into Mercer County Baseball Hall of Fame in 1987.

Students from Jamestown Elementary School participated in a "Thinking Skills" Consortium in 1989 and came away with the best nationwide gains for their performance.

RAILROADS
By Frederick Houser

For the Erie Lackawanna Railroad, the failure of the Penn Central Transportation Company, coupled with the robust trucking industry on the interstate highway system, had been dragging it toward the brink for some time. The final straw was the immense flood damage inflicted on the Erie Lackawanna by Hurricane Agnes in June 1972. On June 26, the Erie Lackawanna officially followed Penn Central into bankruptcy. Suddenly, except for the very profitable Bessemer & Lake Erie (which was then owned by U.S. Steel Corporation), all of Mercer County's remaining rail mileage belonged to railroads in receivership. The federal government planned and financed a rescue of the two railroad's vital operations, along with those of several other bankrupt northeast railroads. The rescue attempt combined those bankrupt carriers into Consolidated Rail Corporation (Conrail) on April 1, 1976.

Conrail had a formidable task of taking several impoverished railroads and creating one profitable enterprise that could some day compete again in the private sector. Survival was the first order of business, and Conrail had to quickly make considerable use of mergers to cut duplicate facilities and overhead on a massive scale. The railroad landscape in Mercer County would not be spared from widespread job cuts and track removals of a railroad consolidation. During the next twenty-three years of Conrail's existence, but particularly in the early 1980s, many rail lines in Mercer County were abandoned and removed. Virtually all of the former Erie Railroad's New Castle Branch was torn up from Sharon, south. The old New York Central branch through Jamestown and Stoneboro completely vanished from the county, as did the NYC Sharon Branch. Most of the former Pennsylvania Railroad Erie & Pittsburgh Branch was retired, although a section was kept between Wheatland and Sharpsville to serve local industries, and short segments were retained near Shenango Yard and Clark to connect with former Erie Railroad track. Even the once very busy Erie Railroad main line lost most of its second main track under Conrail. The fast freight cut-off by way of Orangeville, the original Atlantic & Great Western to Dayton, was retired in place in December of 1980 and lay rusting and unused for over a decade. It became the most recent major track removal in Mercer County when a work train picked up the rails the last week of August 1991.

BESSEMER & LAKE ERIE RAILROAD
By Frederick Houser

By 1973, the entire Bessemer & Lake Erie main line was laid with continuous welded rail, which eliminated the maintenance headaches of rail joints every 39.5 feet. The Bessemer & Lake Erie was the first Class I railroad in the nation to have an all-welded-rail main line.

The final quarter of the 1900s saw much of the Monongahela Valley's steel production come to an end due to competition and recession. This change had a drastic effect on the levels of freight traffic moving over the Bessemer & Lake Erie. It also coincided with a cessation in much of the on-line coal mining, which further depressed carloadings. After U.S. Steel and Marathon Oil joined to form USX in 1986, controlling interests in the former U.S. Steel transportation properties, including the Bessemer & Lake Erie, were sold in 1988 to New York holding company Transtar, Incorporated. Despite the Bessemer & Lake Erie's reduced affiliation with its former steel industry ownership, its fortunes are still heavily dependent upon that industry's remaining traffic. The Bessemer & Lake Erie remains noteworthy, however, for being among only a very few American railroads that reached the end of the 1900s with its corporate name unchanged from its original charter.

FARMING
By Vonda Minner

In the 1970s, the Reynolds School District was the last school to quit offering an agriculture program.

The Poole Farm (Lake Township) was one hundred years old in 1971; the Campman Farm (Shenango Township) and the Smith Farm (Millcreek Township), in 1973; the Callahan Farm (West Salem Township), in 1976; the Marsh Farm (Coolspring Township), in 1980; the Reimold Farm (Delaware Township), in 1984; the Hoffacker Farm (Perry Township), in 1987; and the Steckler Farm (Lake Township), in 1988.

On August 7, 1976, Arthur and Shirley Moore of Amoore Farms (Springfield Township) with their children Dale, Debbie, Beverly, Ralph, and Bob hosted the first Mercer County Town and Country Day. The purpose of the day was to promote better understanding between the farmer and his urban and suburban neighbors.

LAKEVIEW SCHOOL DISTRICT
By Serena Ghering, Jerry Drew, John Hamelly

The 1970s were a time of change for Lakeview School District just as they were for the rest of the world. A change in leadership resulted when Leroy A. Nutt retired and Sam Wilson, the high school principal at the time, assumed the role of superintendent. Bruce Rice was then hired to administer the high school. The dress code relaxed as girls went from wearing skirts to slacks, and eventually all students were permitted to wear blue jeans. Oakview Elementary gained an addition containing twelve classrooms and a new art room in 1972.

RAILROAD-RELATED INDUSTRIES
By Frederick Houser

The economic importance of the railroad industry to Mercer County from the 1860s has represented more than just the activities of its operating railroads. Several of the early coal mines were affiliated with the first railroads to be built in the county. Locomotive fuel remained a major source of business for numerous county mines as long as steam engines were used. Greenville Steel Car Company and its successor, Trinity Industries, have been turning out freight cars since 1916. Trinity has significantly expanded the production capacity of its Greenville plant in the past decade and has, at times, been the county's largest employer.

Cooper-Bessemer, Grove City's largest industry for years, survived the Depression primarily by producing diesel engines for locomotives, including a turbo-charged model.

General Electric used Cooper-Bessemer's engines to power export locomotives and early demonstrator locomotives, and General Electric's Erie plant became the nation's leading producer of railroad motive power. General Electric ultimately undertook manufacture of its own prime-movers for both domestic and overseas locomotives. In 1970, General Electric built its own diesel engine plant at Grove City, which now produces a series of engines that include the highest horsepower diesels used in locomotives.

Other railroad suppliers have been major county employers, although they closed in the latter quarter of the 1900s. The National Castings Division of Midland Ross in Sharon designed and produced cast-steel coupling devices and other heavy railroad equipment parts. One of its products was even known as the "Sharon coupler," named for the city where it originated. The Sharon Works of Westinghouse Electric Corporation produced transformers of all sizes and supplied power equipment for electric locomotives, an application that the firm's founder, George Westinghouse, had pioneered in the 1890s.

Despite vastly reduced infrastructure, the railroads of Mercer County continue to be vital to the local economy.

Athletes and musicians continued to refine their respective activities during the 1970s. The band and choral departments both gave their usual splendid performances under Ray McCallister's direction. Lakeview's athletics department continued its tradition of hard work. Lakeview continued to expand throughout the 1970s with the addition of a girls' basketball team in 1973, a boys' cross-country team in 1974, and a girls' track team in 1977. Despite the expansion, only two championships were won during the 1970s. Not until 1978, after Lakeview left the Tri-County Athletic League and joined the French Creek Valley Conference (FCVC), did another title come. Finishing the decade in 1979, the girls' track team won the Mercer County Athletic Conference (MCAC) Championship. The girls' basketball team won the first district championship of any Lakeview team.

In the 1980s, Lakeview School District again faced major construction challenges with several additions and modifications. The former Stoneboro high school and the Gilmore building in Sandy Lake were still being used as elementary classrooms. Time had taken its toll on both buildings, and they needed major repairs. Also, the high school needed to be expanded. The decision was made to add a middle school facility onto the existing high school. An area, which was once a breezeway, was enclosed and made into a hallway containing more classrooms, a second story was added over this area, and several other small additions were made. This area of the building was then used to house the high school, while the middle school moved into the area formerly occupied by the high school. Oakview Elementary also received three more classrooms, a new gymnasium, and a special education room. These renovations were completed in 1981.

These renovations were done under the leadership of Samuel Wilson, superintendent, Bruce Rice, high school principal, and David Alexander, elementary principal. With the completion of the renovations, another administrator was needed for the middle school. Fred McConnell was hired to fill this position, which he still holds now. All four men played a key role in determining the structure of the district today.

Both the high school and the elementary building lost their principals during this time period as a result of retirements. Alexander had filled the elementary position for so long that the affects of his direction are still being felt at Oakview now. Rose Stellman, the district's first and, to date, only female principal, was hired to fill the position. William Carlson was hired to assume Rice's position upon his retirement.

Throughout the 1980s, McCallister was still bringing out the best in his music students. "Mr. Mac," as he became known, was one of the most effective musical directors the high school music program has ever had. Many of his former students still believe that, although he was stern, his bands were the best they could possibly be due to his dedication and commitment.

As for athletics, the only new sport of the 1980s was girls' volleyball, which debuted in 1986. However, the decade was by far the most notable for championships. The girls' track team won seven MCAC titles, three district championships, and a 14th place finish at the state track meet. The Lakeview matmen took the conference six consecutive years, two sectional team championships, and one District 10 championship. The girls' basketball team contributed nine titles, including five FCVC Championships, one FCVC Co-Championship, two District 10 Championships, and a PIAA Western Championship. The girls' cross-country team won five cross-country championships. The boys' football team won two titles, but the most notable event was the addition of lights to the football field in 1989. On the diamond, the baseball team won the conference in 1985.

Three of Lakeview's five state champions to date came out of this decade: Virginia Wilson, discus in 1982; Rodney Wright, wrestling in 1985, 1986, and 1987; and Brenda Bindas, high jump in 1989.

ALLIED NEWS
By Teresa Spatara

In June 1971, Allied Newspapers was purchased by Ottaway Newspapers, a wholly owned subsidiary of Dow Jones & Company, when that group purchased Sharon Herald Co. for $4.5 million. Now, the Grove City area paper is known as the *Allied News*, a combination of four hometown newspapers: *Grove City Reporter-Herald*, *Sandy Lake Breeze*, *Slippery Rock Signal*, and *Mercer Dispatch*.

While the *Mercer Dispatch* was dominating the news in central and eastern Mercer County in the mid-1800s, Pine Grove (now Grove City) did not have a newspaper. However, the *Mercer Dispatch* took note of some of the events occurring there. On December 30, 1870, the *Dispatch* wrote about construction of the bridge at the Lower Dam in Pine Grove, saying that "as well as improving the area's appearance, the new bridge facilitates crossing the river." The bridge at the Upper Dam in Slabtown (now the area around North Street) was erected later. On December 1, 1871, the *Dispatch* touted the newly built railroad's quest for business and its effect on Grove City: "The Shenango and Allegheny Railroad between Pardoe's Station and Pine Grove is ready for the track, one mile already placed, and four miles mostly completed and ready for ties, seeking to haul Pardoe's coal to Pine Grove."

At about this period, Grove City saw the advent of its own newspaper, *The Pine Grove Telephone*. The *Telephone* began at Karns City in Butler County when that town was at its height as an oil town. J. Borland started it in the interest of the Greenback Labor party. But he did not get the support he wanted, so he changed it in 1881 to an independent journal and added a column to each page. Karns City was having economic problems as the oil excitement waned, so Borland looked for a new home for his paper. He decided on Pine Grove because it was doing much better economically as a community. The first copy of the *Pine Grove Telephone* appeared in 1882. M. W. Moore came with Borland as foreman of the new paper. The *Telephone* was well received in the community and began to prosper.

The *Telephone* continued to operate with few changes under Borland's management until 1884, when A. C. Ray, editor of the *Mercer Dispatch*, bought a half interest. Two weeks later he bought the other half and immediately transferred it to A. A. Little (Millbrook) who still held his interest in 1907.

At that time the *Telephone* was housed in the office of the Union Heat and Light Company. In 1885 the paper was moved to the upper rooms of W. A. Young's harness store at the corner of Broad and Pine Streets. Also in 1885, Little bought Ray's interest in the *Telephone* and transferred it to Maggie C. Moore, who was represented in business by her husband. He brought into the *Telephone* office his job printing business, which he had at Sandy Lake before joining the Grove City enterprise.

Little did the editorial work for the *Telephone* from 1887 until 1891 when he sold his interest to M. A. Lowman who published the paper with Moore until December 1892. At that time, the Mercer County sheriff shut down the paper for nonpayment of debts. Publication was suspended for almost a month until C. F. Lawrence bought Lowman's share of the paper. He and Moore paid off the debts and resumed publication in 1893. In 1894 Lawrence bought out Moore and, with his son, Harry W., published the eight-page paper as the *Grove City Reporter* until 1912.

H. K. Daugherty bought the paper from Lawrence in 1912 and later sold it to J. B. Robinson, Sr. (Jamestown), who operated it until his death in 1922. Then, E. R. Robinson operated the *Grove City Reporter* as business manager with J. B. Robinson, Jr. as editor.

During that time, the *Grove City Reporter* was a stereotype of the small town press. The July 19, 1917, issue carried the serialized fiction, "I'll Come Back to You," complete with illustrations, written by Larry Evan. Pages 6 and 7 carried the stereotype news of World War. But the paper was devoting more and more space to local news. Page 1 featured a story on Company M being honor guests of Sharon Chamber of Commerce. But it also carried five obituaries at the top of the page, a poem that was a tribute to "Our Soldiers" for the Red Cross, two weddings, and a farewell party. Inside pages carried news columns from Clintonville, Fairview, and Liberty, news from the courthouse under the heading "Court House Town," and, for whatever reason, a complete financial statement from Grove City Creamery, including salaries of named employees.

The masthead listed J. B. Robinson as editor and publisher, E. F. Robinson as assistant manager, J. B. Robinson, Jr. as assistant editor, and E. W. Cross as superintendent of printing. It boasted that the paper "covers Mercer County like a blanket" and ran several columns of personal notes, such as "Florence Payne of Mobile Street visited in the home of Jerry and Jennie Jabins last week." It ran classifieds, three lines in three columns three times for fifty cents, but advised, "Don't ask to have it charged. We keep no book accounts of these columns."

Although the *Grove City Reporter* was the major newspaper of the borough at that time, Grove City's early history records two competing newspapers, both of which went out of existence after 1917. Robert D. "Dick" Young published both on a foot-pedal-powered press in a loft above Monroe's Drug Store at the corner of Broad and Main Streets. Young edited and printed *The Occasional*, true to its name—occasionally—spiced with cracker-barrel philosophy. His first edition, published in the spring of 1891, went so far as listing the town's most eligible bachelors. In 1905, Young bought an electric printing press described as "the size of two rooms." He composed as he set all the 10-point type by hand. Operating the press one day a week, he hand-fed sheets four times the size of the newspaper into the flatbed press, that is, a press with type lying flat and the paper rolling over it. (Now the paper is in rolls and the type rolls over it.) Helping Young in setting the type, running the press, folding and distributing the paper were his wife and four children, among them Edward M. Young (later state legislator and mayor of Grove City).

Young published his other paper, *The Outlook*, a weekly, from 1905 to 1907 for some one thousand subscribers. This newspaper was not a political organ. *The Outlook*'s six pages contained national and some blunt local news. Back then, newspapers did not worry about libel lawsuits that they do now. Young "wrote them up" as he saw them. He wrote about a local man who refused to remove his hat when the band played "The Star Spangled Banner," calling him an "old skinflint who, through the mercy of God and a long-suffering public has managed to eke out an existence."

The demise of Young's two papers may have accounted for some changes in the *Grove City Reporter*. In 1920 the paper, which had been a weekly published on Fridays, became a semi-weekly, published on Tuesdays and Fridays. In one issue that year, the *Reporter* touted itself as "the official paper of Grove City" and listed at the top right of Page 1 that it was "seeking better schools and improved roads." Cost of a subscription was $2 annually. It was published by Robinson Print Shop in the Craig Building on Broad Street. The paper was still running display ads on its front page, including one advertising shoes from Montgomery & Sons at $12 a pair. Ads inside gave prices of the Hupmobile as $1,335 for touring or roadster, $2,210 for a coupe and $2,260 for a sedan. Its big news story was that the new Grove City Hospital on Hillcrest Circle would be dedicated November 11.

However "official" the *Grove City Reporter* may have considered itself, the borough also had the *Grove City Herald*, also an eight-page paper, which had originated in 1903 as the *Mercer County Herald*, published by the Moore Brothers. Reverend A. P. Hutchison edited the paper as a prohibition weekly. R. P. Allen succeeded Hutchinson as editor and continued until the Eighteenth Amendment was passed in 1919. Then a company consisting of Dr. C. A. Platt, Ormond Dean, G. G. Forquer, and Howard Archer bought the paper and kept it until 1922 when they sold it to J. P. and Edgar S. "Ted" Hassler who changed the name to the *Grove City Herald*.

In May 1926, the *Reporter* merged with the *Grove City Herald*. An issue of the merged papers as *Grove City Reporter-Herald* listed E. S. Hassler as publisher, Floyd McClymonds as editor, and J. M. McDonald as advertising manager. This edition had dropped the weekly romantic serial and the heavy, stereotyped world and national news and concentrated primarily on local news. A feature that appeared under the masthead was a one-column box listing Grove City's needs, for example, wider RFD (rural free mail delivery) coverage, municipal advertising, new industries, municipal beautification, a jun-

GROVE CITY AIRPORT

By Richard Christner

The Grove City Municipal Airport, located west of Grove City on Oakley Kelly Drive in Springfield Township, is a full-service airport for small planes. The airport was built on land donated by Mr. and Mrs. Walter J. O'Connor. Although already in operation for several years, the airport was formally dedicated in 1975 before a crowd of eight hundred. The fixed-base operator at that time was Beaver Aviation Service, Inc., succeeded by Wings, Inc.; Corporate Wings; Quality Aviation, Inc.; and Silent Wings Soaring, the present operator and lessee of the property from the Borough of Grove City.

(The facility now includes two hangers with space for twenty-five planes, an administration building, and one paved runway 4,500 feet long by 75 feet wide. Silent Wings Soaring, owned by Steve Rhule and Doug Thomas, provides a number of services for users of the airport: hanger rentals, a mechanics shop with inspection service, flight instruction with three FAA-certified instructors, antique and classic aircraft fabric restoration, gasoline sales, western Pennsylvania's only gliding operation, and limited plane rides particularly during the airport's annual fly-in and car cruise event with breakfast provided by the Springfield Volunteer Firemen Association. Of interest in the administration building and large hanger are over thirty miniature model airplanes and seventeen paintings of airport-based or famous airplanes, all crafted or painted by Buzz Winder.)

---

ior high school, resurfacing of the Mercer-Grove City road, a parent-teacher association, four hundred commercial club members, widening Broad Street and removing poles and wires, a community house with recreational facilities, and a municipal airport.

With this merger in 1926, Allied Newspapers began. The paper had moved from its Broad and Pine Streets location to South Broad Street. It moved again in the late 1940 to North Broad Street, and now is located on Erie Street. A large window at the front of the room, facing the sidewalk, allowed passers-by to watch the skilled operators.

During the ensuing years, Hassler bought the *Mercer Dispatch*, *Sandy Lake Breeze*, and *Slippery Rock Signal*.

Other than what is known about the *Sandy Lake News* and the *Lake Local*, which were published in the late 1800s, the progression of the Sandy Lake and Stoneboro newspapers is sketchy after that time, but Glenn R. Scofield was honored by his wife at a dinner in 1952, at the Sandy Lake Hotel, on the occasion of his fiftieth anniversary in newspaper work. What is known is that Scofield founded the *Sandy Lake Breeze*, possibly as an offshoot of one of the early papers, and operated it himself for many years. He had drawers full of type which he hand set. He gathered the news, sold the advertising, wrote the articles, and put the paper together himself. Hassler bought the *Sandy Lake Breeze* from Scofield in 1945.

In 1946, Hassler bought the fourth paper in his chain, *The Slippery Rock Signal*.

After he acquired these weeklies, Hassler decided that four papers could be printed on one press in a central location instead of on four different presses. The Grove City office became that central location. However, the *Mercer Dispatch* retained its offices for news and job printing. The *Sandy Lake Breeze* still had an office on the main street where Scofield typed the news and ads and sent them to Grove City to be set in type. In Slippery Rock, the publisher hired a reporter who gathered news and sent it to the Grove City office. Grove City's advertising staffers went to each of these communities weekly to sell advertising.

Hassler later gave up his position as both editor and publisher to devote himself to his role as publisher. He had Floyd McClymonds as editor for many years. McClymonds' front-page column, "As We See It," was extremely popular. It was taken over by Hassler after McClymonds left the paper.

A devastating fire in 1958 destroyed all five of Hassler's linotypes, in addition to a Ludlow typesetter, the composing room tables, the paper's first press and valuable records and newspapers which dated back to 1870. Loss was estimated at $100,000 to equipment and $20,000 to $30,000 to the building. But Hassler had the very next issue of his paper on the streets a couple of days later with the help of publishers of other newspapers. The news and business offices had only smoke damage.

Hassler continued to publish the four papers as the county became less agriculturally oriented. As the population grew, so did retail stores with more advertising and a better financial situation for the paper. Women now were taking their place with men as advertising managers, editors, and publishers. No more would they be confined to writing only stories of teas and weddings and doing the bookkeeping. In the late 1950s, he had an all-woman staff, including editor, advertising manager, reporters, business managers, and correspondents.

Hassler was owner and publisher of Allied Newspapers for forty-three years, more than any other owner, and had worked for the papers for many years before that. The *Pennsylvania Newspaper Publishers Association Bulletin* in 1953 noted that Hassler was a "builder of weekly newspapers, journalism instructor, and outstanding civic leader."

In 1965, Hassler sold his four papers to the Sharon Herald Publishing Company, but remained with the company as a consultant until his death in 1968. With the change in ownership of Allied Newspapers, came many changes in the papers. They were combined into one paper called *Allied News*, which is now published on Wednesdays.

HERMIT OF INDIAN RUN
By Ruth Woods

In 1973, Alma Carmichael, the "Hermit of Indian Run," died of cancer, having spent sixty-two years trapped in her world of fear and distrust.

The Carmichael family rented an old frame home on Rodgers Road in East Lackawannock Township, having moved from the Sheakleyville area around 1927. The father Orville was a skilled blacksmith who modestly supported his family in his shop behind the house. He had two sons and a daughter, Alma. When his sons were of school age, they received the required smallpox vaccinations from which one son had a severe reaction and died. Grieving, Mrs. Carmichael resolved never to let her daughter Alma suffer a similar fate. Thus, she kept Alma out of public school, claiming she was not bright. Educated at home, Alma, however, quickly mastered reading, writing, and skills in rug-making and wood-carving. The one thing Alma learned best was to fear people. She hid behind her mother's skirts when shopping at the country store. If anyone visited the Carmichael home, Alma darted out of sight. She was rarely heard to speak; and when she did, her voice was hushed and low.

When Alma was sixteen, her mother died, and Alma's world was void of all she trusted. She sealed herself off in an upstairs room. The father, by then an alcoholic, occupied the first floor. Seldom sober, he rarely saw his daughter. Sleeping by day, Alma would

JOHNNY OAKES

By Gail Habbyshaw

In the mid-1970s, 18-year-old accomplished musician Johnny Oakes (Mercer) met Frankie Yankovic at Stroussmeyer's Picnic Grounds near Vienna, Ohio. "Somebody introduced me to Frankie and I got to perform with him. He let me play his accordion," Oakes recalled. In 1978, Yankovic asked Oakes to became a regular on his TV show "Polka Varieties," which was produced at WEWS in Cleveland, Ohio, and broadcast weekly to a nationwide audience. He remained with the show until 1981. The two were good friends and kept in touch until Yankovic's death in 1998.

Oakes also had the opportunity to meet Myron Floren in 1989 when Floren was a headliner at an event at Westminster College (New Wilmington). "We started to correspond and have kept in touch ever since," said Oakes, who grew up watching Floren on the Lawrence Welk Show.

As a professional full-time freelance musician, Oakes works whenever he has gigs. Since he is hired to provide entertainment at over two hundred functions yearly, such as for weddings, reunions, receptions, churches, fairs, festivals, bazaars, nursing homes, and senior citizen centers, he keeps busy. In addition, his many fans in western Pennsylvania can hear Oakes's annual warm-up performance for the Mercer Community Band and all of his four albums, which are frequently played on the Youngstown area radio stations.

hunt and trap for food by night, unseen and unmolested. Her rifle seldom missed its mark. She foraged the fields nearby for grain, which she ground in an old coffee grinder. Her stove was a rusty oil drum set in her room with the smoke pipe curving out of a broken window. The once cozy home deteriorated from a lack of repair. Rain leaked into Alma's room until she wired a spout from the ceiling to drain the rain out of the broken window.

When her father died in 1943, Alma refused to attend his funeral. For protection from intruders, Alma had devised a prop that dropped into place when she closed the door to her room, anchoring the door firmly against outside forces. She received some supplies from her brother Earl, who lived near Leesburg. Also, the owners of the Carmichael property, Brant and Zella Cooper, charged her no rent and would occasionally place boxes of food on her porch. Later, they would drive past and note that the boxes were gone, assuring them that she was still alive.

During the severe winter of 1944, the neighbors became concerned for Alma's survival in the bitter cold. Brant Cooper notified Mercer County detective A.C. Barnes and members of the state police of her plight. Together, they went to the Carmichael home. Cooper shouted to let Alma know who was there. Curious of her uniformed visitors, Alma warily stepped out of her room to see them, dislodging the inside prop that slammed the door shut behind her, locking the 33-year-old hermit out of her sanctuary. Approaching her gently, the rescuers assured Alma that she would not be harmed. She was wearing men's ragged clothes, her legs were wrapped in newspaper, and her feet were bound in rags for warmth. Her hair was tightly matted. She shook her head vigorously at being led away, yet offered no physical resistance.

Alma was moved to the county jail, where she refused to eat on the first day and was unable to sleep at night. However, Alma was cleaned up, given proper clothing, and appeared to be more comfortable.

For years before Alma's exit from the Carmichael home, neighbors had reported various tools and articles missing, many of which were discovered in Alma's home. Also recovered were two pulpit Bibles lifted from the White Chapel Church, and another Bible taken from Indian Run Grange. Although she was arrested for larceny, charges against Alma were dropped, and she was placed in the Mercer County Home. There she roomed alone for twenty-nine years, remaining aloof and making no friends, except for the carefully tended guppies and window plants given to her by the nursing staff. She was taught to work in the laundry and iron clothes. She ironed willingly for many years; however, she said that ironing "just wears the clothes out for nothing."

Conrail
By Frederick Houser

As railroad freight traffic also declined through the middle of the 1900s, in the face of expanding interstate highways and rising costs, the financial health of both the Pennsylvania and the New York Central Railroads led them to seek cost savings through a merger. "Salvation through merger" was not to be, however, and the newly formed Penn Central Transportation Company was bankrupt in just over two years. In 1972, the Penn Central and Erie Lackawanna Railroads were still handling 53,629 annual car loads (an average of 147 loads per day) of local freight traffic to and from Farrell, Sharon, and Sharpsville. The majority of this volume was iron ore for the Sharon Steel furnaces along the Shenango River. During this period, both railroads also handled even greater through traffic on trains that merely crossed Mercer County en route to distant destinations.

The final blow for the Erie Lackawanna came in June 1972 when Hurricane Agnes caused millions of dollars of damage to the main line in part of New York. The company entered bankruptcy later that month and was never successful in reorganizing as an ongoing enterprise.

In 1976, the Penn Central and Erie Lackawanna were folded into Consolidated Rail Corporation (Conrail), along with several other bankrupt northeast railroads. Soon after, the Erie & Pittsburgh Railroad was finally dissolved. The Erie & Pittsburgh had survived as a separate corporation since its 1870 takeover by the Pennsylvania Railroad.

Conrail gradually diverted nearly all through freight trains from the former Erie Lackawanna route and downgraded it to primarily local service. Most of the line west from Youngstown to Chicago was abandoned. The main line trackage between Orangeville and Pymatuning Junction was taken out of service the day after Christmas 1980, not long after the old Erie Railroad's New Castle Branch had also carried its last train. Conrail abandoned the Erie & Pennsylvania between Jamestown and Sharpsville, and from Wheatland to the county's southern border in 1981.

(In 1999, Conrail's assets were divided between the two major trunk lines that now dominate the eastern United States: Norfolk Southern and CSX Transportation. The surviving 5.6 miles of line between Wheatland and Sharpsville continues to serve local industry and became part of the Norfolk Southern Railway. The surviving line of the old Atlantic & Great Western Railroad from Hubbard through Sharon and Greenville to Meadville also became part of Norfolk Southern.)

The double-track mainline of former Pennsylvania Railroad's Erie & Pittsburgh line south of Wheatland had been reduced to one track by 1973. However, huge structures like this three-span truss bridge over the Shenango River were still part of the fixed facilities of Pennsylvania Railroad's successor, Penn Central Railroad. The southbound freight train pictured was headed for New Castle on former northbound track. By 1976, this track was part of Conrail and soon abandoned. (Photo: Vinson Skibo; caption: Frederick Houser)

Coal had come to constitute virtually all of the traffic moving on Conrail's route through Stoneboro by the early 1980s. Only a few thousand carloads annually were being handled by the unit trains as nearby mines closed. The figure was down from over 20,000 loads annually only a decade earlier and from 50,000 yearly during World War II. The last unit train ran in early 1988 after which time the line was abandoned. (Contributor: Frederick Houser)

460

A train wreck between Osgood and Greenville in the 1970s. (Contributor: Richard Sherbondy)

Reverend A. M. Keiffer served Zion's German Reformed Church of West Greenville (now Greenville) for ten years around the beginning of the 1900s. He retired from that post to become superintendent of St. Paul's Orphan's Home, an institution, complete with farm, school, and chapel, which had been built by the Reformed Church to accept orphan children of Civil War soldiers. During Keiffer's tenure, Zion's Church bonded firmly with St. Paul. Men and women spent many hours working in the gardens and orchards, canning fruits and vegetables, and tending the hogs and cattle raised on the farm. It continued as an orphanage in the ensuing years, but since 1967, the home at St. Paul has developed into a large campus with focus on the older generation. It closed out the children's services in 1972. Still under the auspices of the church, now the United Church of Christ, the facility includes a colony of private homes; the Ridgewood, for supervised living in separate apartments; and a 250-bed extended-care and skilled-nursing unit. Although the ties with Zion's congregation are strong, the home is open to every race, creed, and religion. (Aerials: **The Herald***; caption: Gwen Lininger and Janet Hills)*

The Helen Black Miller Memorial Chapel, formerly Grace Episcopal and later Saint Edmund's Martyr Episcopal Church, is now nondenominational. Built about 1884, the church was originally on Venango Street. It was purchased by the Mercer County Historical Society and moved next door to the society's office and museum on South Pitt Street. The restored church (pictured, in 2000) contains the original pews with doors. It was dedicated in 1973 as a memorial to Mrs. Miller (pictured), a local musician and vocalist. The church is used for weddings and other special services. Anna Lydia Black Bass (Helen's cousin) visited the chapel when she was ninety years old in 1998. She lived next to Saint Edmund's as a young girl. Her family could hear the music from the church in their home. She remembers playing in the church with the pastor's daughter when they were about ten years old. (Chapel photographer: Marilyn Dewald; caption: 1998 interview with Bass)

The McClain Print Shop (Mercer), which once set ads for the Saturday Evening Post, was owned by Squire T. W. McClain and later by his son T. W. McClain, Jr. (pictured, about 1931). The younger McClain operated the business until his death in 1965. Donated by the McClain family to the Mercer County Historical Society in 1973, the print shop was moved from its original location on South Diamond Street to the backyard of the society. The building (pictured, in 2000) has been restored, and some of its equipment put back into working order. (Photographer in 2000: Marilyn Dewald)

The original Ebenezer Presbyterian Church was built in the village of Centertown (Wolf Creek Township) in 1893. It was not large enough to support a minister so it was linked with two other churches in the community. The officers of the church were elders and trustees. When a man was elected elder, he served for life. The songbook of the early church was the Psalter. At one time in the early 1900s, some of the younger members persuaded the elders to buy some Bible songbooks. When those books were used, some of the members would not sing. In addition to an active children's program, the church also has had ladies' Bible classes, men's Bible classes, and classes for young married couples. About 1937, the church needed more room so the building was jacked up and a basement was dug out by hand. A well was drilled, and a kitchen and more Sunday school rooms were added. In 1958, the church was completely destroyed by fire. The congregation accepted the Springfield Church's invitation to worship with them and use their facilities while Ebenezer was being rebuilt. However, the Presbytery refused to approve financing for a new building at the original site and recommended the church move to a larger site near a major highway, which would give the church more potential for growth. The new building was constructed on Scrubgrass Road just east of Route 173 on land donated by Mr. and Mrs. Robert Ferguson. The first event in the new church was the 1959 Christmas party. Flooring, pews, and furniture were installed in January and February, and the new church was dedicated on March 6, 1960. An addition with a fellowship hall and Sunday school rooms was added in 1974 (pictured, in 2000). The church had good ministers, including Reverend H. Walter White who has served Ebenezer Church since 1989. (Photographer: Vonda Minner; caption: Ellsworth and Raymond Jamison)

In 1974 Fisher Field was dedicated not only as a ball field, but also as a testament to one man's vision. Enos Fisher had the notion that the area needed a softball field. With the blessing but no funds from the township supervisors, he solicited contributions from county businesses and almost single-handedly turned a briar patch into the field named after him. As a result, next to the Otter Creek Municipal Building, a large grass area now includes a backstop, four poles, benches, bases, and a pitching rubber, used mostly by the local church softball league. (Contributor: Joyce Young)

On August 26–27, 1975, the first Ag Progress Days were held on the McDowell Farms, Route 62, Mercer. The hosts were Mr. and Mrs. John McDowell, Sr.; Mr. and Mrs. John McDowell, Jr.; and Mr. and Mrs. Robert McDowell. (Contributors: the McDowells)

Jesus '78 was the third and last evangelical festival of this magnitude held on the Ralph Watson Farm (East Lackawannock Township). Approximately 45,000 attended the three-day event. Many of the featured performers had appeared at the second event, Jesus '76 (pictured). In addition, Princess Shining Star (Pam Thum) performed with Big Bird and Yogi Bear to appeal to the children in the audience. This interdenominational event had its inception in 1970 when a group of Mennonite youth in Morgantown, West Virginia, wondered why the Woodstock concert could not have a Christian alternative. The first "Jesus" concert was held on a potato farm near Morgantown in 1973, attracting 15,000. Meanwhile, in 1972, Ralph Watson had a vision: Looking out the kitchen window at his fields, he saw "thousands of people gathered to worship the Lord." Within two years, and much hard work and planning, Watson and many volunteers held the first event, Jesus '74. (Contributor: Ruth Woods)

Three of the many businesses with floats in Grove City's 1976 National Bicentennial parade were George J. Howe Company, promoting prices for its brand name "Daily Delight" from its early years in the 1920s; Cooper Brothers, offering concrete products (now under the name of R. W. Sidley Inc.); and General Electric, hauling one of the large turbines produced at its local plant. (Contributor: Grove City Community Library)

The current jail complex was opened in 1976, but it was too small from the start. The original population, including one female, was twenty-four inmates and twelve work release prisoners. The cells contained double bunks. In 1990, the jail was expanded when new housing was built in the old yard and a new yard was added (pictured, in 2000). Now, the complex can hold up to 114 inmates, including women. (Photographer: Marilyn Dewald; caption: Jeff Gill)

"I will never forget the snow that hit in February 1977. The radio was on most of the day giving the weather report about how bad it was getting. I wondered whether my husband would be able to make it home from work at Mercer. He called before leaving and said, 'If I'm not home in the next hour and a half, send the boys after me on the snowmobiles.' Without taking any side roads, he made it only as far as Henry Road, where he had to leave the car. He walked home, changed his clothes, and rode to the township building on a snowmobile. Otter Creek Township had two trucks and a grader at the time, and they were all out on the roads. As soon as Henry Road was opened, my husband brought the car home. Men in the township worked around the clock trying to keep the roads open; but it kept snowing hard, and the wind was so strong that they just couldn't keep ahead of the drifting. Our son Tom went out during the night with the backhoe and was working on making a path down Babcock Road. He said he had gone some distance when he turned and looked behind him. 'I couldn't even see where I had been. It was frightening.' The following day the weather broke, but the radio was still calling for more snow with high winds. My husband called from a neighbor to inform me that Baker Road was now open. If I needed bread or milk, now was the time to get it and get right back home because the break in the weather wouldn't last long. Sure enough, we were hit again. The township then received special funding for large equipment to come in and help clear the roads. After several days, we went through the township taking pictures. It was hard to believe how high the snow was piled up along the roads, for example, at the intersection of Donation and Mack roads (pictured)." (Contributor: Joyce Young)

David and Gene McDowell (Otter Creek Township) raised prize-winning Cheviot sheep in their barn (pictured, in 1976). Suddenly, in July 1977, the barn caught fire, and people rushed to the scene to rescue the sheep and watch the destructive blaze. A timing device is believed to have been used to set the fire, which was one of several barn burnings at that time. The McDowell Farm (pictured, in 1990s) survived the tragedy fortunately. (Contributor: Joyce Young)

Discovered in 1977 beneath the veneer of an East State Street house being razed in Hermitage was a log cabin dating back to the early 1800s. The Mercer County Historical Society restored the cabin with the help of Bob Bechtol and Neil Snyder under the supervision of Frederick Raisch, a director of the society. The cabin was eventually relocated to a ledge on the slope overlooking the Pierce Lock in Sharpsville. The Frederick Raisch Log Cabin (pictured, in 2000) is now open to visitors. (Photographer: Marilyn Dewald)

Opened in 1978, the State Regional Correctional Facility (Findley Township) is an open campus setting on 304 acres, thirty-seven of which constitute the main compound enclosed in a twelve-foot-high fence. Inside the main compound, the housing for the all-male inmate population consists of fourteen units (four modular dormitory, three traditional cellblocks, six campus living units, and one maximum security restricted unit). The other buildings are used for administration, medical and food services, chaplaincy, education, vocation, industry, parole, and psychology. Although designed to hold 579 inmates, the average number of inmates exceeds that capacity due to overcrowding throughout the state correctional system. Built as part of a 1971 Pennsylvania Department of Corrections plan to establish community corrections centers, this facility is the only such center still operating and serves twenty-three counties, including Mercer. (Contributor: Gilbert Walters)

Timeline 1971—1980

The World

1971 "Happy Face" buttons debut selling 20 million; the voting age is lowered to 18

1972 The Watergate break-in occurs; American troops leave Vietnam; the Nixon Administration eliminates the $104 million school milk program

1973 The US Supreme Court rules in favor of a woman's right to personal privacy in the Rowe vs. Wade decision; Oil Embargo causes long gas lines; many US POWs come home; Billy Jean King defeats Bobby Riggs

1974 Nixon resigns and Ford becomes the 38th president; Patty Hearst is kidnapped; Hank Aaron exceeds Babe Ruth's record; "streaking" is popular

1975 The first episode of Saturday Night Live airs

1976 America celebrates its 200th birthday; Legionnaires Disease kills 166; Apple Computers is founded with $1,300

1977 The New York City black-out occurs; Elvis dies; Jimmy Carter becomes 39th president

1978 First class postage rate increases to $.15; mass suicide/murder results in the death of 918 at the People's Temple in Jonestown, Guyana (South America); the Unabomber sends the first bomb

1979 63 Americans are taken hostage in the American Embassy in Iran; Three Mile Island experiences a meltdown; the Pope makes his first visit to the United States

1980 The population of the United States is 227,224,681; Mt. St. Helens erupts; John Lennon is assassinated; Cuban refugees arrive in Florida

Mercer County

1971 "Flameless cooking" or the electric stove is introduced; Citizen Band Radio operators organize 3 local member clubs; Jefferson Township increases road tax and gives laborers a $.25 wage hike to $2.25 per hour; the Pennsylvania Crime Commission awards a federal grant of $16,800 to the county for crime-fighting funds; Lake Wilhelm is formed

1972 Westinghouse employs more than 5,000; residents can no longer be committed under a civil petition to a mental institution without a hearing; construction of the Mercer County Vo-Tech Center (now Mercer County Career Center) is on schedule; Sharon police end "sick-out"

1975 The Buhl Mansion is put up for sale; Art Linkletter visits the county for Head Start's 10th anniversary

1976 Hickory Township becomes the Municipality of Hermitage (the change is supported by 93 percent of the voters); Fredonia holds a Bicentennial Ball for the county to celebrate the nation's 200th birthday and Fredonia's 100th birthday; current county jail opens

1978 State Regional Correctional Facility opens in Findley Township

1980 Sharon's Connelly Manor is built; manufacturers employ about 16,600 workers in the county

Timeline 1981—1990

The World

1981 The Iranian hostage crisis ends; the disease known as AIDS is identified; Reagan takes office as the 40th President and survives an assassin's bullet; the first test-tube baby is born; Personal Computers (PC) are named "Machine of the Year"

1982 Unemployment tops 10%; John Belushi is found dead; National Football League (NFL) is on strike; the first permanent artificial heart implant is used

1983 The US Embassy in Lebanon is bombed

1984 David (the Bubble Boy) dies at age 12; PG-13 ratings begin; first class postage rates increase to $.22; the Macintosh Computer is introduced

1986 The US Space Shuttle Challenger explodes 74 seconds after take-off killing seven crew members; Coke goes Classic; the Chernobyl disaster occurs

1987 Evangelist Jim Bakker resigns from the PTL Club; Oliver North testifies at Iran-contra scandal; Black Monday, the largest stock-market drop in Wall Street history, occurs; 18-month-old Jessica McClure is rescued from the well

1989 George Bush becomes 41st president; stand-off in Tiananmen Square in China occurs; the Berlin Wall is torn down; the Exxon Valdez oil spill occurs

1990 The population of the United States is 249,438,712; Nelson Mandela is released from prison

Mercer County

1981 The Columbia Theater in Sharon is closed following a fire; Conrail abandons most of its trackage in the county

1982 Midland Ross Corporation abandons its National Castings foundry in Sharon; the Chicago Bridge & Iron and Greenville Steel Car (predecessor to Trinity) close in Greenville

1983 The Medical Society of Mercer meet at the Temperance Hotel in Mercer; the Vietnam War Memorial is dedicated in the courthouse square (Gen. William C. Westmoreland is the main speaker)

1984 Tony Butala of the Lettermans, places the highet bid of $10,500 and purchases the Columbia Theatre in Sharon

1985 Operations cease at Westinghouse's Transformer Plant in Sharon; a tornado destroys Wheatland (99% of industry)

1986 Sawhill Tubular Division purchases land from Westinghouse Electric Corporation; Sharon General Hospital opens Laser Surgery Center

1987 Sharon Steel files Chapter 11 bankruptcy; the area's mill jobs dwindle to about 8,500; the Historical Society relinquishes lease on the Porter School

1988 Chairman and CEO of Sharon Steel, Victor Posner, avoids prison when sentenced for tax evasion to spend $3 million to help the homeless; The Winner is founded and The Club is invented

1990 The county's population is 121,003; the creation of a new healthcare concept, Sharon Regional Health System, is announced; *The Herald* publishes the first Sunday edition; the local Army Reserve units are called to active duty in the Persian Gulf War

In the 1980s, pipelines were added to dairy barns, and they made the milking process much more efficient. The milk could go right from the cow into a bulk tank, and farmers could milk up to one hundred cows. (Contributor: Vonda Minner)

General James Pierce, a prominent Sharpsville businessman, and his wife Chloe were Universalists. When Pierce died in 1874, he was providing funds to build a church of that faith along Mercer Avenue in Sharpsville. The church (pictured, about 1900) was finished in 1882 at a cost $16,000. In 1884, Pierce's widow donated to the church an organ, which was imported from Baltimore and cost $40,000. The last Universalist service held in the church was in 1935, when a handful of worshippers heard Reverend G. A. Gay of Girard. From 1920 to that time, only two or three services had been held. Meanwhile, the Seventh-Day Adventists had been organized with twelve charter members in 1918 under the direction of Reverend B. F. Keeland. They met in Sharon in Carver Hall at first, and between 1928 and 1944 the meetings were held in the Welch Baptist Church and Congregational Church. During the early 1940s, membership increased steadily. By 1945, the church was meeting in Sharon's Odd Fellows Hall. Needing a place to call home, they bought the vacant Universalist Church in Sharpsville. In 1966, the Seventh-Day Adventist School opened in a former one-room school on property purchased from the James Downing estate. Ten students were in the first class, and the church had ninety-two members. A number of pastors have served this congregation over the years. In 1982, the Seventh-Day Adventist Church celebrated the centennial of its beautiful church building. Barbara Bush was an honored guest. Wife of the then U.S. Vice President Bush, she is also the great-great-granddaughter of the Pierces who were so instrumental in building this church. The Seventh-Day Adventists continued to use the church building until just recently, when they decided they wanted to build a new church. In March 2000, the Sharpsville Historical Society bought the church for $60,000 to serve as the society's headquarters. The borough helped the purchase along in the interest of preserving the landmark building and organ. (Photo: Vinson Skibo; caption: Mairy Jayn Woge and Seventh-Day Adventist Church)

One of Mercer County's few octagon barns (pictured, in 1981) was near the Boy Scout camp by Milledgeville (French Creek Township). (Contributor: Vonda Minner)

In 1982, a humble and enthusiastic group of thirty-four persons became an official congregation in the Evangelical Congregational Church. They bought a lot near Transfer overlooking the Shenango Reservoir and started a building fund. After worshipping for two months in either Holiday or Sheridan Inn, they put up a picnic shelter and used it for the summer months. After bringing lawn chairs each week for a while, each member agreed to buy his or her own chair, and in short order they had 150 new padded chairs. Unusually mild fall and winter weather and other good fortunes allowed the congregation to proceed quickly with its building project. Nearing Christmas and tired from the strenuous pace they had been maintaining, the congregation was inspired to continue by generous donations of a brand-new baby grand piano, twenty gorgeous poinsettias, and two huge pine wreaths. On December 24, members celebrated their first candlelight service in their new home—just eleven weeks and five days after ground had been broken. Soon, the sanctuary that had looked so big at the beginning was bulging at the seams. Designed to hold 150 persons, it now served over 200 for worship services. As a result, two services were offered starting in 1984. The congregation's early faith promise of $3,000 for mission outreach has grown over the years. Now, over $50,000 will be sent out during the year for missions. Over the ensuing years, the congregation has grown, and the facility has been expanded, including a new sanctuary, gym-fellowship hall, and additional nine acres to the south of the original lot. Adversity struck in 1989 when vandals broke into the church and set several small fires, one particularly damaging. However, with their usual zeal and faith, members repaired the damage and soon were able to worship again in a beautiful environment. As the church building grew, so did the ministries of the church. Small "growth group" Bible studies have been organized. "Junior Church" ministers to the youngsters during worship services. Youth groups provide fellowship, training, and service opportunities. Various special needs groups meet people "where they are." Work teams and short-term mission projects have allowed many members to see the world beyond their valley. Volunteer workers continue to be the key to the expanding ministries. Reverend Scott Shaffer was the founding pastor, and he served until 1994, when Reverend James Hansen became senior pastor. Several ministers have served as associate pastors over the years. *(Photographer: Vonda Minner; caption: Eileen Urmson and Pastor Hansen)*

Before buying Tara, the former Koonce mansion, in Clark in 1984, James and Donna (Carey) Winner were the proprietors of the Shenango Inn (pictured) in Sharon. The inn contained over seventy guest rooms. It has since been sold and is a personal care facility.

The Romanenko Chamber Players performed Handel's "Messiah" with the Symphonic Singers of Erie at Tower Presbyterian Church (Grove City) in 1983.

The merger that created Grove City's United Community Hospital in 1978 made The New York Times *when the ground was broken for a new facility in 1980. The novelty of the merger stemmed from a long rivalry between the medical doctors and the osteopathic doctors although such rivalries were not unique to this town. Osteopaths receive the same training as medical doctors, perform surgeries, and prescribe drugs. They also believe in manipulating the body for proper alignment and blood flow. In Grove City in 1907, the first hospital was established by medical doctors in a house (pictured, in 1997). In 1912, O. O. Bashline and Walter Rossman, both osteopathic doctors, opened another hospital. Both hospitals grew and eventually had stately buildings, which by the early 1970s were too much for the community and the owners to support. Up until that time, many Grove City residents had developed strong feelings about which type of doctor was acceptable. The anticipated trouble when the merger was announced never materialized. The current facility on Cranberry Road and Route 173 (pictured, in 1999) has grown to be a great asset to the community and adds new technology each year. (Photo: Nick and Kathy Pompa; aerial:* **The Herald***; caption:* **Reflections of Our Past***)*

Firemen's Old Home Week parade in Fredonia, 1987.

An institution that has existed almost as long as the community itself is the Stoneboro Fair. Organized as the Mercer County Agricultural and Manufacturing Society of Stoneboro, a reorganization in 1876 saw the corporation become the Mercer County Agricultural Society, which then purchased thirty-one hillside acres at the eastern edge of the borough, abandoning its original lakefront site. Since 1877, the fairground has been expanded and frequent improvements have been made. Since 1975, new exhibit structures have gone up on the grounds (pictured, in 1988) while efforts have also been made to preserve some of the most historic buildings. The Fair is now held over the Labor Day weekend; and the 131st fair, in 1999, was again characterized by displays of livestock (pictured are Gary and Sally Oakes in the 1990 Calvalcade), agricultural products, and farm machinery and by horse racing, stage presentations, truck and tractor shows, carnival attractions, and cow-milking contests (pictured, in 1999, as County Commissioner Lazor and Sheriff Romine good-naturedly compete). (Lazor and Romine photos: Vonda Minner; aerial and caption: Frederick Houser)

478

479

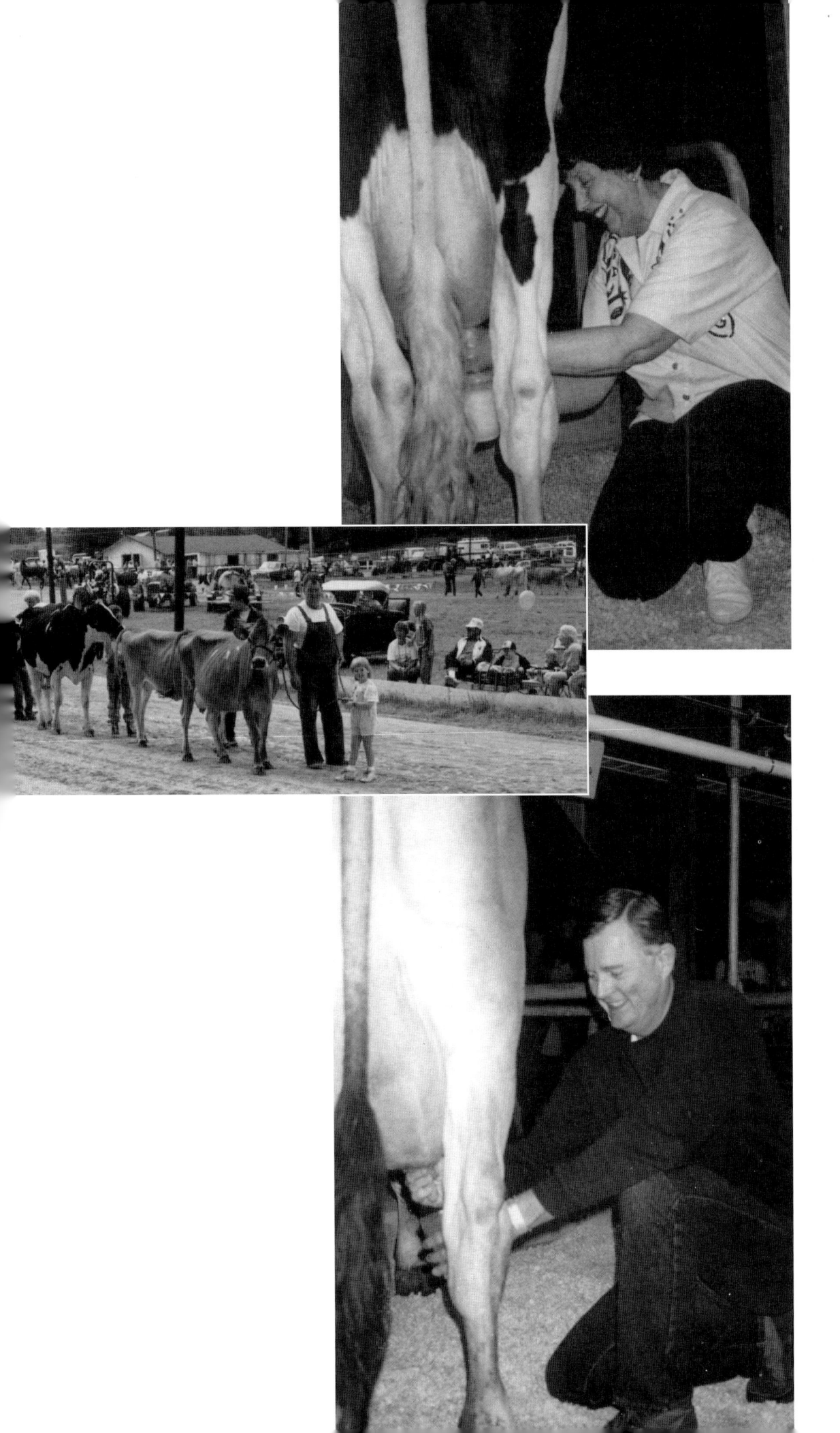

2000

1989

Looking at a jackpot of $115.5 million, hopefuls parked around Grove City retailer Last Minit Mart and waited anxiously for Pennsylvania Super 7 Lottery tickets on April 26, 1989: that night Pennsylvania acquired fourteen new millionaires. (In 1993, the store was purchased by Hirdaypal and Harminder Gill of Grove City and renamed Jiffy Mini Mart, pictured in 2000.) (Contributor: Jimmy Gill)

In 1985, Jamestown Paint & Varnish Company expanded into a new office on Main Street and a research and development laboratory (pictured, with manufacturing plant) facing Liberty Street. The mill had sustained large fires in 1939 and 1951, among other changes and events since it was started in 1885 by V. H. Ehrh. (Now, Jamestown's largest employer, the plant manufactures industrial coatings.) (Photos: Michael Walton; caption: Norma Leary)

Companies used to paint advertising on barns. A common advertisement for many years was for Mail Pouch Tobacco. Toward the end of the 1900s, Mercer County had only a handful of such advertisements still legible. (Contributor: Vonda Minner)

Jamestown Arch. (Postcard: Vinson Skibo)

Chapter 9: 1991–2000

Townships

Coolspring Township was the first in Mercer County to pave all its roads. The equipment used to maintain the roads includes two trucks, snowplows, a mower-ditcher, backhoes, a grader, and a mowing machine. A garage houses all this equipment, and a separate building holds salt. A former grange hall was donated to the township and developed into a community hall. A house next door was purchased for a township office. Once a year, the township supervisors and planning commission sponsor a "Clean Up Day" to rid the roads of junk and litter.

By 1999, of the twenty-seven miles of **East Lackawannock Township** roads, all except four miles have been widened and paved. Township supervisors, in charge of road maintenance, are elected to six-year terms. A wide variety of businesses are located in the township, including building, handcrafting, machinery and auto dealerships and repairs, pets and supplies, food services, health care, and leisure-time facilities.

Surrounding Grove City on all sides, diversified by hills and plains, **Pine Township** is largely agricultural with forests of pine, hemlock, and deciduous trees (some quite dense in areas), and a cranberry marsh. Coal, a great measure of wealth in the township, was mined considerably by different coal companies well into the 1980s. Wolf Creek flows the entire north-south length of the township with numerous small tributaries branching out. By 1959 the population had grown to 2,643; and in the 1990 census 4,193 residents were counted. Pine Township now encompasses 28.65 square miles. Today, coal mining has gone by the way side and the large employers within the township are County Market, General Electric, George Junior Republic, Ivex, Milk Transport Inc. (Hovis Trucking), Fellowship and Orchard Manor (Odd Fellows), United Community Hospital, and Walmart. Now nine churches own real estate in the township: Center Presbyterian Church, Christian Science Society, Church of God of Grove City, Episcopal Church, First Church of God on West Main Street, Galalean Baptist, Grove City Alliance, Mount Olive Baptist, and Scotch Hill Presbyterian Church. Eight cemeteries are maintained in and around the township: Center Church Cemetery, Crestview Memorial Park, Methodist Cemetery, Presbyterian Cemetery, Roman Catholic Diocese of Erie Cemetery, Rose Cemetery, Scotch Hill Cemetery, and Woodland Cemetery.

After the ups and downs in industry and farming felt over the past few decades, **Salem Township** is booming with new homes everywhere, according the Robert Osborn. Few old names are among these new occupants. It seems that Salem Township—so overlooked for so long—is now coming alive.

Jamestown Stone Arch Railroad Bridge

By Norma Leary

The Jamestown Stone Arch Railroad Bridge, constructed in 1873, is historically significant for two reasons: its unique construction and its association with the Jamestown & Franklin Railroad. The structure is an example of stone arch bridge technology, one of the earliest types of bridges in Pennsylvania. They were particularly valued by the railroads for their aesthetics and ability to handle the ever-increasing weight, size, and speed of locomotives and railroad cars. Stone arch bridges are ubiquitous in southeastern Pennsylvania, but they are not as prevalent in the northwestern part of the state. The Jamestown Arch, a deck arch, is 22 feet long and 20 feet wide, with a 10-foot-8-inch clearance. The spandrel walls are coursed, rusticated ashlar blocks with quarry marks and tooling visible. The wingwalls on the north elevation are stepped and flared and on the south elevation, stepped and perpendicular to the bridge. The voussoirs are pointed at the top and have a pick-hammer finish. The edges have a drafted (chisel-axed) finish. Similar finishes are found on the stone coping that tops the spandrel walls.

The Jamestown & Franklin was chartered in 1862 to build a railroad line from Jamestown to Stoneboro and then to Franklin. The line reached Stoneboro in 1865, was opened to Franklin in 1867, and extended to Oil City in 1870. Two years later the railroad was carrying large quantities of oil from the fields surrounding Titusville and Oil City, as well as coal. With the completion of an oil pipeline in 1875, its importance as an oil hauler diminished; but it continued to move coal, passengers, and agricultural and industrial products for the region.

In the late 1960s the railroad became part of the abortive Penn Central Railroad before ownership was transferred in the mid-1970s to Conrail. Conrail, in turn, abandoned the line in the late 1980s. This development spurred the "Save the Arch" committee, chaired by Michelle Valesky Brooks, to seek a decision from the Pennsylvania Public Utilities Commission about whether to remove the arch as recommended by the Pennsylvania Department of Transportation. The latter had declared the arch a traffic hazard and not in compliance with state regulations. About seven hundred signatures were collected from people interested in keeping the arch, some of whom attended a public hearing in Pittsburgh as attorney Robert Walton and several witnesses pleaded to save the structure. The Jamestown Area Historical Society and Jamestown Council agreed to share future upkeep of the arch. In May 2000, the decision was announced that the arch would be preserved.

The Kennard United Methodist Church in *Sugar Grove Township* was built shortly after the Civil War. Now, the pastor is Reverend Fredrick Monk, and Sunday attendance is about eighty-five, which has fluctuated since the church was built. Two ministers who have made lasting impressions on this church are Reverend Ross and Reverend Miliron through their work in developing a strong youth group. Sugar Grove Township's population is now between 900 and 1,000.

Feed and grain businesses, two hardware stores, cabinet and furniture shops, a barber shop, gift shop, golf course, and other activities are active now in *Wilmington Township*. Most of these are individual or family-owned enterprises. Not until 1995 did Wilmington Township have an office building constructed that included a meeting room. Although Wilmington was by 1990 a two-party district, the overwhelming majority of the township is Republican. Now, three schools are in Wilmington Township: Shady Maple, Hillside, and Ligo, which was now Amish-owned.

Fairview Township (by Patricia Jones). "If you travel about seven miles north of Mercer on Route 19, you will pass through two markers that note you are passing through the village of Fairview. Route 19, which is the main thoroughfare in Fairview and Fairview Township, divides the township about in half. As you glance around on this short strip of highway, you will see several businesses and not much more.

In 1964, Laubscher Cheese (Fairview Township) began as a company; however, Robert Laubscher had been selling cheese from his garage since 1957. (By 1999, Laubscher Cheese was shipping fifty million pounds of cheese per year.) (Contributor: Vonda Minner)

"Supposedly the area was named Fairview because of the views one can see from various places in the township in the summertime. Personally I can tell you that these spectacular views do exist, especially looking to the south toward Mercer.

"The businesses as you are traveling north in the township include Palmer Pools established by Virgil and Virginia Palmer and now owned by their son Jeff Palmer, Shelhamer's Energy owned by Gary Shelhamer, Vaughn Chiropractic owned by William Vaughn, Diamond Auto Sales and Notary owned by Joseph McElwain, Laubscher's Cheese Company owned by Bob and Ruth Laubscher, Kenstler's Collision Repair and Notary Service owned by Daniel and Eileen Kenstler, Polar Bear Food and Service, building owned J. C. Moore Industries, Rose's Cake Shop owned by Donna Rose and located just west of Route 19 on Fairview Road. Further west on Marstellar Road is Humphrey's Veterinary Supplies owned by Russell Humphrey. As you continue northwest on Kelso Read, you will find Kelso's Garage operated by Don Rhoades. The American Legion is also located on Kelso Road which is a social club for our veterans. Still going north on Route 19, you will find Fairview Swiss Cheese Company owned by John Koller & Son and Ogelvee Ltd.

"The Amish, who moved into the area in the early 1940s also contribute to the economy of the township with several sawmills and carpenter shops that produce handcrafted furniture. There are over 30 Amish families in the township at this time.

"McCartney's Feed and Hardware located on Airport Road is one of the oldest businesses in the township and continues to be important to the farmers in the area. It was established in 1933 by O. H. McCartney and later run by two of his sons, Howard and Willard, and now run by his grandson, Steve McCartney. Also on Airport Road is the Baurele Greenhouse owned by Richard Baurele along with McKean's Buying Station. Lucille Sykes is an important member of the community with her Cradle Time Birthing Clinic. About 85% of her clients are Amish and she handles from 70 to 120 births a year. She has had 1,650 births at her clinic. She and her husband also operate the B-Well Herb Shop. Both of their businesses are also located on Airport Road.

"Piepenhagen Hay Sales' Meals on Wheels is for livestock located on Schrader Road and is owned and operated by Hans Piepenhagen....

"Route 19 was repaved this summer and the process took

In 1952, Fairview Cheese started. James Koller took over as manager in 1957 when the company was making several kinds of cheese. In the mid-1960s, the entire production was changed to Swiss cheese. Rick Koller, James's son, purchased the business in 1982. The company produces two million pounds to six million pounds of Swiss cheese per year now. This level of production requires approximately one-quarter million pounds of milk each day. Fairview (pictured, in 1999) is now the largest Swiss cheese manufacturer in Pennsylvania. (Contributor: Vonda Minner)

about three months. However, extensive ditching, culvert, and guard rail work was completed to provide a beautiful and much appreciated highway through this section of Mercer County. There are the remains of two bridges on both sides of the village that indicate that at one time Route 19 had a slightly different path than it now has.

"Located on the north side of the village is the township building, which was erected in 1992. The supervisors at that time were Dewitt Palmer, Kermit "Pete" Higbee, and Mont Clark. The supervisors oversaw the construction and donated a great deal or time for the new building. Marjorie Palmer was the secretary at the time and handled the money end of the construction. Marjorie Palmer served as the township secretary for 46 years before retiring. She conducted the business out of her home office. . . .

"Dick and Donna Rose told me that at one time there were five places along Route 19 in the township where you could purchase gas. Beckdol, Kimes, Slater, Schrader, Gehly, and Johnston were the names of some of the people who owned or operated these stations.

Timeline 1991—2000

The World

- 1991 Operation Desert Shield, later renamed Desert Storm (the Gulf War), begins (the United States and 27 allies attack Iraq for occupying Kuwait); Magic Johnson gives up pro basketball
- 1992 Hurricane Andrew hits the coast of southern Florida; Los Angeles riots occur; Garth Brooks tops the charts; Johnny Carson retires after 30 years; Euro Disneyland opens; Barney & Friends air their first television show
- 1993 The tragedy in Waco occurs; several states are affected by the "Mississippi Flood of '93"; World Trade Center in New York City is bombed; William J. Clinton becomes the 42nd president
- 1994 Israel and Jordan sign a peace agreement; the Los Angeles earthquake occurs
- 1995 Oklahoma City Federal building is destroyed in a terrorist bombing; O. J. Simpson's trial is held; the Million Man March takes place; Yitzhak Rabin is assassinated
- 1996 The federal government shuts down due to lack of funding
- 1997 Scientists in Scotland announce they succeeded in cloning an adult sheep named "Dolly"; Lady Diana, the Princess of Wales, is killed in a car accident in Paris; President Clinton begins his second term in office and is sued for sexual harassment and impeached; Unabomber suspect Theodore Kaczynski is arrested; the number of Internet web pages breaks 16 million
- 1999 The world prepares for the international celebration of the millennium
- 2000 US Census Bureau estimates the population at 274,337,000; the Y2K bug, which created widespread concern over a possible computer glitch, causes very few problems; 9 million adults use email at least once a week

Mercer County

- 1994 Grove City Factory Shoppe (now known as the Prime Outlets at Grove City), opens; classes begin a month late for school year 94/95 in the Sharpsville Area School District when State Act 88 sends striking teachers back to work; Gov. Robert Casey visits the Sharon Steel to reaffirm that the state is committing $6 million in loans to allow Caparo, Inc. to buy and refurbish
- 1995 Buhl-Henderson Community Library in Sharon is renamed Shenango Valley Community Library; hundreds of residents travel to Harrisburg to see Tom Ridge sworn in as governor; construction begins to widen Route 18 in Hermitage and Shenango townships
- 1996 US archery team member, Rod White of Hermitage, wins an Olympic Gold Medal
- 1997 Lowe's Home Improvement opens in Hermitage; Western Pennsylvania Civil War Reenactors Society rededicates the Soldier's Monument in front of the courthouse; the 412 area code changes to 724; Hillview Intermediate Center in Grove City receives the national Blue Ribbon School of Excellence award
- 1999 Cooper-Bessemer in Grove City announces its closing; the courthouse is placed in the National Registry for Historic Properties
- 2000 Mercer County Bicentennial Commission plans numerous events for the year: New Year's Eve Gala, Mercer County Birthday Party, July 4th Concert, Mercer County Marching Band, Celebration of Faith, Mercer County Bicentennial pictorial history is published

"Eating places included Laubscher's Restaurant, which closed in 1998; Big Oaks; Ruth's Cottage Restaurant; the Golden Pheasant, a bar and dance hall; and Fenstmaker's Gulf Convenience Store and Lunch Counter.

"Other places of note were Bonnieview Dairy owned by Paul and Isaac Clark, Eckel's Store, Patterson Garage, Neal's Heating & Plumbing, Mecklem's Market and Slaughterhouse, Baxter's Orchard, Little's Fruit Market, and Cheyanne Manufacturing.

"There was a general store, now a private residence, that closed in the mid-1960s. Names associated with this store included McCullough, McCurdy, Nichols, Slater, and Higbee.

"The present home of Jeff Palmer was a stage coach and tavern stop between Pittsburgh and Erie and overnight lodging in the early 1800s."

MUNICIPALITIES

Farrell now occupies 2.5 square miles, three-tenths more land than it had when it was organized. Sharon contains 3.8 square miles; Sharpsville, 1.4; and Wheatland, .82, according to the Shenango Valley Regional Planning Commission.

In 1987, Sharon Steel in **Farrell** once again began to face serious financial problems. It struggled to meet the demands of a local strike and fell into a Chapter 11 bankruptcy. Sharon Steel needed to refurbish one of its blast furnaces. The plant could continue to operate, but it would require various loans and aid from the government. The city of Farrell filed for a "distressed community" to acquire state loans. Sharon Steel continued to struggle out of the Chapter 11 bankruptcy in late 1990, but from 1991 to 1992 it began to slide back down. The end came in late 1992 when Sharon Steel could not meet payrolls and utility bills. Sharon Steel was liquidated. Farrell secured a state loan to bring in needed money that would have come from the liquidated steel plant to pay its city employees and police force. Castro Steel made an attempt in 1994 to rejuvenate the steel plant when it purchased Sharon Steel. In 1998, Duferco Steel bought the plant and by 1999 it was producing steel once more.

The recession half of the boom and bust cycle that gripped **Greenville** in the early 1980s cost the community an estimated 1,500 to 2,000 jobs and forced it into a state of transition that has been anything but painless. However, various bright spots show the enduring hope of the people which leads to the determination of Greenville. The light of hope can be seen in a rapid growth of tourism because of Greenville's wondrous outdoor paradise. Also pride is seen in area businesses, such as Hodge Foundry and R. D. Werner Company, which is known for the world's largest facility for the manufacture of climbing equipment.

Patricia Sowash Potter (**Jamestown**) was the first female Commander of VFW Post 5424 and the first female National Surgeon General in 1994. She has also been serving as the State Surgeon General and on the Governor's State Advisory Council for the past several years. Potter was awarded the National Defense Medal for her service during the Vietnam War and the Medal of Commendation for her service to Pennsylvania veterans. Her husband, Albern Potter, received the Navy Cross for his service in the World War II Hospital Corps in Guadalcanal.

Clark *(by Clyde Moffett).* An article in *The Sharon Herald* in the 1940s said that Clarksville "in recent years has become a popular summer 'playground' for residents of Sharon and vicinity." The article continues, "Jones beach, just north of the town is, perhaps, the most popular swimming spot in the Shenango River. There are several ideal camping grounds bordering the boroughwhich are used each year by Sharon residents. . . ." Actually, the summer recreational facilities of the area were known long before the 1940s and were brought to the attention of vacationers much farther than Sharon. Helen Hall mentioned in her publication that "summer boarders" came from the Valley and as far away as Pittsburgh "and at least two homes were open to them."

The new town of Clark has much more to offer those who enjoy fishing, camping, boating, and other summer fun along the shores of the Shenango Reservoir. Robert Cunningham purchased the former Costar Marina (now known as RC's Marina) and upgraded it to a fine marina. The YMCA has a campground in the borough. The U.S. Army Corps of Engineers maintains a fine campground and boat launch across the lake from Clark. The Shenango Reservoir is well stocked with fish and is famous especially for the crappies, which are caught in large numbers.

In 1995 with the resignation of longtime police chief Francis Dickson, Clark entered into an agreement with Jefferson Township for police services. This arrangement led to the creation of the Jefferson-Clark Regional Police Department.

Fredonia. Betty Stamm, a 1969 Reynolds High School graduate and judo professional, traveled with Team USA to the Olympics as team manager in 1991. She is a graduate of Indiana University of Pennsylvania, where she first started in judo. In the early

1980s she suffered a knee injury which crippled her judo career. However, she operates her own Judo Club in Orlando, Florida.

The Fredonia Volunteer Fire Department has made much advancement within the last decade. They purchased a new rescue vehicle and replaced their water pumper with a larger water tank. The contributions and fundraisers of the community made all of this possible.

Custom Cupolas in Fredonia began as a sideline to Vic Buchanan's heating and plumbing business and his custom fabricating in stainless, sheet metal, and copper. Now retired from the heating and plumbing business, Buchanan works full-time in creating cupolas, each customized to fit a roof pitch and superior to ones designed in wood. Buchanan's cupolas and weathervanes can be spotted throughout Mercer County. Some have been perched on roofs for thirty years now.

Railroads
By Frederick Houser

Despite the apparent decline of railroading in the county toward the end of the 1900s, the Consolidated Rail Corporation (Conrail) finally achieved its goal of profitability in the early 1990s. Other profitable carriers, most notably Norfolk Southern Railway, made attempts to acquire this streamlined and moneymaking property. After a stock bidding war, the Norfolk Southern and CSX Transportation reached an agreement to divide the assets of Conrail between them, effective June 1, 1999. The surviving former Erie Lackawanna and Penn Central lines in the county were all integrated into the Norfolk Southern system, although the CSXT continued to use trackage rights through Sharon east to the Village of Shenango that it had inherited from Pittsburgh & Lake Erie Railroad. (The Pittsburgh & Lake Erie had been granted these rights to interchange directly with the Bessemer & Lake Erie in the early days of Conrail, and CSXT continued to use the rights after it acquired most of Pittsburgh & Lake Erie's operations in the early 1990s.)

Farming
By Vonda Minner

In 1993, an outbreak of bovine viral disease spurred farmers in Mercer County to begin inoculating all their herds.

The Pilgram Farm (Otter Creek Township) was one hundred years old in 1994.

Murphy Dairy has the distinction of being the last dairy in Mercer County to deliver milk door to door. The milk route ended in June 1996.

Farming has always existed at the mercy of nature. On the morning of June 24, 1996, during a severe thunder storm, lighting struck the Chris E. Hostetler barn on Cannery

"Century Farm" Designation

The family farm and rural traditions are important to the continued growth of Pennsylvania. To help preserve farm families, the Pennsylvania Department of Agriculture started the Century Farm Program to recognize farms that have been owned and operated continuously by members of the same family. The farms highlighted in this book for reaching their one hundred-year anniversary have been designated as "Century Farms" under this state program.

Road in East Lackawannock Township and totally destroyed the large structure with its hay, grain, and machinery contents. Local excavator, Merle Cooper, volunteered to halt his busy schedule to bulldoze away the smoldering remains that afternoon and dig a footer for the new barn. Building companies and neighbors hauled in cement blocks, lumber, and supplies so that the day after the fire, a new barn had begun on the same location. Area women prepared meals to feed the barn-raising crew, as the rafters and siding quickly took shape. By evening of the third day, not only was the barn completed, but hay was in the mow and grain in the bins, all donated by neighboring farms. Ironically, fourteen years before, at the same location, the Hostetler barn had burned to the ground by spontaneous combustion from a damp load of hay. The barn-raising was the same then, neighbor helping neighbor to swiftly and skillfully get the job done.

Ronald and Mary Catherine Clark's farm (Green Township) was two hundred years old in 1997 as was Robert and Beatrice Moats and Brian Weimert's farm (Green Township) in 1998.

In 1998, John and Judy Ligo, LiTerra Dairy Farm (Wolf Creek Township), were named Master Farmers. (The last time someone received this honor was in 1929.) Also in 1998, Beckie Kerins (West Salem Township) represented Pennsylvania at the Ohio State Expo Center in Columbus, Ohio, and was crowned queen of the Quarter Horse Association.

The McKean Brothers' farm covers twelve hundred acres, eight times larger than the average farm in Mercer County and in Pennsylvania, according to a May 21, 2000, *Allied News* article. They raise about 1,000 head on their Stoneboro farm and contract-grow about 200 cattle in Colorado and Kansas. In 1998, they registered the most Angus beef cattle in Pennsylvania.

The Joy Cone Company was started in 1918 by Albert George and Albert's sister, Rose Thomas and her husband, Thomas J. Thomas. Now, Albert's son Joe George is the chief executive officer and chairman of the board, and Joy Cone is the largest manufacturer of ice cream cones in the United States.

AVIATION
By Richard Christner

In 1999, W. Michael Hawes, a 21-year veteran of National Aeronautics and Space Administration (NASA) and a 1974 graduate of Greenville High School, was appointed NASA chief and deputy associate administrator of space flight development for the International Space Station project. Scheduled to be manned in 2000, the Space Station is intended for health research.

COMMUNICATIONS

In this decade alone, communication expectations have changed exponentially. Beepers and cellular phones are carried by more and more people. Many cars have phones, and some have satellite positioning systems. Cable television and home satellite dishes offer more than a hundred stations. Radio, television, microwave, and cellular towers dot the countryside. T-1 lines and fiber optic connections are sought by companies that can afford to install such sophistication. Homes often have two phone lines, either for an extra teen phone or for computer access to the Internet. Many households are eagerly waiting for the cable television companies to advance their networks to include computer connections that would speed up travel in the increasingly popular world of Internet databases and electronic mail and commerce (known as e-mail and e-commerce).

EXPERIMENTAL AIRCRAFT ASSOCIATION
By Richard Christner

Chapter 161 of the Experimental Aircraft Association (EAA) was chartered in early 1963, and its first president was William D. Sparks. The EAA's purpose generally is to keep recreational flying alive by fostering the building and flying of small aircraft (particularly of an experimental design) by private individuals. While membership is open to all western Pennsylvanians, many of the members are from Mercer County. Present membership is about seventy. The home base for Chapter 161 originally was the Slippery Rock Airport, followed by Nelson Run near Mercer. Its present headquarters is the Grove City Municipal Airport.

Popular is the group's Young Eagles program through which children are given free plane rides to introduce them to recreational flying.

Recently, a second local chapter was chartered, the Patrick Michael McGinty Chapter 1287. It is based at Nelson Run.

SCHOOLS

Mercer County now has eleven high schools: Commodore Perry, Greenville, Grove City, Hermitage, Farrell, Jamestown, Lakeview, Reynolds, Sharon, Sharpsville, and West Middlesex.

Lakeview School District *(by Serena Ghering, Jerry Drew, John Hamelly).* During the 1990s, the district hired its first female superintendent, Dr. Paulette Savolskis, who had taught in the district for several years before becoming the Curriculum Coordinator. Her knowledge of the district and its needs made her extremely qualified to fill the superintendent position in March of 1995. The high school had another change in leadership in the fall of 1997 when Alan J. Baldarelli was hired as the principal.

Three new instructors have led the music program in the 1990s. Doug Mays continued where Ray McCallister left off in 1992. Mays also has the reputation for expecting and getting the best from his students, as is evidenced by the wonderful marching and concert band performances he leads. Kristen Dennis currently leads the vocal department in

Built in 1954, Grove City High School underwent major renovations during 1997, 1998, and part of 1999. In October 1999, a dedication ceremony was held in the new auditorium. In addition to an exterior facelift and new lobby, nearly all aspects of the school received a new look, including the administrative office. (Source: Ernie Desu)

the middle and high schools. Andy Mitchell instructs Oakview Elementary's music department.

No renovations or additions were made to the buildings during the 1990s; however, several updates were made to the football field area. A new press box was added to the Lakeview Stadium, and the seating was reworked, made of high-quality, enclosed aluminum.

In 1991, both girls' and boys' track teams won French Creek Valley Conference championships, led by Jonathan Boggs, who won the 400-meter state championship. In 1992, Halle Bretz was crowned state champion in the shot put. The girls' track team won the Mercer County Athletic Conference Championship twice more in 1994 and 1995. The boys' and girls' basketball teams were league champions in 1991, and both the wrestling team and the girls' cross-country team won their conferences in 1999. In 1998, the fourteenth varsity sport came to Lakeview in the form of a girls' softball team.

Forty years after the consolidation, students are still enjoying clubs at Lakeview. Some of the clubs, such as Drama, Library (now Literary Guild), Production Management, National Honor Society, Future Homemakers of America, and Student Council are all still active. But as the times changed, so did the need for many of the clubs, which were so popular, to change also. All the language clubs joined together to form a very successful International Club. Every year, this club hosts the widely anticipated Spaghetti Dinner. The Christian clubs of Tri-Hi-Y and Hi-Y have become simply the coed Bible Club. The Agricultural Club, which was once so important, was disbanded. Also canceled were the Business Club, the Projectionist Club, Future Teachers of America, and the Junior Historians. The Art and Photography Club, Varsity L, Chess Club, Computer Club, Health Careers, Industrial Arts, and Students for Charity were all added to the list. The new additions accurately portray the issues and personalities of students in the 1990s.

In the past few years the music program has joined forces with the drama department to produce school-wide musicals, while the art department has created a strong photography program with the construction of a darkroom. Technology has also been embraced in this school district with the introduction of computer classes and clubs. The 1999–2000 school year has seen the addition of a winning speech and debate team.

Renovations are scheduled for the district's three buildings beginning in the summer of 2001. The facilities will be updated, and much needed space added to these structures that were built in the 1950s, 1960s, and 1980s.

Besides an excellent academic program, which has consistently produced some of the highest standardized test scores in the Intermediate Unit IV, Lakeview School District now supports twelve athletic teams, eighteen clubs, a strong music program, and a progressive art program. On Pennsylvania State Assessment Tests, the eleventh graders scored an average of 1,400 points, 100 points above the state average. Schools of similar size score 1,260 to 1,320 points. These scores place Lakeview School District as one of the top schools in the county academically.

GOLF COURSES

According to *The Herald* (May 11, 2000, issue), Mercer County has fourteen golf courses: Birchwood (Transfer), Borland (Wilmington Township), Buhl Farm (Hermitage), Hickory VFW (Hermitage), Mercer (Jefferson), Pine Grove (Pine Township), Pine Hill (Sugar Grove Township), Spring Valley (East Lackawannock Township), Tam O'Shanter (Hermitage), Willow Hills (Pine Township), Greenville Country Club (Hempfield Township), Grove City Country Club (Pine Township), Oak Tree Country Club (Shenango Township), and Sharon Country Club (Hermitage). (Walnut Creek is also listed with a Jamestown address, but it's actually located in Crawford County.)

In addition to the lovely fairways, ponds, hazards, and greens on all these courses and Tam O'Shanter's unique place in history, Buhl Farm Golf Course is unique for being possibly the only nine-hole course in the world with no green fees. The course is part of Buhl Farm Park, which was started and still funded through the generosity of Frank H. and Julia Buhl and since 1915 has been under the direction of a board of trustees.

COUNTY DEMOGRAPHICS

The population of Mercer County is relatively diverse when compared to other Pennsylvania counties in terms of ethnic background, livelihood, income, and education levels.

Residents boast many ethnic backgrounds, dominated by northern Europe. Ranked by population, the top ten national origins of residents' ancestors are German, Irish, English, Italian, Slovak, Scotch-Irish, Polish, Dutch, Scottish, and Welsh. Britain dominates the list partly because many original settlers were Scotch-Irish farmers from neighboring counties. The diversity of the county was influenced by the Revolutionary War veterans who settled here along with the Scotch-Irish.

The ethnic background of Mercer County would suggest a predominantly white society. Although true, the county has one of the highest percentages of African-Americans in the state. With 5.2 percent of the county African-Americans in 1990, Mercer County placed ninth out of the sixty-seven Pennsylvania counties with regard to this segment of the population.

Agriculture became the basis of the Mercer County economy because its early settlers were farmers. It has remained highly agricultural through its history. According to the 1990 census, 49 percent of the county was considered rural. The other 51 percent of the county is urban and connected with local industry. The coal and steel industries provide employment for many, while meeting the needs of the community through services employs many of the rest.

In 1990 the median annual family income in Mercer County was $29,347, placing it in the middle of Pennsylvania counties when ranked. The unemployment rate was 7 percent in 1990; however, like the rest of the nation, it has declined and stood at 4 percent in 1999, slightly higher than many other Pennsylvania counties.

Although the median family income is above the poverty line, Mercer County has a sizable percentage of the population living below that line: almost 13 percent. This situation is more prevalent in the African-American population where 42 percent live below the poverty line compared to approximately 11 percent of whites, according to the 1990 census. Ten percent of families live below the poverty line placing the county in the top third in the state in that category. The average welfare payment in 1990 was $581.23.

Education is another area where Mercer County shows diversity. About 7.5 percent of teenagers age sixteen to nineteen do not attend high school and have not received their diploma. This places the county in the bottom half of the state for high school dropouts. Over 45 percent of county residents have received their high school diploma, and over 13 percent have some form of a college degree.

Mercer County is a unique cross-section of Pennsylvania. Its residents are primarily of white European descent, but it has a significant African-American population. It is about half rural and half urban. Its average median income is above the poverty line, but a relatively large percentage of the population lives below that line. All in all, the population is well educated and ready to contribute to the future of Mercer County.

Mercer County

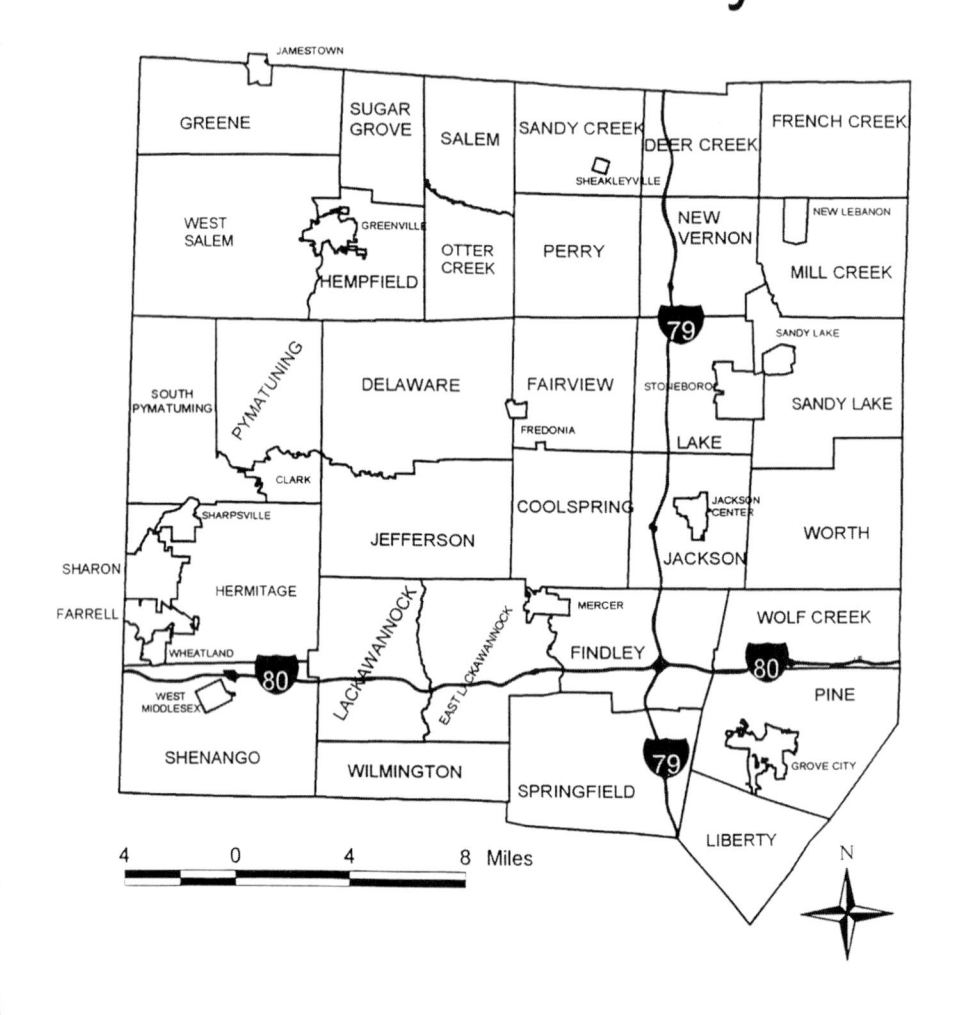

Mercer County
Cities, Boroughs, and Townships in 2000

Cities	Boroughs	Townships	
Farrell	Clark	Coolspring	Otter Creek
Hermitage	Fredonia	Deer Creek	Perry
Sharon	Greenville	Delaware	Pine
	Grove City	East Lackawannock	Pymatuning
	Jackson Center	Fairview	Salem
	Jamestown	Findley	Sandy Creek
	Mercer	French Creek	Sandy Lake
	New Lebanon	Greene	Shenango
	Sandy Lake	Hempfield	South Pymatuning
	Sharpsville	Jackson	Springfield
	Sheakleyville	Jefferson	Sugar Grove
	Stoneboro	Lackawannock	West Salem
	West Middlesex	Lake	Wilmington
	Wheatland	Liberty	Wolf Creek
		Mill Creek	Worth
		New Vernon	

SHARPSVILLE QUALITY PRODUCTS
By Mairy Jayn Woge

The stacks of Douglas Furnace were torn down in 1970. Douglas was the seed for Shenango Furnace Company and Shenango Penn Mold, which became Shenango Incorporated at Sixth and High streets in Sharpsville until the 1990s when Snyder heirs began downgrading the industry.

After the first Sharon Steel Corporation bankruptcy in 1987 made it necessary for Shenango Incorporated to import molten iron from Republic Steel Corporation in Youngstown, operations and some employees were transferred to the Snyder plant in Buffalo, New York. Equipment was moved to the plant in Buffalo and a Snyder industry on Neville Island near Pittsburgh. By 1991, the fourth generation of Snyders had closed all the family businesses. Shenango Incorporated in Sharpsville was out of business. The employees were out of work.

Some of the former employees launched a campaign to collect funds for buying the ninety-year-old Snyder buildings and keeping the machinery left in them running. Organizations and individuals in the Shenango Valley joined the effort. The drive raised enough money to purchase the buildings, buy some parts for abandoned machines, and keep the industry in operation. In 1993, Sharpsville Quality Products opened as an employee-owned company. As of February 2000, its work force totaled eighty.

THE HERALD
By Teresa Spatara

The Herald's home base has always been Sharon. It is established as an afternoon daily, Monday through Friday. *The Herald* switched Saturday's edition to a morning publication when it introduced a Sunday edition in 1990. The newspaper in 1994 had an average daily paid circulation of 25,432 and an average Sunday paid circulation of 24,714. Now, paid circulation is about 23,000 daily and 24,000 on Sunday.

In 1994, *The Herald* had a base of 180 full- and part-time employees, including 31 full-time newsroom staffers. Now, those figures have dropped to 150 full- and part-time employees and 25 in the newsroom. Some of the decrease is due to more technology. In 1998, *The Herald* went to full pagination, producing all of its news, display advertising, and classified ads electronically on the computer screen. The manual process of pasting up pages in the composing room was minimized. At its peak, the composing room had forty-two employees. Now it has four.

In addition to its main office in downtown Sharon, *The Herald* had bureaus in Greenville, Grove City, and Mercer before closing them in 1999.

Although it has become the largest and the leading newspaper in Mercer County, *The Herald* was late in making its local appearance. Started as *The Sharon Herald*, it debuted in 1864, the effort of R. C. Frey and his brother, James H. Frey.

Sharon was a growing community then, and the people were more than ready for a newspaper of their own to tell of their rapidly growing economy. Mercer and Greenville had more than their share of newspapers by then, with a total of eighteen between them. And here was a thriving Sharon with a population that doubled from 500 to 1,000 in one year, its iron-making blast furnaces, coal mining, and the new railroad that was to replace the Erie Extension Canal, and no newspaper of its own.

To remedy the situation, several Sharon merchants went to Conneautville (Crawford County) and offered to pay the Ruperts, publishers of the *Conneautville Record*, to move their paper to Sharon. The Ruperts were not interested, but they suggested that the businessmen approach the Frey brothers who were publishing the *Courier*, rival newspaper to the *Conneautville Record*. The Freys saw a better opportunity in Sharon, and they sold their *Courier* to the Ruperts who merged it into the *Record*. The arrangement worked well for both parties.

The Freys moved to Sharon, and with their brother Joseph and sister Lizzie, just fifteen, a talented typesetter, set up shop on the south side of East State Street. They bought a No. 4 Washington hand press and began publishing *The Sharon Herald* from the banking house of Porter and Perkins. They sold it for $1.50 a year, paid in advance (as was the custom of newspapers in that day). Subscribers who wanted their weekly edition delivered by carriers were charged an additional twenty-five cents. The first edition of nine hundred copies sold out, netting the Freys $75.

Their seven-column sheet followed the newspaper tradition of the times with Page one fiction stories that were serialized and various and sundry items that had nothing to do with news. That first newspaper carried only two columns of local news, although it did better in subsequent editions. Page one also carried advertisements, including one for the packet boat, "Crystal Palace," which was making daily trips between Sharon and New Castle. A business directory also was featured on the front page. The Freys charged fifty cents a week for ten lines of advertising and $5.50 for an entire column of advertising, allowing a 10 percent discount for advance payment.

During their first year of publication, the Freys reported that the annual delivery of coal and iron within five miles of Sharon had a value of $3.2 million, including $1.2 million from the annual sale of 35,000 tons of iron produced at the blast furnaces.

Republican in principle, the paper continued its advocacy of that party's philosophy, stating in its first editorial that it would "support those principles which we believe are essential to the preservation of our federal union and liberty," which then were in jeopardy because of the Civil War.

The Frey brothers then moved the paper to a building occupied by S. C. Yoder and Company on West State Street. In 1865, R. C. sold his interest to Dr. John Winter, a Baptist minister from Sharon; and in 1866 Frey bought Winter's interest and became the sole owner.

Just six months later, Calvin W. Ray bought a half interest in the paper, and the newspaper firm became known as Frey and Ray. The two partners bought some new equipment, enlarged the paper into an eight-column journal, and raised the subscription price to $2 a year.

Although the paper thrived under that partnership, the firm did not last long. In 1869, John L. Morrison (Pymatuning Township) bought Frey's interest. Morrison was far-sighted and wanted further expansion. In 1870, *The Sharon Herald*'s plant was moved to the third story of "Prindle's Block" where it remained for five years, undergoing more improvements throughout that time. In 1871 the owners enlarged the paper to a nine-column sheet and bought a new Cottrell and Babcock power press with an eye to further improvements. The owners branched out, buying a new half-medium Universal Press for their job shop as their business grew. The shop printed such items as posters, show cards, business cards, programs, letter heads, and bill heads and statements. Because of the increased business, the owners were able to reduce the subscription price in 1874 to $1 annually, to be paid strictly in advance.

The Sharon Herald moved again in 1875, this time to the basement of the First National Bank Building. It added a new one-eight medium power press for jobbing work and a B. W. Payne and Sons Eureka engine to run the various presses.

Despite the success of the Sharon Herald Publishing Company, Morrison decided to run for county recorder, was elected, and sold his share of the business to Ray who became sole owner.

Disaster struck the paper in 1878 when four days of rain ended the severe late summer drought, but resulted in what Ray described in his paper as "the greatest flood ever witnessed in this place or the Shenango Valley." *The Sharon Herald*'s offices were flooded with several feet of water, and the paper had to accept aid to publish from two papers that had been started after *The Sharon Herald*: the *Sharon Times* and the *Sharon Eagle*. The flood also suspended railway communication, causing late delivery of the previous edition of *The Sharon Herald*.

In 1879, when Morrison finished his term as county recorder, he returned to *The Sharon Herald*, which he purchased as sole owner. Ray accepted an appointment by President Hayes as Sharon's postmaster, a position he kept for eight years. His second four-year appointment came from President Arthur. Ray completed his postal duties and bought an interest in the *Sharon Eagle* in 1887.

Meanwhile, the *Sharon Times*, the only Democratic paper ever published in Sharon, had been started in 1868 by John A. Lant and George D. Herbert. The first issue was published on June 17 of that year from the second story of T. J. Porter's bank building on State Street, across from the Shenango House. In 1869, Lant left the firm, leaving Herbert as sole proprietor and editor. The *Times*, too, was printed on a Washington hand press and started as a seven-column folio. In 1875, Herbert added a Potter cylinder press and the following year added a steam boiler and engine. But, by 1878, Herbert became financially strapped and sold the paper to P. L. Kimberly with Herbert continuing as managing editor until 1879 when he went to Philadelphia. Reuben Williamson was then business manager and T. W. McClain, editor. After the presidential election of 1880, the *Times* was sold to J. R. McNabb of the *Sharon Eagle*, ending the duration of Sharon's only Democratic paper.

The *Sharon Eagle* had originated as a large nine-column weekly in 1875 as the *Mercer County Eagle* with J. R. McNabb as editor and proprietor. He called it "independent in all things and neutral in nothing." Also in 1875, McNabb began publishing a daily, the *Evening Eagle*, and conducted both papers until his death in 1883. His son, Scott R. McNabb, took over and ran the paper until 1885, when James L. Ray and Walter Whitehead, two printers, bought it. As the paper grew, the owners converted it into a Republican organ. They took Calvin Ray as a partner, changed the name of the firm to Eagle Printing Company, and published the paper in the basement of the First National Bank Building.

About 1901, Morrison constructed a three-story brick building at 13 River Avenue although, in 1894, Morrison had been appointed stationery clerk of the U.S. House of Representatives, had moved to Washington, D.C., and had left the paper in the care of his nephew Joseph Buchholz as managing editor. In 1907, Morrison sold *The Sharon Herald* to The Sharon Herald Publishing Company, owned by Buchholz, William Organ, A. Walter (Dude) McDowell, and William B. Ramsay. (McDowell later became publisher and chairman of the board of *The Herald*.) The new owners bought the equipment and "good will" of Morrison's newspaper for $8,000 and stipulation to lease the building at 13 River Avenue for $65 a month. At that time, $8,000 was a large amount of money, representing double the price of a six-room home.

Plans were to start publishing daily, but with the Panic of 1907 as a public concern, they waited until 1909 to produce that long-awaited daily edition. But just as the daily was enjoying success, the Shenango River again overflowed its banks and *The Sharon Herald*'s home on Herald Square (now Elks' Square) was devastated by the Great Flood of 1913. Three Linotype machines, housed on the second floor, were swept into the swollen river. Building debris fell onto the big Duplex press that was battered but intact. Other presses and equipment fell into the flooded basement and were damaged severely.

The flood wiped out four editions. The newspapermen worked day and night to salvage what they could with reports that Billy Organ finally had to be carried out of the building as the waters reached the building's door. C. B. Lartz, *The Sharon Herald*'s first full-fledged daily news reporter, reported the devastation of the flood. The newspaper accepted the offer for use of the Farrell News Plant as Ramsay prepared a flood edition. Other offers for help came from Beaver Printing Company and from the *New Castle News*. *The Sharon Herald* printed its first edition after the flood at the Farrell Press and the other three at the *New Castle News*.

On April 1, 1913, *The Sharon Herald* established permanent quarters in the Willsonia Building on Chestnut Avenue and started to move in machinery that had been salvaged. A few days later, despite the problems, the newspaper celebrated its fourth birthday in print as a daily. On April 21, the paper announced that it expected to resume publishing from its new home on April 28. Three new Linotypes were rushed in by express. An expert from the Duplex Printing Press Company in Battle Creek, Michigan, overhauled and re-erected the Duplex press, which had been damaged, but was repairable. When *The Sharon Herald* resumed publication, it had the latest Linotypes, a reconditioned Duplex press, a Miller saw trimmer and router, a Dexter folder, a power paper cutter, a power stapler, a Potter cylinder proof press, a casting box and other modern furniture and fittings, all designed to save time. The newspaper had emerged from its adversity in better shape than ever, with power-driven machinery, equipped with individual motors; new composing room; presses in a separate two-story building; special room for carriers; and offices for the business and editorial departments, connecting with the composing room.

As *The Sharon Herald* continued its progress, it had keen competition from a rival newspaper, the *News-Telegraph*, an offshoot of the weekly *Sharon Telegraph*, Sharon's second daily paper that Charles A. Hazen founded in 1892 with James L. Ray. After several changes in ownership, the *Telegraph* was purchased in 1906 by Addison C. Dickinson (Mount Vernon, Ohio), publisher of the *New Castle Herald*, who sold the latter to go to Sharon. W. T. Baines, founder of Baines Realty, was business manager of the *Telegraph* at various times between 1907 and 1918.

Tom Perjol, retired business writer of *The Sharon Herald*, noted that in 1913, the *Telegraph* published both daily and weekly editions. Dickinson expanded his holdings by merging the *Farrell News* with the *Telegraph*. The paper became known as the *Sharon News-Telegraph*. (The *Farrell News* had been organized in 1901 as the *South Sharon News*.)

Competition between the two papers was keen, but not until 1935 did the *News-Telegraph* merge into *The Sharon Herald*. Officers of the new newspaper were McDowell, president; Dickinson, vice president; Buchholz, secretary; William A. Aiken, treasurer; Lartz, business manager; and Ramsay, editor.

Circulation price of fifteen cents a week by carrier, the same price charged by both papers, was continued until 1937, when it was increased to eighteen cents per week. Three additions were built after the Sharon Herald Publishing Company took over the News Telegraph Building on South Dock Street, increasing its frontage along the busy thoroughfare. When the papers merged, *The Sharon Herald* had a twenty-four-page Goss press and the *News-Telegraph*, a thirty-two-page Hoe press. Within two years, the paper bought an almost new sixty-four-page press.

The Sharon Herald received its first ink shipments by tank truck carrier in 1937. Previously ink was delivered in containers. In May of that year, *The Sharon Herald* captured two first prizes for advertising and editorial excellence and second prize for the excellence of its photoengraved pictures in the third annual press conference sponsored by

Pennsylvania State University and the Pennsylvania Newspaper Publishers Association. (*The Herald* and its editorial and advertising staffs have won other awards in the competition that has continued annually since then.)

Also in 1937, *The Sharon Herald* announced that it would start filming all news editions for posterity. It was the first nonmetropolitan newspaper in the nation to adopt the microfilm process, which eliminated the need to bind the editions in three-month volumes.

In 1955, Editor Harshman proclaimed *The Sharon Herald* "an independent newspaper." He noted that, "although, the *Herald* was designated an 'independent Republican' paper for some 20 years, newspapers have ceased to exist as party organs and today seek to reflect the views of that great body of independent voters who now control the political tides."

The Sharon Herald introduced color advertisements in 1957. Pre-printed "hi-fi" four-color advertising appeared in the paper for the first time in 1960.

With an ever-increasing circulation base and in recognition of its regional news coverage, the newspaper dropped Sharon from its name and became *The Herald* in 1970. It now served the entire Mercer County area, including Lawrence County and eastern Ohio.

Throughout its history, *The Sharon Herald* branched into other business areas. It helped pioneer the operation of Radio Station WPIC in Sharon in 1938. The radio station, with an FM affiliate is the area's dominant station today. *The Sharon Herald* also owned and managed a Metal Decorating Division and a Commercial Printing Division.

Additional expansion came in 1965 when *The Sharon Herald* bought the four weekly newspapers in the eastern part of Mercer County. These weekly newspapers eventually combined into one twice-a-week newspaper, *The Allied News*, based in Grove City. That successful newspaper continues now as a weekly publication.

Meanwhile, a unique ownership change had occurred with *The Sharon Herald*. In 1946, the newspaper's management decided to sell stock to the employees. Neither the McDowell nor the Lartz families had heirs who could take over the property. McDowell wrote that the stock distribution was the first step in a "move to guarantee that ownership and control of *The Herald* shall remain with those who create it. Under the program the employees as well as the community, will be safeguarded against the danger of outside interests purchasing control and substituting outside management."

The employee ownership plan extended to all departments and all jobs. Employees bought stock by payroll deductions at book value which was computed annually. Higher-paid employees were able to accumulate more stock than others. Seventy-eight individuals immediately became stockholders. Seven in management positions and forty-four other active employees held stock in 1971, when *The Herald*'s employee stockholders voted to become the tenth newspaper in the Ottaway Newspapers Group. (Ottaway is a wholly owned subsidiary of Dow Jones.) It was an ideal merger in that the philosophies of both organizations were similar in emphasizing editorial quality. The agreement was that the Sharon Herald Publishing Company would merge with Ottaway in an exchange of stock that would give shareholders four shares of Dow Jones for each share of Sharon Herald.

The merger became effective on June 30, 1971. That historic step provided *The Herald* with resources to progress into the realm of electronic newsrooms and computer assisted production.

Farming Changes
By Vonda Minner

In 1900, the farmer was tending the land with horses—much like the Amish of the 1990s. In fact, one only has to visit an Amish neighbor to go back in time. Now the farmer has four-wheel-drive tractors, combines, and choppers.

For many years the soil was prepared by plowing, harrowing, and planting. Crops were gathered with horse-drawn machinery with the help of a thrasher powered by a belt-driven steam engine. People would go from farm to farm to thrash (gather crops). The whole neighborhood would participate. At the meal everyone would sit down to one great meal—thus the phrase "eating like a thrasher." Now much of the land is prepared with no-till or minimum tillage. Farmers are the caretakers of the land and have learned a lot through conservation.

Years ago, farmers grew all the feed for the animals and in nice weather would put them out to pasture. Now, although oats, corn, alfalfa, soybeans, and barley are still grown, many dairy farmers feed their animals "TMR" (total mixed ration) to achieve the best nutrition for the animals. In fact many farms have a nutritionist who visits the farm daily. Feed is sent away for testing to ensure it has the right balance, and supplements are added to the feed. A hoof trimmer trims the cows' feet: when a cow's feet hurt, she doesn't want to milk.

In early times, the necessities were produced on the farm: meat, potatoes, vegetables, and fruits. Women made the clothing (on a treadle sewing machine) and washed the clothes on a washboard (until the wringer washing machine was introduced). When using a washboard, the women had to first heat the water on a fire and then march off to the clothesline to hang the laundry to dry. The cooking was done on a wood stove. She gathered the eggs; hoed the garden; canned the meat, vegetables, and fruits; tended the children; helped to milk the cows (by hand) and feed the animals; and often went into the field to help.

In the 1990s, the modern farm wife still knows how to milk the cows (some do it all) and may do it while the husband is doing other jobs or the couple may milk together to spend some "quality" time. Many women still garden and preserve their food by canning

Under the new ownership established in 1971, **The Herald** *and the weekly publication,* **Allied News,** *became the first and only Ottaway newspapers to be printed at a Dow Jones & Company printing plant. With* **The Herald's** *Scott letterpress in need of replacement and the Dow Jones plant in Cleveland in need of major improvement, Dow Jones built a new printing facility (pictured, in 2000) seven miles from Sharon near West Middlesex, providing the printing capabilities of its TKS offset press to* **The Herald** *and its associated publications. With that offset press and its color capabilities,* **The Herald** *emerged into the forefront of color photography and graphics. (Photographer: Marilyn Dewald; caption: Teresa Spatara)*

Livestock on Farms (1929)

	Number	Value
Horses	9,090	$1,054,440
Mules	210	27,720
Milk cows and heifers	18,500	1,887,000
Other cattle	16,120	830,670
Swine	14,170	221,050
Sheep	17,500	218,750
Chickens	304,500	377,580
Hives of bees	2,500	15,280
	TOTAL	$4,632,490

Farm Statistics (1996)

Commodity	Farms	Cash Receipts
Dairy products	260	$ 24,731,000
Field crops	600	8,961,000
Cattle, hogs, sheep	1,060	8,621,000
Horticulture	31	10,116,000
Vegetables and potatoes	69	1,215,000
Poultry	105	340,000
Fruits, nuts, berries	38	54,000
Other		982,000
	TOTAL	$55,020,000

A double-ten, rapid-exit, herringbone milking parlor, 1990s. (Contributor: Vonda Minner)

or, now, freezing. In fact, they cook, clean, can, and milk plus drive equipment, taxi their kids, and pick up supplies at the feed mills and the parts store. With the time left over, they pay the bills and keep the books. The clothes are put in the automatic washer and dryer, and dishes in the dishwasher. Groceries are bought at "Giant Eagle" and clothing at "Walmart."

In early times, if you were lucky enough to have a gas well or a gas line on your property, you had gaslights. Otherwise, not until President Roosevelt started the Rural Electric Service was electricity extended to the rural areas. Now, in addition to telephones, many farms have fax machines and use computers for bookkeeping and access to the Internet.

Sunday remains for many people a day for visiting friends and family (after chores and church).

In the early days, small dairies existed every few miles and owned five to ten animals. The milking was done by hand into buckets. The milk was poured into cans and set at the end of the lane to be picked up by a hauler and taken to the creamery. If the milk was not sent to the creamery, it was processed on the farm and taken by cans door to door where people could dip the milk they needed right out of the can. This milk went through a separator and after separated, the women would make cream, butter, and buttermilk. Murphy Dairy was the last to deliver milk door to door.

With electricity came the marvelous invention of the milking machine. Milk was dumped into the can, then into a dumping station, and then through a pipeline. Now, many farms in the county have milking parlors where the cows come to the milker—no more bending over. Milk is now picked up in a semitanker and hauled to the dairy for processing.

Even as late as 1966, manure was pitched with a pitchfork onto the manure spreader. Now, the manure may be pumped into a holding pond and spread a couple times a year by a manure pumping company, which may be a partnership with two or more families.

In the early days, the average farm was about one hundred acres. Now one dairy farm in Mercer County tends over one thousand acres: LiTerra, owned by John and Judy Ligo, in Wolf Creek Township. Near Stoneboro, the McKean Brothers raised Angus beef on their twelve-hundred-acre farm. Farming is diversified in the county: horses, pigs, cattle (many breeds, including the Scottish Highlander), poultry, maple syrup, honey, potatoes, buffalo, elk, sheep, fruit, and vegetables.

Farming remains a labor of love, and a farmer is a special "breed" of people. Yet, to survive and compete in the future, the "family farm" has evolved into a "family farm business."

DAY IN THE LIFE OF A DOCTOR, 1999
By George Reeher, DO

"My day begins about 6:45 a.m. after having a couple of calls during the night about hospitalized patients. I arrive at the hospital about 7 a.m. and visit my most seriously ill patient, a young adult male who attempted suicide from a combination of drug and alcohol overdose. He is in intensive care and still comatose. He suffers from alcoholism, as do multiple family members, including his brother and father. One of the drugs he overdosed on, Acetaminophen, can be quite toxic and can have late onset of serious liver problems. However, first, I have to deal with the coma and any substances he may have inhaled into his lungs while comatose. Whether he will survive is still doubtful.

*Dr. Harry Elston built the Shenango Valley Osteopathic Hospital on land abutting Farrell City Park, and it opened in 1958. In 1992, the Farrell hospital joined Greenville Hospital (pictured, in 1999) and formed Horizon Health System. In 1998, Horizon joined the University of Pittsburgh Medical Center network and is now named UPMC Horizon. (Aerial: **The Herald**; caption: Mairy Jayn Woge)*

"My second patient in the hospital is a female in her thirties who has had a lifelong struggle with a disease similar to muscular dystrophy. She has reached the point where her breathing is affected by muscle weakness and is trying to deal with the terminal nature of her circumstance. We are giving her as much respiratory support as she can tolerate. But, she does not want to be on a ventilator to sustain life.

"The third patient in the hospital is a diabetic with an ulcer on her foot. She has been hospitalized to get good control of her diabetes and provide optimum environment for healing the ulcer, which are usually slow and tedious to heal.

"The last adult patient in the hospital is an Amish female in her thirties with an unusual heart problem. She came in with a high heart rate, 250 beats per minute, and has a 'short circuit' in her heart's electrical system. She has been stabilized with medication, and the rate has been controlled. However, she will be transferred to a center in Erie that can map out the short circuit and destroy the offending tissue. Her chances of having this problem resolved and not even requiring medicine in the future are good, given the technology available for mapping and ablating these pathways.

"Next, I go to the nursery where I have two newborns. Both of them have single, teenage mothers, who were also my patients; therefore, we have preestablished relationships. The babies are doing well and should not have problems surviving in the world. I arrange for follow-up home visits by a nurse to help these girls adjust to motherhood and make sure the babies continue to do well.

"I get to the office about 9:30 a.m. and see a variety of patients: some for well care, including babies, and some with mild illnesses, such as ear infections and upper respiratory infections. I see a young adult with asthma; discuss her medications; and adjust them to try to prevent her asthmatic episodes.

"Another patient, a 10-year-old girl, is having academic problems due to Attention Deficit Disorder and learning disabilities. She tries her heart out, but has great difficulty in school. I can only hope the treatment I am using for her attentional problems will help.

"In the afternoon, I also see a variety of patients with relatively minor problems.

"In the course of the day, the young adult male with the drug overdose comes out of his coma. Except for signs of aspiration pneumonia and the possibility of long-term liver problems, he is stable and should survive.

"After completing my office hours in the afternoon, I return home."

Entrepreneurs
By Vonda Minner

An entrepreneur organizes, manages, and assumes responsibility for a business or other enterprise. Many Mercer County men and women have seen the vision, taken the risk, and forged ahead. From its beginning in 1800, the county was blessed with entrepreneurs: shop owners, bankers, blacksmiths, farmers, just to name a few. Through their visions, the county grew and became successful. The benefits have been cultural, financial, and social.

In 2000, Mercer County has many entrepreneurs who are still taking the risk every day and giving back to the county through good paying jobs and excellent products. The county has the largest shoe store in the world, the largest ice cream cone manufacturer in the nation, and the largest Swiss cheese company in Pennsylvania plus nationally known candy manufacturers, farms, steel building manufacturers, and "the Club." This list acknowledges only a few of the privately owned companies in the county. Every such successful entity—no matter the size—has its very own entrepreneur.

One couple, James and Donna (Carey) Winner are individuals who have gone the extra mile. Through their vision and generosity, Mercer County has benefited in culture, with the Vocal Hall of Fame and Art Gallery (Sharon); financially, by providing many jobs (from the Winner, a discount department store, to Winner Steel); and socially, through tourism, including restoring and opening up to the public Pennsylvania's only southern plantation mansion, "Tara, A Country Inn."

Mercer County owes thanks to all the entrepreneurs in the past two hundred years for taking the risk and going the extra mile!

Charles Koonce, son of pioneer Samuel Koonce, became the first burgess when the borough of Clarksville (now Clark) was incorporated in 1848. At one time the Koonce family owned thousands of acres of land. Charles became a coal and real estate tycoon, using some of his wealth to build a huge mansion for his third wife in 1854 on a hill overlooking the Shenango River. The Koonce house boasted sixteen rooms and seven fireplaces. Sitting now on only four acres, the home was handed down through three generations of the family. In the 1920s, the resident owner went on tour of the South. He was so impressed with the southern plantations that, when he returned home, he had the red-brick, federal-style home painted entirely white. He added the twenty-foot-plus wooden columns, akin to the Greek revival style of architecture, to each side of the mansion. In 1929, the sun porches were added. After 1949 when the last member of the Koonce family died, the house passed through several owners. In the 1950s, it was known as the Shadow Lawn Manor; in the 1960s, the Golden Eagle Tavern. Over the years, the tenants included a cable TV company and the Girl Scouts. Eventually, the government became tenants and lowered the ceilings, made small offices out of large rooms, and glued carpeting to the hardwood floors. After the government left, the structure fell into decay. In 1984, James and Donna (Carey) Winner bought it for $70,000. They renovated and expanded it for overnight accommodations, dining, and tours. Now known as "Tara, A Country Inn," the mansion remains as a major landmark in Mercer County. (Photographer: Marilyn Dewald; caption: Tara tour script and Clyde Moffett)

Solid Rock Assembly of God was started by Pastors John and Rhonda Leslie, who came to Grove City to work with a handful of families sharing an identical vision for a church in their town. In 1995, at 124 South Center Street, Solid Rock Assembly of God conducted its first Sunday morning service with eighty-six worshippers. A small second-floor room over what was then Muzo International Gold Distributors served as the meeting location. Later that year, Solid Rock Assembly of God moved to the warehouse formerly housing Ishmael's Baskets on the corners of Grant and Erie Streets. The increased space enabled growth to about two hundred people. In 1997, the church expanded its ministry staff to include Kevin Wilson, minister of youth and music. Also in 1997, the congregation purchased the downtown building at 145 South Broad Street. Previously a shoe store, the building needed much renovation to become a church. Meanwhile, Limberg Brothers (Grove City) had purchased the warehouse where the church had been meeting. The new owners needed warehouse space so Solid Rock Assembly of God had to relocate again while it was renovating its Broad Street facilities. The YMCA allowed the church to use its facility on Erie Street. During the ensuing sixteen months, the church grew to over two hundred people, ministering mostly to young people, young families, and college students, while the renovation progressed. The temporary arrangement at the YMCA required setting up for church each Saturday night and tearing down immediately after each Sunday morning service. Near the end of 1998, the church was given occupancy permits for the Broad Street facility, and its first service downtown was on Christmas Eve. The lively music and open atmosphere of Solid Rock Assembly of God make this church unique. People readily participate in the services rather than simply observe. The church offers a full schedule of services and ministry throughout the week, including Friday night revival and renewal services. LIFE groups (small group ministry) meet throughout the week and most also gather on Sunday evenings. GeNext Youth also meet on Sunday evenings. For children the church offers nurseries and childcare during all services. Sunday mornings feature "Kids on the Rock," which is ministry to kids age six to twelve. (Photographer: Vonda Minner; caption: John Leslie)

Central Community Church, a nondenominational church affiliated with the Willow Creek Association in Barrington, Illinois, originated in 1994 when a dream of becoming a spirit-enabled, seeker-sensitive, salvation-targeted, spiritually maturing church, as found in the New Testament, was awakened in an adventurous group of thirty-five members of Maysville Community Church (West Salem Township). They reorganized and began their quest of turning that dream into a reality when they voted to sell their facility and move to another location. In 1995, they purchased the Transfer Feed Store located on Route 18 in Transfer, along with over ten acres. Within four weeks, the interior of the building was totally renovated and an addition built. The first service, under the name of Central Community Church, was held on April 8, 1995, just in time for Easter. Within two months, the new church doubled in attendance and has been growing ever since. In 1998, Pastor David Kevin Chapman and his family became the church's first missionaries when they moved to Sussex, Wisconsin, to begin a new church. Later in 1998, Tim Kauk accepted the position as pastor of the church and moved from San Jose, California, with his wife Patty and their four children, Matthew, Jordan, Andrew, and Ashley. They now live in Greenville. Weekly attendance now averages 150, with two Sunday services. Central Community Church offers contemporary music; entertaining dramas; relevant and practical teaching; multimedia presentations; and youth, children, and athletic programs (three softball teams in 1999), all in a relaxed environment. (Photographer: Vonda Minner; caption: Autumn Buxton)

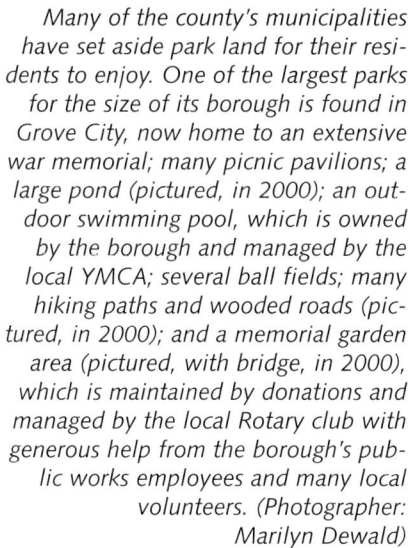

Many of the county's municipalities have set aside park land for their residents to enjoy. One of the largest parks for the size of its borough is found in Grove City, now home to an extensive war memorial; many picnic pavilions; a large pond (pictured, in 2000); an outdoor swimming pool, which is owned by the borough and managed by the local YMCA; several ball fields; many hiking paths and wooded roads (pictured, in 2000); and a memorial garden area (pictured, with bridge, in 2000), which is maintained by donations and managed by the local Rotary club with generous help from the borough's public works employees and many local volunteers. (Photographer: Marilyn Dewald)

A diner was moved to Mercer in the 1950s; it took about thirty days to transport it by truck, in one piece, from Elizabeth, New Jersey. In 1996, Pat and Marl Bradley sold the restaurant, and the dining car (sixteen feet by fifty feet) left Mercer by truck and then by ship to Germany, where the new owner refurbished and sold it to a shopping center owner. It is now operating in Hochberg as a piece of Americana. This diner is the second diner the German entrepreneur has bought and moved to Germany and the second diner to have been on the North Erie Street lot owned by Michael Metelsky, who also owns the Texaco station next door. The first diner was moved to the lot in 1942 and then to West Middlesex in the 1950s. For now, the lot is empty. (Photos: Bill and Judy Finney; caption: Gail Habbyshaw)

In the late 1990s, a Super Walmart was built on land formerly owned by Ervin and Dolly Payne in Hempfield Township outside of Greenville. The Paynes had had a miniature golf course on the property and, in their barn, held the largest horse and livestock auctions in this part of the state for a number of years. (Mercer County now has two other "regular" Walmarts, in Hermitage and Grove City.) (Photo: Joyce Young; caption: Robert Osborn)

This restored railroad station in Jamestown is now the Vanderstappen Wood Carver's Museum. (Photo: Vinson Skibo)

In 1796, Isaac and William Moreland left their family in Ireland to find a new life in the United States. The brothers secured 850 acres of land for their family near West Salem for $2,000. In 1798, the rest of the Moreland family arrived from Europe. They established a home in this part of West Salem that became part of Greene Township in 1844. Through the past two hundred years, the Moreland family has served Mercer County in positions ranging from farmer to church officer. For example, many Moreland generations attended and worked for Jamestown's First United Presbyterian Church. A 1926 church newsletter includes thirty-four Morelands on the membership roll. C. C. and T. S. Moreland were on the session that year, with C. C. acting as the clerk. C. C. was also the superintendent of the Sabbath School, and Mrs. C. C. Moreland was vice president of the Woman's Missionary Society. T. S. Moreland was one of the church's trustees. Louise Moreland served as the vice president of the Young Women's Missionary Society as well as the treasurer of the Young People's Christian Union. In 1996, the Moreland family (pictured, at the church) celebrated their bicentennial. Seventy-two family members from eleven states attended a three-day reunion held on a piece of the original Moreland settlement. The property is still Moreland property, now belonging to Henry Moreland (third row, left, plaid shirt). Andrew and Mary Ellen Moreland (last row, far right) were president and secretary of the reunion.
(Contributor: the Moreland family)

Grove City businessman gets out of 'circulation'

By WENDY HAWTHORNE
Herald Staff Writer

GROVE CITY — A longtime Grove City businessman will get a well deserved break.

James E. Karfes, 92, ended his nearly 68-year business career when he retired Nov. 29. He started in business on the town's Broad Street in 1918.

Karfes, who came from a family of 10 children, was born in Greece in 1893. He left his home at age 15 and went to Lamia, Greece, where he worked two years. In 1910, he boarded a ship for America.

He arrived in New York City in April 1911 and went to Pittsburgh, where he stayed with relatives. After working there for six years, Karfes decided he didn't want to live in the city any longer. He took train rides through western Pennsylvania — Beaver Falls, New Castle, Sharon and Greenville. On one of his travels, Karfes passed through Grove City, where he would later settle.

Karfes set out to establish a shoe shine business in the borough. In 1918, he rented a storefront in a building that Harshaw's Real Estate had at South Broad Street and Majestic Alley, now part of the parking lot of Riverside Market.

Karfes bought the building in 1926. Besides the shoe shine parlor, Karfes also operated a hat cleaning business. He rented space in the building to other firms, including a plumbing firm, insurance agency and a dry cleaner.

Grove City Community Library got its start in a back room of the Karfes building. He gave the library's founders the room without charge for the first three months.

In 1928, Karfes married the former Mary Linderman, whose father had owned a confectionary and ice cream parlor in Grove City for four years before the family moved to Youngstown. Mrs. Karfes joined her husband in business.

In June 1952, Karfes took over The Herald news agency. He started with six newsboys who delivered 600 papers a day.

Retired

James E. Karfes, 92, stands in front of the magazine rack at his former newsstand on South Broad Street in Grove City. Until his retirement at the end of November, Karfes was in charge of The Herald's in-town carriers and dealers.

Wendy Hawthorne/Herald

"The paper cost a nickle then, and it seems that every time The Herald had to increase the price of the paper — to 7 cents, then 10 cents, then 12 cents, then 15 cents, then 20 cents, and now 25 cents — we gained 50 to 75 new customers," Karfes said.

At one time, he distributed 1,400 Heralds in the borough and was in charge of as many as 22 newspaper carriers.

In 1968, Karfes' South Broad Street building was torn down as part of the borough's urban renewal project. Karfes moved his business to a rented storefront in the Allied News building, 113 N. Broad St. The building is owned by Mrs. Caroline Wherry, Grove City.

Besides the newspaper dealership, Karfes sold magazines, pop and candy at his North Broad Street store.

Because of Karfes' retirement, The Herald has hired Mrs. Ann Davis, Grove City, as a part-time district manager in Grove City. She is in charge of The Herald's 20 paper carriers and six dealers.

Mr. and Mrs. Karfes, who live on Carrie Way, Grove City, have two children. Their daughter, Theo, is administratvie assistant at Mercer County Juvenile Probation Office. Their son, Dr. Frank J., is an oral surgeon in Cleveland.

"We're going to spend time at home," Mrs. Karfes said.

James Karfes retired in November 1996 and passed away in January 1997. The article from **The Herald** *summarizes the ventures Karfes ran during his sixty-eight-year business career in Grove City. (Contributor: Theo Karfes)*

Hadley Presbyterian Church (pictured, in 2000) is in the village of Hadley in Perry Township. (Photographer: Marilyn Dewald)

Jackson Center Presbyterian Church, 2000. (Photographer: Marilyn Dewald)

1999

In 1998, Dean Dairy (aerial, in 1999, in Sharpsville) started producing the Milk Chug, a handy container of milk for people on the go. Now, the company employs eleven thousand employees in thirty-eight plants in fifteen states and has annual sales of over $3 billion. The business was originally Brookfield Dairy in Hickory Township, started in 1931 by Louis Yourga and his sons, Michael, Henry "Hank", Joseph, and John. In 1957, they started using the Vacu Therm process. The dairy was purchased in 1966 by Hawthorn Melody and in 1984 by Dean Dairy, a subsidiary of Dean Foods. (Contributor: Vonda Minner)

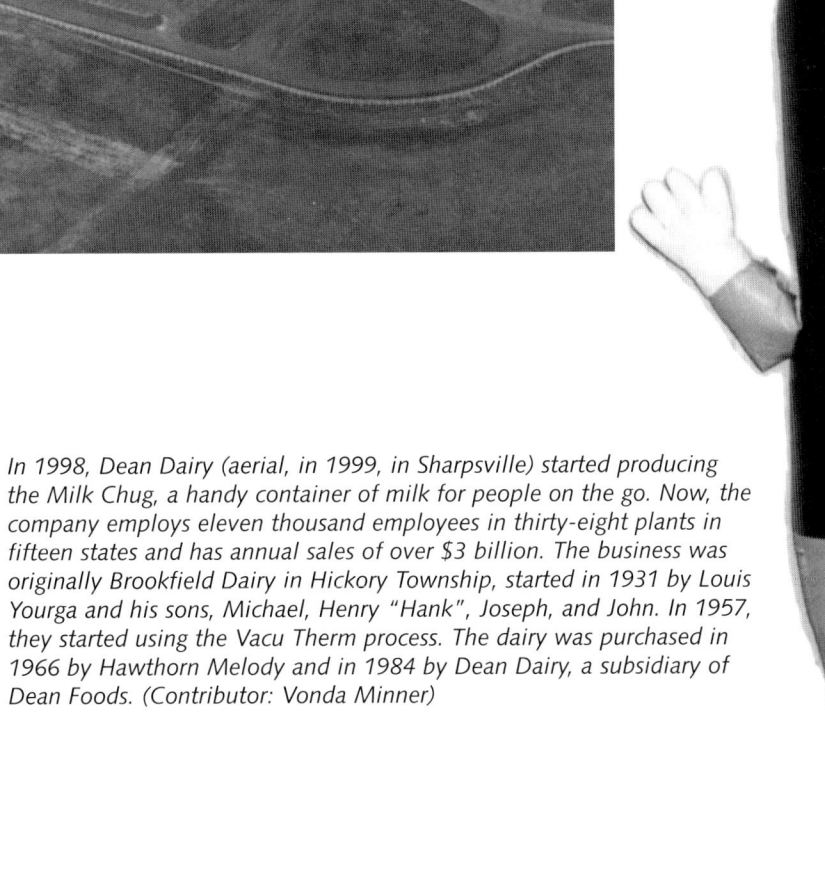

Speeds of the Filling Room at Dean Dairy (1999)

Quart (Chugs)	15,000 per hour
Pint and half-pint (Chugs)	21,000 per hour
Gallon (plastic containers)	9,000 per hour
Half-gallon (plastic containers)	5,400 per hour
Half-pint (paper cartons)	10,000 per hour
Half-gallon (paper cartons)	7,200 per hour
Quart (paper cartons)	9,600 per hour

Founded in 1866 as Thiel Hall in Monaca, Pennsylvania, the college moved to Greenville in 1871 and has developed into a picturesque 135-acre campus. As a liberal arts college, it offers associate and bachelor degrees with about thirty-five majors and twenty areas of study. For the 1999 fall term, 980 students enrolled, 72 percent of which were Pennsylvania residents, 19 percent from Ohio, 4 percent from other states, and 5 percent from seventeen other countries. Thiel has recently installed state-of-the-art campuswide networking that provides Internet access, cable television, and enhanced telephone services, including voice mail, to all residence halls, classrooms, and offices. A new fitness center has been installed, which offers strength training, cardiovascular equipment, aerobics/kick boxing space and a social center. Residence halls have been improved with the addition of new lofted dorm furniture. The student center has been renovated and expanded, and the interior is scheduled to be finished in mid-2000. (1999 aerial: **The Herald***; caption: www.thiel.edu)*

The Shenango Campus of Pennsylvania State University is on 14.5 acres in downtown Sharon, making it the only urban campus in the Penn State system. Over one thousand students are enrolled here pursuing bachelor degrees in human development and family studies, business, and nursing and associate degrees in electrical and mechanical engineering technology, information sciences and technology, occupational and physical therapy assistance, among others. Students may also complete the first two years of nearly all of Penn State's 180+ degrees and then move to University Park or another campus to complete their studies. (1999 aerial: **The Herald***; caption: www.shenango.psu.edu)*

As a sign of the ever-changing landscape due to development in Mercer County, ground was broken in 2000 for a new shopping center and gas station in the open field on Route 58 west of Grove City (lower right corner of aerial). The existing plaza across the street is anchored by County Market and Ames. Behind the supermarket is Walmart, and across the highway is George Junior Republic, a special school for troubled boys. (1999 aerial: **The Herald**)

In this history project, people were eager to identify who had the first car in their communities or to describe the first time they rode in a car. What folks take for granted now are all the new and used car dealerships that dot the county, not to mention all the choices in automobiles available now. As just one example, pictured is the Mel Grata Chevrolet and Toyota Dealership on State Street in Hermitage. (1999 aerial: **The Herald**)

Kraynak's is promoted as a "store for all seasons" and is much more than a greenhouse. In its sprawling facility in Hermitage (pictured, in 1999), one can shop for gifts, decorations for Christmas and other holidays, and miniature trains in addition to lawn and garden enhancements. The store is now well known for its animated holiday displays of Easter Bunny Lane and Santa's Christmasland. (Aerial: **The Herald**; caption: www.kraynaks.com)

In the late 1800s, photography was a still novelty. Shopkeepers probably enjoyed watching photographers set up their tripods and hide under the black curtains as much as the shutterbugs enjoyed showing off their new technology. As a result, photos of business people in front of stores, livery stables, mills, hotels, and banks abound from that era. With today's hectic lifestyles and array of photographic options, however, it's unusual to find such posed shots of current establishments. One such rare moment shows Todd Shillito (pictured, at left) in 2000 showcasing samples from his Custom Signs business in Worth Township with (right from Shillito) Robin Lewis, Brigitte Vogan, and his wife Rita. Of course, the technology used to make such signs has changed dramatically over the past century, too. (Contributor: Idella McConnell and Lucille Eagles)

Members of the Shenango-Pymatuning Chapter of the National Railway Historical Society help maintain and develop the Greenville Railroad Park (pictured in part, in 2000). In 1999, the park acquired a former Erie Railroad flat car due to the alertness of Gordon McClearn (Grove City) and the cooperation of Cooper-Bessemer (Grove City) and Trinity Industries (Greenville). Cooper-Bessemer had started to cut back its foundry and machining operations in 1998. As part of the cut-back, it disposed of its in-plant railroad rolling stock used to move engines, engine parts, and foundry moulds. McClearn then saw the "ERIE" identifications cast on the truck parts and stake pockets of one flat car and realized it must be survivor of early steel-car construction (the exact date unknown). It has a "fish-belly" center sill instead of the deep side sills that characterize contemporary flat cars. McClearn approached Rich Runkle (Fredonia), head of plant maintenance at Cooper-Bessemer, who convinced management to contribute the car to the Greenville Railroad Park and arranged for its transport via Bessemer & Lake Erie Railroad and Conrail to Trinity Industries for restoration. Trinity management and workers repainted and stenciled the car, installed a new wood deck, transported it to the park, and placed it on the new track for permanent display. (Photographer: Marilyn Dewald; caption: Frederick Houser)

As early as 1836, a log school operated at the end of Pilgrim and Straub roads in Otter Creek Township, and the Baptist Society used it as a school for a number of years. Snyder School was built in 1850 at the end of Snyder and Kitch roads. Linn School was at the intersection of Linn-Tyro and Baker roads on property now owned by Robert and Paulette Young. In 1868, a brick building replaced the original log one, built by David Linn in 1843. Charles Freeland built Tyro School in 1875 at the intersection of Linn-Tyro and Kitch roads on property now owned by John and Georgine Knauff (Greenville). It was considered one of the prettiest country schools in the county with dark green blinds, patent seats, and all the modern conveniences; but nothing remains of it now. The Kashner School was located on Donation Road and is now John Browser's house (pictured, in 2000). Over the years it has undergone extensive remodeling, and one would not guess that it had ever been a one-room school. (Contributor: Joyce Young)

Now used by the Community Church, a nondenominational congregation, the building (pictured, in 2000) for an institute in New Lebanon was constructed in 1880 for $7,000. It was incorporated as McElwain Institute in 1883, honoring its most liberal supporter, John McElwain. The academic school was for both men and women and continued until shortly after 1909. (Photographer: Marilyn Dewald)

In the 1950s, a traveling bus came around to each home in Worth Township and supplied groceries to anyone wishing to buy. The gentleman who owned the business was "Whitey" Farrell. Living in Sandy Lake Township, he established a weekly route to which he delivered groceries from his huckster bus. The children along the route always looked forward to his visits because they could buy penny candy. The price of bread was 28 cents a loaf, coffee was 49 cents a pound, and Procter & Gamble laundry soap was 8 cents a bar. After giving up the huckster bus, he purchased the old Presbyterian Church in Sandy Lake and opened Farrell's Browse Shop (pictured, in 2000). Farrell is now ninety-one years old, and the shop is owned by his son and daughter. (Photographer: Marilyn Dewald; caption: Idella McConnell and Lucille Eagles)

McClung Auto Body (Worth Township) is a family-owned collision repair facility now entering its third generation in business. The facility has eight large work areas and state-of-the-art equipment. In addition to offering rental cars, they have a Binks paint booth and mixing room, 360° bench rack, Goff prep area, FMC alignment equipment, Dupont Master tint mixing system and Dupont color net matching system, Trist paint curing system, and a CCC pathways collision-estimating and digital-imaging system. (Contributors: Idella McConnell and Lucille Eagles)

Built in 1845, the building in New Lebanon that now houses the Ginger Snap Junction used to be C. G. Westcot's General Store. The Junction sells antiques and curios. (Photographer: Marilyn Dewald)

The Old Martin General Store in Sheakleyville now sells antiques. (Photographer: Marilyn Dewald)

Chocolate did not catch on with the public until the 1920s—not because people did not enjoy its delicious taste, but rather because the debut of air conditioning then helped prevent chocolate from melting. (Before then, it was uncommon for stores to carry chocolate past April because of the warm temperatures.) The original family store was started in 1903 by George Daffin in Woodsfield, Ohio. Two generations and two moves later, George's grandson Paul "Pete" built a new store in Sharon in 1947, which also served as a candy factory. Eventually, Pete and his wife Jean moved to a bigger, 20,000-square-foot store in Sharon and built a 30,000-square-foot candy factory in Farrell. The Daffin's Chocolate Kingdom and Swizzle Stick Day are popular attractions for tourists and customers. Since Pete passed away in 1998, Jean and their daughter Diane are running the business. Each piece of Daffin's candy continues to be hand-decorated, which is becoming a rarity in the candy business. Now, in addition to the Sharon flagship location, Daffin's has retail stores in Greenville; Oil City; Franklin; and Warren, Ohio. Daffin's Candies has gained a national name for its chocolate candy, including its gourmet Jean Marie Collection. (Source: www.daffins.com)

Built in 1868, Kidd's Mill bridge (pictured, in 2000) spans the Shenango River south of Greenville between Routes 58 and 18 and is the only covered bridge in the county now. (It was also known as the Smith-Cross-Truss bridge.) (Photographer: Marilyn Dewald)

After a successful capital campaign in the mid-1990s, the Grove City YMCA built a new facility (pictured, in 2000, from the highway and from the side) next to Hillview Elementary Center (grades three through six) on Route 58 east of town. The sculpture in front, titled "Family," was created and donated by James E. Myford, a local sculptor. With an indoor pool, full-size gymnasium, recreation room, daycare center, fitness center, and spacious locker rooms, the complex contrasts boldly with the former facility (pictured, in 1997) on Erie Street. That building was originally designed and dedicated in 1908 as an armory. A new armory was built on George Junior Road in 1969, and the old armory was bought by the borough in 1988 to serve as a Recreation Center. Since the new YMCA has opened, the old facility has been vacant. (Photographers, of old YMCA: Nick and Kathy Pompa; of new YMCA: Marilyn Dewald; caption: **Reflections of Our Past***)*

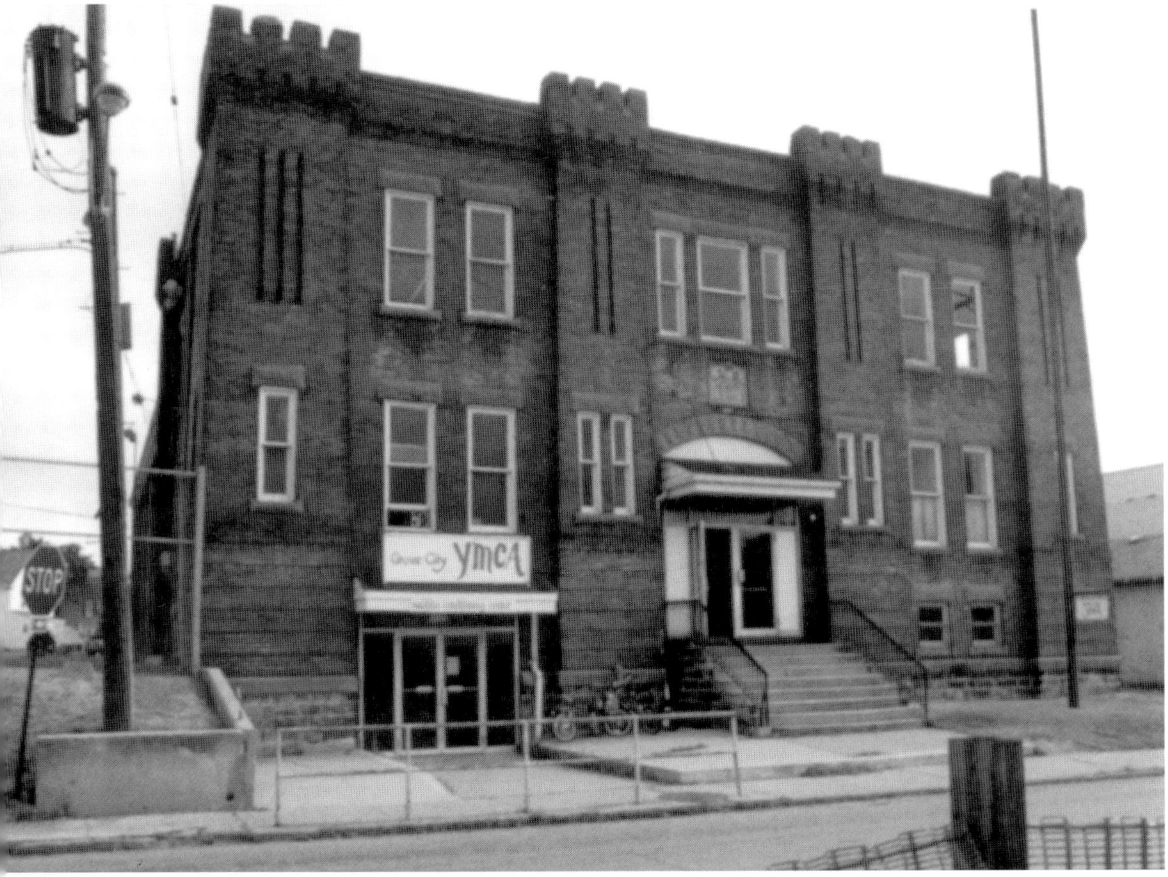
STOP
YMCA

Sheakleyville

The following municipalities are pictured: Sheakleyville, Stoneboro, Grove City (Broad Street and West Main Street, with Howe's Coffee on the right, 1997). (1999 aerials: **The Herald***; Grove City photographers: Nick and Kathy Pompa)*

Stoneboro

524

Broad Street, Grove City

West Main Street, Grove City

West Middlesex

*The following municipalities are pictured: West Middlesex, downtown Sharon, and Greenville. (1999 aerials: **The Herald**; Grove City photographers: Nick and Kathy Pompa)*

Greenville

Sharon

North Diamond Street, Mercer, 1930s.

Appendix A: Government

COUNTY GOVERNMENT OFFICES
By Jeremy Shankle and Josh Grubbs

The political structure of Mercer County is typical of government in western Pennsylvania. Three commissioners run the county, and one of them is the chairman. The commissioners also have a clerk, who is not an elected official, but hired by the office. The sheriff, district attorney, coroner, controller, register of wills, and recorder are some of the other offices that Mercer County citizens elect. All the offices are elected every four years, and there are no term limits. The absence of term limits allows individuals to serve for many years, some as long as twenty to thirty. The Republican Party has primarily controlled Mercer County government. The vast majority of elected officials in the county have been Republicans; however, the Democrats have served more years in only one political office.

The county commissioners are by law elected three at a time. No more than two commissioners may be from any one party. Therefore, minority representation is guaranteed. While it is possible, never have three different parties elected one commissioner each. From 1908 to 1976, an overwhelming majority of the commissioners were Republican. The commissioners act as the legislative and executive arms of county government. Administrative assistants, chief clerk, and county solicitors assist them in their role.

The district attorney's office represents the Commonwealth of Pennsylvania in the criminal justice system. This scope involves out-of-court preparation and appearances at all levels of the criminal justice system, including five district justice offices, three common pleas courts, Pennsylvania courts, and federal courts, including the Supreme Court. The district attorney office also involves appearances at preliminary hearings, routine case processing hearings at common pleas level, pretrial suppression hearings, trials, post verdict motions, and collateral attacks on convictions. The Republican Party has held the office of district attorney about 75 percent of the time, including multiple-term district attorneys such as Leroy Rickard, Edwin Moon, and John Q. Stranahan.

The position of clerk of courts/register of wills in Mercer County is one of few such offices in Pennsylvania because it combines the two offices. Its duties include being in charge of docketing for the court of common pleas and district justice courts. Also as clerk of the orphan's court, the office is in charge of applications for marriage licenses and processes adoptions, guardianships, and trustee accounts. As register of wills, the office administers estates and grants letters of administration. Since 1908, only two clerks have been Democrats.

One office that has not been largely Republican is the county controller, which was not established until 1942. Neither party have ever had two consecutive, different controllers elected; but, with Mary Stevenson's twenty-year term, the Democrats have an advantage in amount of time in the office. The controller is a watchdog of all the county's fiscal affairs, including the county's annual fiscal report and general accounting functions of the county (that is, payroll, invoices, and general bills of the county).

The prothonotary records actions of the civil division of the court of common pleas, such as writs of summons and subpoenas. The office also processes all naturalization records for the Bureau of Immigration and Naturalization Service and passport applications for the U.S. Department of Justice. The Democrats have only held the position twice since 1908. One of the terms was in 1936, and the other is the prothonotary now.

The coroner investigates and reports all deaths of a sudden, violent, or suspicious nature, including where no physician has been in attendance twenty-four hours before death. He investigates and determines whether a death is accidental and determines what should be done with the body. The coroner is a partisan, elected office, and the Republicans have held the position since 1908.

The county recorder keeps track of anything to do with real estate dating back to 1803, including all legal documents such as deeds, mortgages, agreements and assignments, subdivisions, and state highway plans. In addition, the duties of recorder include collecting state and local transfer tax, condemnations of property, and powers of attorney. Democrats have only held the position twice, for a total of sixteen years; and Republican Stephan Lukacs alone held 8 four-year terms.

The county treasurer is in charge of all county funds, including all county taxes collected by municipalities, all grants, and payment for services of the county. The treasurer disperses and invests all county funds and keeps all receipts. In addition the office sells all licenses, such as for hunting, fishing, and dogs. This office is also strongly Republican and no Democrat has been elected county treasurer since 1908.

The office of jury commissioner mails out summons, signs people in when they appear, and screens the jury questionnaires. Each party gets to elect one jury commissioner; therefore, one Republican and one Democrat always hold the position at a time.

The sheriff is the chief law enforcement official of the county. He possesses the position to keep the peace and is largely discretionary. Since 1908, nine Republicans have been sheriff, compared to three Democratic and one "other," making it one of the most diverse offices in the county. The "other" candidate was a member of the Prohibition party, and he was elected during the 1920s.

BENCH AND BAR

The history of the bench and bar of Mercer County is as rich and diverse as the history of Mercer County itself. It has seen one of its members serve as a U.S. Supreme Court Justice, two others as chief justices to the Pennsylvania Supreme Court, and the home of one of its district attorneys bombed.

Attorneys were sworn in as members of Mercer County Bar on February 16, 1804. John W. Hunter (Meadville) was the first to take the oath, followed by twelve other men from Pittsburgh, Butler, Beaver, Mercer (Joseph Shannon), and Meadville. These men practiced law in the 6th Judicial District that included the present-day counties of Crawford, Erie, Mercer, and Venango. Since 1804, over five hundred lawyers have been admitted to practice law in Mercer County.

Of this first group of men sworn in, two advanced their political careers by becoming recognizable figures in state and national politics. John Bannister Gibson later served as a chief justice of the Pennsylvania Supreme Court for ten years. He was appointed to the bench in 1827 by Governor Schultze and presided over six thousand cases. Chief Justice Gibson was known for his instinct of grasping the crucial points of cases and his independence in deciding cases. Another Bar Association member, Henry Baldwin, advanced his political career by serving as an associate justice of the U.S. Supreme Court for fourteen years. President Andrew Jackson nominated Baldwin in 1830, and the Senate approved him only two days later. During Justice Baldwin's time in the Supreme Court, the most famous case to come before him was the *Cherokee Nation vs. Georgia.* Baldwin agreed with the majority opinion and denied the injunction filed by the Cherokee Nation.

Mercer County held its first two sessions of court during the months of February and May of 1804. The tavern home of John Hunter was utilized as a makeshift courtroom and was described by John Pearson in his diary as, "a tolerable good house, but covered with boards which the water thro' it when it rained." Mr. Hunter was paid $1 a day for the use of his house.

These first sessions of court were presided over by President Judge Jesse Moore, who was appointed to this position by Governor McKean. Moore wore his hair long, powdered, and tied back in a ponytail while silver buckles adorned the knees of his black breeches and the tops of his black shoes. Two associate judges, Alexander Wright and Alexander Brown, also served with Judge Moore on these first cases. Twenty-one men served as associate judges, a position that lasted from 1803 to 1871. In addition to Wright and Brown, the following men served as associate judges: William Anderson, James R. Wrick, John Mitcheltree, John Findley, Thomas Wilson, John Newell, Thomas Cunningham, William Leech, William Waugh, Samuel Kerr, William McKean, Thomas J. Brown, David T. Porter, Joseph Kerr, Robert Patterson, David W. Findley, John Lightner, Milton A. Leech, and Richard Carr.

Judge Moore would start court by calling out to his court crier, John Morrison, "Crier, open court." Morrison would then blow on a large tinhorn and call the court to order by proclaiming, "O yez, o yez, o yez. In the name of the Commonwealth of Pennsylvania, I now declare this honorable court open for the transaction of business. The honorable Jesse Moore presiding. God save the Commonwealth and this honorable court." Court criers still use the same language to open court today, but do not blow the horn.

After the court crier opened court in Hunter's home, the first civil case to be heard was the matter of *Jacob B. Hilderbrand vs. Robert McClure*. The case involved claims of trespassing and ejectment, but was eventually withdrawn by the plaintiff's attorney, the aforementioned John Hunter. The cost of the entire case, including attorney's fees, was $26.25.

May 1804 marked the first criminal case in Mercer County. In this case, the defendant, James King, was indicted on charges of forcible entry. The jury found King not guilty. On the same note, the second criminal proceedings were against Henry Gilmore, who was charged with assault and battery. Again, the jury reached a not-guilty verdict. This year also marked the first grand jury, which was made up of eighteen members.

Although the county has generally had a courthouse since 1807, it was not always easily accessible. Until the completion of the Erie Extension Canal, the Pittsburgh Pike (Route 19), and Meadville Road, people had to depend on the sometimes undependable horse paths and back roads. "Riding the circuit" is one good example of this unfavorable journey. The phrase was given to the judges and lawyers who traveled from county to county to carry out their business. This difficult and often dangerous trek navigated through the unsettled wilderness and caused many judges and lawyers to miss their respective cases. These men were also forced to carry law books with them on their trips since the county had no central law library.

In the 1840s a second court served Mercer County to provide relief from the overcrowded dockets. A district court was established in 1839 and originally included only Crawford, Erie, and Venango Counties, but ultimately extended to cover Mercer and Warren Counties. This district court lasted six years and held only one judge, James Thompson. In addition to serving as a judge on the district court, Judge Thompson also served in the state legislature as Speaker of the House and on the Pennsylvania Supreme Court for fifteen years, the last four as chief justice.

Many men followed Judge Moore as judges of the Mercer County Court, but none were as interesting as Judge Leo H. McKay in the early 1900s. Judge McKay's biggest disappointment was losing the appointment of president judge to Judge Rodgers. Both McKay and Rodgers were appointed to replace a deceased president judge; however, only one could hold this high-ranking position. To determine who would hold this office, numbers one through twenty were placed in a cigar humidor and each man picked a number. Judge McKay drew sixteen while Judge Rodgers drew twenty, defeating McKay. This event was not the beginning of McKay's troubles, however. While serving as district attorney in 1929, McKay's home had been bombed and sustained $2,000 worth of damage. The bombing occurred after McKay had investigated several raids on speakeasies in Mercer and Trumbull Counties. Moreover, while serving as judge, McKay was assaulted during a nonsupportive hearing by an irate wife. When the ruling favored the husband, the wife charged Judge McKay and attempted to hit him with her purse. Two deputies grabbed the women, but she overpowered them and fled the courtroom. She was later found and arrested. While in jail the woman broke every window in the women's section of the jail with her shoe. Eventually the contempt charge against the woman was dropped when the husband paid for the damages and the woman apologized to Judge McKay.

William Scott Riddle (pictured in his office) was Mercer County sheriff from 1896 till 1899. William Romine (pictured above) has been the county sheriff since 1988.

Samuel S. Mehard was appointed district judge of Mercer County in 1883. According to a December 14, 1883, article in the **Sandy Lake News**, *"The appointment is a good one and gives as general satisfaction as would be that of any Democrat in this Republican District. Mr. Mehard is a young man, being about 35 years of age, in the prime of life and vigor of his bodily and mental powers. He brings to the Judicial Bench a cultured mind and a good and clean reputation, both as a man and an attorney. He is a native of Butler County, grew to manhood in Mercer, and has spent his life there except so much as was lived at college and in foreign travel and study." Mehard was retired by the time of the dedication of the third courthouse in 1911, but participated in laying the cornerstone.*

Judges (from left): Samuel S. Mehard, Samuel S. Miller, Albert H. Williams, and James A. McLaughry.

The 50th Annual Township Supervisors Convention was held in Philadelphia in 1972 and attended by thirty-seven Mercer County Township supervisors. (Contributor: Joyce Young)

Route 19 splits Fairview Township and the village of Fairview in half. Supposedly the area received its name because of the spectacular views from various places in the township, particularly in the summertime. On the north side of the village is the township building (pictured, in 2000), which was constructed in 1992. One of the overseers of the construction project was DeWitt Palmer, who has served as a township supervisor for fifty-two years and plans to retire as such at the end of his current term. The building contains the township office, a garage for township equipment, and a social area for parties and receptions.

Comparison of Mercer County Voting Percentages to National and State Percentages

	National Voting Percentages				Pennsylvania Voting Percentages			Mercer Voting Percentages		
Year	Republican		Democrat	Other	Republican	Democrat	Other	Republican	Democrat	Other
1996	40.7% Dole, Bob		49.2% **Clinton, Bill**	10.1%	40.0%	**49.2%**	10.9%	37.6%	**50.0%**	11.0%
1992	37.4% Bush, George		43.0% **Clinton, Bill**	19.5%	36.1%	**45.1%**	18.7%	32.3%	**46.7%**	21.1%
1988	53.4% **Bush, George**		45.6% Dukakis, Michael S.	1.0%	**50.7%**	48.4%	0.9%	46.4%	**52.9%**	0.7%
1984	58.8% **Reagan, Ronald**		40.6% Mondale, Walter F.	0.7%	**53.3%**	46.0%	0.7%	49.1%	**50.0%**	0.9%
1980	50.7% **Reagan, Ronald**		41.0% Carter, Jimmy	8.2%	**49.6%**	42.5%	7.9%	**48.5%**	42.8%	8.7%
1976	48.0% Ford, Gerald R.		50.1% **Carter, Jimmy**	1.9%	47.7%	**50.4%**	1.9%	46.6%	**51.9%**	1.5%
1972	60.7% **Nixon, Richard M.**		37.5% McGovern, George S.	1.8%	**59.1%**	39.1%	1.8%	**59.4%**	38.4%	2.2%
1968	43.4% **Nixon, Richard M.**		42.7% Humphrey, Hubert H.	13.9%	44.0%	**47.6%**	8.4%	**47.1%**	46.5%	6.4%
1964	38.6% Goldwater, Barry M.		61.1% **Johnson, Lyndon B.**	0.3%	34.7%	**64.9%**	0.4%	35.9%	**63.7%**	0.4%
1960	49.5% Nixon, Richard M.		49.7% **Kennedy, John F.**	0.7%	48.7%	**51.1%**	0.2%	**54.4%**	45.3%	0.2%
1956	57.4% **Eisenhower, Dwight D.**		42.0% Stevenson, Adlai E.	0.7%	**56.5%**	43.3%	0.2%	**59.1%**	40.6%	0.2%
1952	55.1% **Eisenhower, Dwight D.**		44.4% Stevenson, Adlai E.	0.5%	**52.7%**	46.9%	0.4%	**55.6%**	43.7%	0.7%
1948	45.1% Dewey, Thomas E.		49.6% **Truman, Harry S**	5.4%	**50.9%**	46.9%	2.2%	**52.7%**	44.9%	2.4%
1944	45.9% Dewey, Thomas E.		53.4% **Roosevelt, Franklin D.**	0.7%	48.4%	**51.1%**	0.5%	**53.9%**	45.6%	0.6%
1940	44.8% Wilkie, Wendell		54.7% **Roosevelt, Franklin D.**	0.5%	46.3%	**53.2%**	0.4%	**55.1%**	44.4%	0.5%
1936	36.5% Landon, Alfred M.		60.8% **Roosevelt, Franklin D.**	2.7%	40.8%	**56.9%**	2.3%	45.9%	**51.8%**	2.3%
1932	39.6% Hoover, Herbert C.		57.4% **Roosevelt, Franklin D.**	2.9%	**50.8%**	45.3%	3.8%	**53.5%**	41.7%	4.7%
1928	58.2% **Hoover, Herbert C.**		40.8% Smith, Alfred E.	1.0%	**65.2%**	33.9%	0.9%	**72.7%**	26.4%	0.9%
1924	54.0% **Coolidge, Calvin**		28.8% Davis, John W.	17.1%	**65.3%**	19.1%	15.6%	**65.3%**	16.4%	18.3%
1920	60.3% **Harding Warren G.**		34.1% Cox, James M.	5.5%	**65.8%**	27.2%	7.0%	**60.3%**	25.1%	14.6%
1916	46.1% Hughes, Charles		49.2% **Wilson, Woodrow**	4.7%	**54.3%**	40.2%	5.5%	42.7%	**46.5%**	10.8%
1912	23.2% Taft, William		41.8% **Wilson, Woodrow**	35.0%	22.5%	**32.5%**	45.0%	14.7%	31.8%	53.5%
1908	51.6% **Taft, William**		43.1% Bryan, William	5.3%	**58.8%**	35.4%	5.8%	**47.3%**	39.8%	12.9%
1904					Data not available					
1900	51.7% **McKinley, William**		45.5% Bryan, William	2.8%	**60.7%**	36.2%	3.1%	**55.9%**	39.6%	4.5%

(source: Michael Coulter)

Office of the Commissioners

Beginning year of term served	Names
1911	John Hassel, Thomas Beatty, Frank McGrath
1915	A.W. Beil, Thomas Beatty, W.E. Cossitt
1920	Thomas Beatty, James Gamble, J.W. Black
1923	Thomas Beatty, David J. Jarrett, Pierce G. Minner
1928	W.A. Bone, Harry Hunter, Harry Gibson
1931	J.C. Wilson, Harry Gibson, D.K. Callahan
1935	Robert Jamieson, D.K. Callahan, Geo. W. Boyd
1939	D.K. Callahan, James Bailey, Albert E. Moses
1941	James L. Bailey, Frank D. Fair, D.K. Callahan
1942	D.K. Callahan, R. Roscoe Simons, Lawrence J. Wilhelm
1955	Charles B. Lytle, Arthur E. McCarthy, Lawrence J. Wilhelm
1959	Lawrence J. Wilhelm, Charles P. Minner, Walter E. Cochran
1964	Charles P. Minner, Lawrence J. Wilhelm, John Russell
1968	John G. Johnson, Charles L. McCracken, William Coleman
1972	Frank L. Swogger Jr., William M. Coleman, Charles L. McCracken
1976	Frank L. Swogger Jr., Peter J. Joyce, Charles L. McCracken
1978	Peter J. Joyce, Josephine D. McCutcheon, Harold E. Bell
1980	William M. Reznor, Harold E. Bell, Josephine D. McCutcheon
1984	William M. Reznor, Harold E. Bell, Les Cattron
1988	William M. Reznor, Harold E. Bell, Joseph F. Fragle
1992	Joseph F. Fragle, William M. Reznor, Olivia M. Lazor
1995	Joseph F. Fragle, John G. Johnson, Olivia M. Lazor
1996	Richard R. Stevenson, Cloyd E. Brenneman, Olivia M. Lazor
2000	Cloyd E. Brenneman, Olivia M. Lazor, Brian W. Shipley

County Judges in 2000

Court of Common Pleas

Francis J. Fornelli, president judge
Michael J. Wherry, judge
Thomas R. Dobson, judge

District Judges	District
James E. McMahon	2-1
Henry J. Russo	2-2
Ruth M. French	3-1
Lawrence T. Silvus	3-2
William L. Fagley	3-3

County Officerholders During the 1900s

County Controller	From	To
Arthur B. Collins	1942	1950
Walter E. Coleman	1950	1958
Ida A. Ralya	1958	1966
Mary L. Stevenson	1966	1986
Wanda A. McCamey Oman	1986	1994
Dennis M. Songer	1994	-

Prothonotary	From	To
William Paden	1908	1911
William S. Hirst	1912	1915
William H. Jones	1916	1923
Belle W. Davis	1924	1927
Virginia Lee Davis	1928	1929
Daisy T. Moore	1929	1931
S. Earl Hoagland	1932	1935
John H. Barnes	1936	1939
Harry W. Kremis	1940	1947
William A. Elder	1948	1963
James C. Griffin	1964	1977
Mary E. Griffin	1978	1991
Elizabeth F. Fair	1992	-

Recorder	From	To
J. Allison Keck	1908	1911
Charles Stewart	1912	1915
Sherman E. Mattocks	1916	1919
Edward J. Schadle	1919	1919
D. B. Findley	1920	1923
Myron W. Jones	1924	1927
William G. Jones	1928	1931
Robert G. Campbell	1932	1935
John Nicholls Service	1936	1939
Stephen Lukacs	1940	1971
Marilyn L. Felesky	1972	1979
Georgene Brown	1980	1983
Marilyn L. Felesky	1984	-

Treasurer	From	To
W. H. Simons	1912	1915
U. A. Hanna	1916	1917
John F. McConnell	1917	1919
David Lewis	1920	1923
Malcolm M. Simons	1924	1927
G. Ralph McQuiston	1928	1931
George W. Lawrence	1932	1935
Albert E. Moses	1936	1939
C. G. Scowden	1940	1943
Alex Elliott	1944	1947
Kathryn Campbell	1948	1951
Elizabeth Nicholson	1952	1955
Charles P. Minner	1956	1959
Robert G. Hunter	1960	1962
Frank L. Davis	1962	1965
Irene L. Nicholson	1966	1981
Nettie. J. Pantall	1982	1993
Virginia S. Richardson	1994	-

Clerk of Courts-Register of Wills	From	To
William D. Reznor	1912	1915
George A. Stambaugh	1916	1919
George D. Bagnall	1920	1924
Belle N. Emery	1925	1932
Marvin R. Loutzenhiser	1933	1936
Frank D. Fair	1937	1940
Fred L. Hutchinson	1941	1948
Charles B. Lytle	1949	1952
Kathryn E. Campbell	1953	1956
Elizabeth Nicholson	1957	1960
Marguerite Furey	1961	1971
Freda L. Griffith	1972	1976
Marie Forsyth	1977	1995
Kathleen M. Kloos	1996	-

Sheriff	From	To
Martin T. Crain	1911	1916
J. W. Gibson	1917	1919
David J. Jarrett	1920	1923
William Bone	1924	1927
D. K. Callahan	1928	1931
Frank D. Fair	1932	1935
C. G. Scowden	1936	1939
Alex Elliott	1940	1943
W. T. Courtney	1944	1955
J. R. Knowles	1956	1959
George J. Bryan	1960	1963
Paul H. Ague	1964	1979
Donald A. Marenchin	1980	1987
William H. Romine, Jr.	1988	-

Pioneers first settled in what is now Hempfield Township in 1796. Some of the more prominent early families included Christy, Loutzenhiser, Keck, Klingensmith, and Williamson. James Kamerer, originally from Hempfield Township in Westmoreland County, was instrumental in forming a township in 1856 from parts of Salem, West Salem, Pymatuning, and Delaware townships. Therefore, the name Hempfield was chosen for the new township out of respect for Kamerer. The township building (pictured, in 2000) is on South Mercer Street near Greenville. Now, the supervisors are Russell Dawes, Gary Hittle, and Don Marshall.

Established in 1851, New Vernon Township remains primarily rural and agricultural, with zoning for business, travel, and industrial areas. Camping, boating, and fishing are enjoyed due to Lake Wilhelm and Goddard State Park, which traverse this township. The township building (pictured, in 2000) is on Sheakleyville Road near the village of Clarks Mill. Now, the supervisors are (from left) John Martin, Bob Greggs, and Albert Law.

First used in 1972, the Otter Creek Township building (pictured, in 2000) contains the office and the garages for the backhoe-loader, road grader, and other township equipment. Most of the large equipment was purchased through a revenue sharing program. The township has nearly twenty-three miles of road to maintain. As finances become available, the roads are being tarred and chipped. Already about eight miles have been finished. Now, the supervisors are Richard Straub, Carl Swartz, and Robert Shollenberger. (Contributor: Joyce Young)

West Salem Township was created in 1805. The township building (pictured, in 2000) is on Vernon Road. Now, the supervisors are Ken Sherbondy, William Wingard, and Charles Murrin.

As an eighteen-year-old in 1952, Cloyd E. "Gene" Brenneman moved from Clarion County to the Shenango Valley seeking a good job in the steel mills. He stayed on at Sharon Steel while advancing his education and eventually went into business for himself in home remodeling, drywall, real estate, banking, and now public service. Brenneman was elected Mercer County Commissioner in 1995. Looking back in the fall of 1999 over events spanning nearly half a century, Brenneman reflected, "Through the years, every opportunity that came along, I seized upon it. As my success developed, I also developed a real appreciation for Mercer County and its people. With my wife, Erma, our six children and their spouses, and our twelve grandchildren, we are now a family of 20. I look forward to taking my family and Mercer County, as chairman of the board of commissioners, into the 21st century."

In 1991, Olivia M. Lazor became the first Democratic woman elected and only the second woman to serve as county commissioner. She also became the first woman to chair the board of commissioners.
Her many responsibilities include working on federal legislative issues as a member of the Human Service and Education Subcommittee of the National Association of Counties and working on state legislative matters that affect counties as a member and chair of the Human Services Committee of the County Commissioners of Pennsylvania (CCAP). She has also served as president and board chair for CCAP. Lazor has received numerous awards, including honors from the Pennsylvania Association of Human Service Administrators and from CCAP. The latter was the "1999 Outstanding County Commissioner" award from a nomination by Lazor's Mercer County colleagues.

Brian Shipley first became involved in government while a sophomore at Reynolds High School and helped to found the school's chapter of the Pennsylvania Youth and Government Program. At age 16, he served as student representative to the school board and, at age 18, became the youngest elected school board member in the history of Pennsylvania. By age 20, he was the president of the board! Shipley went on to work as a legislative aide to both State Senator Robert Robbins and U.S. Congressman Phil English and was elected Mercer County Commissioner in 1999.

542

Color Pictures

543

Houser Store, Stoneboro, late 1800s.

Fairfield Presbyterian Church (New Vernon Township) was established in Mercer County in 1799. The original hewed pine log building was replaced in the mid-1800s with a new structure, the first frame church building in the county. In 1903, again a new church was built, on the same site. However, the area surrounding the church has subsequently changed drastically as a result of interstate highway construction and flood control messages undertaken primarily in the late 1960s. Fairfield Church now sits atop a hill that affords a magnificent view of Lake Wilhelm and Goddard State Park with easy access to the rest of country. What a contrast to the frontier that greeted the church's founding fathers. (Photographer: Vonda Minner)

Old Salem United Methodist Church (Leech's Corner in Sugar Grove Township), organized in 1798, now meets in a structure built in 1850, which retains its original architecture. One of the key founders was Bishop Robert Richford Roberts. (Photographer: Marilyn Dewald)

545

The oldest remaining structure on Thiel College's campus, Greenville Hall was built in 1872–74 after the citizens of Greenville induced the fledgling Thiel Hall directors in Pittsburgh to move their school to northwestern Mercer County. Now, Thiel College offers academic programs to students annually. (Photographer: Marilyn Dewald)

Built in 1839 by Robert Hanna of locally fired bricks, this house on South Pitt Street in Mercer was occupied later by Edward Small, an abolitionist minister of the United Presbyterian Church, and his wife Mary, daughter of Robert Hanna. They operated an underground railroad station for escaping slaves, which was confirmed years later when a secret room hidden under the kitchen was discovered. The Yeager White family lived in the house later, and the house still stands. (Photographer: Marilyn Dewald)

Mercer County in 1909 had thirty-one townships, although not quite the same thirty-one it has now. (Photographer: Marilyn Dewald)

Buhl Farm Park (Hermitage) was conceived by Frank H. Buhl in 1907 and now provides picnic shelters, picnic groves, the Casino (pictured), a swimming pool, Lake Julia, playgrounds, bocce and tennis courts, ball and kite fields, a rose garden, a free golf course, a driving range, ponds, and the Performing Arts Center. Concerts are held at the Center almost every Sunday during summers and on Buhl Days. Ice skating was allowed on Lake Julia until the 1960s. (Artist: John Milan)

Caldwell School (Delaware Township) was the last of Mercer County's more than 225 one-room schoolhouses to close, in 1960. Now property of the Mercer County Historical Society, the schoolhouse is open for tours, which have been given for the past forty years by Mae Beringer who was Caldwell's last teacher. (Photographer: Frank Lord)

In Mercer, the Pennsylvania Railroad station was on what is now Route 58 at the foot of Butler Street. It was served by "livery" service to the courthouse on the "Diamond" at the top of the hill. By the second decade of the 1900s, a taxi cab, a new motor bus, and the traditional horse-drawn livery were competing for train riders headed for Mercer's central business district. (Contributor: Frederick Houser)

Nestled in Perry Township is the village of Hadley where the new post office contrasts against its neighbor, the old Gilger & Son Store (now a residence). Gene Jordan (Hadley) related a story about Paul McClain who was born about 1909 and lived nearly all his life in Perry Township. About 1925, McClain lived in Clarks Mills and walked the Lake Shore Railroad to Hadley High School. When he passed Gilger's Store a couple of days before Thanksgiving, Wall Gilger stood on the porch of the store, which his great grandfather had founded in 1867, and called to McClain, "Hey, Paul, you didn't get your ticket for the turkey giveaway." So, McClain gave Gilger a quarter. After school that day as McClain passed the store, Gilger called, "You won the bird, Paul. Come around back and get him." The turkey was still alive so McClain wrestled it under his arm the four miles home east along the railroad to Clarks Mills. (Photographer: Marilyn Dewald)

Further contrasts of the old and new can be seen everyday as the Amish farmers and carpenters live with their traditional and humble ways side by side with the modern trappings of the "English" with their electricity, automobiles, and telecommunications. (Photographer: Marilyn Dewald)

Southeast of Grove City, this airport (Pine Township) was used from the early 1940s until the new Grove City Airport was built in Springfield Township in the mid-1970s. The old airport's principal users were the Cooper-Bessemer Corporation and other local businesses as well as individuals who enjoyed flying as a hobby. One paved runway ran east-west for about 1,500 feet and the other north-south for about 2,500 feet. The line of flight for the latter went directly over the screen of the Larkfield Drive-In Theater, which still stands although is no longer used as a theater. (Photo: William Menzies; caption: Richard Christner)

In 1959, the Sandy Creek Conservancy was established to help solve the problems that the towns of Sandy Lake and Stoneboro were having due to Sandy Creek's periodic flooding. A dam built in 1971 for flood control and wildlife conservation created the 1,860-acre Lake Wilhelm (Mill Creek, New Vernon, Deer Creek, and Sandy Creek Townships), now filled with bass, walleye, and pike. The lake represents the Conservancy's success in coordinating seventeen agencies over a decade. The adjacent Maurice K. Goddard State Park offers picnic areas, hiking trails, and hunting opportunities. In 1974, the McKeever Environmental Learning Center opened nearby to encourage better stewardship of natural resources. (Photographer: Marilyn Dewald)

Chicago-bound intermodal train of the Erie Lackawanna Railroad traversed the former Erie Railroad main line south of Shenango, pictured here in 1974. Two years later, the Erie Lackawanna was folded into Conrail, and its traffic in both directions between New York City and Chicago diverted to Conrail's other routes. Within a few years, almost all former Erie trackage west of Youngstown had been abandoned. (Photo: Vinson Skibo; caption: Frederick Houser)

The Avenue of the Flags at Hillcrest Memorial Park in Hermitage was originally started to mark the duration of captivity for the American hostages in Iran between 1979 and 1981. As the hostage situation wore on, Tom Flynn, Hillcrest owner, with help from unemployed steelworkers in the Shenango Valley and flags donated by the families of veterans buried at Hillcrest, raised one flag for each day of captivity. Now, these 444 flags serve as a symbol of American hope and pride. (Photographer: Marilyn Dewald)

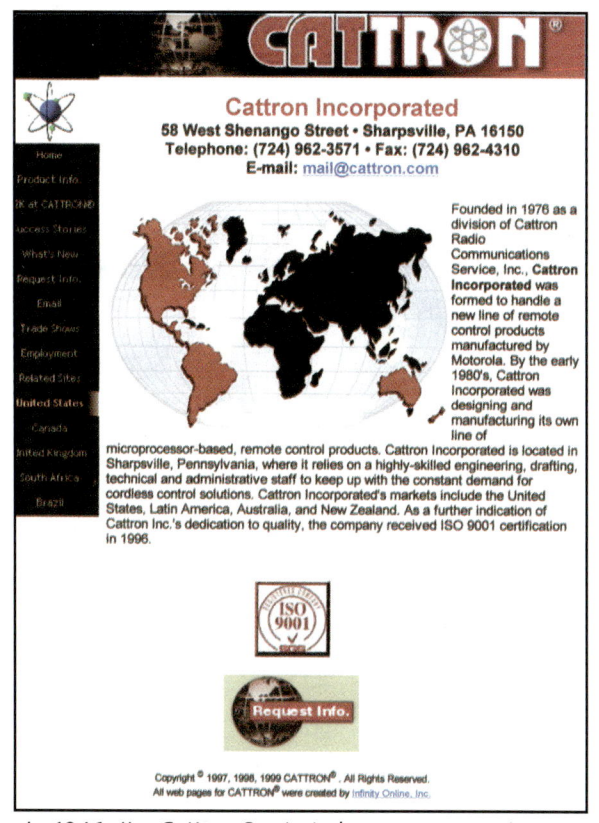

In 1946, Jim Cattron Sr. started a one-man service company to install and maintain a taxi radio system in Hermitage. Cattron Radio Communications Service grew and now, as the Cattron Group, has branched out into diverse markets, including industrial portable remote control systems, and is known worldwide. Cattron Incorporated is one of several companies that now constitute the Cattron Group Inc. (Source: Cattron's Web site)

In Farrell, in the midst of the old steel mill sites, which operated as late as 1992, Duferco Steel Corporation opened in late 1998 with 115 employees. The new plant has continued to grow and now employs about 500. (Photographer: Marilyn Dewald)

West Branch Holstein Farm (Shenango Township) is owned by David, Vonda, Robert, and Ann Minner. In 1966 (see inset), the cows were milked with a milking machine, and the milk dumped into 10-gallon cans, carried into the milk house, and placed in the cooler. By 1999, after gradually adding more technically advanced equipment and techniques, this "family farm" has evolved into a "family farm business" with a milking parlor and the workers and equipment to milk 300 cows three times a day. (Contributor: Vonda Minner)

At the 1999 Stoneboro Fair, (from left) Tammy Hanna (1999–2000 Mercer County Dairy Princess), Samuel Hayes (Pennsylvania Secretary of Agriculture), and Pennsylvania Senator Bob Robbins (far right) pose with representatives of the following, newly recognized Century Farms: the Lackey Farm (established in 1835 in Perry Township), McFarland Farm (established in 1868 in Wilmington Township), and McDowell Farm (established 1838 in Pine Township). (Contributor: Vonda Minner)

In addition to the Mercer County Historical Society, several communities have organized their own historical societies: Greenville, Grove City, Hermitage, Jamestown, Sharon, Stoneboro, and Wheatland. Nine years after organizing in 1974, Jamestown Area Historical Society purchased the Dorothy Simons Snyder home (pictured, in 1999), which dates back to the 1870s. The society participates annually in the Pioneer Festival held at Pymatuning State Park and in the Jamestown Fair. The officers now are Sandra Laurie, Norma Leary, Mary Lou White, Evelyn Anderson, Esther McClimans, Jeff Amon, and Neva Agney. (Photographer: Cynthia Snodgrass Jones; caption: Evelyn Anderson)

In 1994, the complexion of Springfield Township began to change as the Grove City Factory Shops opened. With subsequent expansions and now called the Prime Outlets at Grove City, this shopping mecca boasts over 140 stores and attracts thousands of customers daily. Near the interchange of Interstates 79 and 80, much of the surrounding land, formerly farmland, is being developed to offer new hotels and restaurants. (Contributor: Bruce Engelhardt)

Among all the manmade changes imposed on Mercer County over the past two hundred years, the natural aspects of the countryside can still be observed and enjoyed. Fishing, hunting, boating, and hiking are popular pastimes. Here, in October 1998, the beauty of fall foliage can be seen on Route 965 about halfway between Jackson Center and Perrine Corners. (Photographer: Robert Lark)

Now, Mercer County is crossed by Interstates 79 and 80 and has two large reservoirs created by manmade dams, Lake Wilhelm and Shenango River Lake. (Photographer: Marilyn Dewald)

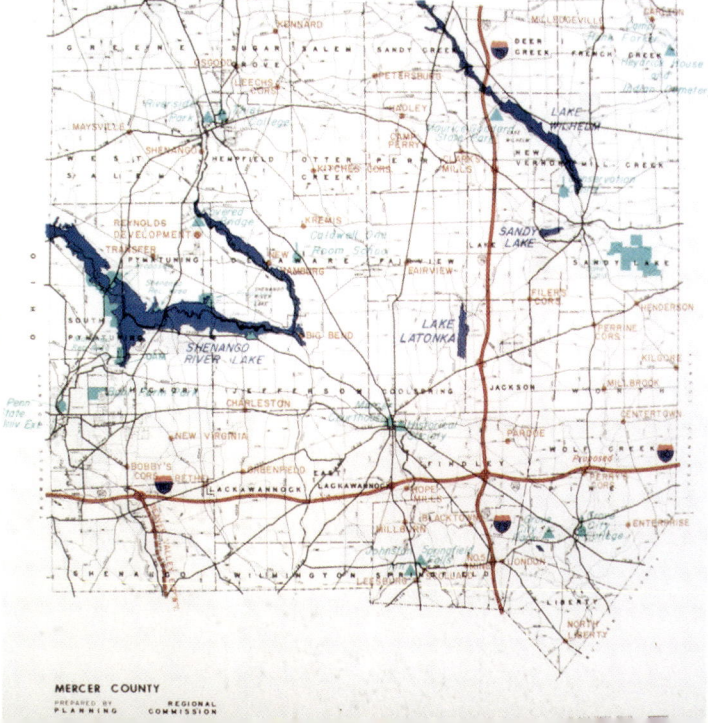

The Mercer County Courthouse at dusk, 1990s, represents the end of a prolific two hundred-year history and the continuation of the institutions of law and order that have prevailed in this county since it was created in 1800. (Photographer: Frank Lord)

561

730
LEROY E. WILLIAMS WT 3/C
USS COLLETT
With Honor I Served in World War II
CARGO
SUB
PLANE
BRONZE STAR 1; SILVER 5; BLUE 10; GREEN 50; RED 100

Appendix B: Military

MERCER COUNTY VETERANS
By Edward Hoagland

Since the beginning of Mercer County, the young men and women have generously given of their time and talents in serving the United States in time of war and peace. Even before the county became official, thirty-six veterans had served during the Revolutionary War: thirty-four in the Army and two in the Navy. During the War of 1812, 187 men served, all of them in the Army. In fact, two of these men were my relatives: Colonel Henry Hoagland and his son, John, helped Admiral Peary get his ships over the sandbar in Lake Erie.

The Civil War showed a significant increase in the number of citizens enlisting. Of those men, 2,080 were killed in action and are buried in various cemeteries of the county. These men served their country well, and those who survived the ordeal came back home to begin life anew.

The next conflict was the Spanish-American War, in which 499 soldiers lost their lives and are buried in the county.

Then came the war to end all wars: World War I. In 1917, many of Mercer County's young people went to France and Germany to carry out their assignments. We lost 1,063 men and women in this tragedy.

World War II saw the great surge of young men and women being drafted and enlisting in the various services. I was one of those who went and served. I was fortunate in that I came back to begin my life again. Of all who served from Mercer County, 6,582 citizens lost their lives in this great struggle. This war marked the great expansion of Mercer County, and we continue to grow in peace and harmony.

The Korean War saw many of our young men serving in the Armed Forces. We lost 976 in this struggle, and they are buried in various cemeteries in the county.

The Vietnam War era saw many of the sons of World War II veterans serving in the Armed Forces, with a loss of 416 men and women.

It is a known fact that Mercer County boys and girls, men and women, have contributed a great deal to the general well-being of each of us throughout the years and we continue to be very proud of them. We can only hope that the next two hundred years will prove to be good ones and that we do not have to send any of our citizens into any conflict.

Work on moving the granite boulder from the Wishart farm started in January 1930. Eventually estimated to be around twenty-six tons, the stone was loaded onto a strong sled (pictured, with Harry Reichart, Harvey Reichart, and Leonard Lawton) and towed down the hill to the Sharpsville & New Wilmington Railroad. It was then loaded onto a flatcar and brought to town. The stone arrived in Sharpsville on March 4, 1930, and was placed in the town park on April 30, 1930, by contractor A. W. Bombeck. A month later, the war memorial was unveiled by S. C. Foster and Watson Rood, Civil War veterans. Several thousand people were assembled near the Legion Home to witness the dedication and watch the parade that followed. At the close of the program, a salute to the dead was given by the Sharpsville Legion Rifle Squad. Fine music was furnished by the Sharon, Greenville, and Grove City bugle and drum corps. The memorial (pictured, about 1999) was erected by the citizens of Sharpsville by their contributions. (Contributor: Peter Joyce)

COUNTY'S LAST CIVIL WAR SOLDIER DIES AT AGE OF 98

2-28-42

Served Throughout War, Marched With Sherman Through Georgia.

LIVED IN SANDY LAKE 73 YEARS

William Bailey, last surviving Civil War veteran in Mercer County, lacking less than two years to reach the age of 100, died at his home on Broad Street, Sandy Lake, Monday evening, Oct. 4, 1943, at six o'clock. Mr. Bailey, had he lived until next Feb. 28, would have completed his 99th year, his birth date being Feb. 28, 1845. Despite his age and failing health for the past year he was bedfast only since Wednesday of last week and a Greenville friend who called on him less than two weeks ago found him alert and interesting which was a characteristic of this remarkable man.

His native town was Weathersfield, O., his parents being Obadiah and Annabelle Kiscald Bailey. He was one of 11 children and is the last to pass away. He spent his youth in Ohio but at his death had completed 73 years of residence in Sandy Lake, 72 years of which he was a member of the Christian Church and a regular attendant as long as health permitted. He served as elder and also as deacon for many years.

He had a fine record as a soldier in the Civil War. "I am proud that I served my country in the Civil War, under General Burnside and later under General Sherman," he told a representative of this paper on his birthday in 1942. "I was with Sherman "from Atlanta to the sea." Four brothers of us in that war and now I have a grandson carrying on in the Medical Department, of the 15th Infantry."

He enlisted when he was 18 and served all through the Civil War, his campaign including Atlanta, Washington and points in Kentucky, Tennessee, South Carolina, North Carolina, Virginia and Maryland.

After the war he engaged in farming in Mahoning County, O., and later worked in a blast furnace at Mineral Ridge, O. He came to Sandy Lake to help open the coal banks on Coal Hill and was engaged there until 1906. For many years he has made his home with his son, Harry, and his granddaughter, Mrs. Dorothy Brown.

He kept up his interest in public affairs and had a hobby of collecting curios and antiques, chiefly guns and revolvers of which he had about 60 rare specimens. He was a great reader and his favorite book was the Bible.

He married Elizabeth Barker, Dec. 1, 1868, who preceded him in death 20 years ago. He is survived by a son, Harry of Sandy Lake, and by a daughter, Mrs. Ernest McCalmont of Ellsworth, O. Another son, Angus, died 31 years ago. Four grandchildren survive Mr. Bailey.

Funeral services will be held Thursday at 2 p. m. at the Christian Church, conducted by his pastor, Rev. F. A. Bright. Interment will be in Oak Hill Cemetery where he will be laid to rest with military honors.

Friends may call at the family home at any time.

William Bailey and patriotic young friends on Mr. Bailey's 97th birthday.

(Source: Mercer Dispatch, February 28, 1942)

A group of Otter Creek Township residents, known as the Willing Workers and led by Mrs. Thomas Whitlatch, organized an effort to place a monument on land donated by Mr. and Mrs. Albert Williamson to honor the soldiers the township lost in World War II. In 1947, the monument (pictured, in 2000) was dedicated, and it has been maintained by the township ever since. In 1984, a group of young people from a local church planted the shrubs. (Contributor: Joyce Young)

Enlarged in 1997, the Grove City Community Roll of Honor (pictured, in 1997) in the community's Memorial Park now lists all known servicemen who died during World War I, World War II, and the conflicts in Korea, Vietnam, Panama, Grenada, and Desert Storm. (Photographers: Nick and Kathy Pompa)

Honor Roll Report: WORLD WAR I

KIA*	Last	First	M	Branch of Service
K	ADDIS	THOMAS	A	USA
K	ALEXANDER	MERLE	C	USA
K	ALEXANDER	STERLING		USA
K	AMON	FRANK	0	USA
K	BAILEY	WILLIAM		USA
K	BATES	CLEMENT	C	USA
K	BEATTY	ROBERT	F	USA
K	BELL	THOMAS	H	USMC
K	BORLAND JR	RALPH		USA
K	BRANDT	DELBERT	C	USA
K	BROCKLEHURST	FRANK	V	USA
K	BUCHANAN	DEAN		USA
K	CARROLL	PRESTON	H	USA
K	CHINN	RUSSELL		USA
K	DAVIS	DANIEL		USA
K	EVANS	WILLIAM		USA
K	FLEMMING	JOHN	L	USA
K	FOUST	JOSEPH		USA
K	FOUST	ROBERT	W	USA
K	GILMORE	WILLIAM	F	USN
K	GOODALL	GROVER		USA
K	HAMLIN	RAYMOND	L	USA
K	HARBULACK	ANDREW	S	USMC
K	HARRIS	WILLIAM		USA
K	HETTRICK	JACOB		USA
K	HOFFMAN	HAROLD	W	USA
K	HOOPES	JOSEPH	B	USA
K	HORN	T	J	USA
K	HUNT	THOMAS	E	USA
K	JACKSON	JOHN	M	USA
K	KELSO	RAY	E	USA
K	KEOUGH	JOHN		USA
K	KINGAN	JAMES	B	USA
K	KINGAN	ROBERT	S	USA
K	KISHLER	EDWIN	P	USMC
K	KLEIN	NORMAN	H	USA
K	LEIPHIEMER	CARLTON	D	USA
K	LEPEY	JOHN		USA
K	LETSKO	MARTIN		USMC
K	LEWIS	WARD		USA
K	LOCKE	FRED	B	USA
K	LUNGER	WILLIAM	G	USA
K	LYNCH	EDMUND	W	USA
K	MAGARGEE	JOHN	R	USA
K	MAHAN	EARL		USA

Honor Roll Report: WORLD WAR I

KIA*	Last	First	M	Branch of Service
K	MAXWELL	DANIEL	H	USA
K	MAYS	JOHN	E	USA
K	MCCAUSLIN	CLARENCE	A	USA
K	MCCONVILLE	JAMES	F	USA
K	MCCONVILLE	JOHN	H	USA
K	MCGINNIS	JOHN	H	USA
K	MCGRANAHAN	CLAIRE	R	USA
K	MCGRANAHAN	JOSEPH	H	USAC
K	MERRITT	CHARLES	B	USA
K	MILLER	FRED	H	USA
K	MILLER	WILLIAM		USA
K	MILLSOP	JOHN		USA
K	MITCHELL	NORMAN	M	USA
K	MONTGOMERY	MERRITT	E	USA
K	MOST	THOMAS	S	USA
K	MULLINS	VERNER	M	USA
K	MURRIN	WILLIAM	L	USA
K	NEEDHAM	PETER		USA
K	PARSONS	HARVEY		USA
K	PATTERSON	ALEXANDER		USA
K	PENCE	FRED	L	USA
K	PENRY	WILLIAM	I	USA
K	POPP	ISADORE		USA
K	RAY	FRED	B	USA
K	REARDON	CHARLES		USA
K	RICHARDS	CLYDE	E	USA
K	ROMANO	VINCENZO		USA
K	ROSE	ESPY	J	USA
K	SAYLOR	VERNON	W	USA
K	SCHADT	FLOYD	D	USA
K	SCHMITT	EDWARD	H	USA
K	SHUPIENES	JOHN		USA
K	SMERIK	GEORGE		USA
K	SMITH	CHARLES		USA
K	SMITH	WILLIAM	A	USA
K	STAFFORD	JOHN	E	USA
K	SWARTZ	RAY	I	USA
K	TAYLOR	EDWARD		USA
K	TROUTMAN	WILLIAM		USA
K	VAN EMAN	CLAIRE	L	USMC
K	VANAERSCHOT	JOHN	V	USA
K	VICKERMAN	CHARLES	M	MERM
K	WRIGHT	CHARLES		USA
K	WRIGHT	SHANNON		USA
K	ZAKRZEWSKI	SYGMUND		USA

Honor Roll Report: WORLD WAR I

KIA*	Last	First	M	Branch of Service
N	BELL	JAMES		USA
N	BOWERS	RALPH		USA
N	BOYD	LEROY	B	USA
N	BURTORS	MICHAEL		USA
N	CALLAHAN	JOHN	J	USA
N	CALLAHAN	SYLVESTER		USA
N	CARFOLI	NICK		USA
N	CLARKSON	ROBERT	W	USA
N	COAKLEY	JOHN	A	USA
N	COWAN	DEWITT	C	USA
N	CUMMING	CHARLES	C	USA
N	ELLIOTT	HARRY		USA
N	FAUST	ROBERT		USA
N	FITCH	JOHN	K	USA
N	GARRIFFA	PASQUALE		USA
N	GILLILAND	WILLIAM	W	USA
N	GLANCEY	DANIEL	J	USA
N	GRAHAM	CURTIS	L	USA
N	GRIFFITH	RALPH	L	USA
N	HARRY	VIRGIL	H	USN
N	HATTON	ERNEST	J	USA
N	HECKMAN	RALPH	L	USA
N	HIGHWAY	JAMES		USA
N	HOFFMAN	WADE		USA
N	KEITH	JOHN	F	USA
N	LARY	RALPH	P	USA
N	LAWRENCE	ELMER	E	USA
N	MCCUTCHEON	J	M	USA
N	MILES	FRED	I	USA
N	REZNOR	RICHARD	C	USA
N	RICHAEL	LAWRENCE	L	USA
N	RODAHEAVER	FRANKLIN		USA
N	ROWE	WILLIAM	T	USA
N	STEWART	WILLIAM	H	USA
N	TOBIA	PETER		USA
N	VIROSTICK	MICHAEL		USA
N	WALTERS	CARL	M	USA
N	WILLIAMS	VERNE	E	USA
N	ZUSCHLAG	ELMER	G	USA
N	ZUVER	EDWIN	P	USA

Information collected as of March 28, 2000.
* KIA column: K = Killed in action as a result of hostile activity; N = Death not as a result of hostile action, for example, accidental discharging a rifle while in a foxhole or being run over by a tank.

Honor Roll Report: WORLD WAR II

KIA*	Last	First	M	Branch of Service
K	ABERNATHY	ISRAEL	E	USA
K	ADAMS	WILLIAM	J	USN
K	ADLER	CARL	J	USA
K	ALBERTSON	ALBERT	J	USA
K	ALTHAM	WILLIAM	H	USA
K	ANCTILL	PAUL		USA
K	ARGENZIANO	JOSEPH		USA
K	ARGENZIANO	JOSEPH	A	USA
K	AXTELL	SAMUEL		USN
K	BACKMAN	JOHN		USAC
K	BALHUT	STEPHEN		USA
K	BALTUS	FLOYD		USA
K	BALUT	MITCHELL	E	USA
K	BARBER	GAIL	L	USA
K	BARNHART	JOHN	E	USA
K	BARR	CLIFFORD	H	USA
K	BARR	ROBERT	N	USN
K	BARTOLO	EDWARD	J	USA
K	BARTON	DAVID	B	USA
K	BECKER	EDWARD	P	USN
K	BEES	GEORGE		USMC
K	BELMONT	AL		USA
K	BENETIN	ANDREW	J	USA
K	BENNETT	CHARLES	W	USAC
K	BENYA	MATTHEW		USA
K	BESTWICK	JAMES	E	USA
K	BESTWICK	ROBERT		USA
K	BIANCO	THOMAS		USA
K	BIGGINS	EDWARD	W	USA
K	BILLIG	WILLIAM	G	USAC
K	BITTLER	LEWIS	W	USA
K	BLACK	FREDERICK	E	USA
K	BLACK	FREDERICK	J	USA
K	BLAKE	HAROLD	W	USAC
K	BLATT	RICHARD	C	USA
K	BLOSE	JAMES	W	USAC
K	BOBBY	ELMER		USA
K	BOCA	ANTHONY		USA
K	BOLLINGER	RICHARD	H	USN
K	BONN	HERBERT	S	USN
K	BOYLE	RICHARD	C	USA
K	BROWN	HERBERT		USA
K	BURLCH	IGNATIUS		USA
K	BURNS	JAMES	T	USMC
K	BUTCHKO	JOHN		USMC
K	BUTTERFIELD	DAVID	B	USN
K	CALBRESE	ANTHONY		USA

Honor Roll Report: WORLD WAR II

KIA*	Last	First	M	Branch of Service
K	CAMERON	JOHN	C	USA
K	CAMINITI	HARRY		USA
K	CAMPBELL	DAVID	A	USN
K	CAMPBELL	PAUL	L	USA
K	CAMPBELL	PHILLIP	G	USN
K	CATALDO	ROCCO	A	USA
K	CHANEY	VICTOR	G	USN
K	CHINTELLA	JOSEPH		USA
K	CHIODO	JOHN		USA
K	CHIZMAR	JOHN	R	USA
K	CLONE	MELVIN	J	USA
K	CLARK	WILLIAM	H	USN
K	COAN JR	DENNIS	J	USA
K	COLES	RICHARD	S	USMC
K	COOK	HOWARD	P	USAC
K	COOKSON	LYLE		USA
K	COOPER	GLENN	E	USA
K	COSEX	JOHN		USN
K	COX	WILLIAM	R	USA
K	CRAFT	RICHARD	E	USA
K	CRAIG	ROBERT	J	MERM
K	CRILL	RONALD		USA
K	CRISAN	NICHOLAS		USA
K	CROSBY	MURRAY	W	USA
K	CROSS	WALTER		USA
K	CURTICIAN	DAN		USAC
K	D'AMORE	WILLIAM	N	USN
K	DARR	GERALD	L	USAC
K	DATKO	JOHN	J	USN
K	DAVIDSON	EUGENE		USA
K	DEMUTH	ROBERT	L	USN
K	DERENCIN	MARIJAN		USA
K	DIGHT	PAUL	N	USN
K	DISILVIO	SAMUEL	A	USA
K	DIXON	ROBERT	L	USA
K	DOHERTY	ROBERT	L	USAC
K	DONALDSON	BERT	W	USN
K	DOYLE	WILLIAM	C	USAC
K	DRAVIS	EDWIN	D	USA
K	DUFFEY	ALLEN	W	USA
K	DUNHAM	CLARENCE	L	USA
K	DUNKERLEY	HOMER		USA
K	DURISKO	JOHN		USA
K	DZURINDA	NICHOLAS		USA
K	EASTON	WILLIAM	H	USAC
K	ELLIS	THOMAS		USAC
K	ERICKSON	FRANK	C	USAC

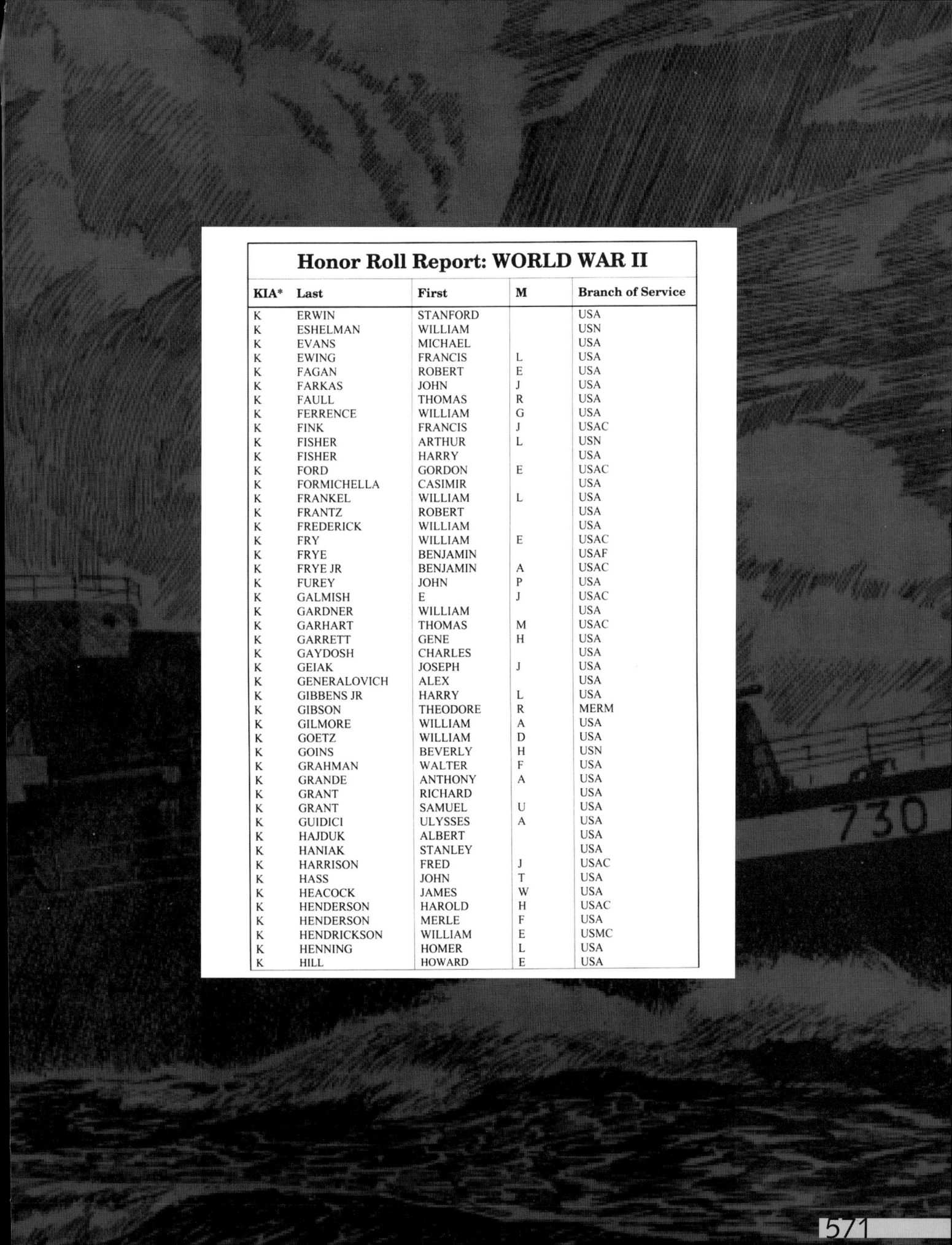

Honor Roll Report: WORLD WAR II

KIA*	Last	First	M	Branch of Service
K	ERWIN	STANFORD		USA
K	ESHELMAN	WILLIAM		USN
K	EVANS	MICHAEL		USA
K	EWING	FRANCIS	L	USA
K	FAGAN	ROBERT	E	USA
K	FARKAS	JOHN	J	USA
K	FAULL	THOMAS	R	USA
K	FERRENCE	WILLIAM	G	USA
K	FINK	FRANCIS	J	USAC
K	FISHER	ARTHUR	L	USN
K	FISHER	HARRY		USA
K	FORD	GORDON	E	USAC
K	FORMICHELLA	CASIMIR		USA
K	FRANKEL	WILLIAM	L	USA
K	FRANTZ	ROBERT		USA
K	FREDERICK	WILLIAM		USA
K	FRY	WILLIAM	E	USAC
K	FRYE	BENJAMIN		USAF
K	FRYE JR	BENJAMIN	A	USAC
K	FUREY	JOHN	P	USA
K	GALMISH	E	J	USAC
K	GARDNER	WILLIAM		USA
K	GARHART	THOMAS	M	USAC
K	GARRETT	GENE	H	USA
K	GAYDOSH	CHARLES		USA
K	GEIAK	JOSEPH	J	USA
K	GENERALOVICH	ALEX		USA
K	GIBBENS JR	HARRY	L	USA
K	GIBSON	THEODORE	R	MERM
K	GILMORE	WILLIAM	A	USA
K	GOETZ	WILLIAM	D	USA
K	GOINS	BEVERLY	H	USN
K	GRAHMAN	WALTER	F	USA
K	GRANDE	ANTHONY	A	USA
K	GRANT	RICHARD		USA
K	GRANT	SAMUEL	U	USA
K	GUIDICI	ULYSSES	A	USA
K	HAJDUK	ALBERT		USA
K	HANIAK	STANLEY		USA
K	HARRISON	FRED	J	USAC
K	HASS	JOHN	T	USA
K	HEACOCK	JAMES	W	USA
K	HENDERSON	HAROLD	H	USAC
K	HENDERSON	MERLE	F	USA
K	HENDRICKSON	WILLIAM	E	USMC
K	HENNING	HOMER	L	USA
K	HILL	HOWARD	E	USA

Honor Roll Report: WORLD WAR II

KIA*	Last	First	M	Branch of Service
K	HOCHADEL	CHARLES	B	USA
K	HOFFENBERG	JENNINGS	L	USA
K	HOFFMAN	WILLIAM	A	USA
K	HOLAUS	CHARLES	R	USA
K	HOUTZ	DONALD		USA
K	HOWARD	DONALD		USAC
K	HOWE	RICHARD	T	USA
K	HUSBAND	ELMER	W	USA
K	HUTMACHER	HAROLD	W	USN
K	JAWORSKI	ROBERT	S	USA
K	JENNINGS	RUSSELL		USA
K	JEWELL	DANIEL	B	USN
K	JEWELL	MELVIN	W	USA
K	JOHN	ANTHONY		USA
K	JOHNSON	BRUCE		USA
K	JOHNSTON	PAUL	E	USA
K	JONES	RICHARD	W	USMC
K	JONES	SIDNEY	B	USA
K	JONES	THOMAS	A	USA
K	JONES	WILLIAM	C	USN
K	JORDON	JAMES	O	USA
K	KALAGHER	TIMOTHY		USA
K	KALTENBAUGH	WILLIAM	P	USA
K	KEFURT	GUS		USA
K	KELLAR	DONALD	W	USA
K	KELLY	JOHN	D	USA
K	KELLY	WILLIAM	L	USN
K	KELSO	THOMAS	R	USA
K	KENNEDY	DONALD	W	USN
K	KERSCHNER	JACK	A	USA
K	KETTERING	C	E	USA
K	KIBASH	JAMES	P	USN
K	KISTOPAD	JOHN	T	USN
K	KITCH	HARRY	L	USAC
K	KLOTZ	ANDREW		USMC
K	KLUSHANK	JOHN		USA
K	KNOTTS	CLARK	L	USA
K	KOERTH	GERARD		USA
K	KOLSKY	RICHARD		USMC
K	KOLTZ	ANDREW		USMC
K	KOSEC	JOHN		USN
K	KOSS	JOSEPH		USAF
K	KOSTECKI	HENRY		USA
K	KOSTKA	BENJAMIN	T	USA
K	KOVACH	NORMAN		USA
K	KOVACH	STEPHEN		USA
K	KROUSE	ELLSWORTH		USA
K	KUDIAK	ANTHONY		USA

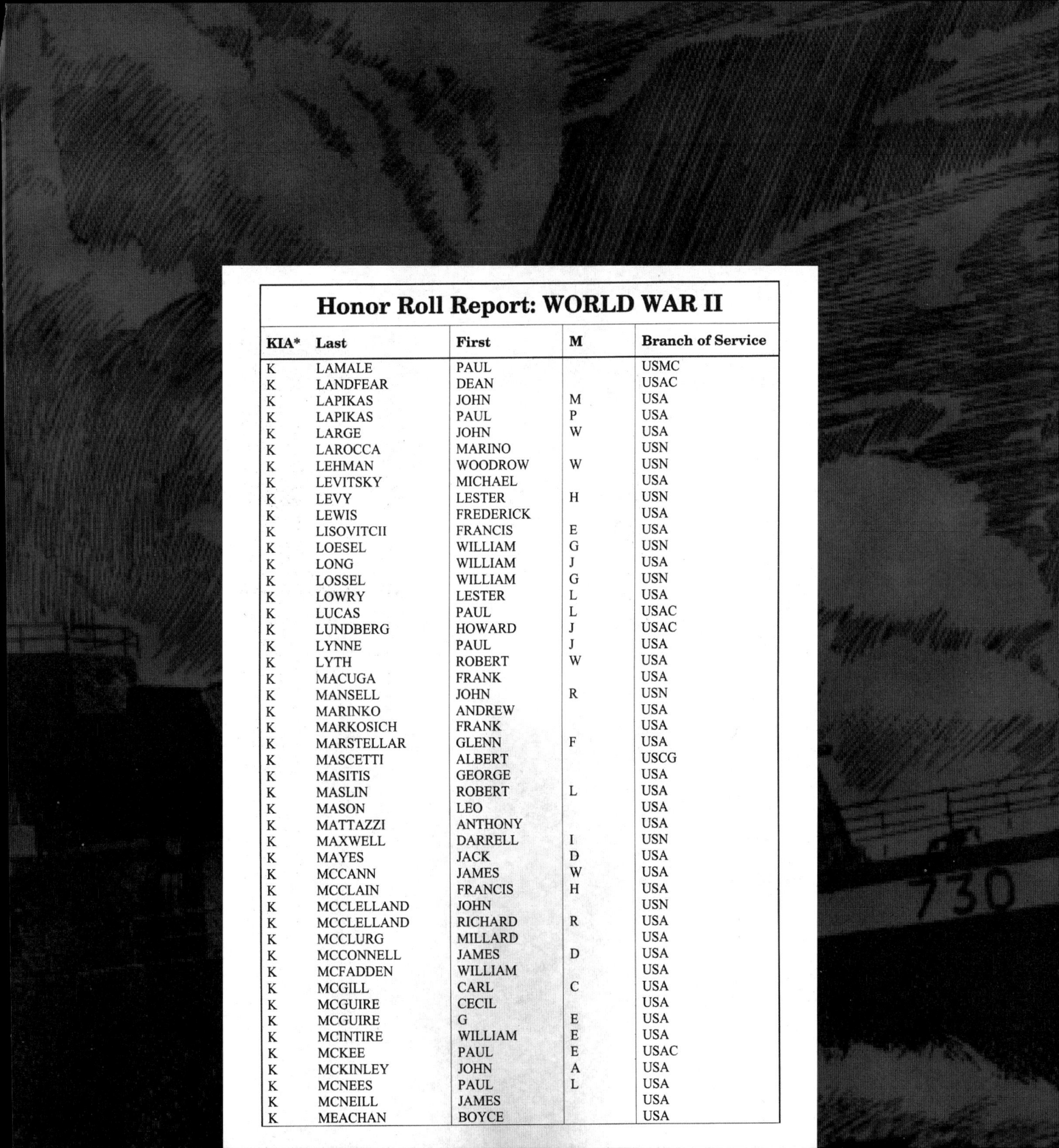

Honor Roll Report: WORLD WAR II

KIA*	Last	First	M	Branch of Service
K	LAMALE	PAUL		USMC
K	LANDFEAR	DEAN		USAC
K	LAPIKAS	JOHN	M	USA
K	LAPIKAS	PAUL	P	USA
K	LARGE	JOHN	W	USA
K	LAROCCA	MARINO		USN
K	LEHMAN	WOODROW	W	USN
K	LEVITSKY	MICHAEL		USA
K	LEVY	LESTER	H	USN
K	LEWIS	FREDERICK		USA
K	LISOVITCII	FRANCIS	E	USA
K	LOESEL	WILLIAM	G	USN
K	LONG	WILLIAM	J	USA
K	LOSSEL	WILLIAM	G	USN
K	LOWRY	LESTER	L	USA
K	LUCAS	PAUL	L	USAC
K	LUNDBERG	HOWARD	J	USAC
K	LYNNE	PAUL	J	USA
K	LYTH	ROBERT	W	USA
K	MACUGA	FRANK		USA
K	MANSELL	JOHN	R	USN
K	MARINKO	ANDREW		USA
K	MARKOSICH	FRANK		USA
K	MARSTELLAR	GLENN	F	USA
K	MASCETTI	ALBERT		USCG
K	MASITIS	GEORGE		USA
K	MASLIN	ROBERT	L	USA
K	MASON	LEO		USA
K	MATTAZZI	ANTHONY		USA
K	MAXWELL	DARRELL	I	USN
K	MAYES	JACK	D	USA
K	MCCANN	JAMES	W	USA
K	MCCLAIN	FRANCIS	H	USA
K	MCCLELLAND	JOHN		USN
K	MCCLELLAND	RICHARD	R	USA
K	MCCLURG	MILLARD		USA
K	MCCONNELL	JAMES	D	USA
K	MCFADDEN	WILLIAM		USA
K	MCGILL	CARL	C	USA
K	MCGUIRE	CECIL		USA
K	MCGUIRE	G	E	USA
K	MCINTIRE	WILLIAM	E	USA
K	MCKEE	PAUL	E	USAC
K	MCKINLEY	JOHN	A	USA
K	MCNEES	PAUL	L	USA
K	MCNEILL	JAMES		USA
K	MEACHAN	BOYCE		USA

Honor Roll Report: WORLD WAR II

KIA*	Last	First	M	Branch of Service
K	MEALS	CHESTER	L	USA
K	MELEKY	JOSEPH		USAC
K	MIHALCIN	ANDREW		USA
K	MILLER	CHARLES	M	USA
K	MISINAY	MICHAEL		USA
K	MONKS	WILLIAM	H	USA
K	MORRISON	THOMAS	D	USA
K	MOSS	RICHARD	P	USMC
K	MOTTS	ROSS	E	USAC
K	NANKOFF JR	DANIEL		USA
K	NAUGLE	ANDREW		USA
K	NEMETZ	GEORGE		USA
K	NIMBELETT	DONALD	L	USAC
K	NORRIS	RICHARD	V	USAC
K	NOVOSAL	FRANK		USA
K	O'CONNER	JAMES		USA
K	ORR	LYLE	N	USA
K	PALMER	JAY	W	USAC
K	PALMER	WILLIAM		USA
K	PALMER	WILLIAM	E	USA
K	PANASEWICZ	EDWARD	J	USA
K	PARIMUHA	JOHN		USA
K	PARRY	MICHAEL	O	USN
K	PATRICK	CARMEN	A	USN
K	PATTERSON	LESTER	J	USA
K	PAULO	STEVE		USA
K	PAVLICH	JOHN		USA
K	PENDEL	ANTHONY	D	USA
K	PERRY	GEORGE	Y	USA
K	PERSCHKA	CHARLES	D	USA
K	PHERSON	ROBERT		USAC
K	PHILLIPS	ROBERT	A	USA
K	PHYTHYON	WILLIAM	E	USA
K	PRIZANT	BENNY		USA
K	RAMSEY	RICHARD	A	USA
K	RAU	WILLIAM	L	USA
K	RAYHAWK	PETER	R	USAC
K	READSHAW	RICHARD		USA
K	REDDINGER	QUENTIN	L	USMC
K	REED	DONALD	K	USN
K	REED	NORMAN	R	USA
K	RHODES	WILBUR		USN
K	RICHARDSON	JAMES	R	USAC
K	RIGGS	DEAN	J	USA
K	RILEY	GEORGE	E	USA
K	ROBBINS	DAVID	A	USAC
K	ROBINSON JR	ROBERT	E	USA

Honor Roll Report: WORLD WAR II

KIA*	Last	First	M	Branch of Service
K	RODECKER	ALBERT		USA
K	ROHA	FRANK	J	USA
K	ROTH	RICHARD		USN
K	ROWBOTTOM	GEORGE	J	USA
K	ROWE	GEORGE	F	USA
K	RUPERT	MARTIN		USAC
K	RUPP	ALLAN	C	USAC
K	RUST	STANLEY	W	USAC
K	SANDERS	PHILLIP	M	USA
K	SCHELL	GEORGE	L	USA
K	SCHEPP	ANTHONY	F	USA
K	SCHUMACHER	HENRY	J	USA
K	SCOTT	CARL	H	USA
K	SCOTT	WILLIAM	C	USA
K	SEABURN JR	HARRY		USA
K	SHANK	ESEKIAL		USA
K	SHEDD	ALBERT	H	USMC
K	SHEEHAN	EUGENE	F	USA
K	SHIELDS	CLARENCE		USA
K	SHINGLEDECKER	HOWARD	T	USAC
K	SINGER JR	GEORGE	A	USMC
K	SINKUS	JOSEPH	J	USA
K	SMITH	THOMAS	P	USAC
K	SNODGRASS	ROBERT	N	USA
K	SNYDER	STANLEY		USA
K	SPATIG	ROBERT		USA
K	SPAULDING	ARDEN		USA
K	SPAULDING	ROBERT	E	USAC
K	SPON	JOHN	C	USA
K	SPON JR	GEORGE		USN
K	STARR	JOHN	C	USA
K	STAUFFER	JAMES		USA
K	STEARNS	GEORGE	A	USA
K	STEELSMITH	HENRY	A	USAC
K	STONER	JAMES	W	USA
K	STRANGE	HOWARD		USA
K	STRAUSE	ROWLAND		USA
K	STUBBS	ARTHUR	R	USMC
K	SULLIVAN	JAMES		USAC
K	SWARTZ	JAMES	W	USA
K	SWOGGER	CLARENCE	J	USA
K	SWOGGER	WOODROW	W	USA
K	TEARE	BUDD	W	USAC
K	TEARE	MERLE	K	USA
K	THOMAS JR	WILLIAM		USA
K	THOMPSON	WILLIAM		USN
K	THUT	GEORGE	A	USAC

Honor Roll Report: WORLD WAR II

KIA*	Last	First	M	Branch of Service
K	TOMKO	WILLIAM	J	USAC
K	TRENCHARD	HAROLD	R	USA
K	TROPE	FRANK		USA
K	TRUCHAN	HENRY		USA
K	TURNER	JAMES		USA
K	TUTTLE	MAURICE	W	USAC
K	UBER	DAVID	V	USAC
K	UBER	FRANK	J	USAC
K	VAN HORNE	LESLIE		USAC
K	VAN RYN	JOHN	G	USA
K	VAN TASSEL	CRAWFORD		USA
K	VATH	HOWARD	B	USN
K	VELLENTE	LOUIS	J	USA
K	VETE	ARTHUR	P	USA
K	WALTER	KENNETH	E	USAC
K	WALTERS	HARRY	L	USA
K	WARD	ROBERT		USA
K	WATTERS	EDWARD		USA
K	WEAVER	CLIFFORD	E	USAC
K	WEAVER	HOWARD	J	USA
K	WEBB	FRANKLIN	K	MERM
K	WEBER	ANTHONY	N	USA
K	WERNTZ	HOWARD	M	USA
K	WHITE	HARRY	J	USA
K	WILLARD	EARL	B	USA
K	WILLIAMS	JAMES	R	USA
K	WILLIAMS	JOHN	T	USA
K	WILLIAMS	MORGAN	D	USA
K	WILSON	GERALD	R	USA
K	WILSON	HOWARD	S	USA
K	WILSON	THOMSON		USA
K	WINGROVE	ALLEN	E	USAC
K	WLODARSKY	HARRY		USA
K	WOLFE	WILLIAM	C	USAC
K	WOLFE	WILLIAM	C	USA
K	YARABENIC	JOSEPH		USA
K	YEZ	GEORGE	F	USA
K	YOUNG	MAURICE		USA
K	YUENGERT	GEORGE	R	USA
K	ZUPEN	PAUL		USA
N	ANDERSON	RALPH	O	USN
N	ARKILANDER	JOHN	E	USN
N	AUGUST	ROBERT	C	USA
N	BARR	ROBERT	E	USN
N	BASHER JR	HARRY	A	USA
N	BELL	JOHN	E	USA
N	BENNETT	GERALD	S	USN

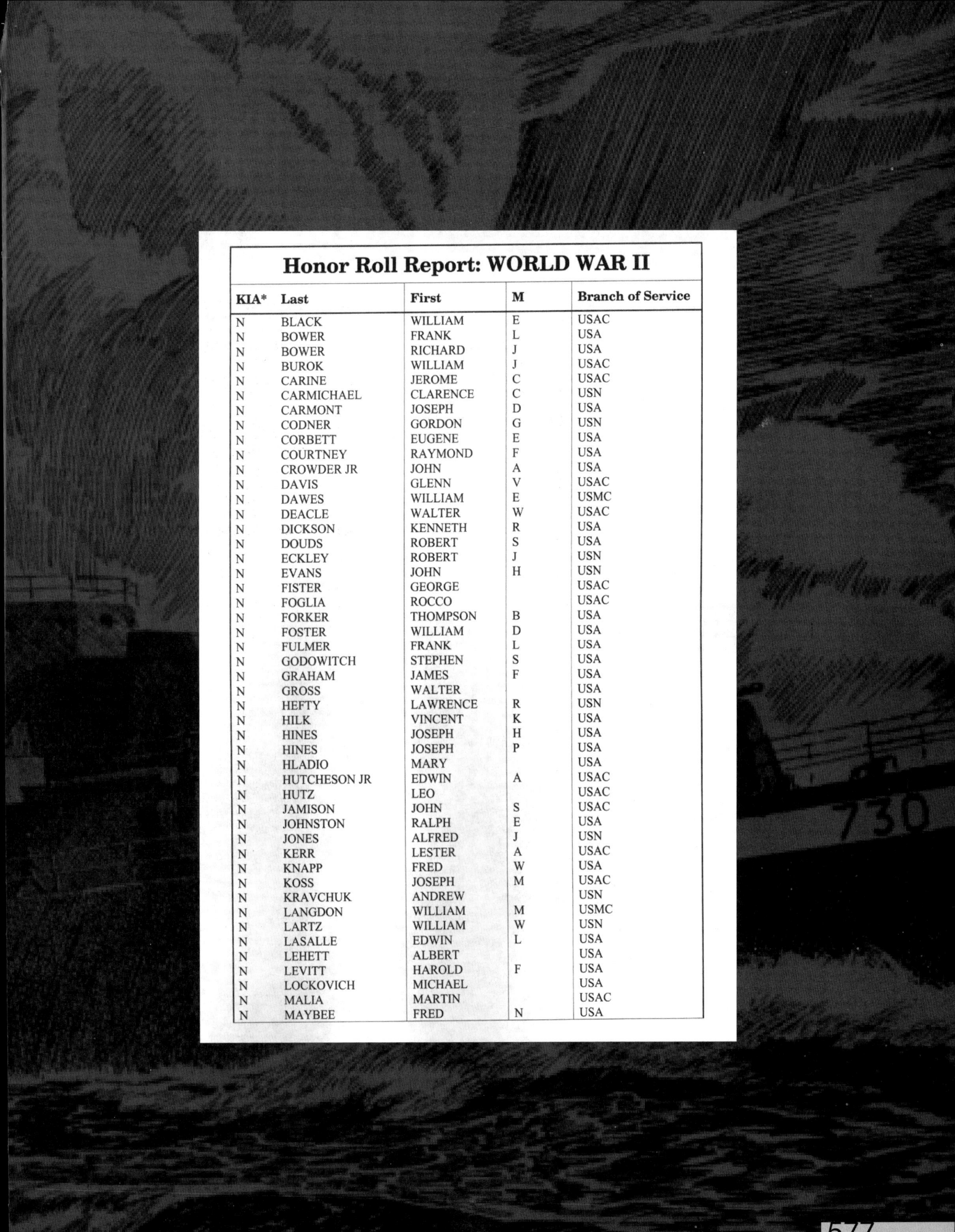

Honor Roll Report: WORLD WAR II

KIA*	Last	First	M	Branch of Service
N	BLACK	WILLIAM	E	USAC
N	BOWER	FRANK	L	USA
N	BOWER	RICHARD	J	USA
N	BUROK	WILLIAM	J	USAC
N	CARINE	JEROME	C	USAC
N	CARMICHAEL	CLARENCE	C	USN
N	CARMONT	JOSEPH	D	USA
N	CODNER	GORDON	G	USN
N	CORBETT	EUGENE	E	USA
N	COURTNEY	RAYMOND	F	USA
N	CROWDER JR	JOHN	A	USA
N	DAVIS	GLENN	V	USAC
N	DAWES	WILLIAM	E	USMC
N	DEACLE	WALTER	W	USAC
N	DICKSON	KENNETH	R	USA
N	DOUDS	ROBERT	S	USA
N	ECKLEY	ROBERT	J	USN
N	EVANS	JOHN	H	USN
N	FISTER	GEORGE		USAC
N	FOGLIA	ROCCO		USAC
N	FORKER	THOMPSON	B	USA
N	FOSTER	WILLIAM	D	USA
N	FULMER	FRANK	L	USA
N	GODOWITCH	STEPHEN	S	USA
N	GRAHAM	JAMES	F	USA
N	GROSS	WALTER		USA
N	HEFTY	LAWRENCE	R	USN
N	HILK	VINCENT	K	USA
N	HINES	JOSEPH	H	USA
N	HINES	JOSEPH	P	USA
N	HLADIO	MARY		USA
N	HUTCHESON JR	EDWIN	A	USAC
N	HUTZ	LEO		USAC
N	JAMISON	JOHN	S	USAC
N	JOHNSTON	RALPH	E	USA
N	JONES	ALFRED	J	USN
N	KERR	LESTER	A	USAC
N	KNAPP	FRED	W	USA
N	KOSS	JOSEPH	M	USAC
N	KRAVCHUK	ANDREW		USN
N	LANGDON	WILLIAM	M	USMC
N	LARTZ	WILLIAM	W	USN
N	LASALLE	EDWIN	L	USA
N	LEHETT	ALBERT		USA
N	LEVITT	HAROLD	F	USA
N	LOCKOVICH	MICHAEL		USA
N	MALIA	MARTIN		USAC
N	MAYBEE	FRED	N	USA

Honor Roll Report: WORLD WAR II

KIA*	Last	First	M	Branch of Service
N	MCANALLEN	FREDERICK	E	USMC
N	MCCLENAHAN	KING		USN
N	METRICK	STEVE	T	USAAF
N	MINK	CLAIR	E	USA
N	MINNER	EUGENE		MERM
N	MINNER	IRWIN	L	USCG
N	MITCHELL	RICHARD		USA
N	MYERS	CLYDE	E	USAC
N	NASSAR	NICHOLAS		USA
N	NATHAN	JONAS		USAC
N	NORRIS	RICHARD		USMC
N	NOVAK	ALBERT	M	USAC
N	ODONNELL	CHARLES	J	USN
N	OWENS	NELSON		USA
N	PATRIZI	DAVID		USAC
N	PATTERSON	FREDERICK	L	USAC
N	PEARCE	RAYMOND	J	USA
N	PETERS	RICHARD	C	USA
N	PHIPPS	FLOYD	C	USN
N	PIERCE	HARRY	W	USA
N	PRITCHARD	DONALD	F	USN
N	RACKETA	SAMUEL		USA
N	RANKIN	ELVIN	G	USAC
N	RICHARDSON	EDWIN	W	USN
N	RILEY	OWEN	E	USA
N	RODE WALT	KENNETH	E	USA
N	SARISKY	ANDREW	P	USCG
N	SCHULTZ	JOHN	D	USA
N	SEPIK	FRANCIS	J	USA
N	SIMON	JOHN	R	USAC
N	SOLOMON	NORMAN	W	USAC
N	SOLTESZ	JOSEPH	G	USA
N	SORRELS	ROTHIER	L	USA
N	SUBASIC	JOHN		USN
N	SUHAR	WALTER		USAF
N	TALLARICO	JOSEPH		USA
N	TOMKO	WILLIAM		USAC
N	TROWBRIDGE	CLARENCE		USA
N	VESPER	ALBERT	R	USAC
N	VINCEK	STANLEY		USA
N	VOGAN JR	DAVID		USA
N	WASSELL	GEORGE		USA
N	WEAVER	JOHN	D	USAC
N	WELLER JR	JOSEPH	B	USAC
N	WHITE	THOMAS	A	USN
N	WISHART JR	JOHN	R	USAC
N	YELOVACH	JOSEPH		USAC

Information collected as of March 28, 2000.

* KIA column: K = Killed in action as a result of hostile activity; N = Death not as a result of hostile action, for example, accidental discharging a rifle while in a foxhole or being run over by a tank.

Honor Roll Report: KOREAN WAR

KIA*	Last	First	M	Branch of Service
K	BAILEY	PAUL		USA
K	BANCROFT	EDWARD	B	USA
K	BENTON	JOHN	E	USA
K	BURNS	RICHARD	N	USMC
K	CAUTION	WILLIAM	E	USA
K	CHRISTY	ALBERT	K	USA
K	CLAWSON	PAUL	E	USA
K	COGSWELL	JOHN	O	USA
K	DINGER	FREDERICK	G	USA
K	EATON	GEORGE	R	USA
K	KINGJR	CHARLES	J	USA
K	KINGJR	JOHN	E	USA
K	LEWIS JR	WILLIAM	G	USMC
K	LOUTZENHISER	JACK		USA
K	MCBRIAR	CHARLES	H	USMC
K	MOORE	CURTIS		USA
K	MUSHRUSH	EDWARD	D	USA
K	OLUICH	LOUIS		USA
K	RICHARD	NORMAN	B	USMC
K	SMITH	FREDERICK	O	USA
K	SPON	RICHARD		USA
K	TULIP	JAMES	G	USA
K	TURNER	RICHARD	C	USA
K	WINKLE	FRANK	N	USA
N	BARNES	JAY	L	USAF
N	BELL	THOMAS		USA
N	BRICKLEY	CLIFTON	K	USMC
N	BRIGGS	CHARLES	R	USAF
N	GAISER	DARRELL	J	USAF
N	GOLUB	WILLIAM	E	USN
N	HILL	WILLIAM	T	USAF
N	HOLLOWAY	JAMES	W	USA
N	HUCK	PAUL	F	USA
N	JONES	LOUIS	B	USA
N	KING	DONALD	G	USMC
N	KNAUFF	SHIRLEY	A	USMC
N	KROPP	BILLIE	G	USAF
N	LAWRENCE	RAYMOND	H	USN
N	LINZENBOLD	JOHN	E	USAF
N	PERRINE	GRANT	L	USA
N	POPESCU	JOHN	A	USA
N	PORTERFIELD	JAMES	W	USA
N	SCHILLER	THOMAS	M	USA
N	THOMPSON	JANICE	L	USMC
N	WILSON	RICHARD	A	USN

Information collected as of March 28, 2000.
* KIA column: K = Killed in action as a result of hostile activity; N = Death not as a result of hostile action, for example, accidental discharging a rifle while in a foxhole or being run over by a tank.

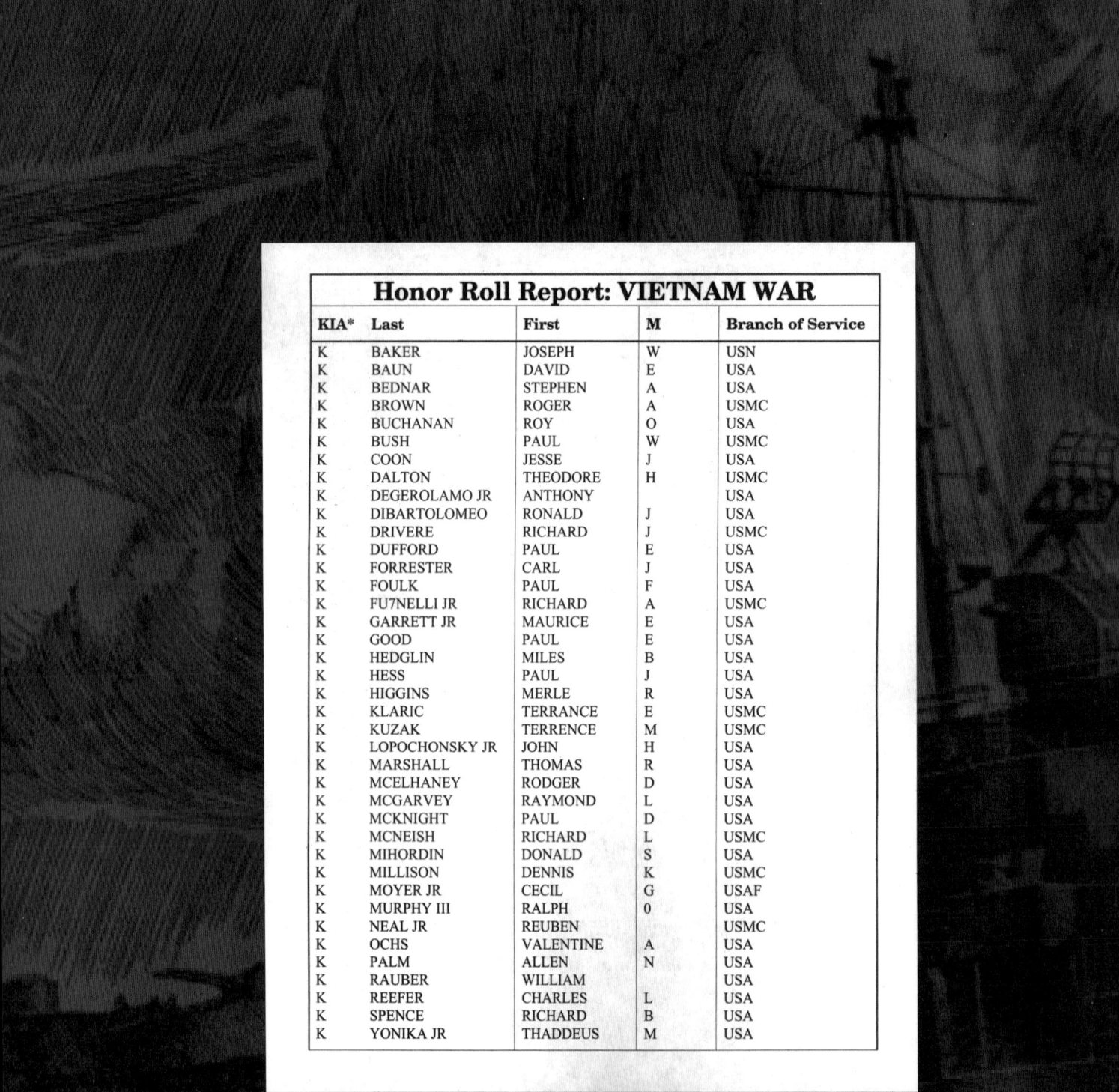

Honor Roll Report: VIETNAM WAR

KIA*	Last	First	M	Branch of Service
K	BAKER	JOSEPH	W	USN
K	BAUN	DAVID	E	USA
K	BEDNAR	STEPHEN	A	USA
K	BROWN	ROGER	A	USMC
K	BUCHANAN	ROY	O	USA
K	BUSH	PAUL	W	USMC
K	COON	JESSE	J	USA
K	DALTON	THEODORE	H	USMC
K	DEGEROLAMO JR	ANTHONY		USA
K	DIBARTOLOMEO	RONALD	J	USA
K	DRIVERE	RICHARD	J	USMC
K	DUFFORD	PAUL	E	USA
K	FORRESTER	CARL	J	USA
K	FOULK	PAUL	F	USA
K	FU7NELLI JR	RICHARD	A	USMC
K	GARRETT JR	MAURICE	E	USA
K	GOOD	PAUL	E	USA
K	HEDGLIN	MILES	B	USA
K	HESS	PAUL	J	USA
K	HIGGINS	MERLE	R	USA
K	KLARIC	TERRANCE	E	USMC
K	KUZAK	TERRENCE	M	USMC
K	LOPOCHONSKY JR	JOHN	H	USA
K	MARSHALL	THOMAS	R	USA
K	MCELHANEY	RODGER	D	USA
K	MCGARVEY	RAYMOND	L	USA
K	MCKNIGHT	PAUL	D	USA
K	MCNEISH	RICHARD	L	USMC
K	MIHORDIN	DONALD	S	USA
K	MILLISON	DENNIS	K	USMC
K	MOYER JR	CECIL	G	USAF
K	MURPHY III	RALPH	0	USA
K	NEAL JR	REUBEN		USMC
K	OCHS	VALENTINE	A	USA
K	PALM	ALLEN	N	USA
K	RAUBER	WILLIAM		USA
K	REEFER	CHARLES	L	USA
K	SPENCE	RICHARD	B	USA
K	YONIKA JR	THADDEUS	M	USA

Honor Roll Report: VIETNAM WAR

KIA*	Last	First	M	Branch of Service
N	ANTHONY	JOHN	E	USA
N	COOPER	RALPH	A	USA
N	CRAWFORD JR	JOHN	W	USAF
N	CULLEN	CHARLES	T	USAF
N	DILLAMAN JR	HAROLD	D	USA
N	DODGE	RALPH	H	USA
N	DUMBROSKI	DAVID	J	USA
N	GROCE	DARRELL	E	USA
N	HODGE	RONALD	L	USN
N	HOWARD	FRED	D	USN
N	KILGORE	JAMES	D	USA
N	MCCLUNG	MICHAEL	C	USMC
N	MCCRACKEN	ROBERT	W	USN
N	MCNEES	JOHN	R	USMC
N	ONEILL	BENJAMIN	H	USCG
N	OSBORNE	LARRY	L	USAF
N	PACILLO	PALMER		USA
N	SHAFER	CHARLES	D	USA
N	SHAFFER	ROBERT	J	USN
N	SLAUGHENHOUPT	EMMET	L	USA
N	STOWE	DAVID	R	USAF
N	STUYVESANT	KENNETH		USA
N	SUTTON	THOMAS	H	USAF
N	WEST	JOHN	E	USAF
N	WHITE	JACK	H	USN

Information collected as of March 28, 2000.

* KIA column: K = Killed in action as a result of hostile activity; N = Death not as a result of hostile action, for example, accidental discharging a rifle while in a foxhole or being run over by a tank.

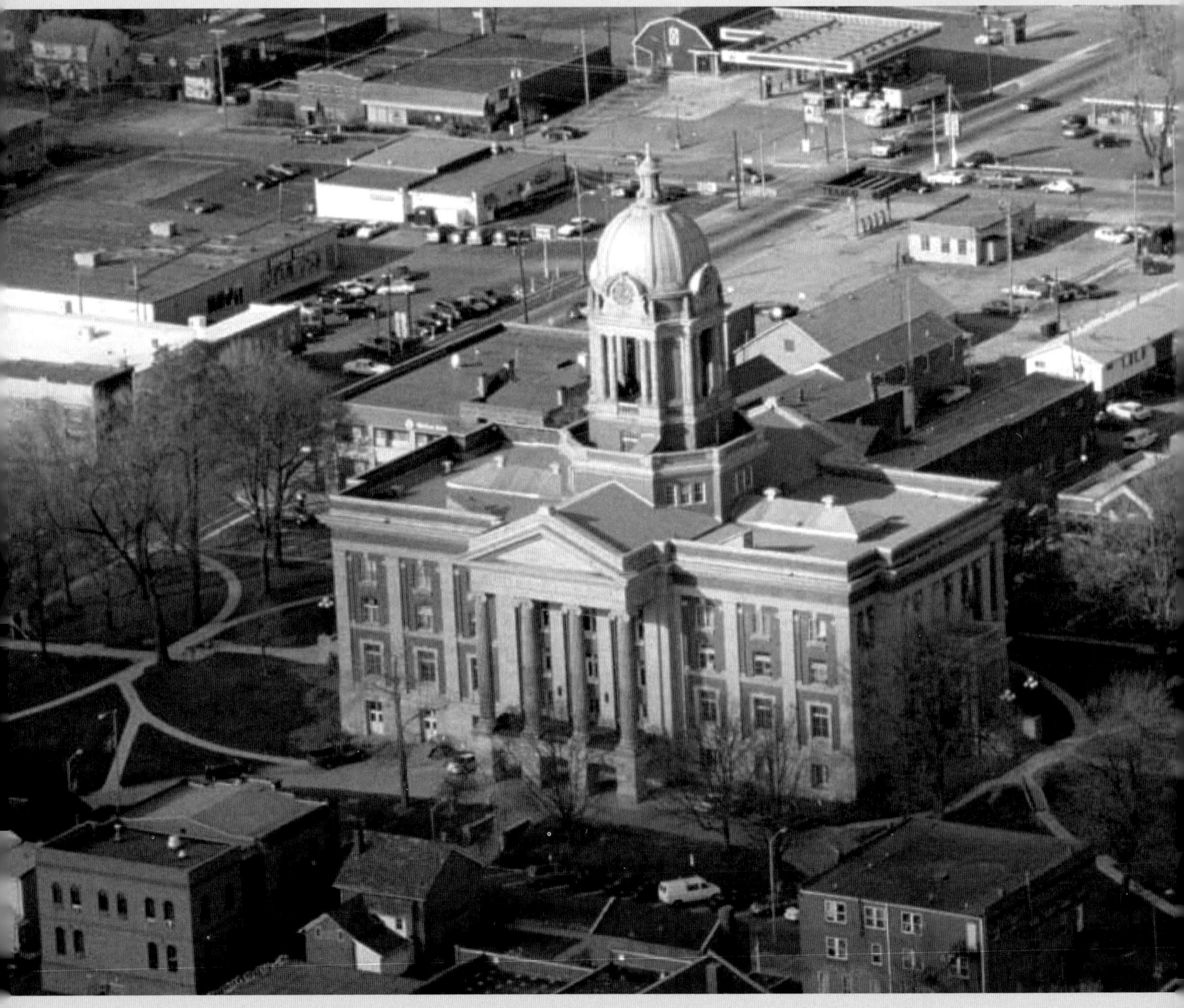

Mercer County: Index

∞—Aa—∞

Achre, Judy, 189
Adams' Mill, 307
Adams, Bertram, 276
Adams, Burt, 307
Adams, Edie, 339
Adams, Gene, 319, 341, 348
Adams, Joe, 194
Adams, John, 194
Adams, Mathias, 273
Adams, Milt, 309
Adams, Sye, 339
Adams, Vic, 340
Advance, 403
African Meth. Episcopal Zion Church of Sharon, 237
African-Americans, 72–73, 134, 163, 179–180, 237–242, 238, 377, 493
Ag Progress Days, 466
Agnew, Charles E., 60
Agnew, David, 64
Agnew, John P., 64
Agney, Neva, 557
Ahonen, James N., 235
Aiken Farm, 231
Aiken, William A., 499
air-conditioning, 246–247
airports, 237, 288, 304, 340, 349, 352, 358, 395, 434, 446, 456, 491, 551
Albin's Corners, 164
Alden, F. A., 45
Alden, F. S., 45
Alexander Farm, 135
Alexander, David, 397, 453
Alexander, Dean, 93, 446
Alexander, Emma Thorne, 320
Alice Furnace, 61, 141
All Saints Catholic Church, 97, 117
All-American Aviation, 289
Allen, Charlie, 59
Allen, Francis, 65
Allen, George, 436
Allen, R. P., 455
Allen, Robert, dust jacket
Allied News, 326, 453–457, 500
Alltel Pennsylvania, Inc., 230
Amasa, 171
American House, 43
American Steel and Tin Plate Co., 133, 134, 163, 178–179, 205, 241
American Steel and Wire Co., 133, 205
Ames, 386, 515
Amish, 34, 131, 273, 345–347, 445, 485, 486, 550
Amity Presby. Church, 38
Ammer, Dortha, 389
Ammer, Otto, 389
Amon, Jeff, 557
Amon, Jerry, 386
Amoore Farm, 451
Ampeo, 277
Amsterdam, 33, 428
Amy, John, 266
Amy, Robert, 392
Anderson Coach and Tour, 389
Anderson's Barber Shop, 307
Anderson, Conrad, 30
Anderson, Ethel Fyffe, 389
Anderson, Evelyn, 557
Anderson, George, 75
Anderson, Harry, 389
Anderson, J. W., 169
Anderson, Mont, 114
Anderson, Orval, 270
Anderson, Orville D., 389
Anderson, Orvis, 33
Anderson, W. V., 213
Anderson, Walter, 270
Anderson, William, 531
Anderson, Zella, 114
Andrews, Elizabeth, 180
Andrijanic, Spiro, 250
Angell School, 34
Anjelic, Karolina, 250
Anti-Saloon League, 195
Anti-Slavery Society, 54, 56
Applegate, Colin, 189
Appleseed, Joannie, 311
Arbuckle, Joseph, 63
Archer, Howard, 455
Armistice Day, 232–233
armory (Grove City), 522–523
Armstrong Grocery Co., 169
Armstrong, Elliott "Alec," 266
Armstrong, John, 432
Arnold, Margaret Mary Bowser, 132
Artherholt, Arleigh, 288
Artherholt, Eileen, 275
Artherholt, Glenn, 288
Artman, Betty Lou, 406
Artman, U. S., 289
Aschman Steel Castings Co., 351
Ashe Confectionery Store, 178
Ashe, Elsie, 405
Askerneese, Michael S., 238
Associate Presby. Church, 432
Associate Reformed Church, 436
Atkinson, Hazel Allen, 59
atomic bomb, 352–354
Atwell, Clyde, 316
Austin, Sara Dillard, 73
Avenue of the Flags, 554
aviation, 181, 225, 232, 237, 238, 288, 289, 336–337, 347–350, 394, 490
Ayers, Ralph, 309

∞—Bb—∞

Babcock Farm, 336
Babcock, Frederick R., 328
Babcock, Russell, 101
Baer family, 33
Bail USA, 402
Baines, W. T., 499
Baird, Absalom, 25
Baker Farm, 394
Baker, Dr., 441
Baker, Grover, 152
Bakmaz, Barko, 250
Baldarelli, Alan J., 491
Balm, 422
bands and orchestras, 229, 239, 270–271, 275, 276, 381
Banic, Stefan, 225
Barber Farm, 394
barber shop, 278
Barca, Fay, 425
Barkeyville, 35
Barnes, A. C., 458
Barnes, John Robert "Jack," 390
barns, 470, 475, 481
Barr, Mrs. William, 150
Barr, William B., 147, 150
Barris, William, 431
Bartholomew Farm, 445
Bartholomew, Elmer, 30
Bartholomew, Genevieve, 435
Bartholomew, Harry, 30
Bartholomew, Jane, 156
Bartleson, P. J., 45
Barton, David Barbour, 368
Barton, Dunham, 326, 368
Barton, J. B., 326
Bashline, Don, 298, 434
Bass, Anna Black, 76, 463
Bassick, Pete, 275
Battey, Dick, 385
Baurele Greenhouse, 486
Baxter's Orchard, 487
Beach, Martin Luther, 379
Beach, Oliver, 379
Beachler, Mrs. H. A., 405
Bear, Jack, 286
Beard, James, 73
Beardsley, Elmer O., 238
Beatty, Kenneth, 334
Beatty, Rutherford, 334
Beaver Aviation Service, 456
Beaver Printing Co., 499
Bebbington, John, 276
Bechtol, Bob, 471
Beck, Lucy M., 402
Beechwood Improvement Co., 133, 134, 139
beer, making, 245
Bell Furnace, 66
Bell School, 32
Bell Telephone Co., 54, 136
Bell's Store, 120, 126, 322
Bell, Dan, 59
Bell, G. W., 169
Bell, J. B., 169
Bell, J. M., 169
Bell, Sam, 309
Bell, Saul, 194
Bell, William, 120
Ben Lemon's Shoe Repair, 307
Bend School, 34
Benedictine Sisters of Erie, 97
Bentley, Ida, 114
Berg, Patty, 302
Beringer, Mae, 40, 548
Bessemer engines, 136, 314
Bessemer Gas Engine Co., 296
Best, William, 317
Bestwick, Bert, 114
Bestwick, Kate, 114
Bestwick, Lester, 114
Bestwock, Bob, 337
Bethel, 32, 34, 197
Bethel School, 32
Beulah Church, 432
Bevan, Anne, 36
Beverly Farms Dairy, 394
Big Bend, 56, 61–62, 120, 326
Big Drift Mine, 71
Big Oaks Restaurant, 487
Bigler, John, 40
Bigler, Susan, 40
Bigler, William, 40
Bindas, Brenda, 453
Bingham, John A., 42, 94, 95
Bishop Farm, 394
Bissett's Garage, 308
Black, Billy, 59
Black, Charles, 418
Black, H. A., 266
Black, Harry, 270
Black, Joseph, 56
Black, Mr. (Osgood), 390
Black, William, 354
Blackstone School, 32
Blackstone, James, 156
Blacktown, 108, 230, 422
Blaine, Scott, 386
Blair, Ralph, 310
Blair, W. S., 318
Blake, Dr. Karl, 43
Blanche Furnace, 63–64
Blaney Farm, 318
blast furnaces. See individual names
block coal, 71
Blood, Col. Henry B., 41, 215
Bloomfield, James, 409
Blooming Mill and Scrap Yard, 188
Boak, Dr. Gordon, 152
Boak, Jay, 114
Boal, Mary, 402
Bobby Run, 62
Boggs, Jonathan, 492
Bollinger, David, 385
Bonafiglia, Peter, 274
Bonani, Mary Ann, 253
Bongiovanni, Guy, 274
Bonner, Jeremiah, 42, 215
Bonnieview Dairy, 487
Book's store (Farrell), 398
Borchert Store, 316
Borchert, Jim, 316
Borchert, Mary, 316
Borden Co., 217
Borland, J., 454
boroughs, Mercer County, 495
Borthwick, Dora, 114
Boston Tavern, 79
Bower School, 75
Bower, Lulu, 37, 75, 212
Bower, Ralph, 75, 202
Bowers, Frank, 238, 352
Bowie Coal Co., 54
Bowman's Store, 310
Bowman, H. A., 403
Bowman, James, dust jacket
Bowmers, Harry, 120, 124
Bowser, Anna Mae Wesner, 132
Bowser, Clarance Albert, 132
Bowser, Edith Florence Lever, 132
Bowser, James, 132
Bowser, James William, 132
Bowser, Mabel, 132
Boy Scout camp, 138, 475
Boyce and Rawle Furnace, 62
Boyce, George, 70
Boyle, Helene McDermott, 146–147
Boyle, James A., 146–147
Bracey, Robert M., 402
Braden and Rigby's Grocer Store, 306
Bradford, David, 401
Bradley, Pat & Marl, 508
Bradshaw, Guy, 337
Brady, Capt. Samuel, 21
Braggins, F. H., 403
Braham, W. Walter, 24
Breckenridge, Elizabeth, 56
Brennan, John, 277
Brenneman, Cloyd E. "Gene", 397–399, 540
Brest, Robert, 355
Brest, William, 355
Bretz, Halle, 492
bridges, 49, 62, 106, 184, 186, 315, 322, 323, 521
Bridget, Thomas, 407
Bridget, William, 407
Bridgett, Ethel, 30
Brisco Springs, 164
Broad, Bill, 309
Broadbent, H. A., 169
Brookfield Dairy, 383, 513
Brooks, Michelle Valesky, 484

583

Brown and Beachler Publishers, 403
Brown and Weir Publishers, 402
Brown, Alexander, 531
Brown, David, 98
Brown, E. Joel "Brownie," 349
Brown, James C., 402–403
Brown, Mary Fruit, 75
Brown, Mrs., 276
Brown, Thomas J., 531
Brown, William P. "Pat," 62
Browser, John, 517
Brugennan, David, 409
Brumbaugh, Forrest, 378
Brumbaugh, Homer, 441
Brumbaugh, Joyce, 355
Brunner family, 310
Brunner, Josephine, 309
Buchanan Farm, 394
Buchanan Mine, 131
Buchanan, Baxter, 52
Buchanan, James, 52
Buchanan, Richard L., 392
Buchanan, Vic, 489
Buchanan, William, 35, 52
Buchholz, Joseph, 498, 499
Buckham's Restaurant, 325
Budd, Daniel, 196
Budd, William, 32, 196
Buhl Armory, 182, 183, 197, 200
Buhl Co., 71–72
Buhl Day, 188
Buhl Farm, 188–189, 190, 305, 318, 547
Buhl Independent Rifles, 144, 181–183, 188, 200, 267
Buhl Iron Co., 139
Buhl Water Co., 72
Buhl, Christian H., 70–71
Buhl, Frank H., 27, 70–72, 138–139, 142, 147, 182–183, 188–189, 230
Buhl, Julia A. Forker, 71–72, 188, 287
Bulick family, 366
Bums, R. J., 349
Bundy, Rachel, 275
Burchert, Bill, 386
Burke, Sr., George W., 73
Burnett, Mildred, 275
Burns, Cheryl, 402
Burns, Whitefield, 399
Burrows Farm, 394
Burrows, Helen Artman, 436
Burton, Ed, 151
Busch Church, 203
Busch, Andrew, 203
buses, 116, 435
Bush Farm, 394
Bush, Andrew, 96
Bush, Barbara, 58, 474
Bush, Paul, 409
Butler, Charles S., 241
Butler, Eva, 230
Butler, P. M., 169
Butz, J. G., 422
Byerley, Marilyn McCutcheon, 414
Byers Plumbing Shop, 178
Byers, C. G., 169
Byers, Charlie, 161
Byers, D. C., 30
Byers, E. L., 161
Byers, F. P., 161
Byers, G. W., 161
Byers, J. M., 178
Byers, J. W., 161, 323
Byers, James W., 266
Byers, William, 27, 165
Byler, Jacob H., 273
Byler, Sadie A. Turner, 273

∞—Cc—∞
C. A. Black Funeral Home, 197
C. G. Westcot's General Store, 519
C. G. Wilson & Son, 261
Cablevision Communications, 392
Calderwood family, 150
Caldwell One-Room School Museum, 202, 265, 412, 548
Calkins, D. L., 45
Callahan Farm, 451
Calumet Lodge, 73, 239
Cameron, Allen, 401
Cameron, Steve, 401
Camp Corn Tassel, 212
Camp Oliver, 33
Camp Perry, 294
Camp Reynolds, 334–335, 357, 359
Campbell's Pioneer Dairy, 135
Campbell, A. M., 403
Campbell, Bruce, 446
Campbell, Capt. John W., 158

Campbell, Earl, 33
Campbell, Ernest, 30
Campbell, James, 390, 442
Campbell, John J., 151
Campbell, Newton, 135
Campbell, Robert, 317
Campman Farm, 451
Candlewood, 79
Canon Farm, 288
Canon, Myrtle, 402
Canon, Thomas, 34
Carey Dairy, 336
Carley, John, 189
Carley, William, 46
Carlson, Edward P., 397
Carlson, William, 453
Carlton, 66
Carmichael School, 38
Carmichael, Alma, 457–459
Carnegie Hero Fund Commission, 290
Carnegie Illinois Steel Co., 178, 180, 292, 301
Carnegie Steel Co., 39, 69, 137, 139, 142, 186, 197, 205, 214, 277, 283, 417
Carnegie, Andrew, 40, 69, 142, 179, 401, 405
Carnegie-Illinois Steel Co., 291
Carr brothers, 27, 33
Carr, Richard, 531
Carroll, Mary, 275
Carruthers, Mr., 296
Carter Brothers Store (Transfer), 120, 121
Carver Community Center, 73, 286
Carver, C. G., 66
Carver, Gene, 274
Casino at Buhl Farm, 547
Castro Steel Co., 488
Cat Nation, 19–20
Cathers, Leslie, 114
cattle testing, 231
Cattron Group Inc., 555
cemeteries, 26, 32, 104, 164, 177, 183, 203, 236, 237, 250, 390
Centennial Organ Co., 108
Center Coal Co., 53
Center Presby. Church, 37, 260, 483
Centerbrook Grange, 399
Centertown, 380, 399, 465
Central Community Church, 506
Central Farms, 135, 180, 231, 288, 336, 394, 451, 489, 556
Central Furnace, 205
Century Farms, 135, 180, 231, 288, 336, 394, 451, 489, 556
Chadderton, Earl, 324
Chadderton, Edward, 446
Chalfant, W. F., 403
Chalmers, Joe, 397
Chanadet, Albert, 152
Chapman, David Kevin, 506
Charleston, 54, 156
Chess family, 285
Chess, Glen, 39f
Chester family, 285
Chestnut, Nellie, 275
Chestnut Ridge, 53
Chestnut Ridge School, 37
Cheyenne Manufacturing, 487
Chicago Bridge and Iron Co., 277
children's games, 255–257, 258, 337–341
Childs, Harvey K., 402
Chinn, Maria, 73
Christ Community Church, 265
Christian Science Society, 427, 483
Christman; J. Fred, 405
Christy, Andrew, dust jacket
Christy, Wayne, 436
Church of God, 266, 483
Church of Our Lady of Fatima, 415
Church of the Beloved Disciple, 296
churches, see individual names
churches in Shenango Valley, 238
cities, Mercer County, 495
Citizens Telephone Co., 54
Civil War, 33–34, 62, 98, 169, 322, 401, 462
Civilian Pilot Training Program, 337, 347
civilian plane spotters, 348
Claire Furnace, 61
Clar, John, 194
Clark, 446, 450, 488. see also Clarksville
Clark Farm (Ronald & Mary Catherine), 490
Clark House, 425
Clark's Barber Shop and Beauty Shop, 307
Clark's Mill, 27, 138
Clark's station, 391
Clark's Town, 391
Clark, Glenn, 389
Clark, Isaac, 487
Clark, Jeff, 301
Clark, Mary Custer, 90
Clark, Mont, 487
Clark, Mrs. Allen, 370
Clark, Paul, 487

Clark, Samuel, 38, 90–91
Clark, Samuel B., 404
Clark, Susannah, 90
Clark, Thomas, 27
Clarkboro, 391
Clarke, Esther McMaster, 442
Clarke, Riley, 442
Clarks Mills, 194, 261, 336
Clarksville, 33, 38–40, 49, 59, 61, 62, 90, 120, 191, 260, 294, 391, 425, 505. see also Clark
Clarksville Fire Department, 103
Clarksville United Presby. Church, 435
Claud family, 285
Clause, William L., 329
Clauson, Mary, 275
Clawson, A. M., 169
Clawson, Charles, 169
Clay Furnace, 60
Clendenin, Samuel, 272, 440
clerks of courts, county, 529, 537
Clinefelter, John, 169
Clover Farm Store, 391
Co. B., National Guard, 159
Co. C., National Guard, 159
Co. E., Pennsylvania Volunteer Infantry, 158
Co. F., National Guard, 158, 291
Co. G Pennsylvania Infantry, 407
Co. G., National Guard, 181–182
Co. M, National Guard, 116, 158
Cochran, Homar, 176
Cochran, John, 35
Cochran, Norman, 386
Cochran, Ruth, 386
Cochran, T.C., 297
Cochranton Telephone Co., 230
coffin factory, 92
Coleman, Fred, 176
Coleman, Westerman and Co., 67
Collier, Katherine, 385
Colonel Hunter Farm, 180
Colonial Trust Co., 277
Colored Literary Society, 72
Combee, Jerry H., 329
commissioners, county, 399, 529, 536, 540–541
Commodore Perry, 278
Commodore Perry High School, 491
communications, 490
Community Church (New Lebanon), 518
Conococheague, 20
Conover family, 138
controllers, county, 530, 537
Cook family, 138
Cook, Betty, 355
Cook, Nancy, 355
Cook, Philip, 355
Cook, Richard, 355
Coolspring, 137, 369
Coolspring Presby. Church, 29, 156
Coolspring Township, 29, 202, 288, 311, 327, 340, 437, 483
Coombe, Dr., 306
Cooper Brothers, 468
Cooper, Brant, 458
Cooper, Frank, 275
Cooper, Merle, 490
Cooper, Zella, 458
Cooper, Zella Garrett, 354
Cooper-Bessemer Corp., 328, 349, 434, 452, 517, 551
Corbett, Nancy M., 220
Cornplanter Indians, 22, 33, 38
Cornwell, J., 41
coroners, county, 530, 536
Corporate Wings, Inc., 456
Cossitt, Epaphroditus, 323
cost of living, 147
Costar Marina, 488
Costes, Dieudonne, 238
Coulter, Mable, 217
Country Chapel, 391
Country Home, 262–264
County Market, 483, 515
court, county, 41, 530–532
courthouse, 98, 100, 143, 560, dust jacket
Courtney Farms, 231
Courtney, Anna Maria, 164
Courtney, D. G., 164
Covert, Stanley, 385
Coyer, I. P., 157
Coyer, Robert, 157
Cozadd family, 30
Cozadd, Betsy, 32
Craig, Mrs., 78
Craig, Ted, 213, 341
Cramer, Wilbur, 266
Cranberry Plain, 35
Cranberry School, 37
Crill's Hardware Store, 306, 340
Crill, John, 79

Crill, L. H., 266
Croatian immigrants, 250
Crompton, Marge, 198
Crosman, Hannah Blair Foster, 236
Crosman, Henrietta, 236
Cross Roads Church, 432
Cross, E. W., 454
Cross, George, 116
Crossgates Inc., 406
Cubbison family, 39
Cubbison, Mr., 217
Culbertson, 41, 165
Cullen, John, 317
Cumberland Presby. Church, 37–38
Cumming's Garage, 308, 309
Cummings, Michael, 189
Cunningham, Margaret, 32
Cunningham, Mr., 290
Cunningham, Thomas, 531
Cunningham, Valentine, 25, 27, 35
Currier Meat Market, 178
Currier, J. M., 178
Curtis, Joel B., 34, 62, 70, 138
Custaloga, 21, 26
Custaloga Camp, 26
Custaloga Town, 21, 24, 138
Custer, Samuel, 41
Custom Cupolas, 489
Custom Signs, 516
Cutler, John D., 46
Cuttler, David, 407–408
Cuturic, Fr. Francis, 251
Cvikovic, Fr. Vincent, 253

∞—Dd—∞
D. R. Thompson Farm Supply, 232
Dab, Ferd, 62
Daffin's Candies, 520
Dahlburg, Mr., 217
Dairy Herd Improvement Association, 181
Dairy Princess, Mercer County, 394, 556
Dairy Queen, 430–431
Dalo, Ferdinand, 183
Dandoy, Dr. William O., 152
Darby family, 135
Darr, D. W., 138
Dart, J. P., 352
Daugherty, Clyde, 323
Daugherty, H. K., 454
Daugherty, Robert Martin, 349
Daugherty, William, 35–36
Davenny Millinery, 120, 126
Davenny, Carrie, 120
Davidson, C. M., 399
Davidson, Carl, 176
Davis, Grace, 402
Davis, H. M., 193
Davis, Herbert, 194
Davis, James, 404
Dawes, Russell, 538
Dean Dairy, 513
Dean, Ormond, 455
death penalty, 244
DeBrakeleer Grocery, 178
Dedendifer, Lucinda, 275
Deer Creek, 21
Deer Creek Golf Course, 400
Deer Creek Township, 255
Deeter School, 259
Deeter, Emma, 259
Delamater, Victor, 139
Delane, Rev., 376
Delaware Grove, 77–78
Delaware Township, 37, 40, 46, 60, 75, 202, 212, 265, 336
Demifonte, Marco, 289–290
DeMine, William, 341
Democrats, 529–530, 536
demographics, 493
Dennis, Kristen, 491
Dent, Frederick R., 336
Dent, Jenny Hoon, 336
Dent, Jr., Frederick R., 336–337
Deramo, Donald, 397
Derr, Naomi Meyer, 412
DeSantis, Rose, 234, 292
Dewey Park, 189
Deweyville, 64, 189, 304, 390
DeWitt & Nichols, 45
Diamond Auto Sales, 486
Diamond Coal Mine, 54
Diamond Corners, 52
Diamond Restaurant, 307
Dick, Col. S. B., 69
Dickinson, Addison C., 499
Dickson, Bobby, 385
Dickson, Francis, 488
Dickson, Harriet, 328

584

Dickson, William T., 328
Dieffenbacher, C. R., 405
Dietrich, William, 277
Dikeman, Evelyn, 385
Dillard, Thomas, 73
Dillon, Charles, 266
distilleries, 92
district attorneys, county, 529, 536
Dixon, Alta Dorothy Bowser, 132
Dodds, Lawrence, 391
Dodge City, 391
Dollar Title and Trust Co., 267, 277
Donaldson School, 34
Donaldson, Alex, 169
Donnell, Charles, 335
Donnell, Max, 283
Donnell, Paul, 283
Douglas Furnace, 61, 64–65, 65, 496
Douglas, William, 425
Douthett, Rev., 432
Dow Jones & Co. printing plant, 501
Drennan & Phipps Drygoods Store, 306
Drenning's Grocery Store, 308
Drenning, George, 266
Dresch, Edward P., 52
Driggs-Seabury, 168, 180
drive-in theaters, 413, 434, 551
drive-in theatres, 386
Duby, Helen M., 446
Duferco Steel Corp., 488, 555
Dukelow, Donald & Valeria, 25
Dumars and Co., 403
Dumars, William H. H., 46, 403
Dumbroski, Frances, 385
Duncan, Mr., 258
Dundore, Paul, 405
Dunham, Adeline, 66
Dunham, Albin, 66
Dunham, J., 33
Dunkle, Alvin, 409
Dunkleberger, Robert E., 156
Dunlap, Jack, 152
Dunlap, Thomas, 35
Dunn, James, 418
Dunn, Rose, 131
Durisko Egg Production, 333
Durst, Maynard, 275
Durst, Stanley, 275

∞—Ee—∞
Eagan, Daniel, 71
Eagle Printing Co., 498
Eagleson, John, 169
Earhart, Amelia, 303–304
Earhart, Edwin S., 303
East End Fire Department (Mercer), 216
East Lackawannock Township, 29, 56, 104, 177, 181, 333, 354–356, 389, 457, 483
East Main Presby. Church, 103, 147, 150–152
East Ward Elementary School, 146
Eastlick, W. A., 169
Ebbert, Harvey, 266
Ebenezer Presby. Church, 380, 465
Eckel's Store, 487
Eckles, W. R., 45
Eckman, Claude, 79
Edmunds, John, 241
Ehrh, V. H., 481
Ehrhart, Wilbur, 181
Ekker, Katie, 189
electricity, 136, 242–243, 246, 333
Elia, Louis (Luigi), 186, 188
Elia, Margaret, 188
Elliott School, 34
Ellis, Jack, 266
Ellison, William "Cappy," 402
Elston, Harry, 503
Emanuel Evangelical Lutheran Church, 203
Emerson, George, 335
Emerson, Raymond, 441
Emery's Drug Store, 306, 309
Emmanuel's Church, 422
Empire automobile, 132, 277
Empire Milk Products Co., 180
Empire Planing Mill, 66
English family, 150
English, R. E., 151
Enke, Ada Dorothy Adams, 339
Enke, Sheldon Adams, 339
Enke, Sheldon Alonso, 339
Enterline Farm, 394
Enterprise Mine, 53
entrepreneurs, 504–505
Episcopal Church, 483
Epstein, Lewis, 189
Erb, James, 402
Erb, Sara E., 402
Erie & Pittsburgh engine No. 1, 65

Erie Extension Canal, 38–39, 40, 45, 48, 49–51, 56, 59, 61–63, 67–68, 90, 93, 97, 276, 283, 404
ethnic diversity, 73–74, 241, 493
Evan, Larry, 454
Evangelical Congregational Church, 475
Evening Eagle, 498
Evening Record, 403
Everett, C. D., 56, 57
Everett, Charles, 56
Everhart, E. F., 401
Everhart, Susan, 401
Exchangeville, 41, 165
Experimental Aircraft Association, 181, 304, 491
Express, 402
extras (newspapers), 248–249

∞—Ff—∞
F. H. Buhl Club, 138, 183, 286, 304
Fahnline, John, 163, 281
Fahrner family, 370
Fairfield Presby. Church, 156, 336, 545
Fairman and Campbell Publishers, 403
Fairman, John S., 403
Fairview, 38
Fairview Friendship Club, 281
Fairview School, 279, 333
Fairview Swiss Cheese Co., 486
Fairview Township, 29, 281, 327, 333, 389, 394, 485–487, 535
Faith United Presby. Church, 435
Fannie Furnace, 204
Farm Bureau, 441
Farmers and Mechanics National Bank, 141
Farmers and Merchants National Bank, 165
Farmers and Merchants Trust Co., 165
Farmers Bank, 307
farming, 135, 180–181, 231–232, 288, 333, 335, 336, 394, 451, 474, 489, 501–503
Farrell, 34, 73–74, 133–134, 178–180, 186, 188, 197, 230, 236, 239–242, 283, 286, 291–292, 299, 377, 391, 487–488. see also South Sharon
Farrell Christian Assembly, 274
Farrell City Park, 503
Farrell High School, 297, 326, 491
Farrell News, 499
Farrell News Plant, 499
Farrell Works, 206–211
Farrell's Browse Shop, 518
Farrell, "Whitey," 518
Farrell, J. A., 205
fashion, 76–78
Fay, Frank, 132, 277
Fay, Wells, 277
Feare, Carol, 385
Feeney, James, 189
Fellowship Manor, 135, 483
Fenstmaker's Gulf Convenience Store, 487
Fenton, Beverly, 355
Fenton, Joyce, 355
Ferguson, Robert, 465
Ferver, W. C., 156
Ficocelli brothers, 276
Fields, Ernest, 179
Filer, 137
Filer, Enoch, 52, 54, 136, 174
Filer, Frank, 52, 136
Filer, Raymond "Rocky," 434
Filer, Rocky, 288
Filer, Ruth, 381
Filson, F. A., 169
Filson, Harry, 266
Filson, Mr., 217, 309
Findley Township, 47, 79, 269, 325, 372, 415
Findley, David W., 531
Findley, John, 531
Finney, F. M., 41
Finsthwaite, J. M., 401
fires, 100, 103, 143, 169, 177, 178, 234, 470, 475
First Baptist Christian Academy, 428
First Baptist Church, 237, 428
First Church of God, 483
First Meth. Church, 73, 97
First National Bank, 165, 213, 221, 229, 287, 306, 309, 322, 405
First Presby. Church, 54–56, 432
First Seneca Bank and Trust Co., 427
First United Presby. Church, 150, 510
First, Ray, 391
Fisher Field, 465
Fisher, Neil C., 396
Fisher, P. P., 197
fishing, 307
Fister, Stephen, 418
Fithian, Dr., 296
Fitzgerald Hall, 182
Five Filer Brothers, 284
Fleet, Clyde "Ike," 304
Fleet, Samuel, 304

Fleming, Linda, 385
floods, 102, 183–187, 230, 283, 284, 420–421, 425, 450, 498, 499, 552
Floros, Nick, 244
flu epidemic, 183, 196–198
Flynn, Tom, 554
Foltz, Nancy Thomas, 402
Forbes Farm, 231
Forbes, Russell, 266
Forker, Henry, 72, 138
Forker, Joseph, 139
Forker, Selina Porter, 72
Forker, Thomas J., 183, 189
Forney Arc Welders, Inc., 395
Forquer, G. G., 455
Forrest, Mr., 23
Forrest, Paul, 418
Forrester family, 407
Forrester, Carl James "Jimmy," 407
Forrester, Emma, 407
Foster, Alexander William, 236
Foster, Caroline, 323
Foster, Elizabeth, 236
Foster, Hannah Blair, 236
Foster, James, 32
Foster, S. C., 564
Foster, Samuel, 236
Foster, William, 33
Fox, George, 114
Fox, Hezel, 311
Fox, Maude Cook, 114
Fox, Will, 114
Frampton, Frank E., 402
Frampton, Helen Thorne, 402
Frampton, Wade, 275
Franek, Joseph, 241–242
Frankenberry, Thomas H., 181
Franklin Manufacturing Co., 177
Frantz, Doris, 386
Frazier, Joel, 101
Frazier, Priscilla, 101
Frederick Raisch Log Cabin, 471
Fredonia, 25, 132, 136, 192, 198, 327, 335, 391–392, 445, 478, 488–489
Fredonia baseball team, 161
Fredonia Fire Department, 103
Fredonia Institute, 37, 218, 279, 440
Fredonia Meth. Church, 40
Fredonia National Bank, 165, 286
Fredonia Pet Parade, 440
Fredonia United Presby. Church, 40
Fredonia Vocational School, 218
Fredonia Volunteer Fire Department, 286, 489
Fredonian, 218
Free Church, 435
freed slaves, 56–59
Freed, Florence M., 189
Freeland family, 33
Freeland, Charles, 517
Freeland, Edwin, 33, 281
Freeland, John, 33, 281
Freeland, William, 33, 229
French and Indian War, 20
French Creek, 21, 66
French Creek Township, 26
Frey, James H., 496–497
Frey, Joseph, 497
Frey, Lizzie, 497
Frey, R. C., 496–497
Friedman and Keller Store, 403
Friendly Tavern, 282
Friendship Grange, 135, 400
Fritz Farm, 394
Frogtown School, 32, 315
Fruit Growers Association, 288
Fruit's Valuable Scholars, 218
Fruit, Frank A., 218
Fruit, James S., 138
Fruit, John, 38
Fruit, William, 38–39, 62
Fry's Barber Shop, 306
Fugitive Slave Act of 1850, 54–55
Fuller, Dave, 446
funerals, 247–248

∞—Gg—∞
Gable Glen and Hollow, 286
Gable Hotel, 235
Gable, Charles E., 235
Gable, Florence, 235
Galalean Baptist Church, 483
Galinac, Fr., 253
Galloway School, 37
Gardener, K. C., 277
gardens, 291
Garlic, Laura, 386
Garner, H., 217
Garner, Philip, 406

Garrett, Aldene, 402
Garrett, Anna Bevan Pearson, 36
Garrett, Janet, 402
Garrett, Russell, 402
Garvin, David, 407
Garvin, John, 407
Garvin, William, 323
Gehser, Herman, 75
General American Transportation Corp., 301
General Electric, 452, 468, 483
Genger, Raymond, 402
Genger, Wilma, 402
George J. Howe Co., 468, 524, 525
George Jr. Republic, 37, 220, 310, 342, 483, 515
George, Albert, 490
George, Joe, 490
George, William R., 220
Georgetown, 41, 165
Gerberich, Marian E., 405
Ghost, A., 217
Ghost, H., 217
Ghost, Isabel, 276
Gibson family, 35
Gibson Farm, 425
Gibson House, 442
Gibson, Baird, 442
Gibson, Charlie, 161
Gibson, Fred, 161, 309
Gibson, Jim, 161
Gibson, John, 161
Gibson, John Bannister, 530–531
Gibson, Paul, 161
Gibson, Susan Beatty, 442
Gibson, W. F., 169
Gibson, William, 442
Gibson-Byers baseball team, 161
Gilbert, Frank, 241
Gildersleeve, Mrs., 217
Gilger & Son Store, 550
Gilkey's Livery, 120, 122
Gilkey, James, 92
Gilkey, John, 436
Gill, Hirdaypal & Harminder, 480
Gillespie, A. D., 46
Gillespie, T. J., 169
Gilliland, Edna, 402
Gilliland, Ed & Alice, 333
Gills, Cecil, 217
Gilmore, Henry, 531
Ginader's Candy Store, 307
Ginger Snap Junction, 519
Girsch, John, 244
Gist, Christopher, 24
Glenn Mill, 27
Glenn, James, 35
Glenn, Mary Stewart, 270
Goddard State Park, 538, 545, 552
Godfrey School, 333
Golden Eagle Tavern, 505
Golden Pheasant bar and dance hall, 487
golf courses, 188, 189, 298, 302, 303, 492–493
Goode family, 75
Goodsell, John, 152–154
government, county, 529–530
Grace Episcopal Church, 463
Grace United Meth. Church, 164
Grace, Alvin, 176
Grace, Charles, 386
Grace, Dr., 194
Grace, Lloyd, 176
Graff Stove Works, 351
Graham, Bill, 309
Graham, James, 27, 35
Graham, Janice, 342
Grajciar, John, 301
Grand Army of the Republic, 144, 169, 183
Grandle, Johnson, 169
granges, 399–400
Gravatte, Dorothy, 355
Great Depression, the, 97, 188, 236, 250, 282, 284, 286, 291, 292–295, 298–299, 306, 318, 329, 365, 426
Great Migration, the, 240, 376
Greek Orthodox Church (Farrell), 237
Greek Orthodox Church of the Annunciation, 74
Green, Frances, 275
Greenfield, 30, 52, 131, 436
Greenfield High School, 30
Greenfield School, 32
Greenville, 19, 39, 40–41, 44–46, 50–51, 55, 66, 68–69, 71, 137, 164, 165, 170, 180–181, 186, 196, 198, 220, 225, 229, 236, 275, 314, 333, 334–335, 402–404, 405–406, 406–410, 488, 526
Greenville Businessmen's Association, 359
Greenville Fire Department, 168
Greenville Hall, 546
Greenville High School, 491
Greenville Historical Society, 238
Greenville House, 406

585

Greenville Industrial Parade, 214
Greenville Iron Co., 277
Greenville newspapers, 44–46, 45, 403
Greenville Railroad Park, 277, 517
Greenville Sea Scout Troop, 317
Greenville Steel Car Co., 132, 277, 295, 452
Greenville-Reynolds Industrial Development, 358–359
Gregg School, 37
Greggs, Bob, 538
Gregory, Roy C., 367
Griffith, Caroline Foster, 236
Griffith, George P., 43
Griffith, Samuel, 236, 323
Grill, Ronnie, 337
Grimm's Hall, 183
Grimm, Mrs. James, 405
grist mills, 27
Grout Steam Runabout, 163
Grove City, 52–54, 68, 71, 112, 136, 150, 157, 160, 164, 197, 203, 233, 236, 284, 289, 291, 296–298, 314, 315, 339, 454–457, 511, 525. See also Pine Grove
Grove City Accredited Dairy Cattle Show and Sales Organization, 268
Grove City Alliance Church, 483
Grove City College, 53, 108, 114, 162, 204, 222–223, 267, 297, 328–331, 337, 394, 422–423
Grove City Commercial Club, 217
Grove City Creamery, 181, 217, 454
Grove City Fire Department, 103
Grove City High School, 113, 297, 491
Grove City Limestone Mine, 53
Grove City newspapers, 454–457
Grove City Sesqui-Centennial, 381
Grove City Victory ship, 379
Grove Coal Co., 53
Gruber Farm, 394
Grundy, Sara, 402
Gruwer, H., 276
Guitar's Restaurant, 307, 309
Guitar's Service Station, 308
Gumfory, John, 42
Gundy brothers, 92
Gundy family, 401
Gundy Farm, 432
Guyasutha, 21–22, 26
gypsies, 236–237

∞—Hh—∞
Haag, LeRoy, 288
Haag, Leroy, 446
Hackney Tavern, 42, 374
Hackney, Aaron, 43
Hackney, Major, 43
Hadley, 195, 286, 550
Hadley Presby. Church, 512
Hagar, William, 266
Haggarty, William, 189
Hall, Helen, 425, 488
Hall, Norman, 189
Hall, Sr., Clarence, 73
Hallsville Mine, 53
Hallville, 35–36, 52–53, 296
Hallville School, 37
Hamburg Dam, 212
Hamilton, George, 56
Hamilton, George E.and, 169
Hammond, Dr., 298
Hammond, Orpha, 403
Hanna, Mark A., 65
Hanna, Robert, 546
Hanna, Tammy, 556
Hanna, William P., 403
Hanna-Small-White House, 546
Hansen, James, 475
Harbin, Dave, 301
Hardesty, Andy, 386
Harker, J. Stanley, 329
Harmon, Dr. H. W., 151
Harmond, Keith, 409
Harmony, 147
Harpst, W. F., 46, 403
Harrison, Dutch, 302
Harrison, Gladys, 386
Harrison, Helen Traposso, 32
Harrison, Mrs., 386, 387
Harry, Eleanor, 402
Harsha, R. B., 432
Harshaw, Ed, 296
Hart, Lewie, 385
Harthegig, 47
Hartman, Henry, 405
Hassel Farm, 394
Hassell Mine, 53
Hassell, Jacob & Elizabeth, 407
Hassell, Pete, 53
Hassler, Edgar "Ted," 326, 455–457

Hassler, J. P., 455
Hause, Quincy, 418
Hawes, W. Michael, 490
Hawthorn Melody, 513
Hawthorne family, 63
Hawthorne, Mary Jones, 63
Hayes, Bert, 157
Hayes, Watson & Margaret, 156
Haynes, Larry, 274
Haywood family, 138
Haywood, B. J., 326
Hazen Farm, 231
Hazen Pharmacy, 120, 122
Hazen, Charles A., 499
Hazen, S. W., 43
Hazen, Z. O., 184
Head School, 34
Hedglin, Hosack H., 259
Hefius, Paul, 238
Hefling, M. K., 266
Heile, Dorothy, 275
Heile, Emerson, 275
Heile, LeRoy, 275
Heilig's Bakery, 307
Heilman, Ralph, 46
Heini, Michael, 355–356
Helen Black Miller Memorial Chapel, 463
Hell's Hollow, 47, 49
Hemlock School, 37
Hempfield Township Fire Department, 103, 389, 538
Henderson, 37
Henderson Clover Farm Store, 37, 305
Henderson Historical Area, 413
Henderson Hotel, 380
Henderson School, 38
Henderson, Carroll, 37
Henderson, Dr., 151
Henderson, Earl, 37
Henderson, George, 138
Henderson, James, 380
Henderson, Jon, 37
Henderson, Lowrie, 380
Henderson, Nancy, 380
Henderson, Rhoda, 305
Henderson, Robert, 37
Henderson, Roy, 37, 305, 380
Henderson-Taylor Park, 446, 450
Hendersonville, 37, 43, 131, 380
Hendersonville United Meth. Church, 37
Hendrickson, Samuel, 96
Henrick's BP gas station, 428
Henry, James, 229
Herald, The, 46, 248, 358, 363, 496–500, 500, 501, 511
Herbert, George D., 498
Hermitage, 29, 71, 189, 274, 302
Hermitage High School, 491
Hermitage Hills Plaza, 386
Hermitage Historical Society, 318
Heydrick farm, 21
Heydrick, Charles, 26
Heylep, Ollie, 217
Hickory, 52, 60, 71
Hickory High School, 383, 384
Hickory Homecoming Parade, 444
Hickory Township, 29, 34, 52, 58, 59, 64–65, 67, 71, 97, 135, 168, 198, 205, 281, 326, 351, 383, 386, 389, 445
Hicks, Betty, 302
Higbee, Kermit "Pete," 487
Higgins, Merle, 409
Higgs family, 138
Hildebrand, Ed, 317
Hilkirk, John, 395
Hill, Helen, 402
Hill, Milt, 229
Hill, Richard, 45
Hill, Tib, 217
Hill, William, 73
Hillcrest Memorial Park, 554
Hillside School, 485
Hillview Elementary Center, 522
Hilton, Fred, 336
Himrod, Mr., 59, 60, 63
Hinckley, George, 25
Hines, John P., 41
Hines, Samuel, 215
Hippee, L., 403
Hirst, J. T., 164
Hittle, Gary, 538
Hoagland, 104
Hoagland family, 168
Hoagland General Store, 104–105
Hoagland School, 34
Hoagland, Alf, 182
Hoagland, Don, 152
Hoagland, Henry, 34
Hoagland, Seth, 104

Hodge Foundry, 488
Hodge, Ed, 277
Hoelzle, Corwin, 304–305
Hoffacker Farm, 394, 451
Hoffman, Nancy & Sally, 413
Hogue's Shoe Store, 307
Hogue, Earl M., 266
Hogue, John F., 41, 55
Hogue, Rose, 275
Hollebaugh, Forrest, 176
Holliday, Cyrus K., 49
Holly Rice and Milk Co., 135
Holstein, Fred, 151
Holy Ridgers, 56
Holy Trinity Evangelical Lutheran Church, 203, 422
home brew, 245
Home Coal Mine, 71
Home Mine, 426
Homer, Neil, 275
Hood, Isobel, 325
Hood, Joseph, 280, 306–311, 319, 324–325, 337–341, 348, 350–352
Hood, Okkie, 308, 310
Hoon and Stewart Appliances, 307
Hoon family, 336
Hoon, Philip, 35
Hoover Farm, 425
Hoover, Thurman, 336
Hope, Dr., 307
Hopkins, Joseph, 436
Horam, Judy Lynn, 385
Hordisty, Louise, 386
Horizon Health System, 503
Horvath Dairy, 232
Horvath, Emil, 390
hospitals, 73, 113, 197, 204, 249, 296, 298, 349, 357, 363, 382, 398, 415, 455, 477, 483, 503
Hostetler, Chris E., 489
Hostetter, George, 178, 205
Hotel Shenango, 447
Houck, C. T., 286
House on the Hill, 440
Houser Store, 544
Houser, Frederick, 352–353
Houston, John & Sara, 73
Hover family, 138
Hover Farm, 336
Hover, Thurman, 231
Hovis Trucking, 483
Howe, Dr., 306
Hoyt, Dr., 155
Huebert, Jacob, 276
Huey, Norris, 266
Huey, Will, 114
Hughes, Fred, 253
Hugo, Julia Stamm, 143, 147
Huling, Frank C., 46
Hull, Agnes Logan, 120
Hull, Beshara, 189
Hull, Daniel, 34, 189
Hull, John, 189
Hull, Mary, 304
Hum, S. D., 165
Humes Hotel, 43, 308, 322, 374–375
Humphrey's Veterinary Supplies, 486
Hungarian Holy Trinity Church, 250
Hunt, Cressy, 380
Hunter School, 355
Hunter, Barbara Kilgore, 386
Hunter, Don, 446
Hunter, Donald, 189
Hunter, John W., 530, 531
Hurst, J. T., 35
Hurst, Reed, 101
Huskin, Miss, 297
Hutchison, A. P., 455
Hutchison, Carlton, 189

∞—Ii—∞
Iacella, Mrs., 289
ice cream salesmen, 295
ice salesmen, 246
iceball business, 246–247
Idlewild Park, 202
immigrants, 73–74, 117, 250, 415
Independent of Greenville, 46
Independent Press, 402
Indian Run, 56, 58–59
Indian Run Grange, 459
Indians in western Pennsylvania, 19–23, 29, 32–34
Ingram, John H., 241
Ingram, Joseph, 183
Interstate 79, 278
Interstate 80, 388, 438–439
interurbans, 112, 305
Irishtown, 60
Iron Banking Co., 60
Iron City Furnace, 30

Iroquois, 19–20, 34
Irvine, Dr. John, 32
Irwin Presby. Church, 37–38
Isaly stores, 247, 306, 427
Italian immigrants, 415
Ivex, 483

∞—Jj—∞
J. C. Moore Industries, 335, 486
J. I. Case Farm Equipment, 288
JA Farrell, 205
Jabins, Jerry & Jennie, 455
Jack's Store (Worth Township), 316
Jack, Carl, 386
Jackal, Jimmy, 308
Jackson Center, 24, 69–70, 370, 394, 559
Jackson Center Presby. Church, 336, 512
Jackson Grange, 400
Jackson Township, 22, 29, 52, 191, 390, 394, 437
Jackson, J. Y., 152
Jameson, Erie, 386
Jamestown, 50–51, 55, 132, 134, 177, 180, 190, 198, 286, 448–449, 488
Jamestown Arch, 482, 484
Jamestown Area Historical Society, 484, 557
Jamestown Area Recreation Board, 392
Jamestown Community Fair Association, 335
Jamestown Elementary School, 450
Jamestown Fire Department, 103
Jamestown High School, 335, 491
Jamestown Institute, 75
Jamestown newspapers, 45, 404
Jamestown Paint & Varnish Co., 481
Jamestown Seminary, 442
Jamieson Farm, 394
Jamieson's Photo Studio, 306
Jamisen, Paul, 176
Jamison, Lillian, 266
Jamison, Marguarite "Toots," 270
Jarrett, Benjamin, 446
Jarrett, Sylvia, 198
Jazwinski, Richard, 418
Jazwinski, Robert, 189
Jeffers, James, 47
Jefferson Township, 27, 54, 60, 97
Jefferson-Clark Regional Police Department, 488
Jennings Farm, 231
Jennyburg Hill, 62
Jereb, Frank, 250
Jesus festivals, 467
Jewell, Lauren C., 395
Jewell, Mr., 120
Jiffy Mini Mart (Grove City), 480
Johnson, A. LeRoy "Spike," 46
Johnson, Boel, 61
Johnson, Bruce, 368
Johnson, David L., 428
Johnson, Edward, 73
Johnson, H. Clay, 368
Johnson, Hal, 240
Johnson, Jerry, 353–354
Johnson, John, 232
Johnson, Margaret, 56
Johnson, Stephen T., 61
Johnston Tavern, 92, 138
Johnston, Arthur, 92
Jolly, Thomas, 33
Jones Beach, 488
Jones, Arthelia, 134
Jones, Elias, 196
Jones, H. C., 151
Jones, Mary Catterson, 63
Jones, Myron W., 224
Jones, Victor, 46
Jones, William, 63
Jordan, Gene, 550
Jordan, Mr., 217
Joslin, Mr., 217
Jovic, Slobodan, 134
Joy Cone Co., 490
Joyce, Peter, 389
judges, county, 530–532, 537
Julia F. Buhl Girls Club, 183, 267, 286
Julian, Bernice, 395
Julian, John, 395

∞—Kk—∞
Kalfman, Alice, 385
Kamerer, James, 538
Kantner, Harry I., 157
Karfes, James & Mary, 284, 511
Kashner School, 517
Kaufman, Mary, 402
Kauk family, 506
KDKA radio, 196
Keaney family, 138

Kearns, Carroll D., 292
Kearns, Nora Lynch, 419
Keck, Joseph, dust jacket
Keck, Robert L., 181
Keeland, B. F., 474
Keen, Ed, 75
Kees, John, 402
Kefurt, Gus, 356
Kegel Farm, 394
Keiffer, A. M., 462
Kelley, Oliver Hudson, 399
Kelly, Dr., 391
Kelly, George D., 64
Kelly, George family, 386
Kelly, Hazen, 177
Kelly, John, 44
Kelly, Oakley G., 237
Kelso's Garage, 486
Kennard, 34, 283, 390–391
Kennard Grange, 400
Kennard United Meth. Church, 485
Kennard United Presby. Church, 177
Kenstler's Collision Repair, 486
Kerins, Beckie, 490
Kerins, John, 302, 440
Kerins, Richard, 440
Kerins, Rick, 302
Kerr School, 37, 52, 54
Kerr, J. P., 215
Kerr, Joseph, 531
Kerr, Samuel, 531
Kerr, William, 418
Ketler, George, 296
Ketler, Isaac C., 328
Ketler, Weir, 296, 328, 329
Keystone Ordinance, 334, 335
Kiefer, A. M., 405
Kilgore, 38
Kilgore family, 386
Kilgore Farm, 386
Kilgore, James, 56
Kilgore, John J., 38
Kilgore, Ralph, 386
Kilgore, Samuel D., 38
Kilner, John, 309
Kimberly Memorial Nurses Home, 382
Kimberly Mills, 39
Kimberly Rolling Mills, 277
Kimberly, Peter L., 97, 189, 498
Kimberly, Samuel, 52, 66
Kimes, Lee, 53
Kimes, Walter, 53
King, Henry, 370
King, James, 531
King, T. W., 307
Kitch and Mower Hardware, 110–111
Kitch, Robert W., 295
Kitch, Walter, 295
Klecic, Frank, 250
Kleffel, Geraldine, 405
Klenovich, Mickey, 352
Kline, Charles, 266
Klingensmith, Daniel & Peter, dust jacket
Knauff, John & Georgine, 517
Knights of Columbus, 296
Knights of Pythias, 238–239, 287
Koehler, Frederick, 189
Kolbrick, Eva, 275
Koller, James, 486
Koller, Rick, 486
Koonce, Charles, 62, 505
Koonce, Samuel, 38, 505
Korean War, 579
Kranz, Pastor, 422
Kraynaks Nursery & Garden Center, 516
Krem, Dorothy Campbell, 333
Kremis, 137, 171–173
Kresinski, Daniel, 97, 253–254
Kroger Grocery, 246
Ku Klux Klan, 178
Kucan, Jerome, 252–253
Kuhn, Charles, 397
Kuhn, John C., 224
Kurpe, Michael Thomas, 447
Kuskuskies, 21
Kyle, Ralph, 355, 389
Kyle, Timothy, 389

∞—Ll—∞

L. Bash Clothing Store, 74
Lackawannock Crossing, 27
Lackawannock Township, 29–30, 32, 52, 63, 131, 156, 197, 231, 232, 315, 333, 390, 445
Lackey Farm, 288, 336, 556
Lackey, Janice, 336
Lackey, Kathy, 288
Lackey, Norman, 336
Lackey, Steve, 288
Lafayette, Marquis de, 42, 374

Laird Opera House, 132
Lake Julia, 189, 547
Lake Latonka, 437
Lake Local, 45, 456
Lake Side Park, 43–44
Lake Township, 29, 52, 191, 394
Lake Wilhelm, 538, 545, 552, dust jacket
Lakeview Church of God, 43
Lakeview High School, 43
Lakeview School District, 38, 268, 279, 333, 386, 394–397, 451–453, 491–492
Lamb School, 38
Lambrose family, 386
Landon, Alfred Mossman, 302–303
Langdon's Department Store, 307
Langdon, C. R., 266
Lant, John A., 498
Larry, Frank, 309
Large Railroad Mine, 53
Larson, Helen, 275
Lartz, C. B., 184, 499
Last Minit Mart (Grove City), 480
Latshaw, Paul, 217
Laubscher Cheese Co., 485, 486
laundry methods, 242–243
Laurie, Sandra, 557
Lavine Hotel, 178
Law, Albert, 538
Law, James, 405
Law, John, 385
Lawrence Grange, 33
Lawrence, C. F., 454
Lawrence, Harry W., 454
Lawton, Leonard, 564
Lazor, Olivia M., 478, 479, 540
Leary, Jim, 392
Leary, Lloyd, 450
Leary, Norma, 557
Lebanon Presby. Church, 336
Lebanon United Presby. Church, 436
Leech and Beachler Publishers, 403
Leech's Corner, 390–391, 545
Leech, Milton A., 531
Leech, William, 531
Lees, Don, 114
Lees, Howe, 114
Lees, Lottie, 114
Lees, Ray, 114
Leesburg, 69–70, 92, 290, 320
Leesburg Falls, 24
Leisher, Frank, 266
Lennon, M. S., 180
Leoffler, Emil, 302
Lescher, John George, 109
Leslie N. Firth Learning Center, 441
Leslie, John, 506
Leslie, Rhonda, 506
Lever family, 39
Lever, William, 39
Levine, Lewis, 292
Lewis Dairies, 217
Lewis, Anna, 146
Lewis, Dave, 270
Lewis, Donald, 311
Lewis, James, 317
Lewis, John L., 301
Lewis, N. S., 144
Lewis, Robin, 516
Leyde Automotive Machine Co., 116
Leyde, Barbara Ann Hollibaugh, 116
Leyde, David, 23
Leyde, James H., 116
Leyde, Joseph, 116
Leyde, Old John, 23
Liberia, 41
Liberty Township, 32–33, 34, 36
Librix, Joseph, 238
Lightner, E. W., 403
Lightner, John, 531
Ligo School, 34, 485
Ligo, John & Judy, 490, 503
Limber, Elsie, 194
Limberg Brothers, 506
Lincoln School, 168
Lindbergh, Charles & Anne Morrow, 238
Linderman, George, 284
Lininger, Lillian, 275
Lininger, Owen, 275
Linn School, 517
Linn, David, 517
Linn, William, 317
LiTerra Farm, 490, 503
Little family (Kennard), 283, 391
Little Jim Church, 43
Little Neshannock Creek, 30
Little Shenango Creek, 229
Little Shenango River, 33, 40, 171
Little's Fruit Market, 487
Little, A. A., 454

Little, Marcia, 386
Little, Penny, 386
Livermore, Elmer, 114, 337
Livermore, Walter, 418
Living Word Church, 445
Loch, William, 405
Locust Grove, 318
Loesel, Mrs. William, 405
Loesel, William, 405
Logan, John, 266
London Grange, 400
London School, 202
Long, Bussell, 179
Loomis, Rod, 413
Love School, 32
Lowe's Home Improvement Center, 384, 386
Lowman, M. A., 454
Lukacs, Stephan, 530
Lydel, William, 101
Lyon's School, 229
Lytle, John, 169

∞—Mm—∞

M. Anne, Sister, 251
M. Bernadette, Sister, 251
M. L. Beach Store, 379
M. Paula, Superior Sister, 251
Mabel Furnace, 61, 157
MacBride-Dexter, Edith, 312
MacKenzie, Charles, 329
Madden, Edward, 189
Madenoff, Emery, 151
Madge Mine, 131
Magaree, Kelly, 386, 387
Magaree, Scott, 386, 387
Magoffin House Museum, 413
Magoffin, Dr. James, 42
Magoffin, Montrose, 198
Mahaney, George F., 287
Mahle, Professor, 30
Mahoney, Jim, 385
Mallot, Lester, 217
Manison, R. J., 66
Maple Drive High School, 52, 383
maps, 31, 494, 546, 559
Mark Twain Restaurant, 442
Marquis School, 32
Marrie, Philip, 189
Marsh Farm, 451
Marshall, Don, 538
Marstellar, Carl, 446
Martin, Grace, 276
Martin, John, 244, 538
Martin, Ken & Marlene, 274
Martin, Susan, 244
Mason and Miller, realtors, 133
Mason, J. W., 402
Masons, 73, 239, 241
Masson Farm, 288
Master Farmers, 232, 490
Masters, Charles, 290
Masters, George W., 290
Mathay, Mrs. D. H., 405
Mathews, Cheryl Maria Hess, 379
Mathews, Mayes, 379
Mathieson, Mr., 217
Matter, Buster, 355
Matter, Donald, 355
Matter, Robert, 355
Matthews squaring shear guides, 163
Matthews, Mr., 217
Maxwell, Melvin, 114
Maxwell, Mont, 114
Maxwell, Norman J., 233
Maxwell, Riley, 114
Maxwell, Ruby, 114
Mayer, Richard, 418
Mayne School, 59
Mays, Doug, 491
Maysville Community Church, 506
McAllister, Ray, 397, 491
McBride family, 428
McBride, C. G., 441
McBride, George, 400
McBride, Jr., Milford L. "Miff," 379
McBride, Madeleine, 379
McBride, William, 35
McCain, Frank J., 440
McCallister, Ray, 452, 453
McCann, Hughie, 309
McCann, Tom, 309
McCartney's Feed and Hardware, 486
McCartney's Ice Cream Plant, 307
McCartney, A. L., 178
McCartney, Howard, 294
McCartney, O. H., 294
McClain's Print Shop, 307, 464

McClain, Paul, 550
McClain, T. W., 464, 498
McClelland family, 150
McClelland Homestead, 231
McClester, R. P., 150
McClimans, Esther, 557
McClintock, George, 189
McClung Auto Body, 519
McClure family, 59
McClure, John, 63
McClure, Joseph, 63
McClure, R. J., 215
McClure, Samuel, 71, 189
McClymonds, Floyd, 455, 457
McConkey, Marian, 114, 267, 315
McConnell School, 37
McConnell, Fred, 453
McConnell, George, 383
McConnell, H. E., 180
McConnell, James, 92
McConnell, John, 35
McConnell, Wendell, 275
McCormick, W. A., 169
McCowell, Alexander, 189
McCoy, F. W., 45
McCoy, Hiram, 36
McCoy, James, 35
McCoy, Mable, 217
McCoy, Olive, 381, dust jacket
McCoy, Thomas, 36
McCoytown, 36
McCoytown Mine, 54
McCoytown School, 37
McCracken family, 318
McCracken Farm, 394
McCracken, Don, 270
McCracken, Mr., 194
McCullough, Frank, 269
McCullough, Glennie, 30
McCullough, John, 20–21
McCune, Jack, 296–297, 298
McCurdy Farm, 394
McCurdy, Charles, 182
McCurdy, Samuel, 370
McCutcheon, Henry, 36
McCutcheon, Thelma Barrows, 414
McDonald, J. M., 455
McDougall Farm, 288
McDowell Bank, 287
McDowell Farm, 288, 556
McDowell Farm (David & Gene), 470
McDowell Farms (John, Sr.; John, Jr., & Robert), 466
McDowell, A. Walter "Dude," 46, 498, 500
McDowell, Andrew, 232
McDowell, David, 35
McDowell, Ed, 192
McDowell, John, 232, 260–261
McDowell, Joseph, 75
McDowell, Mary, 75
McDowell, Matthew, 35
McDowell, Nellie Eliza Dygert, 75
McDowell, Robert, 35
McDowell, William C., 46
McElwain Institute, 518
McElwain, Joseph, 486
McFadden, Kathy, 385
McFarland Dairy, 135
McFarland Farm, 394, 556
McFarland, Reed, 135
McGilvery, William, 66
McGilvray, William, 230
McHale, James, 450
McKay Works, 328
McKay, Leo H., 43, 532
McKay, Robert, 341
McKay, Samuel, 138
McKean Brothers Farm, 490, 503
McKean Farm, 33
McKean's Buying Station, 486
McKean, Harve, 334
McKean, Roy, 334
McKean, Thomas, 169
McKean, William, 531
McKenna, James, 114
McKenna, John, 114
McKenna, Less, 114
McKenna, Margaret, 169
McKenna, Minnie, 114
McKnight family, 39
McKnight, Carl, 413
McKnight, Jane, 385
McKnight, John, 275
McKnight, Margaret, 275
McKnight, Marian, 275
McKnight, William, 45
McLain, Muggs, 309
McLaughry, James A., 534
McLaughry, Mary, 270

587

McMaster, William, 442
McMichael, H. P., 232
McMillan, Mont, 114
McMillen, William, 276
McMullen, Freeland, 397
McMullen, John, 164
McNabb, J. R., 498
McNabb, Scott R., 498
McTaggert, Mr., 324
McWhorter, Blanch, 114
McWhirter, Blanche, 402
McWhirter, J. H., 316
McWhirter, John, 407
Meade, Janifer D., 73
Meadowgold Dairy, 231
Meadville Telephone Co., 230
Mecklem's Market and Slaughterhouse, 487
Medic, Leo J., 250
Mehard, Samuel S., 533, 534
Mehler Block Coal Mine, 135
Mel Grata Chevrolet and Toyota dealership, 515
Melcher, Pastor, 422
Mellon Bank (Mercer), 309
Mellon, Pete, 309
Memorial Park (Grove City), 260, 268, 284, 289, 507, 565
Menzies, William & Jane, 434
Mercer, 22, 29, 42, 44, 47, 52, 58, 62, 69–70, 77, 79, 94, 95, 108, 134, 154, 169, 197–198, 202, 240, 280, 306–311, 337–341, 348, 374
Mercer Academy, 273
Mercer African Meth. Episcopal Zion Church, 72
Mercer Avenue School, 259
Mercer Bowling Alley, 306, 309
Mercer bus station, 307
Mercer Chamber of Commerce, 266
Mercer Coal and Manufacturing Co., 174
Mercer County Genealogical Society, 32
Mercer County Agricultural and Manufacturing Society of Stoneboro, 215, 478
Mercer County Agricultural Society, 478
Mercer County Cooperative Extension, Penn State, 441
Mercer County Eagle, 498
Mercer County Grange Fair, 177
Mercer County Herald, 455
Mercer County Historical Society, 43, 153–154, 181, 404, 407, 413, 463, 471, 548, dust jacket
Mercer County Home, 182, 262–264, 459
Mercer Diner, 508
Mercer Dispatch, 279, 307, 313, 326, 403, 453–454, 456
Mercer East Elementary School, 416
Mercer Fair, 337–338
Mercer Forge, 311
Mercer Gas and Water Co., 306
Mercer High School, 216, 258, 273
Mercer Iron and Coal Co., 41, 52, 136, 137, 177, 190, 215
Mercer Library, 306, 311
Mercer Livestock Auction, 425
Mercer Luminary, 326
Mercer Milling Co., 141, 437
Mercer Mining and Manufacturing Co., 68, 137
Mercer Old Home Week, 164, 274
Mercer Opera House, 178
Mercer Poor House, 262–264
Mercer Republican, 326
Mercer Sanitarium, 306, 339
Mercer School, 34, 324
Mercer Silk Mill, 324
Mercer Tube Co., 301
Mercer Whig, 326
Mercer, General Hugh, dust jacket
Mesin, Ann, 253
Metelsky, Michael, 508
Meth. Episcopal Church, 228, 432
Metz, Laurence, 402
Meyer, Frank, 412
Meyer, Lloyd, 412
Meyer, Margaretta, 412
Meyer, Samuel, 412
Micheals, Dennis, 385
Micro Midgets, 389
Miglin, John, 60
Miglin, Ruth, 60
Miles, Thomas, 432
Miliron, Rev., 485
military records, 563–581
Milk Chug, 513
Milk Maid, Pennsylvania, 394
Milk Transport Inc., 483
milk trucks, 256
Mill Creek, 22
Mill Creek Township, 27, 394
Millbrook, 38, 131, 316
Millbrook Grange, 399, 400
Millbrook Park, 176
Millbrook Presby. Church, 38

Millbrook Schoefield United Meth. Church, 38
Millbrook School, 38, 386–387
Milledgeville, 475
Miller and Sons Funeral Home, 390
Miller's Furniture Store, 306
Miller, C. Earl, 402
Miller, Charles, 30
Miller, David, 408–409
Miller, Don, 270
Miller, Helen Black, 463
Miller, Jacob, 403
Miller, Jacob L., 189
Miller, James, 35–36
Miller, John, 35–36
Miller, Lena, 237
Miller, Priscilla, 30
Miller, Richard, 302
Miller, Samuel S., 534
Miller, Walter, 418
Milliken, Harry W., 237
Milliken, James, 189
mills, 27. See also steel industry
Miner's Patch, 53
mining, 52–54, 68, 70–71, 101, 135–136, 157, 174–175
Minner family, 556
Minner, Frank, 220
Minner, Helen, 341
Minner, Ralph, 220
Minor, Bob, 386
Minor, Gary, 386
Minor, Ronnie, 386
Miss Mercer, 274
Miss Milkmaid, Pennsylvania, 181
Mitch's Laundromats, 73
Mitchell, Andy, 492
Mitchell, Clarence, 73
Mitchell, Coydon, 417
Mitchell, Donald, 417
Mitchell, Dr., 138
Mitchell, Gerald, 73
Mitchell, Howard, 417
Mitchell, LeRoy F., 417
Mitchell, Salvador P., 418
Mitcheltree, John, 531
Moats, Robert & Beatrice, 490
Mohney, D. Lee, 396
Mohney, Ruth, 396
Mongiello Apartments, 307
Mongiello property, 309
Monk, Fredrick, 485
Monkey Run Mine, 174
Montgomery & Sons, 120, 455
Montgomery Drug Store, 306–307
Montgomery, Eva, 399
Montgomery, Pat, 386
Moody, J. H., 241
Moon, Ed, 338
Moon, Edwin, 529
Moore brothers (Grove City), 455
Moore family (Springfield Township), 451
Moore Farm, 37
Moore, Arthur, 181
Moore, J. C., 335
Moore, Jesse, 531
Moore, John H., 330
Moore, M. W., 454
Moore, Maggie C., 454
Moore, Robert, 35
Moreland, Andrew & Mary Ellen, 510
Moreland, Henry, 510
Moreland, Isaac, 510
Moreland, Lillie, 355
Moreland, William, 510
Morgan, George, 403
Morgan, J. Pierpont, 142
Morisuye, Masanobu, 343
Morrell, William, 342
Morris, David D., 53
Morrison, Daisy Thorne, 402
Morrison, Gwendolyn, 275
Morrison, John, 275, 402, 531
Morrison, John L., 404, 497–498
Morrison, Joseph, 61
Morrison, Levi, 403–404
Morrison, Mayme, 275
Morrison, Pauline, 275
Moser, Fred D., 46
Moser, Fred W., 289
Moser, Marvin, 46
Moss, Paul, 276
Moss, Silas, 352
Mother Black's boarding house, 440
Motivation Air, Inc., 395
Mount Hickory, 59, 61
Mount Hickory Furnace, 64
Mount Olive Baptist Church, 483
Mount Pleasant, 177
Mount Pleasant Grange, 177, 400, 440

Mount Pleasant Meth. Episcopal Church, 101
Mount Pleasant Mine, 52
Mowry, Mary, 337
Mowry, Vista, 275
Moyer, Clyde, 355
Moyer, Violet, 355
Mt. Hickory Dairy Farm, 232
Mt. Hope United Meth. Church, 102
Mulhern, Paul, 309
Mulvey, Joseph, 276
Munnell, William C., 335
Murphy Dairy, 489
Murphy, James, 97
Murrin, Charles Charles, 539
Myers family, 138
Myers, A. L. "Spike," 266
Myers, Arthur, 181
Myers, Edith, 396
Myford, James E., 522

∞—Nn—∞

N. N. Moss Store, 276
NAACP, 73, 238
Nace, Robert K., 406
Narlee, Margaret, 114
National Air Mail Week, 1938, 289
National Black Nurses' Association, 73
National Castings Division of Midland Ross, 452
National City Bank, 60
National Guard, 158
National Iron and Steel Co., 139
National Malleable and Steel Castings Co., 180, 301, 351
nationality churches, 134
natural gas, 136
Nazarene Church, 285
Neal's Heating & Plumbing, 487
Neely, Bob, 151
Neely, Cecil, 397
neighborhood stores, 246, 305–306
Nelson organ, 108
Nelson Run, 491
Nelson, J. W., 169
Neolithic Period, 19–20
Neshannock, 34, 101
Neshannock Creek, 22, 280, 307, 325, 337, 437
Neshannock Township, 29
Neshannock Woods Refinishing, 24
Neuroh, A., dust jacket
Neville's Shop, 120, 127
New Castle Christian Assembly, 274
New Hamburg, 212, 265
New Lebanon, 394, 519
New Logic Inn, 92
New Vernon Grange, 400
New Vernon Township, 102, 231, 336, 394, 538
New Virginia, 34, 52, 101
New Virginia Church, 101
New Virginia Meth. Church, 400
New Wilmington Livestock Auction, 333
Newell, John, 531
News-Telegraph, 248, 499
newspapers, 44–47, 140, 248–249
Newton Farm, 425
Newton, Harold, 104
Newton, Laverne, 104
Nicklin, Homer, 282
Nicklin, William, 381
Nickum, J. B., 169
Nickum, John, 341
No. 1 Mine, 41, 52
No. 2 Mine, 51, 52, 71, 136, 289–290
No. 3 Mine, 52, 136
No. 5 Mine, 71
Nolan, J. C., 41
Noll, Josephine, 154
North Carnegie Works, 292
North Farm, 231
North Liberty, 32–33
North River Flats, 336
North, Cliff, 114
Northcote, Elizabeth McFarland, 38
Norton, Mary Brown, 36
Novak, Christopher, 254
Nutt Farm, 336
Nutt, Leroy A., 395, 451
Nych Farm, 445
Nystrom, Elise, 229

∞—Oo—∞

O'Connor, Walter J., 456
O'Donnell, Jack, 447
O'Keefe, John, 97
O'Mahoney, Mary Vanatta, 274
O'Mahony, Dennis, 117
O'Neill's Coffee Co., 92
Oakes, Gary, 478, 479

Oakes, Johnny, 458
Oakes, Sally, 478, 479
Oakland Junction, 325
Oakview Elementary School, 394, 397, 451, 453
Occasional, The, 455
Odd Fellows, 135
Odd Fellows Home, 53
Ogelvee, Ltd., 486
Old Martin General Store, 520
Old Salem United Meth. Church, 29, 545
Old Stone Jail, 95
Olive McClure's Beauty Shop, 306
Olsen, Nels, 232
Olson, Audley, 396
Optimist Club of Sharon, 287
Orangeville, 66–67, 450, 459
Orchard Manor, 135, 483
organ grinders, 295
Organ, William, 182, 498, 499
Ormond, Alexander T., 328–329
Ormond, Grace McCune, 298
Ormond, Roger, 284, 297–298
Ormsby, James W., 60, 65
orphans, 322, 406, 462
Orr, Jr., William, 45–46
Orr, Robert, 169
Orrs School, 333
Orvis, William, 402
Osborn family, 285
Osborn Farm, 394
Osborn, Charles, 283
Osborn, James, 283
Osborn, Robert, 33, 229, 281, 483
Osborne, Florence, 316
Osborne, Jack, 316
Osgood, 68–69, 137, 171–173, 390, 434, 461
Osgood School, 333
Ostojich, Zoran, 252
Otter Creek, 22, 285, 437
Otter Creek Township, 27, 29, 33, 96, 295, 349, 377, 465, 539
Outlook, The, 455
Owen, Olive, 76
Owen, Russell, 392

∞—Pp—∞

Packard, Daniel Berry, 40
Page's Restaurant, 307, 309
Page, Robert H., 394
Painter, Carl, 370
Palmer Pools, 486
Palmer, Dewitt, 487, 535
Palmer, Jeff, 486, 487
Palmer, Marjorie, 487
Pandenarium, 56–59
Pardoe, 68, 117, 136, 137, 174–175, 197
Pardoe Mine, 53
Pardoe School, 269, 372
Parker's Ford Garage, 306
Parquette, Leora, 385
Passavant Center, 409
pastimes, 76–78
Patagonia, 34, 182, 304, 366
Patterson Garage, 487
Patterson, Isaac, 34, 70
Patterson, Myrtle Bower, 212
Patterson, Robert, 531
Patterson, Wade, 270
Patton, Thomas, 436
Paxton Farm, 135
Paxton, Harold, 442
Paxton, Nancy Lee, 151
Payne, Ervin & Dolly, 509
Payne, Florence, 455
Peacock, L. K., 144
Pearson Mill, 27
Pearson, John, 36, 114, 531
Peirce, Walter, 65
Peirsol, Clara, 113
Peirsol, Rexford, 113
Pence, Fred, 183
Pendel, Marco, 250
Penn Grove Hotel, 150, 267, 315
Penn High School, 276, 333, 334, 356, 406
Penn Power Co., 308, 309, 371
Pennsylvania State University, Shenango Campus, 514
Pennzoil gas station, 306, 309
Pepe, Johnny, 281
Perjol, Tom, 499
Perkins family, 138
Perkins Furnace, 65
Perkins, Simon, 65, 189
Perrine Corners, 216, 316, 559
Perrine School, 38, 216
Perrine, Harold, 176
Perrine, Vernin, 176
Perry Highway, 278

588

Perry's Blacksmith Shop, 164
Perry, John, 35
Perry, L., 217
Perry, Samuel, 73
Perry, William, 35
Persch Garage, 363
Perska's Garage, 340, 341
Peters, John, 418
Peterson, Charles, 317
Petroleum Iron Works, 301
Petz, Verne, 409
Pew, J. Howard, 329
Pew, J. Newton, 328
Pew, Mary Ethel, 329
Pew, Samuel, 47
Peyser, Miss, 297
Philips Oldsmobile garage, 391
Philips, Emily Church, 75
Phillips, Isaac, 76
Phillips, M., 217
Phillips, Mary, 251
Phillips, Mrs., 217
Phipp's Drygoods Store, 306, 307
Phythyon, Dan, 30
Piepenhagen Hay Sales, 486
Pierce & Son Store, 318
Pierce Mill, 34
Pierce Opera House, 60
Pierce School, 60
Pierce Woolen Mill, 41
Pierce, Chloe, 59, 61, 474
Pierce, Frank, 59–60, 65
Pierce, General James, 34, 59–60, 64–65, 196, 474
Pierce, James B., 59–60, 65
Pierce, Jonas, 58
Pierce, Jonas J., 59, 64–65
Pierce, Wallace, 59–60, 65
Pierce, Walter, 44–45, 59–60
pig iron, 140
Pilgram Farm, 489
Pilgrim Mine, 131
Pinchalong, 53
Pinchalong Mine, 53
Pinchalong School, 37
Pine Creek, 437
Pine Grove, 25, 27, 34, 120, 129, 147, 453–454. See also Grove City
Pine Grove Meth. Episcopal Church, 164
Pine Grove Normal Academy, 150, 328
Pine Grove Telephone, 454
Pine Grove United Presby. Church of Grove City, 150
Pine Swamp, 22
Pine Top School, 37
Pine Township, 27, 34–37, 52–54, 220, 385, 483
Pine Township Mine, 54
Pinkle, Eleanor, 355
Pinney, Daryl, 450
Pinney, Philip P., 401
Pintar, Anton, 250
Piper, W. F., 238
Pitts, Dorothy, 48
Pivovar, Ronald, 409
Pizor Feed Mill, 169, 240
Pizor, Ira Leigh, 169
Pizor, Isaac Jefferson, 169
Pizor, Zelda Magee, 169, 240
plane wrecks, 232, 238
Plantation Park camping area, 337
Platt, C. A., 455
Pleasant Valley Grange, 400
Pleasantville, 96
Ploski, James, 397
Plummer McCullough Farm, 437
Polar Bear Food and Service, 486
polar expedition, 152–154
polio shots, 416
Polk Junction, 192
Pollard, Bill, 340
Pomona Grange, 399
Poole Farm, 451
Port, William D., 410
Porter and Perkins banking house, 497
Porter Cut-off, 137
Porter, David T., 531
post offices, 92, 323, 420–421
postal service, 44, 45, 134–135, 177
Potter, Albern, 488
Potter, Patricia Sowash, 488
Powell, Clint, 286
Powell, Norman S., 283
Poxberry, Mr., 309
Presby. Church, 435, 518
Pretoria-Delaware High School, 218
Prezgay, William, 252
Price, Thomas J. "Cap," 182
Prime Outlets at Grove City, 72, 558
Prince Hall Masonry, 73, 239
Progress, 46

Prohibition, 195–196, 245
Prospect Free Meth. Church, 177
Prospect Heights School, 363
Protected Home Circle, 46, 144, 322
Protestant Meth. Church, 283
prothonotaries, 530, 537
Pujic, Vinko, 253
Puljic, Ilija, 253
Purvis, W. E., 150
Pymatuning, 33
Pymatuning Creek, 67
Pymatuning Dam, 282, 283, 284, 285
Pymatuning Junction, 67, 459
Pymatuning Lake, 286
Pymatuning Land Co., 283
Pymatuning State Park, 286
Pymatuning Swamp, 283
Pymatuning Town, 24
Pymatuning Township, 33, 34, 59, 275, 359

∞——Qq——∞

Quality Aviation, Inc., 456
Quinby, Achsah, 196
Quinby, Samuel, 196
Quirk, Andrew, 296–297

∞——Rr——∞

R. D. Werner Co., 488
R. R. Wright Education Fund, 229
R. W. Sidley, Inc., 468
Rader, Charles, 374
radios, 249, 300–301
rag salesmen, 292–293
railroad stations, 36, 128, 129, 340, 549
railroads, 34, 36, 41–44, 49–53, 59–60, 62, 64, 66–71, 101, 128–129, 136, 137, 139, 171–175, 189–192, 204, 226–227, 230–231, 268, 287, 327, 344, 356–357, 369, 392–394, 434, 450–452, 459–460, 484, 489, 553
Raisch Log Cabin, dust jacket
Raisch, Frederick, 471
Ralph W. Kyle, Inc., 389
Ramsay, William B., 498, 499
Ramsey, Ed, 389
Ramsey, James, 432
Randall, J., 40
Randall, Judy Borchert, 316
Randolph Young Men's Bible Class, 228
Rapper, Bobby, 429
Raspudic, Fr. Bruno, 252
rationing, 343–345
Rauschenberg, August, 181
Rauschenberg, Carl, 181
Rawleigh man, 281
Rawls, Betsy, 302
Ray, A. C., 454
Ray, Calvin W., 497–498
Ray, Dr. Emerson, 151, 152
Ray, James L., 498, 499
RC's Marina, 488
Rea Farm, 181
Reading Co., 191
Rearick Store, 386, 387
Reash, Elizabeth, 33
Record-Argus, 44–46, 402–404
recorders, county, 530, 537
Red Cross, the, 197, 200, 221, 357, 363, 370
red dog roads, 131
Redic family, 325
Redic's Barber Shop, 306
Redmond, Kenny, 374
Reed Packet Line, 48
Reed, D.C., 156
Reed, James H., 69
Reed, John Fountain, 72
Reeher, Frank, 418
Reeher, George, 503–504
Reese, Dwight, 276
Reformed Presby. Church, 426, 432
Reformed Society, 428
refrigeration, 246–247
registers of wills, county, 529, 537
Rehoboth Presby. Church, 38
Reichart, Harry, 564
Reichart, Harvey, 564
Reimold Farm, 451
Reimold, Augusta, 275
Reimold, Gayle, 275
Reimold, Mary, 275
Rema Christian Academy, 445
Renshaw, James, 241
Republican headquarters, 94
Republicans, 529–530, 536
Revolutionary War, 21–22, 25, 26, 181
Reyers Shoes, dust jacket
Reynolds High School, 218, 491
Reynolds School District, 451

Reynolds, James, 392
Reynolds, Sherry, 396
Reznor Hotel, 43
Reznor Manufacturing Co., 309, 310–311, 326, 340, 418, 437, 441
Reznor, George, 169, 309
Rhoades, Don, 486
Rhoads, Lori, 152
Rhodes Farm, 288
Rhodes House, 377
Rhodes, Gary A., 335
Rhodes, Ralph, 341
Rhodes, Wilber "Dusty," 350
Rhule, Steve, 456
Rice, Bruce, 451, 453
Rich, Mr., 41
Richards, Crosby, 169, 240
Richards, Guy, 390
Richards, Roxy, 240
Richards, Roy, 240
Rickard, Leroy, 529
Riddle, G. W., 169
Riddle, William Scott, 533
Ridgewood, the, 462
Riley School, 229
Riley's Corners, 34
Riley, Norman, 355
Riley, Ralph, 283
Ringer, Floyd, 309
Ringer, Guy, 270
Ringer, Weldon, 309
Ristvey family, 298–300
Ristvey, Michael, 298–300
Ritchey's Poultry Farm, 217
Ritchie, John, 32
Ritz automobile, 168
Riverside Park, 40, 317
road maintenance, 231, 294, 295, 486–487
Robbins, Austin H., 46
Robbins, D. B., 46
Robbins, John, 54
Roberts, Lottie, 33
Roberts, Robert Richford, 545
Robinson Print Shop, 455
Robinson, Charlie, 59
Robinson, D. Homer, 151
Robinson, E. R., 454
Robinson, Ellen, 59
Robinson, Ernest, 164
Robinson, J. B., 45
Robinson, John Robert, 349
Robinson, Martha, 164
Robinson, Sr., J. B., 454
Robinson, Terry, 385
Robinson, Wally, 59
Rockwell, Norman, 417
Rodgers, Jim, 385
Rodgers, Judge, 532
Roemer, Henry A., 292
Rogers, Thomas, 440
Roko, Fr., 252
Rollinson, James, 101
Romanenko Chamber Players, 476
Romanian Orthodox Church, 237
Romine, William, 478, 479, 533
Rood, Watson, 564
root beer, making, 245
Rose, A. J., 277
Rose, Dick, 487
Rose, Donna, 486, 487
Rose, Ephraim, 35
Rose, James, 35
Rosenberg, Carl, 405
Roses, Isaac, 23
Ross, Rev., 485
Rossman, Dr., 298
Rotary Club of Grove City, 507
Roth, Michael, 397
Roux Feed Co., 240
roving street salesmen, 292–295
Rowbottom, George, 337
Rowe, Harry, 164
Rowe, Robert, 418
Rowley, George, 277, 317
Rummel, George, 266
Runkle, Rich, 517
Runser, Andrew, 65–66
Runser, F. D., 66
Runser, Sebastain, 61, 65–66, 76–79
Rural Argus, 403
Russell L. Chinn American League Post, 73
Russell, Paul W., 337
Ruth African Meth. Episcopal Church, 72–73
Ruth's Cottage Restaurant, 487
Ruyechan, Matt, 254
Ryder, Melvin, 418

∞——Ss——∞

S. J. Gully Bank, 287
S. Runser and Co., 66
Sacred Heart Church, 97, 196
safety in steel industry, 141
Saint Cloud Hotel, 79
Salem Township, 29, 33, 229, 281–286, 333–335, 335, 390, 483
Sambo Restaurant, 386
Sample, David, 436
Sampson, Thomas A., 368
Sandt, Lewis Earle, 204
Sandy Creek Conservancy, 552
Sandy Lake, 38, 42–43, 55, 135, 136, 153, 190, 198, 215, 231, 258, 298, 332, 342, 392, 394, 443
Sandy Lake Breeze, 456, 457
Sandy Lake High School, 268, 396–397
Sandy Lake Hotel, 456
Sandy Lake News, 45, 456
Sandy Lake Presby. Church, 336
Sandy Lake Township, 29, 41, 55, 394
Santa Claus Project, 287
Saterfield, Flannagan, 77–78
Satterfield family, 62
Satterfield, James, 156, 432
Satterfield, Samuel, 304
Satterwhite, Samuel "Bo," 429
Saul Farm, 394
Savage Arms Co., 168, 177, 197
Savolskis, Paulette, 491
Sawhill Tubular Division, 447
Schaffer, Earl, 354
Schmidt, Gerald, 402
Schmidt, Gertrude, 402
Schoolhouse No. 6, 60
schools, 131, 142–143, 229, 254–255, 311, 383, 491. See also individual names
Schuller, Richard, 445
Schweiss, Eva, 275
Schwelling's store (Farrell), 398
Scofield, Glenn R., 456
Scotch Hill, 147
Scotch Hill Presby. Church, 483
Scott Farm, 181
Scott, Walter, 275
Scott, William, 59
Scurry, Michael D., 50
Sea Scouts, 317
Searchlight, The, 45
Seely, James M., 422
Seiple, Stanley J., 405
Select School, 328
Semple, Cunningham S., 44
Seneca Indians, 21–22, 26, 38, 61
Service, Fred, 46
Seventh-Day Adventist Church, 474
Sewall, Mary, 385
Shadow Lawn Manor, 505
Shady Maple School, 485
Shaffer, Esther A., 258
Shaffer, Scott, 475
Shalow, Alvah & Elizabeth, 440
Shank's Tavern, 40
Shannon family, 96
Shannon Farm, 181
Shannon, Hallie, 181
Shannon, Joseph, 530
Shannon, Sandra, 181, 394
Shannon, William, 181
Shannon, William Earl, 181
Sharon, 46–47, 48, 50–51, 54, 67–68, 74, 107, 112, 115, 136, 144, 155, 163, 170, 177, 180–182, 184–187, 195–196, 202, 205, 214–215, 221, 224, 229–230, 234–236, 267, 277, 281–282, 287, 298–299, 322, 336, 343, 362–363, 389, 487, 496, 527
Sharon & Greenfield Railroad, 34, 426
Sharon & Limestone Co., 197
Sharon African Meth. Episcopal Church, 73
Sharon Blast Furnace, 64
Sharon Boiler Co., 351
Sharon Boiler Works, 66, 230
Sharon coal, 71
Sharon Coal & Limestone Co., 51
Sharon coupler, 452
Sharon Exchange Hotel, 120, 124–125
Sharon Fire Department, 97, 103
Sharon Furnace, 61, 62, 66, 67, 77–78
Sharon High School, 160, 358, 491
Sharon Iron Co., 34, 70, 72, 426
Sharon Iron Furnace, 189
Sharon Meth. Church, 101
Sharon newspapers, 44, 46, 184, 496–499, 498, 499
Sharon Presby. Church, 101
Sharon Savings & Loan Bank, 276
Sharon Steel Castings Co., 71, 142
Sharon Steel Co., 27, 133, 138–139, 142, 168, 180, 398
Sharon Steel Corp., 139, 292, 301, 417, 488
Sharon Steel Hoop Co., 133, 292, 293

Sharon Tube Co., 230, 301
sharpener salesmen, 294–295
Sharpsburg, 59
Sharpsville, 53, 58, 59–61, 62, 64–67, 77–78, 93, 110, 112, 118, 141, 157, 166–167, 189, 191, 196, 197, 221, 235, 236, 238, 259, 272, 389–390, 487
Sharpsville Advertiser, 44–45
Sharpsville African Meth. Episcopal Church, 72
Sharpsville Boiler, 301, 446
Sharpsville Furnace, 61, 63–64
Sharpsville High School, 299, 491
Sharpsville Historical Society, 474
Sharpsville National Bank, 60
Sharpsville Penn Mold Co., 301
Sharpsville Plaza, 446
Sharpsville Presby. Church, 318
Sharpsville Printing Co., 45
Sharpsville Quality Products, 496
Sharpsville Service Club, 287
Sharpsville Times, 45
Shaw's Dam and Mill, 27, 35, 37
Shaw, J. C., 35
Shaw, Mr., 217
Shawnee Indians, 20
Sheakley, George, 165
Sheakley, James, 165
Sheakley, John, 165
Sheakley, Moses, 165
Sheakley, William, 165
Sheakleyville, 27, 41, 55, 75–76, 165, 190, 193, 196, 198, 285, 524
Sheakleyville Baptist Church, 192
Sheakleyville Fire Department, 103
Sheakleyville High School, 373
Shelhamer's Energy, 486
Shelley, David, 151, 152
Shellito, Ralph, 151
Shenango, 61, 68, 137, 174, 344, 553
Shenango Dam, 62, 420–421, 425, 435
Shenango Furnace Co., 65, 496
Shenango Incorporated, 496
Shenango Inn, 358, 476
Shenango Iron Works, 71, 142
Shenango Penn Mold, 496
Shenango Personnel Replacement Depot, 359
Shenango Reservoir, 425, 488, dust jacket
Shenango River, 20, 27, 34, 40, 50, 62, 70, 90, 92, 93, 116, 138, 183–187, 191, 204, 212, 229, 260, 283, 284, 317, 322, 420
Shenango River Dam, 184, 282
Shenango River Flats, 292
Shenango River Reservoir, 61
Shenango Town, 20, 24
Shenango Trail, 62
Shenango Township, 34, 181, 390
Shenango Township Grange, 399
Shenango Trail, 62
Shenango Valley. See individual communities
Shenango Valley Argus, 403
Shenango Valley Community Library, 138
Shenango Valley Freeway, 386
Shenango Valley Library, 299
Shenango Valley Mall, 253, 383, 384
Shenango Valley News, 46
Shenango Valley Street Railway, 112, 304
Shenango Valley Urban League, 73
Shenango Yard, 450
Sherbondy, Ken, 539
Sherbondy, Virginia Mitchell, 391
sheriffs, county, 530, 537
Sherrard, R. C., 152
Shields, Peter, 139
Shields, William, 41, 55
Shilling, Andrew, 118
Shilling, George, 118
Shilling, Salina Satterfield, 118
Shillito, Todd & Rita, 516
Shipler, J. E., 169
Shipley, Brian, 541
Shipton, Roy, 229
Shipton, Sara, 229
Shollenberger, Robert, 539
Shumaker, Paul, 406
Sicilian, Nick, 289–290
Signal, 45
Silent Wings Soaring, 456
Simmons, Lawrence, 75
Simmons, Leslie, 75
Simmons, Mabel, 75
Simmons, William, 40, 391
Simmonsville, 40
Sine's Grocery Store, 307
Sixteeners Association, 322
Skelton, Amy, 333
Skelton, Richard, 333
Skelton, Tom, 333
Skelton, W. D. "Nute," dust jacket
Skelton, Warren B., 289, 337
Skelton, Zana, 333

Slabtown, 35, 454
Slater Farm, 336
Sleingrave, Charles, 309
Slippery Rock Signal, 456
Sliskovich, Anselm, 250–251
Sloan, Edward G., 318
Sloss, Wesley, 146
Small, Edward, 546
Smathers, C. Blaine, 291
Smith family (Grove City), 150
Smith Farm, 451
Smith, Bernice, 275
Smith, David & Esther, 131
Smith, Joseph, 42
Smith, Minnie, 399
Smith, Russell, 276
Smith, S. S., 266
Smith, Stan, 270
Smoyer, Maude, 405
Snead, Sam, 302
Snodgrass, W. J., 432
snowstorms, 202, 319, 357–358, 360–361, 469
Snyder School, 517
Snyder, Dorothy Simons, 557
Snyder, Elmer, 283
Snyder, Esther, 422
Snyder, Neil, 471
Snyder, Ralph, 283
Snyder, William A., 65
soldiers killed in war, 566–581
Solid Rock Assembly of God, 506
Somerville, Olive, 30
Sommerville, Doris, 333
Sommerville, Sandy, 333
Sopher, Sue, 386
Sopher, Tom, 386
Soul, David, dust jacket
South Pymatuning Township, 29, 425
South Sharon, 133–134, 139, 180, 205, 326, 389. See also Farrell
South Sharon Fire Department, 103
South Sharon News, 499
South Sharon Works, 179
South Ward School, 107
Sowers, J. Edwin, 417
Sowers, Jess, 30
Spangler, Bill, 436
Spanish-American War, 144, 158
Sparks, William D., 491
Spaulding, Leslie, 189
Spearman Furnace, 61, 65, 67
Spearman, John J., 64–65, 66, 138, 139, 189
Spears, Agnes, 217
Spears, James, 53
speed limits (World War II), 343
Spence, Betty Harter, 347–350
Spears, Floyd, 131
Springfield, 147
Springfield Furnace, 92
Springfield Presby. Church, 465
Springfield Township, 23, 129, 202, 290
Springfield Volunteer Firemen Association, 456
St. Anthony de Padua's Church, 415
St. Anthony's Croatian Roman Catholic Church, 250–254
St. Charles Hotel, 401
St. Cloud Hotel, 374
St. Columbkille Roman Catholic Church, 371
St. Edmund's Martyr Episcopal Church, 463
St. Elizabeth's Church, 415
St. Etheridge's Catholic Church, 117
St. George Lodge No. 64, 134
St. George Serbian Orthodox Church, 134
St. Hermengild's Church, 117
St. John School, 38
St. John's Episcopal Church, 72, 305
St. John's Lutheran and German Reformed Societies, 265
St. John's United Church of Christ, 265
St. Paul Homes, 406, 462
St. Paul School, 38
St. Paul's Primitive Meth. Church, 43
stagecoaches, 45, 47, 487
Stambaugh, Mary L., 189
Stamm Farm, 394
Stamm, Betty, 488–489
Stamm, Jean, 406
Stampha, Joe, 282
Stanton family, 138
State Police Barracks, 307
State Regional Correctional Facility, 471
steam engines, 220
Stearns, Frank B., 405, 406
Steckler Farm, 451
steel industry, 68, 133–134, 138–142, 351. See also Buhl, Frank H.
Steele, Helen, 442
Steele, John, 442
Steen, William, 193

Steese, William, 47
Stefanak, Katherine, 250
Stellman, Rose, 453
Sterling gas station, 308, 316
Stevens, Mrs., 386
Stevens, Richard, 391
Stevenson Bill, 284
Stevenson family, 285
Stevenson, Clyde, 418
Stevenson, Gail, 391
Stevenson, Glen, 391
Stevenson, Harold, 283
Stevenson, John, 402
Stevenson, Jr., John, 97, 115, 138–139, 142, 168, 277
Stevenson, Lawrence, 283
Stevenson, Mary, 530
Stewart & Son, 156
Stewart House, 318
Stewart Iron Co., 138, 168
Stewart, John, 56
Stewart, Margaret Pierce, 164
Stewart, Minerva, 30
Stewart, Robert, 318
Stewart, T. D., 156
Stoeber, John B., 337
Stokely School, 114, 202, 311
Stokely, Benjamin, 22–23
Stokely, Drayton, 114
Stokely, George, 114
Stone, Jr., Amasa, 41
Stoneboro, 41–44, 51–52, 69–70, 132, 136, 137, 153, 177, 190–192, 198, 225, 232, 287, 336, 371, 392, 394, 524
Stoneboro and Chautauqua Lake Ice Co., 202
Stoneboro Citizen, 404
Stoneboro Fair, 42, 215, 478, 556
Stoneboro Fairground, 55
Stoneboro Fire Department, 103, 254
Stoneboro First Church of God, 43
Stoneboro High School, 396–397
Stoneboro Industrial Parade, 214
Stoneboro Meth. Episcopal Church, 41
Stoneboro Presby. Church, 42
Stoneboro Strawberry Association, 202
Stoneboro United Meth. Church, 41
Stoneboro United Presby. Church, 42
Stony Point Grange, 181, 400
Stotz, Charles M., 92
Stranahan, III, James Alexander, 367
Stranahan, John Q., 529
Stranahan, Robert, 169
Strange, Auntie, 55
Straub Farm, 288
Straub, Richard, 539
Strawbridge Bank, 120, 123
Strawbridge House, 383
streetcars, 112, 277, 304–305
Streit, William, 195
strikes, 52, 180, 301
Strosser, John, 339
Stroud, Jacob, 25
Strouss, Bill, 386
Strouss, Ruth Ann, 386
Student Army Training Corps, 222–223
Subway Sandwich Shop (Mercer), 273
Sugar Grove Township, 34, 171, 177, 229, 333, 390–391, 434, 485
Summerville, Pam, 402
Sun Oil Co., 329
Sunday, Billy, 144–145, 164, 436
Sunshine Society, 183, 287
supervisors, township, 535
Sutherland School, 31
Sutherland, John, 35
Sutherland, Mike, 286
Swarts, Evert, 151, 152
Swartz, Carl, 539
Swartz, Mildred, 355
Swartz, Walter, 355
Sweesy, Hilda, 402
Swickard, Clayton, 270
Swirl Arena, 358
Sycamore Park, 229
Sydney, Janet, 385
Sykes, Lucille, 486

∞—Tt—∞

T. A. Houston Store, 306
T. A. Walker Hardware Store, 120–121
Taflin, John, 181
Tait Farm, 288
Tait, Festus, 288
Tait, Karl W., 181
Tait, Margaret, 288
Tait, Nancy, 288
Tait, Samuel, 29
Tait, Samuel F., 288
Tait, William, 288

tanneries, 92
Tara, A Country Inn, 505
taxes, 131
Taylor Farm, 394
Taylor, George, 164
Taylor, K. Melvin, 73
Taylor, Mae, 275
Taylor, William, 169
Teachers Institute, 201
Teare, William, 54
telephones, 136, 230
temperance movement, 195–196
Temple Beth Israel, 336, 358
Templeton, Edwin, 277
theaters, 132, 147, 178, 234–236, 235, 236, 299, 307, 309, 320, 340
Thiel College, 46, 276, 303, 317, 337, 406–410, 514, 546
Third Island, 35
Thomas D. West Foundry Co., 141
Thomas, Doug, 456
Thomas, Dr., 441
Thomas, Rose George, 490
Thomas, Thomas J., 490
Thompson Grocery Store, 307, 309
Thompson's Farm Equipment, 232
Thompson, Adam, 27, 33
Thompson, Akin, 169
Thompson, Arlene, 386, 387
Thompson, Carl, 395
Thompson, Charles, 275
Thompson, David, 59
Thompson, Delmont, 232
Thompson, Donnell, 275
Thompson, Francis, 232
Thompson, Ginny, 386
Thompson, Harry, 30
Thompson, Hayes, 30
Thompson, Howard C., 232
Thompson, James, 532
Thompson, M. W., 45
Thompson, Richard M., 328
Thorne, John Baskin "Jack," 320–321
Thornton Run, 62, 189
Thorton Farm, 189
Throckmorton, Thomas, dust jacket
Throop, A. S., 41
Tidball, James, 36–37
timelines, 80–89, 133, 179, 231, 285, 334, 392, 424, 472, 473, 487
Tingley's Raiders, 397
Top Notch Products, 445
tornadoes, 335, 336, 362–363, 447
Toski, Bob, 302
Tower Presby. Church, 339, 476
townships, Mercer County, 495
train wrecks, 64, 174–175, 191, 260, 369, 461
Transfer, 50, 62, 67–68, 357, 475
Transfer Feed Store, 506
Transfer High School, 275
transportation, 47–49. See also railroads; train wrecks
Traposso, Paul, 32
trapping, 308
Travis, Richard, 55
Traxler family, 74
Traxler, Jacob, 74
treasurers, county, 530, 537
Trepasso, Joseph & Gloria, 394
Trexler, Aaron, 183
Trinity Industries, 277, 452, 517
Trinity United Presby. Church, 432
Triumph Church of the New Age, 237
trolleys, 112, 277, 304–305
Troop, Frank, 399
Trout Corners, 66
Trout Island, 47
Trout Mine, 52
Troutman, Joseph, 389
Turk, Mae, 217
Turkey Run Church, 432
Turner, Allen, 403
Turner, E. N., 151
Turner, Ella Chamberlain, 273
Turner, John, 273
Turner, Raymond, 152
Turner, William Z., 244
Twin City Elks Lodge, 134, 237–242, 377, 418, 429
Twombley automobile, 168
Tyro School, 517

∞—Uu—∞

U.S. Army Corps School, 337
U.S. Steel Co., 139, 142, 205
U.S. Steel Corp., 137, 142, 291, 292, 451
Uber, Frank, 114
Uber, Jerald, 275
Uber, Maude, 114

Uber, Mont, 114
Ulp Farm, 62
umbrella salesmen, 293–294
Uncles, Joseph, 401
underground railroad, 54–56, 546
Union Church of Mercer, 100
Union Democrat, 403
Union Supply Co., 290
unions, 73, 134, 179, 301–302
United Church of Christ, 462
United Meth. Church, 400–402
United Natural Gas Co., 136
United Presby. Church, 132, 144, 432
Unity Presby. Church, 156
Universalist Church, 474
utilities, 54, 136

∞—Vv—∞

Vactor, Charles, 242
Valley Baptist Church, 376, 447
Van Harlinger, Virginia, 275
Van Miller Ambulance, 349
Vanderbilt, Cornelius, 51
Vanderstappen Wood Carver's Museum, 509
VanEman, Rev., 435
Vannoy, Mildred, 402
Vansitta, Frank, 309
Variety and News Center, 427
Vath's Meat Market, 306
Vaughn Chiropractic, 486
Vaughn, James, 355
Vaughn, Leona, 402
Vaughn, Margaret, 355
Veach Meth. Church, 400
Veach, Hiram, 401
Veg Acres Farm, 336
Venango Trail, 24
Vengold Dairy, 231
Vermeire, Mary McDowell, 41, 75–76, 192–195, 198–200, 373
Vesper, Mr., 276
Veterans, 109, 144, 169, 563–565
Victor Mills, 27
Vietnam War, 406–410, 580–581
Vincent, George C., 436
Vincent, Mr., 59, 60, 63
Virginia Station, 101
Visitor, 45
Vocal Hall of Fame, 505
Vogan, Briditte, 516
Vogan, David, 290, 415
Vone, Jim, 270
Vosler School, 414
Voss, Mr., 217
voting trends, 303, 536
Vulcan trucks, 168

∞—Ww—∞

W. L. Scott & Co., 50
Wachter family, 410–412
Waddell, Robert, 32
Waldorf, Ward, 402
Waldron, Kenneth, 176
Wales, Albert E., 183
Walker, T. Wade, 302
Wallace, Paul A. W., 24
Wallace, William, 30
Wallis & Carley Co., 139, 267
Walmart, 384, 483, 509, 515
Walter's Delicatessen (Sharon), 398
Walton, Robert, 484
Wanger, Bob, 385
Wannock, Chief, 29
war memorials, 335, 564–565
War of 1812, 35, 278
Ward, Gordon, 439
Ward, Janet, 337
Ward, William T., 181
Warren, III, George S., 189
Warren, James F., 163
Washington, George, 20–21, 24, 26, 42
Wasson, Woodrow, 445
Watkins man, 281
Watson, Harry, 165, 403
Watson, P. H., 41
Watson, Ralph, 467
Waugh, William, 531
Waverly Hotel, 340
Wayne, General "Mad" Anthony, 21–22
Wayne, H. Russell, 179
Wayne, Marshall, 179
WCTU, 195–196, 297
Weaver House, 287
Webb, James, 402
Weber, Alma, 270
Weekly Express, 402
Weekly Progress, 45–46

Weimert, Brian, 490
Weinel, Paul, 418
Weinet, Ruth, 340
Weir, Jacob L., 402–403
Weisen family, 404
Weiss, Michael, 244
Welch, George, 317
Weld, Sam, 335
Weller, Will, 56
Welsh Baptist Church, 474
Wendell August Forge, 314
Wentling, Joan, 406
Werner, Richard, 189
Wesleyan Meth. Church, 38, 285
Wesleyan Meth. Church Campground, 52, 132–133
Wesleyan Meth. School, 133
West Branch Holstein Farm, 556
West Greenville, 40, 45
West Greenville Gazette, 45
West Greenville Times, 403
West Middlesex, 20, 27, 50, 62, 64, 67, 92, 112, 116, 160, 191, 196, 198, 204, 219, 236, 257, 302, 304, 323, 327, 390, 526
West Middlesex High School, 432, 491
West Middlesex Meth. Episcopal Church, 400
West Salem, 510
West Salem Grange, 400
West Salem Township, 180, 355, 378, 405, 539
West, Nathaniel, 54
West, Thomas D.and, 141
Westerman Filer Co., 52–53
Westerman Iron Co., 70, 230
Westerman, James, 66, 70–71
Western Press, The, 326
Westinghouse Electric Corp., 168, 177, 181, 196, 299, 404, 452
Westlake, Anna, 229
Westlake, Fred, 176
Westlake, John, 386
Westrac Co., 437
Wettig, Patricia, dust jacket
Weygandt Farm, 394
WFAR radio, 391
Wheat, Mr., 309
Wheatland, 27, 34, 67, 118, 230, 287–288, 304, 376, 389, 427, 446, 487
Wheatland Tube Co., 291, 447
Wheeler, E. A., 53
Wheeler, Hiram, 73
Whenry, Richard, 99
Whig and Dispatch, 326
Whispering Pines, 318
Whistler House, 374
Whistler, C. W., 169
Whistler, Charles, 45
Whitaker School, 37
White Chapel, 56
White Chapel Church, 34, 59, 459
White School, 333
White, Bell Chalfant, 262
White, Bill, 217
White, D., 217
White, H. Walter, 465
White, James, 36
White, John, 35
White, Mary Lou, 557
White, T.C., 262, 264
White, Yeager, 546
Whitehead, Walter, 498
Whitla, Billy, 146–147, 148–149
Whitla, James, 144, 146–147, 189
Whitlatch, Mrs. Thomas, 565
Whitmer, Roy, 398
Whittaker School, 385
Whittenhall, Mr., 217
Whyte, Harry A., 241
Wigley, James E., 156
Wilkins, Archelaus, 30
Wilkinson, Merle, 352
William C. Munnell & Sons, 335
Williams, A. W., 169
Williams, Albert H., 534
Williams, Alfred W., 147
Williams, Edward, 244
Williams, Lucille, 406
Williams, Mary E., 164
Williamson, C. G., 213
Williamson, James, 33
Williamson, Mr. & Mrs. Albert, 565
Williamson, Mrs., 386, 387
Williamson, Ruben, 498
Willis Chevrolette, 306
Willis's Garage, 308
Wilmington Township, 34, 59, 131, 177, 198, 231, 333, 445, 485
Wilson Aviation, 434
Wilson Farm, 338, 341–342
Wilson School, 432
Wilson, Catherine Hoagland, 341

Wilson, Charles, 385
Wilson, Donald P., 436
Wilson, Everett, 338, 341–342
Wilson, Finley, 434
Wilson, Frank, 180
Wilson, George, 390
Wilson, Helen Crawford, 341
Wilson, Jesse, 318
Wilson, John, 156
Wilson, Kevin, 506
Wilson, Mary Rearick, 386
Wilson, Roberta, 385
Wilson, Samuel, 451, 453
Wilson, Thomas, 531
Wilson, Virginia, 453
Winder, Clarence "Buzz," 303–304, 434, 456
winemaking, 245
Wingard, Charlie, 33
Wingard, J. M., 169
Wingard, William, 539
Winger, G. Leo, 189
Wings, Inc., 456
Wininsky family, 364–366
Winner Art Galleries, 71
Winner Steel Co., 505
Winner, Donna Carey, 71, 476, 505
Winner, James, 71, 333, 476, 505
Winner, The, 505
Winter, John, 497
Wise, Bertha Batman, 257
Wishart Co., 62, 183, 184–185, 404
Wishart Farm, 564
Wolf Creek, 25, 27, 35, 150, 315, 483
Wolf Creek Rangers, 33
Wolf Creek Township, 34, 380
Wolff, Bruce, 406
Wolgast, Al, 445
Woodland Place, 262
Woods Farm, 318
Woods, Benjamin, 35
Woods, Harry E., 318
Woods, William, 37
World War I, 34, 72, 73, 177, 181, 182–183, 192, 196, 197, 224–225, 232, 329, 566–568
World War II, 46, 188, 192, 267, 281–282, 309, 329, 569–578, Ch. 6
Worley, Lewis, 114
Worsham, Lew, 302
Worth Township, 37–38, 131, 216, 229, 281, 316, 379, 386, 394
WPA projects, 26, 218, 286, 295, 297, 317, 326
WPIC radio, 281, 301, 500
Wrick, James R., 531
Wright, Alexander, 531
Wright, G. W., 169
Wright, R. R., 229
Wright, Rodney, 453

∞—Yy—∞

Yankee Ridge, 47
Yanowitz, Meyer, 230
Yarboro, Theodore L., 73
Yarian family, 32
Yarian, F. F., 47
Yeakel, Amos A., 403
Yeakel, Mr., 46
Yellow Breeches Farm, 25
Yellow Horse, 33
YMCA, 506, 507, 522–523
YMCA campground, 488
Yoder, S. C., 497
Yoho, Edrie, 392
Young family, 30
Young, Amanda, 441
Young, Betty Cooper, 405
Young, Cora, 241
Young, Edward M., 455
Young, Harvey, 152
Young, Irene, 275
Young, James, 32
Young, John, 27, 33, 56
Young, Jonathan, 32
Young, Joseph, 134, 241
Young, Joyce, 377, 441, 469
Young, Martha, 349
Young, Robert, 349
Young, Robert & Paulette, 517
Young, Robert D. "Dick," 455
Young, Terri Walter, 441
Young, Tom, 441, 469
Young, Virginia, 441
Young, William, 328, 349, 377, 418, 441
Yourga Co., 447
Yourga family, 513

∞—Zz—∞

Zahniser, Dan, 213

Zahnizer, Stuart, 181
Zarecky, Rudy, 352
Zenobi, Libby, 385
Zimmerman, Ralph, 277
Zion Reformed Church, 405–406
Zion's Evangelical and Reformed Church, 406
Zion's German Reformed Church, 405, 462
Zook, Catherine, 273
Zook, J., 377
Zook, Noah, 273
Zrno, Dr. David, 251–252
Zuschlag, Hilda, 275
Zuschlag, Robert, 275
Zuschlag, Sara, 275
Zuver School, 32
Zwikert family, 324

592